THE CHALLENGE

Andrew Lambert is Professor of Naval History at King's College, London. His books include *Nelson: Britannia's God of War*, *Admirals: The Naval Commanders Who Made Britain Great* and *Franklin: Tragic Hero of Polar Exploration*. His highly successful history of the British Navy, *War at Sea*, was broadcast on BBC2.

Further praise:

'One of the most eminent naval historians of our age.' Amanda Foreman

'An excellent read . . . I must recommend the work most highly to the widest possible range of readers.' Eric Grove, *Navy News*

Trincomalee: The Last of Nelson's Frigates
War at Sea in the Age of the Sail
The Foundations of Naval History
The Crimean War: Grand Strategy against Russia 1853–1856
Nelson: Britannia's God of War
Admirals: The Naval Commanders who made Britain Great
Franklin: Tragic Hero of Polar Navigation

The Challenge

America, Britain and the War of 1812

ANDREW LAMBERT

faber and faber

First published in 2012
by Faber and Faber Limited
Bloomsbury House
74–77 Great Russell Street
London WC1B 3DA
This paperback edition first published in 2013

Typeset by Donald Sommerville
Printed and bound by CPI Group (UK) Ltd, Croydon, CR0 4YY

A CIP record for this book
is available from the British Library

ISBN 978-0-571-27320-1

For my Mother

Contents

List of Maps and Illustrations ix

Maps and Illustrations

Plates

16 USS *Constitution*, flagship of the American version of
   1812 (© *USS Constitution Museum*)

Acknowledgements

This book would not have been possible without the support and encouragement of many people. My debts are many and various, and they are recorded in alphabetical order.

Brian Arthur, Robin Brass, Duncan Campbell, Michael Crawford, Bill Dudley, Larrie Ferreiro, Robert Gardiner, Don Graves, Edward Harris, John Hattendorf, Don Hickey, Nola Lambert, the late Jon Latimer, Christopher McKee, Steven Maffeo, Scott Sheads, Joshua Smith and Michael Tapper. I have debated 1812 with many more over the years, and all those conversations have added to my knowledge – I am in debt to you all. Although many have helped, advised and informed, ultimate responsibility for the final text remains mine, as it must.

Research for this book was conducted in many institutions, all of which provided engaged, professional support; in addition all of them offered a positive and rewarding environment in which to study. They include the British Library, the National Archives of the United Kingdom, the National Library of Scotland, the National Archives of Scotland, the National Maritime Museum, Hull University Library, the Suffolk and Devon Record Offices, Cambridge University Library Archives, the Library of Congress, the United States Naval Historical Center, the William L. Clements Library at the University of Michigan and the Perkins Library at Duke University in North Carolina. Where archive material has been printed, notably in the outstanding American collection *The Naval War of 1812*, I have cited both text and archive for the convenience of fellow researchers.

Once again Julian Loose, my editor at Faber, was prepared to embark on a voyage of discovery to unknown seas, and along with Kate Murray-Browne and Donald Sommerville ensured the story of 1812 was ready for the bicentenary of this much misunderstood conflict. I cannot close without thanking my family and friends, colleagues and students for indulging my engagement with this conflict. Their support is beyond price.

Andrew Lambert
Kew, 2011

Introduction

~~~~

Every nation needs a history, a unifying narrative that explains and justifies the present.

This book is about a war and the way it became part of two very different narratives. Wars have been a central concern for historians for close on three thousand years, their causes, conduct and consequences conveying everything from divine judgement to moral lessons. In a crowded field the War of 1812 occupies a curious position. Although often referred to by Americans as a victorious 'Second War for Independence', it is also considered a success north of the border, where a very different view of the outcome has helped shape Canadian identity. In Britain, 1812 is the year Napoleon marched to Moscow; the war with America is a long-forgotten sideshow. The British define the very essence of 'Britishness' by reference to another, contemporaneous conflict, one in which they fought for their very existence against the greatest military genius of the modern age.

In June 1812 the United States, not yet fifty years old, challenged the greatest naval and economic power of the time, invading Canada and attacking British ships. It would be a curious war, fought in the shadow of a far greater conflict. At first the British simply did not believe that the Americans meant to fight about issues of principle, issues which they had no hope of upholding. Eventually they accepted the need to respond, but only after Napoleon began his terrible retreat from Moscow. Eighty years later a great American historian gently reminded his fellow citizens that the War of 1812 had been a disaster; after a litany of defeats all along the Canadian border, the capture and destruction of Washington, bankruptcy and the loss of several warships, including the national flagship; the peace settlement had been a fortunate escape.[1] This begs the question: how could a defeated nation, one that suffered such devastating losses, declare a victory and remain in occupation of the literary battlefield for two centuries?

The answer lies in the smokescreen of words that obscured American aims and objectives throughout the conflict. President Madison went to war demanding that Britain end the practice of stopping and searching American merchant ships and impressing seamen on the high seas. Yet these aims were not even mentioned in the treaty that ended the war; the peace process was dominated by questions of land and the rights of Indians. While this mismatch between rhetoric and reality was hardly unusual, examining British war aims and strategy reveals a very different war. Both sides considered the war in the context of the European conflict. In the summer of 1812 Napoleon was about to invade Russia with over half a million men. The American administration expected that Napoleon would win. They planned to seize British North America – modern Canada – and hold it while Napoleon defeated the British. Former President Thomas Jefferson expected that the Canadians, anglophone and francophone alike, would be happy to join the American Republic, indeed Jefferson opined that conquest would be 'a mere matter of marching'. Instead, invading American armies were repulsed by a handful of British regulars, Canadian militia and their Indian allies.

In fact the only battles the Americans won in 1812 were at sea, despite the Republican administration effectively ignoring the Navy. In three frigate actions that year substantially larger American ships captured smaller, less powerful British opponents. Desperate for good news to bolster their flagging grip on political power, the Republican Party latched on to the sea of glory, claiming these victories had been won in fair and equal combat, and linked the claim to the idea that war had been declared as response to British treatment of American ships and sailors. In reality the seafaring communities of New England

and New York, who suffered most from pre-war British actions, consistently voted against war, a fact which reinforces the charge of partisan opportunism. War was popular with Republican voters in the agrarian Central Atlantic states, and especially in the West, because it offered a golden opportunity to seize land from the British and the Indians.

Although the war would drag on until the end of 1814, its outcome was decided by the failure of the American army to conquer Canada, the defeat of American attacks on British merchant shipping and a devastating British economic blockade that left America bankrupt and insolvent. In case anyone in America had missed the utter helplessness of their government, 4,000 British troops captured and burned Washington DC. The Presidential mansion, where the decision for war had been taken, was one of the public buildings to be torched. In the rebuild it acquired a coat of whitewash. The idea that the British 'lost' the war – in which they secured their war aims by compelling the Americans to stop invading Canada, destroyed their capital city and reduced them to insolvency in the process – is one that requires explanation.

This book examines the origins, conduct and consequences of the war from a British perspective, focusing on the development of policy and strategy in London and the conduct of war at sea. Not only has the war on the Canadian border been studied in depth by some outstanding scholars, but it was, for all the bloodshed and chaos, a strategic stalemate. Early British victories on land blunted the American offensive; American naval victories on Lake Erie in 1813 and Lake Champlain in 1814 restored the balance. British amphibious operations, from Maine to New Orleans, a mix of triumph and disaster, are equally well-known, if less well understood. The decisive theatre was the American Atlantic coast and oceanic sea lanes, where the Royal Navy's North American Squadron defeated the United States Navy, and blockaded the American coast. The American attack on commercial shipping failed and instead most American warships were blockaded in port, leaving the entire coast open to economic and amphibious attack. As Napoleon wryly observed, the Americans had 'not yet succeeded in seriously disturbing the English'. He expected they would do better in the future.[2]

Most accounts of the naval war focus on the three small-scale, intense combats of 1812 and the lives of the American heroes who won. The other three frigate battles of the war tell a very different story. On 1 June 1813 HMS *Shannon* captured the USS *Chesapeake* off Boston in less than fifteen minutes, in an action of ferocious intensity, fought with astonishing skill and courage on both sides. On 28 February 1814 HMS *Phoebe* took the USS *Essex* at Valparaiso, Chile, in a strikingly one-sided action. Finally, on 14 January 1815, the USS *President* was taken off Sandy Hook by HMS *Endymion* in a pursuit battle that pitted the American flagship, and the American naval hero, against a smaller British opponent. After the Americans surrendered, two more British ships came up to stop the *President* escaping – just as President James Madison had fled the scene at Bladensburg only months before. Re-examining these actions, and the way they have been represented in British and American literature, demonstrates that the American victory was internal. This was a war for cultural identity and cultural independence, one that created a continental America focused on land and expansion. And it did so without reconciling the sectional interests or cultural divisions of North and South, thereby setting the scene for an altogether greater catastrophe half a century later.

This book is about events that occurred 200 years ago, and their contemporary resonance. I have attempted, as far as possible, to allow those who took part to speak for themselves, and in their own language. Of late it has become standard practice to refer to ships and nations as neutered, as it. The men and women of 1812 did not see the world in this way; for them ship was she because it was living thing, a sensibility that Byron expressed in the immortal line:

> She walks the waters like a thing of life,
> And seems to dare the elements to strife.[3]

The same held true for the liberal nations involved in this conflict, invariably represented by Britannia or Columbia, armed and dangerous female embodiments of a tradition stretching back to the war goddess Pallas Athene. I have retained this usage, both in quotations and in the text, because it would be absurd to make the romantic heroes of 1812 speak the language of another age, one that has little comprehension of their mental world, their values or their culture.

It is important, lest anyone confuse the point, to stress that reconsidering an old war fought by brave men with pre-industrial warships and weapons has little to do with winning or losing, and less with old notions of right and wrong. This book examines how the past has been created, and why. It ceased to matter who 'won' the War of 1812 over a century ago, when America, Britain and Canada recognised the need to work together to address far greater threats. What matters now is that we recognise the past as an evolving cultural construction. In this respect art and literature did more to make our War of 1812 than cannon and diplomacy. Modern versions of the war still reflect agendas developed to serve the political interests of the men who waged the war. These became enmeshed in emerging national identities in North America, becoming central to the self-image of modern states. Little wonder much of the discussion is handled in emotive terms.

Anxious to secure re-election, the governing Republican Party declared a victory and adopted the ever-victorious *Constitution* as the flagship of their war. In the ultimate act of cultural construction a single successful ship was deployed to disguise a failed war. While the British soon forgot 1812, they retained enough relics of glory to subvert American claims. Every time an American president used memories of 1812 to threaten Canada, the British backed their diplomacy with warships called *President*, *Chesapeake*, *Shannon* and *Endymion*, because they knew the difference between propaganda and power. These symbols worked because the relationship between Britain and

America reflected the lessons of war. After 1815 the United States fortified the coast from Maine to the Mississippi against the Royal Navy. The real result of the war was a century of peace that segued almost seamlessly into co-operation and alliance, as the three nations worked together to defeat more fundamental threats in the twentieth century. That they did so with a clearer sense of what they shared than what they did not may be the ultimate legacy of 1812.

CHAPTER I

Flashpoints

Early on Monday 22 June 1807 the United States frigate *Chesapeake*, 36 guns, sailed from Chesapeake Bay, heading for the Mediterranean, where Commodore James Barron would take command of the small American squadron. With America at peace with the world the *Chesapeake* was heavily loaded with stores, and the new crew had not been drilled for battle. Master Commandant Charles Gordon, *Chesapeake*'s captain, planned to work the ship into fighting order as they crossed the Atlantic. By mid-afternoon *Chesapeake* had left the inland waters, passing two British warships at anchor in Lynnhaven Bay, and Gordon set his men to work, preparing for the open sea. Observing a ship closing from astern at 3.30 p.m., Gordon backed sails, slowing down to speak with HMS *Leopard*. Captain Salusbury Humphreys, acting under specific orders from Admiral Sir George Cranfield Berkeley, Commander-in-Chief on the North American station, sent an officer on board the *Chesapeake* to demand the return of several British sailors who had deserted from the Royal Navy, and enlisted on the American ship.

This was unprecedented, and illegal. Barron rightly refused to comply, only for the 50-gun *Leopard*, significantly more powerful than the American ship, to close in and open fire. Humphreys knew the Americans were in no position to fight, 'the ship being much lumbered', and few of her 36 guns had been secured on their carriages. Finally Lieutenant William Henry Allen brought a live coal up from the galley and fired a single gun, allowing Barron to haul down the national colours and signal surrender after making a token resistance. Three men were dead, and sixteen wounded. Barron offered to surrender his

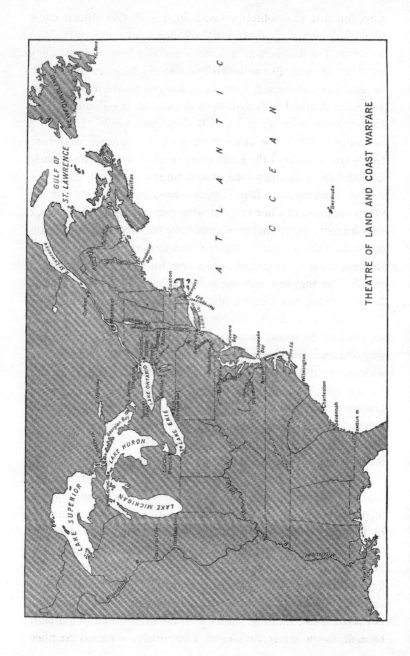

THEATRE OF LAND AND COAST WARFARE

ship, but this was politely refused. Instead British officers came aboard, mustered the crew and took four known deserters, John Strachan, Daniel Martin, William Ware and John Wilson. They were not the only Britons on board, merely the ones who could be positively identified. One man, known to the Royal Navy as Jenkin Ratford, a British-born deserter, had publicly abused British officers ashore at Norfolk only days before. He would be hanged. While the other three were also known deserters, two were black, and the nationality of all three was sufficiently doubtful to ensure they were merely imprisoned.

The *Chesapeake*, her rigging shredded, several feet of water in the hold, her crew utterly demoralised, limped back into home waters, anchoring at Hampton Roads shortly after noon the following day.[1] Humiliated and anxious about their careers, the ship's officers turned on Barron. They requested that he be arrested and tried for dereliction of duty. In the heated atmosphere of a dangerous international confrontation American naval officers were anxious to preserve their collective reputation. They aspired to an international code of honour, and to match the professional standards set by the Royal Navy. This self-proclaimed elite group were proud, yet anxious, many having their image captured for posterity in the full uniform of gold lace, high collars and epaulettes that demonstrated rank and status.[2] Already at odds with the Republican administration, the officer corps feared that the disgrace of the *Chesapeake* might lead to further cuts and loss of status.

The administration and the Navy Secretary had equally good reasons to seek a scapegoat. They were responsible for the feeble state of national defence at sea. When a court of enquiry in October found Barron guilty of negligence and want of judgement a full court martial was inevitable. In January and February 1808 eleven senior officers of the tiny American service gathered on board the *Chesapeake*. Captain John Rodgers was appointed president of the court; only a few years before he had blustered about fighting a duel with Barron, a man he publicly blamed for a litany of slights and insults. Captain Stephen

Decatur had relieved Barron in command of the *Chesapeake*, forming such a low opinion of Barron's conduct that he begged to be excused from the court. The request was refused. The month-long trial proceeded with all the stiff decorum required to preserve the tattered dignity of a deeply embarrassed service. John Rodgers asked a handful of questions, each one carefully calculated to reveal that the ship had not been ready for action. Master Commandant David Porter, a friend of Rodgers and Decatur, focused on the demoralising effect of Barron's supine conduct.[3] Rather harshly found guilty of 'neglecting on the probability of an engagement to clear his ship for action', Barron was suspended from all duty without pay for five years. Mortified and humiliated, Barron would bear a grudge against those who passed that judgment for the rest of his long life. Never again would he command an American warship, even when his country went to war. Nor was he alone in his despair. The tiny, fractious naval officer corps had been dangerously divided by the judgment – Barron's trial and those of the *Chesapeake*'s other officers led directly to three duels, one of which proved fatal.[4] During his years of disgrace Barron earned his bread in merchant shipping. In 1813 he offered his services, an offer that was pointedly ignored.[5]

The shock and humiliation that followed the return of the shattered American frigate to port quickly turned to widespread anger, and direct action against British sailors and stores on shore at Norfolk, Virginia. Yet President Thomas Jefferson preferred a more measured response. He had no intention of going to war with Britain, and by omitting any mention of desertion, the issue that caused the incident, tacitly recognised that the Navy had been unwise to recruit British deserters. Rather than pick a fight Jefferson merely demanded an official explanation, using the distance between Washington and London to cool tempers. The only direct action he took was designed to avoid further friction, denying British warships access to American waters, other than in an emergency. His October Message to Congress harnessed public anger to support his preferred defence preparations: a fleet of gunboats to defend American harbours, ordered only months before.[6]

Yet there were deeper trends in Jefferson's thinking. That July he told the French Ambassador:

If the English do not give us the satisfaction we demand [over the *Leopard–Chesapeake* incident], we will take Canada which wants to join the Union, and when with Canada we shall have the Floridas, we will no longer have any difficulty with our vessels, and this is the only way to stop them.

John Armstrong, the American Ambassador in Paris echoed the thought.[7] Behind Jefferson's carefully contrived rhetoric of outrage lay a deep-seated ambition to make America a continental nation.

In stark contrast, the British response to the *Leopard–Chesapeake* incident was muted. Whatever the legality of the case – and few doubted the Royal Navy had breached international law – most supported Berkeley's action. British seamen were being lured into American service so the chastisement had been necessary. Furthermore, the Admiral was well connected on both sides of the political divide. As the British government reflected on the incident the deciding consideration would be news from Europe. Well aware of the mood at home, Berkeley expected orders to attack New York. Time was of the essence: the Americans were 'hard at work fortifying their harbours' and calling on the exiled French General Moreau for advice, and perhaps to command the army. Berkeley warned the ministers that the Americans would trifle with them until their defences had been put in order, and their merchant ships had returned home.

If I had a few more ships, I certainly should be tempted to run up to New York with the squadron before the harbour is secured and wait there for the issue of negotiations, as having that city under the terror of destruction would insure a favourable issue to any terms you might propose.

As New York Customs provided two-thirds of American state revenue, an attack would be decisive. He reckoned that with four more battleships, two bomb vessels, four large frigates, and six or eight gun-brigs he could 'compel them to any treaty'. After the initial strike he advised exploiting the 'reciprocal hatred' of the Northern and Southern states to split the Union. With a larger squadron and 5,000 soldiers in fast transports he could keep the whole American coast in a state of alarm, bringing them to terms in six months once the revenue fell and taxes rose. The pre-emptive seizure of American merchant ships would cripple the privateer threat before war began.[8]

As Berkeley implied, the early history of Anglo-American relations could be read in the solid angular form of the bricks and stones that formed the coast defence of the new republic. Americans looked to land-based artillery to secure their harbours. New forts were begun in 1794, in case the French Revolutionary War spilled across the Atlantic. Most were simple earthworks, armed with any available cannon. More money was spent during the Quasi-War of 1798–1800, when masonry works like Fort McHenry at Baltimore were constructed. After the *Chesapeake* incident 'the remarkable total of more than three million dollars' was spent. New York and its approaches received more attention than any other harbour, with several new works, including Fort Wood, now the base of the Statue of Liberty. Fort Columbus and Fort Williams on Governor's Island mounted up to 100 guns each; others closed off the narrows. Most American ports had at least one fort by 1812.[9] America feared British naval power.

THE CONTINENTAL SYSTEM

The only problem with Berkeley's incisive strategic analysis was the assumption that Britain, fighting for her very survival in Europe, had an element of choice. The government in London let Jefferson procrastinate and dissemble because Britain simply did not have the men, ships or money to begin another war. Anglo-American relations in this period were dominated by the Napoleonic War, a truly existential conflict that raged across

Europe and the wider world between 1803 and 1815. Britain and France were absolutely focused on a struggle for survival that would only end when one state had been utterly defeated, and its political system annihilated. In this world at war it would have been remarkably naïve for American statesmen to think that the rights and safety of neutral ships that voluntarily sought to profit from the conflict would receive favourable attention from great empires at war. That Jefferson relied on economic suasion to make his case only reinforced the apparent naïveté. American commerce stood to lose far more in a war with Britain than it suffered as a neutral from France and Britain combined. In truth American statesmen were not fools; they saw a quarrel about maritime trade and neutral rights as an ideal opportunity to acquire land, and rearrange domestic politics.[10]

War created opportunities for American expansion. When Napoleon's 1802 campaign to re-conquer Haiti failed he realised that his entire New World portfolio was severely devalued. A hasty, opportunistic sale turned the indefensible territory of Louisiana into ready money, which he used to rebuild his navy to fight Britain, the only state that still defied him. Lord Nelson's sublime victory at the Battle of Trafalgar, 21 October 1805, settled the command of the sea, confining Napoleon to Europe. His global ambitions thwarted, Napoleon turned on Europe, conquering Spain, Italy, Holland and much of Germany. By 1806 he had destroyed nations and shattered the European political system, creating a monstrous super-state that he ruled as the self-crowned Emperor of France and King of Italy.

While Nelson became the war god of the British state, his protégés translated the command of the sea secured at Trafalgar into a powerful strategic tool, enabling Britain to fight for survival against a military colossus with close on a million men under arms. Relying on economic warfare and naval blockades, the British slowly but surely broke the French economy, fostering unrest among subject states and peoples, funding and supporting any who took up arms for their own liberation. They were altogether less friendly to opportunistic neutral traders.

After Trafalgar, the greatest land and sea powers of the age settled into a curiously bloodless conflict, waged by customs houses and patrolling cruisers. In May 1806 a British Order in Council placed the European coast between Brest and the Elbe under blockade, strictly enforced between the Seine and Ostend, the invasion ports. Outside this narrow strategic zone, ships coming from neutral ports were allowed to pass. The object was to destroy French coasting trade, and stop neutrals from carrying French colonial produce to metropolitan France. One side effect was to alienate the United States, which was carrying much of France's West Indian trade across the Atlantic. Jefferson retaliated with the Non-Importation Act of October 1806, which banned British imports. His futile, self-defeating gesture assumed the British would change their grand strategy to suit the economic interests of a minor neutral nation.[11]

In November 1806 Napoleon celebrated his newly won control of Germany by issuing the Berlin Decree, the founding charter of a Continental System designed to exclude British commerce from Europe. Napoleon demanded that Britain abandon the legal regime it had employed at sea for generations, which made the private property of enemy citizens liable to seizure. He knew the British would not surrender this principle short of total defeat.[12] The deeper aims of the System have been widely debated, but the results were clear: it turned Europe into an economic satellite of France, funding Napoleon's military occupation of the continent. The Berlin Decree had far less effect on Britain than on occupied Europe. On the same day, Napoleon ordered the occupation of several German ports, and demanded Denmark cut communications with Britain and demobilise.[13] The Decree also violated French treaties with the United States. Together with the British Orders in Council that followed on 7 January 1807, the Berlin Decree raised the level of economic warfare.[14] The British were trying to cut France's coasting trade, and exclude neutral ships from that trade. Neither Britain nor France achieved decisive results. However, a long war would be advantageous for Britain, which was far better organised for economic war than

France. Superior fiscal systems, public credit and access to long-term loans at lower rates of interest allowed Britain to pay for her war. Napoleon funded his by plunder, forced contribution and the blatant exploitation of his satellite states. During the war London replaced Amsterdam as the world's major money market. Smuggling and new markets helped to lessen the effect of the Continental System on Britain. France simply passed the cost of war on to her conquered territories, using the Continental System as a tool to extend Napoleonic imperium.

Furthermore, the Berlin Decree was something of a dead letter while Russia remained independent, and free to trade with Britain. They were put on hold when a Russian army fought Napoleon to a standstill at Eylau in February 1807. The British began to hope that Russia could distract Napoleon from the sea. Instead, a Napoleonic thunderbolt crushed their feeble hopes. News of the decisive battle of Friedland, 14 June 1807, reached London on the 30th, 'melancholy intelligence' officially confirmed on 10 July. In defeat Tsar Alexander adopted an anti-British tone that King George III found 'very discouraging'.[15] After Friedland, Alexander signed up to Napoleon's system: France and Russia would close the European continent against British business, coercing the last neutrals into the system.

Britain could not afford to sit back and wait for these measures to take effect, or to ignore the longer-term threat posed by Napoleon's fleet-building plans. Effective strategy responds by countering threats, and whenever possible seizing the initiative.[16] Now entirely alone, Britain's only hope of survival lay in the active, aggressive pursuit of a maritime war, using the sea to build economic power while the blockade degraded that of Europe. As Nelson had predicted, a strict blockade of Europe made the inhabitants feel the baneful effects of French fraternity, and rise up in revolt.[17] In any event the British had few strategic options.

The first victims of the economic total war were neutral shipping nations, primarily the United States. For Napoleon, neutrality was not an option. Everyone would have to take sides. For some, like Denmark, that choice would be taken for them;

for others, like the distant United States, the problem would lead to endless debate, frequent legislative change and ultimately an ill-timed war.

When the London *Times* published news on 17 July of a negotiation between Napoleon and Tsar Alexander, the King's Private Secretary pointedly observed: 'We shall again have to carry on the war single handed and I trust we have nothing to dread whilst we continue at open war with those scoundrels.'[18] At the Treaty of Tilsit, signed on 7 July, the two emperors agreed to act together against Britain. This was a dangerous game for Alexander; the Continental System looked remarkably like the last Russian economic war against Britain, which had ended with the murder of his father in 1801. Russia could not afford to wage economic war against Britain; and nothing had changed in the interval. Yet Tilsit committed Russia, and France would now attempt to coerce Denmark, Sweden, Austria and Portugal to make war on Britain. The object of the exercise had become clear on 4 July, when Napoleon bragged: 'Everything points to the continental war being at an end. Our whole effort must now be thrown on the naval side.'[19]

The only common ground between the two emperors was hatred of Britain. While Russia remained hostile, Britain had no hope of defeating Napoleon. Under the cloak of a war against Britain Napoleon completed the conquest of Europe by stealth. The logical conclusion of the process would be a single pan-European empire, and there was no doubting which emperor would rule. That such a state posed a fundamental threat to Britain's security, because it could mobilise massive naval resources, was perfectly clear to Napoleon, and to the British. That Britain responded by attacking the smaller powers at the margins of the conflict, denying Napoleon the first fruits of Tilsit, was no more than sound policy.[20] Fortunately the British government had been hoarding money and manpower against just such an eventuality, using them in a ruthless, dynamic, devastating amphibious operation against Denmark. As Foreign Secretary George Canning observed:

We have now, what we had once before and once only in 1800, a maritime war, in our power – unfettered by any considerations of whom we may annoy, or whom we may offend – And we have ... determination to carry it through.[21]

No longer obliged to debate strategy with allies, Britain would make war in her own, unique way. Canning, like Nelson, looked forward to a time when Europe would rise up and overthrow the dictator. British strategy, based on naval mastery, would secure Britain and her global trading network. Sea control for economic advantage and strategic effect provided the bedrock of British policy; any state challenging that control would find itself at war.

Between Trafalgar and Tilsit British governments had struggled to find a strategy to counter the dynamic expansion of the Napoleonic empire. After Tilsit Britain relied on sea control and economic pressure. A war of money and cruisers might appear indecisive and amateurish alongside Napoleon's titanic campaigns, but it worked.[22] British ministers understood that 'the naval strength of the enemy should be the first objective of the forces of a maritime power, both by land and sea'.[23] That concept underpinned everything successive British governments attempted between 1805 and 1815; it explained Copenhagen, the Peninsular War, and the refusal to compromise with the United States.

News of the Russian defeat at Friedland persuaded the Cabinet to recall and promote George Berkeley, rather than applying further pressure on Washington.[24] Berkeley's suggestion that an attack on New York might be the best way to resolve the impasse was no flight of fancy. The British sent a massive task force to Copenhagen, seizing the Danish capital and taking away the entire fleet and everything of value from the dockyard. The British also persuaded the Portuguese king to abandon Lisbon, then menaced by a French army, and re-establish his dynasty in Brazil.[25] After these stunning successes had re-drawn the basic architecture of the Anglo-French war, Canning hoped the Americans could be brought to reason without relaxing the contentious Orders in Council. Delighted by the deterioration of Anglo-American relations, Napoleon stepped up his seizures of American shipping, unable to resist the temptation of easy pickings from a trade that America could not protect.[26]

MONEY, LAND AND HONOUR

British decision-makers knew, despite the heated rhetoric surrounding the *Leopard–Chesapeake* incident, that the fundamental issues dividing the two countries were economic and territorial. The United States that emerged from the Revolution of 1776 had a population well under four million, a fifth of them slaves. Only 200,000 people lived in large cities; the great majority were engaged in farming, fishing and forestry. It took the new country half a decade to establish a central government, and economic growth remained slow, crippled by a tiny domestic market and the vast distances between population centres. Only coastal and river transport could move bulky agricultural produce to market. Extensive barriers faced American exports and shipping, barriers imposed by all European powers to protect their colonies from competition. American industrial output was minimal. While Britain remained the main trading partner, exports to Britain were significantly lower than they had been before the Revolution. For obvious reasons the British Navigation Laws, designed to protect the British economy and secure a steady supply of sailors for the Royal Navy, gave preference to loyal Canadian and West Indian suppliers, closing inter-colonial trades to American ships. These trades had been the basis of American economic development before 1776. The British government's tough policy was supported by powerful East and West India shipping, colonial and political interests, which controlled a major segment of the House of Commons. British merchants favoured excluding American shipping to protect their own profits. The government listened because those merchants paid the taxes that sustained the state.[27]

Before 1793 there was 'no significant alteration' in American 'carrying trade and exports'.[28] British economist Lord Sheffield publicly condemned any concessions. He anticipated a prolonged period of economic dependence, America remaining a British colony on an 'informal' basis, without the costs of government and protection, rather than the costly 'formal' model. America would serve British commercial interests, increasing British shipping and the strategically vital pool of skilled ocean-going seamen needed to defend the state in time of war.[29] He was right: without significant capital, or many banks, America was an economic dependency. The most obvious American growth area was the agricultural population. With an open frontier, population growth fuelled expansive land hunger, rather than providing cheap labour for industrial development.

America's grim economic prospects would be transformed by the French Revolutionary War. Between 1793 and 1801 the value of American exports and carrying trade earnings increased five times and, after a brief fall caused by the Peace of Amiens in 1801–3, reached a peak in 1807. This was 'primarily a result of the rapid development of the re-export trade'. While exports doubled, re-exports increased by 200 per cent, quickly overtaking domestic-sourced exports in value. Re-exports were foreign cargoes that stopped in American harbours long enough to be classed as American, usually unloading and reloading, before continuing to their original destination. Under this system, American ships carried French goods to France's West Indian colonies, and returned to France laden with Caribbean crops, all despite the British blockade and the annihilation of French merchant shipping. Revenue from shipping services was another major growth area. American freight rates peaked in the late 1790s, just as the Royal Navy cleared European shipping from the seas, leaving European colonies in America, Africa and Asia without commercial transport. American economic growth depended on the European conflict.[30] As the British took control of the oceans, French, Dutch and Spanish colonies, cut off from their homelands by Royal Navy cruisers, resorted to neutral shippers. Suddenly the Americans were allowed into markets that had been closed against them, generating remarkable economic growth.

The meteoric expansion of American oceanic shipping followed the protectionist tariff of 1789, designed to defend domestic shipping routes, and promote overseas commerce. The tariff enabled American shippers to undercut foreign competition, primarily because the next two decades would see every other major shipping nation involved in catastrophic wars. Within a decade 90 per cent of the oceanic shipping using American ports was American.[31] Even allowing for the distraction of Europe this was highly inequitable. One result of this rapid 'artificial' expansion was that half of all skilled seafarers on American ocean-going ships were foreigners. Most were British. Relying on British seafarers at a time when Britain was engaged in an existential conflict risked serious political repercussions; American statesmen chose to complain about the British response, and ignore the root cause. British seafarers powered the expansion of American shipping, the engine of the American economy.[32]

By 1807 the growth of American trade had begun to stall: colonial markets were in decline – the British had seized the most significant French and Dutch colonies, while Spain, soon to be paralysed by a French invasion, left her colonial ports open to British trade. Opportunities for American commercial expansion would have to be sought in more contentious European waters.

ECONOMIC WAR

Napoleon's attempt to defeat the 'nation of shopkeepers' in an economic war between Europe and the British Empire placed America in the firing line. Until then American merchants had used their neutral status to make a fortune out of the conflict. Between the outbreak of war in 1793 and 1807 annual exports increased from $23 million to $108 million, imports (for consumption not re-export) from $32 million to $85 million. Expanding shipping and shipbuilding, the growth of export industries, banking and the extension of agriculture profited large sections of American society. The first American millionaire was a New England ship-owner, and such wealth began to shape American culture.

If the British laughed at American cultural pretensions, the profits of trade did not pass unnoticed. Britain, by a large margin America's best trading partner, began to question American commercial methods. The argument was simple: American ships were carrying French, Spanish and Dutch goods between their colonies and Europe, a trade closed to American ships by the laws of those states in peace. Under the Rule of 1756 the British maintained that any trade closed in peacetime could not be opened in war. Well aware of British law, and the Royal Navy's power to enforce it, Americans off-loaded such cargoes in American ports, paid a nominal duty and then re-loaded them as re-exports.

In a carefully calculated move to pressurise Washington to conform to their views, the British banned the re-export trade. The High Court of Admiralty's *Essex* judgment of 1805 upheld the Rule of 1756, declaring the ship had 'touched in America solely to colour the true purpose', carrying goods from Spain to Havana. This 'fraudulently circuitous voyage' vitiated the ship's neutrality. Ship and cargo were condemned.[33] Lord Sheffield agreed, confident the Americans would not 'deem it expedient' to resort to war; 'a sensible people, not easily diverted from a consideration of their own interests', they recognised no action they might take could compensate for the loss of trade 'and the consequent embarrassment and distress of their maritime towns, in which is centred the greater part of their population, power and wealth'.[34] As a member of the Board of Trade from 1809, Sheffield hardened ministerial attitudes against concession to America.[35] His colleagues included the Prime Minister, the First Lord of the Admiralty, the Secretaries of State for Home and Foreign Affairs, the Chancellor of the Exchequer, the Speaker of the House of Commons, while the Presidents of the Board after 1806, Lord Auckland, Earl Bathurst and Lord Melville were intimately involved in defence, war and empire.[36] Sheffield's belief that economic coercion would force America to accept British practice suggests he had fundamentally misunderstood the United States. He still saw America as a maritime state, but the brief ascendancy of an American seafaring, commercial culture, based on the major port cities of the Atlantic coast, had already begun to fade. America was assuming a new identity.

THOMAS JEFFERSON

At the heart of the growing Anglo-American divergence lay the mind and measures of Thomas Jefferson, third President (in office 1801–9), intellectual, statesman and ideologue of Republican America. Jefferson shaped every aspect of American policy during his Presidency and turned convenient co-operation towards blood-stained confrontation, and his decisions reflected a clear ideology. Where John Adams's Federalist administration (1797–1801) worked with the British when the interests of the two states coincided, Jefferson was profoundly hostile to Britain, the British, and their system of government. After the traumatic experience of being ignored in 1776, Jefferson spent the rest of his days dividing America from Britain. During the Presidential election campaign of 1800 he used explosive rhetoric to charge his Federalist opponents with treasonous intent, and subservience to the old country. He showed no interest in building domestic consensus, preferring confrontation to compromise, pitting the sectional interests of Virginia, his home state, against Federalist New England, repeatedly arguing that political difference was a form of treason. Alongside the elevated sentiments and intellectual insight, Jefferson was, at heart, authoritarian and anti-democratic. The Republican Party was the state; those who held different views were traitors. Not that Jefferson held an elevated notion of the political morality of any party. 'They' threatened to wreck 'his' vision, and must be stopped. The trend towards totalitarianism was clear. In stark contrast to the Anglo/Dutch democratic tradition, driven by the growing cosmopolitan political body to evolve a flexible system of government to share power and compromise, Jefferson drew his politics from Rousseau, who provided little support for practical politicians. Critically, Jefferson tried to recreate

Thomas Jefferson, President of the United States, 1801–9,
ideologue and leader of the Republican Party.

an idealised Roman Republic, where political virtue was linked
to stable agrarian interests, the unchanging rhythm of planting
and harvesting, the natural deference of peasant toward master,
and the untroubled possession of slaves. Desperate for stability
and control, Jefferson tried to preserve his idealised, virtuous
pre-industrial society, only to find that progress and change
were incessant, nowhere more so than in America. His fixed
Constitution only worked while the country remained exactly as
it had been when the document was framed.

Jefferson's political creed made him fear the dangerous
concentration of peoples in cities, which replicated the uneven
division of wealth and power at the heart of 'Old World' politics.
He feared urban mobs, created by manufacturing industry, as

'sores' on the body politic.[37] The danger of foreign influence and political corruption was clear, and the infection was spread by men of commerce: 'Foreign and false citizens now constitute the great body of what are called our merchants, fill our sea ports, are planted in every little town.'[38] He was especially fearful of major port cities, preferring small ports that could be dominated by inland producers, a perspective that ignored the history of commercial and civic development since the dawn of time. Ports connected America to the corruption of Britain, a conduit for dependence and re-conquest. In 1803 Jefferson dismissed the politics of commercial cities as noisy, but inconsequential, contrasting their vicious, foreign influences with the national virtues of the countryside.[39] He had little faith in the political morality of Yankee merchants and shippers, largely because they were Federalists, convinced that their greed made them easy prey to external interests. The only safe course, as he revealed in 1807, would be to close down commercial intercourse, and force the New Englanders back to tilling their stony fields.

Recognising the vulnerability of American shipping to British naval power, Jefferson would be prepared to compromise during the *Leopard–Chesapeake* crisis of 1807; Treasury Secretary Albert Gallatin stressed to him that few places on the coast were safe from British raids, including Washington.[40] While Gallatin advised a pre-emptive strike to seize the British naval base at Halifax in Nova Scotia, Jefferson settled for economic coercion. At first glance such measures appeared futile – how could they protect American ships and commerce from the impact of a titanic struggle that had raged across much of the world for a dozen years? – but the reality was altogether more sophisticated.

In a total war 'neutrality' would only be possible on absolute terms, the complete cessation of all economic intercourse with both belligerents. Much as the idea appealed to Jefferson's agrarian hemispheric nostrums he could not impose such a regime. Too many prominent men made their living in shipping and overseas trade, too much of the national income came from customs dues, and too many seats would be lost at the next election if trade were blocked. The initial attempt to resolve this dilemma was a measure that neither solved the problem nor pleased the people. The 'Non-Importation' Act of April 1806, revealingly timed to take effect in November, after that year's shipping season had ended, attempted to apply economic pressure on London, by banning British imports. Non-importation was more of a shot across the bows than a direct hit. It left the trade to run for another year, and did not stop the importation of key British goods. While the British considered the measure an insult, it was harmless. In April 1807 Rear Admiral Sir Alexander Cochrane advised the First Lord of the Admiralty that non-importation would make the American populace 'disaffected to their Government, which will pave the way for the long expected separation of the Northern from the Southern States, an event which cannot be at a great distance – happen when it may, it must be for the advantage of Great Britain'. Cochrane warned that were Britain to 'submit to American encroachments . . . our Navy will be ruined, and our trade greatly injured'.[41]

Seemingly oblivious to the importance of the Royal Navy to Britain, and the impossibility of manning it without impressment, Jefferson linked non-importation to a demand that Britain cease impressing seamen from American ships. But in the meantime James Monroe and William Pinkney had led a high-powered American diplomatic mission to London, and by the end of 1806 had negotiated realistic solutions to the issues of trade and impressment. In return for legalising the re-export trade, the treaty would have tied America to the British maritime economy, a profitable, secure position, although sacrificing a certain amount of dignity. The British were even prepared to ameliorate the impact of impressment.[42] Jefferson simply refused to put the document before Congress. He did not want a settlement: simmering Anglo-American antagonism served his domestic agenda, polarised American politics, and broke links to the corrupting sea and the Old World beyond.[43]

The opportunity was fleeting; when Napoleon's Berlin Decree stepped up the economic attack on Britain the British responded.

James Monroe, Republican diplomat,
Secretary of State and Secretary for War.

Fresh Orders in Council on 7 January 1807 prevented any ships from trading between ports under Napoleon's control.[44] Since 1803, 731 American merchant ships had been seized by Britain and France, roughly two-thirds by Britain. As the conflict built up to a denouement such losses would only increase. Britain blocked all trade with ports that were closed to British ships; Napoleon's Milan Decree responded by making any ship that passed through a British port liable to seizure as 'British'.

If the economic damage was limited to American trading communities, normally beyond Jefferson's concern, the issue of impressment had the power to shock an entire country. Under British law all British seafarers owed a duty to the Crown, and they could be forcibly impressed into the Royal Navy on the high seas, as well as in British ports. Americans believed that large numbers of American-born sailors were being impressed. In fact rather less than 10 per cent of the American maritime workforce suffered this fate.[45] Furthermore, as Jefferson, Madison and Gallatin soon discovered, American economic expansion depended on British skilled labour. A project to surrender all British sailors in American ships in return for the British ending the impressment of Americans was quietly dropped because half of all skilled seamen in American merchant ships were British.[46] No more than half the men impressed from American ships were actually Americans.

BETWEEN THE MILLSTONES OF WAR

Before Trafalgar, Jefferson seriously considered building an ocean-going fleet, including battleships, as a balancing lever for the international system. After Trafalgar, the British controlled the seas more completely than ever before and, in the absence of allies or armies, used sea power to wage total economic war against France. Jefferson shifted his attention to a force of coastal gunboats. Predictably these failed to satisfy the navalist interests of New England merchants, emphasising the sectional divide.[47] In reality the gunboat navy was built to enforce Jefferson's preferred diplomatic tool, blocking exports of supposedly vital produce from America, and the import of British manufactured goods.

In December 1807 Jefferson unveiled his response to the *Leopard–Chesapeake* incident. The Embargo Act reached Congress before official notification of the British Orders in Council had reached Washington. The Act blocked the American export trade and came into effect only days after Napoleon's Milan Decrees. To punish Britain Jefferson made war on American merchants. The results were disastrous: economic hardship obliged American merchants and seafarers to smuggle, and the New England states, whose ships and men were directly affected by British actions, moved decisively into the Federalist camp. After the Act a merchant community that had funded national warships to defend commerce in 1797–8 systematically broke the law, while the Navy they had helped to create was used to enforce a deeply unpopular measure. Widespread resistance to Federal Law weakened the Union, and caused a dramatic fall in customs revenue, the key source of Federal funding.[48] Not only was 1808 the only deficit budget of the era, but the Embargo brought the law and the administration into contempt. Ironically the Embargo effectively solved the impressment problem: the sharp reduction in American oceanic commerce obliged anglophone sailors to return to British ships, where they could be impressed without diplomatic complications. British ministers were unmoved; they saw no reason to complain, or to make concessions.[49]

Jefferson hoped the Embargo would be a useful adjunct to Napoleon's war against Britain, and that in return a grateful Emperor would give him the prize he really wanted, Spanish Florida. The preposterous claim that West Florida had been part of the Louisiana Purchase dominated Franco-American relations during Jefferson's Presidency. Napoleon considered that American economic measures were more damaging to France than Britain, and he set a far higher price on Florida. He believed that in a total war neutrality was impossible; he wanted an American declaration of war. The Emperor would not give Jefferson a province while American ships were transporting flour to feed British troops in Spain. When French frigates got to sea they systematically burnt American grain ships. The resulting outrage in Washington met blank incomprehension in Paris. Ironically the only defence for American shipping was provided by the Royal Navy, which captured many French raiders. Napoleon bullied and deceived Jefferson and his successor James Madison because America was impotent. Without fleets and armies, their arguments about international law and morality lacked weight. He treated the Americans with contempt because they would not help him defeat Britain; indeed American ships systematically, repeatedly and skilfully violated his 'Continental System', the economic total war he relied on to defeat the British. Napoleon had a hard job telling Americans apart from Englishmen, and he believed that they meekly accepted the British Orders in Council because they were only interested in profit and had no honour. He impounded American merchant ships, and locked up 'American' sailors as prisoners of war – to stop them being impressed into the Royal Navy.[50] Occasional hints that he might relax his regime were self-serving and tactical.

Jefferson's futile Embargo had long antecedents: in 1785 he had argued that America should follow the commercial policy of China 'to practice neither commerce nor navigation'. He knew the idea was impossible,[51] but never changed his view that American merchants were corrupt or corruptible. He dreamt of an agricultural America, relying on others for shipping and industry. Unable to bar his countrymen from the oceans, Jefferson compromised on complete freedom to trade as the least dangerous alternative. He consistently promoted inland expansion, judging that the land would soon outweigh the sea in the nation's political balance.[52] Nor was Jefferson a lone voice: at the height of the 1800 election Virginian ally James Madison publicly linked every British cargo that entered America with the expansion of British influence, connecting Republican politics with an agrarian barter economy.[53] Madison claimed that the fifty or sixty thousand British subjects living in the United States were corrupting the people, preparing the way for re-colonisation through the seaports, the 'reservoirs' that channelled British influence into the country.

The vehemence of Madison's rhetoric, and his reliance on the political wisdom of individual states to save the nation, echoed Jefferson's emphasis on states' rights to secure the nation against the monarchical principles and foreign influence he saw at the heart of Federalism.[54] After 1800, ideology and partisan politics divided the United States along clearly understood, easily drawn lines, separating the commercial seafaring North-East from the slave-owning centre and the growing South and West. The

Louisiana Purchase of 1802 upset the delicate internal balance of power, providing the Republicans with new allies and enabling them to assert that they were the 'national' party, casting their political opponents as servile lackeys of the British. That the Federalists had openly charged the Republicans with Francophilia in the mid-1790s suggests Jefferson's policy platform contained an element of revenge.

For all his hatred of ships and commerce, Jefferson made frequent use of nautical imagery, describing the United States as an 'Argosy' weathering a storm. The link between the sea, storms and periods of acute political stress was clear.[55] For Jefferson the sea was the domain of storm and terror, and not a tranquil, productive element; perhaps he had experienced an Atlantic gale on his European travels. Whatever the cause, it is clear that those who lived by the sea were foreigners to Jefferson, who worked for a hemispheric continental American future, one in which boisterous oceans helped to isolate America from European wars and political contagions. His ultimate object was the spread of republican government across the entire continent by removing foreign rule and influence, while creating a community of agricultural states acting in loose federation. In his view the Louisiana Purchase was only the beginning; Florida and Canada were next. At the same time Connecticut became a foreign country, because it was the last bastion of anglophile Federalism.

REPUBLICAN VISIONS

Economic expansion emphasised regional economic divergence. As the North-East became more urban, and industrial, the South remained wedded to the plantation system, with limited population growth, outside the key port of New Orleans.[56] American economic activity down to 1815 would be driven by external factors, and the way American statesmen responded to them. America had choices, and it would be those choices that transformed an economic boom into an unwinnable war.

The Louisiana Purchase transformed the United States from a medium sized maritime nation into a continental Great Power.

The dramatic increase in territory and agricultural exports that followed the opening of the Mississippi in the 1790s, and the opportunistic Louisiana Purchase in 1803 had a dramatic impact on American policy. The sudden accession of territory, and the development of the cotton gin in the early 1790s, transformed the South from an economic appendage of New England into a politico-economic powerhouse. Cotton sales capitalised the American economy as access to the Mississippi transformed the western lands, and by 1810 over one million Americans lived beyond the Appalachian mountains, people who looked to new land in the West for their economic future, not the ocean. The largest real estate deal in history almost doubled the land area under American control, making America 'a nation of rivers', something that 'changed not only American history in general, but maritime history in particular'. After 1803 America 'would not be a coastal nation trading with the world through Atlantic seaports ... but a great continental empire, trading primarily with itself'. By 1820 the volume of American river and inter-state coastal shipping had outstripped oceanic shipping.[57]

The opening of the West rounded off three decades in which Britain and America had grown apart. Though the two may have shared a common heritage as dynamic, aggressive trading nations, the small island British still depended on external trade, while Jefferson's continental America looked inward. As a result, the early nineteenth century would be both 'the heyday of American oceanic shipping' and 'the last florescence of a waning enterprise'.[58] The War of 1812 merely accelerated an inward turn already evident in 1800. Thomas Jefferson's policies were both responsible for, and more amenable to, this new America than those of his Federalist opponents. He built a political power base among Americans who saw their future in land and agriculture, rather than shipping. He chose the land, not the sea, Republican ideology not national interests.

This became very clear when Jefferson responded to the *Leopard–Chesapeake* incident by stopping American overseas trade. After a decade in which Americans had made windfall profits from the European conflict, Jefferson simply turned his back on overseas trade because, whatever the views of New England, it was inimical to his vision of a Republican America. For a President focused on land it mattered little that, as Albert Gallatin warned, the embargo would hardly affect Britain. He emphasised the positive: it would stimulate American industry, and riverine shipping, and it would do so at the expense of the smaller Atlantic ports, which were devastated by the sudden loss of their dominant economic activity. Ports like Salem lost ground to Boston, which had a far larger economic hinterland. Many small ports reverted to fishing.

The obsession with territorial expansion ensured that America would declare war in 1812 by invading Spanish Florida and Canada, intent on conquest. These were the only wars America could win. Jefferson considered the expansion of American territory and power across the continent the best security for his republic, while seizing Canada would give him the leverage to control Atlantic shipping. The logical conclusion would be to bring Canada under American control: Republican defence policy emphasised land and expansion. That those measures were few reflected over-confidence, not lack of ambition. Jefferson did not 'fear foreign invasion'; he saw America expanding, irresistibly, almost imperceptibly, happily endorsing John Jacob Astor's Pacific North-West project as the germ of a future republican state and natural ally. That New England saw the American future in very different terms did not strike him as an occasion for discussion let alone conciliation. New England was wrong and required correction.[59] The Embargo made war on New England because it suited Jefferson's domestic political purposes to break the link between America and Europe and isolate and bankrupt the Federalists. He was not prepared to mediate on impressment and belligerent rights because these issues served his larger purpose. How far he actively sought a war with Britain remains open to debate; that he did nothing to avert it is beyond doubt.

While the idealist Jefferson dreamt of hemispheric isolation and disengagement, the realist happily exploited any opportunity to advance a continental agenda. His administration proved to be 'aggressively expansionist', despoiling other races and regimes of their lawful property to serve American interests. The Louisiana Purchase fundamentally changed America; it provided apparently endless land for settlement, reinforcing the sense of continental destiny. It also marked the point at which the maritime North-East lost its political ascendancy. The equally problematic settlement of the slavery question laid the foundations for another war, one that would do far more damage to the United States than 1812.[60]

No sooner had Jefferson bought his country an empire – territory that had already been conquered by force and exchanged by treaty on several occasions – than he wanted more. The Floridas would be the next targets of his 'lust for land'. America had no lawful claims so Jefferson manufactured some. After 1807, with Spain seemingly powerless in the New World,

Jefferson, and later Madison, sponsored or connived in the series of quasi-official, wholly illegal manoeuvres that culminated in blatant filibustering.[61]

In all this it is hard to believe that men who could show such cunning and flexibility in other areas of public life chose to make a futile, dangerous stand on a matter of principle when dealing with Britain. Jefferson's hatred of the British and admiration of the French were well-known, but if his Francophilia was more clear-sighted than many have admitted, Anglophobia was surely the one fixed point in his intellectual firmament.

A FLEET OF GUNBOATS

The obvious physical manifestation of Jeffersonian territorial ambition would be the gunboat, a diminutive coastal and riverine warship. Naval historians have found unusual accord in condemning the ships, and the politician who built them, but such judgements reflect modern agendas. When the United States became a major battlefleet sea power it quickly reconstructed its naval past into a morality tale, one in which wise naval officers consistently advised feckless politicians to build such a battlefleet. Military history is peculiarly the province of such judgements, being driven in part at least by the educational needs of contemporary armed forces. In reality Jefferson did not envisage an age of American global power, or the world wars of the twentieth century. He was laying the foundations for a continental hegemony that could be secured without ocean-going warships. An expanded United States would be protected from insult or injury by distance, a universal polity, gunboats, coastal forts and militiamen. The ideology of 'freedom' would be the key to expansion. At New York fifty gunboats provided a vital link between the forts around a harbour too wide to be covered by shore-based guns; gunboat flotillas at New York and Boston could make significant contribution to harbour defence, and escort coastal shipping. It is unlikely Jefferson expected anything more. He opposed the heavy cost of sea-going forces, fearing they could draw America into the Napoleonic conflict. A purely defensive gunboat force, normally hauled ashore for preservation, would uphold local interests without undue cost or risk.

Jefferson's vision of America as an isolated, agrarian democracy, a nation preoccupied with land and continental expansion, diverged fundamentally from the oceanic commercial issues that concerned many of his countrymen. He did not favour using the Navy to defend merchant ships; his gunboats were confined to 'merely defensive operations' in harbours and on the coast, and he was anxious that America might otherwise become excited 'to engage in offensive maritime war'.[62] Jefferson intended to make the tide line into the frontier, impermeable in either direction.

After 1807 Washington used gunboats to collect revenue, stop smuggling, impose the unpopular Embargo, and support filibustering in the Floridas. Popular with Southern Republican land-owning interests, they could be built locally, and provide a first line of defence against pirates – or slave uprisings. In an age when America was without metalled roads, canals or railways, they were the pioneers of conquest, the mobile firepower of expansion. If American particularism has moved on, abandoning the gunboat to the judgement of its critics, along with powdered wigs and knee-breeches, it would be unwise to ignore the logic of these key defensive tools of continental empire. If Jefferson had managed to 'conquer without war' his gunboats would be remembered as a stroke of genius. In shoal water and rivers gunboats were useful, but they were irrelevant to an oceanic conflict.[63]

The Embargo Act prompted a dramatic economic collapse across the American maritime community: insolvency, debt, unemployment and ships laid up in port were only the most obvious indicators of widespread distress. In 1809 Jefferson belatedly admitted that the Embargo threatened to tear the country in half, replacing it with the Non-Intercourse Act in March, averting a civil war without too great a sacrifice of honour.[64] The new measure only barred trade with Britain and

France. Recognising a climb-down in the face of British economic coercion, Foreign Secretary George Canning tried to draw the United States into Britain's economic and political orbit. Cabinet discussions revealed a division of opinion: some suggested making minor concessions, opening some British West Indian trade to the Americans. Colonial Secretary Lord Liverpool objected that this would damage colonial interests only recently stimulated by the Orders in Council.[65] Canning's initiative collapsed when his envoy in Washington misunderstood the mission. The only beneficiary was Napoleon, who hoped the dispute would draw America into a war with Britain. He increased French predation against American shipping, claiming the Americans were fair game because they did not defend their ships, or their flag on the ocean, allowing the British to tax and control their voyages. The Emperor willingly licensed trade with Britain, but absolutely rejected weakening the Continental System in favour of America. Attempts to improve trading conditions in 1809 and 1810 had limited impact.[66] Britain and France were far too busy waging war to consider the finer points of Jeffersonian rhetoric, or the growing divisions within America that the President was attempting to paper over.

THE MANY WARS OF PRESIDENT JAMES MADISON

After the divisive failure of economic pressure, Madison invited Britain or France to secure American friendship by renouncing hostile measures against American shipping. Macon's Bill No. 2 of May 1810 made the intentions explicit. The British had already modified the Orders in Council to reduce their impact on American shipping, seeking a better relationship with the new President. Madison chose to ignore the British gesture, and swallow a blatant Napoleonic lie.

Napoleon wiped out American claims against France for past privateer seizures, set up a tariff barrier that excluded American goods from the European market, and then claimed he would revoke the Berlin and Milan Decrees as they applied to America, if the British revoked the Orders in Council. He had no intention of ending his war on neutral shipping, and did not do so after the British revoked the Orders in 1812. In reality Napoleon was steadily increasing his control of Europe, to wage economic war on Britain. American trade with Russia became the critical issue. American merchant ships in the Baltic were seized and condemned, with American documents denounced as forgeries. Although these measures were primarily directed at Russia, the impact on America was severe. Despite clear evidence from his ministers in Paris and St Petersburg, Madison accepted Napoleon's blatant lie at face value, beginning the descent to war with Britain on the strength of a fraudster's promise.[67] If he stopped seizing American merchant ships outright in 1810, Napoleon simply shifted to the equally damaging nightmare of bureaucratic tergiversation, a tactic that successive French administrations have used to restrict imports.[68] The only significant change in American policy was to

The President who went to war; James Madison,
Republican President 1809–17.

shift the naval priority from gunboats enforcing the embargo to frigate squadrons cruising to protect coastal waters.

LITTLE BELT

Having banned trade with Britain, Madison's administration mobilised the Navy to protect territorial waters, at that date no more than 3 miles from the high water mark. Madison did not provide any fresh resources for the ocean-going cruiser fleet. Instead he sent out ships commanded by officers hell-bent on having revenge for the *Chesapeake*. One Congressman observed, 'send out the navy in its present disposition, and you send it to war'.[69] As the ranking senior officer of the United States Navy at sea Captain John Rodgers took it upon himself to be the agent of that vengeance. Holding the rank of commodore, he commanded the northern detachment of the fleet, two frigates, a brig and a schooner. In any other service Rodgers would have been an admiral but the United States, fearful of military power, by some peculiar land-bound logic decided to restrict the rank structure of the Navy, while proliferating generals, a far more dangerous political commodity. Such slights rankled with Rodgers, and he was not alone in resenting both the implied lack of faith, and the limited pay. Anxious to avenge the humiliation of 1807, Rodgers was looking for a fight; he painted the name of his ship in the largest letters the topsails could carry, to ensure no one mistook her for a British warship. Reminding his subordinates to be ready to uphold the dignity of the flag and neutral rights against Britain or France, Rodgers revealed a deep well of hurt about the *Chesapeake*: 'the inhuman and dastardly attack ... which prostrated the flag of our Country and imposed on the American people, cause of ceaseless mourning'.[70] Rodgers flew his commodore's pendant on the American flagship, the USS *President*.[71]

In 1794 the United States had created a new navy, specifically to deal with the Algerine corsairs who preyed on American merchant shipping in the Mediterranean and held her sailors for ransom.

It would be more economical and dignified to combat the pirates than pay them off with warships and stores. The biggest ships of the new fleet would carry 44 guns, the same as the largest Algerine vessels. Shipbuilder Joshua Humphreys exploited his brief to create super-frigates significantly larger than contemporary European frigates. With the hull strength of a battleship and a large battery of heavy guns, the American ships had a critical edge in battle. Humphreys designed a long, broad-beamed

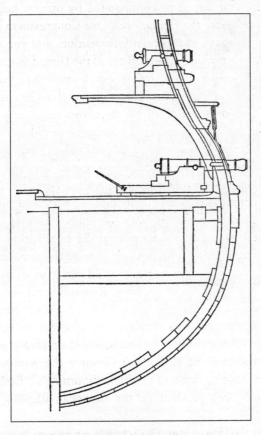

A section through a 44-gun frigate, with long
24-pounder cannon on the gun deck,
and 32-pounder carronades on the upper deck.

ship mounting thirty 24-pound cannon on the gun deck, with space for up to twenty more cannon, or (by 1812) 32-pounder carronades on the extended quarterdeck and forecastle. With an enormous spread of canvas on unusually strong masts, the 44s had the potential for high speed in the hands of experienced seamen, despite their size and weight. And yet the big frigates attracted very little attention. No one considered them the equal of a battleship, and none had seen action with another frigate. *President*, last of the three 44-gun frigates, was launched in New York in 1800 and entered service with an elaborate Federalist figurehead of George Washington. Jefferson's administration replaced this with a simple Republican scroll. Once in service, *President* proved the best of the 44s, very fast going large and before the wind, steady in a seaway and rarely straining her standing rigging. Her sluggish sister *United States* was known as the 'Wagon', and although the *Constitution* was rather better William Bainbridge offered Rodgers $5,000 to exchange into the *President*, 'one of the finest ships in the World'.[72] *President* was the pride of the United States Navy – the flagship of her senior seagoing officer – and the British knew her name.

By one of the many ironies that surround this war, Rear Admiral Herbert Sawyer, based at Halifax, Nova Scotia, had sent the 20-gun ship-rigged sloop HMS *Little Belt* with fresh orders for the frigate HMS *Guerriere*, then cruising along the American eastern seaboard between Charleston and New York. Their pacific import was clear:

You are to be particularly careful not to give any just cause of offence to the Government or subjects of the United States of America, and to give very particular orders to this effect to the officers you may have occasion to send on Board ships under the American flag. You are not to anchor in any of the American ports but in case of absolute necessity, and then put to sea again as soon as possible.[73]

Just as the Americans were hastening to challenge Britain, the British were taking steps to avoid trouble. British warships entering American waters with diplomatic correspondence had strict instructions not to board any American ships: 'you are to be particularly careful to do no Act that may cause further irritation or discussion between the two countries'.[74]

By 1810 the monotonous drip of American vitriol had soured British opinion. Lord Liverpool had favoured conciliation and improved relations, but Madison's policy persuaded him America could be relied on for little more than Francophilia and weakness. Disgusted that America was threatening the very country it depended on for 'security and protection', he had no hesitation sustaining the Orders in Council, and foresaw, 'at no very distant period . . . the Separation of the Eastern from the Southern States'. This would secure British North America from any danger.[75] Even if the British were annoyed by American actions, and their capacity to overlook French duplicity, they had no desire for war.

While Rodgers was temporarily at home in Maryland, the Secretary of the Navy ordered him north, following reports that British and French cruisers were harassing trade off New York. Understandably annoyed by the interruption of a brief period of shore leave, Rodgers sailed on 14 May 1811. He learnt that HMS *Guerriere* had removed Maine native John Diggio from an American merchant brig. Rodgers hoped to recover Diggio in a mirror image of the *Chesapeake* action.[76] Two days later, north-east of Cape Henry, *President* sighted a strange warship, which at first approached, and then fled into the gathering darkness. A lethal combination of unthinking anger and blind ambition led Rodgers to presume he had found the offending *Guerriere*.

In reality he had spotted the *Little Belt*, a tiny Danish vessel seized at Copenhagen in 1807. Captain Arthur Bingham had been looking for the *Guerriere*, and signalled accordingly. When *President* did not answer Bingham recognised the commodore's blue pendant, identified the American ship and turned away. It says much for the collective state of mind on the American quarter-deck that afternoon that Rodgers, and his officers, identified the *Little Belt*, a small, weakly armed vessel, as a 'frigate.'

Unable to out-sail the powerful American, Bingham hove-to and displayed his colours prominently, to ensure there could be no mistake about his nationality. He also prepared for battle, just in case, double-shotting his guns. Rodgers approached the *Little Belt* as if to pass under her stern and rake her, a favoured tactic in single-ship actions, but Bingham had enough way on his ship to defeat such plans. Bingham hailed to ask which ship it was, but Rodgers, unwilling to begin a discussion, merely repeated the question back, and after a second exchange of questions the *President* fired a single gun, possibly accidentally. Clearly Rodgers's gun crews were straining at the leash. Bingham was ready and replied in kind, beginning a lengthy exchange. While the protagonists later disputed who had fired the first shot, Bingham's claim that he did not had the merit of being sensible. Why would he have opened fire on a ship he had already identified as both neutral and vastly superior?

After forty-five minutes the firing ceased. *President* forged ahead, leaving Bingham with thirty-two killed and wounded, his rigging cut to ribbons, shot holes below the waterline and an unanswered question. When Rodgers next hailed he learnt the name of his opponent, and the fact that the British colours were still flying. Bingham thought he heard Rodgers say his ship was 'the United States Frigate', the actual name probably drifting off on the breeze. The ships parted, but at daybreak Rodgers sent over a boat, apologised for the 'unfortunate affair', and admitted he would never have fired had he known the disparity of force. He claimed that Bingham fired first, something Bingham absolutely denied.

Bingham assessed Rodgers's state of mind, his intentions, and American tactical thinking:

By the manner in which he apologised it appeared to me evident that had he fallen in with a British frigate, he would certainly have brought her to action and what further confirms me in that opinion is that his Guns were not only loaded with Grape and round shot but with every scrap of iron that could possibly be collected.[77]

The devastation of *Little Belt*'s rigging was no accident; Rodgers wanted to destroy the British ship's masts and sails, leaving her disabled and helpless.

While Bingham stressed that he had been attacked without provocation, Rodgers had much to 'regret'. Even so his report lamented the unequal contest, not the illegal action. He had chased Bingham because he was 'desirous of speaking' but was unable to ascertain the *Little Belt*'s force before the sun set, when Bingham hove-to and hoisted his ensign. Rodgers claimed he could not discover the nationality of the ensign: in fact there were only three possible options, the Stars and Stripes, the French tricolour or the Union Jack, and they were not in any way similar. Rodgers claimed to have hailed first, and that Bingham fired the first and second shots before he had replied. Determined that 'the flag of my Country' should not be 'insulted with impunity' he finally ordered broadside fire. Despite her diminutive size *Little Belt* was no push-over. By Rodgers's admission she fired very well, hitting two of *President*'s masts in short order, and but for their massive dimensions could have disabled the American flagship. Finally, realising the disparity of force, Rodgers hauled off and stood by until dawn, when he was mortified to see his trifling opponent, and learn of her heavy butcher's bill. With his only defence an exaggerated notion of national honour he requested a court of enquiry.[78] He was anxious to prove the fight had been worthy of his mighty vessel, but attempts to magnify the diminutive ex-Danish sloop into a frigate only served to highlight his poor eyesight, a failing that would dog his career, and that of the mighty *President*.

With Britain and the United States already on the verge of war the bloodshed had surprisingly little impact. While Republicans in the Middle and Southern states were quick to applaud, New England Federalists were critical, making full use of Bingham's account, and those by British deserters from the *President*. Once Rodgers had been cleared by a predictably friendly court of enquiry, Navy Secretary Paul Hamilton ordered new masts to replace those damaged in battle, and offered words of encouragement. Both measures were necessary as he fully expected the action would 'cause you to be marked for British vengeance'.[79] Hamilton's ringing endorsement of Rodgers's valour rings doubly hollow – recent events were hardly heroic, and the Commodore would repeatedly miss the chance to fight ships of smaller force, because he mistook them for vessels superior to his own.[80] A dominating, domineering personality with a will of iron, Rodgers was the unchallenged leader of the United States Navy and, as the senior officer afloat, his flagship was the physical manifestation of national power at sea. Yet he was, as Christopher McKee has noted, deeply flawed:

Rodgers's pre-eminence ran only in administrative and professional matters. As a combat commander his record was equivocal, and the officer corps looked elsewhere for inspiration when it came to war and battle.[81]

Nor were the British prepared to show him any respect. Within days HMS *Guerriere* had painted her name across her fore topsail, in massive letters, to ensure Rodgers did not make the same mistake twice.[82] Perhaps Captain James Dacres knew about Rodgers's eyesight.

The Admiralty published Bingham's report in the *London Gazette*, calmly allowing the public to make up their own minds.[83] Any doubts about Rodgers's intentions were dispelled by British sailor William Burkett, who had been on the *President* during the action. Burkett had deserted from the *President* and gone to Canada after she returned to New York. In sworn testimony Burkett stated that Lieutenant Paulding had plainly seen *Little Belt*'s colours, that the Americans fired first, and that Rodgers put a British seaman in irons for having the temerity to say as much. The British sailors on board were disgusted, declaring they would not fight against their flag. The Admiralty copied the statement to the Foreign Office.[84] While Napoleon hoped Rodgers's indiscretion would lead to war, if only to keep the British off-balance while he crushed Russia, he saw no need to reward the Americans. The opportunity for a suitably grand gesture passed, because he simply did not care about America, as friend or enemy.[85]

Although the British government made little effort to remonstrate, British artists and print-dealers had no such scruples. The *Leopard–Chesapeake* incident had passed without generating a contemporary image, but the *President–Little Belt* action soon appeared in London shop windows. In October and December aquatints appeared 'elucidating the extreme disproportion of Force' between the two vessels, with Captain Bingham 'nobly supporting the Honor of the British Flag'. One represented the ships in action at night, the second the scene the morning after, the emaciated *Little Belt* lying-to, close by the stout *President*. The second image reinforced the representation of inequality, by printing full details of the two ships below the caption. The striking battle scene was created by artist/ engraver William Elmes, better known as a caricaturist; the more measured piece, by second-rank naval artist Joseph Cartwright, was dedicated to the First Lord of the Admiralty. Evidently there was an English market for nationalistic outrage, a third image appearing at a dealer's in Borough High Street, close by the Pool of London.[86] Endlessly reproduced in American texts, these pictures silently subvert John Rodgers's claims.[87]

While many in Britain demanded revenge for the loss of life on the *Little Belt* the government let the matter drop. Two months later another case of trigger-happy Americans was also allowed to pass without comment. On 9 June, off Cape Henry, HMS *Eurydice* was close alongside the USS *United States*, preparatory to communicating, when an American cannon was fired, the shot landing about a cable's length from *Eurydice*'s bow. Captain Stephen Decatur was quick to apologise, 'declaring upon his Honor the Gun fired was an accident and which he much regretted'. Captain Bradshaw received the apology through his first lieutenant, sent on board the American ship 'to demand the cause of such a proceeding'. Satisfied there had been no intention to insult the British flag, Bradshaw decided not to take the matter further.[88] Decatur had burst onto the national stage in 1804 following a daring raid on Tripoli harbour. Immediately promoted captain, he sustained his reputation whenever the opportunity admitted.[89] While Bradshaw's assessment may have been correct, he did not reflect on why the Americans, who had gone to action stations on sighting another warship, were so highly strung. Rodgers, Decatur and the entire American naval officer corps were anxiously expecting a war in which their honour and their lives would be at risk, so it was little wonder their nerves were on edge, or that their men were affected by the heightened tension.

Following the heated public response to the *Little Belt* incident the Admiralty decided not to send Bradshaw's letter to the *Gazette*, reflecting a desire to avoid war. Instead the government relied on 'a well-publicised dispatch of naval reinforcements to the American theatre' to make their point.[90] The *President–Little Belt* incident passed without harsh words, but the dispatch of two British frigates to Halifax caused a brief flutter of alarm in Washington.[91] The Admiralty had ordered two of its best frigates to Halifax: HMS *Shannon* would become the instrument of British retribution.

CHAPTER 2

Going for Broke

If HMS *Shannon* was just another standard British fifth-rate frigate her captain was utterly unique. Philip Bowes Vere Broke had dedicated his career to duty, honour and glory, which he believed would only be secured through superior professional skill.[1] The eldest son of a Suffolk country gentleman and heir to broad acres, Broke had no business being on the quarterdeck. By rights he should have served ashore, in the suitably gentlemanly occupation of an Army officer, with his younger brother. His father had intended him for a life of educated reflection, but Broke wanted to go to sea. Fired as he was by stories of naval ancestors, a major river at the bottom of the garden, and the challenge of the wider world, his determination over-rode parental reservations. The only concession to parental demands was his attendance at Portsmouth Naval Academy, to learn the theory of his profession. At a time when most young gentlemen entered the Navy aged around twelve by joining a ship, and then mastering the practical business of going to sea as they grew up, the Academy gave Broke an edge. The education was systematic, linked theory to practice, and demanded that students work on all aspects of their profession. Broke was a voracious reader and his early schooling meant he was familiar with classical languages and authors. He proved an able student; the 1791 end of term report, 'industrious and well behaved', was faint praise for an officer who would build his career around the twin poles of professional skill and intellectual enquiry.[2]

After going to sea in 1792 Broke rose through the ranks in war, serving under some noteworthy officers, and witnessing the

Battle of Cape St Vincent from the deck of a frigate. In 1801 his father's political connections secured the key promotion to post captain.

When he took his first command in 1805 Broke worked hard to train his ship for battle, demanding the highest standards of gunnery and ship-handling. Everything revolved around the accurate, effective use of artillery. He installed gun sights at his own expense and trained his men to fire at small targets, rewarding them with cash, tobacco and promotion. At a time when many ships made do with one gun drill a month, Broke exercised the artillery five days a week. Not content with technical perfection, Broke constantly studied the tactics of fleet battle and single-ship action. Accurate gunnery would enable him to target different parts of an enemy ship; masts and rigging could be taken down with chain and grape shot, then the gun deck could be cleared by horizontal fire at close range. In an era when ships rarely sank he knew that killing the crew was the key to victory.

In September 1806 Broke's dedication received due reward: command of a new 38-gun 18-pounder frigate – the ultimate test of skill, initiative and leadership. Everything he had learnt went into fitting out HMS *Shannon*.[3] The guns and gun carriages were carefully adjusted to achieve horizontal fire when required; the decks were marked to ensure that every gun on the broadside could be directed at a single point, producing a devastating concentration of destruction. These refinements were paid for out of his own pocket. He drilled the crew to fight in silence, so that any commands could be heard above the din of battle. For five years he kept up the relentless pursuit of perfection, desperate to find and fight an enemy ship of equal force, to prove himself worthy of his profession in an age of outsize naval heroes. Instead he escorted whaling fleets to Spitsbergen, patrolled the French and Spanish coasts, and took his fair share of minor prizes. Although a man of endless intellectual enquiry, self-effacing and averse to public notice, Broke shared the burning desire for glory that propelled so many of his contemporaries on land and sea. In the slightly cramped stern cabin of the *Shannon* Broke shelved a

fine library of professional and classical texts. His midshipmen
benefited from his wisdom, and his culture.

Like any intelligent naval officer, Broke read every scrap of
news that came his way, stopping passing merchant ships to
learn of recent sightings and pick up the latest newspapers. Well
aware of the wider strategic picture, he anticipated the looming
crisis across the Atlantic. Early in 1811 he seized an American
merchant ship off Bordeaux, displaying little sympathy for
the sulky captain, or his country. 'These obstinate, vicious,
kicking Yankees will compel us to chasten them at last – they
appear more insolent than ever by the late papers.'[4] That June
the *Shannon* was refitted, fresh copper sheathing restoring the
speed needed for effective cruiser work. The following month
she was ordered to escort a convoy of lumbering Indiamen
south; Broke only discovered his destination was America when
he opened sealed orders after the convoy was clear of Cape
St Vincent. Captain and crew were disappointed; they feared
Halifax would be a tedious backwater in the world war. The
only Americans they met, New England merchant skippers
making a fortune supplying grain to the British Army, 'will by
no means consent to a war'. Although Broke feared he would
be bored,[5] he realised that the Admiralty had ordered *Shannon*
and *Spartan*, Captain Edward Brenton, to reinforce the Halifax
squadron as a direct response to the *Little Belt* incident. In the
event of war Broke would accept the American challenge; he
would capture the American champions – Commodore Rodgers
and the *President*.

Shannon reached Halifax, Nova Scotia, on 22 September,
joining Herbert Sawyer's tiny squadron.[6] In a strategic backwater
rarely threatened by French cruisers, Sawyer commanded a single,
ancient 64-gun third rate, four frigates and a handful of sloops.
Broke quickly joined Halifax society, a social round of shooting,
dining and visits. The combination of opportunities to relax with
professional camaraderie improved his mood. Cruising off the
American coast for slave ships and contraband traders, Broke
reflected on the looming crisis and assessed American opinion

from local newspapers: 'it appears that their government is determined to make a war with us, but the people in general are equally determined they will have peace'. He concluded that Republicans and Federalists alike were narrowly concerned with agriculture and trade, and neither understood the implications of the vast, existential conflict raging in Europe:

I am really ashamed of the narrow, selfish light in which they have regarded the last struggle for liberty and morality in Europe – but our cousin Jonathan has no romantic fits of energy and acts only upon cool, solid calculation of a good market for rice or tobacco![7]

Even so, he was constantly turning over the prospects in his ever active mind:

If there is an American war . . . our services will be brilliant for a short while and then there will be nothing but *blockade* and I may as well go home. I get very impatient.[8]

Impatient or not the prospect of war kept him busy, refining and renewing the gun drills that set his ship apart from the rest. Every detail was primed and ready for battle. His first American cruise ended at Bermuda, the sunny southern twin of Halifax. The fortified naval base there enabled British ships to refit and refresh before sailing back to the American coast. Once again Broke used his time ashore to widen his social network, and exercise his romantic faculties on the striking scenery of cliffs, trees, shallow water and sunlight. Edward Brenton had ample opportunity to observe *Shannon*'s 'high state of discipline and training', organising the *Spartan* on Broke's example.[9] Brenton had good reason to be prepared. This was personal: he had been born in Newport, Rhode Island, the son of the local customs officer, and his family had been driven into exile by the American Revolution.

By the time Broke sailed northwards along the American coast in early 1812 he had seen quite enough of shore-side society to make him homesick, and join his crew in hoping for war, as a diversion from the tedium of peace. His assessment of the

Americans did not improve, in large part because his information came from Federalist newspapers:

The war party (American) are certainly a wicked and perverse set of men and acting in downright enmity to the welfare of all free nations as well as their natural allies – the mass of the party are sordid, grovelling men who would involve their country in a war for a shilling percent more profit on their particular trade and are perfectly indifferent whether they league themselves with honor or oppression – provided they get their *mammon*. Some of their leaders wish for a war only to get places and commands . . .[10]

While such opinions were common among British statesmen and warriors Broke's animosity also reflected personal concerns.[11] After a decade carrying the strains of wartime command he was desperate to come ashore to his beloved wife Louisa and their children. But he could not do so with honour while he commanded the *Shannon*, and there was a prospect of an American war. At thirty-five, he had served his time in frigates, and was due to be shifted into a battleship, condemned to follow blindly after an admiral. It was not a prospect he relished. Yet the stern call of duty, the obligations of his class and its sense of honour bound him to the wooden wheel of his fate. And the old ambition still coursed through his veins each time he took his men through the gun drills and exercises. If he captured the *President* he could come home with dignity and honour, to assume the obligations of a landed gentleman. A complex and conflicted man, Broke rarely had the luxury of unburdening himself to others; his inner tension only emerged across time.[12]

DIPLOMACY

Despite the *Little Belt* affair the two countries remained at peace through 1811. The *Leopard–Chesapeake* affair would be resolved the following July,[13] but the larger issues of impressment and belligerents' rights remained intractable. Far from the sea, deep inside the Old North-West, the battle of Tippecanoe in November 1811 provided Madison with a minor success, and another excuse to vilify Britain, this time for allegedly supplying the Indians with weapons and encouraging them to attack. The case against the British was flimsy in the extreme, little more than a few second-hand muskets of British manufacture. It hardly amounted to arming and encouraging the Indians – they needed no encouragement to defend their lands and their culture against American land hunger. American frontier politicians pressed for an attack on Canada, ostensibly to stop Indian raids, but in reality to seize the valuable fur trade, destroy the northern tribes and improve market conditions for agricultural produce. The final issue revealed the influence of Westerners; they had no need for Canadian land, but they feared the competition. When Andrew Jackson called for volunteers in Tennessee he linked the looming conflict with the need to secure better markets for agricultural produce. Ports like Baltimore, Savannah and Charleston, serving the central and southern agricultural hinterland and suffering from the Republican trade embargoes, were equally hostile. Orders in Council and Indians unified a majority of American politicians.[14] Napoleon thought that Tippecanoe meant war, only to find the Americans mired in endless, fruitless talk.

While the Congressional 'War Hawks' spoke for the sectional interests of the West and the South (which focused on seizing East Florida), their over-heated rhetoric built a brief coalition of fear and anxiety that led most Americans to see Britain as the enemy. Madison remained anxious for peace, but when Congress assembled in November 1811 the mood was hardly conducive to sober reflection. Presidential attempts to talk and prepare were hampered by the same sectional interests that pushed for war. Navy Secretary Paul Hamilton proposed building twelve battleships and ten more frigates to defend American coasting trade and annoy the enemy; but the very men who most wanted war refused to support the Navy, backing small-government Republicans alarmed by potential tax rises. The frigates were voted down; the battleships were never brought to the floor. America would go to war without new warships. The best that can be said for Madison is that he expected the very public calls for re-armament to coerce the British. In the event the limited results delivered by a fractious Congress left the British entirely unaware of his deeper purposes.

As Americans debated the problem of upholding neutrality in a total economic war, global politics were about to be turned upside down. Frustrated by Russia's evasion of the Continental System, which had created a major trade for American ships, Napoleon decided to settle the issue by force. French diplomacy was reduced to a smokescreen of persiflage, designed to keep Washington at loggerheads with Britain until Russia had been crushed. As Madison girded his loins, and engaged government propaganda to support war he sent a new ambassador to Paris. Joel Barlow's task was to secure an accommodation with France. It proved to be a futile mission. Napoleon rejected claims to indemnify American ship-owners, and America would not sign an alliance. Barlow hinted that America might convoy merchant shipping, which was both illegal and impractical while the Royal Navy controlled the Atlantic. Suitably unimpressed, Napoleon left his Foreign Minister to play the Americans along while he concentrated on Russia.[15] The fraudulent St Cloud Decree of April 1812 only added insult to long-term injury. The vehemence with which Barlow pressed American compensation claims, and the demand to remove French tariff barriers against American imports, reinforced the French Emperor's contempt for American cupidity. He saw no need to reward a nation that had dragged its heels over protecting the rights of neutral trade for a decade, doing little more than issue wordy complaints, and signally failing to defend its interests.[16] Historians have tended to echo Napoleon's analysis, which was not dissimilar to that of British decision-makers, by focusing on the internal and ideological rationale for war.[17]

Quite why the Republican Party thought that it, and the republican principles it claimed to represent, were fundamentally threatened by the unpleasant side effects of seeking windfall profits in a total war is hard to fathom. The alternative causation of American territorial ambition makes much more sense: it is consistent with American diplomatic practice and republican ideology. It also makes sense of the pre-war defence decisions that increased the Army, and not the Navy. If war really was a question of honour then the decision should have been backed by appropriate force, one capable of defending the point. In taking the decision for war American statesmen were doubly blind: they failed to recognise the existential threat that Britain faced in Europe, and they failed to consider their own position if Napoleon had defeated the British. The conquest of Canada and the end of impressments would have been scant compensation for a trade war with all of Europe, and the arrival of Napoleonic legions in Louisiana. As Paul Schroeder concluded:

An American historian of European politics may be permitted to wonder why American historians have made little of the paradox that an infant democratic republic should have entered this titanic struggle on the side of one of modern history's worst tyrants ... perhaps one great emotion linked Jefferson, and Madison, great theorists of democracy, with Napoleon, a great military despot: a visceral hatred of Great Britain.[18]

The question of impressment revealed the depth of cultural estrangement between North and South. Government-sponsored articles and Presidential messages, packed with emotional rhetoric about rights and freedoms, rang hollow in the mouths of slave-owners. Little wonder government claims were dismissed by the very men who were mostly likely to suffer. New England accepted the British position, considering that the rights being fought for by Britain far outweighed the rights being sacrificed by America, damning the Republican party and the quasi-official *National Intelligencer* as little better than Napoleon's puppets.[19] Under British law, and that of every other state in Europe, nationality was permanent; only in America was it transferable. This led to the large scale fraudulent issue of 'naturalisation' certificates for a trifling consideration, often no more than two shillings and six pence, or 'half a dollar' in British slang,[20] by American consuls abroad, and in American port cities desperate for seamen. The precise number of genuine American citizens to be forcibly impressed is uncertain. As every anglophone seafarer in the Atlantic region had known for more than a century the outbreak of war was swiftly followed by widespread impressment. The Royal Navy had to be manned, and losses had to be made good. Impressment was an occupational hazard; the alternative was to go ashore, take up coasting, fishing or river work. Men continued to take the risk because the rewards were high – they preferred American merchant ships because the wages were higher than on British warships.

New England's opposition to war was built on the bitter experience of Embargo and Non-Intercourse. Without trade the region was ruined, and some considered this was the Republican objective, destroying their political rivals by bankruptcy, or by provoking the British to do their work for them. It was little wonder that New England militia would not cross the state line to fight.[21]

When the sloop USS *Hornet*, Master Commandant James Lawrence, returned from Europe on 22 May 1812 the situation was clear: both Britain and France refused to repeal their measures against American trade. Madison set out the case for war with Britain on 1 June 1812. Claiming that British policy had nothing to do with the exigencies of the Napoleonic conflict, but was solely driven by the desire for commercial monopoly, he argued that a relaxation of the British Orders in Council would have given the Americans sufficient leverage to secure the redress of their grievances against France. This was either monumentally naïve or desperately dishonest. He persisted in the absurd fiction that the French had repealed the Berlin and Milan Decrees. Tipping his hat to the War Hawks, Madison claimed to have proof that the British had incited recent attacks by the 'savages'. In reality Governor Harrison had attacked the Indians, ensuring they would fight alongside the British in 1812. Madison's indictment concluded with the fatuous observation that Britain was already in 'a state of war against the United States'. He admitted the

French were equally at fault, but postponed any reflections on their conduct while discussions were held in Paris.[22] This was disingenuous. He knew that no such discussions could be held because Napoleon had invaded Russia, for what many in the Republican administration believed would be the final campaign of the European conflict. This was the most significant factor in Madison's decision. In April 1813 he admitted the war had been based on the assumption that, when Napoleon defeated Russia, Britain would make 'reasonable' concessions. By this he meant an end of the Orders in Council and of impressment. The former was possible; the latter was not. With Britain deeply committed to an all-out war, and her army fighting to liberate Spain from French tyranny, it seemed the time had come to complete the work of 1776, to conquer Canada, which would be, as Jefferson observed, 'a mere matter of marching'. Even if the administration intended to hold Canada as a surety for future British good behaviour, it is hardly credible to argue that once installed an American 'government' would have departed peacefully. Secretary of State James Monroe confessed: 'It might be difficult to relinquish Territory which had been conquered.' Furthermore, the American government had form when it came to filibustering other people's territory, be they Indians or Europeans, and was even then actively engaged in the illegal seizure of Spanish East Florida.

Both Jefferson and Madison favoured expansion without war, by purchase, negotiation or filibuster. If Madison seemed to be more concerned with the growing list of maritime insults suffered at French hands than his predecessor, he still hankered after securing Florida from Spain, with French support. Vulnerable neighbours would be despoiled, by any means. Early in 1812 Georgia militia invaded Spanish East Florida under the most transparent of pretexts, seeking land and the removal of feared free black and Indian populations.[23] While Madison did not order the 'Patriot' war, he selected General George Matthews to 'investigate' the loyalty of a Spanish province that had long been a key target of American diplomacy.[24] Madison, Jefferson and

Monroe shared an entirely unwarranted belief that the United States was entitled to East Florida under the Louisiana Purchase, and developed fictional claims to the territory. There is no reason to doubt that, had the Patriots succeeded, Florida would have become part of the United States. The reason why most accounts assume Madison ordered the attack is that the 'Patriot' War fits the pattern of interaction between the United States and the Spanish American Empire between 1800 and 1898, one of opportunistic despoliation driven by land hunger, internal politics and an aggressive, xenophobic culture of racial superiority.[25]

The invasion of Florida demonstrates that, while American belligerence may have been fuelled by Britain's overbearing, arrogant actions at sea, the key question for American governments was land, land for farming and settlement, land to be taken from the hunter-gatherer Indians, decadent Spaniards and if necessary the British. Then, rather than face Britain at sea, the administration decided to seize Canada. The cultural values of the Republican Party were clear – possession, profitable crops and slaves. Britain, Spain and the Indians all challenged those core values; with Spain in chaos and Britain committed to an existential conflict the Indians would be short of friends. Madison could wrap up the Republican agenda: Florida, Canada and on to Mexico. In an atmosphere that made it possible to stage a filibuster invasion of a sovereign state in peacetime and push the Indians all the way from the Ohio to the Alabama into a corner, the American challenge to Britain would always be military, not naval.

Many have argued that America went to war in 1812 to uphold national honour. If the administration really elected to fight for a nebulous notion without adequate armed forces, in the face of vehement opposition from a substantial minority of the population, they deserved to be hanged. Principles are fine possessions, but without national unity and military power they could neither be afforded, nor protected. James Madison had picked a fight he could not win, ostensibly over issues that few Americans cared about. It is hardly surprising it took the British six months to get round to responding effectively.

In Britain the economic down-turn caused by Napoleon's Continental System, a slump in exports and concerns about the banking system, sparked interest in repealing the Orders in Council. However, by 1812 Russian ports were open and business was booming.[26] The assassination of anti-American Prime Minister Spencer Perceval in May 1812 opened the way for relaxation, but ultimately it was a concern to retain the profitable American market, not fear of American action, that prompted the suspension of the Orders. No sooner had they been suspended than the opposition rallied behind a hard-line interpretation of British maritime belligerent rights. British opponents of the Orders were self-interested, not pro-American. Britain did not fear America, and few doubted that the Americans would reverse the declaration once they learnt the Orders had been suspended. Consequently large shipments were dispatched to American ports, while the outbreak of war between France and Russia gave further cause for economic optimism.

In the event Britain revoked the Orders in Council on 16 June, too late for news to reach Washington before the vote for war. But it is far from certain that an earlier decision would have made any difference: the House of Representatives and the Senate voted on sectional lines. As John Randolph sourly noted, 'Agrarian cupidity, not maritime right, urges the war ... a war of rapine, privateering, a scuffle and scramble for plunder.'[27] How far the War Hawks looked to conquer Canada, and how far they believed temporary occupation would secure British concessions is uncertain. One thing is clear: American expansionists had no history of returning their ill-gotten gains. The War Hawks assumed that the conquest of Canada, and the starvation of the West Indies by American embargo, would be quick, simple and decisive. In truth they overlooked the real British weakness, their dependence on American grain to feed the army in the Iberian Peninsula. In 1812 a million bushels of American wheat fuelled Wellington's march into Spain.[28] Too many Republican politicians had an interest in this trade for any action to be taken: Republican Baltimore was the epicentre of the Iberian grain trade. When French warships burnt American grain ships off the Portuguese coast they reduced American policy to absurdity. Madison was about to make France and America co-belligerents while Napoleon was destroying American ships that carried grain to his enemies. Satisfied that the Americans were finally committed to war, Napoleon saw no need to encourage them; his cruisers burnt more American grain ships later in the year, and he rejected American requests to reduce the French import duties.[29]

The American declaration of war was opportunistic. The filibuster in East Florida and the invasion of Canada leave little doubt that American aims were territorial; the timing reflected Washington's anticipation of another crushing Napoleonic victory. Madison expected that his privateers would be able to use French ports, and he put more faith in Napoleon's vast, largely impotent navy than its creator. Soon after the declaration, news that Britain had repealed the Orders in Council reached Washington, bringing a startled Madison to his senses. Suddenly anxious to end the conflict before it had really begun, he responded positively to the British diplomatic initiative. Once more he offered to exclude British seamen from American ships, if the British would renounce impressment. This was impossible in wartime, and irrelevant in peacetime. The British suspension of the Orders in Council saw War Hawk journals shift the focus of their propaganda to impressment and compensation for past seizures.[30]

Above all the slow descent to war in 1812 provided a stark reminder of the problems that face smaller powers in an age of total war and the irrelevance of diplomacy in the face of blatant, repeated, unblinking dishonesty. America lacked the power to be taken seriously by London and Paris in the midst of an existential conflict. Britain would not surrender the ancient legal right to impress her own sailors; France would not concede the Floridas, or free trade. Both France and Britain were overbearing, arrogant and dismissive of minor neutrals, as great powers have always been in times of national emergency. Fine words and elevated principles were not enough.

AMERICAN STRATEGY

The character of American policy in mid-1812 can be judged by the decisions of the Congress that voted for war: it funded an enlarged Army, but rejected modest naval increases. Fifty of those who voted for war voted against the Navy.[31] In February 1812 the administration had considered how to wage war. Navy Secretary Hamilton, perhaps disingenuously, raised the idea that the fleet might be kept safe in port. Madison declared it should be used, and if ships were lost they must be replaced. Yet he did nothing to prepare any more ships.

In late May, with war looming, Hamilton needed a strategy. Without a professional advisor in Washington, he asked the senior officers afloat, John Rodgers and Stephen Decatur, how the Navy could annoy British trade to 'the utmost extent', avoiding undue risk, and where it should be based. Rodgers argued that British West India convoys, which passed close by Southern harbours, should be attacked by small warships based at Charleston and Savannah. East India and other Atlantic trades should be targeted by frigates and sloops, while a fast squadron operated on the British coast. Any spare cruisers could operate against the traffic between Britain and British North America. American forces must keep moving, and might occasionally combine to attack an East India convoy.

Following the *Little Belt* incident the British *Naval Chronicle* had condemned Rodgers as a 'buccaneer'; evidently he found the remark highly offensive. He wanted revenge, to give the British further occasion for regret. Rodgers recognised that the loss of a single convoy would cause panic in London, damage Britain's credit, and undermine the war effort. It was the only naval operation that might have a significant effect on the war, boosting the prestige of the Navy, and of Commodore John Rodgers in the process. Attacking British trade, Rodgers argued, would deflect the British from attacking American ships. The deep-draught frigates should be based at Boston and Newport, Rhode Island; he believed it would be impossible to blockade Newport for any length of time.[32]

Decatur took a slightly different line. He favoured a commerce-raiding strategy using ships individually, or at most in pairs, on long cruises. Such a force could still attack a convoy. As the junior commodore, he advised Hamilton to give him an independent command, rather than obliging him to follow Rodgers, and share his prize fund. While Decatur preferred bases at defended harbours like Boston, New London, and Norfolk, Virginia, he did not believe the British could blockade the New England coast in winter, and stressed the need to get the ships to sea before war was declared.[33]

The American decision for war raised important questions about the ability of the state to sustain the conflict. Although technically self-sufficient in basic foodstuffs and raw materials, the United States depended on customs revenue for Federal funding, and coastal shipping to exchange primary produce between North and South. In the War of Independence the British blockade had begun to bite by 1782, leading to rampant inflation and funding crises.[34] Nothing had been done to reduce these dependencies since 1782, leaving America even more exposed to British economic warfare. Furthermore, the War of Independence had been waged as a limited conflict, with the parties seeking a negotiated settlement: the Anglo-French conflict was a total economic struggle, and the British would use the same strategy against America that they employed to fight Napoleon. British grand strategy depended on economic blockade. If American merchant ships could circumvent that blockade British strategy would collapse, and defeat and destruction would follow. American re-exports of French Caribbean produce also attracted the ire of the politically powerful British West India planters and their trade committee.[35] British opinions were widely circulated in America, where key British court judgments and political pamphlets were assiduously reprinted.

America was desperately vulnerable to British economic warfare because 92 per cent of Federal income came from customs revenue. Although America was a vital export market for Britain, especially at the height of Napoleon's Continental System, the balance of visible trade was heavily in Britain's favour, as manufactured goods were exchanged for raw materials and food. The invisible sector of shipping and services may have restored the relationship to one of approximate balance or even an American surplus. Brian Arthur has argued that Madison's administration simply did not understand the balance of trade, believing an export ban would do Britain more harm than America.[36] British analysts who saw American merchant shipping as a weapon in Napoleon's armoury were far closer to the fact. When the import ban took effect in 1811 it hit the very capitalists that Treasury Secretary Gallatin looked to for loans; they responded by investing their money in British government bonds. Without access to foreign capital and unable to raise personal taxes, the American administration was hamstrung. The fatal Republican ideological combination of small government and land hunger blocked pre-war attempts to alleviate the inevitable collapse of Federal revenue. Quite simply the United States lacked the economic means to wage war. To make matters far worse it had picked a fight with an economic super-power. Britain had survived Napoleon's economic blockade, and prospered to the extent that she provided her allies with £35 million in subsidies between 1810 and 1815. The economic impact of the American war was minimal, because the British warfare state was already fully mobilised in 1812, generating strikingly high levels of tax revenue and loan capital. Borrowing was easy, while the income tax and other non-customs measures proved resilient. If proof were needed, then the stability of British paper provided a perfect demonstration of British economic power. American bills were soon discounted and the rate kept falling; no one trusted paper dollars. American sailors deserted in droves when paid in paper: British paper money passed at face value.

BRITISH STRATEGY

The British response to America since 1803 had been dominated by the far larger struggle that was raging in Europe. While the Anglo-French conflict frequently threatened to become a truly global one, British naval dominance, diplomacy and money restricted it to the European continent. The British systematically captured hostile cruiser bases, while securing commercial control of the Spanish and Portuguese Empires. By 1810 only a handful of French and Dutch possessions in the Indian Ocean and Asia were still supporting commerce raiders. The economic–strategic need to crush every threat to oceanic commerce ensured they would soon fall. Major amphibious expeditions seized Mauritius and Java in 1811, depriving Napoleon of his last colonies and bases beyond Europe. The British conducted these distant operations with locally based land and sea forces, without detaching units from Europe.[37] The Spanish uprising against Napoleon placed key ports in South and Central America in friendly hands, most colonies remaining loyal to the *junta* at Cadiz. With the cruiser threat largely restricted to European waters, the British could redistribute naval resources.

The campaign in the Iberian Peninsula dominated the military effort; no British troops would be diverted from that theatre before the end of 1813. The Duke of Wellington's 1812 campaign secured two key border fortresses, briefly captured Madrid, and forced the French to abandon Andalusia. By November 1812, despite the recent retreat from Madrid, the initiative in Iberia was firmly in allied hands. Distracted by the Russian campaign and defeated in key battles, French power faltered. Within a year Wellington would be in France. The critical importance of Spain ensured that such troop reinforcements as reached Canada came from the quiescent West Indies and the wider Empire, rather than Europe or Britain. In the last months of peace the British had dispatched three regiments from the West Indies to Canada, as a precaution.[38] However, such regiments tended to be under-strength, weakened by garrison duty in pestilential climates, and even in August 1813 there were more British troops in the West Indies and Bermuda than Canada.[39]

Throughout 1812 the possibility that Napoleon might defeat Russia, creating a pan-European super-state, dominated British planning. Only in January 1813 did authentic intelligence reach London of the disastrous French retreat to the Berezina River and Prussia's switching sides. Good news from Russia and Spain prompted the Cabinet to take active measures against America. The only reinforcements were naval; any spare troops and cash were deployed to support the growing coalition against Napoleon. The European war would dominate British diplomacy and strategy throughout the American war. Napoleon was the real enemy, and Europe the main theatre. American hostility provided an annoying distraction.

INVADING CANADA

The severe mismatch between American strategy and American resources at the outbreak of war only emphasised the degree to which Madison expected British concessions. His selection of the aged, corpulent Henry Dearborn as commander-in-chief symbolised a slow, ineffective build-up of military strength. This proved disastrous because the conquest of Canada – the only way Madison could secure his publicly stated war aims: the removal of the hostile economic measures – required American armies ready to cross the frontier in strength before the British could respond. Instead the American army lacked manpower and training. Most units were short of officers, men, equipment and even common doctrine.

Canada may have been divided by language and administration and sparsely populated, but it was not ready to become American. Most anglophone Canadians were Empire Loyalists, forcibly expelled from the United States, while the staunchly Catholic French-Canadians proved no more enthusiastic for the Republican allies of the atheist French Revolution. This nascent national feeling would be reflected in the wartime performance of locally raised regiments and militia which, together with the small garrison of British regulars, defeated successive American attacks.

Receiving news of the outbreak of war, General Isaac Brock, Governor of Upper Canada, ordered his forces on Lake Huron to capture the American position at Fort Michilimackinac at the narrows that connected Lake Huron with Lake Michigan. The operation was a complete, bloodless, success. The fort surrendered on 17 July, securing British control of a rich fur trade region. More significantly this early success secured Brock the support of Indian leader Tecumseh and his followers.

Madison's strategy followed the advice of General Dearborn and General William Hull, then commanding at Detroit. They suggested a two-pronged attack on Upper and Lower Canada. Madison urged Hull to advance into Upper Canada, but the aged Revolutionary War hero had been rendered mentally infirm by a stroke. After a brief foray across the border Hull pulled back to Detroit. Here he surrendered his army of 2,500 to General Brock and 1,300 Anglo-Canadian troops after a brief artillery bombardment. Brock's master-stroke was psychological: he unsettled his wavering opponent by suggesting he might not be able to control his Indian auxiliaries after an assault. For the rest of the season the North-West frontier witnessed one American disaster after another as each force was humiliated or driven back by British, Canadian and Indian units.

The main thrust of the American attack had been aimed at seizing Montreal, and then laying siege to Quebec, capital of Lower Canada. Madison believed this would secure his war aims. He relied on numbers and enthusiasm to overwhelm the tiny British and Canadian forces. However, his plans were crippled by local politics and the inability of the government to control the individual states. Most states that bordered on Canada opposed the war, reflecting their close economic ties with Canada, and had voted for Federalist governors and congressmen. This seriously weakened the American effort throughout the war. In New England Federalist opposition ensured that the militia was not called out, aborting plans to invade New Brunswick. The administrative and logistical pivot of the American attack on Canada lay at Albany, in the north of New York State. This was the political heartland of the Clinton family, leading Republicans but opponents of Madison and his war. Initially Dearborn signed an armistice with the Governor of Lower Canada, General Henry Prevost, but this was repudiated by the administration. Then Brock paraded Hull's captured army before the American forces gathered on the Niagara frontier, which did nothing to improve their morale. Finally the Americans crossed the Niagara River on 13 October 1812, but most of the militiamen refused to follow the regulars, who were driven back by the outnumbered British at Queenston Heights, before surrendering. A handful of units escaped the debacle, only to disintegrate before the season had ended.

Unfortunately for the British the dynamic, inspirational Brock was killed early in the battle, leading from the front. His loss would be severely felt throughout the rest of the war. By blunting the initial American invasions, Brock and his composite force created a Canadian identity that gave this war a particular importance when the country came of age. The victory was almost immediately turned into a Canadian national myth.

On the other side Henry Dearborn belatedly crossed the frontier at the head of Lake Champlain in November, but returned quickly after an inconclusive skirmish. He had achieved nothing.

The British response to successive American invasions would be dominated by Prevost's view that Quebec was the key to Canada. Anxiously waiting for reinforcements from Britain, he remained on the defensive, and tried to avoid exciting the Americans. Like the government in London he had believed that Madison's government was weak and divided, and would not go to war. Only the conclusion was wrong. The British were convinced that when news of the repeal of the Orders in Council arrived the war would be stopped. When the Americans simply shifted ground to make impressment the *casus belli* the British were convinced that Madison, a typical Francophile Republican, was in league with Napoleon, and bent on the conquest of Canada and Florida. Brock's victories gave the ministers time to send reinforcements. The defence of Canada in 1812 convinced many waverers that it would be possible to hold the country, increasing the support for the war effort.

NAVAL OPERATIONS

On the day war was declared, 18 June, Navy Secretary Hamilton wrote to Captain Isaac Hull, USS *Constitution*, then completing his crew at Annapolis on Chesapeake Bay, with orders to join Commodore Rodgers's squadron at sea off New York. Hamilton expressed no great confidence in his service: observing that HMS *Belvidera* 'is on our coast', he stressed 'you are not to understand me as impelling you to battle, previously to your having confidence in your crew . . . or with a reasonable prospect of success'.[40] By contrast John Rodgers recognised that with so few British warships on station he could defeat them in detail, occupying the mid-Atlantic approaches until British reinforcements arrived.[41] Anxious to capture a rich West India convoy, he slipped out of New York before Hamilton's belated orders of the 22nd arrived. Hamilton wanted to keep his two small squadrons close to the coast, stationed between Chesapeake Bay and New York, to cover incoming merchant ships. He did not want ships detached singly, nor should they 'voluntarily encounter a force superior to your own'.[42] On the 23rd, two days out from New York, Rodgers, commanding three frigates, a sloop and a brig, met the 36-gun frigate HMS *Belvidera*, Captain Richard Byron, about 100 miles south-west of the Nantucket Shoals. Byron had been looking for a French privateer when he fell in with an altogether more formidable foe.[43] Although he knew nothing about war, Byron was understandably cautious. Observing the American squadron approach under a press of canvas he had little doubt that they were hostile.

Rodgers led the chase in the *President*, but superior seamanship kept *Belvidera* just out of reach. By mid-afternoon

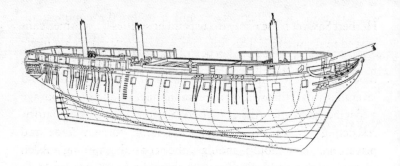

The USS *President*: an American icon.

Rodgers had closed to less than a mile; both ships opened fire. In an action lasting no more than ten minutes both ships suffered slight damage to their rigging, although their speed remained unimpaired. Then *President*'s 24-pounder bow-chaser exploded, and detonated a spare powder charge. Sixteen men were killed or wounded, including Rodgers, who sustained a fractured leg. The forecastle was wrecked, and part of the main deck badly damaged. Unable to mount another bow-chaser, Rodgers put the helm over, firing the starboard broadside into *Belvidera*'s rigging. Since these guns were loaded with round shot, for close action, the broadside did little damage. In the process Rodgers lost ground, and a second broadside proved equally unsuccessful. Meanwhile, *Belvidera* kept up a steady fire from her stern guns, cutting away American sails and rigging. After two more broadsides, Rodgers could see that the British were lightening ship, throwing spare gear overboard and pumping out the water butts. After 2½ hours the British ship stretched out of range; by midnight Rodgers had given up.[44] In an action settled by speed, the American ships, heavily laden for a long cruise, were at a disadvantage. Byron had the skill and the nerve to exploit his advantage.

The British reaction to the American declaration reflected the over-riding importance of avoiding another conflict. On 22 July Augustus Foster, British Minister in Washington, advised

Herbert Sawyer to be ready to suspend hostilities if the Americans agreed to negotiate.[45] This outcome was considered highly likely by Andrew Allen, British Consul in Boston. His local contacts reported that the war was unpopular, and New England would 'eventually overthrow the present administration'. To encourage a pacific outcome Allen advised Sawyer to be conciliatory, restricting his war to American warships, foreign trade and privateers. He should indulge the coastal shipping. Allen recognised that the most damaging thing the Americans could do would be to stop the flow of flour and grain to the Peninsula.[46]

While Foster could offer no insight into American naval plans, he reported that letters of marque had been authorised. Sawyer could anticipate that a swarm of privateers would be at sea before many days had passed. Foster also reported that Hull's *Constitution* lay in the River Potomac near Washington, and offered a prescient warning:

Their Frigates of the largest rate carry 30 long 24-pounders on the main deck and 24 carronades of 32 and 48 pounds on the quarter deck and forecastle . . . It would have a very bad effect upon the general state of affairs here should they succeed in capturing any of our ships even though by superior numbers, and I should hope you would be able to collect your force so as to ensure success in any engagement.[47]

Remaining ashore at Halifax to direct the squadron and await orders from London, Sawyer recognised the importance of American grain and timber for Nova Scotia, the West Indies and the army in Spain. Ship-building materials for Halifax were a priority: repairs would increase exponentially now that war had been declared, and he depended on American supplies. Coming after twenty years of all-out conflict with France this was a curious war: it had only just been declared, yet British diplomats were convinced it would stop, either by government action, or internal uprising. Left to create strategy from political chaos amid considerable uncertainty, Sawyer wisely deployed his scant force on essential defensive operations, to counter the initial American thrust.

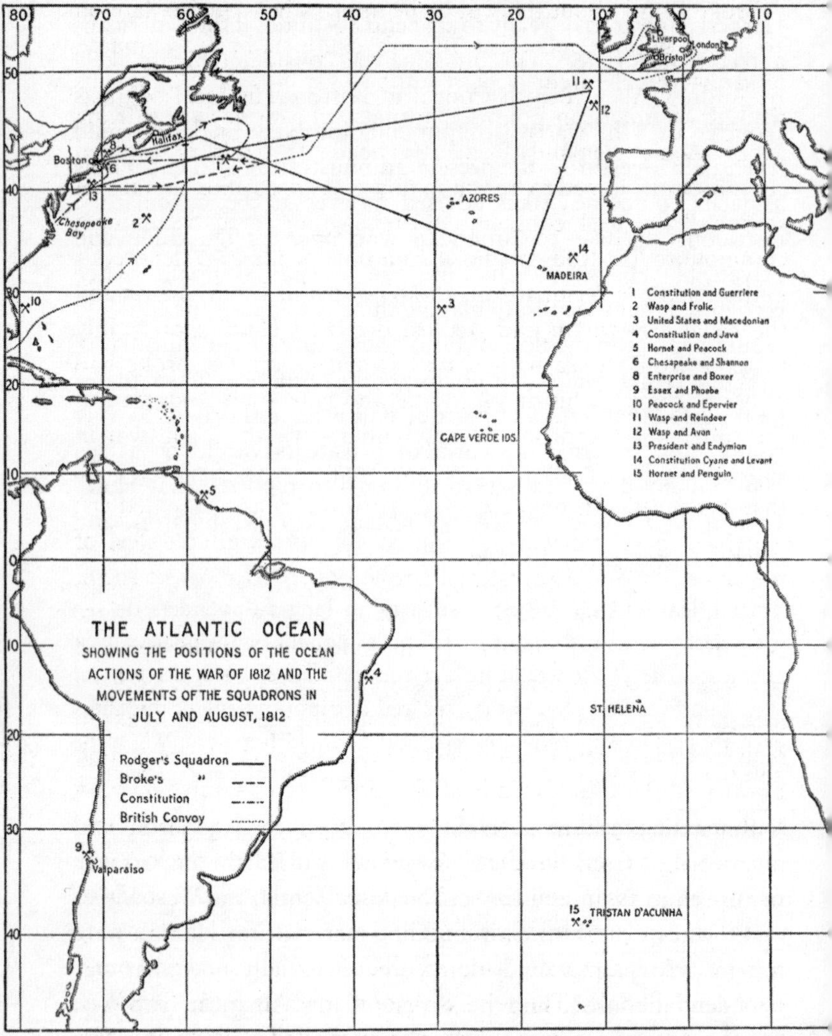

THE ATLANTIC OCEAN
SHOWING THE POSITIONS OF THE OCEAN ACTIONS OF THE WAR OF 1812 AND THE MOVEMENTS OF THE SQUADRONS IN JULY AND AUGUST, 1812
Rodger's Squadron
Broke's "
Constitution
British Convoy
1 Constitution and Guerriere
2 Wasp and Frolic
3 United States and Macedonian
4 Constitution and Java
5 Hornet and Peacock
6 Chesapeake and Shannon
8 Enterprise and Boxer
9 Essex and Phoebe
10 Peacock and Epervier
11 Wasp and Reindeer
12 Wasp and Avon
13 President and Endymion
14 Constitution Cyane and Levant
15 Hornet and Penguin
Liverpool
London
Bristol
Halifax
Boston
Chesapeake Bay
AZORES
MADEIRA
CAPE VERDE IDS.
ST. HELENA
TRISTAN D'ACUNHA
Valparaiso

The war at sea: opening moves.

Broke heard about the war as he approached Halifax late on 30 June. While applauding Byron's conduct, he was amused by Rodgers's apparent lack of spirit to get close and fight. His reading of American political journals led him to expect 'King Mob' would demand Rodgers's head. If Rodgers escaped censure Broke hoped to hunt him down. As the senior captain on station, Broke took command of the seagoing force, becoming a commodore like Rodgers, hoisting a blue pendant to denote his authority. Broke's squadron, the 64-gun third rate *Africa* and the frigates *Shannon* and *Aeolus*, departed Halifax on 5 July to rendezvous at sea with *Belvidera* and *Guerriere*. Broke had only one thing on his mind, to find and fight John Rodgers and the American squadron. Victory would settle the naval war in short order, hopefully bringing the Yankees to their senses. As they headed south towards New York the British checked the American ports for warships and swept up a veritable fleet of merchant ships and privateers. Broke destroyed most of them, to avoid detaching valuable men as prize crew. He was more concerned to secure intelligence. Interviews with fishermen and ship masters, and American newspapers, suggested that Rodgers had followed his instincts, heading north for the Grand Banks in search of a homeward-bound West Indies convoy. Convoys took priority so Broke retraced his route north. On 15 July *Shannon* took the 14-gun brig USS *Nautilus*, Lieutenant William Crane, after a long chase.[48] From the American perspective the loss was wholly unnecessary: Hamilton had despatched *Nautilus* solely to carry vague directions for Rodgers to take care when returning to port.[49] At least Crane had time to destroy his signal and other confidential books. The prize was soon at sea as HMS *Emulous*. Six of her crew were sent to England, suspected of being deserters from the Royal Navy.[50] Five Americans were sent back to be exchanged for British ratings; McDormer, an Irishman, was not a deserter and volunteered for the Royal Navy.[51] Papers found on *Nautilus* confirmed Broke's analysis that if he followed the convoy he might find the enemy, almost the entire American Navy, and wipe it out in one fell stroke.

We were then in a most advantageous situation for the destruction of the enemy's fleet, and for intercepting their ships of war on their return to Port, whether Chesapeake or New York; but having received undoubted information that Commodore Rodgers was gone upon the Grand Banks of Newfoundland to lie in wait for our West India Convoy and considering the vast injury his squadron might do in that point, as well to our trade as to the supplies and reinforcements coming out to Halifax and Quebec it appeared to me the more important duty to abandon the plan we had entered upon of distressing the enemy's trade, for the protection of our own, and I determined accordingly to proceed in quest of the American squadron instead of waiting for their return.[52]

Instead he ran into Isaac Hull's *Constitution* off the New Jersey shoreline on 17 July. After completing a major overhaul, cleaning and repairing the copper and refitting the rigging, Hull had his ship in fine order. Furthermore, the ship was light, having loaded only eight weeks' stores.[53] Recognising the danger at the last minute, Hull turned away, starting a second, equally tense contest of seamanship. In light airs both sides resorted to towing: Broke had the boats of his squadron haul *Shannon* into range, only for Hull to exploit the fact that the action took place in shallow water to kedge ahead. In a fine example of practical seamanship, suggested by first lieutenant Charles Morris, the Americans used the ship's boats to lay out anchors ahead, and then hauled the ship forward on the capstan. Broke could not kedge because the British boats would have been under fire from the American stern-chasers. Hull skilfully exploited the fickle, shifting wind to baffle Broke's attempt to bring on a battle. The following day an equally tense chase under sail developed. Hull finally escaped on the 21st after a brilliant display of seamanship, skill and resolve. Clean copper and outstanding skill ensured Hull, 'escaped by very superior sailing tho' the frigates under my orders are remarkable fast ships'.[54] Hull, Morris and sailing master John Aylwin had few peers as practical seamen.

After a full-scale post-mortem in *Shannon*'s stern cabin, Broke set off for the Grand Banks, hoping to catch 'an active and artful enemy, who will, if he can, do vast mischief to our trade, and perhaps (God forbid) evade after all the vengeance we intend to wreak on him'. He was magnanimous in defeat. Hull had demonstrated the Americans were good seamen; no Frenchman would have handled his ship with such skill, 'but we will have her yet'. On the 29th Broke caught up with what he assumed to be Rodgers's target, a sixty-strong West India convoy escorted by HMS *Thetis*, a worn-out old frigate. Having departed Jamaica on 1 July, Captain Byam only learnt of the war from Broke, who reinforced the escort to 'ensure their safety and I hope our escorting them may lead to a meeting of the squadrons'. This he presumed was 'the prey Commodore Rodgers came to lie in wait for, so we hope by following the game to meet the *poachers*'.[55] In fact Rodgers was a thousand miles to the east, chasing another convoy. Once Byam's convoy passed the Grand Banks Broke planned to return to New York, detaching the lumbering *Africa* to Halifax en route. He entrusted Byam with a report of the current disposition of Sawyer's squadron, his best estimate of the location of the American frigates, sloops and privateers, and the latest news from Canada. He remained optimistic: 'Our squadron is in excellent service order and confident of destroying our Enemy's little navy if we are fortunate enough to meet them.' Then Broke set off after an American ship, heading back to the American coast. He had detached HMS *Guerriere* to Halifax to change her rotten lightning-damaged masts.[56] The Jamaica convoy chased by Rodgers eventually reached Spithead unharmed on 24 August, a major fillip for British morale. Rodgers's cruise may have distracted the British from their own offensive, but the results were singularly unimpressive.

PRIVATEERING

Many Republicans put their faith in the strategic effect of privateering – licensed predation funded by private capital – as an economic, ideologically sound system of warfare to damage and distract the British. However, the results were decidedly mixed. This was a high-risk enterprise. For every successful cruise there were several that failed, leaving owners ruined, and seaman incarcerated. The steady drain of skilled men into privateers weakened the American naval effort, condemning many men to imprisonment at Halifax and Dartmoor. By contrast the cruise of Continental Navy veteran Joshua Barney in the *Rossie* between mid-July and early October 1812 netted 3,600 tons of shipping, 217 prisoners and over a million dollars in prize and ransom. This one privateer did more damage to British commerce than any warship, and Barney made far more prize money than any naval officer.[57]

Nor was the loss of ships and men the only risk to consider when fitting out privateers. Many merchants feared direct reprisals. Within a month of war the merchants of Salem, who had been quick to fit out privateers, became anxious that captured British crews returning to Halifax would reveal the weakness of the harbour defences;[58] they had reason to be fearful. Nonetheless Salem backed the war, hoping to cut into British Asian markets.

Many New England privateers headed north to operate in the Bay of Fundy and further north in the Gulf of St Lawrence. British cruisers and Canadian privateers were soon on station, taking a significant number of American ships. Between 1 July and 25 August the Halifax squadron alone took twenty-four privateers and nearly 1,000 men in the area around Cape Sable, the Bay of Fundy and Shelburne.[59] These captures provided ample human capital to recover the crews of warships and merchant vessels that fell into American hands. Sawyer, however, made a clear distinction between semi-piratical privateersmen and honourable naval ratings. He did not wish to exchange the former.[60]

By collecting the squadron and hunting Rodgers, Sawyer and Broke passed up the opportunity to attack inbound American merchant ships, but they also ensured that a weak force, one small battleship and five frigates, was not dispersed and picked off by locally superior American forces. Sawyer also only received written confirmation on 4 July that Congress had declared war and at this stage most British officers expected that when the

Americans learnt of the suspension of the Orders in Council they would return to diplomatic methods.

CONSTITUTION AND GUERRIERE

After his hard-earned escape, Hull judged the British would already be blockading New York, so he headed north for Boston.[61] Finding no orders in port he decided to set out for the shipping lanes east of the Gulf of St Lawrence, to recapture American prizes heading for England and generally cut up British shipping.[62] On 2 August the USS *Constitution* left Boston harbour, without a British vessel in sight. Passing Cape Sable, Hull cruised in the approaches to the Gulf of St Lawrence, the most promising area for British shipping. Like Broke he was anxious for intelligence, gathering useful information from captured merchant ships and an American privateer, before setting a course to meet a British warship reported to be cruising off Newfoundland.[63] However, Hull had a rather larger scheme in mind. Well aware that orders were en route from Washington to turn over his ship to Captain William Bainbridge, he had purchased charts of the Caribbean, Brazil, West Africa and the River Plate, warning his father 'I may not return for some time.'[64] While his bold decision soon paid dividends he would not need those exotic charts.

On the afternoon of 19 August Hull sighted and pursued the 18-pounder frigate HMS *Guerriere*, Captain James Dacres. Broke had detached *Guerriere*, a lightly built, elderly decayed French prize, from the squadron to replace her masts. Broke was under no illusions about *Guerriere*'s material condition, the accuracy of her gunnery, or the fighting credentials of her captain. While Hull described his opponent as 'a large frigate', he knew he had a major advantage in size, firepower and crew.

When *Guerriere* backed her sails and lay-to, evidently willing to fight, Hull reduced to standard fighting canvas – topsails – and prepared for battle. For almost an hour Dacres manoeuvred. Hull realised Dacres was hoping to secure the weather gauge, but he thwarted every attempt. Well aware that his defective masts

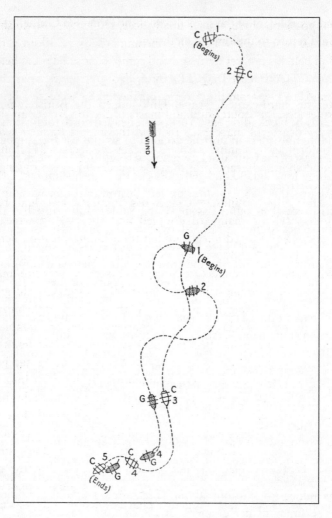

The engagement between the *Constitution* and *Guerriere*.

would not stand any heavy work, Dacres only wore his ship round, unwilling to risk the more stressful manoeuvre of tacking, and he did not use a large spread of canvas. Normally the smaller, faster and more manoeuvrable *Guerriere* would have run rings around the big 44, but rotten masts and an expert opponent blunted her only advantage. Realising the ship-handling duel was going nowhere, Dacres finally accepted battle, only to show his inexperience by wasting his opening broadside at long range. Hull held his fire, set more sail and came to close quarters before replying. Although Dacres's well-drilled gun crews fired three rounds to two from the Americans, the lighter weight of British projectiles, the stouter hull and masts of the big American ship, and a degree of inaccuracy reduced the impact of their work. Conforming to standard American tactical doctrine, Hull fired round shot and grape shot into the masts and lower rigging of the *Guerriere*.

After fifteen minutes *Guerriere*'s mizzen mast had been shot away, the mainyard crippled and the rigging wrecked. *Constitution* ranged ahead, taking up a killing position across her opponent's bow, firing two raking broadsides into the larboard side. At such close range Hull could see his fire 'made great havock amongst his men on the forecastle and did great injury to his fore-rigging and sails'. With the wreck of the mizzen mast dragging off his starboard quarter Dacres was unable to manoeuvre, the helm effectively useless. Even so, *Guerriere*'s fire had not been ineffective. Most of *Constitution*'s braces had been cut; the American ship now unintentionally bore up into the wind, exposing her stern to the enemy. Hull put his helm hard over to starboard and the ship slowly swung back before the wind, just as Dacres was closing to rake. The two ships collided, leaving *Guerriere*'s bowsprit over the American ship's stern. Both captains called up their boarding parties from the gun deck. Facing a much bigger and more heavily manned opponent, this was Dacres's last, desperate chance. Neither side was able to board, however, both suffering heavy casualties in a furious exchange of musketry.

Finally Hull set more sail and drew clear of the *Guerriere*. At this point the British bowsprit snapped and the damaged, defective foremast went over the side, and took the mainmast with it. Seeing his opponent completely disabled, Hull hauled off to repair his rigging. Without her masts the *Guerriere* rolled like a log in the troughs of the swell, her gun ports alternately dipping under water. The ship was defenceless; Dacres consulted his officers, they had no option but surrender. The lightly built ship had been smashed by heavier American shot, with sections of her hull planking literally torn out, leaving many holes on or below the water line. *Guerriere* lost fifteen killed and sixty-three wounded, most, according to Dacres, from musketry and canister when the *Constitution* lay across her bow. The Americans suffered seven killed and seven wounded. Although it is common to ascribe this and other British defeats to poor gunnery, *Guerriere* had fired effectively, leaving the *Constitution*'s massive lower masts so badly damaged that they had to be replaced.[65] This was a creditable performance.

Overnight Hull removed the prisoners and wounded. Daylight revealed the *Guerriere* to be a complete wreck. Without the resources to effect repairs, and little hope of keeping her afloat, Hull blew up his shattered prize. His ship crowded with prisoners and wounded men, Hull had no option but to abandon his cruise after only a fortnight. *Constitution* returned to Boston on 30 August to a riotous welcome. After two months of dismal news the United States finally had something to celebrate. Hull had handled his ship very well, exploiting his advantages to the full. Amid the euphoria, and without the prize to prove otherwise, most chose to celebrate Hull's victory as a fair and equal contest. America's need for success outweighed considerations of equity, amply repaying the decision to build the super-frigates almost two decades earlier. Making this an equal contest allowed a Republican administration, newly alive to the value of the Navy, to shift their propaganda hyperbole from land to sea. As long as no one was so foolish as to bring one of these 'equal' ships home no one need be any the wiser.[66] The British crew, soon exchanged, was worth far more to a hard-pressed Admiralty than a second-hand ship.

Instead of pausing for reflection, an unthinking British press blindly accepted the idea of humiliating defeat; the *Times* blustered that the Navy's 'spell of victory' had been shattered.[67] Broke, who heard the news when he returned to Halifax on

20 September, was more sanguine. The Americans had been fortunate, and he hoped it would make them more confident. He had no doubt the British had the edge in skill and courage, the Americans in size and weight. He took comfort in the news of Wellington's great victory at Salamanca, and envied his brother Charles the glory of battle. Broke knew the best answer to the loss would be taking station off Boston, to seek out the enemy.

When Dacres and his crew returned to Halifax, Broke interviewed the unfortunate Captain over dinner, anxious for every detail of the American ship, her guns, gunnery, tactics and drill. Dacres blamed his defeat on the loss of his masts, which he considered little more than accidental, seriously under-estimating the deliberation with which the Americans had fired into his rigging. It is uncertain how far Broke was convinced by this argument. He did not rate Dacres very highly, reckoning his ship well-painted rather than efficient. Broke hoped this success, although secured by 'a very superior force', would 'make the Yankees so insolent that perhaps they may force their ships to risk a battle'. He pinned his hopes on meeting the elusive Rodgers.[68]

The customary court martial for the loss of his ship, whose members included Broke, honourably acquitted Dacres of blame. His peers accepted the argument that the poor material condition of the ship, and loss of the mizzen mast caused the defeat. There was more than a little truth in the argument: the latest survey of the ship in January 1812 had estimated her effective life at six months.[69] While *Guerriere*'s defects may explain why the action took the precise course it did the result was a foregone conclusion. Facing an opponent 50 per cent more powerful in guns, tons and men, Dacres's only hope of avoiding defeat lay in running away, a tactical choice that would have seen him cashiered, or shot. That Dacres had made the correct choice in fighting, and accepting defeat, became clear when the Admiralty expressed their 'regret at the loss sustained on this occasion'.[70] They were concerned about the men, not the ship.

PRESIDENT

If Broke was sanguine, John Rodgers, who arrived in Boston on 31 August, shortly after Hull's triumphant return, found the situation galling. His five-ship formation had taken a mere seven merchantmen, and not a single warship. While Alfred Thayer Mahan stressed Rodgers's claim that his squadron had distracted the British from American merchant ships this was special pleading by an unsuccessful commander, echoed because it chimed with the opinions of the high priest of American battlefleet sea power. By his own confession Rodgers had not set out to cover returning American shipping; he had been engaged in a single-minded pursuit of a rich West India convoy, following a trail of 'Cocoa nut shells and orange peel' almost into the English Channel. These items would have been useful to the Americans, their cruise being foreshortened by 'that wretched disease scurvy'.[71] The outbreak had indeed been so bad that Rodgers did not regret missing a battle with Broke's squadron.[72] Herbert Sawyer soon received the 'unpleasant information' that Rodgers had returned safely to Boston, albeit after an unsuccessful cruise, 'many of the crews having died of scurvy'. By early September almost the entire active frigate force of the United States lay at Boston: *President*, *Constitution*, *United States*, *Congress* and *Chesapeake*, together with the sloops *Wasp* and *Hornet*. Only the *Essex* had been forced away, while *Constellation* was unable to put to sea. Broke necessarily kept his squadron concentrated while Rodgers was a threat, but British diplomacy, not American sea power, limited the imposition of the blockade. The *Guerriere* action left both commodores to regret that fortune had not smiled on them.

At the outbreak of war a number of British seamen were serving in American warships. While Isaac Hull discharged those who came forward, Captain David Porter allowed the crew of the frigate USS *Essex* to administer the old Revolutionary War punishment of tarring and feathering when a shipmate claimed to be British. Porter justified his action by observing that the victim, John Irving, had American papers. As might be expected the papers were fraudulent; born in Newcastle upon Tyne, Irving had never been naturalised. Secretary Hamilton was not amused.[73] Early prisoner exchanges included six seamen from the USS *Congress*, who had declared themselves British. Sawyer lamented 'this is not generally the case, nearly two-thirds of the American frigates crews are English and manifest a disposition to quit them, but means are resorted to, to prevent it'. He would offer an amnesty to those who returned to the colours, both to weaken the enemy, and reinforce his own hard-pressed rosters.[74]

After the tarring and feathering the *Essex* had sailed from New York on 3 July, for a busy cruise between Bermuda and the Grand Banks. On 13 August the inappropriately named *Alert*, drawn into a close-range action with a vastly superior enemy, was overwhelmed by superior gunnery in eight minutes. With about 500 prisoners from nine merchant ships in hand, Porter sent them into St John's, Newfoundland, on the *Alert*, which was disarmed and treated as a cartel; not for the first time Porter was using his initiative, and violating the rules.[75] The unequal contest deprived Porter of the satisfaction of victory, and any kudos he might have gained as the first American to take a British warship. At least he made some money; the lumbering *Alert* was purchased to serve out her days as a guardship and stores hulk.[76]

Cruising north-east of Cape Cod on 4 September, Porter encountered the *Shannon*, in company with an American prize. Mistaking the vessels for two British warships Porter made off, only to be closed down by the faster British frigate. After dark Porter skilfully put about and bore away to the south-west, losing his pursuer in the process. Unable to slip back into Boston or New York, he headed south to the Delaware River.[77] Despite this close shave Porter's cruise had been a great success, measured in captured ships and seamen, and the distraction of British warships. Whether it should be reckoned at his valuation of $300,000 was less certain.[78]

By this time Sawyer had spread his force along the American coast, with *Shannon* and *Belvidera* off New York. Although the naval news was hardly uplifting, he could send home the American colours from Isaac Brock's triumph at Detroit.[79] Ironically, the delegated general, William Hull, was Isaac Hull's uncle! Sawyer desperately needed a few 74-gun battleships, vessels crushingly superior to the American frigates, to blockade Boston, New York and the Chesapeake. With only a single, slow 64 he simply did not have the firepower to take on the concentrated American force, and could not impose a naval blockade.

CHAPTER 3

Looking for a Way Out

News of the American declaration of war prompted a brief outburst of patriotic anger in London, where most had expected a peaceful outcome. The *Times* regretted the need to carry 'the flame and devastation of war' to America, but did so without fear of the outcome. Even America's best friends were convinced the matter would blow over as soon as news that the Orders in Council had been repealed reached Washington. It would take six months of war, and a number of naval defeats, to make the British take the Americans seriously enough to hate them.[1] Throughout the conflict lack of resources left the British on the defensive, reacting to American initiatives. The invasion of Canada determined the main theatre of the conflict, forcing the British to deploy all available military resources to defend the provinces. The Navy sustained the strategic link between Britain and Canada, defending troopships and oceanic commerce, and slowly built up effective naval and economic blockades. Only the last was a truly offensive, coercive measure, and its application was greatly delayed by lack of resources.

Although he shared the widespread hope that the Americans would negotiate, Lord Melville, the First Lord of the Admiralty, wisely consulted his senior officers about the options if they did not. Admiral Lord Keith responded with information about American harbours.[2] Melville summoned Admiral Sir John Borlase Warren to London on 30 July, offering him command of the combined North American and West Indies squadrons. In a career stretching back to the previous American war Warren had been an enterprising frigate commander, an effective diplomat and a loyal parliamentary supporter of the Pitt/Grenville government.[3]

He had been Ambassador to Russia between 1802 and 1804 and later Commander-in-Chief on the North American Station between 1808 and 1810, specifically chosen to reduce tensions after the *Leopard–Chesapeake* incident. Above all he had considerable experience of America and Americans.[4]

Most commentators dismiss Warren with faint praise, under-estimating the profound problems of controlling a war that stretched from Newfoundland to Mexico with inadequate resources, while his political masters back in London took a very different view of the conflict. London only decided to take the conflict seriously some months after war began. The build-up of resources was therefore slow, while the endless demands to protect West Indian trade, which had high-level support in government and Parliament, compromised theatre strategy. Furthermore, the Admiralty consistently under-estimated the scale of the American threat. Warren addressed the problems with carefully considered defensive dispositions, command choices and offensive initiatives. His eventual removal from command had more to do with political pressure from West India interests than ability.

With Napoleon advancing into Russia the government hoped to avoid an awkward distraction. Foreign Secretary Lord Castlereagh ordered Warren to offer the Americans a cessation of hostilities, and authorised him to negotiate, within limits. On 31 July the Cabinet ordered the detention of all American ships at sea and in port, an effective measure that secured many large American ships.[5] Castlereagh stressed that Warren's primary role was to restore peace. Melville spent more time and effort managing his extensive patronage interests, providing Warren with a list of promotion candidates on all three American stations, and the precise order in which they should be promoted.[6] This was not untypical: Melville's political power in Scotland depended on effective use of patronage; his handling of English and Irish clients would be guided by his Cabinet colleagues.

The First Lord of the Admiralty normally conducted a considerable private correspondence with senior officers holding important commands. This allowed both men the freedom to express opinions and requests that could not be entrusted to public dispatches which, as they might be published, tended to be anodyne. In a relationship based on trust and confidence the First Lord's private letters explained the political and diplomatic basis of official orders, discussed strategy and reflected on the merits of subordinate officers. The two men would assess promotion claims based on merit or patronage. However, Warren and Melville were never close; their letters remained guarded, and rather stiff. The subtext was clear: the American war was an awkward embarrassment for the government, and Melville blamed Warren for not making it go away.

Having accepted the appointment Warren received a rich haul of intelligence, records, charts, drawings of ports, statistics and other data to inform the development of strategy. General Dumouriez's 'Memoir on war with America' offered a carefully argued strategic analysis of the conflict, prepared shortly after the *Leopard–Chesapeake* incident, helpfully marked 'Instructions regarding the war'.[7] The exiled French general, a long-term British resident, made a significant contribution to British strategic planning throughout the Revolutionary and Napoleonic era.[8] Once war had been declared the Hydrographer of the Navy, Captain Thomas Hurd, secured a large supply of North American charts, from Laurie & Whittle of Fleet Street, including fifty sets of Halifax harbour and the Gulf of St Lawrence.[9] Throughout the campaign Warren assiduously collected and processed every scrap of human, cartographic and technical intelligence he could acquire; soon his files bulged with American coastal charts, captured orders and signal logs.

On 3 August Warren received orders to unite the three American stations under his command, to ensure the most efficient use of resources. On the same day Rear Admirals Sawyer and Laforey and Vice Admiral Stirling, respectively commanders of the Halifax, Leeward Islands and Jamaica stations, were directed to place themselves under his orders.[10] To provide a suitable fleet the Admiralty added several ships just coming out of refit to his command. Desperately trying to find additional frigates and smaller cruisers to defend trade against American privateers, Melville could only pray for peace in a trying autumn. He waited anxiously for the seasonal return of the Baltic fleet to provide ships and men. He provided Warren with two 74s and 'nine of our heaviest frigates' to control the American Navy and prevent it 'from making any very formidable efforts by sea. If the war continues, however, we must expect considerable annoyance from their Privateers, as soon as they are able to fit out vessels of that description to any extent.'[11] This had an immediate impact on other fleets. The Commander-in-Chief in the Mediterranean learnt that his time-expired battleships would not be relieved until Warren had enough frigates.

The Admiralty also picked out some of the Navy's best senior officers. In mid-August Rear Admiral George Cockburn was directed to leave Cadiz, hoist his flag on the 74 HMS *Marlborough* and join Warren, along with Captain John Beresford in the 74-gun battleship HMS *Poictiers*.[12] Captain Robert Dudley Oliver in the 50-gun ship HMS *Grampus* was ordered from the Cadiz station to the Leeward Islands, to exchange commands with the captain of the 74 *Dragon*, and join Warren. Combat veterans like these would translate strategy into operational effect.[13] In particular Melville looked to Cockburn to take the offensive onto the American coast to 'accelerate the return of peace'.[14]

However, the opening moves of the naval war would be dominated by diplomacy and the defence of trade. Urgent reinforcements were invariably delayed by the need to escort convoys, while Warren was ordered to base himself at Halifax, the best location to wait for a diplomatic response from the American government. A week later he was directed to convoy valuable merchant shipping, along with vital naval and military store ships heading for Halifax, Bermuda and Jamaica. His subordinates in American waters were directed to station cruisers in the key choke points and dispersal areas where merchant shipping would be especially vulnerable to American cruisers.[15]

Before sailing, Warren reflected on his twin-track mission: although his primary role was to secure peace he needed to prepare for war. If the Americans decided to fight he would need to make sea power felt on land: heavy mortars, the classic naval land-attack weapon, and new Congreve rockets 'would prove of infinite advantage'.[16] An obtuse Admiralty requested details; the resulting delays ensured the rockets were not ready when Warren left Spithead on 14 August.[17]

Arriving at Halifax on 27 September with the 74s *San Domingo* and *Poictiers*, Warren found both Herbert Sawyer and the old 64 *Africa* in poor shape. He decided to send them home, as convoy escort. Recognising that the war had assumed a 'more active and inveterate aspect than heretofore', Warren addressed the threat posed by American sloops, brigs and privateers. His limited resources were already spread thin by convoys and cruising; he had nothing left to meet the challenge.[18] Short of ships, and hamstrung by restrictive rules of engagement designed to facilitate peace, Warren faced a near impossible task with little help from home. As the American crisis deepened the Admiralty had been focused on a major build-up of French naval forces in Aix Roads, leading the more pessimistic Sea Lords to fear that France might be able to out-build Britain.[19] Fortunately, just as the American war added a significant new demand for ships and men, the decline of the French threat released the means without a significant increase in cost. The 1813 Naval Estimates were £20 million, only £700,000 more than in 1812. Little wonder the Admiralty clung to the hope that 'there was some appearance at one time of the American Government being inclined to return to a state of peace' for as long as possible. That dream evaporated on Trafalgar Day 1812.[20]

Warren accepted that defensive tasks must take priority, and at this late season the majority of merchant shipping would be coming from the West Indies, not Canada. Once the Americans had responded to the peace initiative he would head south to Bermuda, the central point of his vast command, and take the 74s with him. This would leave Broke as senior officer on station with a frigate squadron to protect the Nova Scotia area during the winter. While he waited for an American answer, Warren put the Halifax station on a war footing, inspecting the dockyard, meeting his officers and developing the intelligence picture.

In mid-October HMS *Nymphe* returned to Halifax, having fallen in with Rodgers's squadron, three frigates and a sloop, which had sailed from Boston on the 5th. On the 18th Broke sailed with the frigates *Shannon*, *Nymphe* and *Tenedos* and the sloop *Curlew* specifically to cover important convoys about to sail from Newfoundland, the St Lawrence and Nova Scotia.[21] With this defensive task Broke could only hope Rodgers would come to him. This was the right approach. While he waited for the big prize Broke took some small fry, the brand new Marblehead 18-gun privateer *Thorn*.[22] Sweeping up these predators was a basic wartime role for British cruisers; Broke had already taken many French and Spanish privateers. The successes kept insurance rates low, a critical indicator of effective sea control. Such prizes might be bought to reinforce the British cruiser fleet, or sold to local privateers. The crew would be locked up for the duration; British prisons filled with prime American seamen weakened the American war effort.

To Broke's regret Commodore Rodgers was nowhere to be seen. Broke feared each cruise might be his last: he knew that *Shannon* needed a major overhaul, an ideal excuse for the Admiralty to shift him to the boredom of the battlefleet. Returning to Halifax on 24 November, he was far from pleased by the numerous dinners that preceded Warren sailing to Bermuda. Despite being left in local command, which implied he should stay ashore to administer the station, Broke elected to cruise. Any thoughts of returning home perished with the loss of *Guerriere*, which bound him:

. . . to the service until we have restored the splendour of our flag . . . my views are so brilliant and the call of honor so imperious that my only chance of release from the charge is by continued and active pursuit of our enemy, and I trust our next cruise will be a successful one.[23]

He took the squadron back to sea on 12 December.

In mid-November Warren learnt that the diplomatic mission had failed. Recognising that the suspension of the Orders in

Council had negated their chosen *casus belli*, Madison's administration simply switched focus to demand the end of impressment.
Warren understood that the challenge to 'one of the most
essential and ancient supports of the British Naval Power' made
'any further correspondence . . . unnecessary', before Madison
repeated the point in Congress.[24] Aware that London would
not compromise on this point, Warren could concentrate on the
business of war.

The American privateer effort had been highly successful in
the first months of war, when the convoy system in American
waters remained embryonic. At least 150 British ships had
been taken, and more privateers were fitting out. To meet the
combined challenge of privateers and frigates Warren needed
reinforcements, a theme that would dominate his command.[25]
The Admiralty response was distinctly unsympathetic. In January
the Board declared that, as he faced only a handful of warships,
and had a clear superiority in all classes, he should 'quickly and
completely' dispose of the enemy.[26] Such nonsense reflected
growing agitation from well-connected Liverpool merchants like
John Gladstone, a local MP, and the former Foreign Secretary
George Canning for increased naval protection.[27] Without more
ships and men Warren could do little to meet such demands.
The key to success was to control the Atlantic coast of America
through an effective naval blockade, to prevent hostile shipping
putting to sea. More than 2,000 miles long, with numerous
harbours and inlets, the American coast posed a formidable
challenge for Warren's pitifully small force.

While London waited for news, hoping for an early end to an
unwelcome complication, the Admiralty hurried to explain an
unexpected, alarming defeat. On 15 November 1812 the Board
issued a circular to all commanders-in-chief at home and abroad.
An inspection of recent log books had revealed many instances
of ships not being exercised at great guns, or small arms. The
Printed Instructions required ships to be fit for service, ready for
battle, not polished like a yacht. Regular gun drill and tactical
exercises would prepare the crews to act in a 'cool, steady and

regular manner', so every drill should be noted in the log, for the Board's inspection.[28] Before these orders had taken effect two more frigates would be lost.

AMERICAN FRIGATES

Before the second American sortie Secretary Hamilton divided his scant force into three squadrons, each of two frigates and a brig, led by Rodgers, Decatur and William Bainbridge, who replaced Hull in command of the *Constitution*. The three commodores would select the best cruising ground to 'afford protection to our trade & to annoy the enemy'.[29] Despite reports of a steady increase in British strength Rodgers was determined to get to sea.[30] The new orders gave Bainbridge and Decatur an opportunity to earn their laurels, but Rodgers was doomed to disappointment, unable to catch a British frigate, largely because he was desperately anxious to avoid a battleship.

On receiving Hamilton's strikingly general orders, Bainbridge consulted his friend William Jones, Philadelphia merchant and former sea captain, about the best rendezvous and routes for success.[31] Bainbridge reckoned he could stow provisions for four or five months, and water for 100 days. Jones recognised the arrival of British 74s as an unwelcome complication: they were far superior to American 44s. He doubted the British would attack the American coast, which risked unifying the country behind the war. Realising that Bainbridge favoured a cruise to the South Atlantic, Jones focused on the choke points where shipping left the West Indies, and the obvious rendezvous off the Azores, before homing in on the north-east coast of Brazil. Here 'the British derive a valuable trade and the returns are very frequently in a very convenient Commodity viz Gold Bars and Coin and other compact valuables'. Jones also sketched 'a brilliant cruise' to the Indian Ocean, but one full of risk without a friendly port, and the threat of disease. He doubted it was wise to risk a third of the Navy on such a venture. That judgement would change as the fortunes of war turned. Despite his reservations Jones sent Bainbridge the

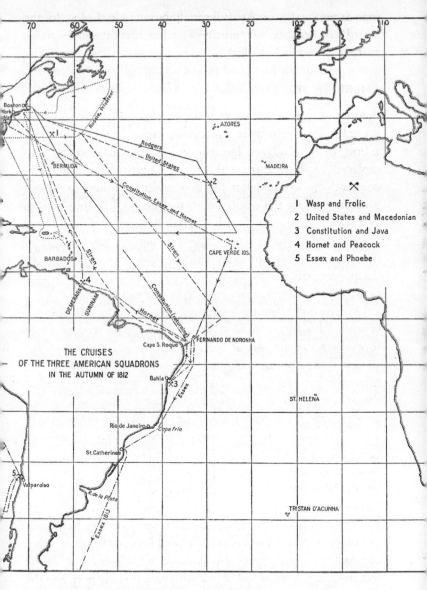

At war on the oceans: round two.

best British books on Asian navigation. He endorsed a cruise to Brazil, returning by way of the West Indies choke points, Cape Canaveral and the Crooked Island Passage in the Bahamas.[32] This was sage counsel: Jones had picked a rich, lightly defended area, beyond Warren's command, where American naval power could be deployed to maximum advantage. Bainbridge's squadron orders and rendezvous conformed to Jones's plan, and left David Porter, sailing from the Delaware with the *Essex*, free to use his 'best judgement' if they did not meet.[33] Bainbridge got to sea with *Constitution* and *Hornet* in late October.

Hamstrung by the lack of cruisers, Warren remained unaware that Bainbridge had left Boston until a week after the fact. He had known Bainbridge planned to sail, and heard that *Constellation* might attempt to join his force from the Chesapeake. To counter the latter he deployed the 74 *Poictiers* and a frigate off the Chesapeake Capes. Distinctly unimpressed by Warren's report, the Admiralty wondered why he had not stationed his flagship, the 74-gun *San Domingo*, off Boston with a frigate squadron to intercept Bainbridge. They demanded a full statement showing the disposition of the entire fleet.[34] In truth the only frigates available, Broke's squadron, had been deployed on the Newfoundland Banks to protect the Canadian trade, and to meet Rodgers.

Bainbridge was in fact the last of Hamilton's commodores to leave Boston: Rodgers (with *President* and *Congress*) and Decatur sailed together on 9 October, keeping company as they passed through the British cruiser patrols. Rodgers took a Post Office packet from Jamaica, laden with specie, but he failed to catch a frigate. He also failed to rendezvous with the third ship of his squadron, the sloop USS *Wasp*, Master Commandant Jacob Jones. *Wasp* sailed from the Delaware on 13 October, only to run into a gale. Five days later *Wasp* encountered a six-ship convoy, escorted by the brig HMS *Frolic*, some 300 miles north-east of Bermuda. The same gale had scattered the convoy and damaged the *Frolic*.

Despite a missing mainyard, a sprung main topmast and other defects, Commander Thomas Whinyates knew his duty. He took in sail and waited for the suspicious ship to approach. The task of a convoy escort was to fight commerce raiders, buying time for the merchant ships to scatter. Whinyates commanded a well-drilled ship, but the damaged rigging seriously compromised her manoeuvrability. Both ships were armed with sixteen 32-pounder carronades, ensuring they would fight at close range.

The larger, more heavily manned American ship closed quickly, and despite having lost her main topmast, mizzen topgallant and gaff in the gale, *Wasp* easily outsailed *Frolic*. *Frolic*'s gaff and head braces were shot away in the initial exchange of fire, leaving her all but helpless. *Wasp* took up a raking position across *Frolic*'s bow, and poured in a heavy fire of cannon and musketry. Having cleared the British upper deck, the Americans boarded and took the ship. Soon after that both *Frolic*'s masts went over the side. With 17 dead and 45 seriously wounded, including every officer, from a total complement of 110, *Frolic*'s defence had been truly heroic. Nor had it been ineffective. *Frolic* had knocked *Wasp*'s masts and rigging to pieces; she could neither chase nor run. In consequence the entire convoy escaped unharmed, and two hours later the crippled *Wasp* surrendered to John Beresford's 74 HMS *Poictiers*.[35] Shattered and dismasted, *Frolic* was never repaired, replaced on the Navy List by the *Wasp*, renamed HMS *Loup Cervier*. Jones may have earned his gold medal, promotion and fame, but the United States could ill-afford such heroism; it would run out of warships and seamen long before Britain.

Nor were successes against minor British war vessels, however glorious, going to affect the big picture. The British blockade soon began to bite. A torrent of complaints from Charleston made it clear that the port was effectively besieged by a few British brigs. Secretary Hamilton ordered Bainbridge's squadron to clear the coast, but the orders reached Boston after the *Constitution* had sailed.[36] Alongside the demonstration of American impotence in the face of overwhelming British naval power, the destruction of coastal shipping shattered the national economy. Coastal states normally exchanged sub-tropical and temperate products, tobacco and cotton for grain and manufactures. The blockade worked because there were no alternative transport systems. By November the U.S. Navy's supply of shipbuilding timber, 'live oak' from Georgia, had been cut.[37]

UNITED STATES AND MACEDONIAN

Having parted from Rodgers on 12 October, Decatur, with *United States* and *Argus*, set a south-easterly course for the Azores, another prominent shipping rendezvous, in search of prizes. (*Chesapeake* was allocated to Decatur's squadron but had not been ready to sail.) By the 25th *United States* had lost contact with *Argus*, and was heading south, midway between the Azores and the Cape Verde Islands. Shortly after daybreak Decatur encountered a strange ship coming up from the south-east, which proved to be the 38-gun 18-pounder frigate HMS *Macedonian*, Captain John Surman Carden. While his ship was in good order, and remarkably fast, Carden lacked the single-minded determination required by successful cruiser captains. Unlike Philip Broke he found cruising on the trade routes 'the most harassing duty I had at any time to perform'.[38] An officer so obviously lacking self-confidence, insight, tactical acumen and leadership was foredoomed to failure.

After spotting the enemy, *Macedonian*'s officers discussed tactics. Convinced he had encountered the *Essex*, which carried only short-ranged carronades, Carden decided to fight a long-range battle, as Decatur noted. *Macedonian*'s superior sailing enabled Carden to secure the weather gauge, and choose his tactics, but he was comprehensively out-thought by Decatur, who handled the sluggish 'old wagon' to make best use of his superior firepower and strength:

Macedonian	46 guns	561-lb broadside	1,081 tons	377 men
United States	54 guns	876-lb broadside	1,533 tons	478 men

Accurate long range-fire from the American 24-pounders proved decisive, shattering *Macedonian*'s masts and rigging. In

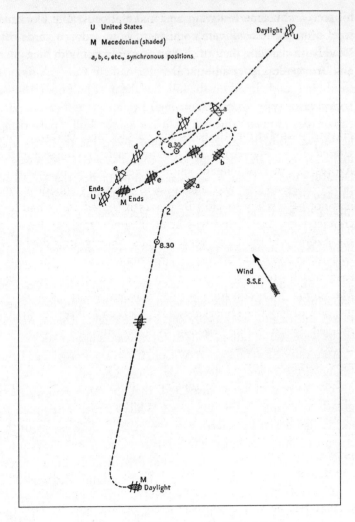

The engagement between the *United States*
and *Macedonian*.

later attempts to explain his defeat, Carden claimed he sought close action, while Decatur kept his distance. In truth he only attempted to shorten the range after his ship had been badly damaged. As the crippled *Macedonian* tried to close Decatur used his newly won superiority in speed and manoeuvrability to hold station on the *Macedonian*'s starboard bow, only 50 yards off, steadily dismantling the British ship's top-hamper with long guns and carronades. After an hour Decatur had cut Carden's rigging to ribbons, and closed for the kill. For the next half hour *United States*' vastly superior battery of long 24-pounders and 42-pounder carronades ripped through *Macedonian*'s hull, pulverising her crew. With the mizzen mast shot away, the topmasts and mainyard gone, and the upper deck guns disabled, Carden was at Decatur's mercy. Then, in a repeat of Hull's tactics, the American sheered off to repair his rigging. He returned an hour later, calmly taking up a raking position across *Macedonian*'s bow. Carden had no choice but surrender. In an action of more than two hours *Macedonian* lost 36 killed, 36 severely wounded, and 32 slightly wounded. The crew fought bravely, but Carden displayed neither skill nor judgement. Even so *United States* did not escape unharmed: 7 dead and 5 wounded. While the American ship's masts and rigging were badly cut up, the mighty *United States*' masts were still standing, unlike *Macedonian*'s lighter sticks.

Admiralty Secretary John Wilson Croker acknowledged the implications: 'This ... heavy and most unexpected blow ... proves what we always suspected, that the American 44's are greatly over match for our 38's.' While Carden attempted to excuse his defeat by referring to the massive dimensions of the American ship, 'her larger guns and crew', he missed the point.[39] He ran a neat and tidy ship, one that fired steadily, but the crew was sullen and unresponsive. A previous captain, who would be dismissed the service for brutality, and the current first lieutenant had thoroughly demoralised the men. The court martial acquitted Carden, but he was never employed again. His judges suggested that close action would have been a better option, but the disparity of force meant that only superb ship-handling or precipitate flight could have saved the *Macedonian* from disaster at any fighting range.[40] Not only did Carden demonstrate little capacity it is likely that his eyesight was defective. Despite being on board the *United States* only months earlier he failed

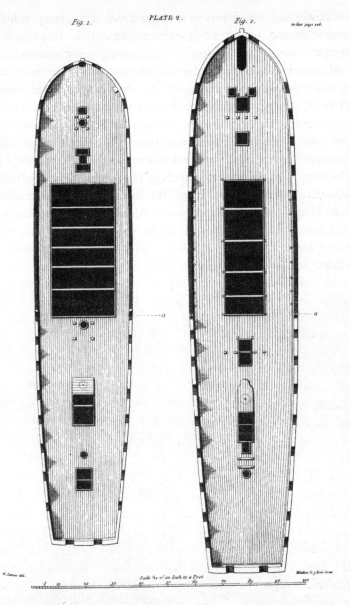

Fair and equal combat? Comparative deck plans
of the *Macedonian* (left) and the *President*, as measured by William
James in 1817

to identify his opponent, confusing her with the smaller, lighter *Essex*. Decatur took the opportunity gifted to him by Carden with skill and judgement, fighting a cautious, considered battle.

Rather than continue his cruise, Decatur 'deemed it important' to bring the prize home to show the American people the fruits of his success. Evading the evolving British blockade, Decatur took *United States* into Long Island Sound and anchored off New London on 4 December. Having lost contact in the fog, *Macedonian* put into Newport, Rhode Island, two days later.[41] The two ships then sailed into New York, cheered by jubilant crowds. It seemed to the Americans that they were winning the war; anxiety turned to euphoria in a welter of public dinners, speeches and celebrations.

CONSTITUTION AND JAVA

Encouraged by the prospect of easy prizes and rich pickings Bainbridge followed Jones's advice, taking his two ships across the Atlantic to the Cape Verde Islands and then south-west to the coast of Brazil. On 13 December *Constitution* and *Hornet*, Master Commandant James Lawrence, reached the Brazilian port of San Salvador, and discovered the very target Jones had mentioned, the British sloop HMS *Bonne Citoyenne*, heading north from Rio de Janeiro laden with specie. Her captain very properly refused Lawrence's insulting challenge to single combat, leaving the frustrated Master Commandant to draw a crumb of comfort from publishing his bombastic epistle. Bainbridge left *Hornet* to blockade the sloop, heading south along the coast on 26 December. Three days later he spotted HMS *Java*, Captain Henry Lambert, and set a course out of Brazilian territorial waters, with the British ship in hot pursuit. This was a random encounter: the newly commissioned *Java* was en route to India, crowded with seventy naval supernumaries as well as the Governor of Bombay and his staff, and laden with shipbuilding stores. The extra passengers had obliged Lambert to stop at San Salvador for water. Despite having made an official complaint about a weak crew before leaving Britain, Lambert had no hesitation accepting battle.

| Java | 46 guns | 535-lb broadside | 1,073 tons | 370 men |
| Constitution | 54 guns | 754-lb broadside | 1,533 tons | 480 men |

As the ships closed both captains tried to gain the weather gauge, a contest easily won by the faster, handier *Java*. Shortly after 2 p.m. the first shots were fired, with *Java* holding a good position on the American port bow, outside the effective range of American anti-rigging projectiles. Bainbridge later claimed he had tried to close, but Lieutenant Henry Chads disagreed: 'our opponent evidently avoiding close action and firing high to disable our masts and rigging'. Instead British fire took effect on the American upper deck and rigging; after twenty minutes *Constitution*'s wheel was shot away, reinforcing *Java*'s advantage. The American ship would be even less agile while Bainbridge had to relay helm orders to the rudder tackles on the lower deck. At the same time Bainbridge was slightly wounded, but he remained on deck and in command.

Henry Lambert exploited his early success to take up a raking position across *Constitution*'s stern, but failed to inflict any serious damage before Bainbridge luffed up to resume broadside action. This time the range was down to pistol shot, the British ship on the American quarter, *Java*'s jib-boom fouling *Constitution*'s mizzen rigging. Just as the ships cleared one another an American shot smashed *Java*'s jib-boom and the head of her bowsprit. This was exactly what Bainbridge needed, leaving *Java* less manoeuvrable than her heavyweight opponent. The speed and agility that Lambert had used to keep his ship clear of *Constitution*'s punishing broadside, preserving the lightly built ship and her crew, were gone. Once again, damaged rigging left a British ship at the mercy of a larger, less agile enemy. Now Bainbridge held all the aces: firepower, manpower, manoeuvrability and time. When the American ship wore, *Java* tried to counter by tacking, but she answered the helm too slowly, receiving a shattering raking broadside through the lightly built stern, and was left to fight at close range. Recognising that, with his masts damaged and men falling fast, he had few options Lambert put the helm over, desperately trying to close and board only to lose the foremast and miss his target. As *Constitution* forged ahead she fired another raking broadside, bringing down the British main topmast. By now *Java*'s starboard battery was largely disabled by fallen rigging, leaving only two or three guns still firing. Soon after Henry Lambert was mortally wounded, leaving the ship to be fought by Lieutenant Henry Chads. The final phase of the battle, close-range broadsides, lasted until 4.35 when *Java*'s mizzenmast fell.

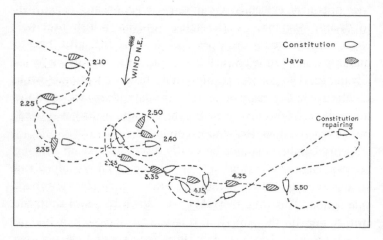

The engagement between the *Constitution* and *Java*.

With the enemy crippled, the American ship forged ahead and lay-to, repairing her rigging, which was 'extremely cut'. After an hour of knotting and splicing, clearing away the dead and wounded and re-roving gun tackles, *Constitution* was ready for action. While the Americans worked, *Java*'s mainmast fell. Seeing his enemy was now utterly helpless, Bainbridge calmly waited until *Constitution* was ready. Then he closed in, taking station across the *Java*'s bow. Chads had no option but surrender. *Java* had been reduced to a dismasted wreck with 24 dead and 100 wounded; the Americans lost 14 and 44 respectively. Despite a scratch crew and limited training, Henry Lambert had been a skilful opponent, making Bainbridge work very hard for his victory. Nor was *Java*'s gunnery in any way discreditable. British shot damaged all three American masts, which only remained standing because of their stout proportions, and massive reinforcing timber splints. Although Bainbridge chose not to mention the damaged masts in the battle report they obliged him to abandon his cruise.

Despite the valuable naval stores she contained Bainbridge could not repair the wrecked *Java* for a passage home. Landing the British crew on parole at San Salvador, he set fire to the dismasted hulk on 31 December, bringing a fiery end to a dispiriting year for the Royal Navy's cruisers. The paroled British officers and men were soon back at sea with a score to settle. The battle made a powerful impression on Henry Chads: he became the Royal Navy's leading gunnery specialist.[42] Because Lambert died heroically, and the ship had been stoutly defended against a more powerful foe, their Lordships were correct to consider the action a matter of some pride.

The twice-victorious *Constitution* reached Boston on 18 February 1813.[43] As if to prove Warren's contention that it was impossible to blockade Boston in winter Bainbridge slipped in when Broke's squadron was driven off station by gales and snowstorms. Only in March did Warren order Broke to maintain a close blockade of Boston.[44]

In all three frigate battles the American captains used superior firepower to cripple the enemy's masts and sails, securing an advantage in manoeuvrability before closing in for the kill. Once the enemy had been crippled they shifted fire to the main and upper decks, knocking over guns and crew.

Of the five British warships which had been captured in 1812, only two, the *Macedonian* and the collier brig *Alert*, reached American ports to be assessed for prize money. The destruction or loss of the *Guerriere*, *Frolic* and *Java* posed a problem: American law provided no means of rewarding the officers and men. Secretary Hamilton recommended that Congress vote a suitable award, and after an interminable delay Hull and Bainbridge and their crews received $50,000 for each action, Jones's men made do with $25,000. The heroic captains also received Congressional gold medals, based on European models. With a bust portrait on one side, a battle picture on the other, and captioned in Latin, they placed the leaders of a new navy in an old lineage.

For all the glory, these successes were, as Mahan observed, illusory. They did not affect the balance of power at sea, impede the reinforcement of the Canadian army, or raise British insurance rates. Instead they provided a potent, unifying demonstration of national determination, one that a desperate administration was quick to harness.

EXPANSION

By the end of the year the very men who had voted down naval increases were trumpeting the glories of the United States Navy, largely because the Army had signally failed to 'march' into Canada. War made the Navy into an American national institution. That this half-starved navy won a series of victories against the Royal Navy said a great deal for the professional skill of its officers and men, and nothing whatsoever for the wisdom of the President, his War Hawk allies or Congress.

Although the Republican administration hastened to exploit the propaganda value of these unexpected naval victories, stressing the moral meaning of decisive contests, not their reality, they faced a gloomy prospect. It required little insight to realise that the British response would be quick, simple, and devastatingly effective. With a handful of 74-gun third rates and frigates Britain could blockade any ports containing American warships and clear the oceans of national cruisers, allowing brigs and sloops to escort merchant shipping convoys against privateers. Once these defensive tasks had been completed, the British could bolster the economic blockade, crush American commerce, and thus annihilate the customs receipts that the Federal government depended on for funds.

It is no surprise that Secretary Hamilton returned to the idea of building battleships to defend the coasts and commerce, and more frigates to harass British trade. He had raised the idea before the war, only to be voted down by the men who demanded war. Men who wanted more land and fewer Indians saw no need to waste money defending coastal cities and their trade. Republican ideology distrusted foreign-going merchants, and ignored their interests. Seizing the moment, Hamilton and the Senate Naval Committee Chairman proposed building 74s and 44s, leading to a three-week-long debate in the House of Representatives in November. A belated recommendation to Congress generated another three weeks of heated exchange. Finally, on 23 December, Congress agreed to build four 74s and six 44s, the first naval building programme of the Republican era.[45] It was also Hamilton's last contribution. Naval officers may have felt vindicated by the programme, but the new battleships and frigates would take years to build.

Everything depended on Napoleon. The Emperor had occupied Moscow, but Russia would not come to terms. Once the French began to retreat the more perspicacious American politicians could see the writing on the wall. With Napoleon in retreat the Americans would have to fight their own war, on land and sea, while Britain could send more ships and men. Some Americans remained optimistic: on 4 December War Hawk Henry Clay told Congress that he expected Napoleon was at that very moment dictating peace in Moscow.[46] Madison opened the New Year by signing the naval programme into law, marking the collapse of his hopes and a dawning realisation that, having taken his country to war utterly unprepared, he, as Chief Magistrate, was responsible for a looming catastrophe.

While the British thought that a Franco-American alliance was the only logical explanation for American belligerence, the reality was very different. Alarmed by Madison's open discussion of an early peace, the French Minister in Washington urged Paris to make concessions. The French allowed Joel Barlow to set off for Napoleon's headquarters at Vilna, carrying a trade treaty that Napoleon would never sign. Unwilling to halt his epic flight back to Paris, Napoleon passed Vilna without stopping. America was irrelevant; he needed 250,000 fresh soldiers. Barlow died at Vilna on 26 December 1812, leaving Franco-American relations on hold for the next six months. American naval success prompted a brief flurry of French interest, and several high-grade aquatints. When the French finally did something concrete, allowing American privateers to use their ports, Madison could not reciprocate. American law prohibited the admission of foreign privateers and, humiliatingly, he lacked the Congressional support to effect a change. Nor would the Americans block the export of grain to Napoleon's enemies in Spain: Secretary of State Monroe admitted that too many politicians were involved for Congress to accept a ban.[47] Monroe's concern for Republican Baltimore became academic when the British took control of Chesapeake Bay in March, ensuring that only Federalist New England grain went to Spain. At this point the British controlled American trade.

Contrary to all expectation the American naval campaign of 1812 had been an almost unalloyed triumph. Yet winning six single-ship actions wrecked the attack on British commerce. The only national cruisers to achieve any success were those, like Rodgers's *President*, that failed to find and fight British warships. Hull, Jones, Decatur and Bainbridge all traded in their commerce-raiding careers for a shot at glory. If the loss of *Guerriere* and *Java* was embarrassing, this was neither dishonourable nor especially disadvantageous. The British got the precious crews back within weeks, and both times *Constitution* headed home to replace her masts – leaving the seas open for British commerce.

WAGING ECONOMIC WAR

In the first days of war Rear Admiral Herbert Sawyer had planned a naval and economic blockade of the American Atlantic coast, but his designs were disrupted by the over-riding obligation to protect oceanic commerce, especially the big West India convoys, from John Rodgers's squadron. Sawyer shifted his wholly inadequate forces to trade defence, abandoning offensive economic warfare. The Foreign Office had provided further grounds for caution; their last instructions had stressed the need to avoid war. Consequently he did not treat the *Belvidera* incident as *casus belli*, simply sending a sloop to New York to request information from the British Minister in Washington.

Once war had broken out, few in Britain doubted that an economic blockade would be at the heart of strategy. London took the first economic war measures on 1 August, banning British ships from trading with the United States and revoking licences to sail without convoy to the Caribbean or North America. The system of licensing American ships to trade proved more complex. With a large number of licences in circulation, and many plausible forgeries, it proved almost impossible to police the system. Warren wanted to ban them outright, but the need for grain, flour and timber from 'friendly' New England prompted a veritable flood of licences in 1812 and 1813. The British continued the practice until Wellington could feed his army in France. Even then, Canada and Bermuda, the hub of the blockade, depended on the licensed supply of food and timber. Any economic advantage the trade gave the Americans was vastly outweighed by the logistical benefits for British strategists waging global war. Economic warfare might be the basis of British strategy, but the American war was a secondary consideration

Warren shared Sawyer's urge to impose an economic blockade, but the rapid development of the privateer threat tied his limited resources to defensive tasks. As the concentration point for Atlantic convoys the area around Halifax proved especially attractive to predators. Although twenty-four privateers were taken in Nova Scotian waters between 1 July and 25 August the threat seemed to be endless. Warren had three options for his tiny force: convoy, patrol and blockade; he chose the first two. He would be widely blamed for failing to blockade the privateer ports.[48] The Admiralty, which determined the level of force on the station, disingenuously joined the chorus of complaint rather than provide extra resources. The Board was equally slow to settle the question of lawful prize – the key to effective economic warfare – as if hoping against the fact that the Americans could still be brought to terms.

The question of ships was critical. On arrival at Halifax Warren found only two ships in port, the worn-out *Africa*, and the frigate *Junon*, which he detached under a flag of truce to New York to ascertain if the Americans were still set on war. This satisfied the key stipulation of his orders. Soon afterwards the frigates *Orpheus* and *Statira* joined him from the West Indies, but they were almost unseaworthy, with weak, sickly crews. The rest of the widely dispersed North American squadron returned to Halifax in the following weeks; most required general repairs, stores, water and above all more men. Clearly Warren's first task would be to make his force efficient, to meet the threat posed by the American frigates. While he waited to discover if he would negotiate peace or wage war the priority was necessarily defensive. In early October Warren had to deploy both flagships, the 74 *San Domingo* and the *Africa* off the Newfoundland Banks to cover convoys carrying troops and stores to Quebec and Nova Scotia, 'but for this protection they would have been destroyed by the enemy's privateers'. To make matters worse, on 27 September the small frigate *Barbadoes*, escorting a convoy from Bermuda to Halifax, ran aground on Sable Island. Warren had to send *Shannon*, the only ship fit to go to sea, to recover the ship's company, stores saved from the wreck and $63,000 to pay the artificers of Halifax Dock Yard. Just as *Shannon* returned, the frigate *Tenedos* came in with a convoy, and with the newly joined *Nymphe* Warren finally had a frigate squadron to search for Rodgers. At the same time he had to escort two convoys sailing from Nova Scotia and New Brunswick to the West Indies, which had been waiting several weeks for protection.

As soon as the newly arrived 74 *Poictiers* was ready, on 10 October, Warren opened the economic warfare campaign by dispatching the 74 with two frigates, a sloop and a schooner to cruise off the Delaware River and Chesapeake Bay, stretching as far south as Cape Hatteras. Captain John Beresford had to combine his primary defensive mission, to intercept the frigate USS *Constellation*, privateers or rumoured French warships, with the destruction of American trade.[49] Though he had a singularly slight force to cover the area, Beresford produced results, taking the USS *Wasp* and several privateers.

After three weeks at sea *San Domingo* and *Africa* now returned to Halifax. *Africa* was patched up to limp home as an ocean convoy escort. And three weeks after departing for New York the *Junon* also returned with news of the American government's determination to fight.

Throughout the first month of his command Warren's main focus had been to defend critical convoys while refitting and maintaining his scant, worn squadron. The small dockyard at Halifax was struggling to meet wartime demands, enlarged forces and harsh winter weather.[50] By early December Warren had refitted his squadron and improved the yard. When Broke returned it took only six days to get *Shannon* ready for sea. Having arranged the northern part of his station, and strengthened the defences of several open harbours along the coast of Nova Scotia and in the Bay of Fundy where the trade sought shelter, Warren now detached the newly arrived frigates *Maidstone*, *Acasta* and *Aeolus* to join Beresford off the Chesapeake. Then he sailed in *San Domingo*, accompanied by *Junon*, *Statira*, *Laurestinus* and *Wanderer* with a convoy for Bermuda. Broke was left in command at Halifax with *Shannon*, *Tenedos*, *Nymphe* and *Curlew* to conduct essentially defensive operations. His orders were to escort a valuable convoy of New Brunswick mast ships, heading for the Royal Dockyards in Britain, to a point 150 leagues east of the Newfoundland Banks, and then look for Rodgers's squadron, also occasionally cruising off St George's Bank. The squadron should rendezvous at Halifax if dispersed. Warren dismissed the obvious alternative; experience in the previous American War convinced him it was impossible to blockade Boston 'between the months of November and March'. While Broke operated out to sea, three frigates, five sloops and several schooners patrolled the Nova Scotian coast and the Bay of Fundy, the smaller vessels covering coasting convoys.[51]

In order to impose an effective economic blockade, the strategic measure that would 'produce a great change in the people of the Country', Warren needed enough battleships and frigates to cover all the key American ports.[52] His reading of the latest intelligence down-played the much anticipated fracturing of the United States: the Southern states might have been composed of 'the most vile materials', but the Union would hold.[53] The decision for an early blockade of Charleston and Georgia reflected British assessment of the innate hostility of the Southerners, and the desire to interrupt the supply of timber to the Northern shipyards.

As fresh forces arrived, Warren faced incessant demands to provide local protection for Caribbean islands and their shipping, and was harassed by subordinate flag officers who viewed the war as an opportunity for personal advantage. Although he was nominally in command of the Jamaica and Leeward Islands stations, the vast distances involved meant he had little real control. Vice Admiral Stirling used the Jamaica command to gather freight money and other inducements from anxious shippers, while encouraging merchants to blame Warren for their problems. Although Rear Admiral Francis Laforey did not break the law, he was notably obtuse about returning ships. Ultimately Stirling would be court-martialled and dismissed from the Navy, but the political influence of West Indian planters provided a powerful distraction throughout Warren's command.

BLOCKADE

The British government finally ordered general reprisals against America on 13 October, news that reached Warren on 16 November, just as he learnt that the Americans had rejected an armistice. In economic terms the first six months of war had

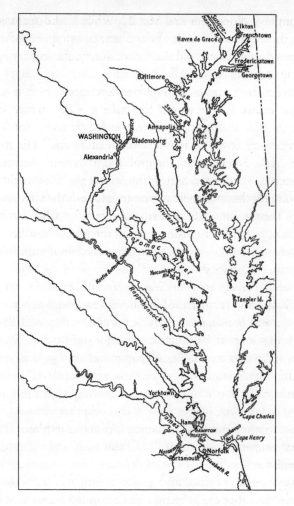

The British target: Chesapeake Bay,
Washington, Baltimore and Norfolk, Virginia.

been wasted. On 21 November 1812 Earl Bathurst, Secretary of
State for War and the Colonies, ordered the Admiralty to impose
an economic blockade, specifically directing that the Chesapeake
Bay and Delaware River be subject to 'a strict and rigorous
Blockade'.[54] He excluded the New England states, hoping

they might secede. Believing the Republican Mid-Atlantic and Southern states, where the slave plantations of the governing class produced cotton, tobacco and rice, were responsible for the war, Bathurst advised finding other sources of supply, and destroying these trades. Lord Liverpool agreed and two days later the Prince Regent signed an Order in Council for General Reprisals against the ships, goods and citizens of the United States.[55] With an effective blockade in place and duly notified, Warren could then deny neutral ships access to American harbours. Lord Castlereagh promulgated the Chesapeake and Delaware blockade to neutral powers at the end of the year.[56]

This was a carrot and stick approach inspired by British needs, and a flawed assessment of American politics. Bathurst's blockade had been designed to achieve maximum impact, at the least cost. To maintain the supply of grain to the army in the Peninsula, provide shipbuilding stores and food for the West Indies and Canada, and exploit internal factional divisions, the British issued hundreds of trading licences. Licensed trade also kept skilled seamen away from warships and privateers. Indeed American owners trusted British paperwork and kept on trading, widening the divisions between maritime and inland states, and weakening the war effort. American merchants happily forged suitable licences to widen their access to other markets.[57] The licensed trade infuriated American officers; Decatur treated licensed ships as lawful prize.[58] Despite such zeal the trade was countenanced by the inaction of the American government.

Britain could protect and promote any trade it chose to sanction, and it could stop that of the United States at will. As a result Britain could borrow and tax to fund an effective war. The United States could not.[59] The American Atlantic coast had to be blockaded both for defence, to protect British West Indian commerce, and to impose economic hardship on America. This posed a formidable challenge for Warren's force, and it proved impossible to achieve absolute control despite a major expansion of the squadron. As Warren stressed in a private letter to Melville, an effective blockade would 'require twice my numbers'.[60] The

Atlantic theatre tested the fabric of his ships, and the mettle of his men, leaving around a fifth of his force in harbour under repair at any one time.[61]

Warren's naval blockade began to take effect in the spring of 1813 when a combination of more ships and better weather enabled him to keep the American fleet largely confined to port. This reduced the threat to convoys, enabling the economic blockade to be imposed with striking completeness. Furthermore, fundamental strategic changes in Europe, especially the opening of the Baltic for large-scale trade in grain and timber, had already ended British dependence on American supplies. In consequence the British could adopt more stringent measures. New York, the largest American port, producing approximately a quarter of the national revenue from customs dues, was effectively closed for business by May 1813. Despite a doubling of the rate of customs duty, American revenues fell to catastrophic levels, making it impossible to fund the war. More easily blockaded than New York, Philadelphia suffered a 90 per cent fall in revenue. Government stock failed to sell at sustainable rates, while the economic impact of war made it increasingly unpopular with many Americans. The British had carefully targeted specific sections of American society, hoping to exacerbate internal divisions. The Americans reinforced the British blockade by stopping 'illegal' imports of British goods on American vessels, cutting customs revenue further. As Henry Adams noted 'the pressure of the blockades was immediately felt'.[62]

SHOOTING THE MESSENGER

The first six months of war proved curious and troubling for the British. While the naval defeats had been embarrassing, the war on land had been unexpectedly successful. Against all the odds the British had held the Canadian frontier, and by the close of the year the first flush of American success at sea was about to ebb. In Europe the news had been bigger, and better. Napoleon's catastrophic defeat in Russia transformed Britain's position from strategic stalemate to expanding success. From Salamanca to Smolensk the French were in retreat. By December Napoleon's fleet was shrinking, allowing the British to redeploy naval power to the New World. The American Navy would only get smaller.

Even so, the British government remained understandably anxious to limit the American conflict. Having repealed the Orders in Council, the Cabinet expected Washington to negotiate, and therefore restricted military action to an active defence to avoid exacerbating the situation. Only in late November did they order Warren to impose a blockade, which was confined to the Chesapeake and Delaware. This localised blockade, targeting Republican decision-makers, was finally established on 21 February 1813. New England remained outside the blockade. The letters of marque necessary for effective reprisals against American merchant ships were only settled at the turn of the year, after Warren's dispatch confirming the American decision for war reached London.[63]

At the time of his appointment Warren must have possessed the confidence of the Cabinet: his mission was complex, and called for a degree of judgement and discretion. After the diplomatic initiative had failed the Cabinet collectively lost interest in the war, leaving strategic management to the Admiralty, which soon lost faith in the Admiral. By the end of 1812 the tone and content of Admiralty dispatches had become distinctly critical. The Board seemingly expected him to produce favourable outcomes with ships that had yet to arrive on station, but the combination of heavy demands for convoy and inadequate forces on station discouraged offensive action. Although 110 American merchant ships had been brought in before Warren offered the Americans an armistice on 30 September only a handful more were taken and condemned before the year ended.[64] While the decision to seek an armistice wasted the best three months for waging economic war under favourable circumstances, the opportunity for peace was too important to be sacrificed for mere strategic advantage.

Warren knew that the greatest threat to British trade came from privateers. As he sailed south for Bermuda he saw several, and managed to take one, reinforcing his concern to convoy British trade passing between the Caribbean and the North Atlantic. In November HMS *Maidstone* demonstrated the point, taking the brand-new Philadelphia privateer *Snapper* close to a convoy, within a day's sail of Bermuda.[65] Far from adopting his insight the Admiralty retorted: 'It is not their Lordships' intention that the trade should proceed without sufficient protection against privateers.'[66]

When Warren reported the failure of diplomacy, and asked for more ships, Melville and his Board turned against him. Melville, who only took up the post in March 1812, had inherited the weak and dismal elements of the previous Board. The new Senior Naval Lord, Admiral Sir William Domett, had been a good second, and a good staff officer, but he had no experience of fleet command and became nervous when faced with decisions. Soon Domett's irresolution turned to despond, infecting the whole Board. He finally departed in October 1813, replaced by Sir Joseph Yorke, who was slightly better.[67] But neither Domett nor Yorke had any command experience, and could offer little useful advice to Melville, let alone the vastly more experienced Warren. Although a tough and capable politician, Melville found his dismal councillors little help when he had to meet the shock of defeat. Desperate for a solution, he turned on Warren. It seems that the collapse of unduly optimistic expectations that America would seek an early peace led Melville to view Sir John with a jaundiced eye. It was, as he explained to Sir Edward Pellew, proving very difficult to find the money to sustain the present scale of naval warfare.[68] The combination of strategic stasis and fiscal crisis made him irritable.

In a deliberate slight the Board refused to confirm Warren's promotions, the easiest way to undermine an Admiral's authority.[69] Dismissing his assessment of the difficulty of blockading the American coast with a certainty more appropriate to an experienced admiral, Melville was 'surprised' Warren had not blockaded the Chesapeake and Delaware, despite the lack of orders, and ships. In a few days the official line had been transformed from seeking peace to waging offensive war. With 'some of the most enterprising Captains in the Navy' under his command, Melville expected that Warren would have 'no difficulty in undertaking any service for the success of which a reasonable prospect may be entertained'. Rather than respond to a general request for reinforcements, he asked Warren for a detailed assessment of types and numbers, because the report could not reach his desk inside two months. Warren had approximately a seventh of the Navy's ships under his orders, and ought to be grateful.[70] On 2 December 1812 the Admiralty demanded a formal statement of how the squadron was disposed.

Although startled by the vehemence of Melville's letter, Warren provided a strong defence of his policy. He recognised that London was attempting to micromanage the station, critiquing the positioning of individual ships that were beyond his control.[71] Knowing who the Board members were, he can have had little faith in their assessment of his problems. In a clear sign of a deteriorating relationship Melville moved from heading his letters 'My Dear Sir' to 'Dear Sir'. Altogether more alarming for Warren was the evidence that political pressure from economic interests was driving government policy. 'We have been assailed from various quarters on the defenceless state of the West Indies', Melville moaned, 'and yet, as far as we know, the force in that quarter is very considerable & amply sufficient.' He also reflected the domestic impact of defeat: 'The capture of the *Guerriere* and *Macedonian* has created a great sensation in this Country, and we look for retribution in the vigorous prosecution of offensive measures and the strict blockade of the Enemy's ports.'

At least the Admiralty had taken steps to limit the danger to trade, stationing a small squadron of battleships and frigates off Madeira and the Portuguese Western Islands.[72] This was critical: the Portuguese islands were a classic landfall for transatlantic voyages, and a common watering stop for the Asian trader, attracting numerous predators, both American and French, national and private. Several actions would be fought in the waters around the Atlantic islands, the Azores, the Canaries, and the Cape Verdes.

Far more significant, although barely registered then or now, was the successful defence of British floating trade. The United States Navy had failed to take a convoy, or break the rapidly evolving convoy system. In 1812 the British won both rounds: they secured Canada and their shipping. Mr Madison's challenge had faltered, his mighty weapons had shattered in his hands.

Ultimately, Admiralty criticism of the failure to defeat or blockade the American fleet was driven by more pressing concerns than mere loss of prestige, or the risk of increased maritime insurance rates. The American conflict might be limited, but it had a significant impact on British naval deployments. In October 1812 the Mediterranean Fleet was cut to twenty-six sail of the line, despite the growing French naval force in the theatre, to reinforce Warren.[73] Three more battleships, another 50-gun ship and five frigates were sent over the winter of 1812–13.

EVOLVING AN EFFECTIVE BRITISH POLICY

As the old year closed the British government finally accepted the time had come to bring home the full implications of waging war on leviathan. On Christmas Day Earl Bathurst directed the Admiralty to establish 'the most complete and vigorous Blockade, of the Ports and Harbours of the bay of the Chesapeake and of the River Delaware'.[74] Before the new orders arrived Warren took stock of the strategic situation. Predictably he wanted more ships and men. The loss of *Guerriere* led him to stress the need to counter the American 44s, which were markedly superior to British frigates, while the Americans were 'seducing our Seamen into their Service and converting them into American citizens by every art and means in their power'.

Nor did Warren restrict his request to existing warships, calling on the Admiralty to create a specific ship type to counter the 44s. The ideal solution would be six or seven old 74s cut down a deck to become razee 50-gun frigates with 32-pounder main deck batteries. These ships would have the same firepower edge over the American 44s that they possessed over standard British frigates. Warren had commanded such ships twenty years before in the Western Approaches. The Admiralty was already thinking about razees. Cutting off the upper deck and repairing an old 74 would create a powerful vessel, one that would last long enough for the current war and, unlike a regular 74, might lure an American 44 into battle. With fewer guns they would require a smaller crew, making them the most economical *President*-killers.

Without such ships Warren had to operate his cruisers in small squadrons, usually of two frigates and sloop, which, along with the need to convoy the West India trade and cover the St Lawrence approaches, reduced the effective cruiser force below the level required for a naval blockade. He also begged the Admiralty to increase the complement of his frigates by twenty-five to thirty seamen and marines. The privateer threat in the West Indies and along the coast of Nova Scotia and New Brunswick was equally pressing. He estimated the Americans had about 600 such vessels. It was little wonder that cruisers were at a premium from Jamaica to Newfoundland.[75] Writing on the day the *Java* was lost, Warren may have feared the news would never improve.

CHAPTER 4

Waiting for the *President*

Although the balance of the war had already turned in their favour, the New Year found the Admiralty anything but satisfied with their Commander-in-Chief on the North American station. Vice Admiral Sir John Warren's decisions and judgement had been called into question, his advice ignored. Even so the Board had little choice but to retain him in command; it was already too late to send out a replacement for the 1813 season. In large measure their annoyance reflected the British government's belated acceptance that they were at war. British aims remained unchanged: an early return to peace without concession. All the evidence suggests that the Cabinet collectively lost interest in America in the autumn, leaving the War Office and the Admiralty to run the war. Everyone else was transfixed by the deep, dark disaster that overtook Napoleon's Russian campaign. Cabinet ministers hardly mentioned America in 1813, filling their letters with detailed discussions of the European situation.[1] Although preoccupied with Europe, the Admiralty had to find ships, men and money to protect trade and convoy troops to Canada. It was a very annoying distraction.

The limits of Admiralty control were set by the immense distance that separated London from Warren's peripatetic flagship, making communication a long-term and often inconsistent process. Official dispatches travelled in warships or Post Office packets, until heavy losses among the packets made Warren unwilling to trust them with anything sensitive.[2] Harsh winter weather added to the delay: in one case vital orders from London, signed on 27 November reached Bermuda on 21 February. Such lengthy, uncertain exchanges obliged London to give Warren general, permissive orders, leaving him considerable latitude to adjust them in the light of the latest intelligence. This mattered because British policy underwent a fundamental change in late November, accepting the need to wage an offensive campaign to secure peace. The first dispatches to reflect this new appreciation did not reach Warren until late February 1813.

Fortunately for the government, Parliament only met for relatively short sessions, and had many issues to discuss. On 3 February 1813 Castlereagh read the Foreign Office's account of the origins of the war into the record.[3] This document established that Britain had tried everything to avoid war, right down to the end of Warren's diplomatic mission. It satisfied the great bulk of members of both Houses. As a result when the Whigs and Radicals criticised the administration they were obliged to make their attack on the narrower ground of the administration of the Navy, which they blamed for demoralising the seamen, and causing the losses. Radical Samuel Whitbread took the lead, but a stout defence by Castlereagh and George Canning secured the necessary votes.[4] This assault seems to have unsettled the Admiralty, leading them to dismiss Warren's assessment that the scale of American privateering required more cruisers as 'in a great degree exaggerated', blaming him for not blockading their bases and ignoring evidence that privateers could operate from almost any port on the American coast.[5] In similar vein the Board accepted Warren's view that Boston could not be blockaded in winter, then criticised him for not doing so when news arrived that Bainbridge's squadron had escaped in October.[6]

Admiralty hostility was largely a reflection of strident public criticism and political pressure from commercial organisations, topped off by the unexpected loss of the three frigates. The only response was to send reinforcements. Rather than strip forces from the European fleets the Admiralty selected more ships newly refitted or commissioned. They included four more battleships, to join the initial deployment of six. Their mission was to control the big American frigates; one 74 would be sent home each time an American 44 was taken. At least the Board accepted Warren's stress on fast ships – several 74s were specifically chosen for superior sailing: *Dragon* and *Superb* were among the fastest ships of their rate ever built – and most were commanded by outstanding officers. Captain Thomas Bladen Capel, in the new 74 *La Hogue*, had been a star frigate commander for a decade. He would use that experience to blockade New England ports.[7] The Board believed that ten battleships would enable Warren to crush the American Navy 'quickly and completely', and impose 'strict' naval blockades of any harbour containing American warships or privateers. This would reduce the need for heavy convoy escorts in the Atlantic theatre, allowing those forces to switch to offensive operations on the American coast. Recognising that all three frigate battles had been settled by 'superior force', the Board urged Warren to avoid operating his 18-pounder frigates singly. Warren would be reinforced to thirty frigates, fifty sloops and two battalions of Royal Marines. The Board also placed a chosen officer at the heart of Warren's command team, appointing Captain Henry Hotham captain of the fleet.[8] While the Board tried to manage the uncertainties out of war at sea Warren knew only too well that ample means, a galaxy of star officers and skilfully judged deployments were no guarantee of success. Finding American frigates would be a matter of chance.

In May the Whigs advanced a more measured critique of the Admiralty in the House of Lords. Melville based his defence on the 'superior force' of the American frigates, and under pressure from the Earl of Galloway to build frigates equal to the Americans he did not rule out the idea. Instead he defended the decision not to do so before the war as a rational act, given that the British government had not planned or started the war. Earl Bathurst backed him up on this point. Prime Minister Lord Liverpool pointed out, in case their noble Lordships had forgotten, that the over-riding naval task was to watch the French fleets, especially the one that lay only 200 miles away at Antwerp. Consequently 'such accidental disasters' could not have been prevented, and were no reason to criticise the administration of the Navy, or by extension the country. The critical Whig motion was comfortably defeated.[9] Although Melville avoided unnecessary disclosure, the Admiralty had ordered two 50-gun super-frigates a week before, along with five improved Endymion-class ships in January.[10] These were purpose built *President*-killers, to supplement the impressive razees.

TAKING CONTROL OF THE CHESAPEAKE

In late 1812 Warren sailed south from Halifax to Bermuda, clearing the coast, driving off the brig USS *Argus*, and destroying the successful privateer *Teazer*. While intelligence suggested the British had been close to Rodgers's squadron, vile weather and snowstorms limited visibility. At Bermuda the 74 HMS *Dragon* joined from Barbados and Warren sailed for New York on 4 January with *Dragon*, *Statira* and *Colibri* in company, hoping to intercept Decatur's frigates heading into Long Island Sound. By the time he returned to Bermuda a second time Warren had cruised the American coast from Nantucket to Cape Hatteras, capturing and destroying twenty-nine vessels. Off the Delaware HMS *Belvidera* finally delivered the Admiralty Secret Orders of 27 November, requiring 'the most complete and vigorous Blockade of the Ports and Harbours of the Bay of the Chesapeake and of the River Delaware'.[11] Warren immediately established the necessary blockade, which he promulgated on 6 February. Having asserted British control of the Atlantic seaboard, Warren moved to crush American trade, a strategy he expected to 'produce some deficit in the Revenue of the United States ere long'. [12]

As the British squadron entered Chesapeake Bay Warren spotted the frigate USS *Constellation* heading for the open ocean after a major repair at Washington Navy Yard. Captain Charles Stewart only had time to hurry into Norfolk, Virginia, hauling the ship into shallow water and grounding her on the tidal flats before the British could get into range. When the tide rose Stewart hauled his frigate into Norfolk, and moored her between the forts that guarded the harbour.[13] Once again Warren had been tantalisingly close to an American warship, but not close enough. Stewart's keen eyes, exemplary seamanship and a favourable breeze saved the *Constellation*. Without a powerful landing force, at least a battalion of soldiers or Marines, to capture the harbour forts and drive off the local militia, Warren could not get at the American ship. He left the frigates *Maidstone*, *Belvidera*, *Junon*, *Laurestinus* and *Statira* to watch the American ship and blockade Chesapeake Bay.

Returning to Bermuda on 13 February, Warren found further reinforcements, Rear Admiral George Cockburn in the 74 HMS *Marlborough*, the 74s *Ramillies*, Captain Sir Thomas Hardy, and *Victorious*. Nelson protégés like Henry Hotham, George Cockburn and Thomas Hardy raised the standard of Warren's fleet. They were men of ideas and action, with proven records in every aspect of naval warfare, from fleet battle to amphibious raids. All three would add to their laurels on the American coast. Warren assigned Cockburn to blockade the Chesapeake and Delaware, with the battleships *Marlborough*, *Poictiers*, *Victorious* and *Dragon*, the frigates *Acasta* and *Narcissus*, the schooner *Paz* and brig sloop *Fantome*. When these were combined with the five frigates already off Norfolk, Cockburn had the assets to combine strict blockade with coastal attacks. Within a month most of Chesapeake Bay was under British control. Cockburn's force precluded American resistance at sea, and brought home the cost of the war to the tidewater communities. With all trade at a stop, and British raiding parties operating on shore almost at will, Cockburn reported that the blockade had made Virginians 'clamorous and anxious for peace'. His actions ended the brief export-led economic boom of late 1812.[14] With *Constellation* securely locked away the only American defences in the Bay were unimpressive local militias. Cockburn's coastal raids demoralised local communities only a day or two from Washington. American merchant ships were snapped up with ease, cutting national revenue and raising insurance premiums.

Anxious for the latest news, Warren waited at Bermuda for the January mail, completing *San Domingo*, *Ramillies* and the sloop *Colibri* for sea. Then he returned to the American coast: 'to harass and alarm the enemy and by capture and destruction of the trade and shipping interests, and if possible his ships of war, to carry all hostile effect into his harbours'. The inevitable attack on *Constellation* failed, compromised by a lack of local knowledge and inadequate preparation. Warren could not risk extended land operations because he had to keep his battleships within supporting distance of Cockburn's squadron to counter the rumoured arrival of a French battle squadron. The British still assumed a degree of coordination with France, the only logical explanation for American action. The false alarm only delayed the detachment of 74s to blockade American harbours.

EXTENDING THE BLOCKADE

As the season advanced and the weather improved, Warren deployed his battleships and frigates to cover the key deep-water harbours used by American warships. The extra 74s were detached singly, operating with one or two 18-pounder frigates, as an ideal counter to the American 44s. No American ship or squadron would dare to engage a 74, while British frigates backed up by a 74 could operate aggressively. As the *Wasp–Frolic* action demonstrated, a lost battle that left the enemy crippled could easily turn into a strategic victory. Recognising the scale of the task, Warren stationed mixed forces of capital and cruising ships north of the Delaware, off New York, Rhode Island and Boston. The first detachment, commanded by Captain Robert Barrie, took station off Sandy Hook in HMS *Dragon* while the frigates *Belvidera* and *Acasta* lay off Montauk Point to complete the blockade of New York. They ensured Decatur's frigates could not get to sea. However, Warren knew he would have to reinforce *Dragon*.[15] In April Oliver was joined by Hardy in *Ramillies*, who attacked the Long Island Sound coastal trade and attempted to blockade the growing number of privateers in New York.

Thus, by early March, Warren had shifted from a defensive strategy of convoys and patrols, the only option with limited forces, to a carefully targeted economic blockade of the middle states and a naval blockade of the remaining harbours, delivered by a reinforced squadron. He expected economic warfare, hitting American incomes, to produce political and strategic change, but his offensive options would remain limited until the dangerous 44s had been taken or blockaded. Their presence meant he needed at least one 74 or two frigates to escort a convoy or blockade a port.

With Chesapeake Bay, the Delaware River and New York harbour sealed, Warren shifted his attention to Boston and Newport, where most of the American frigates were based. Seasonal gales meant Boston would not be closely blockaded until late March, when Broke's frigate squadron moved inshore, with Bladen Capel's 74 as backup. In contrast to the Chesapeake and the Delaware the Boston blockade was purely naval: New York and New England lay outside the economic blockade, still open to neutral merchant ships. Although many of these ships were fraudulently re-registered Americans British officers had little difficulty unpicking such obvious sleights of hand.

Warren constantly adjusted his strategic priorities in the light of successful British intelligence operations. American news-papers proved a rich source, along with the interrogation of captured seafarers, ship's papers and ciphered French diplomatic correspondence. From the state cabin of the *San Domingo* Warren read with interest of the American government's struggles to raise money, by tax or loan, for a war that became ever more unpopular as the burden fell on citizens. This would 'produce more beneficial effects . . . than any other Measure Whatever'.[16]

Thirty years' experience of America and her coast helped Warren process intelligence and anticipate enemy actions. The basic strategic architecture of the conflict was simple. As long as British troops held Canada the focus of American naval efforts would be the critical triangle linking the Gulf of St Lawrence, Halifax and Newfoundland, the area through which all troop and supply convoys must pass. Breaking this threat would enable Britain to maintain an army in Canada and hold the frontier.

However, Britain needed something more than defensive success to force the Americans to make peace: the only strategic offensive option was the economic blockade.

STRATEGY AND CULTURE

In late February Warren received a hostile dispatch demanding to know his 'intentions for carrying on the naval war and for protecting the British colonies and commerce'. He recognised that the tone reflected their Lordships' 'great regret at the escape from Port of the American Squadron under Commodore Rodgers', something 'it was not in my power to prevent'. Having dealt with the headline event Warren outlined his operational decisions since taking command at Halifax on 26 September, four months after the war began.[17] In a robust overview he stressed that threadbare resources, foul weather and ill-luck limited his options, and he saw no reason to regret his choices. He also reflected on the deeper meaning of the war. America wanted to destroy Britain's naval power, seduce her seamen and trim the belligerent rights that were the very basis of British strategy. In short Americans 'entertained the idea at some future time of assuming the Empire of the Sea'. He advised attacking the American centre of gravity, the expansive inland concerns that dominated Republican politics. If the Americans secured their territorial ambitions they would 'render the European nations dependant upon the Continent of America for their supplies of its produce and Bullion'.

Aware that it would be futile to ask for an army, Warren planned an amphibious strike with a very modest force, a battalion of Royal Marines, up to 1,200 men, including a company of artillery, embarked on naval troopships and backed up by the West India Regiment of black soldiers currently stationed in the Bahamas. This force would seize New Orleans, cutting off the trans-Appalachian states from the sea, a devastating economic stroke that would force the Westerners to abandon offensive operations against Canada. Pensacola would provide an ideal base for the operation. A second line of attack ran through Amelia Island off the coast of Florida; the third would be coastal raids inside Chesapeake Bay, destroying public stores at Baltimore and Washington, making local planters fear for their crops, stores and property, and raising the prospect of a servile revolt. The resulting 'disquiet, commotion and distress' might break up the Union, or oblige Washington to make peace on 'solid and liberal' terms.

Warren's 'Secret' letter recognised the critical role of culture in conflict, revealing a sophisticated understanding of the deeper undercurrents of American life, the economic issues, the hopes and fears of an infant nation that he had fought against as a boy, and observed more recently from nearby Nova Scotia. Critical elements of his strategic analysis reflected an intelligence report by Captain James Stirling. During an enforced stop-over at Spanish Pensacola Stirling assessed the strategic and economic importance of the Gulf Coast and the Mississippi River. His economic focus and recommendation to enlist Creek Indian tribes reflected the opinion of locally based British merchants.[18] The report, read by most leading policy-makers, exercised a significant influence on British strategy.

Throughout his campaign Warren had to prioritise defence over attack. Every time a ship sailed he made the best use of the move to escort a convoy, be it regular commerce, troops, supplies or naval stores, or facilitate a refit. In a typical complex interlocking move designed to maximise the value of every voyage, Warren sailed north from Bermuda in early March, to escort the light frigate *Minerva* and vital Ordnance transports heading for Halifax, and seek opportunities 'to annoy the enemy' between Chesapeake Bay and New York. Putting Warren in command of three stations gave him an opportunity to make the most efficient use of his forces, exploiting the seasonal highs and lows of winter storms and hurricanes to shift resources between the Caribbean and the Atlantic, but the extent and complexity of the task made it essential to have a captain of the fleet as chief of staff. Unaware that Hotham had already been appointed he requested Sir Thomas Hardy, Nelson's flag captain at Trafalgar.[19]

Understanding that his campaign had not met the expectations of his political masters and naval colleagues at the Admiralty, Warren reminded them that a thorough blockade of the American coast 'from its extent and number of ports requires more ships of war than are at present with me'. He wanted more large frigates, to extend and reinforce the blockade. He repeated the call for a Royal Marine battalion, for amphibious strikes against key naval targets like the *Constellation*.[20] Fortunately, as he noted:

. . . the Blockade of the Chesapeake and Delaware has already produced a considerable sensation, as flour has fallen from eleven to eight dollars per barrel, and it is supposed will be at even four dollars, as it is acknowledged to be nearly impracticable to send any vessel to sea.[21]

The strategy of carefully targeted operations, one that he had recommended, was bearing fruit. Regional specialisation in the American economy, and absolute reliance on coastal shipping, left economic activity desperately vulnerable to Warren's cruisers. The South, which relied on imported food and manufactures, suffered far more than New England, where manufacturing and smuggling took up some of the slack.[22]

Anchored in Lynnhaven Bay, close to the Chesapeake Capes, Warren discussed a Russian armistice proposal with Mr Swartz-koff, Secretary at the Tsar's Washington embassy. On the surface this seemed to be a helpful gesture: Russia remained neutral in this war, but fought alongside Britain against France. In reality the profoundly Anglophobe Chancellor Nikolai Rumiantsev wanted 'to save the American fleet as a counterweight to British maritime supremacy, and a way of forcing Britain to end its maritime despotism'.[23] With Napoleon in full retreat, Rumiantsev wanted to double the victory by breaking British control of Russian overseas trade. He had a profound concern for Russian economic development, and formed a close working relationship with John Quincy Adams, the American Minister at St Petersburg. Rumiantsev envisioned America becoming an alternative carrier and trade partner, and an ally in legal and naval disputes with London.[24] Russia's long-term interests required Britain to make concessions on belligerent rights. In the event Rumiantsev's influence was limited: he had been sidelined in St Petersburg as the Russian Army and Imperial headquarters marched into Germany.[25] The Tsar was focused on defeating Napoleon; he needed British money and munitions to sustain the war. This was no time to let the American sideshow stand in the way of the bigger issue. Not that Warren was taken in: as a former Minister to St Petersburg he knew the Russians, recognising a blatant attempt to undermine British belligerent rights, an issue that had been at the heart of the brief Northern War of 1801. His only mistake was to think that the Americans had prompted the initiative.[26] Warren's sources also indicated that Madison could not get his measures through Congress, where many were anxious to end the war. With Napoleon in full retreat Madison publicly blamed the French for misleading him. After due consideration Warren informed Swartzkoff that America could have peace, if the administration abandoned its demands on impressment and naturalisation, and all hostile measures against British ships. He was careful to stress that his diplomatic opinions were entirely unofficial: he only acted in a military capacity. Melville approved his cautious response, leaving unspoken the terms the government might consider.[27]

In truth the government was completely focused on the titanic events reshaping Europe, and would have been satisfied with the *status quo ante*. This moderate, conciliatory, statesmanlike approach to diplomacy formed a sharp contrast to Napoleon's double or quits military gambling, and the naïve desperation of Madison. Given the abject failure of land operations in Canada it is difficult to understand why the Americans persisted with a disastrous conflict.

EXTENDING THE ECONOMIC BLOCKADE

By late March 1813 Warren had blockaded the Chesapeake and Delaware and begun offensive coastal operations. At the same time the Admiralty finally accepted the need to extend the economic blockade further north, covering the American coast from the Mississippi to Rhode Island. This would allow British warships to prevent neutral ships entering or leaving the ports under blockade. The decision had been carefully calculated. Ministers were anxious to avoid problems with neutral shippers, notably Sweden, Russia, Spain and Portugal. To explain the new strategy Melville ended a three-month hiatus in high-level correspondence with Warren.[28]

We do not intend this as a mere <u>Paper</u> blockade, but as a complete stop to all Trade, & intercourse by sea with those Ports, as far as the wind and weather, & the continual presence of a sufficing armed force, will permit and ensure. If you find that this cannot be done without abandoning for a time the interruptions which you appear to be giving to the internal navigation of the Chesapeake, the latter object must be given up, & you must be content with blockading its entrance, & sending in occasionally your cruisers for the purpose of harassing & annoyance.

Despite the caveats he thought Warren had the resources to meet the demand: ten 74s, thirty frigates and a proportion of smaller vessels had already been sent; they should suffice for convoy, blockade and inshore operations, and cover reliefs and refits.[29] Given the length of the American coast this was strikingly optimistic. Official orders to extend the blockade were issued on 23 March; three days later a fresh Order in Council gave it legal status, providing ample warning for neutral powers.

Melville emphasised that British war aims remained unchanged: to end the war as soon as possible. Responding to newspaper rumours that the Americans might seek peace, he noted that Warren's diplomatic powers had lapsed when the Americans rejected the initial armistice. Rather than deal in rumour and innuendo the government had extended the economic blockade. This was the core strategic tool. Melville made the priorities crystal clear: coastal raids were subordinate to the economic blockade, and all offensive operations were subordinate to the vital task of defending British trade. While he readily admitted that much of the clamour from Jamaica and Leeward Islands interests about privateers was based on unfounded rumours that Warren had moved 'a large portion of the West India force to the Northward', Melville would not admit that his earlier criticism might have been in error. Reflecting on recent good news from America he implied it was all either too little, or too late. The observation that Warren had, 'at length entered upon active measures, and a rigorous system of blockading the Enemy's Ports', simply ignored the Admiral's cardinal point that without authority to blockade the entire coast he could neither stop neutral trade, nor control access to Boston in the winter. For Melville it was all very simple – Warren must do better: 'We trust that during the remainder of the season, none of the Enemy's ships of war will be able to escape either from those or from any other ports to the southward.' He went on to insult the Admiral's intelligence: reminding a veteran of many trade defence campaigns that the best way to deal with privateers was to make the business hazardous and unprofitable smacked of desperation. At least the First Lord could offer something useful: the Board had revoked all licences for British merchant ships to cross the Atlantic without convoy. Such ships provided the majority of privateer captures – henceforth privateers would have to fight convoy escorts for their prizes.

Warren would have realised that Melville's carping tone reflected the political impact of bad news. The public had been dismayed by the frigate defeats, while the commercial sector pushed for more protection:

The capture of the *Java* has excited a considerable sensation here, and I cannot help thinking that our Captains of Frigates ought to have a secret hint that they are not only not expected to attack those large American ships, but that their voluntarily engaging in such an encounter would be considered here in the same light as if they did not avoid an action with a Line of Battle Ship.

The good news was that the Board would send out the 74s *Sceptre* and *Plantagenet* with the next convoys. Melville had finally provided the ships he had promised earlier. Now Warren would have ten battleships spread across the three stations in addition to those escorting regular West India convoys. By increasing the frigate force to thirty, and with eighty other cruisers available, Melville expected to cover the station and allow a third of the ships to be tied up refitting and repairing.

Melville recognised the strategic value of attacking New Orleans but Britain lacked the military manpower to take or hold the city. The only practical strategy for 1813 was an economic blockade of the Mississippi.[30] The Admiralty intended despatching two Royal Marine battalions, each of 600–700 men, for coastal operations, but the Marines needed to recuperate after arduous service on the north coast of Spain. As if the proposed strike force were not small enough, Melville also demanded they should not be exposed to undue risk. In return for his Marines Warren had to meet the growing demands from the expanding fleet on the Great Lakes. Captain Sir James Yeo's command on Lake Ontario provided critical support for the defence of the frontier, and Governor-General Prevost made frequent demands for seamen, Marines and stores. These became a major drain on Warren's force.

Still fixated on the key control mechanism of regular communication, Melville dismissed Warren's fears about the security of his mail, trusting duplicates, proper precautions and the frequent return of worn-out ships and crews to Britain would keep the 'secret and confidential' correspondence flowing. To enhance his control he urged the Admiral to use the base at Bermuda, 'the most centrical spot within the limits of your station', and sent another rear admiral to command the Halifax station. He promised to replace the unsatisfactory Caribbean admirals. Cockburn and Hotham would relieve Warren of local command and planning tasks and, by implication, enable him to focus on theatre strategy. Furthermore: 'You have under your command some of the most active and intelligent officers in the Navy, and I rely on your rendering them available to the public interest.'[31] He observed that Hardy was too low down the list to be captain of the fleet.[32] Despite his critical tone and imputation of slow proceedings, Melville tacitly acknowledged Warren's contention about the scale of American privateering. Warren decided against sending his letters in a sloop, preferring to wait a fortnight for a convoy carrying the Royal Marine battalion, escorted by the 74 HMS *Asia*.[33]

Between March and September 1813 Warren's forces took 138 American vessels, 2 warships and 136 merchant ships, letters of marque and privateers. Small, low-value craft were destroyed, to avoid detaching prize crews; others became British cruisers. By the time the 1813 wheat harvest had been reaped the grain trade to Lisbon had stopped. Both exports and imports were falling into British hands with increasing regularity. As a result American goods flowed into British factories and markets, fed Britain's armies in Canada, and even repaired British ships at Halifax and Bermuda. The biggest problem was the inability of the Vice-Admiralty Prize Courts at Bermuda, Jamaica, Halifax and the Leeward Islands to handle the volume of business. Well over 300 ships were sent in for condemnation in 1813. If America evaded the full impact of economic blockade in 1813 it only delayed the inevitable.

AMERICAN STRATEGY

Despite the repeal of the Orders in Council shortly after the outbreak of war, which divided the Republican Party, and the pathetic military campaigns of 1812, Madison was re-elected to the Presidency in December 1812, with a sharply reduced majority. This political weakness, and the dominance of local concerns, ensured that Congress rejected the trade embargo he requested, to deny the British army in Canada access to

American food. Unable to secure peace by commercial embargo, Madison had little option but to try another military campaign, enlarging the army over the winter. He also needed men to meet the inevitable British attacks on the American coast. However, financial weakness restricted military recruitment to 35,000 troops. New Secretary for War John Armstrong advised that attacking York (modern Toronto), Kingston and the Niagara frontier were the only realistic options for 1813. These plans were given particular urgency by gubernatorial elections in New York State at the end of April. When the British reinforced Kingston, York became the only target within American capability in the time available. The deflection of strategy, from destroying the critical naval dockyard at Kingston, which would have wrecked the British position below Montreal, to a strategically insignificant provincial capital, was a heavy price to pay for a domestic political advantage. Navy Secretary Paul Hamilton had preferred further operations on the broad oceans to developing naval power on the Great Lakes in support of the land war. His replacement, William Jones was more attuned to the strategic needs of the lakes, using extra funds to encourage seamen to serve there, rather than construct 74s. He preferred smaller vessels to carry the war to the British in their own waters.

The failure of Russian mediation left Madison with no option but to continue the war for Canada. The land frontier, and the Great Lakes that were the key to strategic mobility in the area, would remain the core of the war. Powerful navies were created on Lake Erie and Lake Ontario. In March 1813 Secretary Armstrong ordered General Harrison to secure command of Lake Erie, supporting Master Commandant Oliver Hazard Perry's efforts to build a fleet of warships at Presque Isle, and collect transports at Cleveland for his army. The size of Harrison's force alarmed General Procter and, anxious for his supply lines, he pressed the young Captain Barclay, commanding the British flotilla on Lake Erie, to give battle to Perry's superior force. The struggle in the far west took a decisive turn when Perry captured the British squadron

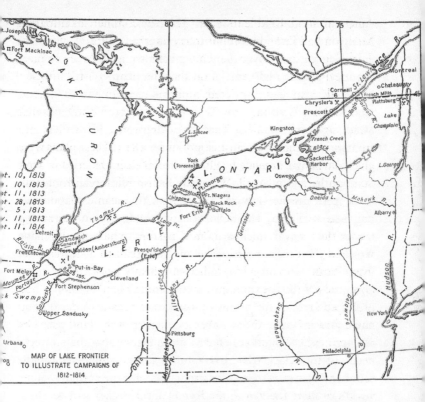

War on the Great Lakes, 1812–15.

after a savage action near Put in Bay on 10 September 1813. His success was quickly followed up: within two weeks Perry had transported Harrison's 7,000-man army across the lake, forcing Procter to evacuate Detroit. Harrison pursued Procter, wiping out his 900-man force at the Battle of the Thames on 5 October. The American triumph was complete when the mutilated body of Tecumseh was paraded. The last hope of the Indian nations fell in a minor British debacle. The battle settled control of the Detroit area for the rest of the war, and destroyed the last vestiges of Indian power in the region.

On Lake Ontario General Dearborn's forces, carried by Commodore Isaac Chauncey's fleet, captured York on 27 April, burning the public buildings. The army then re-embarked, crossed the lake and landed on the Niagara Peninsula, capturing Fort George in late May, and advancing west along the Niagara frontier. On the night of 6 June a smaller British force attacked the American camp at Stoney Creek. In a confused action the Americans drove off the British, but both their generals were captured, negating their tactical success. With their lake communications now cut by Commodore Yeo's squadron, the Americans retreated. On the 24th 600 Americans were surrounded by Indians and forced to surrender at Beaver Dams. This fresh disaster ensured Dearborn's retirement. Once again the American army would wither away by the end of the season under the pressure of low morale, poor logistics and ill health. York had been a vital political success, securing victory in the New York elections, but failure on the Niagara frontier left upstate New York exposed to British raids.[34]

For the rest of the war the two fleets on Lake Ontario spent their time building and skirmishing, neither side being prepared to fight when inferior. The astonishing shipbuilding efforts, respectively at Sackett's Harbor and Kingston, progressed rapidly from sloops to frigates, and culminated with the commissioning of HMS *Saint Lawrence*, a 100-gun three-decker in late 1814, which gave the British undisputed command of the lake. At the end of the war she had sisters on the stocks at Kingston, and two American rivals building at Sackett's Harbor. These were colossal vessels to build in wilderness outposts, but they only served to reinforce the mutual caution of Chauncey and Yeo.

The American army fared no better to the east. A two-pronged advance against Montreal came to nothing. In October 1813 General Wade Hampton's 4,000 men moved north-west from Lake Champlain and crossed the frontier along the Chateauguay River, heading for the St Lawrence. They were driven back by a far smaller force of embodied and sedentary Canadian militia at the battle of Chateauguay on 26 October. Hampton then retired across the frontier and took up winter quarters. In November General James Wilkinson led nearly 8,000 men from Sackett's

Harbor down the St Lawrence towards Montreal, pursued by a small British force. When Wilkinson turned to engage the 800 British, Canadians and Indians at Chrysler's Farm on the 12th his troops were beaten off. The following day, learning that Hampton's force was retreating, Wilkinson crossed back into American territory and went into winter quarters. Another season had passed without any worthwhile achievement by the American army, bolstering the morale of the Canadian and British forces. In late December British troops even crossed the frontier to capture Fort Niagara and sack the villages of Buffalo and Black Rock.

On 29 December 1812 Paul Hamilton, a man of limited organisational ability already facing a Congressional investigation, had offered his resignation.[35] Madison accepted without demur, offering the post to William Jones, Philadelphia ship captain, merchant, Congressman, and above all loyal Republican. Well aware this would be no easy task Jones pondered the offer for several days before accepting. He well understood that he would have to re-organise the department while waging war against the most powerful navy the world had ever seen.[36] A rare War Hawk with maritime experience, Jones knew the British would tighten their blockade, harass the coast and intercept privateers. He had been examining the strategic options for several months, having advised Bainbridge on cruising grounds and trade routes in October.[37] Once in office, Jones proposed sending his warships out singly to cruise against British commerce anywhere between southern Ireland and the Cape of Good Hope, 'to draw the attention of the enemy from the annoyance of our coast, for the protection of his own rich & exposed Commercial fleets'. He sought a 'powerful diversion' by spreading the handful of national warships individually across the North and South Atlantic.[38] Recognising the morale value of naval glory, Jones was prepared to risk battle with equal foes. Such operations would oblige the British to concentrate their forces, facilitating the privateer operations that would inflict real economic damage.

Unable to protect the American coast from overwhelming British naval power, Jones believed that the destruction of commercial shipping would distract the attackers. Confident in his own expertise, Jones issued his captains with precise orders, orders that many found unduly restrictive in an age without reliable communications.[39] Jones set American naval strategy for the rest of the war, as far as the British blockade, convoy system and patrols allowed. American warships captured very few merchant prizes, and if the privateers were more single-minded in their pursuit of profit, their success declined sharply after early 1813. British commercial losses fell as many prizes were recaptured, leaving British insurance rates effectively unchanged. This made a striking contrast with the situation in 1810, when French privateers had prompted a sharp increase in rates. Effective trade defence reduced British losses to manageable levels, levels that Britain could absorb. Furthermore, when American privateers did reach the distant waters off China they found the British ready and waiting.[40] This was hardly unexpected; after all they had been engaged in a truly global war for the past twenty years. Commerce-destroying had a long history of failure as a decisive strategy.[41] For all the profit and glory of predation it was the last resort of weak nations unable to contest command of the sea, the ability to use the ocean for trade and war. Such powers lacked the resources to win a naval war; they could not stop the movement of merchant vessels, merely subject it to a level of attrition that obliged the dominant sea power to employ effective trade defences. Such campaigns by French and American privateers between 1688 and 1815, and German U-boats between 1917 and 1945 proved costly and occasionally embarrassing, but never decisive. It helped that, by the spring of 1813, the peak of French commerce warfare had passed. Even so Britain had the resources to meet both threats.

Despite his defeat in Russia Napoleon did not make it any easier for his co-belligerents. He allowed American privateers to sell prize ships in French ports, but they had to re-export British goods that could not be legally imported under the Continental

System, primarily to allow France to retain desperately needed specie. At least the Americans were treated better than French privateers, who could only watch as captured British goods were burnt. Indeed several French privateers operated under the American flag. Napoleon even blocked the release of American sailors who were willing to join privateers, believing most of them were British. Eventually the sloop *True Blooded Yankee* was commissioned at Brest with an all-American crew; it proved highly successful, taking $400,000 worth of prizes on three voyages before falling to British cruisers in the Straits of Gibraltar.

HORNET

The USS *Hornet*, Master Commandant James Lawrence, had accompanied the *Constitution* on the cruise that culminated in the capture of HMS *Java*. When Bainbridge headed home he left Lawrence to blockade HMS *Bonne Citoyenne* at San Salvador. Lawrence, a tall, elegant man of refined manners, was widely admired by his peers, not least for his heightened sense of personal and professional honour. Furthermore, he bore the Royal Navy a deep and abiding grudge. In 1805 he had been humiliated when three men deserted from his gunboat at Gibraltar, and Admiral Lord Collingwood refused to return them because they were British citizens. In the autumn of 1812 Lawrence threatened to resign when Charles Morris, first lieutenant of the *Constitution*, received a unique double promotion for the *Guerriere* action, overtaking him in the race for the coveted rank of captain. Navy Secretary Hamilton told him to get on with his job. Little wonder he was so anxious to fight. Having earned his previous promotion by bravery in battle, Lawrence had no illusions about the best way to become a captain. Acutely sensitive to the finer points of precedent in a tiny officer corps, Lawrence was clearly bursting to get on.[42]

On 24 February, off Demerara, Lawrence engaged the smaller, less heavily armed and manned British brig HMS *Peacock*. A brig, with only two masts, would be at a serious disadvantage against a three-masted American sloop if both ships suffered any damage to their rigging, a fact only too well known to Lawrence. To make matters worse *Peacock*, widely known as a 'yacht', had not exercised her guns with any regularity. Both ships carried a main armament of carronades, with only one or two small long guns, so there was no possibility of a complex manoeuvring battle, like those between frigates. The British ship had 24-pounder carronades, the American 32-pounders, a British crew of 122 faced 165 Americans.[43]

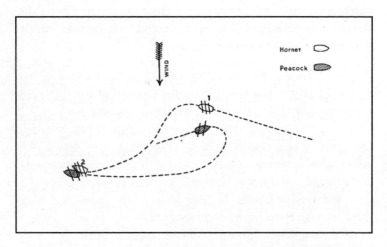

Ill-matched creatures: USS *Hornet* versus HMS *Peacock*,
24 February 1813.

Lawrence's approach to battle has been described as a combination of 'cockiness and excessive self assurance'. Despite the odds *Peacock* was game enough, sailing into battle without hesitation. An initial exchange of broadsides on opposite courses left *Peacock* winged, her main topsail and gaff halyards cut by American dismantling projectiles. The British broadsides were equally high, scything through the *Hornet*'s sails, but without damaging her heavier three-masted rig. *Peacock* did not use any dismantling projectiles: the Royal Navy had stopped issuing them. Having crippled his opponent Lawrence manoeuvred into a killing position close on her starboard quarter, where only two British guns would bear. Exploiting superior manpower, Lawrence also kept up a heavy fire of musketry and small shot from the tops to clear the exposed British quarterdeck, leaving Commander William Peake among the dead. Soon after, *Peacock*'s mainmast fell, leaving her crippled and overpowered, wallowing in the swell. Finally Lawrence shifted his guns from clearing the British upper deck to solid shot. At close range 32-pounder solid shot tore through *Peacock*'s hull, and the hold began to fill with water. After little more than fifteen minutes of close action the shattered, waterlogged brig surrendered. *Peacock* was hastily abandoned, sinking soon afterwards.

The *Peacock* action reminded the British that a dangerous minority of officers still emphasised paintwork and polished brass over gunnery. After news of the loss reached London the Admiralty ordered captains to attend to the 'expert management of the Guns', essential to preserve 'the high character of the British Navy', through the necessary instruction and practice. To ensure they were obeyed the orders would be repeated.[44]

Lawrence had earned his promotion: bold, aggressive tactics and a well-handled ship proved him a man of mettle, and he took up his next post with the advantage of experience in single-ship combat. In his next battle he would repeat the tactics used to take the *Peacock*.[45] The emphasis on close-range action distinguished him from other American frigate captains, who preferred to fight with long guns, disabling the enemy before closing to decisive range. Because *Hornet* had a short-range carronade battery Lawrence began with a heavy fire of anti-rigging projectiles at close range. Once the enemy lost manoeuvrability he turned *Hornet*'s armament to clear the enemy upper deck, decimating the British gun crews, and then sank her in short order. While Peake has been blamed for failing to exercise his men at the guns, a far more serious fault lay in his rigging. Peake adopted the overly tidy, minimalist rigging of a 'smart' vessel. Too many British officers took pride in reducing the number of rigging blocks to a bare minimum; such ships looked smart but they were easily disabled. On the other hand experienced, thoughtful officers like Broke rigged extra shrouds and spare gear to counter the threat.

Returning to New York in late March 1813, Lawrence became the latest to have his name inscribed on the patriotic banner, receiving praise, dinners and promises in equal measure. His report of the action, and informal comments were widely reproduced by sensation-hungry newspapers. As befitted a man of honour Lawrence's treatment of the captured British officers was exemplary, eliciting a public letter of thanks on the occasion of their exchange.[46] While it seemed this latest success had established the naval character of the nation few realised that it marked the high tide of oceanic glory.

Despite his victory, and his promotion, Lawrence remained a highly strung, sensitive man, acutely aware of the dignity of his calling. Broke must have read Lawrence's famous challenge to the *Bonne Citoyenne*, and his insulting rejoinder when refused. This makes the letter Broke later sent into Boston a masterpiece of psychological warfare. Recognising the character of his opponent, Broke carefully contrived the most insulting combination of remarks based on Lawrence's own published utterances delivered with the studied politeness of a gentleman. He wanted an affair of honour – a duel. Evidence for Broke's understanding of his opponent can be seen in his decision to revisit the question of how long it took to defeat the enemy. Lawrence had observed: 'My clerk reported the time of action as eleven minutes, but I thought fifteen minutes was short enough, so I made it that in my report.'[47] While cruising off Boston, Broke picked up the latest American news from prizes and fishing vessels, reading Lawrence's speech at the public dinner given by the Common Council of New York on 6 April.

BRITISH STRATEGY

By March 1813 the British were committed to a strategy of close blockade, both to bottle up American warships and privateers, and conduct economic warfare, supported by convoys to protect British trade. The economic blockade from the Mississippi to the Rhode Island took precedence over offensive operations. While the Admiralty accepted Warren's explanation that bad weather in winter made a close blockade of Boston impossible, they expected him to interrupt Rodgers's free access until the weather improved. As the French threat had evaporated he could spread his ten battleships singly along the coast. The Board argued that they recognised the peculiar difficulties that Warren faced, assigning him a significantly larger force than would normally be deployed to deal with this level of threat.[48] While this may have been a backhanded compliment to the impact of American naval and privateering activity, it ended the successes of 1812.

By late March Warren's forces were deployed along the Atlantic coast, with a major concentration in Chesapeake Bay. Baltimore, Charleston and Savannah. The Southern ports, home to 'the most implacable and virulent people in the whole Union', were blockaded to bottle up the privateers. New York, the second privateer centre, would soon be blockaded, using anchorages that the Royal Navy had last occupied in the Revolutionary War. Warren's planned dispositions included Broke's squadron of three frigates cruising to defend Nova Scotia. In March he anticipated shifting Broke out onto the Grand Banks, to cover troop convoys heading into the St Lawrence River with vital reinforcements and stores for the Canadian front. When the weather improved Warren would place a squadron to watch Boston and Rhode Island, cutting communications between Boston and Long Island Sound.[49] Broke chose the post of honour off Boston, the only place where he could see American frigates, and hope to meet them in action.

These were well-judged, effective dispositions. Once Warren had an adequate force, the United States Navy found itself pinned down, unable to get to sea, and increasingly drawn into local defensive operations. Just as Secretary Jones feared, the British had the initiative, and they knew exactly how to make it count. A century of high-intensity naval conflict, refined by twenty years of war with Revolutionary and Napoleonic France had refined the methods of naval and economic blockade, convoy and coastal raids. They were so familiar that neither Warren nor the Admiralty bothered to discuss details. There would be no more unpleasant surprises, because everyone knew what was expected. Warren seized the initiative at several locations, pinning American resources to costly local defences that made no positive contribution to the war effort. It did not take the British long to translate command of Chesapeake Bay into a devastating strategic offensive, one that obliged the American government to respond.[50]

FEELING THE PINCH

Navy Secretary Jones recognised that demands for additional defences in the Chesapeake and the Delaware would divert resources away from the offensive at sea, and the Great Lakes. Powerful British forces probed the navigational and military hazards of the maritime highways leading to America's major cities. Alarmed civic leaders looked for help to a government that lacked the manpower, artillery and money to act. All Jones could do was praise local enthusiasm, and attempt to talk down the threat. He argued that the British failure to destroy the *Constellation*, the city of Norfolk, or any other population centre on the Chesapeake indicated their only intention was to distract:

[After attempting Norfolk] they then moved off and proceeded to menace Baltimore in the same way exciting a great alarm and expense in preparation for defence ... Their plan of operation appears to me clearly to be that of a rigorous Blockade and harassing exciting and depredating with the hope of diverting our attention from the Oceans and the Lakes by employing our troops and our Seamen in the preparation for the defence of our Sea port towns and innumerable Bays harbours rivers and creeks, and surely if they could reduce us to act on the defensive only while they vary the scene of action by their superior force and keep up the excitement, alarm and constant preparation from North to South their object would be gained. For it is idle to suppose we can be prepared at all points to meet the concentrated force of the enemy, and also act with vigour upon the Ocean and the Lakes.

Jones proposed creating limited local defences based on gunboats and block ships.[51] Whatever the merits of his proposal the lack of resources left the coast wide open.

In a typical operation between 29 and 31 May the boats of three British warships swept the Delaware River, taking or destroying more than twenty vessels.[52] Warren tempered his applause by advising captains to be careful to keep down casualties.[53] There was no need to take risks.

While Warren's operations appeared to confirm Jones's deductions, the Admiral was developing his coastal operations into a fundamental threat to the economic life and internal cohesion of the middle states, and raising the prospect of a race war. He played on the deepest fears of the plantation states – a servile revolt following the horrific genocidal precedent of St Domingue not two decades before. Sounding the Patapsco River confirmed that naval forces could only approach Baltimore to attack the town and shipping if the forts and batteries on the river had been captured. This would require enough troops to disperse the local militia; he would not risk precious seamen on such an enterprise. However, there were other ways of waging war without an army. Warren took most of his supplies and additional manpower from the enemy. 'I never saw a country so vulnerable, open to attack, or that affords the means of support to an enemy's force, as the States.' To reinforce his landing parties he recruited from a slave population that demonstrated the 'most ardent desire to join any troops or seamen acting in the country', a desire he was happy to oblige.[54] British law was quite clear: no man who trod the deck of a British warship remained a slave. The 'Colonial Marines' were volunteers serving for pay. Local knowledge and acclimatisation made them excellent reinforcements, while the moral effect on tidewater planters of a disciplined force of heavily armed black men in red jackets, backed by the overwhelming firepower of the Royal Navy, added a frisson of existential terror to an emerging economic catastrophe.

THE ESCAPE OF *PRESIDENT* AND *CONGRESS*

When he returned to Boston on the last day of 1812 with the frigates *President* and *Congress* John Rodgers seemed astonished that he had sailed several thousand miles through the very heart of the British global trading network, and hardly saw a ship. He took only two prizes. Apparently unaware just how effective a well-run convoy system could be, he had little more to show for his pains than worn-out rigging and damaged copper. For his next cruise Rodgers planned a demonstration off Halifax before attacking British army supply ships on the Grand Banks, then proceeding towards the Azores and on via the coast of Ireland to the Baltic.[55] Navy Secretary Jones rejected his plans to head for the China Seas, restricting him to the North and South Atlantic.[56] Rodgers sailed from Boston in the *President* in company with the *Congress*, in case they were intercepted by the British frigates. The post of honour was held by Philip Broke in *Shannon*, supported by his friend and Suffolk neighbour Hyde Parker in *Tenedos*. Broke made it very clear that the British ships were willing to fight, challenging Rodgers to a battle between the two pairs of frigates. Having nothing to gain by such heroics Rodgers ignored the letter, but this very public challenge clearly got under his skin, just as Broke had intended.

The Americans dropped down to President Roads on 23 April, and after a week of head winds sailed on the 30th, but were held up by more adverse winds and only cleared Boston Bay on 3 May. Never one for an even fight Rodgers slipped out during thick squally weather. The sheer hard work of beating out had its reward; the British frigates had been forced to work out to sea by the easterly gales.[57] While Rodgers's escape was hardly glorious it was a strategic success. Only six American frigates got to sea in 1813; most were penned in by superior force.

Broke was mortified. He had been desperate to get hold of one of the big American 44s, to prove that the British had been out-matched in the three engagements of 1812. Bladen Capel, the senior officer at Halifax, stressed that no blame attached to Broke: 'it is impossible for more zeal and perseverance to have been shewn by any Officer'. Capel hurried out to sea in *La Hogue*, 74, and redistributed the squadron to intercept the Americans. Once again Rodgers's luck held: Capel saw the *President* on the afternoon of the 3rd near St George's Bank, but could not close on the American flagship.[58] Rodgers had spotted *La Hogue* and the frigate *Nymphe*, and pressed on with his mission. He would return to Newport in September after a five-month cruise that netted only a dozen prizes, and no glory.

DECATUR'S DEBACLE

Secretary Jones directed Commodore Decatur to take his squadron, *United States*, *Macedonian* and *Hornet*, to sea from New York and clear British light forces blockading South Carolina and Georgia. Later the orders were altered to raiding West Indies trade. The large privateer schooner *Scourge*, Captain Samuel Nicoll, elected to accompany Decatur to sea.[59] Whatever his destination might be, by late March Warren knew Decatur would try to leave New York in the next few weeks, and accordingly set about reinforcing the blockade of both exits. By April 1813 Captain Robert Oliver in the 74 *Valiant* waited off Sandy Hook with the heavy frigate *Acasta*, while Captain Sir Thomas Hardy, *Ramillies*, 74, held station between Montauk Point and Block Island with the frigate *Orestes*, controlling Long Island Sound. Hardy had already stopped the local coasting trade.

In late May Decatur tried the Sandy Hook exit, only to be frustrated by foul weather that left his ships anchored under the forts in plain sight of the British blockading squadron. Decatur returned to New York, intending to pass the difficult Hell Gate and leave by Long Island Sound, believing Hardy's squadron to be less powerful than Oliver's. On the 24th Decatur and Nicoll took their ships through the Hell Gate without incident, only for the *United States* then to run aground, and be struck by lightning. In the event Oliver, forewarned by intelligence sources ashore, outfoxed Decatur, switching stations with Hardy to ensure that the *Acasta*, the largest and fastest British frigate on the American station, and his fast 74 were waiting. Despite his precautions Nicoll's privateer slipped out on the 27th.

On 30 May Oliver saw the American warships anchored west of Fisher's Island. Decatur, who could only see the 74, still reckoned he could get out. On the morning of 1 June Oliver rounded Montauk Point, spotting the Americans 7 or 8 miles dead to windward. On sighting the two British ships ahead Decatur convinced himself two or three more were loitering behind Block Island. All three American captains believed they had been ambushed by a superior force. In fact there were only two British ships, but they did constitute a superior force, and they had been kept very light, with only the minimum water and stores, to preserve speed for a chase. Oliver immediately crowded on every stitch of sail, while Decatur was flying for home with studding sails set, his heavily laden 44 lagging well behind his faster consorts. *Acasta* got up close enough to exchange a few shots with the *United States*, but without effect, and on reaching the Race Oliver had to call off the pursuit: no one on board had the necessary knowledge of local navigation.

Decatur rushed into the Thames River at New London, which proved to be a strategic disaster. One quarter of America's frigates had been locked up by an intelligence-led operation. They were, as Oliver concluded, 'in a situation where perhaps they can be more easily watched than in most others'. Oliver summoned Hardy round from Sandy Hook, hoping to attack the Americans in the river, but Hardy was delayed by light winds giving Decatur time to get his ships 5 or 6 miles upriver and build shore batteries. The British captains decided against an attack; the charts showed little water in the Thames River, and they lacked a suitable landing force to assault the batteries. Well aware that local sympathies were decidedly Federalist Decatur tried to stop communications with the British. He did not find much support from a local community opposed to the war that found his presence a major impediment to their shady business dealings.[60] Robert Oliver's skilful interception demonstrated that the British had all the intelligence they needed. Loose talk on the New York waterfront betrayed Decatur's plans; it would do so again. For all his bravado Decatur had no answer to a 74 and a frigate anchored off New London, nor was Secretary Jones in any hurry to send the New York gunboat flotilla to help him, once he had taken up residence so far inland.[61] Not that the civic leaders of New York were prepared to send 'their' gunboats so far afield to help the Navy.[62] The British had bottled up three American warships in a narrow river; they would be easy to blockade. Although Decatur's hasty retreat was not the worst thing to befall the United States Navy on 1 June 1813, it did mark a fundamental change of fortune. Oliver's success proved the wisdom of Warren's strategic assessment: the British needed enough heavy ships to pin down all the major American warships, and close the key ports. Once those forces arrived Warren shut down the Chesapeake, the Delaware, New York and ultimately Boston. America's glory days on the oceans were over.

THE CRUISE OF THE *CHESAPEAKE*

After Rodgers put to sea the only seaworthy frigate left in Boston[63] was the USS *Chesapeake*, Captain Samuel Evans. Built at Norfolk, Virginia, in 1798–9, the *Chesapeake* was the last and smallest of the original six frigates, a standard 18-pounder ship almost identical to *Shannon*.[64] Evans had sailed from Boston in mid-December 1812. He returned after a modestly successful cruise against British trade on the Equator in early April with a short sick list, and a long catalogue of defects. Exhausted and troubled by an old wound, Evans requested shore service. Secretary Jones evinced no great concern to keep him afloat.

Evans wanted time to refit, and new masts. Jones, anxious to keep his scant force active, and unimpressed by the meagre results of the four-month cruise, pressed him to refit quickly and cheaply, pointing to the 'highly extravagant' fittings of Evans's cabin. At this time Jones could not have known that the cautious Evans would be the most successful American officer when it came to taking British merchant ships.[65]

After refitting *Hornet* James Lawrence proposed cruising in company with the sloop USS *Argus*: one option was to head north, seeking out ships bound for Quebec, before heading to the Orkney Islands, then past Greenland and back home by September. He expected to cut up the Arctic whaling fleet. Alternatively he advised exploiting his local knowledge off Surinam and Demerara.[66] Such plans ignored the fact that newly promoted Captain Lawrence was too senior to command the *Hornet*. Jones ordered Master Commandant James Biddle to relieve him on 1 May. If Lawrence hoped for a period of shore leave, as his biographer implies, his reputation made it unlikely the Navy could spare him. The occasion for him to return to sea came sooner than anyone expected.

On 6 May Jones, anticipating that the *Chesapeake* was ready, ordered Evans to sea. He may have intended to push Evans to resign: a carefully constructed paragraph offered him an honourable transfer ashore. Jones stressed the strategic purpose of the cruise was to destroy 'ships with Military and Naval Stores, destined for the supply of his armies in Canada, and Fleets on this station, and the capture of transports with troops destined to reinforce Canada, or invade our own shores'. *Chesapeake* should sail along the coast of Nova Scotia, the Gulf of St Lawrence and Strait of Belle Isle, the coast of Labrador or the east coast of Newfoundland, before heading for Greenland, 'where the entire whale fishery of the enemy, being without protection may be speedily and completely destroyed'. The nature of the war had changed. Jones emphasised it was almost impossible to bring prizes back to American ports so that captured ships, especially those laden with military stores, must be destroyed to prevent the British recapturing them. He argued that a single ship could cut the Canadian lifeline because the convoys broke up close by Cape Race, leaving the entrance to the St Lawrence unprotected. Expecting the *Hornet* would also be ready for sea Jones sent the same orders to Biddle.[67] That this was the very cruise Lawrence had proposed only two weeks before suggests that what followed was anything but coincidental. Lawrence would conduct the very cruise he had planned, accompanied by his old ship *Hornet*.

After his promotion, Lawrence was initially detailed to command New York Navy Yard. A week later fresh orders gave him command of the *Constitution*, a ship in which he had served as first lieutenant. The *Constitution* was undergoing a refit at Boston. Having written to Evans on 6 May, effectively ordering him to put to sea or come ashore, Jones changed his mind. Later the same day he ordered Evans to New York Navy Yard, exchanging commands with Lawrence. Evans had not shown the enthusiasm that the Secretary expected; his health and concerns over the refit suggested he was the wrong man for the job. Steady, reliable peacetime managers and navigators had to be replaced by men like Lawrence, heroic killers with a reputation. Only days after being promised the *Constitution*, Lawrence found himself ordered to the smaller *Chesapeake*, which was ready for operations. Secretary Jones trusted to his energy and enthusiasm to get the ship to sea.[68]

Bitterly disappointed at losing his preferred command, Lawrence claimed to be concerned about his wife's health, and tried to exchange the *Chesapeake* for *Constitution*. He hoped Captain Charles Stewart would be anxious to get to sea.[69] After the frustrations of fitting out the *Constellation*, only to be blockaded in Norfolk, Stewart may very well have been looking for action, but not so anxiously as to exchange down to a smaller ship. Furthermore, Stewart, the senior officer, had every right to command the bigger ship.

Many modern accounts dwell on Washington Irving's idea that the *Chesapeake* was an unlucky ship, as if the humiliation of 1807 reflected something rotten in her fabric. This nonsense only gained currency after 1 June 1813. The implication that *Chesapeake* had a defective crew was equally unfounded. After *Chesapeake* returned to Boston in April, ninety-two officers and men, including the captain, were replaced from a complement of 387. This was no ordinary ship's company: the muster book reveals that there was not a single landsman, and only thirteen boys. Lawrence commanded a remarkably experienced team of deep-sea mariners. Many had served under Samuel Evans; others had moved from other American warships. Some were British; at least thirty-six would be identified by the British authorities.[70] Nineteen fresh Marines took the place of Scots and Irish privates sent ashore before the ship sailed. This rate of turn-over was not uncommon for a ship in harbour after a long cruise; some men were sick, some had made themselves undesirable, while others' terms of enlistment had expired.

Lawrence relieved Evans in command of the *Chesapeake* at 1.00 p.m. on 20 May. Within hours he made his intentions clear: 'At 6 p.m. beat to quarters & exercised the guns. Loaded them with round and grape.'[71] Over the next eleven days Lawrence paid close attention to gun drill and the action stations of his crew. He obtained flintlock firing mechanisms for his heavy guns, the sure sign of a professional fighting sea officer.[72] Six times he had the men 'Beat to Quarters', three times he 'Exercised the Guns' and once exercised the boarders. Having an experienced crew, three-quarters of them veterans of Evans's command, Lawrence used the drills to fine-tune the ship for battle. He anticipated using the tactics that had served him so well in his last command.

Reporting his assumption of command to Secretary Jones, Lawrence was very clear about his ship: 'I found her ready for sea.' Once he was on his new quarterdeck the thought of an exchange quickly faded; he would 'proceed to sea at the first favourable opportunity', and set a rendezvous for *Hornet*.[73] Other officers were equally clear that *Chesapeake* was ready for sea. Only a week after Lawrence took command, new first

Tragic hero of the United States Navy:
Captain James Lawrence.

lieutenant Augustus Ludlow reported 'the ship is in better order for battle than I ever saw her before'.[74] This was no offhand remark: like everyone else in Boston Ludlow knew all about the British frigates in the Bay, the name of their senior officer, and his habit of burning prizes. If the American frigate sailed there was every chance of a fight.

The most important improvement Lawrence effected on his new command was to replace several officers, especially the divisive Acting Lieutenant Pierce, 'at variance with every officer in his mess'. With a better set of young gentlemen on the quarterdeck, and a fortnight of drill to ensure the ship recognised the hand of the new master, Lawrence happily reported, on the very morning of battle, 'my crew appear to be in fine spirits, and I trust will do their duty'.[75] Having stowed the ship for a long cruise on the 27th Lawrence's gunners spent the 28th fitting spare breeching ropes for the guns, a sensible precaution reducing the risk the cannon would be disabled by damage to the control tackles. The following day, 29 May, *Chesapeake* loaded 130 bar shot, 52 chain shot and 8 langridge projectiles. Evidently Lawrence intended to fight another '*Hornet*' action, crippling the enemy's rigging before taking up a killing position on the bow or quarter, clearing the upper deck with grape and canister, and then perhaps boarding. At sunset Lawrence had the yards sent down and beat to quarters.

On 30 May Lawrence conned the *Chesapeake* down from the Long Wharf to the anchorage at President Roads, to give his men a few days to prepare for sea, stow the last of their provisions for an extended cruise, and tighten down the rigging. The following day, 31 May, with a British frigate in the offing, he prepared for action.[76] Unlike James Barron he had no intention of being caught napping as he left the American coast. Unlike John Rodgers he had no intention of skulking out in a fog. First he had to settle a bitter legal dispute with William Bainbridge, who claimed a commodore's share of the prize money for the *Peacock*. This unseemly squabble was only resolved the evening before the ship sailed.[77] Having resolved the money question Lawrence dined with Bainbridge and other naval officers at Charlestown Navy Yard, the talk was inevitably about the British ship that lay so close. This silent ship posed a moral challenge, one that occasionally arrived in written form. American officers had already received a splendid example of Philip Broke's elegant prose, challenging John Rodgers, but Rodgers was long gone.

While it has been customary to examine the *Chesapeake*'s battle as a heroic duel, with little more purpose than an affair of honour between gentlemen, Secretary Jones's orders were imperative, and they conveyed a clear strategic purpose. The war on the Canadian border was the heart of the conflict; with the American army in chaos the Navy must make every attempt, at any risk, to reduce the flow of British troops and stores up the St Lawrence to Quebec and Kingston. Naval stores were equally important: command of the Great Lakes would determine the outcome of the land war. It was for this reason that James Lawrence set sail, accepting battle with an enemy ship of equal force. Indeed, without a specific order not to engage equal force, Secretary Jones's reference to 'honour and advancement' could be read as a direction to give battle. This reading is reinforced by the fact that the orders had originally been drafted for Captain Evans, whom Jones considered unduly cautious. Knowing Lawrence's record it might have been wise for him to remind the new captain that such actions were not in the best interests of the state. Win, lose or draw, a naval battle off Boston would do no harm to the British shipping off the St Lawrence, or the whalers off Greenland. John Rodgers's furtive escape was a far better model; indeed at the end of May there were opportunities to slip through the fog.

BROKE ON BLOCKADE

For Philip Broke the winter had been anything but glorious. By early 1813 he could see that his ship desperately needed a complete refit, a job for a British dockyard. When that happened he would be shifted into a battleship, ending any prospect of single combat and individual fame. A career dedicated to the pursuit of glory through scientific seamanship and gunnery could end with a whimper. It is likely he would have preferred long overdue leave, and gone home to his other life as a country gentleman. Yet the New Year found Broke resolutely holding station in appalling weather: halyards and braces froze in the blocks; his men suffered the agonies of frostbite. There were few rewards. In company with *Tenedos*, *Nymphe* and *Curlew Shannon* took an American privateer before returning to Halifax on 23 February 1813.[78]

In late March, during a brief interval replenishing stores and water in Halifax, Broke released the pent-up anxieties of command in letters to his beloved Louisa, half a world away, who knew little of ships and wars. He wanted to come home, even if the war went on. The endless monotony of cruising in difficult waters, waiting for Commodore Rodgers, was beginning to wear, but once the squadron was refreshed they would set out again, taking station off Boston and Rhode Island. He would apply more pressure: 'and if our adversaries will not come out and dispute the ground fairly with us, we shall punish him by harassing the trade & feel confident we shall not have such a dull cruise as our last'. The Army had defended Canada:

. . . had we done as well, these spiteful renegados would be cringing for peace – but our blockades are forming, & they will soon learn who commands the ocean – it will be a pious work to chastise them – for it will soon lead to peace –, & after tasting the miseries of war they will recollect that they were the only people who might have enjoyed the blessings of peace without danger or dishonour. They are most absurdly wicked – God mend them![79]

A month later he learnt that his friend Hotham would be captain of the fleet; he would ask him to arrange his relief.[80]

For all his heated rhetoric Broke didn't have the stomach to make grim and cruel war on local seafarers. Reckoning them peaceful enough, he let their small coasters pass.[81] He was well aware that American strategy had shifted focus, their cruisers heading for distant stations where British trade was not convoyed. It was time to extend the economic blockade to Boston, and end the licensed trade: 'to make them all feel the war'.[82] His next cruise off Boston proved more profitable, recovering the French privateer *L'Invincible* from the beach off Cape Ann on 16 May.[83] However, the weather was appalling, low temperatures froze the rigging and covered the ship in ice.[84] The escape of the *President* and *Congress* made matters worse.

Anticipating that only the *Chesapeake* would be ready for sea before he had to replenish at Halifax, he now sent in a second, explicit challenge.[85] But he would have to adjust the blockade, to level the field of combat. Broke recognised that the sole American frigate ready for sea was unlikely to come out while two British ships continued on blockade and so he ordered his friend Hyde Parker to take HMS *Tenedos* out past Cape Sable on 25 May. Parker would watch in case *Chesapeake* slipped out at night or in a fog. This station had been occupied by Bladen Capel's 74 *La Hogue*, but she had recently returned to Halifax to replenish stores. Broke took fifteen tons of water from *Tenedos*, leaving Parker to replenish at the nearest Canadian harbour.

The last week of May witnessed a succession of gales, rain and fog. Even so Broke took or re-took several prizes; they provided him with fifteen British seamen from prize crews, and twenty young Irishmen. The new hands were quickly integrated into the ship's company; the seamen took part in musketry drill and the raw Irish lads were given less demanding posts. On the wet, squally night of 31 May *Shannon* hove-to about 7 miles south of Cape Ann.

The next morning dawned bright and clear, with *Chesapeake* in plain sight, lying close by Fort Independence. Anxious to get his battle before his supplies ran out, or his worn-out ship went home to be rebuilt, Broke compiled another challenge.[86]

H.B.M. ship *Shannon*, off Boston,
June, 1813 Sir,

As the *Chesapeake* appears now ready for sea, I request you will do me the favor to meet the *Shannon* with her, ship to ship, to try the fortune of our respective flags. To an officer of your character it requires some apology for proceeding to further particulars. Be assured, Sir, that it is not from any doubt I can entertain of your wishing to close with my proposal, but merely to provide an answer to any objections which might be made, and very reasonably, upon the chance of our receiving unfair support.

After the diligent attention which we had paid to Commodore Rodgers; the pains I took to detach all force but the *Shannon* and *Tenedos* to such a distance, that they could not possibly join in any action fought in sight of the Capes, and the various verbal messages which had been sent into Boston to that effect, we were much disappointed to find the commodore had eluded us by sailing on the first chance, after the prevailing easterly winds had obliged us to keep an offing from the coast. He, perhaps, wished for some stronger assurance of a fair meeting. I am therefore induced to address you more particularly, and to assure you, that what I write I pledge my honour to perform, to the utmost of my power.

The *Shannon* mounts 24 guns upon her broadside, and one light boat gun; 18-pounders upon her main-deck, and 32-pound carronades on her quarter-deck and forecastle; and is manned with a complement of 300 men and boys, (a large proportion of the latter), besides 30 seamen, boys, and passengers, who were taken out of recaptured vessels lately. I am this minute, because a report has prevailed in some of the Boston papers, that we had 150 men, additional, lent us from *La Hogue*, which really never was the case. *La Hogue* is now gone to Halifax for provisions; and I will send all other ships beyond the power of interfering with us, and meet you wherever it is agreeable to you, within the limits of the undermentioned rendezvous, viz.

From 6 to 10 leagues east of Cape Cod light-house; from 8 to 10 leagues east of Cape Ann's light; on Cashe's ledge, in latitude 43 north; at any bearing and distance you please to fix off the south breakers of Nantucket, or the shoal on St. George's bank.

If you will favor me with any plan of signals or telegraph, I will warn you (if sailing under this promise) should any of my friends be too nigh, or any were in sight, until I can detach them out of my way; or I will sail with you under a flag of truce to any place you think safest from our cruizers, hauling it down when fair to begin hostilities.

You must, Sir, be aware that my proposals are highly advantageous to you, as you cannot proceed to sea singly in the *Chesapeake*, without imminent risk of being crushed by the superior force of the numerous British squadrons which are now abroad; where all your efforts, in case of a *rencontre*, would, however gallant, be perfectly hopeless. I entreat you, Sir, not to imagine that I am urged by mere personal vanity to the wish of meeting the *Chesapeake;* or that I depend only upon your personal ambition for your acceding to this invitation: we have both noble motives. You will feel it as a compliment if I say, that the result of our meeting may be the most grateful Service I can render my Country; and I doubt not that you, equally confident of success, will feel convinced, that it is only by repeated triumph in even combats that your little navy can now hope to console your country for the loss of that trade it can no longer protect. Favor me with a speedy reply. We are short of provisions and water, and cannot stay long here.

I have the honor to be, Sir,
Your obedient humble servant,
P. B. V. BROKE, Captain of
H.B.M. ship *Shannon*.

N.B. For the general service of watching your coast, it is requisite for me to keep another ship in company, to support me with her guns and boats when employed near the land, and particularly to aid each other, if either ship in chase should get on shore. You must be aware that I cannot, consistently with my duty waive so great an advantage for this general service, by detaching my consort, without an assurance on your part of meeting me directly; and that you will neither seek or admit aid from any other of your armed vessels, if I detach mine expressly for the sake of meeting you. Should any special order restrain from thus answering a formal challenge, you may yet oblige me by keeping my proposal a secret, and appointing any place you like to meet us (within 300 miles of Boston) in a given number of days after you sail; as, unless you agree to an interview, I may be busied on other service, and, perhaps, be at a distance from Boston when you go to sea. Choose your terms, but let us meet.

On the envelope Broke wrote:

To the Commander of the U.S. frigate *Chesapeake*.

We have 13 American prisoners on board, which I will give you for as many British sailors, if you will send them out: otherwise, being privateersmen, they must be detained.

Broke knew his opponent, carefully exploiting Lawrence's freshly won laurels and well-publicised challenge to the *Bonne Citoyenne* to stress the honourable nature of the proposed encounter. Broke deliberately set out the precise number and weight of his guns, the number of his men, and the advantage he was offering. If Lawrence did not risk single combat the *Chesapeake* would have to brave two or three British opponents to escape from Boston. He closed by stressing that his was no mere lust for glory; both men served a national purpose. A British victory would 'be the most grateful Service I can render to my Country'. Pointedly and provocatively he offered Lawrence the chance of a victory to 'console' his country 'for the loss of that trade it can no longer protect'.

Broke sent the letter into Boston on a fishing boat, in the hands of an American merchant captain. In the event Lawrence never received the letter. He did not need a British challenge;

he had imperative orders from the Secretary of the Navy that made it a matter of honour and duty to put to sea, backed by the exaggerated expectations of a nation whose emotions had been worked up to fever pitch by a triumphalist press and the growing realisation that the war could not be won. Having issued an almost identical challenge of his own only six months before Lawrence would have been stung by Broke's letter, but such personal considerations could only add to the reasons why he decided to sail that day.

There was something Homeric in the classical combat of two hand-picked champions, hastening to battle on board their closely matched wooden warships. It was as if Achilles and Hector were once again before the walls of Troy, the fate of great empires in their hands. This was no ordinary frigate action: the hopes and fears of entire nations – literate, engaged nations – rested on the outcome. The cultural impact of previous battles had transformed the trivial details of tactical encounters into the stuff of legend.

CHAPTER 5

Many Ways to Die

THE GLORIOUS FIRST OF JUNE

Early on the morning of 1 June Lieutenant George Budd, officer of the watch, hurried below to James Lawrence's spacious stern cabin to report the presence of an enemy ship. On reaching the deck Lawrence climbed aloft to look for himself. Satisfied it was a frigate of *Chesapeake*'s rate he sent a pilot boat out to check that no more British vessels were loitering in the offing, and ordered the crew to prepare to unmoor. Before they sailed the men received their prize money from the last cruise. With his men in motion Lawrence sent a final letter to Secretary Jones:

I am now getting under way to carry into execution the instructions you have honored me with. An English frigate is now in sight from my deck; I have sent a pilot boat out to reconnoitre, and should she be alone, I am in hopes to give a good account of her before night. My crew appear to be in fine spirits, & I trust will do their duty.

Having ascertained that the enemy frigate was indeed entirely alone, Lawrence, perhaps reflecting on the unfortunate Captain Peake of the *Peacock*, wrote a final letter, entrusting his brother-in-law with the care of his wife and children.[1] By 10 a.m. the ship was ready.

The previous day Broke had checked the *Chesapeake* was still in Boston, hoping his carefully crafted challenge might yet produce the desired result. He had closed a letter to his beloved Louisa with relief, anxious, but not desponding. The following morning dawned calm and bright, giving Broke a fine prospect of the approaches to Boston; in these conditions no one could get to sea without being seen. He took the *Shannon* closer, spotting

Chesapeake at anchor in President Roads: the American was ready for sea, her rigging set, sails furled, hull freshly painted with a broad yellow band below the gun ports. He fired a single gun, a challenge, almost an insult, so close in to the harbour.

Despite being so close to Boston the *Shannons* maintained their regular routine, after breakfast they cleaned and dried the ship, and at 10.00 Broke mustered the crew at action stations for the daily gun drill; this might be the last opportunity to integrate the recent arrivals into his finely honed fighting teams. Taking station in the maintop Broke could see the Americans were preparing to sail and to fight: he observed two boats pull inshore from the *Chesapeake*, landing a number of women close by the lighthouse. As Broke knew, these were the 'wives and sweethearts' beloved of sailors in every port – some may have been genuine, most were not. Their departure was a promising sign, but by 11.30 there was still no indication the Americans would sail. He returned to the quarterdeck, standing the men down from action stations. Dinner was piped, although the ship remained in all other respects ready for battle. He trusted the American captain would not be so amateur as to interrupt his men at their dinner.

Shortly after midday the *Chesapeake* fired a single gun in reply to Broke, hoisted a large white flag emblazoned with the emotive, challenging words 'FREE TRADE AND SAILORS RIGHTS', and waited for the pilot boat to return. The banner represented the core of America's challenge, the demand that Britain abandon age-old, time-honoured ways of raising men and waging war, at the behest of her former colonial subjects. Not to be outdone Broke had John Dunn, his clerk, write another copy of the challenge, sending it ashore with an irascible fishing skipper detained the day before. The challenge did not name the *Chesapeake*'s captain. Neither copy ever reached Lawrence; he needed no such encouragement. The messenger landed at Marblehead, and tamely posted the letter. It reached William Bainbridge at Boston Navy Yard the following day.[2] Still the British crew waited, some, like Broke, anxious for battle, others worried that they might be wounded, or worse still, disgrace themselves in the eyes of their messmates.

After what must have seemed like an eternity the American ship finally got under way, leaving President Roads accompanied by a swarm of small craft, the shore crowded with spectators. Boston had caught the 'victory disease', assuming success was preordained, planning a celebratory dinner for that very evening with a seat reserved for Captain Broke. To meet the occasion, Lawrence unmoored with a flourish, all sails sheeted home together, a smart, seamanlike, professional manoeuvre, exploiting the ebbing tide. Once *Chesapeake* began to move through the water Lawrence set the studding sails, a truly spectacular display so close to port. As if relieved of a great burden Broke turned to first lieutenant George Watt and observed, 'I hope to have the pleasure of shaking hands with Captain Lawrence today.' Although Broke could plainly see that his last challenge had not arrived in port he made sail and steered for the suggested rendezvous off Cape Ann, which lay some 12 miles north-north-east. He had no intention of engaging so close to Boston, where American gunboats could join the fight. While the ship prepared for action Broke went down to his cabin to pray, asking God to look after his family, his men, and his honour.

With time on his hands Broke had a section of the quarterdeck screened off with canvas partitions so he could dine with his officers, using his silver and fine glasses before they were packed away below deck, out of harm's way. This was no mere pleasantry: he had many agendas to address. Reminding those present that they were about to risk all, that they needed to follow orders and work as one, he exploited the occasion to reconcile two officers whom he knew had recently quarrelled over a toast and handshake.

While the elegant decorum of gentlemanly war was being played out on the quarterdeck, Surgeon Alexander Jack was preparing the tools of his trade, laying out simple steel instruments ready to cut, probe, saw and stitch the wounded, while battle lanterns were lit, and a table but recently used for lunch was scrubbed up for operations, water butts filled, bandages wound, and tourniquets laid by. Nearby Gunner Richard Meehan set up the damp screens that would cover the handing-up area where charges were passed up to the guns from the magazine deep in the bowels of the ship. His men were hard at work filling flannel cartridges with set charges. At some stage Lieutenant Provo Wallis, ranking third in command, gave Meehan his watch for safe-keeping. Meehan would use it to time the action.[3]

On the gun deck the divisional officers ensured every super-fluous item had been cleared away. The guns were loaded alternately with two 18-pounder round shot, or one shot and one stand of grape shot. The flints in their locks were checked and the tackles carefully laid out to ensure a smooth recoil. The deck was wetted and sanded, to reduce friction, prevent fire, and provide barefooted gun crews with a decent purchase. Fire hoses were run out, and connected to the pumps. Alongside each gun were three water butts: one to douse a fire, one to refresh the crew, and a third dry, holding the lit slow match that would be needed if the flintlock failed. On the upper deck the 32-pounder carronades were prepared in similar fashion, with stands of muskets, pistols, tomahawks and boarding pikes laid by in case it came to close-quarters fighting. Aloft the topmen prepared the rigging for battle, all lashed up with the yards slung in chains. The last was a vital detail. A yard falling from aloft could wipe out the upper deck guns, or disable a significant part of the crew. A stout boarding net was stretched above the deck, over head high, to stop rigging blocks and chunks of timber hitting the crew. Such injuries were so common that Broke, like many another officer, wore a stout leather top hat in action.

The *Shannons* had ample opportunity to transform their home into a battlefield. Broke kept heading out to sea for around three hours, finally taking in sail when the ship was 15 miles from Boston, out of sight of the city. The dining screen and table were struck down and stowed below deck, the men were piped to their grog ration, the goats thrown overboard. *Chesapeake* was closing on a converging course, and less than 4 miles off.

SHANNON
— AND —
CHESAPEAKE
June 1st, 1813.

The battlefield – Massachusetts Bay. In order to reach the
Atlantic Lawrence had to escape from Boston.

With the provocative white banner at the foretop and a national
ensign at each masthead the American seemed anxious to be
noticed, perhaps slightly too anxious.

As *Chesapeake* closed Broke hardly took his eye off her
rigging, noting every time Lawrence housed a yard or struck a
sail. He copied most of the changes, but left his topgallant yards
across, as he expected the breeze to fall in the evening, and he
might need a little extra canvas to get out of Boston Bay.

At 5.10 p.m., satisfied the ship was ready for battle, and the
enemy closing, Broke mustered the crew on the main and quarter
decks, where all could see him. The men were stripped to fight,
with cotton waste ready to stuff in their ears, and scarves ready

Old England Forever: Philip Broke in all his glory,
the enemy ensign underfoot.

to hold it in place; the officers had dressed in worn, old uniforms,
and buckled on their fighting swords. The Royal Marines made
a fine contrast in scarlet jackets and white crossbelts, stood
to attention at their quarters. Broke spoke to the men with a
quiet, imperturbable confidence. He stressed they would have
an opportunity to demonstrate their skill, and reverse the tide
of defeat. He reminded them that nothing but the 'disparity of
force' had given the enemy their success, urging them to show
'that there are Englishmen in the frigate who still know how to

fight'. Ever the professional, Broke stressed the cool performance of duty, discipline and the years of sustained training. There was not a hint of bravado, or bombast:

Don't try to dismast her. Fire into her quarters: main deck to main deck; quarter deck into quarter deck. Kill the men and the ship is yours. Don't hit them about the head, for they have steel caps on, but give it them through the body. Don't cheer. Go quietly to your quarters. I feel sure you will all do your duty; and remember you have the blood of hundreds of your countrymen to avenge.

It was a most auspicious day to fight: the anniversary of the 'Glorious First of June', Lord Howe's great victory over the French fleet in 1794. Broke's themes of honour and glory, heritage and hurt, pride and above all professionalism provided a potent message. When Jacob West, a veteran from the *Guerriere*, asked if they would have revenge, Broke made a promise, and he insisted that they needed only one ensign, unlike the three that fluttered from the masts of the enemy. *Chesapeake* flew ensigns at the mizzen royal masthead, at the mizzen peak and in the starboard main rigging, while Lawrence had hoisted the white flag emblazoned with the legend 'FREE TRADE AND SAILORS RIGHTS' to the fore royal masthead. The merits of that argument would soon be settled. Of course Broke had three spare ensigns triced up and ready just in case the Blue at the mizzen peak was shot away. Then he sent the men to their quarters in silence, because they were professionals. With battle imminent, Broke's first thought was for the 9-pounder bow chasers mounted forward; these had been detailed to shoot away the American ship's wheel.

Chesapeake had cleared Boston Lighthouse under all sail at 1.00 p.m., steering to close with the *Shannon*, then standing off and on under reefed topsails. According to second lieutenant George Budd, Lawrence already knew his opponent was the *Shannon*, a familiar sight to all Bostonians. He may not have realised exactly what that information meant. As *Shannon* pulled away from the coast Lawrence made sail in chase and cleared for action.[4] At 3.40 *Chesapeake* fired a single gun, challenging

Shannon to stand and fight, but Broke, cool-headed to the last, had no intention of engaging in sight of Boston. He would fight out to sea, so that when he had won his battle he could secure the prize and withdraw without the hostile attention of American gunboats armed with long 32-pounders. The hopes of a great navy and great nation rested on his shoulders. He had to win, and win well, bringing home his prize in triumph, giving the *Gazette*, the *Times* and the rest of the British media ample occasion to celebrate the restoration of naval glory.

Around 4.00, as *Chesapeake* came on, Broke bore away on the light westerly breeze, and Lawrence followed; the two ships remained in sight, about 7 miles apart. When *Shannon* reached the chosen ground off Cape Ann, Broke reduced sail, braced his main topsail back against the mast, cutting *Shannon*'s speed to a minimum, and prepared for battle. Every man was at his station, every gun loaded. When the *Chesapeake* arrived all hell would break loose, but until then they would wait in silence, each man thinking of what was to come, how well they would meet the test of combat. Some, like Broke, thought of loved ones far away, of wives and children; for others the solid camaraderie of the main deck was the only thing that mattered, as messmates bound together by arduous service and shared skills exchanged confidences and promises. In the close-confined spaces of a fifth-rate frigate there was no room to hide; any man who ran, skulked or shirked his duty would become an outcast. Social barriers and distinctions of rank that separated officers and men slipped away; all were going into harm's way, standing shoulder to shoulder on the quarterdeck, crouched in expectation over the sleek, black 18-pounders on the gun deck or, aloft in the tops, ready to fight or furl sail, as the situation required. After long years of drill and training every man knew his job, each tightly knit team had loaded and fired until the movements became unthinking automatic routine. Deep in the gloomy spaces below the waterline the gunner and his mates, the carpenter's crew, the surgeon and loblolly boys were prepared to feed the guns, plug shot holes and patch up the inevitable tide of mutilated humanity that would flow down the companion-ways once the guns began to roar. Although time hung heavy, seconds draining through the sandglass one grain at a time, no one flinched. Anxiety and fear had been suppressed by drill, discipline and exemplary leadership. All through the languid wait Philip Broke stood alongside the ship's wheel on the quarterdeck, the deadly space where command was exercised, leadership shown, and decisions taken. If he seemed lost in thought, those thoughts were critical to the outcome of the battle.

After seven years commanding the *Shannon* Broke was finally going to have his battle. Everything he had learnt since he left his beloved Nacton as a child was about to be tested. He waited and watched as the enemy closed. His cool demeanour and unhurried movement communicated calm and confidence to officers and men who waited on his every word and gesture, putting their faith in his judgement. He wore full uniform, to ensure everyone recognised him amid the smoke and chaos of battle, so that he would be obeyed without hesitation. In the eerie silence of the occasion all eyes focused on the post of honour where the command team waited.

Broke, George Watt and sailing master Henry Etough watched the set and draw of the two suits of sails, computing the speed and angle of the American ship as she bore down on them. The battle would be decided by manoeuvre and firepower. Despite having the absolute minimum of sail set Broke had to prevent the American ship getting across his flimsy, unarmed stern, and avoid the long-range bombardment of anti-rigging projectiles that had settled the last three actions. He wanted to get his enemy in close, relying on the rapid, accurate point-blank fire of his guns and carronades, and musketry.

In the eerie silence both ships creaked and strained, the fabric of wood and rope twisting and wracking as they moved. At 4.30 George Budd observed *Shannon* hove-to, with her head to the south-east, waiting for *Chesapeake*. At 4.50 Lawrence took in sail, bringing the royal yards down to the deck, furling the royal and topgallant sails, to reduce his speed through the water and prepare for battle under a reduced sail plan, 'fighting canvas'. This freed most of his topmen, his best sailors, to man the upper deck guns. Broke followed suit, stripping away everything save the jib, topsails, topgallants and spanker, retaining enough power to steer and move, with the minimum number of men aloft. *Shannon* lay ahead and just to port of *Chesapeake*, which was closing from astern. They were about 18 miles out from Boston Lighthouse. At 5.30 Lawrence hauled up his courses, and closed for battle.

Watching from the *Shannon* Lieutenant Provo Wallis assessed Lawrence's ship-handling during the approach to contact. He judged the American captain manoeuvred with great skill, to avoid being fired on as he approached from the *Shannon*'s quarter. However, Broke had no intention of opening fire while *Chesapeake* continued to close.[5] He wanted to bring the enemy in very close before firing, to ensure his first and best broadside would be decisive.

With battle imminent, Lawrence, like Broke, had addressed his people. He reminded them of their patriotic duty, that the Americans had won every action of note since the war began, and ended with a striking reference to his own exploits, demanding '*Peacock* her my lads, *Peacock* her!' This was no mere rhetoric. Lawrence fully intended to reprise the tactics of his last engagement; he would fight the same battle.[6] This was why he ordered the gun crews to load canister and bar shot on top of the round shot and grape already stowed and waiting. We have no way of knowing what Lawrence was thinking as he sailed into battle, but like Broke he knew the risks. Within minutes it would be death or glory; neither man would back away. It would be the defining moment of the war.

At 5.30 *Chesapeake* steered for *Shannon*'s starboard quarter. Watching from the stern rail, Broke responded by filling his main topsail to gather a little momentum, then checked the topsails and lay-to, brailing up his spanker at the throat, ready to release if he needed steerage way. Broke had held his ship ready to counter any move the enemy might make, and ready to fight. At this point Lawrence had the option of trying to cross

Shannon's stern and engage from the port side. A slight change of course suggested he would try. Broke responded quickly, had the jib sheeted home and put the wheel over to starboard, before dividing the gun crews to fight both batteries, ordering any men who were not needed to fire the guns to lie down, to avoid the devastating impact of raking fire through the stern. He knew a manoeuvre across his stern would be difficult to execute in battle; even the best-drilled ships would struggle to change course while heavily engaged, and at the same time lose speed to bring up alongside. Where a novice might have been tempted to change course, Broke coolly countered the threat and held on; he needed a steady gun platform for effective gunnery.

Despite Broke's precautions it is unlikely that Lawrence intended to cross *Shannon*'s stern. Having loaded his guns to dismantle the British ship's rigging he needed to retain the weather gauge, choosing the simpler, safer option of engaging broadside to broadside. At 5.40 he altered course to starboard, only 50 yards off the *Shannon*'s stern, and squared his mainyard as the American crew gave three rousing cheers. Ominously the British did not reply: Broke insisted on the silent execution of duty. Battle was inevitable. *Chesapeake* closed from astern, making 3–4 knots, brisk walking pace, slightly faster than *Shannon*'s 2–3 knots. If he meant to 'Peacock' his new opponent Lawrence needed to fire a crippling broadside into the *Shannon*'s lower rigging, and then take up a commanding position on her bow or quarter, where he could use his full broadside against a fraction of the enemy guns. Had he known just how skilled and professional an opponent he was facing he might have made a different choice.

Having studied the previous frigate actions in detail, Broke expected a long-range attack on his rigging: this was the first threat he countered. As Lawrence closed he knew the chances of success were improving with every yard. By holding his nerve, Broke won the battle of manoeuvre, bringing his opponent into the ideal position, broadside to broadside, at point-blank range. As the ships closed, shouted orders were audible across the last 40 or 50 yards that separated the otherwise silent crews. Lawrence may have expected the British ship to alter course to meet his attack, as *Peacock* had, but he would be disappointed. This was not gallantry, it was cool calculation. Only a steady gun platform and well-laid guns could deliver the killing stroke.[7]

Broke had loaded his main deck guns alternately from the stern with two round shot and round and grape. Not content with the finest gunnery team the Royal Navy had ever produced he added more specific weapons to maximise his chances of success. The key to battle would be the ability of the two ships to manoeuvre, and the effective leadership of their officers. While Lawrence planned to open his attack by crippling the British rigging Broke preferred to lay his main battery on the American gun crews, while special weapons targeted the steering gear and command team. He had a small gun on a travelling carriage on the poop deck, and the two 9-pounders forward, which were ordered to destroy the American ship's wheel, and kill anyone standing near by. The Marines were ordered to pick off the American officers. Nor was he going to leave all the work to others: he kept a small bucket of hand grenades in easy reach, close to the ship's wheel. As *Chesapeake* ranged up, Broke picked up a grenade and carefully trimmed the quickmatch fuse to length with his penknife. It was a very short fuse.

Down on the gun deck William Mindham, captain of the fourteenth and aftermost gun had orders to fire into the second gun port of the American ship. By holding his course Broke provided his gunners with an ideal platform, a steady, upright ship on a straight course. The guns had been levelled for accurate horizontal fire, and the gunners were trained to hit small targets. Mindham carried out his orders to the letter, waiting as the American ship's bow crossed his sights, and then the first gun-port, which posed no threat, because it pointed forward. As the second port, a 3-foot-square target, came into view Mindham gripped the lanyard and snapped the lock. Two balls were seen to smash through the American ship; shortly after a tin case full of musket balls scythed through the port, destroying the gun crew. It was 5.50. *Shannon*'s aftermost quarterdeck carronade fired fractionally later, at its opposite number on the American bow. The remaining guns of *Shannon*'s starboard battery fired in succession into the American gun ports as they ranged alongside. Within two minutes most of the gun crews of the American forward division had been destroyed, and several guns disabled. Edward Ballard, fourth lieutenant, officer in command of the fore division, lost a leg in the opening exchange. He died shortly afterwards. The shattered remains of eight men from the first two American gun crews were heaved overboard. It is unlikely that any of their comrades were still capable of fighting. Men stationed in *Shannon*'s tops reported the withering effect of *Shannon*'s gunfire on the American upper deck, where a storm of splinters and projectiles hacked down men and equipment, cut ropes and shattered solid structures. A haze of dust and wood chips hung in the air, scented with powder and blood, hot iron and sweat. The Royal Marines and seamen, directed by Broke, his officers and petty officers, poured a heavy fire of musketry into this maelstrom, concentrating on the command team around the wheel.[8] At 25 yards even a smoothbore Brown Bess musket was accurate.

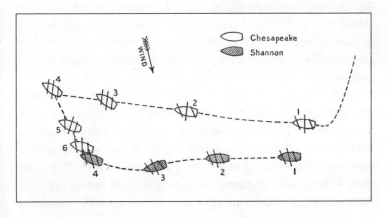

Tactical finesse: note how Lawrence squared his mainyard to lose speed, while Broke had already taken in sail – on such details battles are lost and won.

Within a minute Lawrence had lost the battle: he had come into action too fast. As the *Chesapeake* came alongside her sails blanketed *Shannon*'s canvas, reinforcing the speed differential. Despite Lawrence hastily luffing up to cut his speed through the water *Chesapeake* still passed ahead of her opponent, exposing the ship's wheel and backstays to carefully directed British fire. The American gunners returned fire smartly, but their ship was heeling towards the enemy, and most of the first broadside smashed harmlessly into the *Shannon*'s waterline, just above the copper, the overloaded guns unable to drive more than a single round shot through the British hull, while the anti-rigging and anti-personnel projectiles so carefully loaded before the action began were wasted. There were some hits on the British gun deck, but far, far fewer than the British had scored. The American carronades proved more effective, slashing through the *Shannon*'s lower rigging with potentially decisive effect.

As George Budd observed, 'the first broadside did great execution . . . damaged our rigging, killed among others Mr. White the sailing master, and wounded Captain Lawrence'.[9] William White had been decapitated; alongside him two midshipmen and Lieutenant James Broom of the Marines were also dead. Bosun Peter Adams had been hit, and would not survive the day, while first lieutenant Augustus Ludlow was taken below with a serious, but not fatal wound. Within a minute the American command team had disappeared, only Lawrence, with a musket ball in his leg just below the knee, remained on deck.

In the opening exchange *Chesapeake*'s jib sheets were shot away, the fore topsail yard lifts, which had not been secured, were cut, along with the spanker brails, allowing the spanker to blow out into the mizzen rigging. Just when Lawrence needed to settle on a parallel course the spanker amplified his luff into the wind, bringing *Chesapeake* further up into the wind, exposing her stern to *Shannon*'s eager gunners. At this point the wheel was smashed, the backstays cut and the American quarterdeck became a 'slaughter pen' of smashed bodies, bloodstains, smoke and wreckage. Lawrence, 'colossal in figure' and 'fatally conspicuous by the white vest and habiliments he had assumed', was leaning on the compass binnacle, with his wounded leg. With the wheel smashed, the tiller ropes cut and all three quartermasters out of action the Americans were in serious trouble.

As *Chesapeake*'s bow swung away from her opponent, the American guns that were still firing, from the midship and after ports, hit *Shannon*'s starboard bow, the carronades again proving more effective than the long guns. On *Shannon*'s forecastle Able Seaman Thomas Selby was decapitated, Neil Gilchrist cut in two by a 32-pounder ball, and Boy Thomas Barry by a star shot. At this point Broke must have thought the enemy was trying to escape; he went forward to direct the two 9-pounders to take out *Chesapeake*'s yards. No sooner had he arrived than a 32-pounder ball smashed into one of the small guns, driving the iron directing bar into the knees of the gun captain, Royal Marine Corporal William Driscoll, and mortally wounded another member of the gun crew. Broke escaped unhurt.

With *Shannon*'s after guns no longer bearing, the quarterdeck carronade crews came forward, picked up muskets and joined the Royal Marines, who were firing at their American counterparts. Then *Chesapeake* suddenly lost way. Her turn into the wind had left the sails flapping uselessly, and she began to drift astern towards her tormentor. This allowed the British guns to pound the exposed, defenceless American stern, shattering the after gun crews and scything down any who tried to carry on fighting. In a few short minutes the massive disparity of manpower – 320 to 387 – between the two ships had been reversed; now there were more Britons fit and ready to fight than Americans.

Broke could see the enemy ship was out of control; he had won his battle in only seven or eight minutes. Directing the forecastle 32-pounder carronades to fire into the American Marines he prepared to finish the job in a properly scientific manner, with accurate close-range cannon fire. At 5.58 a cartridge box on the American quarterdeck exploded, adding to the chaos, probably hit by one of Broke's hand grenades. Anxious to complete the battle in full control of his ship Broke altered course slightly and shed speed, both to keep his guns bearing on the American stern and quarter, and avoid contact as the enemy drifted downwind, out of control and seemingly without a commander. But by now the ships were very close and damage to *Shannon*'s jib-stay and foresails meant she answered the helm too slowly.

Realising the ships were going to collide, giving him one last chance to turn the battle, Lawrence called up the boarders from the gun deck, where they were no longer able to bring their cannon to bear on the target. Neither captain favoured boarding – it was a desperate course, and something of a lottery – but neither could prevent the ships from colliding.

Precious few men answered Lawrence's call: the forward gun crews had been decimated by the opening broadsides, the after by raking fire in the last few minutes. Lieutenant Ballard, leader of the fore division was dead, while a shockingly large contingent of badly wounded officers and men waited for the attention of Surgeons Richard Edgar and John Dix. Only the midship division responded to Lawrence's order, following Acting Lieutenant William Cox up the main hatchway. There they met a tide of mangled human misery flowing in the opposite direction. Few men remained standing on the upper deck, and when Cox struggled up he found Lawrence was the only officer on the upper deck. Just as Cox reached his side the captain was hit a second time.

Royal Marine Second Lieutenant John Law had identified the tall American from a vantage point on one of *Shannon*'s quarterdeck carronade slides, taken deliberate aim and hit him in the groin with a musket ball.[10] Seeing his captain and mentor fall, Cox, still only an acting lieutenant, apparently unaware that he was the last officer on the quarterdeck, sent his men aft to meet the British boarders while he accompanied Lawrence below. As he staggered down the gangway, Lawrence called for more boarders, unaware that very few of his men were fit to fight. Carried down to the surgeon's table in agony, Lawrence continued to urge his crew, yelling 'Tell the men to fire faster! Don't give up the ship!' As Dix prepared to operate, Lawrence demanded he go on deck, to instruct the senior officer standing to fight the ship until she sank. He was persuaded that a loblolly boy should carry the message. This was wise; there was not one officer on deck to receive the order.

Through a dark sea of pain James Lawrence experienced the anguish of defeat, and the agony of responsibility. His wound was mortal: he did not need Edgar or Dix to tell him that a musket ball in the groin would end in the fatal, lingering agony of peritonitis. He had served long enough to have seen such cases. From this point, stretched out on the table, Lawrence was no longer involved in the fighting. His last words, however many times they are retold to encourage his successors, were those of a distraught dying man, wrapped up in hopes and fears, thinking of his wife and family, friends and enemies, a life passing in review between episodes of searing pain. Ten minutes earlier he had begun the battle in high spirits, nervously watching his opponent, trying to out-think and out-fight the enemy just as he had done so spectacularly only scant months before. Instead he had met his match, out-thought, out-manoeuvred and out-performed by the most single-minded perfectionist ever to command a ship in battle.

With the rigging crippled, *Chesapeake*'s crew could not stop her sternward drift; at 6.00 she crashed into *Shannon*'s starboard bow. Her shattered port quarter hooked on to one of the British ship's anchors, stowed on the gangway before the battle above the fifth main deck gun port. The American spanker boom swung over the British forecastle, and Broke grabbed the opportunity, ordering the ships lashed together. While carrying out those orders veteran boatswain William Stevens was terribly wounded by American grapeshot. Broke seemed to bear a charmed life. Clerk John Dunn and Purser George Aldham were killed by grape shot while standing beside him, but he remained unhurt despite American musket fire, round shot and grape. With the ships tied together it was time to finish the job. He called away the quarterdeck and main deck boarders. This was not the random act it might appear. Specific men had been pre-selected for the task, led by their divisional officers.

With the American quarterdeck effectively empty Broke had no hesitation in leading the attack; *Chesapeake* was swinging round and would soon break free from the *Shannon*. Yelling 'Follow me who can!' Broke clambered over the hammock netting and the anchor, and stepped down via a carronade onto American territory. He was followed by the last survivors of his personal retinue, Midshipman John Samwell, Marine Sergeant Richard Molyneux and Coxswain William Stack.

The boarding action begins.

When the battle began forty-four American marines stood on the quarterdeck and poop, but they had been virtually annihilated by British fire. The officer commanding and all but one NCO had been killed or wounded. Only a dozen stunned men remained and they were rapidly overwhelmed by the impetuous charge of the British tars. Acting Chaplain Samuel Livermore foolishly snapped a pistol in Broke's face, only to be knocked aside by a back-handed stroke from the Englishman's fighting sword, a heavy Spanish blade mounted in a regulation hilt. Livermore's arm was practically severed. With men swarming up from the after guns, which no longer bore on target, the *Shannons* overwhelmed the brave remnant of the American crew who made a stand at the midships gangways. George Budd, who commanded a division on the gun deck, had been called up by one of Lawrence's aides just as the British began to board, because there were no officers left standing on the upper deck. Reaching the spar deck he ordered the men to haul on the fore tack, to get the ship clear of the *Shannon*, and then led an attack on the quarterdeck.

Budd and Ludlow, his wounds hastily patched up, rallied the gun crews and tried to recover the ship. Any trifling success they had was quickly reversed by sheer weight of numbers. Budd was knocked back down the fore hatchway by a cutlass blow on his arm, while Ludlow was left stretched out and unconscious on the deck by a savage sword cut across the head. Several Americans surrendered, hoping to be spared by the onrushing British boarders. The rest were driven to the forecastle, where the last few Marines and some British deserters continued to resist. Realising what was happening Lieutenant Cox attempted to reach the upper deck, but was unable to stem the tide of defeated demoralised men streaming below. A few American sailors in the mizzen top continued to fire on the British, mortally wounding Midshipman Samwell and hitting Lieutenant Watt in the foot, until *Shannons* led by Midshipman Philip Cosnahan drove them out with accurate musketry, the last of them grappled and thrown to the deck by a British topman.

In two minutes the British had taken control of the *Chesapeake*'s upper deck. When he reached the cockpit for treatment Budd found both Lawrence and Ludlow lying grievously wounded. Alerted by the musketry and commotion Lawrence heard the ship had been taken. His response was chilling: 'Then blow her up! Blow the ship up!'

With the battle over the two ships drifted apart, after little more than a minute in contact, leaving seventy British boarders aboard *Chesapeake*. The speed and ferocity of the attack had been decisive, the shattered American crew unable to hold their ground. With all resistance apparently at an end, Broke moved quickly to control his men, saving several Americans from his over-enthusiastic tars by standing between the two groups. At this point three of the men who had been spared took up arms again. They attacked Broke with a pike, a cutlass and an empty musket.[11] Alerted by a shout, Broke turned in time to parry the thrust of the pike, but was hit over the head by the butt end of the musket, which knocked away his stout leather top hat, and then struck by a cutlass from behind and to the left. The cutlass inflicted a terrible wound, splitting open the skull and exposing the brain cavity. He was fortunate that William Mindham, the gun captain who had opened the battle, was close enough to parry a second stroke and then kill his man. His accomplices, who had also killed a British rating, and wounded two more, were hacked to pieces by enraged British seamen. Provo Wallis had no doubt all three were Royal Navy deserters, men who had no hope of surviving an American defeat.[12]

Stunned and covered in blood, Broke slumped into a heap of quicklime. While British historian William James enjoyed claiming that Lawrence had planned to use the corrosive powder to blind his opponents the truth is altogether more prosaic. Americans used quicklime as a disinfectant; the barrel, which had not been struck below when *Chesapeake* sailed, was smashed by a random cannon ball.[13] The quicklime probably saved Broke's life, preventing infection. Despite his wound Broke did not forget his sword, and was helped to his feet by Mindham and Midshipman Smith in time to see the British ensign raised over his prize. In the interval a second tragedy unfolded at *Chesapeake*'s poop rail. *Shannon*'s men had already hoisted a small blue ensign, but Lieutenant George Watt, hobbling with a musket ball in his foot, had brought a large white ensign for the occasion. Seeing an officer haul down the British ensign, *Shannon*'s number seven main deck gun, mistaking the gesture for an American rally, opened fire. Watt was killed instantly, the top of his head smashed by grapeshot; five more Britons were

Philip Broke, attacked by three seamen, was cut down in the
moment of victory; only the timely arrival of William Mindham,
rushing past the mast, saved his life.

killed or wounded. The blue ensign went back up very quickly,
and no more guns were fired. At this point Provo Wallis left
Shannon's gun deck to see what was happening.

With the two ships drifting apart, the British boarders drove
the remaining American crew off the gun deck and below into
the hold, barricading the hatchway with stout gratings. When an
American on the berth deck shot and killed William Young, the
Royal Marine sentry posted at the hatchway, the British opened
fire. They were only stopped by fourth lieutenant Charles
Falkiner, who put a pistol to the nearest man's head. Having
silenced the din, Falkiner coolly told the Americans that he had
300 men on board, demanded that they surrender and stressed
that he would shoot them one by one if they did not send up the
man who had killed Young. Hearing the firing, Broke directed
that the Americans be driven into the hold and then collapsed,
from shock, loss of blood and the release of tension. The battle
was over: a lifetime's work had lasted little more than eleven

minutes, timed on Provo Wallis's watch by Gunner Richard Meehan.

With Watt dead and Broke incapacitated, Charles Falkiner found himself in command of a small prize crew, on a ship that had not formally surrendered, with an unknown number of armed men below deck. To make matters worse he was less than 20 miles off the American coast. He had every reason to expect trouble, but a boat-load of Marines soon arrived to secure the prize. Broke was gently lifted into the boat and taken back to the *Shannon*. Surgeon Jack cleaned the wound and stripped away the blood-soaked clothes; neither he nor Provo Wallis, now senior officer of the two-ship formation, dared hope Broke could live. The gash, about 4 inches long, ran from behind his left ear down toward the corner of his mouth, leaving the outer membrane of the brain exposed, pulsing slowly. There was nothing the surgeon could do, save clean and dress the wound, and pray. Wallis took a small bloodstained bag containing a lock of Louisa's blond hair from around Broke's neck; his sister made a fresh bag after the ship reached Halifax.

When some Americans continued to shout and threaten from below, Falkiner shipped some across to the *Shannon* suitably shackled with the very handcuffs Lawrence had intended for British prisoners. The rest were cowed when a loaded 18-pounder was pointed down into the hold. As evening drew on *Shannon*'s surviving crew scrambled aloft to repair the standing and running rigging of the two ships, both of which had suffered severely. More than half of *Chesapeake*'s shrouds had to be replaced. The lower standing rigging on *Shannon*'s starboard side had been cut to pieces by the *Chesapeake*'s fire and would, in a seaway, have allowed her masts to roll overboard, despite Broke rigging extra shrouds.

Boats loaded with American spectators hurried home astonished and alarmed by the speed of the action, and the entirely unexpected result. The celebratory public dinner was hastily cancelled. A funereal pall settled over Boston; dreams of glory passed in an instant. Men suddenly rendered sober remembered that Lawrence had gone out to fight a ship of the hitherto invincible Royal Navy. The American victories of 1812 had been a brief disturbance in the natural order of things – normal service would now be resumed.

Not that the victors were celebrating. As day ended the victorious *Shannons* committed the bodies of the dead to the deep, an ancient naval ritual, the liturgy of the Church of England intoned over men who, scant hours before, had been in the first flush of youth and vigour. The sun setting over the land to the west rendered the scene truly sublime as victor and vanquished, shattered and torn, slowly passed in easy sight of Gloucester and Cape Ann. Having honoured the fallen, and tended the maimed, the crew returned to repairing the rigging, cleaning the decks and pumping the bilges as the two ships slowly stood away into the eastern darkness.[14] A light south-westerly breeze helped the two cripples set a course for Halifax away to the north.

The pilot who took *Chesapeake* to sea that morning returned to Boston in the evening, having witnessed the action, and reported to William Bainbridge. Bainbridge informed Secretary Jones that the ship had been taken, 'after a terrific bombardment', and although he had neither seen the action nor had a report from anyone on board either combatant, declared the loss 'entirely due to some fortuitous event happening on board of her, and not to any superiority of skill or bravery in the enemy'. The only 'event' had been the explosion reported by the pilot. Desperate to sustain the glory of 1812 Bainbridge closed with a classic example of the ridiculous hyperbole that would characterise American accounts of the battle for more than a century: 'We have lost one frigate, but in losing her I am confident we have lost no reputation'.[15] In the years that followed Americans created a heroic myth, desperate to sustain the fleeting successes of 1812 by deifying the conveniently dead captain, while demonising Lieutenant Cox, a black bugler, a Portuguese mate and the very fabric of the lost ship.

That night 22-year-old Provo Wallis found himself in command of two crippled ships close by the enemy's coast, facing a long voyage to Halifax. He scarcely left the deck until it was completed. The two ships travelled in silence; both carried horribly wounded captains. The two principals in the battle were fated never to meet. At daylight on the 2nd Wallis encountered two large warships, which he feared might be *President* and *Congress*. After an anxious wait while the vessels exchanged numbers he realised they were the 74 HMS *Sceptre* and the frigate HMS *Loire*. Wallis received permission to pass on to Halifax with his cargo of wounded.[16]

Lieutenant Provo Wallis,
temporary captain of the *Shannon*.

During the day it was possible to estimate losses: *Shannon* had 26 killed and 58 wounded; many of the latter, including Broke, were not expected to survive.[17] The Americans had at least 48 killed and 99 wounded; many of the latter, like Lawrence and Ludlow, were severe cases. It has been estimated that 20 men fell in every minute of this astonishing battle.[18] Such unprecedented devastation bore testament to the skill and determination of

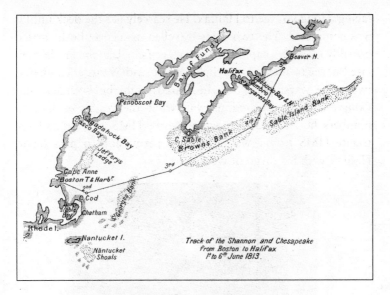

The slow way home: *Shannon* and *Chesapeake*
limp back to Halifax.

both crews. Several *Chesapeake* men disappeared during the battle, some jumping overboard; they were almost certainly British deserters. One deserter from *Shannon* had even been recognised amid the chaos of battle; he leapt overboard.[19] Of the 325 prisoners entered into the Melville Island naval prison at Halifax, 32 admitted to being British, including the gunner.

Written a fortnight after the battle, Lieutenant George Budd's account did not mention that any of the American crew had misbehaved, or that they were in any way sub-standard. His assessment of the American combat performance was clear and positive. He stressed that the initial exchange did great execution 'on both sides', attributing the loss of the ship to the fact that not one officer was left standing. Somewhat disingenuously he also pointed to the presence of men from *Belle Poule* and *Tenedos* on board the *Shannon*, without noting the substantial disparity in manpower between the two ships, or the presence of men from *Constitution* on the American frigate.[20]

James Lawrence in all his finery.

Delirious and wracked with pain, Lawrence occasionally writhed and waved his arms, shouting 'Don't give up the ship!' Despite a horrific cutlass stroke across his skull Augustus Ludlow seemed to be on the road to recovery. Installed in George Watt's cabin, he was able to discuss the action with Provo Wallis, admitting the battle had been lost fair and square, although he hoped for another opportunity. Wallis kept the ship quiet to ease the suffering of the other wounded hero. On the deck above Ludlow, Broke lay in his cot, as weak as a kitten. He had the fifer play 'Yankee Doodle' to raise his spirits, and was perfectly capable of reading the anxious expressions of Surgeon Jack and Provo Wallis. It appeared his case was hopeless. He had won the greatest victory, and turned the tide of the war in an afternoon, yet he was listless and anxious for his family as he struggled to regain some degree of control over his faculties. The cost of honour and glory had been terrible, but Broke wanted to live, to go home and spend the rest of his days beside the Orwell with Louisa and his children. The unrelenting willpower that had seen him through the long years of waiting now focused on survival and return: Philip Broke wanted to live, because he had much to live for.

Sunday 6 June 1813, Provo Wallis in HMS *Shannon* leads the captured *Chesapeake* into his home port, Halifax, Nova Scotia.

Closing on Halifax early on the 4th the two ships were delayed by a fog that obscured the harbour. Lawrence's losing battle with peritonitis ended that morning. He was spared the humiliation of entering the British port. Finally, on Sunday 6 June, the fog lifted and the two frigates stood into the harbour under full sail, *Shannon* leading her prize, Halifax-born Wallis in command, to be greeted by an entire population running from home or church to catch a glimpse of the greatest glory. Fearful any noise would affect Broke, Wallis would not let any spectators on the ship; they inspected the *Chesapeake* instead. He sent Broke ashore to the quiet comfort of the Commissioner's house, where his old friend Captain Philip Wodehouse would care for a man few dared hope could live. Surgeon Rowlands of the naval hospital found the patient weak, unable to converse beyond monosyllables.

On the 8th Lawrence's body was brought ashore and given a full ceremonial funeral, attended by British officers, the Army garrison and any American officers able to stand. He was buried with all the honours due a hero who had fallen defending his ships and his flag. After what had seemed to be a miraculous recovery Augustus Ludlow suffered a sudden relapse and died on the 13th. He was buried alongside his captain, with the same honours. The two men deserved to rest in peace, but they would be removed, taken to Salem and reburied. Salem ship-owner George Crowninshield arranged the first removal. The remains were reburied on 23 August, the day they arrived in the once prosperous port. Among the pall bearers were Isaac Hull, William Bainbridge and Charles Stewart, the three wartime captains of the *Constitution*. Finally Lawrence's family persuaded the Navy Department to bring the bodies back to New York, and although Robert Oliver agreed that Crowninshield's vessel could pass the blockade with this cargo, the bodies were moved by land, at a cost of $533.[21] The remains reached the city on 13 September, and were taken on board a warship at the Navy Yard. Three days later the whole city turned out – military guard, civic dignitaries and a large crowd – for a funeral procession and interment in Trinity Churchyard on Broadway. By now they were regarded more as totems than men; the memorial erected in 1816 was inscribed with a suitable verse that ended with the line 'DON'T GIVE UP THE SHIP'. A second, more durable monument was set up by public subscription in 1847, the first having become dilapidated. Lawrence's wife would join him in 1865.

As befits the age, the American crew received rather less consideration, installed in Melville Island prison with captured seamen from privateers and other warships. Those with severe wounds joined *Shannon*'s wounded at the naval hospital where seven died, including Ludlow. Another five passed away at the prison: one of pneumonia, another of syphilis. Two prisoners managed to escape during the winter of 1813–14.[22] The Americans were unable to exchange their men as quickly as they would have wished, enabling the British to inspect their captives, and check for deserters.

Well aware of the importance of the victory, Thomas Bladen Capel, as senior officer at Halifax, compiled an account of the action, with the help of Broke's officers, and dispatched it to England on the 6th. There were significant errors of detail, but the bigger picture was clear. The tide of disasters had been reversed in the most comprehensive manner imaginable. By the 11th Broke was well enough to write a short letter home. By the time he wrote again on the 19th the American propaganda machine was already trying to reverse the verdict of the battle:

The foolish Americans have been publishing a thousand absurd lies. Not liking to believe that their ship was bigger than *Shannon*, and got such a terrible beating by *fair play* as she did, the simpletons say we used *infernal machines*. They are sadly disappointed.[23]

It is not clear what evidence was used to write the early American accounts of the action. Commodore Bainbridge only received George Budd's account of the battle on 23 June, when a cartel carrying officers and men from *Chesapeake* arrived from Halifax. Purser Thomas Chew carried Budd's letter. Gloom and despair marked the collapse of bright hopes, and a dawning realisation that the infant United States Navy could not defeat the mighty British.

When Charles Falkiner reached the Admiralty with Bladen Capel's garbled despatch on 7 July the whole country went wild with joy, a heady mixture of relief and pleasure.[24] Long perplexed by the run of defeats and desperate for good news, the Admiralty quickly turned the news to account in the House of Commons. For a year Admiralty Secretary John Wilson Croker had been obliged to endure the taunting mockery of Whig opponents who attributed every defeat to Tory mismanagement, which they claimed had disheartened British seamen. The fortuitous arrival of such unalloyed good news allowed Croker to round on his tormentors with a measured display of sarcastic vitriol that rose to new oratorical heights as he destroyed the standing of his most dangerous political opponents, Captain Lord Cochrane and Sir Francis Burdett, the Members for Westminster. The *Courier* considered his speech:

. . . distinguished for argument, eloquence and fact, the particulars of the action between the *Chesapeake* and the *Shannon*, which were brought yesterday afternoon to the Admiralty. It is impossible to conceive a more enthusiastic effect than the statement produced. It was repeatedly cheered from all parts, and Mr Croker well said 'came most opportunely to confound the statements and confuse the misrepresentations of "*Westminster*'s *Pride and Britain*'s *Glory*"'. (Oh! what Pride! And what Glory!) meaning Burdett and his colleague Lord Cochrane.

The *Chesapeake* was superior in size, superior in weight of metal, superior in numbers to the *Shannon*. She came fresh out of her own port, in all the completeness of preparation, in all the consciousness of superiority and in all the confidence of conquest. She was attended, as we have heard, by several American barks and boats, laden with the friends and countrymen of her crew, eager to witness the battle and the victory. In fifteen minutes after she came into action, she was no longer American property. Twelve minutes after the action began, our gallant seamen boarded, and three minutes were sufficient to complete the business.[25]

After goring his opponents with the relish of a wounded bull, Croker went on to praise Broke's skill, courage and resolve in this unequalled action, a theme picked up by every media outlet. Broke kept a copy of the newspaper report. The following day Croker, clearly enraptured by the news, and euphoric after his oratorical triumph, sat down at the Board table to compose the official response. Although he wrote as the servant of the Board Croker might be forgiven a little personal and institutional self-congratulation:

My Lords have before had occasion to observe with great approbation the zeal, judgement and activity which have characterised Captain

Broke's proceedings since the commencement of the war, and they now receive with the highest satisfaction a proof of professional skill and gallantry in battle which has seldom been equalled and certainly never surpassed; and the decision, alacrity, and effect, with which the force of H M's Ship was directed against the enemy, mark no less the personal bravery of the officers, seamen, and marines, than the high discipline and practice in arms to which the ship's company must have sedulously and successfully been trained.

My Lords to mark their sense of this Action have been pleased to direct a Medal to be presented to Captain Broke, Lieutenants Wallis and Falkiner.

Broke would be the first British officer to receive a naval gold medal for a frigate action. His lieutenants were rewarded because they had commanded the ship and the prize after action. The Board concluded by hoping that Broke's wound 'is not likely long to deprive his Country of his valuable services'.[26] Such hopes were quickly dashed.

On the same day Croker penned an altogether more sober response to the frigate actions. Acutely conscious of the need to avoid further embarrassment, the Admiralty directed that individual British frigates should not engage 'the larger class of American ships, which were closer to battleships in size, complement and weight of metal'. This followed an idea Melville had floated after the loss of the *Java*.[27] Frigates meeting American 44s should avoid combat, but hold station, hoping another British warship would appear.[28]

Far from a concession of American superiority, as many have implied, the logic was irrefutable. Frigates did not engage battleships. It is unlikely that this wise precaution would have stopped Broke engaging the *President*, a prospect he still seemed to relish as he sailed home four months later, his skull held together by little more than a crepe bandage and blind faith. It should also be noted that the American response to the loss of the *Chesapeake* and later of the sloop *Argus* was identical. President Madison favoured instructing commanding officers not to engage equal forces, but to concentrate on commerce-raiding.[29] Secretary

Jones agreed 'commerce is our true game', seemingly oblivious to the obsessive lust for glory that tormented his captains.[30]

While the Admiralty had been happy to join the public celebrations, Melville's private judgement was markedly cooler:

On the subject of the *Chesapeake* I have felt as you do. The achievement was brilliant, and complete in all its parts, but I never admitted the previous nonsensical idea of superiority or even equality on the part of <u>any</u> foreign ship or seamen. I felt indignant at such an unfounded supposition, unauthorised by anything that had happened.[31]

Much as he disliked the spotlight of celebrity, Broke had solved many problems that fatal afternoon off Boston; he would have to bear the burden of his triumph in the interest of an entire nation. For him the congratulations of professional friends like Henry Hotham, and an after-dinner toast by the victorious Duke of Wellington, his brother Charles among the guests, would be far more to his taste. Hotham knew that Broke had prepared his ship for battle by ensuring it was 'perfect in the use of the guns'. He had copied Broke's methods on his own ship, and wished 'all our brother officers had given as much of their attention to the important part of the service of the management of the guns that you have, we should not then have made so poor a figure as we have done before you set us up again'.[32] Long before the war ended, every captain with eyes to see, and a brain to think adopted Broke's methods, trying to make their ships into *Shannon*s. Although few had a chance to follow the path to glory, one would match, or even surpass Broke's achievement.

By mid-August the Admiralty had to accept that their hero was gravely injured, ordering the *Shannon* home for a long-overdue refit as escort of the first Halifax convoy.[33] By the time these orders had arrived Broke's wound had largely healed over; his strength was returning. The men of money had recognised his services in the usual way: the Freedom of the City of London, the ultimate reward for a naval hero who had served the economic interests of the nation, accompanied by a suitably ornate sword worth 100 guineas. The insurance underwriters of Halifax matched their London brethren with a silver dinner service worth another 100 guineas. The connection between capturing American warships and steady insurance premiums was very clear. On 4 October Broke resumed command of the *Shannon* for a voyage that brought two battered warriors back to their repose, shepherding a slow convoy of merchantmen. Even so he was not without hope that Rodgers, skulking elusive Rodgers, would make an appearance, to attack the convoy and seek revenge. Re-energised by the sea and the ship Broke buckled down to the business of gunnery, ensuring the unique, obsessive drill was carried out, just in case. Whenever the guns fired his head filled with pain, and he left the day-to-day management of the exercises to others. The *Shannon* reached Portsmouth on 2 November, to find her captain had been made a baronet, but the voyage left him weak. Melville came to greet him at his hotel in London, and realised the hero would not be ready for active service any time soon. He was lauded by the gentlemen of Ipswich and Suffolk, who presented him with fine plate worth £1,000. Over the winter Broke recovered much of his strength, but resisted the offer of a large new 50-gun frigate specifically built to catch the *President*: he owed his family some time ashore.

THE VERDICT

Years later American diplomat Richard Rush recorded how news of this battle stunned America. Only twelve months before no one would have been surprised by a British victory, but a year of success had turned many heads. Consequently American despair exceeded British exultation.[34] The *Shannon–Chesapeake* action had been the deadliest action yet fought by the American naval officer corps. While larger butcher's bills were common in the Royal Navy, the tiny American force was deeply traumatised by the savage arithmetic of death and defeat.

By a curious coincidence Stephen Decatur, another man defeated by the British on 1 June 1813, presided over the

Chesapeake court martial. Even allowing for the heightened emotions and strained days of war the court martial was truly bizarre.[35] It sought excuses for a defeat that needed none, a defeat that shed nothing but glory on the men who had given their lives fighting their ship. Stating that *Chesapeake* won the gunnery action, that she was disabled accidentally, and that the British had more men and guns was simply wrong in point of fact. Blaming the only black man on board for failing to blow his bugle with sufficient vigour, and disgracing Acting Lieutenant William Cox for neglect of duty and un-officerlike conduct was vindictive and perverse. The black bugler was given 100 lashes and lost his pay. Cox lost his career. Claims that *Chesapeake*'s crew were untrained, drunk, or mutinous were deliberately mendacious. The ship's muster book proved the crew were largely veterans of the previous commission. Furthermore, James Lawrence, a fine seaman and an experienced warrior, would not have gone into battle with a ship of equal force with a crew he did not trust. The court martial and other posthumous attempts to turn Lawrence into a martyr, or excuse his defeat by all manner of implausible excuses, from 'jinx' ship and 'raw' crew, to the dereliction of black or Portuguese ratings reflected 'a great amount of self-deception'.[36]

Chesapeake was beaten because *Shannon* fired first, fired more accurately, and more effectively. Her command team was annihilated, key men were killed, her rigging and steering gear were disabled, and the upper deck cleared. Before the ships collided *Chesapeake* had been hit more than 40 times with 18- and 32-pounder shot, *Shannon* only 10 or 11 times. Together with the accurate demolition of *Chesapeake*'s steering gear, head stays and other key elements of the rigging, the battle had been won long before Broke boarded. Indeed his instinct had been to keep his distance and bombard the enemy until they surrendered. This would have been truly scientific. However, Broke's ship had also been crippled by accurate, effective fire from *Chesapeake*. The opening American broadside had been well trained, it hit the target; but not well laid, it hit far too low. Under the slight press of the wind the ship had heeled over towards the enemy, sending a storm of star shot, bar shot, grape, canister and solid ball into the *Shannon*'s water line, where it did little damage. Broke's men did not waste a round; they hit the American gun and quarterdeck with remorseless precision, killing, wounding and dismantling. The effect on the exposed quarterdeck was such that few men remained standing to meet the British boarders. The Americans had nothing to be ashamed of, their gunnery was good, and they fought bravely, but they were beaten by better men, perhaps the best fighting crew that ever went to sea.

As he convalesced in Halifax, Broke inspected HMS *Chesapeake*. With characteristic precision he noted every round and grapeshot that had hit the American ship, and discussed the details with other survivors. Lieutenant Richard King counted the hits. His findings were clear:

	Shannon	*Chesapeake*
Hits by 32-pounder ball	13	25
Hits by 18-pounder ball	12	29
Hits by grape shot	119	306
Hits by bar shot.	14	
Hits by 9-pounder shot	2*	
Total:	158	362[37]

* *other rounds had hit the ship's wheel, killed the sailing master and cut the backstays*

Overall *Shannon* scored twice as many hits as *Chesapeake*.

The British were astonished by the number and variety of anti-rigging projectiles on the captured ship, double-headed shot and star shot, the latter comprising a number of foot-long iron bars connected by chain links, and neatly folded to be fired from the 18- and 32-pounder guns. When fired, the bars opened out into four sections, which were linked to a central ring.

The object of this novel artillery was to cut away the shrouds, and facilitate the fall of the masts; and the plan was to commence the action with the bar and chain shot, so as to produce, as early as possible, that desirable result, after which the American ship could play round her antagonist, and cut her to pieces with comparative impunity.[38]

A small supply of these projectiles had been issued to British ships for a century. The contrast lay in the scale of the supply: the Americans deployed large numbers of dismantling shot as the key to their tactical system. In 1811 the Royal Navy had stopped issuing them, although a few were still at sea.[39] Having pre-selected his tactics Lawrence had been caught with his guns loaded with the wrong munitions for the opening broadside. The impact on American combat effectiveness was stunning. In battle, of the fourteen bar shot that hit the *Shannon*'s hull, only one penetrated the gun deck, and even that one remained lodged in the hull. The others gouged the exterior planking without causing any damage.[40]

British naval gunnery expert Sir Howard Douglas was the first to realise that the American captains had, Lawrence apart, fought their battles with considerable caution, emphasising considered manoeuvre over aggression. British captains had been over-confident, simply careless or slightly unlucky in their tactical choices. Broke admitted that, after two decades spent chasing elusive French ships, speed in pursuit had become the acme of naval skill, with combat a mere formality. Furthermore, frigate design had reflected the change, emphasising speed and losing handiness.[41]

William James argued that this was the only 'fair and equal' frigate action of the war. After reading the absurd whitewash court martial James was inclined to mock the quality of *Chesapeake*'s crew, if only to expose the absurdity of the conclusions, and the over-hyped reputation of the American service. With the benefit of greater distance and detachment Broke's biographer Peter Padfield took the opposite view, stressing their quality, and argued that, had Lawrence been able to bring his ship squarely alongside, the action would have been far closer, and even more costly for those who fought that day. James's heated rhetoric had much to do with lingering post-war tensions, and Padfield is the better guide.[42]

DESERTERS

The British were not surprised to find deserters and other British subjects on board *Chesapeake*. Some were traitors, and fought desperately against their own countrymen, knowing that 'if captured, they could not expect a better fate than death'.[43] To be classed as traitors these men had to be known deserters from the Royal Navy. Others had been discharged from the Royal Navy, and some knew the surgeon at Halifax Hospital. After the battle several men came forward, or were betrayed to the British authorities. On 22 June Captain Robert Oliver, then senior officer at Halifax, reported the names of those who had already surrendered. Four men freely confessed to being British, claiming they had been coerced into American service, or refused the opportunity to leave. They had neither served in nor deserted from the Royal Navy. They were: Londoner Thomas Jones, aged 23; Liverpudlian Henry Simpson, 27, who had been nine months on the ship, recruited dead drunk at New York; John Pearce, 21, and like Broke from Ipswich, had been in the American coasting trade for many years before shipping in the *Chesapeake* seven months previously; Lancastrian Thomas Arthur, 24, had joined the ship at Boston some eight months before. Arthur named other Englishmen belonging to the *Chesapeake* in prison. George Williams came forward later; although English-born he had lived in America from the age of seven. He claimed that ten or twelve Englishmen had been killed on board the *Chesapeake* during the action, 'and that a great many more are now in the Prison'. Anxious to recruit for his short-handed ships Warren wanted to offer a pardon.[44] In October the four men who gave themselves up as British nationals were sent home as disposable to serve in other Royal Navy vessels.[45]

Chesapeake's crew included a number of British deserters; they faced the death penalty for serving the enemy in war, which explains the treacherous attack on Broke, and the fact that several men jumped overboard. The ship's muster book, however, did not record a single British sailor.[46] That did not mean there were no Britons on board, only that none were recorded. One known deserter was caught, sent to Britain, tried and executed. Lancashire-born Joseph Warburton was a deserter from HMS *Aeolus* and a mutineer, having carried a prize into an enemy port. He was tried by court martial, condemned and hanged at Portsmouth on 18 November 1813.[47]

The Navy's insatiable need for skilled seamen meant that Britons who gave themselves up, and were not naval deserters, were pardoned and employed. Hanging the occasional deserter served as an example of the terrible fate that awaited all traitors.

SECRETS

Because the *Chesapeake* was taken so quickly, and with such heavy loss of life among her officers, the orders, confidential papers and signal books were taken. Capel sent copies direct to England, distributed the signals to his squadron and detached a force to intercept the *Hornet* at the rendezvous set by Lawrence. In British hands the American signal code had the potential to confuse and mislead.[48] British warships received copies of the American signal book from early July.[49] But Purser Chew had warned Bainbridge of the loss and the Commodore quickly created a new code with Secretary Jones, comprehensively changing the meaning of existing flags.[50]

By the summer of 1813, British strength on the American stations had risen from 83 vessels at the outbreak of war to 129, with the most marked increase in battleships and frigates. This force was adequate to sustain a close blockade of all significant American harbours, those that contained warships, and to convoy merchant ships against privateers, which became increasingly ineffective as controlled sailings denied them easy prey. To secure this result Warren needed ten 74s, the 58-gun heavy razee *Majestic*, sixteen frigates and a host of brigs and gun vessels manned by 14,300 men. At this stage Warren had approximately 10 per cent of the British fleet by numbers and manpower under his command.[51] Even so British forces in the Channel and the Mediterranean were twice as big.

CHAPTER 6

Securing the Seas:
The American Attack on British Trade

—∞∞∞—

The American naval threat to British shipping was decisively defeated on 1 June 1813. Philip Broke and Robert Oliver had thwarted two attempted break-outs, and by the end of the day a third of America's frigates had been taken or placed beyond use. Very few American warships would get to sea after that day, and those that did achieved very little as commerce raiders. The failure of the United States Navy to achieve any significant strategic effect as a commerce-raiding force has led many analysts to argue that 'victory' was secured by American privateers, a naval 'militia' coming to the defence of the state, destroying British shipping and humiliating the Royal Navy. While examples of financial success, seafaring skill and handsome profits abound the reality is more complex.

Republican ideologues placed great faith in the ability of privateers, a cheap, ideologically sound auxiliary fleet, to damage the British economy and distract the Royal Navy. Privateers, state-licensed predators, employed armed merchant ships as an auxiliary naval force in wartime, supplementing state assets on a strictly commercial basis.[1] In the Revolutionary War American ship-owners and merchants returned to a trade they had practised under the British flag for the previous eighty years. Successful privateer operators from Baltimore and Salem, which largely escaped British blockades, turned windfall profits into post-war commercial leadership. Salem owners opened Asian markets, while Baltimore's economic expansion reflected a large, productive hinterland and close proximity to the West Indies. During the Revolution Baltimore combined profitable trade, over

700 privateers, and a key role in the logistics of the Continental Army. Merchant, soldier and privateer owner General Samuel Smith exemplified Baltimore's war, making money, serving the cause and taking control of the local militia.[2] Baltimore's privateering depended on locally built schooners, a specialised development of fore-and-aft-rigged ships of between 100 and 200 tons, ideally suited to the short distances and perishable cargoes of West Indian trade. After 1793 the windfall profits of the re-export trade generated a step-change in economic expansion. Registered American shipping tonnage doubled in the next six years, while profits averaged 40 per cent. The questionable legality of the re-export trade put a premium on fast ships, ideal for conversion into cruisers. Heavy losses to French privateers before the Quasi-War ensured a suitably named local warship was built for the Federal Navy.[3] In addition Baltimore fitted out seventy-four privateers. Once again Samuel Smith took a leading role. The 1797–8 'mobilisation' sustained skills and expertise that would be harnessed in 1812. Despite their Republican politics, most Baltimore owners violated Jefferson's Embargo in the search for markets and profits, supplying the British Peninsular army with wheat and flour. Long exposure to aggressive, high-risk business ventures predisposed Baltimore's commercial elite to privateering, while the explosion of shipping ensured the city was amply supplied with ship-builders, timber, ropewalks, forges and canvas to build, operate and repair ships.

By 1812 Baltimore was the New World centre for fast ships and quasi-legal activities.[4] Little wonder the town fitted out privateers as soon as war was declared. Congress delegated authority to license privateers to State Department and Customs officials.[5] Owners competed to get the first licences, and hasten their ships to sea. Baltimore took 175 of the 1,100 licences issued, the largest number for a single port. Such enthusiasm was welcomed by a cash-strapped government that charged for licences and took sureties from guarantors, often close connections of the owners: it would also take a cut of any profits. Privateers would subsidise the state, damage the enemy and refresh the national coffers.

Investors risked significant capital, unlike the state. Accordingly, investors were anxious to maximise profits. The prospect of prize provided an ample inducement for American investors, captains and crew, while the government share of sales would provide useful wartime revenue. Privateering would keep the seafaring community in business in wartime, and supplement the woefully inadequate national navy.

In Baltimore ownership was spread across some 200 investors: 100 small operators took shares in a single ship, another fifty picked up shares in two or three ships, but the critical players were the fifty active investors with shares in more than four ships, each risking capital of between $10,000 and $40,000. The higher figure equalled the cost of a single, large, purpose-built privateer. Forty of the active investors were merchants, most had previous privateer experience, and most were linked to a handful of large firms. Once again Samuel Smith played a leading role. Marylanders expressed few qualms about the conflict; Baltimore Federalists happily invested alongside Republicans because privateering was good business.

Alongside privateer licences the American government also issued letters of marque, which allowed merchant ships to continue external trade, with the possibility of taking lawful prize. Investing in both forms allowed active investors to spread risk, a typical wartime insurance technique.[6] Many investors also stood surety for the privateer bonds of business colleagues, interlocking risk, ownership and profits. In addition to the 200 investors some 7,000 men eventually served on privateers and letters of marque, from a total population of 50,000. While 7,200 individuals took risks in the trade, 10,000 more earned their livelihood from support operations ashore. The collapse of alternatives for capital and labour at the outbreak of war forced investors, seamen and workers alike into the privateer trade. Quakers could assuage their religious scruples by taking letters of marque.

Most vessels taken up in the initial rush were schooners from the West Indies trade, vessels that operated close to port, were easily manned, and fast. Very few Baltimore square-rigged vessels served as privateers; they had been built for cargo capacity, not speed. New York, Salem and Boston privateers often used square-rigged or hermaphrodite ships because they faced more demanding operating conditions, and had a good supply of suitable seamen.

American privateering has frequently been portrayed as a 'patriotic' response to war, transforming commercial activity into a noble national effort, a 'naval militia'.[7] In reality privateering was an attractive commercial opportunity that needed no patriotic encouragement. For every genuine patriot, like Joshua Barney, there were a dozen speculating on the profits of predation. Most active investors spread their risk by taking British grain licences, to feed Wellington's army. Patriotic privateers like Barney contested the practice, sending licensed ships in for adjudication. Others sent them in hoping for a quick profit. Just as the administration decided the licensed trade was legal, because it needed the revenue, the British stopped it. By September 1812 good domestic harvests and Russian grain had ended British dependence on American supplies, and simplified the economics of war. This was a serious blow for the owners of square-rigged ships, which had no other wartime use.

With Chesapeake Bay blockaded from February 1813 'normal' trading activity ceased. Flour quickly piled up in Baltimore, half a million dollars' worth lying idle when the blockade began, paralysing trade. Attempts to use land transport proved futile and prices dropped rapidly. With commerce in limbo local investors shifted their funds into manufacturing industry, if only to keep their money working. Economic conditions steadily worsened during 1813.[8]

Far from accepting their fate as a patriotic sacrifice, local capitalists pressurised Congress to improve the financial returns of privateering, the last remaining profitable seafaring business. In August 1813 Congress lowered the duties payable on the sale of prize goods, sacrificing national revenue as an incentive to sustain a 'strategic' industry, a decision that reflected the political weight of Baltimore's fifty active privateer investors. The incentive arrived at a vital moment, because the character of the business was changing. In 1812 investors had rushed to fit out existing 100- to 200-ton schooners, to operate on the American coast and the West Indies choke points. This had been a relatively cheap activity. By mid-1813 these areas were controlled by British blockades, convoys and cruisers. The second half of the war witnessed a steady shift towards larger, heavily manned purpose-built privateers, designed to operate in distant waters, seeking profitable hunting grounds. For the same reasons the number and proportion of ships operating as letter of marque traders declined. By late 1814 the remaining privateers were ranging far afield in the search for prize. Often they were forced to choose between returning home without a profit or attacking dangerous targets like British armed transports, small warships and packet vessels. The decision to attack could be a simple case of mistaken identity.[9] The same financial imperatives would inform the defence of Baltimore in August 1814.

The British identified Baltimore as an uncommonly hostile city, while a harbour packed with privateers, prizes, cargoes and shipyards was a tempting target for retaliation. Early in 1813 the *London Evening Star* suggested Baltimore deserved to share the fate of Copenhagen in 1807, a terror bombardment by rockets and bombs.[10] When the attack came 60 per cent of privateer investors joined the defenders, under the command of militia major general Samuel Smith. These men were protecting extensive personal investment in ships, tobacco, flour, prize goods, buildings and shipyards. While investors provided ships to block the harbour, two privateersmen died defending Fort McHenry. The British attack came at a critical moment for Baltimore: small firms and investors had begun to fail; confidence and credit were steadily draining away. While Americans were told about the patriotism of Baltimore, the link between Smith's millions and his strategy should be obvious to more detached analysts.

THE MECHANICS OF PRIVATEERING

The privateer schooner became the enduring Baltimore icon, an image of man-made perfection. Hezekiah Niles described the privateer *Chasseur* as 'perhaps the most beautiful vessel that ever floated in the ocean, looking for all the world like she was about to rise out of the water and fly in the air'.[11] *Chasseur*, a late-war-built 356-ton schooner, was among the largest of her type. Only exceptional ships could get to sea and operate effectively in 1814, when this vessel alone did more damage to British trade than the entire United States Navy. It was no wonder the Royal Navy put so much effort into the capture or destruction of large privateers. The speed of the Baltimore schooner came at a price: they were remarkably dangerous. With a vast cloud of canvas spread on heavy masts and yards they capsized easily, even at anchor, if the wind shifted or increased suddenly. In inexperienced hands they were lethal, easily driven under water by the sheer press of their sails. Good captains and men were critical. These sharp-lined locally built schooners were 'effective but dangerous instruments to operate in rough waters and best suited for the more temperate zones where their unique characteristics were utilised to the greatest advantage'. A modern replica based on *Chasseur*, the *Pride of Baltimore*, was knocked over and sunk by a Caribbean storm in 1986, with the loss of four lives. Her successor, *Pride of Baltimore II*, was built to a less extreme design.[12] Despite the danger the Royal Navy added several captured schooners to its inventory.[13] With smaller crews and less experienced officers they rarely matched their original performance, but they were a useful local reinforcement for hard-pressed squadrons on the American coast.

In addition to special ships, privateering was a manpower-intensive industry. Initially Baltimore was able to provide plenty of sailors, a large draft of landsmen, who made up about a third of the crews, and around 125 captains. Experienced officers were essential to a successful voyage; few men had the commanding personality required to drive a ship hard, and discipline a large, aggressive crew. A handful excelled, others failed and were soon replaced; investors anxious to protect their capital offered premiums to proven winners. About 10 per cent of privateer captains were successful, mostly the men who ran their ships like naval vessels and chose how and where to operate. The mid-Atlantic and the Caribbean were the natural home for the fast but tricky schooners. Similar letter of marque vessels carried the Iberia trade, where speed was equally important. Despite their speed, insurance on letters of marque quickly rocketed to an uneconomic 50 per cent, forcing most owners to spread their risk across multiple investors. Indeed, for most of the War of 1812, American ships and seamen had other economic outlets: the licensed trade and letter of marque voyages provided better returns on investment than privateering, an option the British deliberately maintained.

There were never enough men to crew Baltimore shipping. Instead, sailors were drawn from other ports, by adverts and editorials in *Niles' Weekly Register*. Landsmen came from local farms. The Navy closed the recruiting depot at Baltimore early in the war; few men were choosing Navy gunboats over the prospects of a privateer windfall. When the British blockade increased the risk of capture, volunteers became harder to find. Letter of marque traders had large crews, about double the peacetime complement, to man the guns, and possibly a prize or two. Their crews were generally acknowledged to be a better class of men than the 'desperados' attracted to privateering. By October 1812 some 1,538 men were serving in privateers, and about as many again in letters of marque, a remarkable figure given that the city recorded only 1,000 sailors in 1806. As the trade demanded a steady influx of men British prisoners were encouraged to sign on; some of them were later caught and prosecuted. In part these new recruits made good losses by storm and capture: at least 300 Baltimore men were imprisoned in Jamaica, Bermuda and Halifax, many more ended up at Dartmoor.[14] By 1813 few privateers operated in American waters, where British cruisers were ubiquitous. Relying on intelligence about convoy routes and sailing dates to shape their course, agents operating in other American ports and profitable markets for prizes, they tended to take a circuit of North Atlantic trade routes via Barbados, Madeira and the African coast. They then headed home through British and Irish waters, Newfoundland and the Grand Banks, obliged to keep moving ahead of the inevitable British response.

The actual taking of a prize was carefully contrived to minimise risk and maximise profit. Usually a warning shot and displaying the American flag sufficed. If the enemy refused to heave-to a heavy fire was directed into the rigging and across the upper deck, to cut the control ropes and demoralise the crew. If necessary the ship could be boarded. The tactics were determined by the need to secure an undamaged ship to send home as a prize.[15] The prize remained at risk during the voyage home: many were recaptured, some by their own crew, many more by Royal Navy warships – which received attractive payments to stimulate their efforts. Around 750 American prizes were re-taken. Only a third of American prizes reached home to be adjudicated by a court; fewer still were condemned and sold. Some were stripped of valuables and scuttled, or released as prisoner cartels, lost to the weather or re-captured. Some vessels were ransomed, but this was illegal under British law and many ransoms were dishonoured.[16] Privateers also earned a bounty for prisoners. In 1812 this stood at $20 per man, rising to $25 in 1813 and $100 in 1814. The prisoner bounty was the only state reward to private investors.

Most of the prize ships and goods sold at auction were purchased by the investors who owned the privateers. Privateering was integrated into the wider American–West Indian–European trade network; owners used prize money to speculate in prize goods for further profits. Prize agents received and distributed sale funds, offering investors credit on sales already in hand. In effect many investors took goods in lieu of cash, as part of a complex web of commercial profits. Wartime demand for West Indies produce and European manufactures was high. Both state and national governments imposed court fees and customs dues on these sales. Owners complained that the double customs dues levied from July 1812 to fund the war reduced their income by 30–40 per cent, while making the government, which did not share the risk, a major beneficiary of the trade. If prize goods were re-exported by linked letter of marque traders customs dues would be recovered. Numerous letter of marque voyages carrying West Indies sugar and coffee to Napoleonic Europe only served to emphasise the inextricable connection between these activities. Privateer investors exploited their ability to export to increase the profits of predation.

By mid-1813 the combination of an effective British blockade and falling returns made privateering significantly less attractive as a business investment. Vociferous protests by investors persuaded Congress to reduce customs dues by one-third in August 1813. Philadelphia ship-owner, Navy Secretary and acting Secretary of the Treasury William Jones understood the connection between private capital, profit levels and investment.[17] It was hardly a coincidence that he acted only weeks after the naval campaign had been wrecked. After 1 June 1813 privateers were the only offensive arm of American strategy. With a large privateer costing over $40,000, the government had to encourage investment when declining prices for prize goods reflected a glutted market and limited opportunities for onward sale. Perishable goods often had to be sold cheaply. While Jones's attempt to stimulate privateering by lowering customs dues may have encouraged investors to keep trying, increasing returns on the best prize cargoes by up to $30,000, capital costs and the risks of war continued to rise. The government had to be flexible. It had been taking up to 40 per cent of gross receipts from sales, but 1 June 1813 shifted the balance of power in the relationship decisively in favour of privateer investors. The government desperately needed them to keep their capital in the trade.

Baltimore and New York were the leading privateer ports, with Boston and Salem a very distant third and fourth respectively. When the Chesapeake was firmly blockaded several Baltimore privateers shifted their base to New York.[18] New York owners favoured larger vessels. Among the best known were the *General Armstrong*, which measured over 300 tons and was heavily armed. She began her career in 1812 and was finally destroyed by a British squadron at Fayal in the Azores on 26 September 1814.[19] Also highly successful was the French-owned and -commanded New York brig-schooner *Prince de Neufchatel* taken on 28 December 1814 and purchased for the Royal Navy; she measured 328 tons and carried sixteen 12-pounder carronades and two long 6-pounder guns.[20] The success of two New York privateers against the British Archangel trade in 1813 demonstrated both a detailed understanding of British trade networks, and remarkable confidence. At least twenty British ships were taken and many condemned and sold in Norway.[21] Even larger New York vessels, such as the 550-ton ship-rigged *Hyder Ali* and *Jacob Jones*, went to Asian waters.[22] The connection between the naval and privateer wars grew ever closer as the war continued. When the Navy needed new sloops for commerce-destroying it bought some privateers and turned to New York shipbuilders Adam and Noah Brown, who had built the *Prince de Neufchatel* and *General Armstrong*. Using their experience the Browns built the 500-ton USS *Peacock*, which proved equally successful as a destroyer of shipping.[23]

Unlike Baltimore, Charleston and Savannah, which combined Republican fervour with private profit, the Northern ports took an altogether more equivocal view of the privateer war. New England investors and operators often combined privateering with smuggling, working with the British to thwart their own administration. In the harsh northern waters of the Bay of Fundy, where America met Canada, predation worked both ways, with at least forty Canadian vessels, and rather more Americans, operating against trade. Very few satisfied the 'patriotic' model beloved of older histories. Most were happy to engage in illegal activity: smuggling, raiding the shore and attacking neutrals. Yet many in New England saw Britain, not the plantation South, as their natural ally, thwarting their own government, and

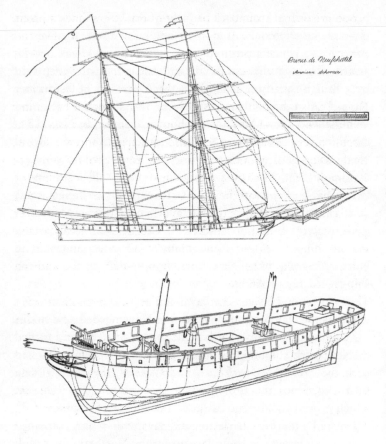

Prince de Neufchatel, the ultimate privateer.
A fast, powerful and efficient ship,
built for one purpose.

occasionally burning American privateers because their presence attracted unwelcome attention from British cruisers. By 1814 so many New England privateers were using licences to cover smuggling that Madison revoked the licences of any with fewer than twenty crewmen.

During the war Baltimore would operate 122 private armed vessels; 30 were pure privateers, and another 15 operated in either category. They took over 500 prizes and brought home

1,600 prisoners. Around 58 per cent of privateers made a profit, defined as prize money of more than $50,000. Overall, investors made a 200 per cent profit, although the rewards were unevenly distributed. Active investors with more than five investments did very well, but half of those with a single investment lost money. Samuel Smith probably made $400,000 – no wonder he wanted to defend his city, ships and warehouses in September 1814. The largest investor, banker and insurance agent Andrew Clapper, made $800,000, about a third of the total profits. Some 55 Baltimore licensed ships were taken or wrecked, including 19 privateers; 11 were captured by the Royal Navy or driven ashore in coastal waters, some $760,000 worth of shipping.[24] However, privateering could not absorb all of Baltimore's disposable capital. Money moved into industry and government stock. Privateering was better than stagnation, but peaceful commerce had been more profitable.

While Jerome Garitee has argued that local patriotism was a significant motivation, the evidence is unconvincing. Both Jean Ordronaux, captain of the *Prince de Neufchatel*, and his owners were French.[25] The nefarious post-war careers of privateersmen and their ships support the conclusion that profit was the real motivation. Many ships and men ended up privateering in the Spanish American Wars of Independence, or joined the slave trade. Half of all privateer vessels were sold into foreign registry, very few for 'legitimate' purposes. Within half a decade these activities were widely condemned, by Samuel Smith among others, as piratical.[26] Post-war Baltimore suffered a major financial collapse, abandoning the sea for a new role as a communication hub and industrial city, mirroring the landward shift of national culture.

THE DEFENCE OF TRADE

In stark contrast to the high drama of privateering – the battles, lucky escapes and valuable prizes that made up the substantial profit and loss columns of the American attack on British floating trade – the underlying purpose of commerce-raiding was strategic. By the time the Americans declared war the extensive French privateer campaign that began in 1793 was faltering. Faced by well-organised British defences French privateers averaged less than two prizes per ship and ran a high risk of capture.[27] Only ships and men with no other economic outlets would run the risk; that they did so at all was a testament to the astonishing impact of Britain's economic blockade. Despite this salutary lesson the American government looked to privateers as a significant part of its war effort. Whether their aims were achieved by the total destruction of British commerce or by rendering that commerce uneconomic was relatively unimportant. The object was to oblige the British to negotiate.

In early 1812 this strategy appeared rational. American ships would join an extensive French effort in European, Caribbean and Asian waters. Furthermore, privateering was self-financing. Britain was fortunate America attacked just as the tide of war turned in Northern Europe. The vital Baltic trade had been re-opened in 1810, reducing dependence on American supplies and markets, and Atlantic shipping, by providing alternative sources of grain, timber and other forest products, and alternative consumers of sugar, coffee and spices. At the same time the British had broken the back of the commerce war outside Europe, largely by capturing French and Dutch bases at Martinique and Guadeloupe in 1808 and 1809, Mauritius in December 1810 and Java six months later.[28] Reflective Americans must have realised that British success at sea indicated underlying strength, strength that could be turned to meet new threats. For over a century the British state had defeated every privateer and cruiser campaign, even in the darkest days between 1779 and 1782 when the enemy included France, Spain, Holland and the rebellious Colonies. British counter-measures had been refined and reinforced during the existential conflict with Revolutionary and Napoleonic France after 1793. By 1812 the British were extremely well prepared to meet the American challenge, the key mechanisms of effective trade defence tried and tested by decades of war.

This was no accident. Maritime commerce occupied a central place in British economic life, giving the shipping, commercial and financial interests tremendous political leverage. Trade, industry, and even the food supply, depended on successful trade defence. After the 'Glorious Revolution' of 1688 merchants and investors had a firm grip on the levers of national power, through Parliament, the National Debt and the major trading corporations. By 1812 the best estimates suggest there were at least 3,500 merchants with some ability to influence government, and they demanded effective protection for their merchant shipping and cargoes. The merchants had power in the House of Commons, effectively obliging the Royal Navy to convoy their shipping, blockade hostile bases and provide cruiser patrols, while the commercial sector provided insurance cover to spread risk for ship-owners, and supplied alternative sources of intelligence.

The interaction between the Admiralty and representatives of trade was constant, well organised and effective. Lloyd's of London, the main insurance market, maintained daily contact with the Admiralty, exchanging intelligence, and dealing with complaints about escorts, or merchant ships leaving their convoys. Other large trade organisations, notably the East India Company, had ready access to the Admiralty through the Board of Control and Lord Melville's long-term political connection with the sub-continent. More diffuse groups of merchants in specific trades were advised to band together and appoint spokesmen to liaise with the Navy. The British system was flexible, intelligence-driven and effective. The key indicator of success was the maintenance of steady insurance rates.

CONVOY

The basis of trade defence was the legal requirement for ships heading abroad to sail in escorted convoy. By 1812 the British convoy system was well established. After nineteen years of war with France and its various allies and associates no one holding a position of authority in naval, commercial or insurance centres needed any instruction on this subject. Collecting merchant ships sailing to linked destinations in large oceanic convoys, protected by warships, enabled the British to limit risk, keep insurance rates on key routes at acceptable levels, and defeat America's only offensive naval strategy. This demonstrated the futility of the war, and maintained morale in the City of London, where a loss of confidence could have serious repercussions for government interest rates and loans. In October 1812 the Board insisted that all ships were obliged 'to take the benefit of periodical convoys'.[29] Special licences were required for ships to sail alone, permission usually restricted to large, well-armed vessels. Insurance policies also required ships to sail in convoy. Any ship that ignored the law, or deliberately left a convoy at sea, voided the insurance cover and rendered the master and the owners liable to prosecution by the Admiralty. Both Lloyd's and the Admiralty were happy to provide evidence, and to publicise 'exemplary' punishments handed down by the court.[30]

These punishments were well merited. The convoy system provided an effective defence against most threats. Convoy escorts were specifically directed to report on any 'runners' leaving the convoy to reach market ahead of the fleet for commercial advantage, and stragglers, ships that fell out astern. These provided American cruisers with their main source of prizes. While regrettable, these losses were not dangerous. The real danger was the loss of a major convoy, something the Americans signally failed to achieve. The American effort did not break the convoy system, or capture a single convoy. Commodore John Rodgers recognised the political and strategic consequences of taking a big convoy: he began the war by targeting a specific West India convoy. His British opposite number Philip Broke understood the over-riding priority of defending the convoy system, abandoning offensive operations against American trade to reinforce weakly defended convoys. In the event Rodgers failed to find his target.

The main problem for the Admiralty in the War of 1812 was the impossibility of preventing all losses. Because blockades are invariably imperfect, the British had a fall-back position, patrolling the key landfalls and effective convoy escorts with good doctrine. Well organised escorted convoys provided the best answer to the privateer threat. When attacked by hostile ships escort commanders understood their role was to delay the enemy, often by engaging in one-sided battles with superior warships while the convoy dispersed.[31] Often the escorts were markedly inferior to the American raiders. The escorts faced larger ships, more guns and bigger crews, forcing them to fight hopeless defensive battles while the convoy scattered.

The results of such combats could be misleading. On 5 August 1813 the new, purpose-built 240-ton Charleston privateer *Decatur* captured HMS *Dominica*, originally an American-built French privateer, in a savage, close-quarter battle that ended with the large privateer crew boarding the British vessel. Three-quarters of the *Dominica*'s crew were killed or wounded, including the captain. The 'American' captain, Dominique Diron, had been one of Napoleon's privateers.[32] Critically, *Dominica* had been escorting the valuable packet ship *Princess Charlotte*, which escaped.[33] While the human cost had been high occasional defeats of this sort were inevitable. The British would destroy the *Decatur* on the Penobscot River in September 1814. In a forty-five-minute action on 29 April 1814 the brig HMS *Epervier* was taken in a one-sided combat by the American sloop USS *Peacock*. The British ship lost eight dead and fifteen wounded, the Americans two wounded. The British gun mountings had failed and the main topmast had been shot away. While this might be read as a straightforward American success the outcome was more complex. Commander Richard Wales had done his duty as a convoy escort, engaging and detaining the enemy while his convoy escaped.[34] Officers who commanded such defences might receive a reward from the Admiralty, often promotion, and a significant token of esteem from Lloyd's.

The convoy system expanded to meet demand. The Convoys and Cruisers Act of 1708 required the Navy to deploy a substantial proportion of its assets in this role. After 1793 the

British merchant marine expanded steadily with the number of ships rising from 16,079 to 24,418 in 1814, and the average size of ships also increased. The Convoy Act of 1798 made it illegal to venture abroad without convoy, with few exceptions. Compulsion worked because the Admiralty ran an effective convoy system in close liaison with the commercial community, covering almost all needs. Most convoys ranged from ten to fifty ships, although Baltic fleets could exceed 1,000. Discipline was critical: merchant ships had to obey orders, and attend to signals. The Admiralty set convoy sailing dates and departure points. For London shipping these were the well-protected anchorages at the Nore and Portsmouth Roads. Both were in telegraph communication with London, to facilitate postponing sailings, or sending fresh intelligence. Merchants had ample opportunity to join convoys, and take out the relevant insurance. When a merchant ship arrived at the rendezvous the master was obliged to sign for a copy of the written instructions, including signals, rendezvous in the event of dispersal by storm and other points which merchant ships needed to note. Once at sea the escorts spent their time shepherding the convoy, by flag signal, gunfire and even towing slower ships. Seamanship standards varied as many of the merchant crews were under-strength, not least because escorting warships frequently impressed their men. Massive convoys that sailed from Spithead heading for Asia, the Mediterranean and the West Indies, gradually separated out into smaller formations, West Indies-bound ships called at Madeira before crossing the Atlantic, heading for Barbados, and then on through the archipelago. At all major destinations local admirals deployed cruisers to secure convoy termini against predators.[35] Similar cruising stations would be established at all focal points where significant numbers of ships and convoys passed, notably in the Western Approaches and off the Atlantic islands.

The principal convoy routes threatened by American cruisers were those to Halifax, Quebec and the West Indies, where the existence of separate Leeward Islands and Jamaica stations demonstrated the importance of regional trade. Ships heading in either direction would be assembled at specified ports, and pre-arranged times, to meet their escort force. Sailing dates were determined by the demands of the trade, often highly seasonal, in the north because ice and weather conditions made the Gulf of St Lawrence dangerous, or in the south to meet the sugar crop.

Although the declaration of war caught the Admiralty somewhat unprepared it responded quickly. By the second week in August 1812 the Board was liaising with City trade associations to arrange convoys to sail within a week to Halifax, Bermuda and the West Indies, and pressing the Navy's administrative departments to make sure the escorts were ready. Warren received the relevant information on convoys before he sailed for Halifax, 'stating the periods & call his particular attention to the placing some of his cruisers in such situations as he may judge best for affording adequate protection to the trade while within the limits of his station'. These instructions were copied to the Leeward Islands and Jamaica stations.[36] Most convoy escorts were scheduled to make round trips, rather than reinforcing Warren's over-stretched fleet.[37] Issuing instructions was in part a matter of routine, and part to provide a paper trail to meet complaints from insurers about losses incurred at the end of the voyage.

The key weakness of the convoy system was the necessarily wide publication of sailing dates, long before the convoy actually sailed. Any interested parties could gather the intelligence from newspapers, City of London coffee houses and ship chandlers. During the War of 1812 American newspapers frequently reprinted this intelligence, especially in privateer ports like Baltimore, Boston and New York. Such public information determined the course of John Rodgers's first cruise. However, the vagaries of wind, weather, and merchant-ship performance made interception in the open sea a matter of chance and persistence.

The British convoy system in place at the outbreak of war in 1812 was effective, robust and flexible. Losses soon fell to relatively low levels, and remained sustainable throughout the conflict. The occasional alarm generated by specific seizures should not distract attention from the striking success of British trade defence. Indeed occasional 'alarms' in London can be read as part of the process of passing and exchanging intelligence between the state and commercial actors. While the British Army blunted the American drive to conquer Canada, the Navy defeated the war against trade. This joint success mattered because these were the only American strategies capable of coercing Britain.

No system of trade defence could prevent all losses, and the British system was no exception. It survived the shocks of war because a strong marine insurance sector spread risk to minimise individual losses, thereby maintaining the credit-worthiness of ship-owners and merchants. Marine insurance was critically dependent on the law, which gave all parties confidence in the integrity of the system. The rise of Lloyd's reflected the collection of shipping data in *Lloyd's List* from 1734, enabling underwriters to calculate risk with some certainty, noting the age and origins of ships, their masters, ownership and crew. The *List* was equally useful to the Admiralty.[38] London dominated international shipping insurance, helping to keep rates low. The French Revolutionary War witnessed a major increase in the amount of shipping insured, as convoy became compulsory and rates were adjusted to reflect compliance. Under the pressure of war the relationship between Lloyd's and the Admiralty became even closer. The Admiralty provided Lloyd's with convoy lists, reports of proceedings and confidential advice, while Lloyd's could vitiate insurance for convoy voyages on the evidence of the escort commander if in fact the ship sailed independently.[39] By taking an active role in the convoy system, ranging from insurance to advising on the frequency of sailings, punishing masters who 'ran', and providing a constant flow of intelligence about enemy movements, sightings and arrivals, Lloyd's enabled the state to operate an effective, efficient trade-defence system without the massive overheads of a dedicated naval trade division, or networks of agents relaying commercial intelligence.

By 1812 John Wilson Croker, First Secretary of the Admiralty, and John Bennett, the Secretary of Lloyd's, had built an excellent working relationship. This mutually beneficial arrangement moved raw data, commercially useful news and strategic insight between Westminster and the City on a daily basis. Although France remained the main focus American maritime predation quickly reached worrying levels; as losses mounted the two organisations had to calm excitable shippers and investors. Lloyd's sent the Admiralty large quantities of raw intelligence gathered from ships and agents, mixed up with a number of pointed queries about rumoured or reported enemy movements and convoy sailings, seeking official conformation to pass on to owners. Many of the rumours proved unfounded.

A case that unfolded only weeks before war broke out exemplified the speed and efficiency of the relationship. On 25 May Lloyd's complained that HMS *Dauntless* had failed to escort her 32-ship convoy from Jamaica, arriving in England entirely alone, having parted from the convoy a month before. The Committee for Managing the Affairs of Lloyd's was alarmed as only half the ships entrusted to *Dauntless*'s charge had arrived: they would face considerable losses if the rest were taken by the French. The Admiralty immediately sent out enquiries.[40] More significantly they ordered out all available cruisers at Portsmouth and Plymouth to find and escort merchant ships entering the Western Approaches without protection. The Committee promptly sent 'their particular thanks', and on the 28th Lloyd's received a copy of an explanatory letter from the captain of *Dauntless*.[41]

Once war broke out Lloyd's provided a stream of intelligence from local agents and incoming ships. Alongside predictable maritime news were useful insights ranging from an early report of the American declaration of war to military news from the Canadian frontier.[42] Given the uncertain movement of information across the Atlantic in the age of sail there was every chance that some news would first reach the Admiralty from the City. Inevitably some items proved erroneous. Admiralty information enabled Lloyd's to advise owners and insurers about specific convoys. They publicised Admiralty directions regarding convoys, and used their agents at the assembly ports to check that ships' masters reported their arrival to the port admiral.[43]

In a mirror image of the *Dauntless* incident the Admiralty raised a general complaint that merchant skippers were inattentive to signals and voluntarily parted company from convoys. If this happened the Navy could not be held responsible for the protection of trade. The Committee of Lloyd's was very apologetic, enquiring into specific vessels named by an escort commander. If the master's explanation did not 'prove satisfactory, measures may be taken against him for his misconduct as an example to others'.[44] The public prosecution of masters and owners who strayed from convoy made clear that Lloyd's and the Admiralty were doing everything they could to minimise risk and loss. Such punishments were carefully calculated to be exemplary, rather than punitive. In early 1813 Lloyd's backed the Board's decision to have the Admiralty Proctor prosecute William Evans, master of the *Douglas* of Liverpool, for leaving convoy. After reviewing the case Lloyd's prosecuted the owners as well, hoping a suitable public announcement would make masters 'pay proper attention to the signals and orders of the officers of HM Ships appointed for their protection'. Both bodies recognised the real impact of prosecutions was deterrent: once Evans had been imprisoned Lloyd's requested that the Admiralty stop further prosecution because the action had already produced salutary effect.[45]

The following day Lieutenant Fegan, commanding HMS *Kangaroo*, reported another egregious breach: the master of the *Coquette* had left his convoy, homeward-bound from St Thomas. The Admiralty advised Lloyd's that they would make the prosecution public 'for the information of Masters of merchantmen in particular.'[46] A month later Lloyd's sent in a testimonial of 5 April from the masters of the ships under *Kangaroo*'s convoy, praising Fegan. By then all vessels that sailed in the convoy had arrived in Britain. The masters specifically drew the attention of Lloyd's Committee to:

. . . the great care and attention paid by Lieutenant Fegan to every ship of the convoy; he was perpetually on the look out to assist every vessel that stood in need of it, and towing or remaining by the dull sailing vessels by which attention every ship of the convoy has been brought safe into port.[47]

In February 1813 the master of the *Coquette* was convicted of deliberately running from the convoy, spending a month in Marshalsea prison for his pains. A report in the *Naval Chronicle* ensured wide publicity for this exemplary deterrent.[48]

Evidently under pressure from owners, Lloyd's responded to a new wave of Admiralty prosecutions for disobeying signals by suggesting that some losses could be avoided if the Board gave directions to senior officers on the coasts of Spain, Portugal and Brazil 'not to suffer any valuable British vessel to sail without convoy during the present situation of affairs with America, unless loaded with perishable commodities'.

This was unnecessary: general orders had been issued to that effect a year before.[49] The only point of dispute between the insurers and the Admiralty was the appropriate level of protection. When Bennett claimed that the next St Thomas convoy had only one escort, the *Amaranthe*, and requested Croker might suggest to the Board 'the propriety of ordering out some ships to protect them', the Board was not amused. Their Lordships had already sent 'a competent force for the protection of the West India Convoys and ships returning from America'.[50] The only predictable outcome of such correspondence was increased pressure on Sir John Warren to produce results.

Not content with such general observations, the Committee returned to the subject two weeks later with hard evidence that, at the very least, implied inadequate protection. They offered a letter from Halifax reporting that 156 ships had been taken by the Americans. However, even this missive was tempered with good news: a New York paper mentioned that 165 American vessels had been captured.[51]

By late November 1812 more specific intelligence began to arrive, naming 'several American privateers' cruising near the

Leeward Islands.[52] Not only did the Admiralty copy the letter to Warren the next day, but they let Lloyd's know that they had done so, effectively shifting the blame onto the Admiral. In case there was any doubt about responsibility the Board belatedly added the word 'large' to a description of his force.[53] The cycle of gloom was finally broken by news that two privateers had been taken off Barbados by Royal Navy cruisers, and another beaten off by an armed merchant ship. However, the large privateer *General Armstrong* of 19 guns and 120 men captured a prize, and escaped, despite being repeatedly chased by the frigate *Tribune* to the windward of Barbados, where she appeared to be cruising with another privateer.[54] Intelligence continued to flow from Lloyd's for the remainder of the war.

From the first news of the American declaration British policy had been dominated by the search for a quick end to the conflict. However, before the British could implement their chosen offensive strategy of economic blockade they had to defeat a significant threat to their own maritime trade. While the primary focus of American war aims and strategy had been the conquest of Canada, the diversionary attack on seaborne trade posed a more serious threat to Britain. Without trading profits Britain could not continue the existential conflict with Napoleon's pan-European empire, the issue that had dominated every aspect of policy for a decade. British ministers did not discuss the need for economic warfare, or the operational methods needed to defeat a *guerre de course* by warships and privateers. They remembered American prowess in such warfare from the last Anglo-American conflict, and were well informed about the sheer scale of shipping that could be deployed in licensed predation. The nature of the American threat had been clearly demonstrated by Rodgers's squadron cruise, and the rapid appearance of privateers on the shipping lanes. Not only was seaborne trade vital to the British economy, but the merchants, planters and insurance agents who ran the West Indian sector of the economy possessed significant political influence at the highest levels. The government needed their co-operation both to vote for the war, and to ensure the remission of specie – precious metals in the form of coins or bars, to London – to provide the cash subsidies that were vital to Britain's growing network of European allies. Portugal, Spain, Russia, Austria, Prussia and Sweden all received British aid, much of it in the form of weapons and other hardware, because the British were desperately short of hard cash.[55] This only emphasised the need to escort West Indian convoys that brought home gold and silver.

In one sense the American declaration of war changed little: trans-Atlantic trade had been escorted against French cruisers and privateers since 1803. The additional threat merely increased the number and size of the escort force. However, the Admiralty did not have a bottomless reserve, for every ship that crossed the Atlantic escorting a convoy another had to return, sometimes the same ship, but just as often a worn-out, time-served or weakly manned unit ready to pay off. When Admiral Laforey unilaterally tried to reinforce his squadron by sending smaller units home the Board reminded him that the complex mechanics of a global convoy system in an age of sailing ship and shutter telegraph communications systems combined detailed planning with time-honoured doctrine.[56]

Similar issues of doctrine governed the dispatch of outbound convoys. When too few ships assembled for the pre-arranged November 1812 West India convoy the chair of the committee of London merchants trading to the West Indies asked the Admiralty to delay the sailing until more ships reached Spithead. The Board agreed.[57] The same sensitivity ensured that when the Admiralty learned that a West India convoy had dispersed it promised to inquire into the circumstances. This was no empty gesture: if an escort commander had been derelict in his duty he could expect to lose his command, or his career.[58]

The priority accorded the convoy system also affected the rate at which Warren received desperately needed reinforcements. The fast 74s and frigates needed to blockade American warships were delayed by the need to assemble and escort sluggish convoys, each moving at the pace of the slowest, and finally dragged away from the optimum strategic course to see their charges through to the destination. In mid-December 1812 *Ramillies* and *Coquette* undertook a circuitous route to war, convoying the trade to Barbados and Jamaica, before heading north to Bermuda; only then could they move on to take station off New England.[59] The problem was circular. With few ships to spare for a new, expanding commitment the Admiralty had to find a balance between the defence of trade and an effective naval blockade. If the American frigates could get to sea, convoys needed a strong escort, usually a 74, a frigate and some sloops to defend against all threats. Only a tight blockade could keep the American warships in harbour, and it required a naval force about equal to a convoy escort stationed before the port. If the naval blockade worked, convoy escorts could be reduced to the scale needed to deal with privateers, a second-line frigate and a few sloops. While the Admiralty gave clear priority to the defence of oceanic shipping, delaying Warren's reinforcements, they did not provide extra ships and were quick to complain that he had failed to impose an effective naval blockade. Such double standards reflected mounting pressure from the City, regional trade organisations and West Indies planters, as well as the litany of bad news that dominated media coverage of the naval war down to the spring of 1813. When Warren complained about the slow pace of reinforcement the Admiralty attempted to shift the blame, ascribing its diversion of ships to convoy duty to his failure to keep the American cruisers under control. They claimed this obliged them 'to detach more than one squadron for the protection of the trade, but also to increase the force of the outward bound convoys by ships which would otherwise have been ordered to make a direct passage to join your flag'.[60]

The connection between war, trade and insurance was clear. Lloyd's was very anxious to have news of HMS *Bonne Citoyenne*, the ship James Lawrence had been so anxious to fight.[61] As the British ship carried a fortune in bullion and specie from the River Plate and Rio, Lloyd's urgently requested news of her arrival. The Admiralty used the semaphore telegraph across

London to advise the Committee that they had no news.[62] When the Admiralty finally reported her arrival the Committee sent their 'best thanks'. To emphasise the cost of naval protection the Committee was informed that the 74 HMS *Montagu* had convoyed the *Bonne Citoyenne* from San Salvador 'to a certain latitude; and then returned' to the Brazil station.[63] Days later Lloyd's neatly reversed the sense of obligation, by reporting that Admiral Dixon had taken the *Montagu* to join *Bonne Citoyenne* at San Salvador in hopes of meeting *Constitution* and *Hornet*, before convoying the sloop out to the Line.[64]

Reports that British ships had been captured off the Portuguese Western Islands and Madeira by a French frigate and an American privateer prompted the Admiralty to observe that there were two strong squadrons cruising in the neighbourhood '& their Lordships not having granted licence to sail without convoy are surprised that British vessels should be in the situation stated without protection'.[65] The Azores, and Cape Verde Islands were well known locales for hostile cruisers; several were taken there by the British.

Down to the end of November 1812 convoy planning was necessarily *ad hoc*: the Admiralty, like the rest of the government, still hoping the war would be concluded quickly. Bowing to the inevitable, Admiralty Secretary John Croker interviewed a deputation representing the West Indies trade on 2 December, seeking advice on future convoys. Outbound convoys would leave Portsmouth on 12 December, 1 February and in March. Ships concentrated at Cork, a major source for salt meat, butter and other foodstuffs used in the West Indies, would leave on 15 December, 28 January and 15 March. Homeward-bound dates were necessarily less precise; they depended on the vagaries of the season, the completion of cargoes and the availability of escorts. Even so approximate dates were needed, to enable Warren, Laforey and Stirling to factor escort missions into their planning. The Jamaica fleets would depart in 'about April', the middle of June and on 26 July, a date sufficiently far forward that it could be altered. Leeward Islands shipping would sail in March, at the end of May and on 1 August. The admirals would use these general dates to begin planning 'such measures as according to the season may appear best for the security of the Trade'. They should expect further changes. The Admiralty hoped to raise the level of escort for the Portsmouth convoys to include a 74, the best guarantee against American predators, and stressed that Stirling and Laforey should 'attach a Line of Battle ship to the homeward bound convoys'. West Indian political pressure was equally clear in the pointed reminder that all three flag officers should pay 'most particular attention to the Security of the West Indian Islands and adjoining seas from insult by the enemy, who now that the chance of making captures on his own coast, will be greatly diminished, may be expected to make some effort in that quarter'. Finally intelligence suggested two French frigates that lately escaped from the Loire might be heading for America. Their Lordships trusted that Warren's dispositions would 'prevent them doing an injury to the trade of His Majesty's subjects'.[66] The final cutting remark hints at the trade-related anxiety that gripped the Board.

Anxious to defuse domestic criticism, adverse copy in the press, and the subtler influences of the West India lobby, the Admiralty claimed that every loss could be attributed to Warren's failure to blockade the American frigates. In a hostile dispatch they demanded to know what he had done in response, information which, they implied, should have been submitted earlier. Apart from a report that he had detached Broke's squadron, the Board was 'in complete ignorance' of his dispositions. He should rectify this oversight immediately and regularly. The Admiralty's complaint was simple: 'the war has now continued some months without any advantage on <u>our</u> part'. Their Lordships were 'anxious' his next dispatches would provide information of active and successful operations, and although they were well aware that all naval operations were subject to a great degree of uncertainty, especially in 'preventing the occasional excursions of an enterprising enemy', they hoped American luck had run out. Warren must 'restore the natural order of things at sea, vindicating the honor of His Majesty's arms and the pre-eminence of the naval power of the Country'. Rarely have such hopes been so completely fulfilled.

In March 1813 the *Times* criticised the Navy's failure to provide adequate convoy, apparently unaware just how effective the trade protection system, backed by legal constraints and the key trade organisations had become.[67] The convoy system demanded constant attention, balancing escort and blockade with relief, refits and other tasks.[68] Once again the Board had already acted: in early January it sent a captain of the fleet – a chief of staff – to help Warren organise his large station, four subordinate flag officers and complex interlocking convoy sailings, blockade stations and reliefs for his hard-pressed cruisers. The need was urgent, and the distance great, so the Board selected an officer for the post without consulting the Admiral. Fortunately the selection was made on professional grounds: Captain Sir Henry Hotham was an experienced and supremely capable officer on the verge of his flag promotion.[69] Warren proved equally professional: taking the appointment in his stride, he quickly delegated much of the hard, tedious planning work to Hotham.

Warren addressed the Admiralty's convoy plans of 2 December on 20 February, an indication of the length of time it took correspondence from London to reach the flagship. His assessment was clear, correct and thorough. He would add a battleship to each convoy, station a frigate and sloop to the windward of Barbados with the escorting battleship while the convoy was assembling to protect the concentration point from French or American frigates, and place a small squadron off the coast of Demerara to protect the substantial Brazil trade. He had ordered Stirling to station a small squadron off New Orleans and the mouth of the Mississippi. Warren noted that the home-bound trade would benefit from the Admiralty's decision to place a fast battleship and frigate cruising to the north-west and south-west of the Portuguese Western Isles, to escort convoys near to the chops of the Channel. This measure would go a long way to ensure the safe arrival of home-bound commerce. The

Commander-in-Chief was less impressed with the judgement of his divisional subordinates in the West Indies. The threat in that quarter was almost entirely from privateers, which he expected them to deal with under his general instructions, rather than looking to him for direction. He stressed that Stirling's dubious treatment of merchant convoys at Jamaica, which caused serious concern in London, had taken place without his knowledge. Success against American warships and privateers provided Warren a useful supply of smaller cruisers, but he would only be able to employ them if he could raise men.[70]

Before this exchange of barbed dispatches, with its anxious attempts to apportion blame, went much further it became clear to all concerned that the convoy system had solved the fundamental problem. After mid-1813 American privateers were responding to British measures. Fewer privateer commissions were taken up as the war progressed, profit margins declined, and operations were conducted at ever greater distance from the home base, requiring more costly vessels, further reducing the profit margin, and the chance of selling the ship and goods.

COUNTER-MEASURES

Despite the occasional outburst of alarmist hyperbole in London newspapers, the British understood commerce-destroying rather better than the Americans. Their response to privateering reflected over 200 years' experience operating and combating privateers. They understood that privateering was almost impossible to eradicate, but it was relatively easy to limit. Close control of enemy coastal waters, blockading key ports, escorted convoys and the maintenance of economic insurance rates kept the ships moving, and sustained the confidence of the commercial community. British officers who spotted a privateer would pursue it relentlessly, until it was taken or escaped over the horizon. One chase lasted eleven days, many more between two and six days. Such single-minded determination paid dividends.[71] Other ships were taken by cutting-out expeditions, including four handsome units on the Rappahannock River on 3 April 1813. Attacked by boats from two battleships, two frigates and two brigs the privateersmen abandoned ship; three became British cruisers.[72]

British losses were largely among ships sailing alone, often after convoys had dispersed to sail for smaller ports, or as they headed for convoy assembly points. American cruisers soon found the ocean empty, and began to range ever further afield. Time, distance and the sheer difficulty of bringing prizes home for adjudication quickly ruined the economics of commerce warfare. American privateers did not win the war; their failure is obvious from the stability of British insurance rates – the standard indication of a successful defence of commerce.[73]

TURNING THE SCREW

In little more than twelve months the Royal Navy had solved the major strategic challenge posed by America; it had secured British floating trade, blunting one of the strategic pillars of the American war effort. The failure of the United States Navy in this campaign has led many to argue that the American 'victory' was secured by privateers that took British commercial shipping, and humiliated the Royal Navy. In 1812 privateers were 'an inexpensive but influential second navy' which served the national interest; after June 1813 they were 'the Republic's only maritime force', 'succeeding where the national government had failed in intimidating the British'.[74]

Despite the financial success, seafaring skill and handsome profits of individual privateers, the reality is more complex. Successful predation does not equal strategic effect. No one made this point more cogently than Captain Alfred Thayer Mahan, USN, America's pre-eminent naval strategist. In 1889 Mahan demolished the privateer myth:

It is not the taking of individual ships or convoys, be they few or many, that strikes down the money power of a nation; it is the possession of that overbearing power on the sea which drives the enemy's flag from it, or allows it to appear only as a fugitive; and which, by controlling the great common, closes the highways by which commerce moves to and from the enemy's shores. This overbearing power can only be exercised by great navies.[75]

For Mahan privateering was a weak, indecisive form of war. With or without the support of a handful of national cruisers it could not coerce Britain. It was a sure sign of American weakness that the privateers steadily shifted ever further from their home ports, ending up off Canton. Such operations were utterly irrelevant to the war.

Having defeated the twin commerce-raiding threat of warships and privateers Sir John Warren shifted the naval effort from the defence of floating trade to an economic blockade, the core of Britain's offensive strategy. The naval blockade had confined most American cruisers, national and privateer, to harbour. It was a simple step to transform it into an economic blockade that would wreck the American economy. At the outbreak of war the lucrative re-export trade simply disappeared. In 1813 only a third of American ocean-going merchant ships got to sea; in 1814 the figure fell to a twelfth. As customs revenues made up 90 per cent of Federal income in peacetime the collapse of maritime trade proved catastrophic. Both revenue and exports fell by over 80 per cent in two years, leaving the administration unable to raise cash or obtain credit.[76] With American oceanic trade falling from $40 million in 1811 to $2.6 million in 1814 only ports with alternative economic activity survived into 1815. Abandoned by their government, maritime communities acted in their own interest, with responses ranging from privateering to smuggling. The impact of economic stagnation was predictable: unemployment, bankruptcy and inflation. It was just a question of how long it took the American administration to acknowledge the reality of their defeat.

CHAPTER 7

The Price of Folly

---∞∞∞---

By the time the sun set on 1 June 1813 the American naval challenge was over. After twelve months of relatively easy access to the Atlantic American cruisers had been bottled up by superior force; now they would be closely watched and slowly stripped of key personnel for the war on the Lakes. The price of folly proved to be a steadily tightening economic blockade. For all the euphoria prompted by American naval victories in 1812, and the morbid reflections that followed the sudden reversal of fortune, American national warships had achieved very little in material terms. One frigate had been brought home, but a frigate, a sloop and a brig had been lost, several ships failed to get to sea, and those that did had precious little to show for their efforts. The United States Navy did not win the War of 1812, nor could it possibly have done so. Naval heroics did not delay the reinforcement of Canada, the devastating economic blockade or destructive amphibious raids on the Chesapeake.

Capturing the *Chesapeake* and bottling up Decatur's squadron shifted the balance of power at sea decisively in favour of the British. The troops and stores Warren shepherded into Canada had secured the two provinces, despite the American advantages of location and numbers. Once there were more professional soldiers north of the border than south it would be very hard for Madison's generals to seize Quebec. Escorting military convoys, an unending drain on Warren's resources, was one of the unseen costs of maritime strategy. Yet the scale of the escort could be reduced: with few American cruisers at sea privateers could be seen off by small frigates and brigs. Warren could spare frigates for convoy duty because he had more battleships, while a long summer of relatively mild weather and excellent intelligence gave the King's ships control of American coastal waters. American merchant ships were captured in large numbers, not just those engaged in high-seas commerce, but also the small coasters that connected the suppliers and markets of a vast, under-developed economy. Ultimately it was not victory at sea that mattered, but the effect the victorious navy would exert on hostile American territory and national life. Sea power worked by making those who lived on land feel its weight.[1] British warships anchored off major ports reinforced economic hardship with a growing sense of unease. What would come next, an invasion, or a destructive raid?

Even the swarming privateer threat was slowly but surely crippled, as more and more privateersmen found their cruise ended in a British prison. With the threat from cruisers and privateers ebbing, Canada still in British hands and Napoleon in full retreat the Americans had little leverage for peace. Madison had no alternative strategy, and would not risk the political consequences of surrender. Instead the focus of American commerce-destroying shifted from taking prizes to destroying ships and attempting to divert British ships away from the exposed coastal states. Sending raiders to distant stations was a confession of abject weakness. Unable to operate on their own coasts, or the Atlantic shipping lanes, American cruisers ran to the furthest reaches of the globe, seeking merchant vessels without convoy. This activity had little impact: British warships in distant seas did not come from Warren's force. The cost of distant operations soon outweighed the consequences. A close naval blockade, linked economic blockade and convoys left the ocean empty of all but hard targets. American warships could not relieve the pressure.

SIR JOHN'S DILEMMA

Writing to Warren in early June 1813 Melville's primary concern remained the need to avoid further disasters. The Admiralty, and by implication the government, was anxious that New York and

Boston should be blockaded by a naval force equal to the enemy: 'any more naval disasters, more especially if they could fairly be ascribed to want of due precaution, would make a strong impression on the public mind in this country'. Any frigates that escaped must be pursued, and suitable reinforcements were on their way. Melville's priorities were clear: the primary mission was 'blockading the enemy's ships of war in their Ports'. Economic blockade and coastal raids were secondary.[2]

Warren had to hope his luck would change. Fortunately the economic blockade was a relatively straightforward task. He had advised the ministers to apply economic sanctions selectively, hitting regions that had voted for the war, while leaving Federalist New England free from economic pressure. He believed differential treatment would exacerbate sectional differences and weaken the overall American war effort. Indeed American trade and cash quickly flowed north, to states where licensed trade, smuggling and other illegal measures were rife. Warren hurt the enemy without depriving the army in Spain of vital grain and flour, or the West Indies of lumber and fish. The initial blockade of Chesapeake Bay was extended by Admiralty order in March 1813 to cover the coast from Rhode Island to the Mississippi delta. Once in place, the blockade desiccated American commerce; ships stopped moving, and every port city began to suffer a devastating combination of glut and drought, as exports piled up unsold and imports failed to appear. While desperate merchants turned to other activities, the administration persisted in attacking Canada.

In May the Admiralty tightened the blockade, restricting neutral ships to ports that were not blockaded, and restricting the licensed trade to American ships returning home from Britain.[3] As Cockburn's operations in the Chesapeake and the economic blockade of the Delaware, Charleston and Savannah were beginning to bite, New York and Boston remained open to neutral ships not carrying contraband. If trade volumes were low they still generated Federal income to sustain the war. The closure of the northern loophole was long overdue, not least because the existing naval blockade needed little reinforcement to stop trade. When Warren extended the blockade north to Narragansett Bay on 16 November he closed New York for business.

America had no alternative to sea transport: the distances involved and the absence of integrated canal or interstate highway systems made inland transport uneconomic. For port-to-port carriage interstate land transport costs were 100 times higher than by sea. Bulk produce like flour, timber, sugar and cotton was left to rot where it lay, while shortages elsewhere led to rampant inflation. The British could read about the effect of the blockade from an unfettered American press.[4] *Niles' Weekly Register*, the *National Intelligencer* and other journals gave British admirals and American citizens unrivalled access to the commercial impact of the war on the trade pages, and in the editorials.

HARRYING THE BAY

Although the British government needed every man to defeat Napoleon, Earl Bathurst, Secretary of State for War and the Colonies, provided Warren with a strike force of 2,400 men for diversionary operations. Warren focused the amphibious war on the warlike states surrounding Chesapeake Bay. He picked his targets by consulting the Congressional division list, another consequence of an unfettered press. The British amphibious force of two battalions of Royal Marines, 300 soldiers from the Bermuda garrison, 300 French ex-prisoners of war, with sailors and Royal Marines from the fleet, proved ample. The keys to success were absolute command of the sea and George Cockburn's incisive strategic intellect. Contemporary American newspapers characterised Cockburn and his campaigns with all manner of opprobrious epithets: they were little more than the futile fulminations of a frustrated, frightened, feckless foe, happier penning squibs than firing muskets. Cockburn exploited the superior agility of sea-based troops to confuse and confound, striking enemy depots and weak points, keeping the tension high all along the Chesapeake shoreline. Military targets and privateers were captured or destroyed while the British exploited the freedom to roam, fill their water casks, gather fresh food and receive escaped slaves. An extensive range of prize goods flowed out of the Bay, including tobacco, cotton and rice. Cockburn's war was economical, effective and very nearly self-sustaining.

Cockburn pushed into the James, Rappahannock, York and Potomac rivers. He met little effective opposition. Although intended to divert American military efforts away from the Canadian frontier, the operations had little success in this respect. The Americans preferred leaving the defence of the Bay to local militias. The Chesapeake campaign was popular in London, where the steady stream of good news and hopes it might relieve Canada made better copy than the embarrassing fiascos of the previous year.[5] The campaign was largely self-sustaining: the ships and men were fed, watered, refitted, and provided with coastal craft from American sources. Cockburn's 'Colonial Marines' recruited from former slaves, proved strong, loyal and highly effective at unsettling the minds of their erstwhile masters. In effect every ship taken and every prize seized ashore was pure profit. The British understood the unwritten rules of war: they paid market price for food if the Americans were willing to sell, and took what they wanted if they were fired on. Cockburn's coastal operations made many Americans anxious for peace; the tidewater and smaller ports were simply abandoned.

OCEANIC WARFARE

In 1813 only six American warships escaped the British blockade and put to sea. The *Chesapeake* hardly counts; *President*, *Congress*, *Enterprise*, *Argus* and late in December *Constitution* were the others. The outstanding American operation of the year was William Henry Allen's cruise in the brig *Argus*. Allen had fired the only shot from the *Chesapeake* in 1807, using a live coal from the galley. He had been promoted to command *Argus* after serving as first lieutenant of the *United States* when she captured the *Macedonian*. Jones ordered Allen to deliver new Ambassador William H. Crawford to the first French port he could access without risk, before carrying the war into British waters, concentrating on 'the commerce and light cruisers of the enemy, which you will capture, and destroy in all cases, unless their value, and qualities shall render it morally certain, that they may reach a safe, and not distant port'. Tacitly acknowledging the Royal Navy's domination of the oceans, Jones stressed that prize crews would be taken prisoner when prizes were recaptured; detaching them left the ship short-handed. He wanted the enemy to 'feel the effect of our hostility, and of his barbarous system of warfare; and in no way can we so effectually accomplish that object, as by annoying and destroying his commerce, fisheries and coasting trade'. The last was Allen's special target, exploiting *Argus*'s size and handiness. Cruising between the west coast of England and Ireland he could cut up coasters and pick off incoming West Indies and Iberian shipping. Crawford would advise him if prizes should be sent into French ports, and if the French would provide provisions to extend the cruise.[6] These orders shifted the focus of American strategy from a commerce war funded by captures to a war of destruction, the methods of U-boat warfare.

Argus escaped from New York, passing Sandy Hook on 18 June. After a fast, boisterous passage, which included taking and burning the *Salamanca*, London-bound in ballast from Oporto, Allen delivered Crawford to L'Orient, quickly refitted and put to sea on 20 July. Between 23 July and 13 August *Argus* swept across the Western Approaches from the chops of the Channel to the south-west coast of Ireland, and raided up the River Shannon. He took twenty prizes and caused a minor panic, but such audacity had an inevitable consequence. Allen should have shifted his cruising ground, but he hung on, entranced by the rich harvest that appeared on the horizon every morning. Of the twenty vessels captured he sent two, the *Matilda* and *Betsey*, to France; both were re-taken, with prize crews of twenty

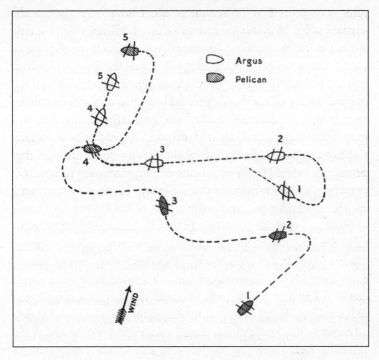

Fire and manoeuvre: superior ship-handling and gunnery enabled
HMS *Pelican* to capture the USS *Argus* on 14 August 1813.

irreplaceable seamen. Allen also released five ships as prisoner
cartels and burnt twelve; the last ship simply disappeared.

On 14 August *Argus* encountered the British brig HMS
Pelican, Commander John Maples, off St David's Head in St
George's Channel. Thoroughly roused by the barrage of bad
news, Admiral Thornborough, commanding the Irish station,
had ordered Maples to find the predator two days earlier. The
sheer scale of destruction left Maples with an easy trail; he found
Argus close by a blazing merchantman. Instead of fleeing, as
his instructions required, Allen calmly took in sail and waited
for the enemy, willingly engaging in a close-quarter broadside
action. The range and tactics were dictated by the carronades
that both ships relied on for their combat power. This time

Pelican had a clear advantage, mounting 32-pounders to the American 24s. After forty-five minutes Maples had worn down American resistance by superior gunnery; her rigging disabled and raked from astern the Americans surrendered just as Maples prepared to board. Early in the action Allen's left knee had been shattered by a round shot and his leg was amputated. With the captain down, two midshipmen killed, the first lieutenant, the boatswain, boatswain's mate and carpenter wounded, the *Argus* had little chance. All told 11 men died, and 18 were wounded: *Pelican* lost 2 dead and 5 wounded. Allen initially survived his injuries, and the horrific treatment, only to die in Plymouth's Stonehouse hospital on the 18th.[7]

There can be little doubt the *Argus* had been well drilled: Allen had trained the gunnery team that took the *Macedonian*, and so many have sought an explanation for his defeat. While Petrie, Roosevelt and Henry Adams argued that detaching prize crews fatally weakened the ship,[8] the explanation is far simpler. Allen chose to fight, suggesting he was confident of victory. Fighting a ship with superior weight of broadside at point-blank range was always going to be a lottery. Once the command team had been destroyed, the main braces and after running rigging shot away, *Argus* stood little chance. With only two masts, such damage left her at the mercy of her opponent. Just like *Chesapeake*, albeit on a smaller scale, the loss of command and control settled the action. The capture of *Argus* was a heavy price to pay for fleeting success.

Soon after the battle John Maples provided artist Thomas Whitcombe and engraver Thomas Sutherland with information for a painting and a coloured aquatint.[9] Such eyewitness endorsements became a key feature of naval celebratory art: the market no longer tolerated the generic battle scenes and re-used images that were perfectly adequate two decades before. In an age increasingly insistent on accuracy the best British prints were suitable companions for the precise histories of William James.

PRESIDENT

Desperate to cut the British supply line to Canada and weaken the blockade, Jones wanted his cruisers at sea. He consulted senior captains about suitable cruising grounds. John Rodgers picked out five for *President*, stretching from the north of Norway to the Equator. He favoured crossing the Atlantic, entering the Baltic, replenishing stores in Denmark, and then heading for China. Jones decided that China was a step too far for such an important ship, restricting him to the Atlantic side of the Cape of Good Hope.[10] Accompanied by John Smith's *Congress*, Rodgers slipped out of Boston Bay on 3 May, while easterly gales forced Broke and Hyde Parker to beat offshore. After chasing the brig HMS *Curlew*, and being chased in turn by Capel's *La Hogue* and *Nymphe* near St George's Bank, Rodgers and Smith headed south-east, parting company about 600 miles east of Delaware Bay on 8 May. Rodgers had hoped to find a valuable British West India convoy south of the Grand Banks, but a combination of sightings earlier in the voyage, and the effective convoy system, ensured he saw nothing but the occasional American grain ship inbound from Iberia. Shifting his ground to east of the Banks Rodgers ran in fogs, and saw even less. When an American merchantman provided intelligence about a British convoy sighted four days before, the avaricious commodore hurried off to the north-west, on another wild goose chase. He was lucky not to find the convoy, escorted by the 74-gun HMS *Cumberland*. Finally, on 9 June, Rodgers began to meet solitary, unescorted vessels, taking four in as many days, including the Post Office packet *Duke of Montrose*. Three prizes, laden with cod, were sent to France; the packet was used as a cartel.[11] The British government rejected Rodgers's irregular cartel, did not exchange any Americans for the prisoners sent home on the packet, and kept the ship.[12] Under international law the British were entirely within their rights, having banned ransom payments. Rodgers's blustering fulminations spoke eloquently of his chagrin.

Having warmed up the area Rodgers crossed the Atlantic in high latitudes, passing north of the British Isles. Once again he had chosen barren ground, only meeting Danish vessels with British trading licences. On 26 June he stopped at Bergen for food and water. As Norway was strictly blockaded by the British, Bergen offered little beyond water and rye meal. Sailing on 2 July Rodgers headed for the Orkney Islands, and then the North Cape, looking for the Archangel convoy. Instead he found two isolated ships heading for Russia in ballast: not worth sending in for adjudication they were burnt. On the 18th he linked up with the New York privateer *Scourge*, agreeing to share prize money.

The following day Rodgers revealed his usual ocular failing, or the less glorious aspect of his character. In hazy weather the Americans spotted two ships, and after chasing for three hours were about 5 miles off when Rodgers convinced himself they were a battleship and a frigate. Having placed an affidavit to that effect, signed by his officers, in the ship's journal he turned tail. Captain Nicoll of the *Scourge* had identified the enemy accurately and slipped away; he realised there would be little profit to be had hanging on the Commodore's coat tails.[13] The two British warships then chased Rodgers through the almost permanent daylight for two full days. Only on the 23rd did *President* finally escape.[14] As Nicoll had known all along, the pursuers were a small frigate, HMS *Alexandria*, and the sloop HMS *Spitfire*, easy prey for a mighty 44 with 24-pounder long guns and 32-pounder carronades. Captain Robert Cathcart's petty 660-ton fir-built fifth rate, armed with 12-pounders and 24-pounder carronades, had a laughable broadside of 300 pounds.[15] Rodgers convinced himself he could see the 74 *Plantagenet*, a ship that seems to have haunted the imagination of several American officers. The ancient 400-ton fireship *Spitfire*, a typical small convoy escort, offered little additional firepower, mounting fourteen 18-pounder carronades, and could not run away. With Rodgers flying before him Cathcart assumed the enemy was an equal or weaker force, and the harder he tried to catch up, the more certain Rodgers became that he faced a superior foe. At least that is the usual story.

However, the day after his 'escape' from a superior force, Rodgers used the name of his pursuer to seize the British whaler *Eliza Swann*. Rodgers tricked the master by claiming to be the *Alexandria*.[16] Ordered to accompany a 'British' officer on board with the ship's papers, the master only learnt of the deception when safely inside Rodgers's cabin. It is likely that newspapers taken from earlier captures had provided Rodgers with details of convoys and escorts. The question remains how he can have come so close to his 'shoe box' sized antagonist and still run away.[17] A decade later British historian William James ridiculed Rodgers, aided by the testimony of British ship masters on board the *President* at the time, and some of the American officers who signed Rodgers's statement about seeing a battleship. Rodgers, they reported, made 'ludicrous' preparations for battle, issued treble rations of grog, and served out an immense quantity of dismantling shot, evidently hoping to cripple the enemy and make his escape. He was equally spooked when he met the lumbering whaler *Eliza Swann* the following day, making 'a very cautious approach'.[18] Duplicity had its reward: the owners of two of the three prizes ransomed refused to honour the bills of exchange, and his irregular cartels were ignored.

Like many American cruisers *President* ran out of food. Having eaten their way through everything that could be stowed in the hold in little more than two months, the huge crew were reduced to scratching out a living from prizes. Anticipating that the British would soon be on his trail Rodgers changed his cruising ground. He headed back across the Atlantic, taking two prizes off the Banks. One of the prizes summed up his war: he took the *Shannon*, not Broke's famous frigate, but a small merchant brig laden with rum, sugar and molasses, bound from St Kitts to London. Then he skulked back home with little to show for his voyage but a scorbutic crew, and petty prizes. Even so his luck held.

On 23 September, close by the Nantucket Shoal, Rodgers encountered the ex-privateer schooner HMS *Highflyer*. A tender to Warren's flagship *San Domingo*, *Highflyer* had been stationed to warn the blockading squadrons of inbound American warships. Using a captured signal book Rodgers persuaded Lieutenant George Hutchison that his ship was HMS *Sea Horse*. *Highflyer* hove-to under the stern of the big 44.[19] An officer in a British uniform ordered Hutchison to take his signal books on board, to exchange for updated copies. Once on board Hutchison blithely informed his host that Warren was particularly anxious to take the *President* and Commodore Rodgers, 'an odd fish and hard to catch'. Having acquired an intelligence windfall, Rodgers dropped the disguise. Hutchison's credulity ruined Warren's carefully laid plan to intercept the home-bound American flagship. Rodgers abandoned plans to make for Boston, entering Newport on the 26th. Alert to the very real threat of a British amphibious attack, he quickly took the ship further up Narragansett Bay to Pawtucket, and then Providence. Hutchison's embarrassment continued when Rodgers discovered he had been among the raiding party that torched the Commodore's house at Havre de Grace earlier in the year.[20] Hutchison never served afloat again.[21]

In almost five months at sea Rodgers took 12 vessels, and 271 prisoners. The cartels and three ransoms had not been honoured, three vessels were sunk, and three each sent to France and the United States. One of the early prizes was recaptured, and only 55 prisoners remained when Rodgers reached Newport. Even so only *Argus* and *Essex* were more successful in 1813, and both were taken, but that still left the mighty *President* as a modest mid-table predator. Rodgers had avoided congested shipping lanes, and reduced risk, but the American flagship remained the ultimate prize for the British. It is doubtful if Rodgers diverted any British ships from the blockade; those that chased him in the North Sea and the Arctic were from the European station, fighting an entirely separate war.

Rodgers reached harbour in a predictably grim mood. Acutely conscious of his failure to match his peers, and stung to the quick by the publication of Broke's challenge and the loss of the *Chesapeake*, he apologised for not adding 'any additional lustre to the character of our little navy'. Fortunately Secretary Jones provided another soothing response, largely because the ship was still American, and he wanted it back at sea as soon as possible.[22] Rodgers would make a fourth cruise later in the year.

The other Boston escapee, *Congress*, finally returned to Portsmouth, New Hampshire, in mid-December 1813. A long, desperately unproductive South Atlantic cruise secured four small prizes.[23] The slow, labouring *Congress* had been fortunate to make three cruises without being in any danger.[24] Soon Hyde Parker's *Tenedos* was blockading the port anxious to repeat Broke's achievement, but *Congress* did not dare come out. She needed extensive repairs, which, together with the expiry of crew enlistments and a desperate need for men elsewhere, saw her towed 4 miles up river and laid up without guns. Her remaining men were deployed to Lake Ontario.[25]

Although Jones issued precise orders on 4 October Rodgers's fourth cruise did not begin until 4 December, when the bad weather dispersed the blockading squadron off Block Island.[26] After recapturing the American schooner *Comet*, lately a prize to Hardy's squadron, he slipped past the British on the 6th, following another hesitant encounter with an unidentified British warship. On the 10th HMS *Loire* took the heavily manned 118-ton Baltimore privateer *Rolla*, a day out from Newport. Captain Thomas Brown's prisoners revealed they had been destined for the Brazilian coast, to rendezvous with *President*. He also found the recognition signal: '*Rolla* to hoist two American Ensigns, and he will answer it by three ensigns.'[27] Rodgers was heading south, via the Canary Islands, and on to the West Indies. En route he fell in with two French frigates, which he chased on the perfectly valid assumption they were British. Not only were French-built warships (which had a distinctive appearance) rarely found at sea, but most that were, like *Guerriere* and *Java*, flew the Union Jack.[28] Cruising to the windward of Barbados in early January Rodgers picked up two British merchantmen; they were plundered and burnt. On the 16th he was off Cayenne, and then cruised past Surinam, Berbice and Demerara, then on to the north-east past Puerto Rico and through the Mona Passage, along the north of the Bahamas to reach the Florida coast at St Augustine. He took another prize on 4 February while heading north along the Atlantic seaboard. Running into the blockading squadron off Charleston he was obliged to keep moving. Once again the opposition was trifling. When the sloop HMS *Morgiana* reported being chased off Charleston by a frigate, which her commander suspected was French, Warren sent his flagship, the 74 *San Domingo* in chase.[29] The *President* met another ship in thick weather off the Delaware, but Rodgers left her when he heard signal guns, convinced she must be part of a blockading squadron. On the 18th he spotted a British schooner and a warship off Sandy Hook. The larger ship approached cautiously, and then retreated. Rodgers, always predisposed to see a superior force looming out of the haze, convinced himself she must be a battleship. The local revenue cutter confirmed his suspicions, and the sails of another British ship could be seen, so Rodgers hurried across the bar and headed into New York. Rodgers mistook a frigate for the 74 *Plantagenet*, which did not have the normal poop deck aft.[30] In fact the *Plantagenet* was close to Barbados at the time. Rodgers's British 'battleship' was Thomas Brown's *Loire*, and Brown had good reason to avoid the big American. He had only 220 effective men on board, 130 under-strength. With 75 seamen absent in prizes, 40 too sick to do duty, and 20 boys, Brown could only man half his guns. Furthermore, *Loire* was entirely alone. Once again Rodgers fled from the phantoms of his imagination.[31] *President* returned to the city of her birth.

What are we to make of John Rodgers, leader of the American Navy? A century ago his biographer carefully set him apart from other war heroes: 'his services had been less brilliant and picturesque than those of some of his fellow officers', naming Hull, Perry, Macdonough, Decatur and Bainbridge. This was a trifle rich: Rodgers carefully avoided battle with anything that might possibly be a superior force, and ended up fleeing from petty craft. Charles Oscar Paullin tried to place such conduct in the best light: 'It would appear, however, that the commodore was more cautious than some of his naval colleagues, and that in one or two instances his caution led him into error and lost him a capture.'[32] At least his caution preserved the American flagship to fight another day, a matter of no small moment in a war that turned on impressions and isolated incidents.

COMMAND

By the summer of 1813 the Royal Navy had 129 warships in American waters, a massive increase on pre-war levels, not just in numbers, but more especially in the size of the ships and the quality of their officers. On the American coast Warren deployed ten 74s and a razee 58, each of which would make short work of any American warship, and 16 standard frigates. The Leeward Islands and Jamaica stations each had two 74s and six or seven frigates, Newfoundland had a 74 and four frigates.[33] British power was limited, though, by a permanent shortage of men. As Melville explained to Scots political ally Sir Alexander Hope:

We have several frigates ready for commissioning, we have four or five sail of the line and nearly a dozen frigates which have been for sometime in commission, but which we cannot send to sea for want of men. We intend therefore to abstain from bringing forward any more till we have some prospect of being able to man them.[34]

Hope's client Captain Pipon was appointed to the frigate *Tagus* in September and got to sea in November, suggesting that the manpower crisis may have passed. The speed with which Pipon turned his ship's company into an effective team demonstrates that Hope's patronage was not misplaced. On 6 January 1814, while escorting a convoy to South America, *Tagus* took the French frigate *La Ceres* off the Cape Verde Islands.[35]

Having made significant sacrifices to win the naval war, the Admiralty, unaware of the decisive actions off Boston and Long

Island, became frustrated by Warren's inability to crush the Americans. Another querulous dispatch pointed to the apparent paucity of ships north of Halifax, in the Gut of Canso (between Nova Scotia and Cape Breton) and the Gulf of St Lawrence. The Board was concerned because large troop convoys would pass through those waters any day, heading for Quebec and New Brunswick. Furthermore, they wanted to see 'a more considerable force off Boston' where most of the American frigates lay. The complaint was already out of date. *President* and *Congress* had escaped, while *Chesapeake* was heading for Halifax under the British Ensign. Not that the blockade took absolute priority: Warren was reminded, in a somewhat patronising manner, that he could move heavy ships between Caribbean escort duty and Atlantic blockade in tempo with the changing seasons.[36]

It is unlikely anyone around the Board table believed Warren needed reminding about such basic issues as the movement of trade, the pattern of convoys and seasonal changes in the weather. Their Lordships let off steam because Warren had not wrapped up the naval war, offering him advice suitable for a novice. Such documents would 'prove' that the Board was 'doing something' to answer criticism in Parliament, from the trade associations and the press. It was no accident that Melville penned a long overdue private letter on policy the next day, after three months' silence.[37]

In late May the Admiralty, somewhat belatedly, had recognised that the 'present extended scale of naval operations on the Coast of America' required an admiral permanently stationed at Halifax 'to superintend and expedite the refitting and completion of HM Ships & vessels that must necessarily resort to that Port', oversee the defence of the province, and local shipping. They appointed Rear Admiral Edward Griffith.[38] The Admiralty had chosen well; Warren knew and trusted the new man.[39] He proved a steady hand, meeting the many demands of an inadequate dockyard, a backlog of repairs and even a hurricane.

THE POLITICS OF DEFENCE

Increasing British strength all along the coast caused considerable alarm among seafaring communities, especially those, like Baltimore, with a large stake in privateering. Early in June, Samuel Smith, privateer investor and chair of the Senate Naval Committee, requested information on the number of gunboats in service. Secretary Jones listed over 100 in service: 20 at Norfolk, and 31 at New York, with the rest spread thinly. With other local-defence craft built or building he had little concern for harbour defence and no desire to waste Federal funds on more such craft, which could not be manned. He was more concerned to replace three brigs lately lost at sea, to cover the coast of New England, as 'depredations have greatly increased there and gunboats are not applicable to that coast'.[40] For all the rigour and insight that informed Jones's opposition to creating small, dispersed, weak forces he had no answer to the political pressure Republican interests used to demand local naval defence. As American trade shifted south from the heavily blockaded Chesapeake the British simply followed it to North Carolina. Wilmington received six gunboats from the Charleston station, Ocracoke two and Beaufort one. Politically inspired dispersal of effort left the Americans exposed everywhere, whenever the British chose to attack. At least Jones was able to pull his gunboats out of Spanish East Florida to protect Georgia.[41] The problem of balancing the needs of the Lakes, cruisers and local defence proved insoluble: Jones simply did not have the ships, men, guns or money to provide effective forces anywhere. This made the pressure to increase local defence irresistible. In mid-June Congress approved a bill to purchase hulks, to be scuttled as harbour defences, and prepare booms.[42] Philadelphians built six gun barges to defend the city, effectively forcing the Navy to pay for them in September.

Such measures were futile while the British had the initiative. On 12 July Cockburn raided Ocracoke and Plymouth Islands with seven ships and 500 men, seizing the shipping, and occupying towns. Although well prepared for defence, and scuttling, the privateer brig *Anaconda* and 240-ton letter of marque schooner *Atlas* were taken, the Americans simply overwhelmed by the speed of the attack. The merchant ships in harbour proved to be neutral. Cockburn harvested local food supplies, worked out that the area contained nothing else worth raiding, and withdrew with his prizes. *Anaconda* was purchased and given to attack leader Lieutenant George Westphal, a Cockburn protégé.[43] The Admiralty approved Westphal's promotion to commander. The Board appreciated the publicity value of such successes.[44] Warren supplied Cockburn with men and materials through the autumn, maintaining pressure on the American centre.[45]

IMPROVISED EXPLOSIVE DEVICE

Unable to defend their coast, the Americans resorted to ingenious methods. In March 1813 Congress enacted legislation that offered to pay half the value of enemy ships destroyed by private individuals. The 'torpedo act' prompted a spate of improvised explosive devices, floating bombs and booby-traps. The squadron blockading Decatur's force off New London was the main target. On 25 June a booby-trapped schooner loaded with naval stores was abandoned, in the hope it would be taken alongside Thomas Hardy's *Ramillies*. The bomb was meant to sink the 74. The British fell for the trick and the IED detonated alongside, killing one officer and ten men, and wounding three more. The normally mild-mannered Hardy was incandescent. The dead officer, Lieutenant Geddes, a promising young man, had been his follower for eight years. He threatened to burn down the nearest town if anything similar was attempted again. Reflecting on the 'Diabolical and Cowardly contrivance of the Enemy' Warren directed that prizes and American vessels attempting to communicate with the blockaders should be kept at a safe distance.[46] Such indiscriminate terror weapons, ever the last resort of the weak and desperate, accorded very ill with the notions of chivalric combat and personal honour espoused by officers like Decatur. Yet Decatur was actively involved in the project, offering his inventive friend Robert Fulton 'any aid in my power'.[47]

When Hardy heard about another torpedo attempt he sent a party ashore, seizing Joshua Penny, the prime suspect, in his bed in East Hampton. Dismissing local protests, he announced he had ample proof of complicity and he warned the townspeople 'against permitting the torpedo to remain anywhere near them.'[48] President Madison and Secretary Jones, untroubled by the morality of an indiscriminate, murderous mode of warfare, thought random acts of terrorism committed by civilians were acceptable, but putting a man in irons for planning them was not.[49] The American retaliation of placing a prisoner in the same situation was ridiculous: the British had not planned to use an IED. American citizens resorted to such indiscriminate weapons because the government and the Navy Department could not defend them.

When Warren reported the descent into terrorism, the Admiralty had no answers, simply issuing futile instructions to caution officers to be 'on their guard against attempts of this description'.[50] Although there were no more lethal incidents, torpedo warfare continued to excite men in London. In the autumn they sent Warren the latest American plans, along with a copy of Fulton's 1810 pamphlet on torpedo warfare. The motto Fulton gave his work, 'The Liberty of the Seas will be the Happiness of the Earth', and the demonstration he afforded Jefferson, Madison and other Republican leaders showed his political agenda.[51]

FEELING THE PINCH

Acutely aware of the opportunities provided by economic hardship and Federalist sympathies, the British continued trades that funded their war effort, exacerbated internal divisions, and provided unrivalled intelligence. This last had little to do with espionage: it was merely the collection and collation of newspaper reports, gossip and unguarded remarks ashore. There were, as both British and American observers noted, always a few men ready to sell their country for cash or consideration. Captured mail provided a distinctive source. In mid-July Melville received an amusing insight into the delusional quality of Republican thinking. On Christmas Day 1812 John M. Taylor of Philadelphia had written to David Baillie Warden, American Consul in Paris. While admitting the fiasco at Detroit, Taylor boasted that Canada would fall the following year, because there were 8 million Americans against 350,000 Canadians. He observed that a long war would benefit America, protecting her nascent industries from British competition. He assumed Napoleonic victories in Russia and Spain would oblige Britain to accept American terms, and hoped Napoleon would settle American maritime compensation claims.[52] By contrast, Boston Federalist newspaper the *Columbian Centinel* reported that, in late 1813, 200 square-rigged vessels were laid up in port, and insurance rates had reached 50 per cent. This was the reality of Madison's war: winning a few frigate actions and even the odd land battle offered no compensation for the utter devastation of the American economy.[53]

Although hemmed in by British power America's frontiers proved remarkably porous. The constant flow of intelligence and contraband out of American harbours, and across the Canadian frontier, fed and forewarned the foe, without replenishing the national coffers. In late July the President ordered the Army and Navy to stop such 'criminal intercourse'.[54] The need to remind men of basic patriotic duties spoke eloquently of the political turmoil and disarray that cramped the American war effort. Master Commandant Jacob Lewis noted that leaving New Haven open for 'neutral' trade secured the British an ample supply of food while Long Islanders, 'fast friends of the administration' were 'suffering prodigiously'.[55] The legal complexities of proving intent, and the responsibility in the civil courts that naval officers potentially had for any actions they took, hampered counter-measures. Even the most blatant cases of trading with the enemy were hard to prove, and without an official legal indemnity officers were unwilling to apply the law rigorously.[56]

Isaac Hull, commanding Portsmouth Navy Yard, observed that, with the blockade in place, there was little point trying to protect local trade. He advised sending his naval brigs to harass the British at sea, but local political pressure kept them on station.[57] Hull used his force to protect local trade against British privateers and cruisers, and counter trade with the enemy. The brig USS *Enterprise* (commanded by William Burrows) captured the similar HMS *Boxer* off Portland. Both captains were killed, along with three or four men on each ship, and four times as many wounded. With her captain dead and her masts reduced to useless lumber, *Boxer* had little option but surrender. The American ship had fired more effectively.[58]

BRITISH STRATEGY – AUTUMN 1813

With Britain straining every nerve to find men, money and materiel to support her growing list of allies in the critical task of defeating Napoleon, resources for America remained tight. Canada would be defended by regiments spared from distant garrisons. Fortunately Napoleon's defeat in Russia led him to drain marines, gunners and shipyard workers from his vast, dispersed armada. This allowed the British to reinforce Warren, and extend the scope of his operations. Without an army in North America, the British had to rely on naval power to coerce the United States, and get her troops off the Canadian border. Alfred Thayer Mahan described the British blockade of America as 'the most systematic, regularized and extensive form of commerce destruction known to war'. As the Russian Minister told Warren in April, the blockade 'does them more harm than all the hostilities'.[59]

Desperate to prevent the escape of even a single American warship from Boston, the Board sent orders direct to Griffith at Halifax. As Warren correctly observed they should have been sent to him in the first instance as Commander-in-Chief.

Understandably irritated by the obvious lack of confidence in his judgement, and the deliberate slighting of his authority, Warren offered a robust defence to the specific complaint that Boston had only been blockaded by Broke's two frigates, observing that the 74s *Valiant* and *La Hogue* had been stationed on the Grand Banks.[60] To add to his displeasure an Admiralty dispatch of 19 June demanded to know how the American ships in Boston and New York had been able to get to sea, when he had an adequate force on station and the season was favourable. With more than a hint of sarcasm Warren declared: 'I very much regret that their Lordships have given credit to intelligence so unfounded,' and explained that he had blockading formations based around a 74, at least one frigate and a brig off Sandy Hook, Long Island Sound and Boston. Capel's squadron blockading Boston had been more than adequate, but the Americans had slipped out in a fog. Once he knew Rodgers had escaped Warren had 'detached Sir John Beresford with *Poictiers*, *Maidstone* and *Nimrod* in search of the enemy's Squadron off the Tail of the Great Bank of Newfoundland in the stream of the River St Lawrence', covering the military convoys. Later intelligence on Rodgers's movements had prompted him to send Capel with *La Hogue*, *Tenedos* and *Recruit* off the Banks of Newfoundland and to the eastward. He closed by stressing that he would 'send every ship that can be spared, to close the eastern Ports, in the expectation of the Enemy's return into Port'. To emphasise the merit of his dispositions Warren enclosed Robert Oliver's account of driving Decatur's squadron into New London, and his plans to attack the Americans in port.[61]

When the intelligence indicated Rodgers was homeward-bound Warren 'made the best disposition in my power to intercept his return'. This was no idle boast: Warren deployed six 74s, a razee, ten frigates and many smaller units between Newfoundland and the Chesapeake Capes, to cover every conceivable deep-water anchorage. This was in addition to keeping Decatur, *Constellation* and *Constitution* in port, dealing with the privateers, providing a succession of convoys with escorts and rotating weak and defective units back to Britain. Only Narragansett Bay had not been closely blockaded. Yet, once again, Rodgers had eluded him. At this stage Warren knew Rodgers had captured the *Highflyer* with his orders on board. He did not know the exact, embarrassing circumstances.[62] The Admiralty had already criticised the decision to rate *Highflyer* as a tender, because tenders 'weaken the companies of H M's ships without giving to the squadron any adequate increase of power'.[63] This was unfair: Admiralty Orders of 18 November 1812 authorised Warren to reinforce his cruiser force by purchasing captured American privateers.[64] Rather than face the fact that controlling the American coast required a larger force the Admiralty lambasted Warren. They ordered that no more tenders were to be allowed.[65] The tone of the correspondence suggests the Board had heard enough of his complaints.

After Rodgers's evasion Warren was left to extend the blockade, humiliating the enemy by crushing their maritime economy. On 16 November 1813 he placed the American coast from Long Island Sound to New Orleans under blockade. The British army had crossed the Pyrenees, and no longer needed American grain, while the final defeat of Napoleon was now only a matter of months and marching as his armies melted away before overwhelming allied legions. The blockade was never perfect. Ships avoided capture, but the effort and risk made most trades uneconomic. The success of Warren's campaign can be measured in the remarkable fortune made by his secretary and prize agent. In less than two years George Hulbert acquired £100,000 as his cut from every capture made between the Gulf of Yucatan and the Gulf of St Lawrence.[66] Between 20 April and 11 November Warren's squadron alone sent over 100 vessels to Halifax for condemnation.[67]

DIVINE INTERVENTION

On the evening of 12 November Halifax harbour was crowded with warships, merchant vessels and transports when a hurricane of almost unprecedented force and duration swept through. To make matters worse the wind swung round from south-south-east to north-west during ninety chaotic minutes. The next morning between fifty and sixty ships were ashore, including Warren's flagship, Capel's *La Hogue*, the frigate *Maidstone* and six smaller warships. Fortunately only the frigate and one smaller vessel needed to be hove down and repaired; the rest came off without serious injury, but several ships lost masts and yards. Of the merchant ships gathered for convoy to England only one was ready to proceed.[68] With the resources of the yard already stretched to breaking point this was the last thing Warren needed.

Despite the hurricane Warren extended the blockade in line with his instruction from the Admiralty. He unilaterally stretched the area to include New London, which became a 'Naval Station' when Decatur's squadron entered the Thames. Warren's proclamation stressed he had 'adequate and sufficient' ships to 'enforce and maintain the blockade thereof, in the most strict and rigorous manner'.[69] The purpose of the blockade was to ruin America and secure peace.

The same day Warren wrote to Prime Minister Liverpool, complaining about British banks weakening the economic blockade by helping to float another Federal loan. He wanted additional military and naval forces for 'decisive strokes against the enemy'. With the Royal Navy now firmly in control of the Atlantic coast he advocated two lines of attack:

. . . either upon the Lakes at his principal Depot of Sackett's Harbour: or by a vigorous attack to the Southward in taking possession of New Orleans and bringing forward the Indians and Spaniards in that quarter and a division of Black Troops to cut off the resources of the Mississippi; and alarm the states of Kentucky, Ohio, the Carolinas and Virginia for their own safety and independence.[70]

How far Warren's advice influenced Cabinet decision-making is unclear, but additional resources were sent.

On the New England coast excellent coasting pilot books and willing accomplices ashore provided the British with food, water, lumber and intelligence, while smuggling through Halifax emphasised the weakness of the Federal government.[71] The British found the situation highly amusing, but Bainbridge at Charlestown Navy Yard lamented that such 'familiar intercourse' would enable the enemy to sustain the blockade through the winter.[72]

BRITISH SUPER-FRIGATES

The American war forced the British to re-think their cruiser fleet. The success of the big American 44s, and the demanding winter conditions off New England left the standard 18-pounder fifth rates looking slightly inadequate. Bigger, faster, more seaworthy, and above all more powerful ships were needed. Warren stressed the short-term solution, creating a force of razees, old 74s cut down by one deck. This would create 58-gun super-frigates with a main battery of long 32-pounders, more than enough to demolish the *President*.[73] The Admiralty followed plans prepared by Captain John '*Magnificent*' Hayes,[74] one of the finest seamen ever to tread the quarterdeck, to convert the *Majestic*, *Saturn* and *Goliath*. *Majestic* sailed for America in May 1813, with Hayes in command: the final unit followed at the end of the year. Armed with twenty-eight 32-pounder long guns, twenty-eight 42-pounder carronades and two 12-pounder bow chasers these were the most powerful frigates at sea and, with 495 men, the most heavily manned as well. The Admiralty stressed that such ships would replace 74s, making a major saving in manpower.[75] Hayes reported *Majestic* fast and seaworthy, with outstanding heavy-weather performance, holding on to far more canvas than conventional frigates, and translating that power into speed through the water. The captain of a standard frigate left trailing in *Majestic*'s massive wake was awestruck by her speed, and stressed her deceptive appearance. He hoped Hayes could lure Rodgers's *President* under his guns.[76] *Majestic*'s superb heavy-weather performance made her ideal for the Boston blockade. The razees had one major defect: poor performance in light airs, when the bulky battleship hull, with the greater surface area below the waterline, significantly increased frictional resistance.

The ideal solution to the American problem would be new purpose-built ships, but these would take years to construct. Instead the Admiralty turned to the only British 24-pounder frigate. HMS *Endymion* was an unusual ship, built in the 1790s to a French design, with light scantlings.[77] In service her original 24-pounder battery had soon been exchanged for lighter 18-pounders; the heavier guns were unnecessary to fight French ships, and damaged the hull structure. Even so the large, lightly built ship proved expensive to maintain, her repair costs double those of a typical British frigate. Such expense was justified by her remarkable performance: a superb sailing ship, combining astonishing speed, over 14 knots going large, and handiness in a near perfect combination. However, *Endymion* had been built to fly, not to fight the far larger and more heavily built American 44s. While *President*'s massive frames were separated by a mere 2 inches, 3 inches separated *Endymion*'s lighter timbers. At close range this would be decisive, allowing shot to penetrate more easily. Furthermore, the American ship mounted four more main deck guns. Even so *Endymion* was the Royal Navy's only big frigate. When war broke out she was in the middle of a major repair, returning to sea in May 1813, with 24-pounder long guns and an extra pair of 32-pounder carronades on the quarterdeck.[78] The heavier 24-pounder guns cost *Endymion* almost a knot, and she required careful stowage and handling, but her performance was never matched by a British frigate under canvas in the French and American wars. Even in the 1840s she made over 13 knots going large and remained the bench-mark against which all new frigates were tested.[79]

Captain Henry Hope took command of *Endymion* in May 1813. Although a proven frigate captain he was given the prize command on the recommendation of his cousin, Admiral Sir William Johnstone Hope, a Naval Lord of Admiralty. Hope worked the ship up in the Channel before heading for America, capturing the large privateer schooner *Perry* on 3 December

1813. From the moment she arrived on station *Endymion* was assigned to the most demanding posts, taking several more privateers.[80] Initially Hope served under Sir Thomas Hardy, blockading the USS *United States* and *Macedonian* in New London. When Decatur dismantled his ships *Endymion* moved to the Sandy Hook station.

To complement the *Endymion* and the razees the Admiralty ordered new super-frigates. Five, based on *Endymion*, were built at Wigram's yard at Blackwall on the Thames, the largest commercial firm in the country. Hastily built in fir, *Severn*, *Forth*, *Liffey*, *Liverpool* and *Glasgow* entered service between September 1813 and August 1814. Two larger purpose-designed ships, *Leander* and *Newcastle*, were added to the list, and offered to outstanding frigate captains. After Broke turned down one command they were given to Sir George Collier and Lord George Stuart. The last pair, like the razees, were '*President*-killers'. They went to sea in the spring of 1814.[81] Melville hesitated to build any more of this 'new and cumbersome description of ships ... merely because the Americans have three of them; we may more easily supply line of battle ships'.[82] By 1815 the British had eleven frigates at sea with 24- or 32-pounder long guns. These ships, the only units with the speed, seaworthiness and firepower to counter the American 44s, were deployed to the squadrons blockading Boston, New London and New York. They were supported by the fastest 18-pounder frigates, including *Tenedos*, *Pomone*, *Acasta* and *Nymphe*. Slower frigates were detailed to patrol or escort convoys.

DESPERATE MEASURES

In December 1813 Secretary Jones issued cruising orders to the brigs *Siren*, *Enterprise* and *Rattlesnake*. His over-riding concerns were to attack British commerce, and avoid combat. *Siren* would head for Madeira and the African coast, where there were many rich, unescorted prizes, and the Indian Ocean, operating between Mauritius, Bourbon and India, looking for homeward-bound East Indiamen. If the prizes provided food and water the cruise should be extended because, Jones stressed, no prizes were to be taken.

A Single Cruiser, if ever so successful, can man but a few prizes, and every prize is a serious diminution of her force; but a Single Cruiser, destroying every captured vessel, has the capacity of continuing in full vigour her destructive power so long as her provisions and stores can be replenished, either from friendly ports, or from the Vessels captured. Thus has a Single Cruiser, upon the destructive plan, the power perhaps of twenty acting upon pecuniary views alone; and thus may the employment of our small force, in some degree compensate for the great inequality compared with that of the Enemy.

Not only were the chances of any prize reaching port slim, but the prize crew would end up in 'a loathsome prison in the hands of a perfidious and cruel enemy'. If he found adequate provisions off Mauritius Master Commandant George Parker should try to head for Chile, where Porter had found adequate provisions. At Valparaiso he could decide his next step. Jones placed a high value on securing British prisoners, expressly forbidding cartels and ransoms. Finally he demanded there were to be no foolish challenges: 'His Commerce is our true Game, for there he is indeed vulnerable.'[83]

Master Commandant John Creighton was directed to take *Rattlesnake* and *Enterprise* on a cruise from Portsmouth, New Hampshire, through the West Indies, avoiding the obvious British stations, and returning to Wilmington. The two brigs should keep company. Once again, taking prisoners and destroying shipping were 'the great object', only prizes of great value, or those 'morally certain' to reach port were to be manned.[84]

Siren got to sea and destroyed the merchant brig *Adventurer* off the coast of Africa before being taken by the 74 HMS *Medway* on 12 July 1814 after an eleven-hour chase. She lasted three weeks longer than *Rattlesnake*, which was taken by the super-frigate HMS *Leander* off Cape Sable on 22 June, having thrown most of her guns overboard in a futile attempt to escape. *Rattlesnake* and *Enterprise* had followed Jones's directions, taking eight vessels, of which three were burned. Only *Enterprise* survived the summer.[85]

That one American brig managed to complete her voyage suggests that Warren was still short of ships: hurricanes at Halifax and Jamaica, the need to carry specie home from Jamaica, and other distractions left the Leeward Islands and West Indies inadequately covered. He urged 'the extreme necessity of increasing the force in every part of the West Indies'. The latest intelligence offered a worrying portent. The Americans were rapidly building large corvettes of 600 tons and 24 guns: 'I am very apprehensive of the mischief their Cruisers will do to our Trade.' To make matters worse two American battleships would be launched in the spring. He needed more ships, especially fast ones, to catch and kill the new generation of American corvettes and privateers.[86]

Even if they were not winning the war, privateers were, by early 1814, 'the nation's only effective offensive force', a force entirely dependent on private capital, rewarding investors on a 'no-win, no-fee' basis. The parlous condition of national revenue and the lack of credit made privateering doubly attractive. Yet the impact of the campaign was declining: British counter-measures had cleared the seas of easy prey, and made it hard to bring home captured ships for adjudication. In April 1814 French courts stopped selling American prizes. Successful privateers were left to plunder high-value items, and destroy vessels. This approach reconnected private and national war. From the outbreak of war Baltimore men had argued that privateering should become national strategy: Samuel Smith and Hezekiah Niles consistently urged the government to invest in a strategy of schooner-based commerce-raiding. In February 1814, with economic returns slumping, Baltimore interests sought a government bounty for destroying British commerce, because they could not get the prizes home to operate the usual reward system. Well aware that private capital would only support the war if it received a regular dividend, Baltimore investors offered to compromise with the government for a payment by results system that rewarded privateers for destroying ships. Nothing came of these proposals: the administration lacked the money to fund either scheme – because it had grossly mismanaged the economic war effort.[87] This made the government ever more dependent on major capitalists like John Jacob Astor, Stephen Girard and David Parish for loans and securities.[88] It had no interest in subsidising Baltimore.

Smith supported the dividend and state schooner models; he argued that cutting British West Indies commerce would secure American victory. His own aims were a return to peaceful trade. War was not good for business and hard as Smith worked his capital between 1812 and 1814 the returns fell short of those he made in peacetime. Few either then or now have reflected on the salient fact that Baltimore's pre-1812 prosperity was built on an artificial commercial bubble, the re-export trade, the result of wartime economic dislocation. As a result the return of peace in Europe would ruin Smith and other privateer investors.[89] Smith had opposed the war, which he called the act of 'madmen', but voted for war along party lines. He had little faith in Madison, unlike local political rival and Madison supporter Joshua Barney.

MEN WANTED

Throughout the war the Admiralty was acutely conscious of the problems of raising and retaining qualified seamen. The Board stressed the need for humane and consistent punishments, and avoiding expensive small-scale actions where the results did not warrant the human cost. While Warren tried to stretch his resources, using prizes like the *Highflyer* as tenders, the Board disagreed, preferring fewer but more efficient ships. They regretted 'excessive punishments' on *Acasta*, *Plantagenet*, *Dragon*, *La Hogue*, *Martin* and *Tenedos* where five dozen lashes had been inflicted on at least two occasions. They disapproved all such punishments, along with the six dozen lashes awarded to one man on the *Laurestinus*. Instead they praised the exemplary record of the schooner *Paz*, which reported no corporal punishment. The Board wondered why Warren had not commented on the quarterly punishment returns. Not content with this steely rebuke, the Board added the 74 *Albion* to the list of flogging ships a few days later.[90]

Despite the endless search for skilled manpower, Warren earned official praise for his generous response to Governor-General Prevost's demand for seamen for the ever expanding Lake fleets. The American victory at Lake Erie had reminded Prevost that the defence of the frontier was primarily a maritime issue. Warren met the demand by paying off worn-out cruisers and stripping men from ships heading to Britain.[91] Warren also sent his second Royal Marine battalion to the Lakes, a serious reduction of his tiny amphibious strike force.

Although the Royal Navy was plagued by desertion, the American service was by no means immune to the problem; open spaces and alternative options provided bored, frustrated men serving in wet, uncomfortable gunboats with ample inducement to leave.[92] Many more Americans found themselves locked up in British prisons. By late 1814 Halifax was running out of space for prisoners, and those allowed out on licence were abusing their privileges by sending information home on cartels. To make matters worse Prevost sent 500 prisoners from the hulks off Quebec, confident they could be accommodated at Halifax.[93] Warren accepted Governor Sir John Sherbrooke's recommendation that the entire prisoner depot be moved to the old French settlement at Louisbourg.[94] Edward Griffith solved the intelligence leak, placing all seventy American officers under close confinement in retaliation for the American decision to lock up forty-six British officers. The Admiralty gave their 'perfect approval'.[95]

WARREN'S WINTER OF DISCONTENT

Despite the growing success of his campaign, Warren never escaped the overwhelming demands of the European war. In early 1814 the need to send specie home from the West Indies distorted the disposition of forces, leaving the West Indies squadrons unable to meet the basic needs of convoy escort and insular protection. The Halifax hurricane only made the situation worse. Frustrated and over-stretched, and annoyed by constant criticism of his actions emanating from Jamaica, Warren advised separating the three stations, going back to the pre-1812 position when Jamaica and the Leeward Islands reported directly to London, retaining overall control only in an emergency.[96] This was wise: the two West Indian squadrons had been less useful than had been hoped, and less co-operative. Sir Francis Laforey on the Leeward Station was slack, paying little attention to commercial needs, while Sir Charles Stirling had been unduly swayed by planters, merchants and personal greed. The barrage of complaints and a desperate need for hard cash and treasure to subsidise the growing list of European allies swayed the ministers.

Warren was also troubled by his health. Cold voyages aggravated his rheumatism, his eyes hurt and his spirits were anything but buoyant. Melville used Warren's dispatch as grounds for his removal, arguing that complaints from Jamaica were the key reason. He was equally annoyed by Warren's attempt to control the patronage of all three squadrons.[97] The Board was little better pleased by his decision to send specie home from Jamaica and Bermuda in two frigates when the 74 *Poictiers* was also making the passage.[98] Because Warren was too senior to hold a separate North American command Melville would replace him with either his Scots political connection Sir Alexander Cochrane or Nelson favourite Sir Richard Keats. When the news of his recall reached Warren at Bermuda, although clearly annoyed, he carefully avoided unseemly recriminations. He would retain command until April 1814.

BLOCKADING THE AMERICAN FLEET

While the American frigates had been dealt a heavy blow, Warren's squadrons were equally successful against the privateer threat. While Beresford was searching for Rodgers he took the 20-gun privateer *York Town*, and recaptured her latest prize, the Post Office packet *Duke of Manchester*. Such news provided useful fodder for the *Gazette*.[99]

Further successes on the Halifax station saw the *Nymphe* take the 12-gun *Thomas*, while the *Young Teazer* was destroyed by *La Hogue* in Lunenburg Bay. This steady attrition kept the sea lanes into Quebec and Montreal clear, and locked up increasing numbers of prime American seamen.

In mid-October Warren set out his plans for the winter campaign. He entrusted major operational roles to key subordinates. Griffith would blockade Boston and Rhode Island, while cruiser patrols protected New Brunswick, secured the Bay of Fundy and escorted convoys.[100] Griffith's squadron comprised *Nymphe*, *Majestic*, *Junon*, *Tenedos*, *Raleigh*, *Wasp*, *Fantome*, *Martin*, *Curlew*, *Epervier*, *Arab*, *Manly*, *Thistle*, *Shelburne*, *Muquidobit* and *Bream*.[101] On 16 October Warren learnt that Rodgers had got into Newport 'despite the best dispositions in my power to intercept him'. All his hard work since the early summer had been undone at a stroke. Anticipating another round of ill-informed carping criticism from Whitehall, Warren explained his plans in detail.

The effort required to stop a solitary frigate getting into an American port was striking. Warren had spread his 74s and frigates in powerful combined forces, linked by smaller cruisers to cover all approaches to the main American harbours. From north to south *La Hogue* and *Tenedos* took station on the tail of the Grand Banks off Newfoundland, with *Poictiers* and *Maidstone* positioned between Sambro Lighthouse and Sable Head cruising south-easterly from there some 20 leagues and back by way of Cape Sable. *Ramillies* and *Loire* stood from Cape Sable south-east along the edge of St George's Bank as far as

Lat. 42.00 with Sir Thomas Hardy in command off Boston with an inshore squadron comprising *Nymphe*, *Majestic*, *Junon* and *Wasp*. *Orpheus* and *Loup Cervier* operated between Tuck a Nuck passage and Block Island, where they linked up with *Valiant*, *Acasta*, *Atalanta* and the gun brig *Boxer*, controlling the waters between Block Island and the entrance to Long Island Sound, from their blockade station off New London. The 74 *Plantagenet* lay off Sandy Hook. *Belvidera*, *Statira* and *Morgiana* controlled access to the Delaware, while *Dragon*, *Lacadaemonian*, *Armide*, *Dotterell* and *Mohawk* held the entrance to the Chesapeake. It was only reasonable that Warren 'entertained the most confident hope that Commodore Rodgers would not have been able to escape through all these ships'. Unfortunately human error and damaged rigging wrecked his calculations. As Rodgers headed for Tuck a Nuck passage he took the *Highflyer*, which had been placed to warn the blockading ships. To make matters worse the frigate *Orpheus* had sprung her mainmast and returned to Halifax for repairs, leaving a gap in the patrols. By the time the 74 *Albion* took over her station it was too late.

It would be hard to fault Warren's arrangements, and for once the Admiralty was not minded to try. Silenced by Warren's well-crafted dispositions the Board listened to the dispatch in silence: it entered the archive without the usual carping minute.[102] News that Rodgers had captured *Highflyer*'s signal book and orders only added to Warren's dismay.[103] After a boisterous passage south Warren arrived at Bermuda on 18 December, to find that the October and November mails had not arrived.[104] Hoping to pre-empt further criticism from London he dispatched a record of his dispositions.[105]

CONSTITUTION

On 9 September Secretary Jones ordered the *Constitution* to sea from Boston. Unsuitable weather and a close blockade delayed Charles Stewart's departure for three months. He needed a north-easterly wind to get away. While he waited, Stewart built a furnace to heat red-hot shot, which he proposed to fire from his stern battery, if engaged with an enemy of superior force. With Hayes's powerful razee *Majestic* frequently in the offing Stewart advised fitting the gunboats with furnaces.[106] The British were soon aware of the new equipment.[107]

When Warren headed south he left Griffith to repair hurricane damage and watch the American 44s. The combination of long nights, blowing weather and a shortage of suitable ships made it unlikely he could prevent them getting to sea. Rumours abounded, and he had to check every report. John Hayes took command of the inshore squadron, securing useful intelligence from the friendly inhabitants of Province Town. In November Hayes reported *Constitution* 'perfectly ready for sea', her enlarged crew exercised at their guns and sails. If the American escaped Hayes hoped to mount an intelligence-led pursuit. Warren agreed, directing Hayes to pass any intelligence he had to British warships he fell in with; if they headed north-east intelligence could be shared with the consuls at St Michael's in the Azores, Tenerife or Madeira. If he drew a blank he should return to Halifax for fresh orders.[108]

On 15 December a Swedish merchant ship reported *President* had left Newport on the 4th, intelligence soon confirmed by a British midshipman recovered from a prize taken by *Loire*.[109] When HMS *Wasp* looked into Boston on 2 January she confirmed that *Constitution* had sailed, while a corvette-built ship was preparing to sail for the East Indies. The rest of the harbour was almost deserted. While Griffith waited for confirmation he assessed the reports that Decatur had escaped to be less credible.[110] Hayes reported Rodgers had sailed on 4 December, escaping Boston Bay in a north-west gale early in the New Year: 'notwithstanding the most zealous and persevering blockade our squadron endeavoured to maintain of that port'. He was not surprised; 'in fact for the last fortnight we have had such repeated gales with frost and snow it would have been extraordinary if she had not made her escape'. Hayes followed *Constitution*, certain her course was to the eastward, expecting

President to follow a similar course. Warren also learnt that *Congress* had reached Portsmouth after a prize revealed the presence of a superior force off Boston.[111] Amid a chaotic intelligence picture of truth, half-truth and complete fable, Hayes's decision would pay dividends.

After crossing the Atlantic in pursuit of *Constitution* Hayes encountered the Philadelphia privateer *Wasp* late on 2 February. Chasing the American he ran into three ships and a brig between the Azores and Madeira early the following day. There were two frigates, a Spanish ship and a merchant brig. Reckoning that he had found *Constitution* and *Essex*, Hayes abandoned the privateer, making for the new enemy. The frigates were French. Captain Mallett in the *Atalante* hastily abandoned his compatriot, and after a hectic pursuit Hayes brought *Majestic* close alongside the 44-gun *Terpsichore*, which promptly surrendered. Hayes was unable to pursue the other frigate: the prize was in a chaotic state and the sea was rising. The prize was swiftly added to the Royal Navy.[112] Once again the action had taken place close to the Azores, the Atlantic crossroads where convoys bound for the East and West Indies passed. It should be noted that French frigates did more damage to British trade in 1813 and 1814 than the Americans, and fought many more actions.

By the time Hayes set off in pursuit of *Constitution* Griffith's cruiser force had been seriously eroded. Manpower demands from the Lakes fleet forced him to pay off four sloops and send the men to Kingston by the arduous overland route.[113] He could only hope to man these ships in an emergency.[114] Warren requested another 300 seamen and 150 Marines to make up numbers.[115] Griffith's force was further eroded when HMS *Wasp* went to Bermuda to report that *Constitution* was out, another sloop carried Prevost's ADC to Britain, and HMS *Bramble* took important diplomatic correspondence to Annapolis.[116] Fortunately the remaining small cruisers maintained a steady run of success against American privateers. On 23 February 1814 HMS *Epervier* encountered the privateer brig *Alfred* 'about 220 tons' of 16 guns, 110 men, on her return to Salem after a twelve-week cruise that yielded only three small prizes. The Americans surrendered as soon as the *Epervier* opened fire. The sloop *Prometheus* brought in two more Salem privateers in March, and news that Rodgers had returned to New York after an unsuccessful cruise of nearly three months.[117]

Throughout the winter Warren's squadrons maintained the unceasing pressure of blockade and capture along the American coast. Off the Delaware *Belvidera*, *Recruit* and *Dotterel* captured the schooner USS *Vixen* heading for the river, and drove the letter of marque *Inca* ashore, saving part of her valuable cargo. Between September 1813 and the end of the year Barrie's squadron in the Chesapeake destroyed dozens of coasters and at least seven big letter of marque schooners headed abroad. In this period *Plantagenet* destroyed twenty-five small ships on the Sandy Hook blockade station, while waiting for an American 44 to come her way.[118] In late January the new fir-built 24-pounder frigate HMS *Severn*, Captain Joseph Nourse, arrived at Bermuda after a disastrous voyage in which the valuable transport *Blendon Hall*, part of an outbound Bermuda convoy under her protection, was taken and sunk. On 18 January, at approximately 24° North 53° West, Nourse had encountered the French frigates *Étoile* and *Sultane*. Once he realised they were hostile Nourse signalled his convoy to scatter and drew the enemy into a long stern chase, in which the *Severn* easily held her distance. The following morning the French ships broke off; they would meet more British ships when they touched at the Cape Verde Island five days later.[119] Warren immediately dispatched *Plantagenet* and the brig *Childers* in pursuit.[120]

CONSTITUTION'S THIRD CRUISE

Charles Stewart was a canny operator: he spent six months getting his ship ready for sea, shifting and cleaning her copper. He was not going to rush out of Boston at the first opportunity to pick a fight. Not only had Madison and Jones strictly prohibited any such affair of honour, but Stewart needed no trophies.

The decision to wait paid off. At 3 p.m. on 31 December 1813 *Constitution* put to sea after a winter gale had cleared away the blockading squadron. While Hayes expected him to head for the Azores, Stewart set a course for the Brazilian coast, and then followed his orders to cruise in the Caribbean. After a frustrating month chasing shadows and neutrals he encountered the brig HMS *Mosquito* off Guyana on 3 February, which evaded capture by the simple expedient of running into shoal water, and going aground. Five days later another brig, HMS *Columbine*, simply sailed away. Realising that the British ship would alert Admiral Sir Philip Durham, Stewart changed his colour scheme to mimic the British on the 14th and the following day he took a merchant ship and the schooner HMS *Picton*. The brig was burnt, the prize used as a cartel. More schooners were taken and destroyed on the 17th and 18th. Having carefully measured the force of the 18-pounder frigate HMS *Pique*, Captain Anthony Maitland, which he encountered west of Puerto Rico on the 23rd and 24th, Stewart declined battle on both days. In his official account Stewart claimed that the British ship sailed away from him the first night they met, but this claim is not supported by *Pique*'s log book. Although Durham was appalled by Maitland's apparently pusillanimous conduct, much as his crew had been, the Admiralty had explicitly ordered captains not to engage the American 44s single-handed.[121] In March a defective mainmast compromised *Constitution*'s sailing qualities and Stewart decided to return to Boston. Early on 3 April 1814, as he neared home the wind dropped and he spotted *Tenedos* and *Junon* of the blockading squadron closing quickly from astern, having caught the wind. Stewart pumped out the remaining water, threw overboard spare stores, and ran into Marblehead just before noon. Leading the pursuit Hyde Parker planned to follow the American into the undefended harbour, but he was recalled by his superior officer, Clotworthy Upton, in *Junon*. Upton's decision was never explained. With two frigates in good order he had no reason not to make the attempt. Intelligence from ashore suggested the Americans had expected an attack.

As one young officer observed 'without some risk, some dash, very little will ever be done in the navy; prudence has never yet answered. Even if you fail, the attempt will gain you the applause of Englishmen'.[122] The chance proved fleeting. Six hours later a shift in the wind enabled Stewart to get into the fortified port of Salem; soon after he slipped back into Boston to refit.[123]

DECATUR FRUSTRATED

After the failure of the torpedo schemes Stephen Decatur found life on the Thames River increasingly tedious. In January 1814 he suggested a 'fair and equal combat' between his two frigates and two British blockaders, for the prize of getting to sea. Lord Nelson's old flag captain was not impressed by such tomfoolery. Nor did he hold Decatur's notion of 'honour' in high regard: six months earlier the same man had overseen the use of an IED to kill a British officer and ten seamen alongside Hardy's flagship. Hardy had no reason to trust his honour. This was war, and it should be conducted according to the appropriate rules, not tenets of terrorism, or the plot of a romantic novel.[124] Warren agreed, expressly banning the meeting. The 'present great superiority' of the British must be applied with vigour, not risked.[125] For once the Admiralty concurred.[126]

The cruiser squadrons remained active. On 28 January the newly arrived ex-French frigate *Niemen* captured the 285-ton letter of marque packet *Bourdeau*, laden with sugar, mounting five guns and crewed by fifty men, 'pushing for the Delaware'.[127] Captain Henry Hope in the beautiful 24-pounder frigate *Endymion* took another letter of marque, the new 230-ton copper-fastened schooner *Perry*, bound from New York to Santiago de Cuba with a cargo of flour, on 3 December after an eight-hour chase while heading north to join the blockade of New York. The *Perry* had sailed the previous evening. Hope took the similar *Meteor*, 219 tons, 3 guns, and 32 men, bound from Nantes to New York, on 7 February, using her boats as the wind fell away, despite a 'long and fatiguing row' under fire. The American was on the return leg of her maiden voyage, with a valuable cargo.[128] From the Chesapeake Robert Barrie reported that *Constellation* had attempted to escape, only to be driven back into Norfolk by *Dragon*, *Lacadaemonian*, *Armide* and *Sophie*. There was nothing else worthy of notice in that quarter.[129] Before handing over his station, Warren could report one more pleasing success. He had sent his flagship in pursuit of the 'frigate' seen off Charleston, Rodgers's *President;* she returned with the letter of marque trader *Argus*, 13 guns and 65 men, five days out from Savannah bound for Havana.[130]

On 28 January 1814 Warren received official notice of his relief. He reported that the fleet had reached the required strength on most stations, but the Halifax and St Lawrence command remained short by three frigates, while four sloops had been paid off to man the Lakes fleet.[131] Between June and November 1813 Melville's correspondence was, once again, restricted to patronage. He continued to reject Warren's promotions, undermining the Admiral's authority.[132] He only broke his silence on the higher direction of the war to explain that Warren's command was at an end.[133] Melville implied the recall was, in large part, Warren's fault. He had cut across Melville's control of naval patronage.[134] That Melville chose his political ally Alexander Cochrane over the more capable Keats is revealing. Cochrane arrived at Bermuda on 6 March when Warren handed over the ships, orders and intelligence. Soon after he set sail for Spithead.[135]

Most assessments of Warren's command have been critical, linking lack of success to his age, while the destruction of American commerce has become the basis for hostile reflections on personal greed and indecision, but few were disinterested. In reality Warren's command, which only lasted two winters and one summer, began under the most difficult circumstances, trying to negotiate peace at the expense of an effective strategy of economic blockade. The differential economic blockades helped to exacerbate internal American disunity, but this was not decisive. Furthermore, Warren was always short of ships and men, drained away by the Lakes, convoys, and Jamaican interests; the occasional lost ship and savage Halifax hurricanes only reinforced the problem. By the time Broke took an American frigate it was too late. The changing fortunes of the European war did not help; set alongside Wellington's success at Vitoria and the titanic bloodbath at Leipzig, Warren's blockade seemed rather tame. Desperate for positive results, the government was happier lauding Cockburn's small raids than the slow grinding wheels of a war-winning blockade.

In reality Warren's war was effective, economical, and above all successful. By June 1813 the American naval effort had comprehensively failed and the privateer threat was fast fading as effective convoys and well-placed cruisers countered and often caught the predators. Almost 1,000 merchant ships had been taken, sunk or burnt; and with them the basis of American national revenue was lost. But it was left to another officer to carry the war to a conclusion.

CHAPTER 8

World-Wide War

While the War of 1812 was dominated by actions on the North American continent and the adjacent seas, the North Atlantic and the Caribbean, oceanic warfare eventually stretched across the globe. The sheer ubiquity of British floating commerce made all the world's oceans target-rich zones. In 1813 John Rodgers raided the Arctic. More American officers and strategists planned to enter Asian waters, the Indian Ocean routes of the East India Company, the greatest of all trading conglomerates, and the high-profile Chinese trade, ships laden with silks, porcelain, tea, silver and opium. The Americans believed that the further they stretched away from home the less effective British defences would be, the richer the prizes and the greater the strategic dislocation their activities could cause, perhaps relaxing the blockade itself. Such thoughts became ever more attractive in 1813, as the Royal Navy took control of the North Atlantic and Caribbean, convoyed all shipping, patrolled the focal points, and imposed a naval blockade on American harbours. In truth the British anticipated the American effort, having an encyclopedic knowledge of American navigation in Indian and Chinese waters.[1]

American plans to attack Asian trade reflected pre-war ambitions to challenge British dominance of regional commerce. While Asian routes were relatively well-known to American seafarers, the Pacific remained a sea of aspiration and dream – a vast empty canvas waiting for ships and men to make their mark, to impose an American vision. Early whaling and fur trade sorties held out the promise of limitless catches and massive profits. Nowhere were Thomas Jefferson's continental exceptionalism and Federalist commercial expansion closer than on the north-west coast, where settlement and trapping depended on the Chinese fur trade for profits. Aggressive commercial expansion and commercial war provided alternative visions of success, and mutually beneficial skills. Knowledge gained in two decades of Asian trade influenced American strategy. Naval officers considered the China Seas, Indian and Pacific Oceans attractive, relatively lightly held regions where rich prizes could be obtained. Navy Secretaries William Jones and Benjamin Crowninshield possessed extensive experience in Asian trade. This experience dominated Jones's strategy.[2]

Americans sailed the Pacific because the Federal tariff system of 1789 made it economically attractive to operate in China. Designed to promote national shipping, the tariff used financial penalties to force foreign-owned and -built ships out of interstate and international trades, rewarding American owners and merchants who used American ships and crews. By 1812 American ships carried 90 per cent of American foreign trade. Tariffs discouraged foreign merchants from bringing Chinese tea into American ports, a deliberate attempt to control the market. New York, Baltimore and Philadelphia benefited from tariff policies that made American trade with China significantly more profitable than that of any competitor.[3]

Independence had freed American shippers to challenge the East India Company monopoly on British Asian trade, one of the more obvious targets of the revolutionary 'Boston Tea Party'. British rules had not stopped ambitious New Englanders reaching Asia, or carrying on trade, but the removal of legal restraint was a major incentive. Two ships set off for China in 1784, one belonging to Elias Hasket Derby of Salem, the other from Philadelphia. Within a few years American ships were trading directly with India, China, Java and the Spice Islands. Indian trade expanded rapidly during the Anglo-Indian and French Wars; Derby used the trade to become the first American millionaire. In violation of the 1794 Jay Treaty American ships traded directly between India and Europe, and secured the coastal trade in home waters in the absence of other European craft. Similar war profits fell to another Salem family, the Crowninshields, who developed trade with Mauritius, India and Java. The trade was mutually beneficial, so long as Europe was at war and America at peace with Britain. Jefferson's Embargo of December 1807 marked a sudden, devastating shift of fortune. Trade revived after 1809, but the outbreak of war in 1812 brought the business to a complete stop: it never recovered.[4]

Although the United States occupied only a toehold on the Pacific coast in 1812 statesmen and business leaders had been attracted by the economic and expansionist opportunities of the region. Jefferson began systematic exploration of the continent searching for scientific understanding and economic opportunity before the Louisiana Purchase. Reading British fur trader Alexander Mackenzie's journal of an expedition across the Rockies to the Pacific prompted Jefferson to dispatch the Lewis and Clark expedition. Aware that America lacked the military and fiscal resources to occupy such vast spaces he saw the fur trade as a useful way of securing American control in the North and West.[5] John Jacob Astor would follow the President's lead, setting up a fur trade outpost on the Pacific North-West coast in 1811. Astor's plans were driven by windfall profits in Asian commerce – sea otter furs from the North-West were the most profitable imports for the Chinese market. During the war he would loan the cash-strapped government $2.5 million in return for a meaningless promise to defend his settlement.[6]

Astor had developed a global fur trade from his base in New York, taking control of the Canadian trade and then using furs to open the Chinese market, bringing home cargoes of tea and high-value fabrics. This trade was very profitable; a single cargo might be worth $250,000, and most were swiftly re-exported to Europe. By 1800 twenty to thirty American ships a year were going to Canton. By 1803–4 Astor already owned two ships trading with Canton, and had built up excellent political contacts. Treasury Secretary Albert Gallatin was a critical ally.[7]

When Jefferson adopted the Embargo, part of his reasoning was to develop the fur trade as a mechanism to tie the Indians to

America. This prompted Astor to expand his horizons, through closer links with the Canadian-based North West Company, and taking over trade settlements set up by the American government. Jefferson hoped to stop foreign traders from inciting Indian attacks. Suitably encouraged, Astor sought government support for a trading post on the Pacific coast in April 1808. Jefferson remained cautious, withholding official sanction.[8] Even so, Astor's expanding fur trade and vaulting ambition prompted British traders to demand support from their government, prompting a race to the North-West.[9]

The Non-Intercourse Act persuaded Astor to set up a permanent fur trade settlement. The ship he sent to establish a post at Astoria in July 1810 was escorted down to the Equator by the USS *Constitution*, to prevent British ships impressing the crew. This project was part of a complex, but fluid plan Astor had evolved to create an integrated supply and trading network for China trade, linked to Russian America. However, Astor was a poor judge of men, and the initial settlement was attacked by local Indians.[10]

Like most American merchants Astor opposed the war; it would be very bad for business. In March 1812 he was among many New York merchants urging the administration to rely on trade restrictions to leverage the British. Astor had good reason to oppose a conflict, but despite the inevitable problems caused by war and economic legislation he continued trading across the border, albeit in slightly reduced volumes, throughout the conflict.

Once the war began Madison and Gallatin made fur trade expansion part of national strategy. They had little choice; the administration desperately needed Astor's financial and political support. After spending $28.5 million more than it received in revenue in 1812 the administration needed a loan. In February 1813 Congress authorised a $16 million loan; Gallatin looked to Astor and other American capitalists to find the cash. New York financiers were opposed to the war, and found the repayment conditions uncertain. This obliged Gallatin to offer a better deal to three big players: Astor, Stephen Girard and David Parish would pay $88 in cash for each $100 bond, and earn 6 per cent per annum on loans that would be redeemable after 1825. Another $5 million was raised in February, and $10 million in March along with another bond issue of $25 million in March. Astor ignored the last issue, because the administration would not exempt his European trade from the embargo on bond sales and imports. Between 1812 and 1814 the American government issued $61 million in bonds, but only sold $45 million, and less than $8 million of those went at par. Ever the astute man of business, Astor used loan contracting to secure political leverage for his business interests. By late 1814 only New England banks still paid in cash, leading to a significant economic slow-down, discounted bank notes and a collapse in the value of government stock. By late 1814 bond values were down to 66 per cent of par. As Madison would not support Astoria, Astor was not inclined to help.

Desperate to maintain his economic empire, Astor used British and American licences to keep trading with Europe. Even so, he lost two ships to the Royal Navy; one of them was taken despite a Russian pass. In July 1813 the Federal government prohibited the use of British licences, and in December of the same year banned all exports of goods and produce. This legislation was relaxed in May 1814, but these changes left Astor and other prominent merchants facing uncertain, fluctuating trading patterns. Despite the barriers Astor sustained economic activity by exploiting every opportunity to get his ships to Europe.

By contrast the British effectively stopped American trade at Canton, which fell from $31 million in 1811–12 to $450,000 in 1813–14. Astor's *Beaver* remained blockaded at Canton for the duration.

The situation at Astoria proved more challenging. Astor expected the government to defend the post, using his role in promoting the bond issue to leverage official support. When Madison and Monroe ignored his request Astor sent a ship with a government pass; it was wrecked near Hawaii. Astor's

British competitors, the North West Company, proved more successful. It persuaded the British government that the West Coast fur trade had a strategic importance, and secured an East India Company licence to trade direct from Astoria to Canton. Suitably encouraged, the North West Company sent two forces to seize Astoria. The Company-owned armed storeship *Isaac Todd* left Portsmouth on 25 March 1813, escorted by the frigate HMS *Phoebe*, Captain James Hillyar, with orders to: 'totally annihilate any settlement which the Americans may have formed either on the Columbia River or on the neighbouring coast'. He should rendezvous with a second force of 100 men that had set off overland for Astoria between May and August 1814. They would place the American post under British control. This was a secret mission, and Hillyar was given a cipher for his dispatches. Given the unusual destination the Board also saw no reason to miss out on an opportunity for ethnographic and hydrographic research.[11]

When Astor learnt that the North West Company was sending eighty men with heavy guns in the *Isaac Todd* he asked the Navy to send the *Argus* or *Hornet* with stores and men. A Navy project to reinforce Astoria, using the USS *John Adams*, was postponed indefinitely on 26 June 1813, only days after Secretary Jones and Astor had discussed loading stores on the warship. Facing disaster closer to home, Jones had little option but to pay off the ship at New York, sending Captain Crane and his crew to Lake Ontario. America could lose the war on Lake Ontario; Astoria was expendable.[12] In August 1813 Jones ordered the USS *Siren* to prepare for the voyage, only to cancel the orders. While Astor felt abandoned, the government he had supported and funded was powerless. The ubiquitous, all-conquering, omnipresent Royal Navy could stop any ship heading for the North-West. Astor's distant dreams had to be sacrificed when the public buildings of Washington DC were in flames.

When the North West Company's overland expedition reached Astoria with news of the war in the autumn of 1813, Astor's agents preferred business to violence. They sold the post and the furs for $58,000, a fair market value, on 16 October 1813. The deal done, the Americans left. Astor was furious: he had lost a lot of money and, far worse, a business opportunity.

With the relaxation of the American Embargo and the possibility of peace in late 1814, Astor became more ambitious. This suggests that Gallatin kept him informed on the progress of the negotiations at Ghent. Astor bought the merchant brig *Macedonian* for $27,000, spent $15,000 outfitting her for sea and $30,000 on cargo. He expected to make a $300,000 windfall on a return cargo if peace came. Astor's brig put to sea in January 1815 and reached Canton in July.

PORTER, *ESSEX* AND THE PACIFIC[13]

Before the war Captain David Porter had proposed a Pacific voyage of exploration and colonisation to Navy Secretary Paul Hamilton. Although Hamilton did nothing the plans were not wasted. Assigned to Bainbridge's squadron in October 1812, Porter in the USS *Essex* followed the Commodore's schedule, but found no sign of the squadron at Bainbridge's rendezvous, Porto Praya in the Cape Verde Islands or on the Brazilian Coast. While he waited Porter captured the Post Office Packet *Nocton* on 12 December. After stripping out £15,000 in specie Porter sent the ship home as a prize; it was recaptured by HMS *Belvidera* on 5 January. He took another British ship off Rio de Janeiro at the end of December, before falling back on his discretionary orders to act 'for the good of the service'.[14] Porter decided that this felicitous phrase meant following his instincts round Cape Horn. His pre-war study provided useful insight into the vast new theatre where he proposed to operate. He knew the Spanish colonies on the west coast of South America were in revolt, and might give a sympathetic welcome to a warship from the original American republic. The British Pacific whaling industry provided a suitable target, and the well-equipped whale ships could make the long voyage home. Finally the British had no warships in the Pacific.

DIXON'S COMMAND

As Porter realised, American access to the Pacific passed through the extensive waters of the British Brazil station, stretching from the Caribbean to the coast of Chile. These seas supported a large and growing volume of British trade, including vital homeward-bound remittances of specie and bullion. After Napoleon's invasion of Spain and Portugal, Iberian imperial control in South America had collapsed. The evacuation of the Portuguese court to Rio in 1807 and successful rebellions in several Spanish provinces opened hitherto controlled markets to the British. When Rear Admiral Manley Dixon took command of the Brazil station, based at Rio, in early 1812 the main concerns were expanding markets, protecting British interests from local instability, and above all extracting large quantities of specie from the continent. Having served in the Baltic between 1808 and 1811 Dixon was well aware of the over-riding imperative of commerce warfare, both offensive and defensive. United States merchant ships were frequent visitors to the South American ports. On receiving news of war Dixon focused on those that might be fitted out as privateers. Further south British merchants in Buenos Aires, alarmed by a sudden change of government in Argentina, hurriedly loaded their cash onto HMS *Bonne Citoyenne*. Understanding their anxieties, Dixon hastened the brig north carrying 'a considerable sum of money'.[15]

These essentially local concerns were thrown into the shade on 4 January 1813 when Dixon learnt that Bainbridge's squadron was off San Salvador. He hastened north in his 74-gun flagship, HMS *Montagu*, to escort *Bonne Citoyenne* clear of danger. Arriving at San Salvador on the 24th he learnt of the loss of HMS *Java* and arranged to dispatch the crew back to Spithead. Then he headed north, escorting *Bonne Citoyenne* past the Equator before retracing his route to San Salvador, where he arrived in early March. On the 9th a Portuguese Navy sloop reported meeting Bainbridge at sea two months before. Then Dixon received a report that *Essex* had been sighted off Rio at the end of January. Dixon suspected the Americans were looking for the specie-laden frigate *Nereus*, but he was confident Captain Peter Heywood was safely at anchor in the River Plate. Although he believed the Americans had already left the area, he concentrated all available warships to protect trade off Pernambuco and San Salvador.[16] In fact Bainbridge, Lawrence and Porter were long gone, in different directions, so the main threat to British trade came from the privateers congregating off Pernambuco, the centre of British trade with Brazil.[17] On such a vast station the demand for escorts invariably outstripped the meagre forces Dixon could deploy. In early February Dixon received his convoy instructions, created by the Admiralty and the trade association. Convoys would dominate his operations for the remainder of the war.[18] Despite the vast distances, the Convoys and Cruisers Act would be enforced: convoys would leave Rio, San Salvador and Pernambuco on set dates. In late November the Admiralty promised Dixon another battleship and four frigates. By July 1813 his force comprised a single 74, an ancient 24-pounder frigate, four other frigates, three sixth rates and three sloops and two cutters.[19] The frigates had been sent to carry specie home from Buenos Aires and Rio de Janeiro, the over-riding concern. Hard cash was needed to wage war in Europe.

By late April it had become clear that the American warship encountered off Cape Frio in January had been the *Essex*, masquerading as the *Constitution*. Although forewarned that the *Montagu* would sail for San Salvador, Porter had very nearly fallen in with the flagship. While Dixon remained uncertain about the current position of Bainbridge's three ships, he expected at least one of them had gone round Cape Horn.[20] Rather than chase shadows he relied on widely deployed, effective British intelligence-gathering assets: with consuls, merchants, ship masters and warships in several key locations the information flow was relatively rapid. On 3 April Captain Heywood of the *Nereus* at Buenos Aires reported that *Essex* had arrived at Valparaiso on 15 March, intent on a short stay; his sources had been unable to discern her onward destination. Heywood was in no position to chase the American; he had over a million Spanish dollars on board, consigned to England.[21] By the time he heard about the *Essex* Dixon had detached HMS *Cherub* to chase the 16-gun privateer *Argus*. The constant demand for escorts and safe passage for specie prevented him sending the sloops *Cherub* and *Racoon*, lately detached from the West Indies, into the Pacific.

PURSUING PORTER

David Porter's Pacific cruise ended in defeat because the British global intelligence system proved remarkably effective. In May 1813 Heywood forwarded a letter from British merchants Brown and Watson at Valparaiso, reporting the enthusiastic welcome given to the *Essex*, while Porter had 'gone out to take and destroy the English whalers on the coast'. Rumours were circulating that Porter would cross the Pacific to join Bainbridge's squadron on the coast of China, with 'orders to destroy, but capture nothing', or return via the River Plate.[22] Dixon received Heywood's letter on 3 June.[23] Nor was the *Essex* the only problem facing British interests in the Pacific. Letters from merchants in Valparaiso and Lima confirmed pro-Spanish Peruvian cruisers had attacked British vessels.[24]

By early June HMS *Racoon* had returned from the coast of San Salvador and Pernambuco, which was reported clear of American privateers. Having thus secured the main trade arteries, Dixon turned his attention to the Pacific. The shift in priorities coincided with the arrival at Rio of the North West Company expedition, *Phoebe* and *Isaac Todd*, on 10 June. As these ships were heading for the Pacific, Dixon consulted James Hillyar before settling his strategy. He decided to send the sloops *Cherub* and *Racoon* to guard the whale fishery while the *Phoebe* conducted her secret mission.[25] The Admiralty later wished to know why the sloops had not been sent off far sooner.[26] Dixon had prioritised the key tasks – specie transport, convoy, clearing the Brazilian coast of privateers and advancing British trade

– before looking to the Pacific. His decision also avoided the risk that the two sloops might fall in with the *Essex*, which would have made short work of such feeble craft.

Anxious as they were to reach the Columbia River, North West Company factors Donald McTavish and John MacDonald revealed the details of the expedition to Dixon. Concerned that the Americans might have sent reinforcements, making Hillyar's mission doubly difficult, Dixon placed the ship sloops under his command. He had intended sending another frigate to pursue *Essex* but resources failed him. Fortunately the planned American expedition never sailed. The North West Company factors also persuaded Dixon to redistribute some of the stores to the warships, in case the slow *Isaac Todd* was delayed.

Suitably reinforced, Hillyar should be able to deal with the *Essex*, escort the *Isaac Todd*, address complaints about Peruvian privateers and re-open commerce with Peru.[27] Well aware that fresh intelligence would reach the *Phoebe* long before orders from Rio, Dixon properly gave Hillyar complete discretion. The only question to be resolved was that of relations between the Spanish crown and the revolted colonies: Hillyar must remain neutral. Despite the threat to British shipping Hillyar's secret orders took priority over other considerations.[28]

As Hillyar headed south, Dixon, reasonably certain there were no more American warships on his station, shifted his attention to the remarkable advance of British commerce in the River Plate and the imminent arrival of almost 2 million Spanish dollars and £100,000 in cash. Recognising that his first priority was to carry the treasure safely through the North Atlantic Dixon adopted a radical solution. When the frigate *Nereus* reached Rio, Dixon turned her cargo over to *Montagu*, put Heywood in command and sent her home; a 74 was the ultimate strong box. The Admiralty did not send her back, leaving Dixon to fly his flag in a succession of small frigates.[29]

Information security at Rio left a lot to be desired; Dixon feared the secret mission had been widely discussed, not least by the troublesome, garrulous master of the *Isaac Todd*. This gave the American minister at Rio an opportunity to warn Porter via Valparaiso.[30] These fears were borne out: the new station chief at Buenos Aires, Captain William Bowles, intercepted several letters from Rio containing the details of the secret mission. It was common knowledge on the Argentine waterfront, and he feared that the Americans would get the news to Valparaiso.[31]

Bowles, in the small frigate HMS *Aquilon*, had been detached from the Baltic in late 1812, a theatre that had closed just as the American war increased demands elsewhere.[32] At Buenos Aires Bowles harvested the trans-Andean trade routes for intelligence on the American threat, as well as the larger issues of British trade and Chilean politics. All three were of fundamental concern in London. The Chilean ports had been opened to British traders by the newly independent government in 1811. This created significant opportunities for commerce just as Napoleon's Continental System threatened to undermine the economic basis of British power. The trade remained risky, the Spanish authorities in Peru were seizing British ships.

The value of British commerce to local merchants and the long naval arm of the British state meant that when Porter tried to sell some of his prizes at Valparaiso Bowles was able to block sales with a stiff protest from Buenos Aires. Moreover, the fall of the Carrera family from power in the autumn of 1813 shifted the political situation to favour Britain rather than the United States. The 'glorious' news of the defeat and capture of the *Chesapeake* made 'all Englishmen hold their heads very high, and the Americans lower their tone considerably'; American influence at Buenos Aires was 'much on the decline'. The distant resonance of Broke's action echoed across the River Plate, emphasising the remarkable resilience of British power. However, with the war in Spain coming to a close, and Napoleon beaten, moderate rebel leaders in Argentina and Chile looked to mend their relations with Madrid. The presence of a British warship only reinforced the point that the future independence of these states was, ultimately, in Britain's hands. All the British wanted, Bowles pointed out, was stability and liberal trade policies. In Chile

American diplomatic agent Joel Poinsett had endlessly preached the gospel of French success, and opposition to Britain. News from Europe steadily undermined his position.[33]

On 12 July, six days after leaving Rio, Hillyar copied his orders and instructions as sealed orders for the commanding officers of *Cherub* and *Racoon*, to be opened at a given rendezvous, or thrown overboard before capture. Two days later he gave the master of the *Isaac Todd* a series of rendezvous for wood and water that avoided contact with the South American mainland, Juan Fernandez, the Galapagos and Cocos Islands. While rounding Cape Horn the warships became separated from *Isaac Todd*, and in October, as he neared the Equator, Hillyar received intelligence that suggested she had been taken by the *Essex*. He detached *Racoon* to the Columbia River, took *Cherub* in company and headed out to sea to search for the American.[34] *Racoon* reached the Columbia on 30 November 1813 to find the North West Company had already secured the fort, by the commercial transaction discussed above.[35] Meanwhile Hillyar picked up Porter's trail, calling at Juan Fernandez Island, Valparaiso and the Galapagos Islands, without ever being able to fix his position.[36] Through the last months of 1813 Hillyar was acting alone. Bowles picked up what little intelligence could be had from Chile, but facts were scarce.[37] Dixon had standing orders to reinforce the Pacific squadron, but only in early 1814 did he have both enough ships and a suitable opportunity. When an outbound convoy from England stopped at Rio, Dixon placed the ships bound for Buenos Aires under the escort of the *Nereus* and *Tagus*, the latter proceeding to protect the Pacific whale fishery. The *Tagus* had provided Dixon with another frigate, taking the French *La Ceres* on 5 January. Dixon shifted his flag into the prize, freeing the *Nereus* for sea service.[38] He also relieved Bowles after his distinguished service at Buenos Aires.[39]

Captain Sir Philip Broke won undying fame by taking the USS *Chesapeake* in thirteen bloody minutes off Boston. Artist Samuel Lane has posed Broke with the captured American colours underfoot. Broke spent the first year of the war looking for Commodore John Rodgers and his massive frigate USS *President* (below, left), seeking revenge for Rodgers's unprovoked attack on the diminutive British sloop HMS *Little Belt* in 1811.

BRITISH VALOUR and

Britons Strike Home! When HMS *Shannon* took the USS *Chesapeake* an entire nation celebrated; once again heirs of Nelson ruled the waves. George Cruikshank's lively caricature manages to report the battle and reflect most British prejudices about Yankees.

OASTING or, Shannon versus Chesapeake.

American glory: The USS *Constitution* took two British frigates in
1812, HMS *Guerriere* (*below left*) and HMS *Java*. Despite American
rhetoric these were markedly unequal combats, a point amply made
in the British view of the second action (*below*).

The figureheads of *Shannon* and *Chesapeake* were given to Broke. While the British adorned their ships with classical figures, in this case (*left*) a female deity representing the River Shannon, the Americans sent their warships into battle with the stern republican symbolism of a fiddle head.

Pacific warriors: David Porter (*left*) and James Hillyar played cat and mouse across an ocean before their battle at Valaparaiso gave the British their second frigate victory.

The capture of the USS *President* by HMS *Endymion* ranks among the most notable single-ship combats of all time. The complex chase action demonstrated the seamanship and fighting skills of the two protagonists to perfection. This action brought the score in frigate battles to three each.

Commodore Stephen Decatur had been the heroic icon of the US Navy for a decade, but he went down to defeat off Sandy Hook, and fell in a duel with a fellow officer only half a decade later.

The last 1812 frigate: The USS *Constitution* under way. The British still use the name of her sister, the *President*, for a naval HQ in London. The guns (*below*) and ammunition (*below right*) of the old ship, including the dismantling projectiles that proved so effective.

Sent to the Americas with a dual commission as admiral and diplomat, Sir John Borlase Warren secured British command of the Atlantic, convoyed merchant shipping and launched the first coastal raids. Portrait by Captain Mark Oates.

The USS *Constitution*, flagship of the American version of 1812, dressed overall, and brought out to celebrate.

PORTER'S PACIFIC

After a rough passage round Cape Horn, *Essex* reached the Chilean port of Valparaiso on 15 March 1813. The ship and her captain received a warm welcome from the revolutionary regime, which Porter turned into food, water and naval stores. He was preparing for a campaign against the whaling trade. After an eight-day refit he headed north, taking a Peruvian-based Spanish privateer that had attacked American merchant

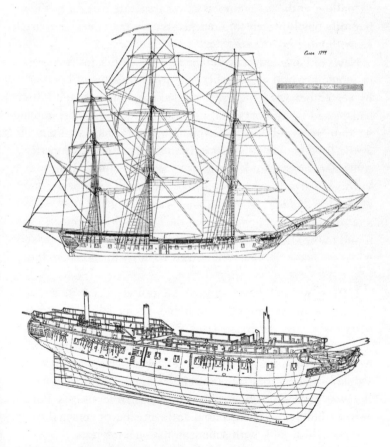

Pacific pioneer: Porter's ship, the USS *Essex*,
was built by Salem merchants.

ships, and recaptured an American whaler on his way to the Galapagos Islands. Once there he took twelve British whalers between 29 April and 18 September. These were easy successes; the powerful frigate was too quick and too strong for any resistance. The prizes provided stores and food, but water was short. To increase the spread of his depredations Porter armed two of his prizes as auxiliary raiders. Two old ships were returned to their captains, carrying the prisoners to Rio. Porter claimed that he inflicted damage worth $5 million, over £1 million at the contemporary exchange rate of $4.4 to the £, but only one captured ship reached the United States, the cartel *Essex Junior*, ex-*Atlantic*.

News of Porter's success reached Bowles at Buenos Aires early in September, and was quickly forwarded to Rio and London.[40] By September 1813 the *Essex* needed a major refit, and Porter had picked up rumours that a British squadron was searching for him. To avoid detection while refitting Porter based himself at the little-known Marquesas Islands, far from the American continent, or any trade routes. He reached Nuka Hiva on 25 October, warped *Essex* into the bay and began a major overhaul of the ship and her rigging. While his crew waged a brief war on a recalcitrant tribe, or sweated at their work Porter annexed the island to the United States, hoping the name of Madison's Island might persuade the Chief Magistrate to ratify the decision. It did not.

Having refitted *Essex*, buried an officer killed in a duel, and prepared his prizes to sail home, Porter fell victim to the besetting sin of American cruiser captains. Desperate for the personal glory of single combat he decided to 'signalise my cruise by something more splendid before leaving'. He sailed back to Valparaiso, expecting to encounter Captain Hillyar in HMS *Phoebe*. Enthralled by the prospect of heroic success Porter appeared oblivious to the fact that the pursuit of personal glory was entirely at odds with American national interests.

When Porter left Nuka Hiva on 13 December 1813 a small squadron of prizes, officers and men remained. Months later the American force collapsed in mutiny and conflict with local people; the last remnants were captured by the British in Hawaii, bringing David Porter's American empire to a chaotic end.

Essex arrived at Valparaiso, *Essex Junior* in company, on 12 January. His friends, the Carrera family, who had controlled Chile when he left nine months before, now languished in jail. A distracted, anxious nation, at war with itself, and facing a Spanish counter-attack, proved altogether less welcoming on his second visit.[41]

News of Porter's return soon reached Buenos Aires, and Bowles reported it to Rio and London, along with reports of the fall of the Carrera family. One rumour suggested that Porter would embark Joel Poinsett and American property before heading home, possibly calling at the River Plate to attack Bowles's ship. Should they succeed, it would 'produce a most prejudicial effect' on local opinion. James Hillyar picked up the rumour, but he gave it rather less credence; he had no intention of letting the *Essex* leave Valparaiso.[42]

CHILEAN STAND-OFF

On 3 February *Phoebe* sailed into Valparaiso, accompanied by the 18-gun ship-rigged sloop *Cherub*. Although originally sent to destroy the trade post at Astoria, Hillyar's mission had been modified at Rio, when Manley Dixon gave him additional force, and additional tasks including destroying the *Essex*. After detaching the ship sloop *Racoon* to Astoria, Hillyar anticipated Porter's next move. As befits a senior officer selected for a secret mission James Hillyar was careful, cautious and capable. He was also a fine seaman, and proven tactician. To make matters worse for Porter, Chile realised Britain offered more useful diplomatic support than America. Having found the enemy, Hillyar's primary duty lay in stopping the Americans putting to sea. He watched the *Essex* and waited. And when it came to waiting Hillyar possessed a major advantage over his aggressive, impetuous opponent.

Captain David Porter: hero of his own tale.

David Porter found sitting still and waiting a torment, one that did nothing to improve his mood, or his temper. Knowing that he had willingly sailed into such an obvious trap only made his situation worse. Waiting for Hillyar to make a mistake was depressingly tedious. The situation might have been different if American reinforcements had been sent to the Columbia River, as Astor wished.

While *Phoebe* was slightly larger than the *Essex*, her conventional battery of twenty-six long 18-pounders gave Hillyar a massive advantage at long range over *Essex*'s all-carronade armament. Porter knew this only too well, having complained vociferously, if ineffectively about the dangers of such a battery. Furthermore, *Phoebe* was a proven battle-winner, having already taken two French frigates, both larger than *Essex*. She had participated in the hard-fought Anglo-French actions off Mauritius in 1811 under Hillyar's command. To make matters worse *Cherub* was vastly superior to the armed whaler *Essex Junior*. Then there was the personal factor. Porter had met Hillyar years before in the Mediterranean, and knew he had little chance of outwitting him.

On his arrival Hillyar found a British commercial community anxious to provide intelligence on the American ship, and on local politics. The *Emily* put to sea to intercept the inbound frigate and her master, one-time naval officer George O'Brien, proved very useful, being well acquainted with the port. Mr Crompton and Andrew Bless kept Hillyar up to date with the fluctuating political situation ashore, along with observations on wind and weather, while seeking Hillyar's support for their commercial concerns.

Most commentators describe Porter's decision to sail for Valparaiso as a mixture of quixotic ambition and sheer folly. In reality he knew that four British ships were coming; he even knew their names. He concerted tactics with the commander of the *Essex Junior* for a two versus two combat, a duel between ships, assigning the prize the job of drawing off the smaller British ship. He planned to negate the disadvantage of his short-range battery by closing under a Spanish flag.[43] Yet, when Hillyar arrived, Porter, at that stage with many of his men ashore, allowed *Phoebe* to come into the harbour, run close alongside and anchor without firing a shot. For his part Hillyar, acting on the advice of George O'Brien, tried to provoke the American to fire first. However, while part of *Essex*'s crew had earlier been ashore they had returned by the time Hillyar came alongside. Porter held his fire, but missed a fleeting chance to get away. Porter claimed that *Phoebe* came very close and that, just as Hillyar enquired after his health, the two ships almost collided. Despite being in neutral waters Porter threatened to engage, calling up his crew and hoisting kedge anchors to the ends of the yards to grapple the enemy.[44] Recognising that *Essex* was fully manned and ready for combat Hillyar hauled off.

Porter's forbearance, if such it was, cost him his only chance of success. The following day the two ships engaged in a boisterous display of nationalistic pride. *Essex* hoisted a large white banner marked 'FREE TRADE AND SAILORS RIGHTS' to the fore topgallant masthead, just like James Lawrence. To counter this 'insidious effort to shake the loyalty of thoughtless British Seamen' *Phoebe* returned the compliment with a rather wordy riposte, sewn onto an English flag, 'God and Country, British Sailors Best Rights. Traitors Offend Both.' Then Hillyar played 'God Save the King' and the crew manned the rigging and gave three rousing cheers.[45] Later Porter paraded his men ashore with flags bearing well-worn American slogans. Hillyar reported that Porter's rather pathetic attempt at propaganda had no effect.

How far the men on board either ship were ready to die for abstract issues like Free Trade was, as Greg Dening has observed, open to question. The close-quarters loyalties that bind together messmates and ship's companies determine how men behave in battle. Camaraderie and exemplary leadership provide positive reasons to fight, but the depth and quality of training, the over-riding impact of drills and routines, and the recognition that any man who ran away would be seen and punished made sure most sailors remained at their posts. Kings and Countries, Republics and Rights were soon forgotten in the maelstrom of danger and death. Hillyar's very public use of the word 'Traitor' in his reply to Porter's squibs reminded the American crew that if they lost the British would be looking for deserters and other British subjects.[46] Such anxieties may explain why they remained at their posts even when fight was clearly lost.

The exchange of words and symbols between two anglophone crews was inevitable, while they were within hailing distance. Both crews had reason to be proud of their ships, and their service. Porter's attempt to engineer a duel through increasingly desperate, wordy challenges proved futile, because imputations of dishonour cut no ice with Hillyar. He had the enemy in a trap, leaving Porter the victim in a deadly game of cat and mouse, looking for a way out. Several times Porter had *Essex* get under way, as if to fight, only to recover his moorings. Taking advantage of the neutral harbour the two captains even met on shore. Hillyar secured the release of several British seamen, whom he promised would not serve on his ships, in exchange for the same number of Americans to be released from British custody. In the process he confirmed *Essex*'s all-carronade battery and the strength of her crew, but failed to ascertain Porter's intentions.

Having replenished his water and victuals and with *Essex* showing signs of moving, Hillyar took both British ships to sea on the 14th.[47] He feared Porter might exploit the neutrality of the port to have his ship detained for twenty-four hours after the Americans sailed.[48] Lying offshore, the British still received fresh beef and water while Hillyar watched and waited, cruising 4 to 5 miles from the *Essex*, normally anchored off the Point of Angels. On 25 February Porter towed the prize *Hector* to sea and burnt her, a very deliberate challenge. The Chilean governor was sufficiently annoyed by this violation of Chilean neutrality to let the British merchants know that his government might turn a blind eye if Hillyar finished the business in the harbour.[49] When, some time after the action, Porter began to complain about violations of neutrality Hillyar pointed to the burning of the prize, the fact that *Essex* fired two shots at *Phoebe* from inside the harbour two days later, and Porter's attempt to board his ship on 12 March to prove the American had been the first to violate Chilean hospitality. Mr Crompton had warned Hillyar about the boarding plan, another reason for the Chilean governor to be annoyed with Porter.[50] Midshipman David Farragut noted that Porter only gave up the attempt when he realised the British were expecting him.[51]

In accordance with contemporary practice Hillyar did not consider anywhere beyond the range of Chilean coastal guns to be neutral, while Porter did not show any intention of placing his trust in such questionable protection throughout the six-week stand-off. Both men were jockeying for advantage. On the evening of

27 February *Essex* and *Essex Junior* had slipped their cables and set sail. Having cleared for action and spoken to the crew, telling them to be 'steady and clear', Hillyar wore ship, denying Porter the opportunity of a close-range engagement. Porter responded by firing a signal gun for his consort, and two rounds at *Phoebe*, before tacking back into the port. Hillyar followed, but held his fire; the American rounds had been ineffective, and by the time he was within range the Americans were anchored under the Fort of the Angels. Porter did not mention this confrontation then or later, but his officers, including Midshipman Farragut did. They believed Porter had responded to a British challenge, in reality the accidental discharge of a gun while clearing for action, and criticised Hillyar for not engaging when *Essex* made sail.[52] On 9 March a letter, supposedly from *Essex*'s crew to their British counterparts, offered single-ship action, the Homeric fair and equal combat of Porter's dreams. While Porter claimed the letter was a response to offensive letters from the *Cherub*, Hillyar was unimpressed by such petty tomfoolery.

Porter's dreams of glory faded. *Essex* was blockaded by a superior force, and a skilful opponent, in a foreign port where most officials were decidedly pro-British. Unwilling to abandon his dreams, Porter hung on, hoping to lure Hillyar into a favourable situation. A seasoned professional with an excellent war record, Hillyar had no need to take risks. He had won glory enough already, and knew the road to flag rank and further employment lay in completing his mission. He must take, sink, burn, or otherwise destroy the USS *Essex*; with a superior force he had no business taking risks. The stalled career of John Carden of the *Macedonian* was ample warning that no one would thank him or any other British captain for another defeat. Porter's subsequent claim that *Essex*'s superiority in speed meant he could have escaped 'at almost any time' suggests the imaginative streak noted by several contemporaries was deep-rooted. If *Essex* was so superior it was Porter's duty to escape, and carry on the task set him by the Navy Secretary. The British found no evidence of superior speed.[53]

While Porter waited for a chance to fight, the noose was tightening around his neck. In March 1814 Dixon sent a third frigate to the South Pacific. The Admiralty detached HMS *Briton* from the Channel on 31 December 1813 specifically for the Pacific. At Rio Dixon directed Captain Sir Thomas Staines to make all speed to Valparaiso, where *Essex* had been reported. He would get more recent intelligence from Bowles, whom he might encounter heading north from Buenos Aires, or from Hillyar returning around the Cape. Dixon also advised Staines that the three American 44s would put to sea in December, and one of them would try to link up with Porter. The Foreign Office informed Staines that a restored Madrid government had ordered local ports to admit British cruisers.[54]

After a month of cat and mouse Porter finally recognised that the only certainties were that Hillyar was not going to waste his decisive advantage, and more British ships would arrive. His sources confirmed that they were the 18-pounder frigates *Tagus* and *Briton*, both larger than his ship. Once Hillyar had two frigates, let alone three, Porter could expect an attack. He had to escape, and soon. Hillyar was equally focused, spending every night under sail only 3 miles to seaward of the Point of Angels, constantly looking for any sign that the enemy was moving. The British merchant community, desperate to resume profitable trade, warned Hillyar that Porter was planning to move on 23 March. It is unlikely Hillyar needed prompting.

Porter was preparing a collection of tricks to mislead his opponent. He began by sending his purser ashore to conduct further business on the 27th, ensuring this was reported to Hillyar. He hoped the British would lower their guard. Then on the night of 27/28 March Porter sent Lieutenant Maury out to sea in a boat, loosing off rockets and burning blue lights to draw *Phoebe* to leeward, clearing the way for *Essex* to escape at daybreak. Maury carried out his mission. Hillyar shortened sail to investigate the lights off to the north-east; finding no ship he 'supposed the signal made by Enemy's boats was a Decoy'. Having spoken to *Cherub*, he resumed station, dead to windward of the

Essex's anchorage, a test of seamanship that required constant adjustment to the shifts and flaws of the seasonal weather.

At daybreak Hillyar could see the *Essex* at anchor. He may not have realised just how disappointed Porter was to see *Phoebe* and *Cherub* 'close to the weather point of the Bay'. He had expected them to be off to leeward, giving him a chance to escape. Hillyar wore inside the point, then wore out again, reminding the Americans that they were being closely watched by well-manned and well-handled ships. As the wind strengthened from the SSW Porter struck his royal masts and yards at 2.45 p.m. Soon after one of the *Essex*'s cables parted, Porter ordered a boat across from *Essex Junior* to take Joel Poinsett ashore while the other cable held. Once Poinsett was over the side Porter cut the cable and made a run for the sea. Hillyar responded immediately, closing to cut off Porter's escape past the Point of Angels. Then *Essex* was hit by a heavy squall, which carried away the main topmast at the lower cap. Two topmen, Samuel Miller and Thomas Browne, were thrown into the sea with the wreckage and lost.

Hillyar observed the Americans putting to sea at 3.10, set his mainsail and bore up in chase with *Cherub* in company. Both ships again hoisted a St George's flag emblazoned with the motto 'God and Country. British Sailors Best Rights. Traitors Offend Both'. As *Essex* attempted to round the point, to weather on the British ships, Hillyar saw the main topmast fall and Porter's change of course. The damage ended Porter's fleeting hope of escape: without the main topmast and yards *Essex* could not out-run her opponent, and Porter had no chance to make repairs. He wore the ship onto the starboard tack, cleared the wreckage and cut away the mainsail and main topsail, which were flying out of control. The sacrifice of canvas was essential; flapping sheets would hamper his attempt to work back into Valparaiso Bay. Judging that his crippled ship would be unable to fetch her old anchorage inside Point of Angels, Porter bore up for a small bay on the other side of the harbour, 5 to 6 miles from the town, and at least 2 miles from the nearest Chilean fort (Castello jel Barren). The fort was not in sight of the ship.

At 3.45 (4.00 on *Phoebe*) *Essex* dropped her spare anchor in the Bay, in 9½ fathoms about 25 yards from the shore. Porter had two ensigns aloft, on the fore and mizzen tops: 'FREE TRADE AND SAILORS RIGHTS' and 'GOD OUR COUNTRY AND LIBERTY. TYRANTS OFFEND THEM'. Hillyar had time to note the mottos; he was in no hurry. With *Essex* crippled there was no need to run any risks. He considered that the enemy lay outside the limits of the port, and was therefore in international waters. At 4.10 he signalled *Cherub* to prepare to fight at anchor, roving additional cables to the anchors, so the ship could be veered round to bring the broadside to bear. This was sound practice. While the crew were working to deploy the cables and springs George O'Brien joined one of *Phoebe*'s boats ashore and pushed for the ship. A second merchant ship master, Mr Murphy of the brig *Good Friends*, also boarded *Phoebe*. This was no ordinary gesture; the sea was running high, and both boats were nearly swamped. Suitably reinforced *Phoebe* was ready to fight.

The initiative was now entirely with the British. They could sail and manoeuvre and *Phoebe* had a long-range main battery, and a more powerful second ship in support. To fail now would be abject, and unlikely. Hillyar headed into the bay, intent on bringing his ship up close under the American stern, the killing position. He may have intended completing the destruction of the American ship's rigging. Instead the squally weather pushed *Phoebe* further off, denying Hillyar his preferred station. He began the battle at 4.20 (3.55 on *Essex*) at half gunshot, about 250 yards, while still under way. *Phoebe* opened with both long guns and carronades on *Essex*'s stern and starboard quarter. *Cherub* fired on *Essex*'s starboard bow, until heavy, accurate return fire from the 12-pounders on *Essex*'s forecastle persuaded a badly wounded Commander Tucker to shift his berth alongside the *Phoebe*. Despite his wounds, Tucker remained on deck throughout the action. Desperate to bring his broadside guns to bear on his tormentors Porter twice managed to get a spring rove onto his anchor cable, but each time it was shot away before it could be used. While he later downplayed the role of his 32-pounder carronades they proved very effective during this phase of the battle. Damaging hits from these heavy projectiles persuaded Hillyar to open the range, and change his tactics. During the initial exchange *Phoebe*'s popular and capable first lieutenant, William Ingram, was mortally wounded by splinters at his post alongside the captain. At 4.40 Hillyar ceased firing, wore round and pulled off the shore, which was very close, and came to on the larboard tack. He had not observed his fire produce any effect on *Essex*. By contrast Porter could see that *Essex*'s shooting, primarily from the 12-pounder cannon in the stern, had been accurate and effective. They had fired into *Phoebe*'s rigging, and by the time Hillyar hauled off his topsails were flying loose, the mainsail was much cut up, the jib-boom damaged and the fore, main and mizzen stays shot away. Once out of range *Phoebe*'s crew quickly mended the rigging and furled the mainsail. Porter's men took the opportunity to reeve a third spring on their cable.

Before renewing the battle Hillyar hailed Tucker, advising him that, while *Phoebe* would fight at anchor, *Cherub* should keep under way and fire as occasion allowed. At 5.35 *Phoebe* closed in again, engaging with her bow chasers, and receiving a steady return from *Essex*. By now the wind had fallen away, occasionally to a dead calm. Once again Hillyar carefully chose his position, off *Essex*'s starboard quarter, where neither broadside nor stern guns would bear. This time he held a longer range, a little under half a mile, close enough to hit the *Essex* with almost every round from his long 18-pounders, but too far for the American carronades to be effective. He had yet to reach the position where he planned to anchor when the wind shifted to the landward. Porter seized one last, desperate chance to level the playing field, setting every remaining sail and cutting his cable, hoping to run alongside the *Phoebe* and board. At 5.50 Hillyar observed *Essex* cut her cable and set the jib, foresail and fore topsail. While the moving target made it difficult to keep *Phoebe*'s broadside bearing, Porter's last gambit failed. Once again the wind played him false, dying away even as he cut the cable. It had always been a forlorn hope. Hillyar had a major advantage in manoeuvrability. *Essex*'s rigging had been shredded, leaving Porter with little control over the ship once under way. Now calm accurate fire from the British 18-pounders turned the action into a carefully controlled demolition job. *Essex* could only reply with three 12-pounders, their crews repeatedly scythed down by shot and splinters.

Throughout the action Hillyar targeted the American upper deck and standing rigging. After the battle Bosun Edward Linscott reported that *Phoebe*'s fire had cut away large portions of *Essex*'s standing and running rigging at the level of the chain plates and dead eyes.[55] This was very good shooting. Having disabled the enemy, Hillyar could edge away, keeping his distance and pounding the shattered *Essex*. The consequences were catastrophic. *Essex*'s sailing master admitted, 'we were now in a most dreadful situation as the enemy hull'd us every shot, and our brave fellows falling in every direction'. The American carpenter's crew, desperately trying to plug shot holes and keep the ship in the battle, were wiped out. Hillyar could see his guns 'gradually becoming more destructive', his crew, 'if possible more animated'. The British guns were well laid; many of Porter's guns had been disabled, and his gunners killed. The explosion of a small pile of powder charges near *Essex*'s main hatchway caused the morale of the shattered crew to falter, the inevitable consequence of the devastating loss of life and limb that turned the ship into a slaughter house.

Always ready with an outsize gesture Porter, like James Lawrence before him, wanted to destroy the ship rather than surrender. He ordered *Essex* run ashore and blown up. Once again the wind let him down, and with many men too badly wounded to abandon ship he had no option but surrender. Even so, he encouraged the able-bodied to abandon ship; sixty or seventy Americans took the opportunity to head for the shore, most by boat. Some drowned, others were rescued from the sea by British boats, and about forty escaped. There must be a suspicion that some of these men were British. *Essex*'s flag came down at 6.00 p.m. by the *Phoebe*'s timepiece, 6.20 in Hillyar's version, and 6.30 according to *Essex*'s sailing master; either this last clock had gained several minutes, or the Master unilaterally extended the duration of the battle to emphasise that the 'resistance had been worthy of the cause'. Such was the chaos and confusion in the American rigging, and the profusion of flags and banners that Porter had hoisted that it took the British ten minutes to realise the colours had been lowered.[56] Once the point had been confirmed Hillyar sent a boat to take possession of his prize, and secure her papers.

Essex's upper deck was a chaotic shambles of broken bodies and detached limbs. Overwrought by his exertions, largely a question of occupying his proper station beside the wheel, to show the men that he was not afraid, traumatised by the casualties, and humiliated by defeat, Porter openly wept as he boarded *Phoebe* to offer the victor his sword. Magnanimous in victory, Hillyar refused the customary gesture. The next morning the captains breakfasted together. By this time Porter had recovered his composure, debating the time the battle began, and the number of men who had swum ashore after the fighting stopped. The civilities of war were resumed.

Porter's account of the decision to surrender composed three months later takes longer to read than he took to make up his mind. It conveys the impression that only an endless succession of misfortunes prevented him from capturing a nervous, effectively beaten enemy. Such statements as 'her capture was owing entirely to accident' required remarkable self-deception, while the accompanying smokescreen of imputations of dishonourable conduct, illegal action and inhumanity cast at James Hillyar reveal a growing anxiety that the court of inquiry might not be satisfied by his explanation of how he came to lose the United States Ship *Essex*. Blaming Paul Hamilton for his all-carronade armament may have been warranted, but much of the rest smacked of special pleading. 'I hope, Sir,' he begged Navy Secretary Jones, 'that our conduct may prove satisfactory to our country.' Having defamed Hillyar throughout his essay Porter then switched tack, trying to ameliorate the abuse by praising his conduct after the battle, before complaining the British had plundered personal property. Praise for the elevated behaviour of his own service read uneasily coming from the pen of an officer who allowed his men to tar and feather foreign sailors. Porter's exculpatory essay ended with a confused section alleging that the American government had a right to claim the restoration of the ship.[57] Curiously these deluded, self-justificatory ramblings have become the basic version of the six-week stand-off and sanguinary combat at Valparaiso.

In marked contrast to Porter's self-serving sour grapes James Hillyar proved a gracious victor, praising the performance of the *Essex* which, 'taking into consideration our superiority of force; the very discouraging circumstances of her having lost her Main Topmast; and being twice on fire, did honour to her brave defenders'. Porter, he stressed, had only struck his colours when heavy casualties and damage to his ship made further resistance futile. As he was entitled to head money for every American sailor he was less than pleased by Porter's decision to urge his men overboard, claiming these men were, in honour, his prisoners. When Porter argued that the men only abandoned ship after the cartridge fire Hillyar dropped the issue. He had to be content with Porter's claim that over 260 men were on board when the battle began, because none of the ship's books or papers survived. He had more luck with the impressive American chart collection.

Attributing success to God, Hillyar praised his officers and men, and echoed Tucker's commendation of *Cherub*'s people, listing those promoted into death vacancies or recommended to their Lordships' attention. Finally he suggested that George O'Brien might be restored to the Navy List.[58]

While the *Phoebe* lost 4 killed and 7 wounded, and *Cherub* 1 and 3 respectively, *Essex* suffered 60 per cent casualties, 58 dead and 65 wounded. At least the butcher's bill proved that David Porter was not James Barron. Both ships were damaged, but perfectly seaworthy.

Porter had directed his fire into the rigging, hoping to cripple the *Phoebe* and escape. Despite their disadvantages the American gunners had fired well, leaving *Phoebe*'s main and mizzen masts:

... rather seriously wounded, – these with a few shot holes between wind and water, which we can get at without lightening [the ship]; and a loss of canvas and cordage, which we can partly replace from our well stored prize; are the extent of the injuries.

Hillyar found the *Essex* fully stored for a six-month cruise, and 'although much injured in her upper works, masts and rigging, is not in such a state as to give the slightest cause of alarm respecting her being able to perform a voyage to Europe with perfect safety'. *Essex* had been hit over 200 times, her stern smashed in, and a hole driven in the counter, the wheel and rudder damaged, all three masts had been hit, the figurehead shot away and the upper works heavily damaged. *Phoebe*'s gunnery had rendered the American ship incapable of further resistance. The guns and gun crews on the larboard side had been devastated, 15 guns disabled, 55 gun crew dead, and 60 wounded.[59] *Essex*'s men paid a terrible price for their captain's obdurate refusal to risk his honour. By a curiosity Porter remained entirely unharmed amid the slaughter. The human cost of battle would be embellished and turned into glorious rhetoric over years: men who fought and died in battle were made to issue grammatically perfect patriotic effusions when they lost limbs. Nowhere was a moan or an expletive allowed to spoil the carefully contrived illusion of willing sacrifice and elegant death.[60]

Throughout the battle *Essex Junior* remained a motionless spectator. Porter must have expected her to draw off the *Cherub*, but even this proved to be beyond the small ship and her tiny crew. Captain Downes of the *Essex Junior* finally boarded *Essex* to ascertain Porter's wishes just as he surrendered.

The day after the battle Hillyar moved the two captured ships into the main anchorage at Valparaiso, embarking forty-six American prisoners on the *Phoebe*. That afternoon they were transferred to a Spanish prison hulk in the harbour. On 2 April Hillyar repaired the shot holes below *Phoebe*'s waterline, heeling the frigate over by moving her guns. On the 13th HMS *Tagus* arrived. On the 26th the British moved their prisoners to the *Essex Junior*, under a cartel agreement, and she sailed the following day. Hillyar followed up his victory by helping to reconcile the Peruvian and Chilean governments, a process rendered more pressing by the growing realisation that the European war was over, and Spanish power might be restored. The Treaty of Lircay proved a useful, if strikingly short-term success, restoring good conditions for British trade.[61] On 21 May HMS *Briton* arrived at Valparaiso and ten days later *Phoebe* sailed for home.[62] There would be no more American operations in the Pacific during the war, leaving the British to police local conflicts, and control their expanding markets.

News of the battle may have reached Buenos Aires as early as 20 March, and Rio on 19 May. Hillyar's despatches, which passed over the Andes, were in Dixon's hands by 20 June. The Admiral praised the 'watchfulness' of the blockade' and the 'small loss . . . compared with the enemy'.[63] Dixon also confirmed the Treaty of Lircay.[64] He ordered Staines to keep *Briton* and *Tagus* in the South Pacific, along with *Cherub*, to protect British whalers from American or Peruvian privateers.[65] The American privateer *Joel Barlow* had been taken by *Briton* on 3 July, completing the rout of American cruisers in Pacific waters.[66] In November Dixon sent HMS *Indefatigable*, Captain John Fyffe, to relive one of Staines's frigates.[67] Soon afterwards HMS *Racoon* arrived at Rio to report her proceedings at Astoria.[68]

Manley Dixon found himself operating at a great distance from the scene of the action, and the Admiralty in London. The Board frequently questioned his judgement, and evinced remarkably little sympathy with the man on the spot. The issues were the same that had troubled Warren, specie, convoys, rotations and promotions. In mid-1813 Dixon was heavily criticised for sending £16,000 of specie in a small schooner, and the commander of another small vessel was required to explain why he had left this convoy at sea, instead of bringing it safely into San Salvador. In this case the Board had a point: as a result of this neglect the merchant ship *Caroline* had been attacked by the American privateer *Comet*.[69] By contrast Captain Tucker of the *Cherub* earned a commendation for using no corporal punishment in the last quarter of 1812.[70] News that Hillyar had been reinforced prompted the question why *Cherub* and *Raccoon* had not been sent sooner, as ordered, to protect the whale fishery.[71] The Board grudgingly approved Dixon's additional orders to Hillyar in October 1813.[72]

The Admiralty finally learnt of Hillyar's success in August 1814.[73] That did not stop them criticising Dixon's decision to purchase and commission the prize, stripping out men from other ships to form a crew, 'particularly as the present enemy has frequently appeared on the Station under your command' and very pointedly refused to confirm the appointment of his flag lieutenant as captain.[74] This was a serious rebuke, calling into question an admiral's authority. Dixon was also criticised for sending *Nereus* with specie when *Phoebe* and *Essex* were also heading home. Once again the imputation was that Dixon rewarded his protégés, in this case his son, at the expense of operational efficiency.[75] Dixon would have been pleased, though, by confirmation that *Phoebe* was acting under his orders when she took the *Essex*, securing a flag share of the prize money.[76]

The *Essex* was quickly refitted and went home as a prize with her captor. The two ships reached Spithead on 13 November, complete with a useful freight of much needed specie. Hillyar, rightly rewarded for his skilful handling of a difficult situation, enjoyed a long career. Initially the British spirit of fair play led many to downplay *Phoebe*'s success, lauding the courage of Porter and his men. Exposure to Porter's self-serving recriminations and exculpatory apologia changed the mood with striking swiftness. His obsessive attempt to prove British bad faith and unfair conduct led most analysts to wish it had been a single-ship action, perfectly satisfied that the result would have been the same. It is hard to disagree. James Hillyar was older, wiser and far more experienced. He had a better ship, longer reach, and no reason to take risks.

By contrast American accounts traded in hyperbole, a currency that reflected the desperate need for good news, even in defeat. Republican journalists printed Porter's words, his every carping complaint adopted and embellished. They transformed Hillyar's considered tactical decision to keep at 'a respectful sneaking distance', making the tactics used by the American 44s in 1812 into a question of personal honour. It is doubtful if any moderately intelligent reader treated such dross as news or comment. However, Porter had coined enough excuses to equip his promoters for an entire season. James Madison even referred to the *Essex* in the 1814 Presidential Message to Congress, claiming her 'loss is hidden in the blaze of heroism with which she was defended'. Little wonder Federalist commentators begged to differ. In *Essex*'s home town the *Salem Gazette* of 19 July went straight to the heart of the problem. A savage lampoon contrasted Porter's prolix, self-serving apologia with Oliver Hazard Perry's nine-word report of his success at Lake Erie.[77]

While the capture of the *Essex* restored British control in the Pacific Hillyar remained anxious to complete his mission. He wanted to get the American sailors out of the Pacific as soon as possible. Unable to refer back to Dixon at Rio, he had *Essex Junior* disarmed and turned into a cartel to exchange the American crew. One hundred and thirty-two officers and men were sent home. Other men, too badly wounded to travel, were provided for at Valparaiso.[78] *Essex Junior* arrived off New York on 8 July 1814, after a voyage of seventy-one days, only to be stopped by the razee HMS *Saturn*. After the boarding officer had checked the ship's papers and returned to his own ship it appears that a member of the boarding party reported that he suspected British a deserter was on the cartel. The British boarded again and the man in question turned out to be an old shipmate of a British sailor, but not a British subject. Porter took the opportunity to make a grandstanding escape by boat, only for the British to allow the ship to pass. In the event the Americans were in more danger from their own nervous coastal batteries, which opened fire as *Essex Junior* approached New York. Porter must have been relieved to receive a hero's welcome. Secretary Jones conveniently bought the *Essex Junior* for $25,000 to provide him with a pecuniary reward.[79] America needed a new hero: the news of the war had been almost entirely bad since Porter had rounded Cape Horn eighteen months before. The seemingly limitless ocean across which American warships had ranged with relative freedom in 1812 was now constrained and controlled by British convoys, blockades, and patrols at key landfalls and rendezvous.

The delusional turn of Porter's mind found further employment at home. Publicly lauded by the press, which accepted his version of events without demur, and in public ovations, dinners and other celebrations, he tried to rewrite his defeat. In Secretary Jones's words Porter and his crew had arrived, 'in triumph though captives'. Such nonsense was a desperate reaction to the parlous news coming in from all other quarters. The Navy had lost its 1812 lustre, and in desperate times even a brave defeat became worthy of note.

For all the public hoorays Porter needed a naval enquiry to acquit him formally of blame for the loss of the ship, and he was far from certain that his conduct warranted such a judgment. Fortunately Secretary Jones was not minded to complain. He ordered Stephen Decatur to convene a court on board the *President*, but suspended proceedings eight days later, before they had begun. This released both captain and crew to travel south to defend Washington. At the same time the American government conveniently decided that the terms of Porter's parole had been violated by the *Saturn*, leaving captain and crew free to serve.[80] The British never accepted this argument. Alexander Cochrane was furious; he wanted to keep this dangerous officer under control.[81] The court of enquiry was never reconvened. Some argued that the lack of formal closure explained why Porter chose to publish an account of the voyage, in effect putting his case before the public.[82] There was certainly a strong strain of ex-post-facto self-justification in his text, reinforced by the 1822 edition which included further 'evidence' of British illegality and dishonour.[83] Although little more than a smokescreen of sour grapes these claims have exercised historians for too long. In truth they matter little. Chile was in no position to enforce respect of her flag, even in her main harbour; both sides were happy to breach the paper restrictions of a neutral port when it suited them. Porter's real complaint was that he lost the battle. The legal issues would have passed without a word had he won.

The Navy rewarded Porter for losing his ship by renaming the new 44-gun frigate building at the Washington Navy Yard *Essex*, and assigning him to command. The incomplete ship was burnt when the British reached the outskirts of the city, which may explain his less than creditable intervention in the operations at Alexandria a week later. Even his biographer rates the attempt to kidnap a British midshipman as 'little short of lunatic'.[84] After that Porter built a battery that failed to stop the British escaping down the Potomac with their prizes, before commanding a regiment of sailors and marines at Baltimore. In October he was assigned to command Fulton's steam battery, imagining a glorious future for the new ship, but pending her completion tried to raise a flotilla of raiding schooners. Once again he would be disappointed; the war ended before he got to sea.

While he waited at New York Porter, assisted by his old friend Washington Irving, marshalled a powerful literary defence. Porter effectively declared himself a hero, repeating the claims made in his letter of 8 July 1814 that he had devastated the British whale fishery, inflicted $2.5 million in damage and cost the British $6 million to counter his cruise, redeploying ships and men that could have been used to attack the United States. In truth the returns from his cruise were negligible: only one prize made it back to the United States. The first three British warships that rounded Cape Horn in pursuit of the *Essex* had all been assigned to that station anyway, making the *Tagus* and *Briton* the only real 'diversions'.[85] The British had ample reason to reinforce their squadron on the west coast of South America, to protect their trade in the chaotic conditions caused by the Spanish–American revolutionary wars. Yet Porter's version of the cruise of the *Essex* became a central pillar in the mythology of commerce-raiding, an antecedent of the *Alabama*, the *Emden* and the *Atlantis*. In fact all four ships were hunted down and destroyed by a dominant sea power; they did not challenge the ability of the British to use the ocean. The cruise of the *Essex* proved the soundness of Secretary Jones's order to avoid fighting enemy warships.[86] Porter had no business sailing to Valparaiso: his mission was to destroy British commerce. Hillyar's task was to stop him and Porter made his job all too easy.[87]

After the war British writers, led by William James, took a studied and considered revenge on Porter, lambasting his honour and integrity, while affecting to be outraged by the salacious tales of promiscuous liaisons with the native girls of the Marquesas Islands.[88] Even in defeat David Porter had a unique facility for making enemies, and he would acquire many more at home after 1815. He was not quite a gentleman, in victory or defeat.

CHAPTER 9

Burning the White House: Punishing the Republicans

The New Year began with a change of command. Facing pressure from the West India Committee, and increasingly annoyed by Warren's litany of complaints, Melville had decided to dispense with his services. His adept political mind quickly conceived a neat device to explain the decision. He simply adopted Warren's suggestion to re-divide the unified command, thereby ending the need for an officer of his seniority.[1] The real purpose became clear from Melville's choice of a new commander for the North American Station. Scots aristocrat Vice Admiral Sir Alexander Cochrane had fought in the War of Independence, losing a much-loved brother at Yorktown, and acquired considerable combat experience, notably directing amphibious operations at Alexandria in 1801, and Martinique and Guadeloupe in 1809 and 1810. He had volunteered for the American command in 1812, but the desire to avoid war made Warren the better choice then. As governor of Guadeloupe since 1810 Cochrane was better attuned to West Indies interests than Warren. He retained the governorship until November 1814, and the considerable salary.[2] Local knowledge was useful, but his key recommendation was a deep, intimate engagement with Melville's Scots patronage network, the constellation of naval and Indian contacts that gave him control of Scottish votes and secured his place in Lord Liverpool's government.[3]

The political relationship between Melville and the Cochranes worked both ways. While Melville controlled the levers of patronage, he needed Cochrane votes. In late 1812 he desperately needed Sir Alexander's son Captain Thomas Cochrane to vote in

Edinburgh. After a lengthy correspondence Thomas Cochrane used his vote in return for a promise that he would not be given an undesirable deployment, making nonsense of Melville's protestations to act in the interests of the service.[4]

Melville knew Alexander Cochrane to be dependable, biddable, and politically reliable. Unfortunately these synergistic factors, which promoted the smooth functioning of a long-distance civil–military relationship, could not compensate for Cochrane's limited abilities and awkward relations with other senior officers, or a marked enthusiasm for his own financial interests. Sir Richard Keats would have been a far better choice: he had worked closely with other Nelson protégés like Cockburn, Hotham and Hardy, the best subordinate commanders on the station, and excelled in every type of naval operation. Melville sent him to the backwater posting at Newfoundland.

On 27 December 1813 Cochrane was appointed Commander-in-Chief on the Coast of North America.[5] He received copies of Warren's correspondence to read himself into the command on the voyage to Bermuda.[6] He was advised not to issue any trade licences, although he should respect those still in force.[7] With amphibious operations a priority Cochrane selected his brilliant, maverick nephew, radical MP Captain Lord Cochrane, to command his 80-gun flagship HMS *Tonnant*. However, the Admiralty suspended Lord Cochrane from command on 14 March: he had been imprisoned in the Tower of London charged with Stock Market fraud.[8] This must have delighted John Wilson Croker, Admiralty spokesman in the House of Commons, for so long the target of Cochrane's partisan attacks. Sir Alexander had better luck with another nominee: Major Edward Nicholls commanded *Tonnant*'s Royal Marines and played a key role in Gulf Coast strategy, collaborating with the Creek Indians.[9]

To direct a war being waged on the American littoral Cochrane requested specialist survey officers, extra chronometers, a portable printing press, paper and a copying machine. He wanted two surveyors, 'one for the coast south of Rhode Island and the other to correct the numerous errors to be found in the Charts'.

Hydrographer of the Navy Captain Thomas Hurd urged the Board to provide the instruments and another surveyor.[10] As the American coast was not well charted, especially south of New England, it made sense to improve the charts while the coast was under British control, both to assist current operations, and secure intelligence for future wars. The Admiralty finally allowed Cochrane a new Boulton & Watt rolling copying machine in October.[11]

Cochrane was not the only officer to benefit from Melville's patronage. The system was open to abuse. On passage across the Atlantic new captain of the fleet Sir Edward Codrington reflected on recent losses,[12] attributing much of the American success to the selection of substandard officers. He thought that the favouritism and political influence, evident in the relationship between Melville and Cochrane, meant that officers were employed and promoted who ought to be 'dismissed the service'.[13] Fortunately most of Melville's appointments combined political value with professional merit.

CHANGING COMMANDS

As if to prove that he could make good appointments Melville sent Rear Admirals William Brown and Philip Durham, two excellent flag officers, to command the newly independent Jamaica and Leeward Islands stations.[14] They would be given a suitable force, and held responsible for the security of shipping on their stations. Durham was a particular favourite, being a Melville candidate at the last elections in 1812. A superb seamen and skilled operational commander, Durham had been appointed in November 1813. While heading out to his station in January 1814 he picked up intelligence that two French frigates were nearby off Madeira, quickly worked out where they would be and hunted them down in his 74 HMS *Venerable*. The new frigates *Alcmène* and *Iphigénie* had already taken two British merchant ships and attacked a sloop. Durham brought the prizes into Carlisle Bay, Barbados, in triumph, heralding a fresh start for a station depressed by Francis Laforey's despondent sloth. To address the endemic shortage of men Durham moved most of the flagship's crew into additional cruisers, replacing them with locally raised black sailors. Efficiency and profit were Durham's twin watch-words. In little more than nine months he cleared the station of American privateers, taking eighty-four and making a lot of money in the process. Local commercial interests were delighted, complaints were replaced by praise.[15] After William Brown's sudden death from yellow fever in September 1814 Durham shouldered the additional burden of the Jamaica station.

The change of command allowed Henry Hotham to give up the thankless task of captain of the fleet.[16] Rather than recall such a talented officer, wasting his hard-won expertise, the Admiralty offered him a junior command.[17] When his replacement, Captain Sir Edward Codrington, another outstanding officer, joined the flagship at Bermuda in mid-July,[18] Hotham left to command the New York blockade.

Despite the infusion of fresh ships and the ties of political sympathy linking London and the flagship, Cochrane remained dangerously short of seamen. In April 1814 the European war ended, and the Admiralty began to demobilise.[19] While they sent out extra seamen they also began to draw down his fleet.[20] By October Cochrane was echoing Warren's lament about the 'great deficiency' of men, and his inability to replace casualties. Having sent 1,100 extra men and boys to his squadron in 1814 the Board was distinctly unsympathetic.[21]

BUSINESS AS USUAL

The change of command did not affect the basic architecture of the blockade. Cochrane arrived at Bermuda on 6 March to discover that Robert Barrie had kept the Americans busy around the Chesapeake through the winter, taking numerous vessels, going ashore almost at will, acquiring stores, intelligence and runaway slaves. Inbound neutral ships were turned away.[22] He also kept the *Constellation*, the only American warship in the bay, tightly blockaded. Warren's plan to occupy Tangier Island was put into effect when Cockburn returned to the Bay in spring. He built a depot, watering station and camp for the runaways from captured American lumber. Cochrane's proclamation inviting all those who wished to leave the United States provided manpower to build the Tangier Island depot, and create a force of Colonial Marines. This was astute. The sight of black men in red jackets advancing inland terrified tidewater planters: they feared their own slaves far more than the British. While many properties were abandoned other landowners entered into illicit supply arrangements with the British. Cockburn kept the Bay in turmoil, exploiting the superior mobility of amphibious forces, and the superior fighting power of his Marines and seamen to overwhelm local militias, raiding towns and depots where military stores had been collected.[23] Cockburn's skilful use of intelligence to destroy American military stores, confound local defences and take privateers left junior officers awe-struck by his energy and acumen. Even American historians cannot avoid a degree of admiration.[24]

Further north British officers followed Cockburn's example; the imminent extension of the economic blockade provided ample encouragement to raid inshore. Relying on local intelligence sources Thomas Bladen Capel, commanding off New London, sent a major raid up the Connecticut River on the night of 7/8 April. His men destroyed twenty ships afloat and on the stocks, including three privateers, totalling an estimated 5,000 tons.[25] The Admiralty not only approved the operation but paid a $2,000 'allowance' to the American citizen who piloted the attack upriver.[26] It was hardly coincidental that Decatur's squadron on the nearby Thames River was paid off a week later.[27] The British had absolute control of the coast between New York and Boston, denying the seas to all but the most audacious, or lucky, American ships.

WAR ON THE FRONTIER

On 30 March 1814 Madison's Cabinet had abandoned the trade ban, the last element of their failed economic strategy. It was a telling reflection on American information security that Cochrane heard the news in Bermuda before the measure became law.[28] He also noticed the Congressional committee report that increased imports into New England would be the main source of revenue to fund the war. It was high time the blockade was extended north.[29] On 25 April Cochrane placed the entire coast up to the Canadian border under economic blockade. To stop the last remnants of American trade the British notified the neutral powers of newly peaceful Europe of the extended economic blockade on 31 May. Unwilling to send a large, costly army, the British pushed their preferred strategy of economic coercion to the limit because it was cheap, effective, and consistent with their way of waging war.

The lack of British troops in Canada gave the Americans one last chance to win. In 1814 their only hope for success lay in another attempt to conquer Canada. While the administration mustered some 27,000 regular troops across the country, and a substantial militia, to face a mere 12,000 British troops in Canada their strategy was ruined by quarrelling commanders. During the spring the Niagara army was drilled into an effective force. Expecting Commodore Chauncey on Lake Ontario would support him, and without waiting for Chauncey's reply General Jacob Brown crossed the frontier on 1 July. He captured Fort Erie on the 3rd and defeated the British at Chippawa on the 5th. However, Chauncey had no intention of subordinating his campaign to the Army, and had no orders to support Brown. Believing control of the lake was critical he considered the British fleet his true objective. Without naval support, Brown fell back, and his army was badly mauled by Lieutenant General Gordon Drummond's troops at Lundy's Lane on 25 July. With Brown and Winfield Scott, one of his principal lieutenants, badly wounded, the American offensive on the Niagara front stalled

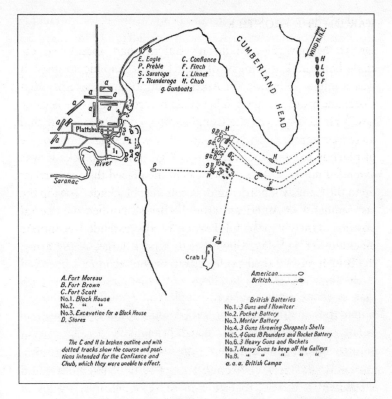

Decision on fresh water: the battle of Lake Champlain,
11 September 1814.

for the rest of war. The failure of the campaign reflected the lack of a clear command chain, and poor inter-service co-ordination. The one redeeming feature was the improved performance of the American army.

Further problems were created when much of General George Izard's army was moved from Lake Champlain to Lake Ontario, leaving the major north–south route into America wide open. The Americans were saved by the ignominious debacle that overtook the largest British land operation of the war. General Prevost, the cautious Governor of Lower Canada, had been ordered to advance south to Lake Champlain with 11,000 regulars, many of them veterans from Spain. Before attacking the heavily outnumbered American defenders of Plattsburg on the lake's western shore, Prevost ordered his naval force to attack the American flotilla. The British were decisively defeated on 11 September by Commodore Thomas Macdonough's squadron. Having demonstrated no enthusiasm for the operation, Prevost retreated to Canada. Failure at Plattsburg brought a sense of reality to British war aims.[30]

PEACE IN EUROPE

Napoleon's abdication had ended the European conflict, but the return of peace forced the British government to face the massive economic costs of a 21-year total war. While peace in Europe might imply that Britain could concentrate its military effort to defeat America, nothing could have been further from the truth. Europe was in chaos, with displaced people and armies to be moved, boundaries and thrones to be settled and a sustainable long-term balance of power to be constructed. Britain still faced far greater security threats than a conflict with America. The main problem was a resurgent, ambitious Russia, ruled by the mysterious, quasi-messianic Tsar Alexander, backed by his Prussian jackal and Austrian client, both anxious to feed from the Romanov table. To satisfy the eastern powers, Italy and Poland would be carved up, Germany refashioned, and the Bourbons put back on the throne of France. In 1814 the central concern for British policymakers was to keep Antwerp, and the menace of invasion it implied, out of French hands, by ensuring the security of Belgium and Holland. These were critical strategic issues. Under treaties signed on 29 June the British undertook to maintain an army of 75,000 troops in Europe until the Vienna Congress concluded the conflict. Fulfilling this onerous but essential undertaking obliged the government to retain several German mercenary formations, and hire 22,000 Prussian troops at £50,000 a month. Unable to meet their European troop commitments, the British were in no position to start a major war in America.[31]

Discussions with the Duke of Wellington, hero of the Peninsular campaign, and a political ally of the ministers, revealed the inner workings of the official mind. The stability of Europe, especially France and Belgium, were far more important than Canada. Any thought of sending a significant military force to America was swiftly abandoned, British troop ships were used to repatriate Portuguese and British soldiers from France, and then paid off. Economy was long overdue. Instead of an army the British sent three regiments from Bordeaux, while another regiment loaded in the Mediterranean.[32] This was nothing like the force needed to 'win' in America, and the ministers knew it. In the event British decision-making proved remarkably sound. Within a year Napoleon had returned to power, while the construction of a new European system at the Congress at Vienna proved to be a long drawn-out, difficult process, one that would ultimately require the undivided attention of the British state to secure acceptable terms.

Not that European concerns were uppermost in American thinking. Although the United States and France had never been allies, the defeat of Napoleon destroyed any last lingering hopes for a timely diversion or French diplomatic assistance. Having declared war when Britain stood almost alone, her economy on the brink of collapse, the United States found itself facing a re-invigorated enemy, with few military distractions and a booming economy, propelled by a massive surge in European exports. The British had no reason to compromise on maritime belligerent rights and impressment – fundamental elements of the strategy that defeated Napoleon. In late June, when Madison's Cabinet discussed peace, the Navy and Army Secretaries, William Jones and John Armstrong, urged the need to end the war, even if it meant accepting impressment. Their colleagues were not ready for such a humiliating *volte face*, but a week later cold reality and further bad news from Europe made them rethink. They conceded impressment, the palladium of British Sea Power. Having failed to conquer Canada, America had run out of strategic options.[33]

When the new command team assembled at Bermuda in late June, Cochrane, Major General Sir Robert Ross and Codrington agreed that coastal offensives were: 'the true way to shorten this Yankee war, whatever may be said in Parliament against it'.[34] Reuben Beasley, the American Commissioner for Prisoners of War in Britain, had warned Madison that the British were sending Admiral Cochrane and his famous nephew, because there was 'a strong war party in this country who cannot bare [sic] the idea of peace', and opposed attempts to negotiate with Bonaparte:

If these people are disappointed in their wishes for a continuance of the war on the continent it is to be feared that they will then exert themselves the more to spin out the war with America; and there are persons in the Cabinet who would lend a willing ear to any suggestion of that sort.[35]

The Post Office 'Black Chamber' quickly decrypted Beasley's letters for Melville's perusal.

NEW ENGLAND BLOCKADED

After escaping from Salem in late April, *Constitution* underwent a thorough repair at Boston; in the meantime Charles Stewart's decision to return home early was examined by a wholly unnecessary court of inquiry, prompted by the envy and malice of that dark soul William Bainbridge. The British were astonished by such foolishness.[36] The fool in question was William Jones, unduly influenced by his old friend. Such actions did not show the Secretary in a very positive light, and reflected deeper tensions within the American administration.

Soon after *Constitution* arrived the Boston blockade was reinforced. On 21 May Sir Thomas Hardy, in the 74-gun *Ramillies,* took command. By 4 June the blockading ships believed the *Constitution* was ready for sea, and stepped up their watch. They also knew about Stewart's red-hot shot furnace.[37] The 74 HMS *Bulwark*, Captain David Milne, arrived on 7 June. Meanwhile Hardy and others had been active further up the coast, using a small military force to seize part of Maine. By

19 July the British knew *Constitution* was ready for sea.[38] Over the next few weeks another 74 and the purpose-built *President*-killers *Leander*, Commodore Sir George Collier, and *Newcastle*, Lord George Stuart, arrived with the fast 18-pounder frigate HMS *Acasta*. This was the standard British response to the American 44s, a close blockade led by 74s, razees or fourth-rate 24-pounder frigates, with fast 18-pounder frigates in company. Anxious that the American prestige ships did not cause any more embarrassment the Admiralty directed that if they did get to sea they were to be hunted down and destroyed.

The after-effects of the Halifax hurricane hampered British operations for months. HMS *Nymphe*, one of the best fifth rates on the station, did not complete for sea until early March because Warren prioritised repairing brigs and schooners. When *Nymphe* finally got to sea, snowstorms and fog made it difficult to take what few vessels came in sight. In May *Nymphe* joined *Tenedos* and *Junon* off Boston, beginning a three-month residency which combined blockading *Congress* and *Constitution* with the destruction of the coasting trade. With a 74 and heavy frigates like *Leander* in the bay there was little chance of an American frigate putting to sea. In June Hardy rejoined the squadron to consider attacking Portsmouth, where an American battleship was approaching completion. After checking the forts and the navigation he decided against. He had no troops. Instead his reconnaissance drew out the gunboats and local militia at Portsmouth, enabling the British to attack Scituate, Massachusetts, burning all but one ship. The sole survivor belonged to a local man who guided their attack. Captured newspapers and garrulous prisoners kept the British up to date with the acute political divisions in Boston. When the Federalists celebrated the downfall of Napoleon the Republicans labelled them Englishmen. On 19 June, the second anniversary of the declaration of war, Bainbridge attempted to launch the 74 *Independence* at Charlestown. When she got stuck 75 feet down the slipway Federalist papers had a field day wringing every last drop of symbolic irony out of a very public failure. By now Boston Bay was thoroughly alarmed, but despite additional defences Sailing Master Charles Goullet got into the port of Boston on the night of 20 June, burning a sloop within a mile of the *Constitution*. He then sent a delightfully irreverent letter to the Republican *Boston Patriot*, which used it to attack the Federalists for failing to defend the harbour. The resulting internecine paper war kept the British amused for weeks.[39]

With agents active on shore, the British had little trouble picking out good targets. Using captured coasters and sloops as tenders they could raid or re-supply at will, picking up fresh meat, fish and vegetables. Occasionally Canadian privateers were stopped to impress a few good men, to maintain crew numbers. This had the added benefit of encouraging the privateers to leave the best cruising grounds to the Navy. Cruising off Salem, Lieutenant Henry Napier noted that the once prominent Crowninshield family had lost all their privateers, and the vehemently belligerent stance of the local women, 'perfect Amazons!' in comparison with their equivocating men folk.[40] With time on their hands, and no opposition at sea, the British kept up a harassing, if minor war on local commerce.

The economic blockade soon brought home the devastating consequences of challenging the masters of the sea. The only limit on the blockade was the weather. Experienced officers back in England, Warren, Captain Sir John Beresford and Broke, agreed that it would be impossible to stop all American commercial traffic in winter, but still expected up to 50 per cent would be taken.[41] New England indeed felt the same hard hand of war that had been harassing the Chesapeake for the past year. Neutral vessels seeking a quick profit were warned off, their log books endorsed so they could be taken if they violated the blockade a second time. Sensing a commercial opening, one that would gain them an advantage over their British rivals, Halifax merchants tried to get licences to trade with America. Cochrane refused, emphasising that he was waging an economic war to the finish, every dollar of import duty the American government obtained would fund their war effort. Now New England was fully in the war.

Britain's grip on America had many effects: the average size of American merchant ships steadily fell, square-rigged ships giving way to agile schooners, which had a better chance of evading British cruisers. So effective was the British blockade that the starving offshore island of Nantucket – the cruising station of two frigates that waited to the south-east of Nantucket Shoal, the landfall and choke point for ships travelling in or out of New England – begged to become neutral. The island's whaling fleet had been decimated by war, while the blockade stopped the import of food. In return for local supplies and a steady delivery of American newspapers, the British allowed them to operate fishing boats.

Out in the Atlantic British cruisers took a heavy toll of American ships. On 22 June George Collier, HMS *Leander*, captured the brig USS *Rattlesnake* off Cape Sable. Returning from an unsuccessful voyage in British waters the American had been out-sailed on every point and threw her guns overboard in a desperate attempt to escape.[42] Samuel Pym was equally pleased with his seamanship in the new French prize frigate HMS *Niemen*, taking the privateer *Henry Gilder* of 195 tons, 12 guns and 50 men after a chase of 14 hours at speeds between 10 and 12 knots.[43]

CONQUERING MAINE

Alongside the blockade and local raids the British conducted a major offensive in northern waters. Recognising an opportunity to rectify the unsatisfactory 1783 border, secure the vital over-land winter route between St John and Quebec and pressurise fragile local loyalties, the New Brunswick administration urged the government to act. In early June Bathurst, Secretary of State for War and the Colonies, ordered General Sir John Sherbrooke, Lieutenant-Governor of Nova Scotia, to occupy northern Maine. Bathurst left the senior officers at Halifax, Sherbrooke and Edward Griffith, wide latitude to plan and execute the operation, which he linked to Prevost's thrust towards Lake Champlain.[44]

The Maine offensive began with a small expedition to test the American defences. A force under Captain Robert Barrie seized the towns of Thomaston and St George on 21 June, destroying the forts lately built to stop the locals trading with the British. An expedition into Passamaquoddy Bay, led by Hardy and Lieutenant Colonel Andrew Pilkington, secured Moose Island on 11 July.[45] The citizens simply switched their allegiance and carried on business. Having thoroughly alarmed the whole coast down to Boston, Sherbrooke waited for additional troops to complete the campaign. Once fresh regiments came in from Gibraltar he led a 2,500-man strike force in ten transports into Passamaquoddy Bay. The original plan to seize Machias was changed at the last minute when HMS *Rifleman* reported the corvette USS *Adams* had limped into the Penobscot River, badly damaged by grounding on the south-west point of Isle au Haut in a fog on 17 August.[46] Once the *Adams* had floated off, Captain Charles Morris had mistaken his position on the sparsely settled coast and headed north, hoping to reach the fortified harbour at Portland. When he realised his mistake, he had no option but to enter the Penobscot. Recognising the over-riding naval imperative, Sherbrooke landed at Castine on 2 September. The garrison fired a single salvo and fled, leaving the British in control of the port, fort and towns of Castine and Hambledon.

That evening an amphibious force of 700 troops, led by Captain Barrie of HMS *Dragon* and Lieutenant Colonel Henry John, followed the Americans upriver. Another force secured Belfast on the opposite bank of the Penobscot to secure their retreat. Morris had towed the *Adams* upriver to Hampden, landed his guns to defend the ship and called out the local militia. Early on the 3rd the British, led by a screen of riflemen from the 60th Regiment, attacked through the fog supported by a salvo of rockets. Unsettled by the rockets, the militia broke and ran. The British stormed the American batteries leaving Morris no option but to burn his ship. The British lost ten killed and wounded, the Americans a few more, and over eighty prisoners. Having captured the American guns, stores and powder, the

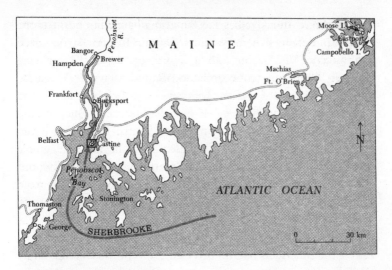

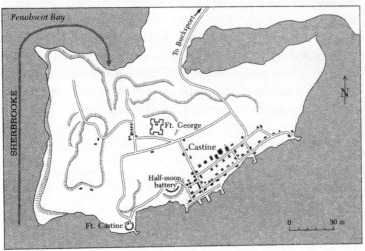

The capture of Castine and Bangor
and the destruction of the USS *Adams*.

British moved quickly to seize Bangor, where they burnt more shipping, including the privateer *Decatur*. Once the strike force had returned to Castine, Sherbrooke sent Hyde Parker and Colonel Pilkington to occupy the original target at Machias, 90 miles west of Castine. This swift, economical campaign secured an overland route between Halifax and Quebec and gave the British undisputed occupation of the Penobscot River line.[47] The conquered territory greatly facilitated smuggling, further reducing American customs revenue and accelerating the export of cash. Without money or political will the American government made no effort to recover the territory: the locals soon renewed their loyalty to an old flag.

The discovery of a copy of the Royal Navy's day signal book among the USS *Adams* stores revealed that it had been taken from HMS *Dominica*, when she was captured by the privateer *Decatur* off Charlestown. This prompted a full-scale inquiry to determine why Lieutenant George Barette had not destroyed the book before the ship was taken. The discovery that sixty of the eighty officers and men on board had been killed or wounded restored a sense of perspective.[48] Otherwise the Admiralty was delighted by Castine, an operation 'performed with so little loss'.[49]

BURNING THE PRESIDENTIAL MANSION

Cochrane hoped that stepping up the tempo of coastal raids would force the Americans to defend the Atlantic coast, rather than reinforce the army attacking Canada, and punish them for burning Canadian towns. In private he explained to Melville and Earl Bathurst that Boston, New York and Philadelphia could be attacked, both to secure a significant strategic advantage, and provide moral chastisement: 'I have much in heart to give them a complete drubbing before peace is made – when I trust their northern limits will be circumscribed and the command of the Mississippi wrested from them.'[50] These targets were too well defended to be taken by naval means alone; he needed a landing force to open the way. With his fleet and troops already at work in

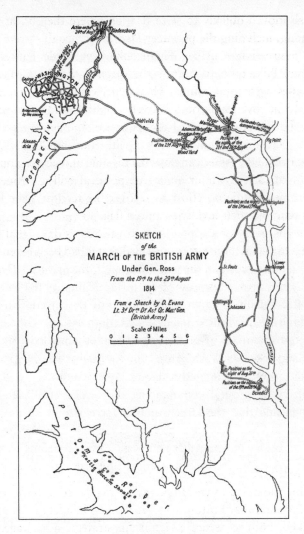

The capture of Washington, August 1814,
a remarkable achievement for a mere 4,000 men.

the Chesapeake, Cochrane favoured attacking Baltimore, centre
of the privateer effort, and an ardently Republican city, before
tackling Washington. Fixed fortifications aside, the Americans
had few defences on the Chesapeake: a handful of oar-powered

gunboats, a solitary blockaded frigate and dispersed militia formations of no great military value.

Taking account of the distinctly unhealthy summer climate of the Bay area – in 1813 over 500 men had been disabled by sickness – Cochrane thought it might be preferable to operate north of the Delaware, possibly destroying the battleship building at Portsmouth, New Hampshire, or seizing Rhode Island. These operations would keep the troops healthy, ready for operations further south when the weather improved.[51] Instead he conducted two major offensive operations in the Chesapeake in the unhealthy months of August and September. This change of priorities reflected the advice of his most experienced subordinate.

Having landed the troops at Benedict, Cockburn witnessed the destruction of the last American floating force in the Chesapeake Bay, when Joshua Barney blew up his flotilla at Pig Point on the River Patuxent. Moving quickly to exploit this success, Cockburn landed his seamen and Marines to join Ross's 4,000 men, mostly newly arrived troops. He persuaded Ross to strike overland towards Washington. On 24 August the vanguard of Ross's army encountered a larger American force, well dug-in on rising ground commanding the bridge at Bladensburg. Recognising that the largely militia force would be unwilling to fight at close quarters, the British vanguard pushed over the narrow bridge under artillery fire. The leading echelons sustained heavy losses, but advanced steadily, supported by a fusillade of terrifying Congreve rockets. By the time Ross reached the field the American army was in headlong flight; only Joshua Barney and his sailors stood and fought, buying their countrymen time to reach Washington before the enemy. After a brief rest the British pushed on, occupied the city, and destroyed all the public buildings, save the Patent Office. The Navy Yard had been burnt by its commandant, destroying the nearly complete 44-gun frigate *Essex*, a sloop of war already afloat, two old warships and a large magazine of naval stores.[52] The Navy Yard alone would cost half a million dollars to repair. After Ross and Cockburn

In ruins: the Presidential mansion was one of many
public buildings destroyed by the British.

had enjoyed the meal prepared at the Presidential mansion to
celebrate Madison's anticipated victory, they torched the building
and withdrew the following day without meeting any resistance.

The American response was predictably florid, and futile.
Republican partisans complained bitterly about 'barbaric and
cruel methods'; *Niles' Register* had already compared Cockburn
with Satan, and not to Sir George's advantage. The sheer
stupidity of these comments can only be attributed to shock
and humiliation. The British operation was perfectly legal, and

The man who burnt the Presidential mansion, and clearly
enjoyed the task, Rear Admiral Sir George Cockburn.

the troops behaved remarkably well.[53] It required only 4,000
British troops to capture the American capital, revealing the
unimaginable folly of a government that deliberately picked a
fight with a global power, allegedly about questions of principle,
without bothering to raise an army or navy capable of defending
the country. In 1814 the only effective American armies were
attempting to conquer Canada. Burning Washington was seen as
a suitable punishment for the American stab in the back of 1812

by a British administration that disliked the vulgar populism of the American political system, especially the Republican Party, and the sustained campaign to undermine British economic war strategy after 1803.[54] The flames of Washington provided a useful strategic diversion, a massive political lesson, and the key to peace.

The Admiralty had no difficulty approving the success, praising:

> the judgement with which the plan was framed, the alacrity with which it was executed; and the bravery of the officers & men employed, are all deserving the highest commendation, and their Lordships' satisfaction is greatly increased by the consideration that a service so honourable to His Majesty's arms and so injurious to the Enemy has been achieved with so little comparative loss on the part of His Majesty's forces.

The Board was especially pleased by the 'zeal and gallantry', of Cockburn, his officers and men.[55] Melville had noted Cockburn as a man of experience, decision and courage.[56]

While Ross and Cockburn secured Washington, Captains James Gordon and Charles Napier, in the frigates *Sea Horse* and *Euryalus*, led a small naval squadron up the River Potomac. Passing the American shore batteries, they seized the Virginian city of Alexandria, as a diversion and potential alternative line of withdrawal for Ross's army. Having completed their primary mission they obliged the locals to surrender twenty-one merchant ships, and load them with local produce. Codrington spoke for many when he observed: 'it is nothing less brilliant than the capture of Washington, and those employed deserve laurel crowns'.[57] A delighted Admiralty agreed, readily endorsing the substantial promotion list.[58]

These operations exposed America's catastrophic lack of central authority, intelligent direction and disposable manpower. They prompted a fatal run on the banks in Washington, Philadelphia and Baltimore, most of the cash moving across the border to buy British government bonds. With no more cash, American paper money was trading at a 20–25 per cent discount.[59] Cockburn had delivered a compact, potent, professional military force onto a weakly defended section of the American coast, taking and destroying a key objective. The speed of the attack caught the Americans flat-footed and they never recovered their equilibrium. While disgruntled British opposition politicians echoed whining American editorials, drawing silly parallels with the 'barbaric' burning of Moscow in 1812, such sentiments only demonstrated the depth of their disquiet at the final fall of Napoleon, and the triumph of the government.

While the Admiralty was delighted by the Washington/Alexandria operations it was highly critical of the other diversionary attack. HMS *Menelaus* had been sent to create a diversion north of Baltimore, but Captain Sir Peter Parker and several men were killed in a futile skirmish at Caulk's Field. Already feeling the financial and manpower effects of the European peace, the Board deeply regretted the loss of a star officer, 'and of the brave men who fell with him'.[60] Recognising that the temptations of peacetime employment in merchant ships made it essential to keep the men happy and confident, the Admiralty condemned heavy butcher's bills, unnecessary or ill-considered attacks, and unusually severe punishment returns.

BALTIMORE

Once their strike force had reassembled, Cochrane and Ross reconsidered the original plan to leave the Bay forthwith. Carried away by their success, Cockburn and Ross persuaded Cochrane to attack Baltimore. For Codrington this 'would have been much better deferred until our return from the northward according to the Admiral's own plan'. That said, the chief of staff remained optimistic; his only concern was for the men's health.[61] Following this last-minute change of plan the task force headed up the Bay towards the final major target in the area. As a fiercely Republican privateer port Baltimore was an obvious objective. Emboldened by success and mindful of a potential prize windfall, Cochrane believed the city 'ought to be laid in ashes'.[62]

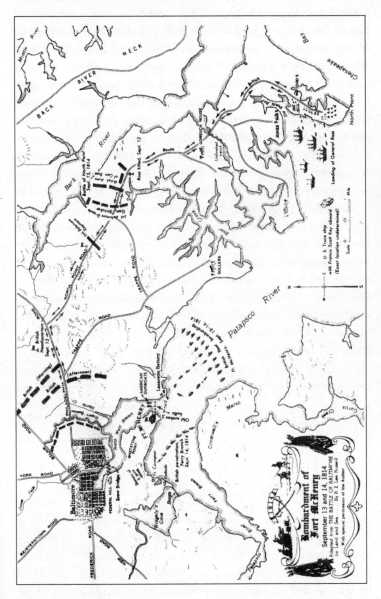

The combined attack on Baltimore met significantly greater resistance.

Cochrane, Ross, Cockburn and Army Deputy Quartermaster Lieutenant George De Lacy Evans quickly produced a plan. The admirals acknowledged that strong sea defences meant ships alone could 'do little either towards capturing or destroying the town'. They relied on the army to open the narrow harbour entrance, by seizing the eastern shore. This would allow naval forces, small cruisers and boats, to attack the waterfront area, burning and sinking shipping. Whatever the merits of the plan, the British had little reliable intelligence on Baltimore's defences. Codrington recognised they were planning on the basis of newspaper reports, and assumed the defences would collapse in panic when attacked. Although the captain of the fleet, now a ranking rear admiral, told Ross that irresponsible hearsay was no basis for a risky operation, especially one undertaken by such a small force, the operation went ahead. Ross landed on 12 September, advancing quickly towards the city as soon as the first echelon troops and naval brigade had formed up. Speed was of the essence. That evening he met and dispersed a large American force at North Point. Up at the front of the attack, in full uniform and one of very few mounted officers, Ross was killed by an American musket ball. His death stunned the British; energy and enthusiasm seemed to evaporate; even the ebullient Cockburn wavered. Despite their differences about the operation Codrington lamented 'a most severe loss to his country'.[63] With the harbour blocked and Fort McHenry still in action, despite a heavy bombardment, Cochrane properly left the final decision to Colonel Arthur Brooke, the ranking field officer. Brooke called off the operation the following day.

This was wise: over the previous three months Baltimore had been transformed into a massive armed camp, the land flank covered by major earthworks and the city packed with armed men. Even if the British defeated the American army, Baltimore was too large, populous and above all hostile to be occupied in the manner of Washington. Instead, the British re-embarked without opposition. Cochrane and Ross had intended using the time while they waited for the proper season to attempt New

Orleans 'making a demonstration upon the city of Baltimore, which might be converted into a real attack should circumstances appear to justify it'.[64] On reflection Cochrane described the operation as an 'Essay . . . contrary to my opinion, but extremely urged by the General, to which I reluctantly consented . . . to preserve unanimity between the two services.' He had suggested attacking Newport, to attract the attention of the northern states away from Canada and refresh his ships and men in the healthier northern waters before attempting New Orleans. In describing the attack as an essay Cochrane emphasised that the British were testing the enemy, to see if the defenders of Baltimore were made of better stuff than the men they met at Bladensburg. Had Baltimore's defenders run, 4,000 troops might have captured the city. By holding their nerve, and their positions, the Americans had called the British bluff. Baltimore was simply too big, something they had known all along. Even so Sir Alexander reckoned that adding the two infantry regiments lately sent to Halifax would have been enough to leave Baltimore in ashes. While Codrington thought these regiments relatively weak, they had performed well on the Penobscot River.[65] The Americans quickly found reasons to claim a victory while the spectacle of rockets and bombs fired from the fleet, their fuses burning brightly as they arched through the night sky, inspired Francis Scott Key to pen 'The Star-Spangled Banner'.

The Admiralty was not minded to contest Cochrane's assessment. While regretting the 'unfortunate death' of Major General Ross, it noted with pleasure:

. . . the defeat of an army so greatly superior in point of numbers, the unmolested manner in which the Troops retired & were again embarked, the good conduct of the seamen & Marines & the perfect unanimity that existed between the two services.

Once again Cockburn and the naval brigade were singled out for praise. The Admiralty accepted that the operation had been a probing expedition, to test the resolve of the defenders, not an all-out assault.[66] A full-scale attack against unbroken American defences would have been suicidal, and highly unlikely given the presence of Cockburn, proven master of skilful, effective, and above all economical warfare. Baltimore survived but the blockade ensured it did not prosper. Suitably chastened, Cochrane left the Chesapeake for Halifax to plan the attack on New Orleans, his rendezvous with destiny in the Deep South.[67]

The setback at Baltimore had no effect on the blockade. A steady harvest of American ships fell to the blockading forces, while neutral ships stayed away, recognising the reality of a close and complete closure of trade. With powerful 74s, razee 58s and an increasing number of British 24-pounder frigates on the coast, there was little prospect of the blockade being challenged, leaving smaller cruisers, many of them former American privateers, to sweep up any trade. Even so Cochrane discovered that American privateers could still inflict embarrassing losses. The Ordnance transport *Stranger*, carrying sixty-six cannon for the fleet on the Great Lakes, had been taken by a small American privateer and carried into Salem. The escort, HMS *Antelope*, had seen the enemy, but chose not to pursue. Before anyone could blame him, Cochrane pointed out that this was the second occasion on which valuable ordnance stores had been taken by insignificant privateers because they had been sent out in an unarmed ship.[68] He was more confident about the prospects of maintaining the blockade throughout the year than Warren, relying on the experience of blockading the French Atlantic ports, a combination of responding flexibly to adverse weather and forming an adequate cruiser patrol 'some distance from the land'.[69] At Halifax Codrington was pleased to see how many frigates had been set up in the Broke style, not least Hyde Parker's *Tenedos*: he had no doubt such ships would be a credit to the country.[70]

THE STRATEGIC PICTURE

After April 1814 the Admiralty had the luxury of focusing its attention on a single enemy, one with distinctly limited resources.

Digesting the stream of intelligence reports, newspaper cuttings and rumours that flowed across the Atlantic, the Board attempted to anticipate American strategy. The task was complicated by the absolute incoherence of the Madison administration. It was hard to understand a bankrupt government that still dreamt of conquering Canada after two years of abject failure. Even so, the threat was taken seriously, drawing manpower and material to Yeo's fleet on Lake Ontario. However, the main problem remained American predation of oceanic trade. While British diplomats tried to close French harbours to American privateers their new method, absolute destruction, limited the need for bases. Successful American cruisers could be self-sustaining, feeding and re-equipping from prizes, even taking fresh men. Peace had seen the end of the European convoy system, so American privateers found the best hunting grounds lay across the Atlantic. Losses drove cargoes onto neutral vessels, which paid lower insurance rates.[71] The only answer to the plague of privateers was to maintain the Atlantic convoy system, patrol key choke points and step up the blockade.

That said, by 1814 privateering was no longer profitable, and few American warships even attempted to put to sea. Battle, convoy and blockade had secured British control of the Atlantic, a success they translated into effect on American territory. Without trade, customs dues, the main source of Federal funds, collapsed. As President Theodore Roosevelt observed a century later, the British blockade:

. . . inflicted a direct material loss to the American people a hundredfold greater than the entire American Navy was able to inflict on Great Britain from the beginning of the war to the end . . . The very fact that the workings of the blockade were ceaseless and almost universal makes it difficult to realise their importance.[72]

By late 1814 the British had won the war: it only remained for a bankrupt enemy to recognise the fact.

By 1814 the British were blockading all major American ports with squadrons based around a 74 or a razee, a few frigates and smaller cruisers. If the Americans completed any battleships the British would have to reinforce the blockade. The squadrons off Boston and Portsmouth, New Hampshire, monitored the progress of the evocatively named *Washington* and *Independence*. Although launched in the autumn of 1814 neither ship would be ready for sea before the spring. Just in case, the Admiralty sent Henry Hotham, commanding the squadron between New York and New England, a new flagship, the 98-gun three-decker HMS *Boyne*. Furthermore, the Board repeated the order about 44-gun frigates: British 74s should not engage the American 74s in single combat. The object, sensibly left unspoken, was to avoid further humiliation.[73]

The most pressing threat came from more conventional forces. As the autumn wore on the Admiralty concluded that the Americans were planning a major operation in Asian waters. Melville warned the East India Company that three 44-gun frigates and two battleships would be ready for sea before the turn of the year. While an American sortie would miss the seasonal convoys, it might pick up a few straggling Indiamen heading home alone. Having watched American preparations for several months Hotham and Griffith reached similar conclusions, preparing for a sortie by redoubling the blockades of New York, New London, Newport, Portsmouth and Boston. Griffith ran the blockade as far south as Portsmouth from Halifax, Hotham exercised command around New York and the Delaware in the fast 74 HMS *Superb*, normally stationed off New London.[74] By mid-August Hotham knew that the *President* was ready for sea, but discounted rumours of a sortie. Hotham was not above a little psychological warfare: using the arrival of Hardy from Boston, and three new frigates joining his command, to create the impression that he planned to attack: 'a general alarm was excited, and they have from 1000 to 1500 men at work every day in improving the defences of New York; and they have added largely to the number of their troops on Long Island opposite to the town.' Just in case the Americans doubted his intentions Hotham had the mortar vessel *Terror* throw 200 bombs and 100

Congreve rockets into the town of Stonington, punishing the inhabitants for a recent torpedo outrage. Hotham stressed the need to keep two frigates off the Nantucket Shoals and asked Cochrane for another frigate and two more sloops.[75]

Having chastised Stonington, Hotham anchored off New London with an impressive armada: two 74s, a razee, several frigates and a bomb vessel. The effect was immediate, and easily observed: 'the inhabitants are removing their property into the country'. Calling out the militia hampered the harvest. Although there were torpedoes and a 'turtle-boat', a crude submarine, in town he had no plans to attack. New London was 'quite beyond our reach and our means', while *United States* and *Macedonian* were 12 miles up the River Thames and no longer ready for sea. He anticipated, however, that the sloop *Hornet* would attempt to escape at the first opportunity.[76]

Hotham intended following up the attack on Stonington with a sortie into Long Island Sound, to bombard another town, 'putting the country in a state of alarm . . . to the great prejudice of the harvest'. Thwarted by calms and fog, he detached Hardy with the bomb vessel *Terror* to join Cochrane. *Terror*'s next target would be Fort McHenry. Hardy also carried the latest information on the defences of New York, to brief Cochrane on a potential target.[77] Under-estimating American determination to get to sea, Hotham assumed Decatur's appointment to command the naval defences of New York made it unlikely *President* would sortie, and adjusted the blockading frigates accordingly. Considering a razee, a 24-pounder frigate, and an 18-pounder frigate would be adequate off Sandy Hook, he brought one 18-pounder frigate back to Long Island Sound. As the autumn wore on the squadron off Sandy Hook faced severe weather, and lacked a safe anchorage. Only the most powerful sailing ships could hold station.[78] They would have to be rotated regularly to ensure they remained fully effective. When Hotham sailed north to load stores at Halifax in late October he persuaded Griffith to supplement his forces.[79]

THE STEAM BATTERY

When the British transformed the naval blockade of New York into an economic attack the effect was immediate. Hotham's squadron took a heavy toll of American merchant ships and privateers from Long Island Sound and Sandy Hook, crippling the economic life of America's greatest port.[80] The ever-present British warships ensured the populace had reason to fear an invasion, or a damaging raid of the type being experienced all along the Chesapeake coastline. The large earthwork thrown up on Brooklyn Heights and additional sea defences hardly challenged the blockade, but something altogether more original sprang from the dangerous, inventive mind of Republican zealot, steam engineer, torpedo pioneer and adopted New Yorker Robert Fulton. Fulton conceived a steam-propelled warship to operate in Long Island Sound, discussing the concept with Decatur. Decatur, Jacob Jones and James Biddle, locked up in New London, considered the new vessel 'more formidable to an enemy than any kind of engine hitherto invented'.[81] On 9 March 1814 Congress funded construction of Demologos, the 'voice of the people'.

At 153 feet long and 58 feet wide, the twin catamaran hulls resembled a shoe box with rounded extremities, propelled by a central paddle wheel. Displacing 1,450 tons, the new ship was little smaller than a 74-gun battleship. Above the waterline the ship had two continuous decks from side to side, apart from the well for the paddle wheel. The 120-horsepower single-cylinder engine sat in the port hull, the two copper boilers in the starboard, with four funnels to carry away the fumes. The framing and planking were on a massive scale, creating a solid body of timber several feet thick, intended to be impervious to conventional round shot. She was armed with twenty-six 32-pounders, but the projected underwater cannon and pumps intended to deliver hot water to the upper deck were never fitted.

In late October Captain James Nash, HMS Saturn, provided a progress report on the battery, although his shore-side source clearly lacked a classical education, rendering her name as '*Demi Locusta*'.[82] Hotham was not impressed.[83] At the same time several reports indicated that American warships, notably *Constitution*, had been fitted with furnaces to prepare red-hot shot.[84] Through the autumn Hotham received a steady stream of dockside gossip, newspaper reports and the uninhibited remarks of American officers, which ensured that his conclusions about the size, armament and function of the battery were strikingly accurate.[85] Henry Hope of the *Endymion* recognised that the battery would 'keep the [Long Island] Sound clear in the spring, with a squadron of gun boats, Galleys etc', and recommended using red-hot shot to burn the monster. Hotham agreed, equipping his flagship to fire carcasses filled with combustibles and red-hot shot from her main deck 32-pounders, and urging the Admiralty to send out several suitably equipped gun brigs in the spring.[86] At the end of the year Hotham reported that the monster mounted thirty long 32-pounders, with a bomb-proof deck.[87]

While massive timbers and independent mobility would have made *Demologos* a dangerous opponent in the confined waters of New York harbour or Long Island Sound, the British were not unduly concerned. Carcasses and red-hot shot would quickly transform the massive hull into a fireball. Launched on 29 October *Demologos* finally made a trial run in July 1815, long after her designer had died. While British observers remained unimpressed,[88] the Danes and the French, who had felt the hard hand of British naval power, expressed a serious interest in the ship.

KEEPING STATION

In late October Henry Hope reported from off Sandy Hook that the ships ready for sea in New York were 'crowded with volunteers'. *President* and the 26-gun corvette *John Adams* were expected to sail before 10 November, while the sloop *Peacock*, 22 guns, had just arrived, along with the notorious privateers *Grampus* and *Chasseur*. He expected they would soon head back to sea. Additional new privateers were planning to cruise via the South-Western Approaches, to Madeira and the Canary Islands and the West Indies. Several letter of marque traders were preparing to run the blockade, picking up cargoes in Lisbon or Cadiz. There were also reports that valuable cargoes were inbound from China for Newport, New Bedford and New York. Well aware that the British were reading their newspapers, Yankee ship owners had begun printing disinformation. Another story gaining traction in New York had the crews of Thomas Macdonough's Lake Champlain squadron manning the frigates at New London, and attempting to link up with Decatur and *President*. A rather more accurate report had Commodore John Shaw taking command at New London.[89]

In late November, with the winter nights drawing in and the weather deteriorating, Hotham and Griffith expected trouble. They had to watch a swarm of privateers, two 74s, five frigates and several brigs. For timely warning they relied on human intelligence, regular inspections by their cruisers, American newspapers, deserters, fishermen, British nationals lately ashore and neutral ship masters. Returning to New London in late December, Hotham found that the enemy had not moved for a month, but he sensed a major sortie was imminent. One report suggested that with the Union on the verge of collapse the government wanted to get the frigates out of the River Thames, lest New England secede. Although *Hornet* had escaped in a gale he doubted the frigates would be so lucky. He also received a report of the Hartford Convention.[90]

CONSTITUTION ESCAPES

When Cochrane headed south, Edward Griffith had been left to blockade Boston. He kept a close watch on *Constitution* as, from early November, she had appeared ready for sea. The 74 *Independence* had her topgallant masts up, but no yards of any kind nor, he concluded, was she armed.[91] In mid-December 'a Scotchman lately at Boston' reported that the Americans were assembling 5,000 men as well as the *Constitution* and *Independence* to recapture Castine, but Griffith had more confidence in another source's suggestion that the 74 'has not got her guns on board, nor has she men'. Even so he spread his cruisers a little further north, for an occasional look into the Penobscot.[92]

However, Griffith had other pressing tasks, not least dealing with the privateer threat. In October he reported a major success: the privateer effort out of Portsmouth, New Hampshire, had been decimated. On 23 October Milne's *Bulwark* took the Portsmouth privateer schooner *Harlequin* of 330 tons, pierced for 10 guns, and carrying 115 men. Milne also recaptured the *Amazon* loaded with flour and biscuit for the army at Quebec.[93] Francis Stanfell, HMS *Bacchante*, took the Portsmouth privateer *MacDonough* on 1 November. His report provided an interesting insight into the economic condition of the port. The 200-ton ship was 'particularly well manned, 19 masters of vessels serving onboard for want of other employment'. George Collier continued his run of success on 9 November, taking the 160-ton 8-gun *General Putnam* after a chase of close on 100 miles in dark, stormy weather. The prize had already been chased by eleven different British cruisers.[94]

The situation at Boston changed quickly. HMS *Arab* found Hotham on Christmas Day with news that the *Constitution* had escaped from Boston in a gale on the 18th, along with *Congress*. Captain Fane had first warned Lord George Stuart at Provincetown and then set off to warn Hotham, meeting Sir George Collier on the 23rd. Collier picked up *Newcastle* and *Acasta* the following day and headed east in pursuit. Sifting the garbled intelligence, Collier concluded that the American ship was heading for a rendezvous with *Congress*, and *President* and *Hornet* if they had escaped. Collier reckoned that the Americans were trying to assemble a squadron to attack a convoy off Madeira, before striking for the British coast. While the assessment proved false, four days later the squadron captured the big privateer *Prince de Neufchatel*, which enabled him to send his dispatches home on the fast cruiser.[95]

Taking advantage of a Portuguese ship heading for London, Hotham sent a ciphered dispatch informing the Admiralty that the Americans had escaped, and that Collier with *Leander*, *Newcastle* and *Acasta* was in pursuit, heading for the Portuguese Western Islands, Madeira and the Canaries, before returning via Barbados and the Carolinas to Halifax. He expected *President*, *Peacock* and *Hornet* would sail from New York and if the warships escaped he thought David Porter would try to follow with six commerce-raiding brigs. Hayes, with *Majestic*, *Forth*, *Pomone* and *Nimrod*, was waiting off Sandy Hook. Having 'received good information that the enemy's ships are to join, to intercept outward bound East India Fleet off Madeira, or Cape Verde Islands', he sent suitable advice after Collier.

By 2 January the intelligence picture had begun to clear: *Congress* had not escaped.[96] Instead Hotham warned Cochrane of the emerging threat to Indian commerce posed by *President*, *Peacock* and *Hornet*. The latest New York intelligence indicated measures had been taken for a very long voyage, with experienced Asian navigators among the crew. While he had a strong force off Sandy Hook, none were prepared for a voyage to Asia.[97] On 6 January Hotham produced additional evidence to support his contention that the American effort had been concerted: 'an officer of the *Constitution* who was left behind at Boston has been ordered on board the *President* at New York, to take a passage to the former ship'. Another privateer squadron, under Oliver Hazard Perry, was expected to sail from Boston. Just in case anyone thought the Americans had given up he reported extraordinary efforts to build privateers. When Hotham's dispatch reached London on 17 February the Admiralty hurried it across town to the East India Company headquarters in Leadenhall Street.[98]

At Halifax Griffith realised that *Constitution* had been able to escape because Lord George Stuart had chosen to anchor *Newcastle* and *Acasta* in an area of Cape Cod Bay where he could not see the enemy ship, and was to leeward of Boston between 12 and 22 December. Such a serious misjudgement required explanation. While he hoped *Bulwark*, *Junon* and *Bacchante* might have intercepted the enemy leaving Boston Bay this was unlikely.[99] A month later Griffith provided some alarming intelligence: 'The spirit of privateering seems at its height, not less than 68 are already gone to sea, or fitting in the different ports.' Yet there was ample evidence that America was in crisis; 'the Government is confessedly bankrupt'. Confidence in public and private finances had collapsed. At the latest Boston sale Treasury Notes were bought at a discount of 27½ per cent, while Treasury Stock raised only 56 per cent of face value, having sold at par only a few months before. Every American bank outside Boston and Essex County had suspended specie payment. New York bank bills were already discounted 20 per cent. The consequences were clear: public bodies had no money. Troops were being paid in depreciated treasury notes:

It seems impossible to conjecture how they can devise means to be ready to meet another campaign – very few enlistments have for some time taken place, the recruiting officers not having the means to furnish the Bounty. All public creditors have for the two last quarters received their dividends only in treasury paper.

The economic war had worked: the American administration was bankrupt, insolvent and utterly without credit. Griffith stressed that the government retained power by the narrowest of margins: 'If the affairs at Plattsburg and Baltimore had fortunately succeeded the General Impression in the United States is that Mr. Madison and his adherents would have been compelled to resign.' It would be necessary for the Army to administer some hard knock to demolish the confidence the Americans had drawn from Plattsburg.[100]

The Americans kept sending out privateers, largely because they had no other use for ships, or seamen. Many were captured; very few made money. The hermaphrodite brig *Guerriere*, 4 guns and 100 men, was taken on 3 January by HMS *Junon*, Captain Clotworthy Upton, four days out from Portsmouth. Stored for a four-month cruise, the privateer had yet to open her account.[101]

The *Tomahawk* was taken by *Bulwark* on 22 January after a ten-hour chase. Typical of the latest purpose-built privateers, the 202-ton schooner mounted 9 guns and carried 84 men. She was only two days out from Boston, without a single success to her name.[102] Griffith's cruisers were overwhelming Halifax with prisoners; most would have to be moved to England.[103] By late February Griffith had concluded that the frigates and the smaller ships from Boston were destined for the North-West coast, to re-establish Columbia, before moving on to join *President* in the China Seas and Indian Ocean. Clearly economics drove strategy: he noted that Astor, 'a German and very rich', had 'subscribed largely to the first and second Government loans and is said to have much influence with Mr Madison and his Party'.[104]

In mid-February Hotham received further insight from the same 'credible source' in New York that had warned him of Decatur's plans:

Captain Warrington of the *Peacock* called on a friend of mine . . . and purchased from him a complete set of Charts and Directions for the Indian Ocean, and China Seas, and observed to him that he hoped in a few months to completely cut up the Country Trade in India, likewise made particular enquiry if supplies could be obtained for ships of war on the coast of Cochin China.

David Porter had also publicly stated that the ultimate destination of the warships at New York had been:

the eastern entrance of the Straits of Malacca between Piedro Blanco and Pulo Aor, he declared they were to cruise ten or twelve days off the Isle of France, and it is believed they are to meet the *Constitution* on a rendezvous near the Cape de Verde Islands; and I observed on his explanation to his friend on the Globe he pointed to those islands.

American strategy had been fatally compromised by David Porter's big mouth, and a canny Federalist chart seller.

Hotham copied the news to Admiral Tyler at the Cape of Good Hope, providing details of armament, manning and store ships used by the Americans, and the dates they sailed.[105] After that he could only wait on events.

DEFEAT IN THE SOUTH

By early summer 1814 Cochrane had blockaded the American Gulf Coast, while Edward Nicholls contacted the Creek Indian confederacy. While these were promising steps, the attempt to seize New Orleans and the Mississippi with an army of 6,000 men was astonishingly ambitious. In reality the plan, based on deeply flawed assumptions, was doomed before it began. With nowhere near enough troops to conquer New Orleans, the British could only make a demonstration in force, and hope the locals would crumble. It would be another Bladensburg.

British assessments of the political situation in Louisiana reflected an underlying assumption that the Washington administration had little control over the region. They assumed that a large number of 'foreign' residents, alien culture and distance were a recipe for disharmony and failure. James Stirling's 1813 report, while reliable on geopolitical issues, economics and racial conflict, fatally misread the past as the present. Stirling did not realise that pragmatic francophone Louisianians had cashed in old identities and loyalties for a share in the spoils of a white supremacist regime that could protect them from the existential threat of slave revolt. Far from seeking old masters Louisianians wanted to be more American than the Americans. While Stirling assumed they would fold under pressure, they had more to fight for than the people of Washington DC, already securely 'inside' the American system. Far from aiding the attack on New Orleans, Nicholls's attempt to enlist Creek Indians, slaves and the Spanish confirmed white Louisianians' worst fears: the British were coming to take away their lands, and their slaves.[106] If America preserved 'the slave regime and the control or elimination of Indians', white Lousianians would stand together and fight the British.[107]

When Napoleon abdicated, the British initially envisaged sending General Lord Hill to America with 14,000 men in a hundred transports, but when they realised that this would strip the country of effective troops the force was halved, and Hill stood down. A smaller force was split between Prevost's army defending Canada, and Ross's amphibious command. When New Orleans was discussed War Office Under-Secretary Colonel Henry Bunbury advised against sending a large force. He stressed the need to retain troops to secure Antwerp; they could be required at any time to 'push over into the Low Countries to support out interests in that quarter'. His assessment that the war faction in France might rise again proved prescient: less than a year later British troops were marching through Brussels. Nor did he favour attacking New Orleans: it was too far from the Chesapeake and Canada for mutual support, while the target looked difficult, with nightmarish navigation, climate and logistics. Bunbury's assessment reflected the thoroughness of British intelligence and reconnaissance. On balance he advised waiting until the spring, when Europe would be settled, and the question of war or peace with America resolved. Then a force of 12,000 might be sent without risk, making a total of over 20,000 to attack in the Chesapeake and occupy Long Island and other coastal targets, because 'pressure upon the centre of American power would produce a quicker result than any distant operation' like Louisiana.[108] Despite Bunbury's incisive critique, an attack on New Orleans was ordered in early September, and another 2,000 men were ordered to join Ross's army.[109] Although he had few extra men the Admiralty did provide landing craft.

While Bunbury favoured concentrating on the east coast, Cochrane preferred to exploit the superior mobility of sea power with a widely dispersed three-pronged offensive to disrupt and distract the Americans. Cockburn, the acknowledged master of the art, would stage amphibious operations on the coasts of Georgia and South Carolina to draw off the Americans fighting the Creek Confederacy. This would enable the Indians to attack Louisiana in support of the main British offensive, while Cockburn continued to lead the Americans a merry dance.[110]

On the way south Cochrane stopped at Guadeloupe, to return the island to French control. While Edward Codrington remained optimistic, expecting the Americans would be forced

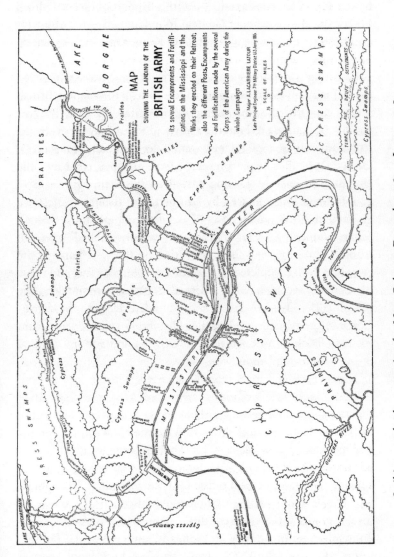

Striking south: the campaign for New Orleans, December 1814–January 1815.

to accept peace, 'whether the Madisonians would like it or not', he doubted if the senior Army officer, General John Keane, was fit for the chief command.[111] As the expedition set sail from Jamaica in late November General John Lambert turned up with two fresh regiments; he was to relieve Keane until Major General Sir Edward Pakenham arrived.[112]

Rejecting a possible slow approach up the Mississippi River, the British chose an overland route. In a heroic action British sailors captured the American gunboats guarding Lake Borgne, enabling Cochrane to land the army and set up a decisive stroke. Unfortunately General Keane wasted a fleeting chance for success. On 23 December, when presented with an open road into the city, he held back.[113] Having passed up the chance for decisive action Keane was replaced by Lambert, and then the aggressive Pakenham. On 8 January 1815 Pakenham compounded Keane's failure, launching a frontal assault on well-entrenched American troops before the vital flank operation on the west bank of the river had been completed.[114] His folly cost him his life, and those of many brave men who deserved a better commander. The British suffered 2,036 killed and wounded. Despite the defeat, Cochrane remained enthusiastic. He simply switched his main focus to Cockburn's operations in Georgia and South Carolina, trying to split the Union.[115]

The defeated British troops departed without opposition. Andrew Jackson's victorious army preferred tracking down fugitive slaves and restoring them to their masters. The Battle of New Orleans was a great victory for the plantation economy, and the Southern political system. The campaign legitimised local interests as American national interests, and ensured they would spread. The people of Louisiana became ardent Republican Party loyalists.[116] The subsequent elevation of the battle to mythic status reveals a great deal about post-war America, the political career of Andrew Jackson, and Southern pride. The real losers that day were the Indians, who lost their land, Spanish Americans who lost Florida, and African-Americans, who would endure another fifty years of servitude as the plantation economy spread westward. Between 1815 and 1861 the United States' slave population more than doubled; slavery won the War of 1812.

Even the mythic Battle of New Orleans revealed the depth of the American economic crisis. Andrew Jackson had been offered access to the personal funds of James Monroe to pay his troops. In any case New Orleans mattered little in the bigger scheme of things: peace had already been signed because a bankrupt United States was utterly unable to carry on paying for the war.

Over the autumn and winter Madison had reconstructed his Cabinet: John Armstrong resigned as Secretary for War, being replaced by James Monroe, while Jones was replaced as Navy Secretary by Benjamin Crowninshield. Jones argued that the Navy could not provide any more men for the Lakes without completely stripping the ocean-going forces and local naval defences. Monroe sought additional troops for a 'decisive' attack on Canada, but the Senate crippled his measures, leaving him to develop a plan for 15,000 regulars and 40,000 volunteers under Jacob Brown to cross the St Lawrence, an operation forestalled by poverty and peace. While Britain waited the Royal Navy pointedly continued the fight. The British had no intention of letting the Americans think there was any other option. As Brian Arthur has demonstrated 'the blockades had brought about decisive commercial, fiscal and financial consequences, and their conclusive political results'.[117]

THE LAST CRUISE OF THE *CONSTITUTION*

The British had kept the *Constitution* bottled up in Boston for six months. Her crew of 450 prime seamen would have been more usefully deployed to the Great Lakes, or at sea in privateers. Finally on 18 December Stewart saw the Bay was empty and exploited a fresh west-north-west breeze to escape. Once at sea Stewart headed south along the American coast, passing the Delaware and Chesapeake, picking up the unfortunate convoy straggler *Lord Nelson*, heading to the Caribbean. While he stocked up on captured provisions Stewart never found the convoy, only the equally unsuccessful privateer *Anaconda* on her way home. Then he crossed the Atlantic to try his luck in the shipping lanes off the Canary Islands. With peace restored in Europe most of the ships he met were neutrals, which he could neither capture nor silence. Cruising off Cape Finisterre on 8 February he heard rumours that peace had been negotiated at Ghent, but until the treaty was ratified he could carry on the war, as a race for glory. Stewart headed south, desperately seeking a 'fair fight' with a British frigate before the war ended. After taking a second prize he stopped the Russian ship *Josef* on the 19th; the master had been in Boston only months before, and was not fooled by his 'British' disguise. Aware that his presence would soon be known to every British warship in the area Stewart hurried south.

The following day, about 180 miles east-north-east of Madeira he encountered the small British cruisers *Cyane* and *Levant*, holding station to cover the seasonal convoys heading for the Caribbean. Stewart set off in pursuit, quickly gaining on the smaller ships, which were manoeuvring to join forces. The contest that followed demonstrated masterly ship-handling, effective tactics, overwhelming force and superior speed. The British ships didn't stand a chance. *Cyane* carried 34 guns, twenty-two 32-pounder carronades, ten 18-pounder carronades and only two long 9-pounders. The *Levant* had eighteen 32-pounder carronades, two 12-pounder carronades and a pair of long 9-pounders. While well armed to fight a privateer, their most likely opponent, they were hopelessly outclassed by *Constitution*'s 52-gun battery of thirty long 24-pounders, two 24-pounder gunnades, and twenty 32-pounder carronades. Stewart's long guns had more than double the reach of the British carronades. He took the larger ship-rigged *Cyane* first. By one of the war's more unusual ironies Captain Gordon Thomas Falcon had boarded the *Chesapeake* back in 1807 to remove the British deserters.[118] The smaller *Levant* attempted to escape into the gathering darkness, but Stewart quickly closed her down and, as the *Constitution* came alongside for the killing stroke,

Captain Douglas wisely hauled down his colours. The British ships lost 35 dead and 42 wounded from crews totalling 340. Stewart's casualties were 4 dead and 14 wounded from a massive force of 451. The British ships had fired well, but few rounds penetrated the American hull. The prizes were refitted and prize crews installed.

Stewart now decided to try his luck further south; the master of his last prize had reported that the small British frigate *Inconstant* was heading home from the River Plate with a million pounds in bullion onboard. On 10 March 1815 the three ships anchored in the Portuguese harbour of Porto Praya in the Cape Verde Islands. Stewart was anxious to get rid of his prisoners, in case he had to fight again. The next morning a heavy fog covered the harbour entrance, but *Constitution*'s crew could see the upper masts and yards of three large ships coming into port. Unwilling to trust to Portuguese neutrality Stewart cut his cables and made sail. Some of the British prisoners ashore rushed to the nearest Portuguese fort and opened fire, without effect. As the Americans headed out to sea past the northern point of the harbour the fog began to lift, giving Stewart a fleeting, hazy glimpse of the enemy rounding the southern point. He reckoned they were two 74s and a frigate. This was a fair assessment: Collier's two big double-banked 50-gun frigates had full upper deck batteries and massive masts and yards. In any case Stewart was greatly outnumbered, his prizes too lightly manned to be combat-worthy, while his own ship had over 200 British prisoners stowed below deck, and nearly a third of her crew absent. The odds were so heavily stacked that several American officers went below to pack their possessions, to secure them from pilferage when the ship was taken.

Collier, one of the outstanding frigate commanders of the Napoleonic Wars, had been appointed to HMS *Leander* specifically to deal with the American 44s. Picking up *Constitution*'s trail from the *Josef* on the day Stewart took *Cyane* and *Levant*, he quickly concluded it was time to visit the Western Islands. Superb strategic anticipation enabled Collier, with *Newcastle*,

Lord George Stuart, and *Acasta*, Captain Mark Kerr, to track down the most skilful and elusive of all American frigate captains. On the morning of 10 March Collier could see, through hazy weather, three ships in company. The latest intelligence suggested they were all powerful 44-gun frigates, John Rodgers's new *Guerriere*, *Constitution* and perhaps *United States*. This made his squadron significantly inferior in firepower. Only two of his ships carried 24-pounder long guns, and both were seriously undermanned.[119] That both senior officers over-estimated the strength of the enemy suggests the weather was far from perfect. In both cases their opinions influenced their tactical choices.

Stewart tried to escape, and the two squadrons quickly settled into a stern chase, with every stitch of canvas set. The *Acasta*, smallest and fastest of Collier's ships, quickly gained on the slow, short-handed prizes. At 1.10 p.m. Stewart responded by ordering the *Cyane* to tack away to the north-west. *Acasta* pressed on, ignoring the distraction of an easy prize. *Cyane* ultimately managed to get back to America. By 3.00 the British were closing on *Levant*; once again Stewart signalled his consort to alter course. This time all three British ships followed the tiny two-masted *Levant*, allowing *Constitution* to escape. Collier recaptured the trifling prize in Porto Praya harbour, in violation of Portuguese neutrality, providing a suitably ridiculous end to the war.[120]

Two years later, historian William James demanded to know what 'untoward circumstances' led to *Constitution*'s 'most unaccountable escape'.[121] Collier had signalled *Acasta* alone to pursue the *Levant*, but a signalling error and uncertainty about which ships they were chasing led all three ships to break off the pursuit of the American talisman to recapture a battered ship-sloop, when *Acasta* was less than three hours from getting alongside the American frigate. Clearly dissatisfied by this version of the story, James kept nagging away. Ultimately he wrote that Collier had disgraced the British flag. 'What could have possessed Sir George Collier to act in this manner?' he demanded. 'What were the capture of the *Guerriere*, *Macedonian*, and *Java*, or half a dozen other such frigates, to the disgrace entailed upon the British Navy by this third and last escape of the *Constitution*?' Mortified by the imputation that he was either incompetent or a coward, Collier cut his throat on 24 March 1824.[122] Subsequent judgements were clouded by his suicide. While the *Constitution*'s log book confirms Collier's account of poor visibility Captain Edward Brenton, who commanded HMS *Spartan* throughout the war, agreed there had been 'some unfortunate misconception'.[123]

While Collier was neither a coward, nor incompetent, such considerations matter little. He had allowed America's new totem ship to escape almost certain capture. The cultural consequences of this blundering finale are still significant. *Constitution*'s three successes became a core element in the American 'victory', conveniently overlooking the loss of her sister ship, and the rest of the naval war. Had Collier handled his ships with common ability, let alone the seamanship and skill that he had been boasting of for the past six months, Stewart had been destined to follow Porter and Decatur, taking tea in a British stern cabin. *Acasta* had the speed to catch *Constitution*, and bring Collier into the battle. Charles Stewart would have recognised such odds were the occasion for honourable surrender, rather than a futile bloodbath. Had *Constitution* ended up in British hands the United States Navy would have had little to brag about.

After his fortunate escape, Stewart stood away and south and then south-west. He was still looking for the *Inconstant*. It proved to be a futile mission. He had been misled: the British frigate did not sail from Rio until May. Stewart landed his prisoners at the Brazilian Island of Maranhão on 4 March, and sailed for home nine days later. He reached New York on 15 May, having finally learnt that peace had been ratified a few weeks earlier. The celebrations that greeted Stewart's triumphant return contained an element of desperation: New York's own frigate, the mighty *President*, was nowhere to be seen.

CHAPTER 10

Taking the *President*

On 14 February 1814 the USS *President* had slipped into New York after another uneventful cruise, and there she remained for precisely eleven months.[1] John Rodgers relinquished command, perhaps hoping his luck would change. By late 1814 the United States capital had been burnt and American coastal and overseas trade annihilated; bankruptcy loomed, and British armies were poised to invade from north and south. While the morale boosting victory on Lake Champlain helped obscure the repeated failures of the Army, America expected more from its star ships, the 44-gun frigates *Constitution*, *United States* and *President*, and successful captains like Stephen Decatur, the celebrity icon of a vainglorious age. Cheap newspapers and mass literacy spread these names across an entire nation.

Decatur had attempted to return to sea in 1813, only to be thwarted by the British blockade. Driven into New London, Connecticut, Decatur accepted his fate, unwilling to fight a superior force. Such circumspection did not please everyone. James Biddle, commander of the USS *Hornet*, became thoroughly disenchanted: 'Decatur has lost very much of his reputation by his continuance in port. Indeed he has certainly lost all his energy and enterprise'.[2] Biddle might have been a hot-headed 21-year-old, but there was more than a grain of truth to the indictment. Decatur, acutely conscious of his public image, would have sensed as much. For all the bravado of his public persona, Decatur was an innovative, reflective officer. In 1811 he successfully tested exploding shells, but decided not to use them in a war with the British 'as he means to have fair play with them'.[3] Such noble sentiments did not last long; as has been seen he helped set off an

IED alongside Thomas Hardy's ship.[4] In early 1814 Decatur paid off *United States*, and took command of the famous *President* at New York.

NEW YORK

New York's enormous sheltered harbour linked major inland waterways like the Hudson River and coastwise trade to New England through Long Island Sound, making it America's dominant port. Yet the seaward approaches were challenging: numerous sand banks lay beneath the 6 miles of water stretching between Sandy Hook and Coney Island. Pilots were essential for ocean-going vessels attempting the narrow navigable channel. These dangerous waters were littered with shipwrecks. A 4-foot tidal range helped ships pass the shallows, while twice-monthly spring tides added a foot more water. The ebb tide swept past Sandy Hook at 3 knots, speeding outgoing ships on their way, but making their return all but impossible. Such information, well known to blockaded and blockader alike, was more useful for those lying in wait outside. The bar made it dangerous to enter New York in poor visibility. At least there were soundings to be had 20 miles out to sea, warning experienced mariners that the coast was near. Once at sea, ships heading for Europe hugged the Atlantic coast of Long Island, which stretched 104 miles from Coney Island to Montauk Point without a single harbour large enough to take a frigate. Once past Sandy Hook a sailing ship had only two options, press on or put back, a choice determined by wind, tide and weather.

The first year of the war barely affected New York; both merchant ships and privateers put to sea with ease. By the summer of 1813 the British had clamped down on these trades, taking station off Sandy Hook and at the entrance to Long Island Sound. Trade quickly dried up as ocean-going and coastal vessels were unable to enter the harbour. Import prices doubled, while export goods found few buyers. The nascent American canal system had helped New York sustain her commercial life in 1813, but by 1814 unsold commodities were piling up on the waterfront. The merchants were heartily sick of Madison's unnecessary war.[5] They had reason to fear a British attack, building batteries, waiting anxiously for Robert Fulton's *Demologos*. They took some comfort from the presence of the *President*, with Decatur commanding the harbour defences.[6]

At the close of 1814 New York was full of prime seamen, and Navy Secretary Jones decided to use them in a last attempt to influence the war. In November Jones discussed the options with Decatur, who suggested a distant cruise. Jones proposed capturing the East India Company's annual China convoy. Not only did the convoy carry wealth beyond the dreams of avarice, but it was critical to the entire British commercial system. Stock Market panics caused by the American privateers in 1812 would be as nothing to bankrupting the East India Company. After such a disaster holding Canada would seem remarkably unimportant. However, the British had excellent intelligence sources in New York, and American officers proved uncommonly garrulous. Relying on his Asian experience, Jones decided that *President*, *Constitution* and a small sloop would rendezvous at Tristan da Cunha to replenish water before heading for the Sunda Strait, picking up the north-west monsoon between Madagascar and Mauritius. The next refreshment stop would be Pulo Aor or Pulo Condore at the Straits of Malacca. This strategic choke point was the ideal place to 'intercept all the trade from and to China'. Capturing local shipping would provide Decatur with the latest intelligence about the convoy. Jones forwarded a letter from Canton, explaining how to capture 'the whole China Fleet', along with a French hydrographic treatise.[7]

After two years locked up in port, his name slowly slipping down the list of American heroes, Decatur was eager. He advised hiring a storeship, to be fitted as a privateer once emptied.[8] Jones agreed and detached *Constitution*, replacing her with the sloops *Hornet* and *Peacock*.[9] While James Biddle, who had brought *Hornet* to New York, considered the change 'a most infamous arrangement', he was in the minority.[10] Decatur purchased the freshly coppered 260-ton schooner *Tom Bowline*. John Jacob Astor offered to take another two or three hundred barrels of stores to the rendezvous without charge.[11] Decatur believed the plan 'cannot fail (barring accident) in my opinion of producing all the effects that this government could wish'.[12] He was wrong. It would be no accident that *President* was taken.[13]

STRATEGY AND INTELLIGENCE

In 1814 British forces on the American coast possessed excellent operational and strategic intelligence on American plans. When Cochrane left the Atlantic theatre for New Orleans Henry Hotham remained in command off New York. In late November the Admiralty warned him that with three American heavy frigates ready for sea he should prepare to meet a hostile squadron, keeping his ships in contact.[14] That these orders reflected an over-riding concern for West Indian trade was obvious: Barbados and Jamaica were the rendezvous if the enemy escaped and their destination remained unknown. If no certain information could be obtained, news of an escape was to be communicated 'by every possible exertion' to all quarters.[15] Admiralty concern reached a crescendo in mid-December. Another battleship was sent to Hotham, along with orders to 'keep the force under your orders collected in such a manner as may ensure your being able to meet the enemy upon equal terms, should they make any attempt on our blockading squadrons'. To avoid any repeat of the disasters of 1812 ships at sea must be fully manned. These directions did not reach Hotham in time to be useful.[16] Fortunately he had reached almost identical conclusions. In mid-December Hotham returned to New London after refitting his 74-gun flagship *Superb* at Halifax. On the 14th he took the opportunity to supply the frigates *Pomone* and *Endymion* with beef, pork, bread, pease, rum, flour, lemon juice, vinegar and sugar.[17] His intelligence network provided copious information on American plans. On the 29th he reported '*Constitution* and *Congress* sailed from Boston and Portsmouth about the 17th', and he expected *President*, *Peacock* and *Hornet* would soon attempt to leave New York.

The squadron off Sandy Hook was led by Captain John 'Magnificent' Hayes in the razee *Majestic*. In early January Hayes shared his vigil with three more ships, the 24-pounder frigate *Forth*, the 18-pounder frigate *Pomone* and the 18-gun brig *Nimrod*. *Forth*, a new Endymion-class ship, was commanded by Nelson's nephew, Captain Sir William Bolton. The French prize *Pomone*, Captain John Richard Lumley, had been very successful picking up privateers and merchant vessels on the coast.

Hotham believed that the Americans planned to intercept an outward-bound East India convoy off Madeira, or the Cape Verde Islands.[18] By 2 January he knew that *Congress* had not sailed from Boston, but '*President*, *Peacock* and *Hornet* are waiting only for an opportunity to sail and the information I have received from New York ... states that they are going to India'.[19]

Intelligence from 'different persons at New York' gave *President*:

a chosen crew, estimated in number at 550 ... victualled and stored for a very long voyage, even to the extent of seven or eight months, with large supplies of Sour-Crout, and other anti-scorbutics; that charts of the East Indies have been bought up by her officers.[20]

A week later he knew that *President* and *Hornet* lay off Staten Island, ready for sea; *Peacock* was in the East River, waiting for bread. *President*'s complement of 420 seamen and officers and 55 Marines included very few boys. Decatur had informed his officers that the squadron would be absent twelve or eighteen months, if war continued. In addition *President* had seven months' provisions stowed – with more embarked on board the storeship. Hotham even knew that Astor's brig *Macedonian* would carry extra provisions to the rendezvous. Furthermore, Decatur's 'instructions are not to man prizes, but to destroy every thing he meets'.[21] There were few secrets ashore in New York. Anticipating that *President* would soon attempt to escape past Sandy Hook Hotham dispatched *Endymion* to relieve *Forth*.[22]

ENDYMION: THE BEAUTIFUL SHEPHERD

At first sight this was a curious decision, asking a lot of a ship that had recently suffered heavy losses. While returning to New London from a refit at Halifax in early October, Henry Hope had spotted a privateer and her prize almost becalmed off Nantucket. As *Endymion* closed in the wind fell away and Hope sent his boats, manned by almost half the crew. As they approached the enemy the tide turned with a vengeance and the enemy opened fire. The second barge had one set of oars shot away and the little flotilla became entangled, making a perfect target for the Americans. Some of the boats got free and attacked, but they lacked the numbers to overwhelm the enemy, and found the ship well prepared. The attack was pressed with great courage, but ultimately beaten off with heavy casualties. The second barge was forced to surrender. To make matters worse the target was the notorious privateer schooner *Prince de Neufchatel*, 340 tons and 18 guns, and only 37 men were on board when she was attacked. Hope lost 62 of his best officers and men, including the first lieutenant, about a quarter of his crew. The high proportion of officers and petty officers among the dead and wounded demonstrated the vital role of exemplary leadership in cutting-out operations.[23]

Depressed and despondent, Hope returned to his post off New London. Doubting he could rebuild the ship's company on the American station, he expected to be sent home. Henry Hotham took a different view: desperate to retain his fastest ship he drafted men from the razee HMS *Saturn*, then heading to Halifax.[24] He knew *Endymion* could catch anything that put to sea, even if the gunnery teams had been decimated. Far away to the south Cochrane, anticipating Admiralty criticism of such heavy casualties, stressed that Hope had been unlucky. The *Prince de Neufchatel* was worth the risk. Despite the savage losses Henry Hope managed to restore the ship to something like perfection in less than two months. Not only had he kept his 'fellows close to their exercise' but the system they followed was that of Philip Broke.

BREAK-OUT

Because he anticipated an American sortie, Hotham had to send a 24-pounder frigate to relive *Forth*. *Endymion* was the only ship available. On 6 January Hope left the anchorage off New London. Once under way he exercised the ship's company at great guns, usually high-tempo loading practice followed by a few rounds of aimed fire at a floating target, using the same drills as HMS *Shannon*. *Endymion* rendezvoused with *Majestic*, *Pomone* and *Forth* at mid-afternoon on the 8th, some 12 leagues off Sandy Hook. Hope quickly lowered a boat to visit *Majestic* where Hayes briefed him on the position of the enemy vessels, the specific problems of Sandy Hook, and the standing orders and signals for battle or bad weather. Then the squadron settled down to cruise in company, approximately ESE of the Hook, briefly disturbed by the need to catch and identify the returning *Nimrod*. On the 9th *Forth* set course for New London, and after a brief stop headed south for Bermuda.[25] Late on the 10th the 14-gun schooner HMS *Pictou* arrived with the latest intelligence. Hotham also detached HMS *Tenedos*, Captain Hyde Parker, from New London, bringing Hayes's squadron up to four frigates. Clearly he was expecting trouble.[26] On the 13th *Endymion* exercised at great guns and small arms before closing the American shore, where Hope observed two ships anchored close under the Hook, waiting for a chance to escape. They were ideally placed for a break-out. Hayes expected they would try soon, exploiting a combination of westerly winds, a high tide and a dark night. The sea was smooth, the weather overcast. Later that day the squadron chased the newly arrived *Tenedos*.

The following day the squadron was struck by a heavy snow-storm, *Endymion* losing sight of the other ships. When the snow squalls passed the four frigates reassembled off Sandy Hook.

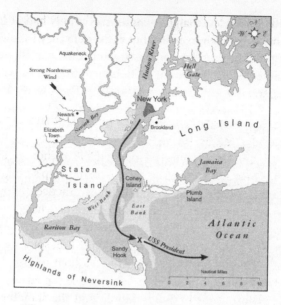

The seaward approaches to New York and the
early stages of the *President*'s break-out attempt.

Hotham and Hayes knew what to expect, and Decatur did not
disappoint.

Confident that the storm had dispersed the blockade, Decatur
decided to leave after dark on the 14th when wind and tide were
favourable. Although the *Tom Bowline* had grounded on her way
down from New York Navy Yard on the 13th, Decatur would
not wait. He would sail that night with Astor's *Macedonian*,
leaving poor *Tom* to accompany *Peacock* and *Hornet*.[27] With
a strong north-westerly wind blowing, intermittent snow
showers and a dark night Decatur needed no second bidding.
Dark and windy nights were ideal for furtive movement, but
not for careful navigation. The gunboats anchored to mark the
navigable channel had been badly placed, and at 8.00 the deeply
laden *President* ran onto the bar. After labouring heavily for over
an hour, breaking several pintles of her rudder, high water and
strong westerly winds drove her into deep water, never again to
grace an American harbour. Unable, or more likely unwilling, to

return to port Decatur set a course along the south coast of Long Island, hoping to evade the enemy in the dark.

After running 50 miles north-east along the Long Island shore Decatur steered SE by S until 05.00 when three ships were seen ahead, one of them within gun shot.[28] They were *Majestic*, *Pomone* and *Endymion*. Decatur quickly hauled up and passed 2 miles north of the enemy. '*Magnificent*' Hayes had anticipated Decatur's every move, making a near-perfect interception just before dawn, leaving a whole day to catch and kill his quarry.

This was Hayes's reward for the sustained grinding effort of holding station off Sandy Hook. Repeatedly blown out to sea by gales, his squadron always clawed their way back as soon as the wind eased, holding station on a point of bearing from the Hook that he judged likely, from existing circumstances, would be the enemy's route. Forethought and skill put Hayes in Decatur's path:

... the squadron was blown off again in a severe snow shower; on Saturday (13th) the wind and weather became favourable for the enemy, and I had no doubt but he would attempt his escape that night; it was impossible from the direction of the wind to get in with the Hook, and as before stated, (in preference to closing the Land to the southward), I stood away to the northward and eastward, till the squadron reached the supposed track of the enemy; and what is a little singular, at the very instant of arriving at that point, an hour before day light, Sandy Hook bearing WNW 15 leagues, we were made happy by the sight of a ship and a brig standing to the southward and eastward, and not more than two miles on the *Majestic*'s weather bow; the night signal for a general chace [*sic*] was made, and promptly obeyed by all the ships.[29]

Observing a strange ship to the NNW at 5.30, Hayes let out the reefs in his topsails and courses and made all sail, lit a blue light and fired three rockets – the night signal for a general chase. He did not detach a ship to chase the brig, preferring to concentrate on the frigate, well aware that the lottery of wind and weather, sails and trim, made it uncertain which of his ships would be best equipped to chase down the flying enemy. In the presence of the mighty *President* the brig was irrelevant.

BATTLE

At first light on 15 January Henry Hope observed a frigate and a brig to the east; he assumed them to be the enemy when they did not answer Hayes's private signals. The wind was blowing hard, north-west by west. When Hayes signalled the general chase *Endymion* bore up and made all sail. With a strong breeze blowing, *Majestic* was the first to close on the enemy; an hour after sighting his quarry Hayes fired three shots at the flying *President*, but they fell short. At dawn *Pomone* and *Endymion* were in company, but Hayes detached *Pomone* to investigate a strange ship seen off to the south. She proved to be the errant *Tenedos*. By 8.00 the squadron was once more in company, in light airs: their quarry was 5 miles ahead bearing east a half north. Anticipating that Decatur might turn south-east, Hayes ordered *Pomone* to leeward, pinning *President* against the Long Island shore with only one course open. Through the morning the wind gradually fell away, and its direction veered between north-west by north and north-north-west. The ships raced eastward; *Endymion* recorded various headings from north-northeast, to south-east.

By midday the American brig had escaped, showing a remarkable turn of speed for a laden transport, and *President* was now 8 or 9 miles ahead.[30] As the wind fell away Hayes's razee dropped behind the lighter, finer-formed frigates. Once *Tenedos* had re-joined Decatur could see British frigates on *President*'s port and starboard quarters, with another pair directly astern. After midday the winds 'became light and baffling'. Having pulled away from *Majestic*, *President* found another large ship coming up. Indeed, as the wind dropped away, Hope noted that *Endymion* 'passed ahead of our squadron fast'. By noon he was closing on two ships, which he took to be *President* and a brig of war.

Decatur responded by sending every spare man to lighten ship, starting the water, cutting away anchors, and jettisoning stores, boats, cables, and anything else that could be sacrificed. Neither Decatur, his officers or the master had ever handled the ship at sea, and it would be very easy to alter the trim and damage the ship's sailing qualities. Decatur also sent men aloft to wet the sails, which he hoped would improve their draw. At least he had the wind almost dead astern, although precious little of it. In light airs the finest form would have a major advantage. Predictably Henry Hope's elegant *Endymion* edged up on her quarry, making considerable distance when Hope anticipated a shift in the wind in mid-afternoon.[31] As the wind dropped all five frigates shook out the last reefs and set studding sails and skysails, adding extra canvas to the immense acreage already spread, desperately searching for every last ounce of effort. Unable to keep pace, Hayes was left to observe the ultimate test of seamanship:

... the chace [sic] became extremely interesting by the endeavours of the enemy to escape, and the exertions of the Captains to get their ships alongside of him; the former by cutting away his anchors, and throwing overboard every moveable article, with a great quantity of provisions; and the latter by trimming their ships in every way possible to effect the purpose; as the day advanced the wind declined, giving the *Endymion* the advantage in sailing.[32]

By 1.00 p.m. *Endymion* was gaining hand over fist and would soon be within range. Hope ordered the crew to their quarters, a well-practised exercise conducted to the rat-a-tat-tat beat of the drums. The last partitions were knocked down, the decks soaked and sanded, to counter fire and blood, rammers and sponges taken down, guns cast loose, magazines manned, charges measured and shot arranged. Finally the gun crews stood by their pieces – each man in his station, and each aware of the vital role that he played in the repetitive, lethal business of loading, hauling out, aiming, firing, controlling the recoil, sponging, ramming home the charge and being ready again. After the savage losses of the *Prince de Neufchatel* action many gun crews had been reformed; some men must have wondered how the new teams would stand up under fire. By the time the two ships were within range the gun deck was a silent study of tension, from the lieutenants in command waiting on barked orders from the quarterdeck, to the powder boys, holding fresh ammunition charges in leather boxes, and the directing midshipmen stationed along the deck. On the upper deck the picture was very different. With *Endymion* straining every nerve to catch a flying enemy most of the gun crews and Marines were hard at work attending to the set and trim of the sails. Most of the best seamen, the topmen, were stationed at the upper deck carronades, which were only used at close range, while the Marines, who provided musketry and boarding parties, were the muscle power for tacking and wearing. The only upper deck gun that was required in a pursuit action was the bow chaser, a very non-standard long 18-pounder bronze cannon on the forecastle. So far nothing had happened that went beyond the usual business of 'exercise at the great guns'. This much was routine drill.

While everyone else went about their business Hope 'observed the chace throw overboard boats, spars casks etc.' at 1.18. *Majestic* and *Pomone*, now a clear second in the pursuit, also recorded this detail. At the same time *Tenedos* exchanged recognition signals with the brig HMS *Dispatch*, and Hyde Parker cleared for action. He was still 5 miles astern.

Action commenced at 2.00 when Decatur opened fire with his stern guns. Hope returned the compliment when his bow chaser bore on target. The two captains had but one idea between them. They wanted to cripple the enemy's rigging and slow the opponent down, but Decatur had the better field of fire. Unable to fire dead ahead, Hope was obliged to choose between closing the range and firing on the enemy. The Americans hit home first: at 2.39 a shot cut through 'the head of our lower studding sail, foot of the main sail, through the stern of the barge in the booms and going through the quarterdeck lodged in the main deck without causing any other damage'. At 3.00 the brig HMS *Dispatch* joined the chase, just as *Endymion* exploited a shift in the wind to close.

Accurate long-range gunnery was difficult in a heavy swell, under full sail. Hope was impressed by the rate and accuracy of the *President*'s fire, but *Endymion* suffered no significant damage. At 4.10 *Endymion* shot away *President*'s jib halyards and the fore topgallant staysail sheet followed ten minutes later. With *Endymion* now hanging on his starboard quarter, a blind spot for his stern guns, Decatur began to luff up into the wind, opening his stern arcs in a desperate attempt to cripple the flying *Endymion*. Confident he had the legs of his opponent, Hope pressed on. Standing at his exposed station on the starboard side of the quarterdeck, he knew exactly what his opponent was trying to do; his observation that *President*'s fire was 'passing over us' tells its own tale.[33]

TACTICAL CHOICE

The British had been profoundly shocked by their defeats in 1812. For the previous twenty years they had hardly lost a single-ship action, easily taking French and Spanish vessels that fought bravely, but with little tactical skill or seamanship. This resulted in complacent tactical thinking, coming to close quarters as soon as possible, firing into the enemy's hull and boarding if necessary. The Americans were much better seamen than their continental contemporaries, but their success flowed from careful, cool-headed tactics. When Decatur fought the *Macedonian* he countered British tactics and superior sailing with anti-rigging projectiles in the opening stages of the action. This reflected a conscious doctrinal choice: American ships carried a far higher percentage of such rounds than British ships – up to 20 per cent of the total.[34] American captains used star shot, bar shot and double-headed shot, along with langridge and grape shot, to dismantle the rigging and immobilise the enemy. By crippling the sails and masts of their opponents the Americans gained a 'decisive advantage from the superior faculties of their long guns in distant cannonade', particularly against opponents anxious to close.[35] Having disabled the enemy, the American captains calmly exploited their superior mobility to take a commanding position for raking fire. These tactics made the best use of superior firepower.[36]

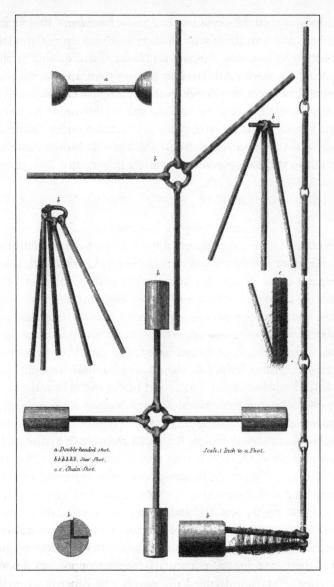

a. *Double-headed shot.*
b.b.b.b.b.b. *Star Shot.*
c.c. *Chain-Shot.*

Scale, 1 Inch to a Foot.

Stars and bars: American dismantling projectiles,
designed to cripple an enemy ship's rigging.

Decatur used the same tactics against *Endymion* that he had employed against the *Macedonian*. He tried to cripple the enemy, to secure his ultimate object, in this case flight. He did not adjust to the circumstances. Hope knew exactly what to expect – the British had learnt their lesson – and he adapted his tactics as the action developed. It was no accident that Hope chose a position that denied Decatur the opportunity to fire broadsides into his rigging throughout the chase. If Decatur would not stand and fight he could be crippled and brought to bay.

CLOSING FOR THE KILL

At 3.00 the frigates were exchanging fire, British bow to American stern. 'The object of each was to cripple the spars of the other', as *Endymion* slowly closed the last 1,000 yards. By 5.00 Hope occupied a near-perfect position on *President*'s starboard quarter, within half point-blank range – little more than 100 yards – where few American guns would bear. This was fine seamanship, and consummate tactical skill. In order to fire effectively Decatur would have to luff up and open his stern arcs. Every time he did so the chasing squadron would gain. If he did not knock *Endymion* out of the chase Decatur knew he would be defeated. He must have realised he was facing a real seaman, a far abler tactician than blundering John Carden of the *Macedonian*, and well-trained gunners: 'The fire of the English ship now became exceedingly annoying, for she was materially within point blank range, and every shot cut away something aloft.' The two ships were heading east by north, the wind now north-westerly, and racing along under every stitch of canvas that could be spread. This was highly unusual: ships normally fought under head sails. Moreover, the relatively poor performance of *President*'s guns led some to think her powder defective.[37]

For half an hour Decatur endured *Endymion*'s galling fire, hoping that his wily opponent would come alongside, where his superior battery and much larger crew (broadsides: 916

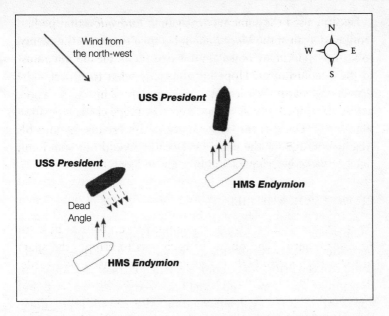

HMS *Endymion*, just abaft the starboard quarter of USS *President*, presents a 'dead angle' for the *President*'s broadside. *Endymion* could engage effectively with her port broadside because of the relative position of the ships and the direction of the wind. Decatur had to choose between continuing to try to run away and turning to fight.

pounds to 676; crew 480 to 346) would shift the balance in his favour. Anxious to end the combat quickly, he prepared his men to board, to exploit another major advantage.[38] Never a man for half measures Decatur told the crew he planned to take *Endymion*, transfer the crew and scuttle *President* before fleeing from the rest of the British squadron.[39] This was desperate and delusional: he must have realised his opponent would not fall for such a simple plan. Well aware of the disparity of force between the two ships, and his increasing isolation, Hope constantly yawed across the American quarter, firing into her rigging: 'every fire now cut some of our sails and rigging'. There could only be one conclusion to this combat: *President* would be disabled and fall easy prey to the British. The *Pomone* was slowly gaining ground; if she joined the action Decatur was doomed. *Tenedos* held station in the middle distance, but *Majestic* had dropped astern, despite Hayes's constant attention to the set and draw of his sails and the trim of the ship – he desperately needed a breeze to push the heavy ship.[40]

Up to this point Decatur may have believed his cagey opponent was just another standard British frigate, well-handled, with well-laid guns, because the only projectiles to hit the *President* had been 18-pounder shot from the bow chaser. Having dropped the razee far astern he might have believed the other three frigates posed little threat. Stepping onto a shot box, to get a better view over the bulwarks, Decatur was almost complacent. It was a serious mistake. Hope had no intention of trading blows, broadside to broadside with the powerful American. His ship was significantly lighter than the American in scantling and frame, and he had no need for heroics. A skilful appreciation of the evolving situation governed his every move. Having damaged the enemy aloft it was time to shift his guns from the rigging to the hull, from catching to killing. To capture a resolute, professional opponent he would have to subdue the enemy in a close-range gunnery duel.

With *Endymion* fine on *President*'s quarter the first British broadside smashed into the American quarterdeck: Decatur was knocked flat by a huge splinter that hit his chest; another cut his forehead. Although stunned and winded he quickly resumed his position, but he had been lucky.[41] Among those standing beside him first lieutenant Fitz Henry Babbit had his right leg cut clean through and was knocked down the wardroom hatch. He died two hours later. Another splinter fractured Lieutenant Howell's skull, with fatal consequences. This was no picnic. Many of those who stood in the 'slaughter pen' beside the ship's wheel that day would die. Hope poured in a succession of broadsides at a range where every shot told.

Between the sharp bark of his own guns Hope would have caught fragments of sound from his opponent, sounds of death and injury, of shattered timber and chaos. Delighted by such accurate gunnery, he 'observed that our shot did considerable execution'. The screams and cries of the wounded would have carried across the interval, along with the heavy stroke of iron balls on solid oak. Every minute he held his position he was levelling the odds; soon he could close for the kill. Struggling to regain his senses Decatur read the situation with equal facility: these were well-matched combatants, experienced, confident and determined. Suddenly aware that the enemy was far more powerful than he had expected, Decatur had to act quickly; even the *President* could not endure such punishment for long. If she lost a mast the action was over, he had to get away. Decatur's only hope was to cripple *Endymion*. He continued to fire high, searching for a killing blow, to smash a yard, cut a backstay or perhaps bring down one of *Endymion*'s masts. He had done it once before.

Just after dusk Decatur changed tactics, suddenly shifting to a southerly course in a desperate attempt to knock *Endymion* out of the race with one or two raking broadsides and escape into the gathering gloom. At 5.30 Hope observed the *President* brail up her spanker and bear away on the wind, as if to cross *Endymion*'s bow and rake. As he made the manoeuvre Decatur had the battle lanterns extinguished.[42] One contemporary concluded that Decatur had expected the *Endymion*'s masts, already damaged by his fire, would go by the board, leaving her disabled.[43] This had been the main reason for the defeat of all three British frigates in 1812. Once again Henry Hope was ready.[44] Well aware that a raking broadside of 24- and 42-pounder shot could cripple his ship, Hope immediately put the helm hard a-weather to counter the threat. No sooner had Decatur begun to change course than Hope followed suit, and *Endymion* was far handier than *President*.

Decatur's sudden change of course brought the two ships broadside to broadside, giving the American one last chance to cripple his opponent and flee into the gathering gloom before the other British ships could get up. This time Hope did not avoid action; he considered the situation 'favourable' and continued to

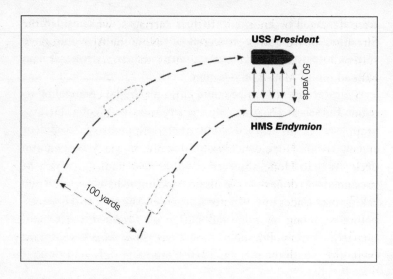

Decatur's attempt to catch Hope unawares by a turn to starboard.
Instead Hope has *Endymion* turn with *President* and accepts a
broadside to broadside engagement.

close the range. His guns had slowed the American, and inflicted
serious damage. With the daylight ebbing away he had no choice
but to engage – unless he was prepared to give up the greatest
prize of the war. He would fight, on his own terms, and not risk
a boarding action. At 6.04 the *President* began firing musketry
from her tops, Hope countered with his Marines. Frequent small
adjustments, edging up into the wind, allowed Hope to close the
range without losing the favourable position he had taken for
broadside fire, just abaft *President*'s beam. The two ships were
now at half musket shot, 50–100 yards, and Decatur's fire finally
began to tell on *Endymion*'s sails and running rigging.

Yet the real story was the terrible beating that *Endymion*
inflicted on *President*'s gun deck. The American ship's fire
visibly slackened as men fell and guns were disabled. Among
the first casualties was fourth lieutenant Archibald Hamilton,
commanding a division on the main deck, cut in half by a
24-pound shot. Many of his men died at their guns, six of which

were damaged or knocked off their carriages, while ten of the fifteen starboard gun ports were hit.[45] Now the American crew suffered the same savage punishment the *United States* had handed out to *Macedonian*'s men.

With the two ships running south on parallel courses, Hope countered Decatur's every attempt to close the range. Unable to grapple with this wary foe, Decatur continued to fire into her rigging, while Hope concentrated his fire on the American gun deck. At 6.40 Hope observed the *President* haul up, which he presumed was done to avoid his fire, and immediately poured two raking broadsides into her stern, with devastating consequences, before resuming his preferred station on *President*'s starboard quarter. At 7.15 *President* shot away *Endymion*'s starboard boat, along with the main and lower studding sails.

At 7.18 the enemy not returning our fire we ceased firing, at 7.30 the enemy shot away the larboard main topmast studding sail and the main brace, at 7.32 the enemy hauled suddenly to the wind, trimmed sails & again obtained the advantage of giving him a raking broadside which he returned with one shot from his stern gun, the enemy much shattered.[46]

Between 7.40 and 7.50 *President* bore away from *Endymion* and ceased fire. At 7.58 she displayed a light in her rigging, the recognised night signal of surrender.

After two and a half hours of broadside fire *Endymion*'s rigging had been cut to pieces and several sails shredded. Hope hauled up to repair his rigging – as Decatur had before finishing off the *Macedonian*. Rather than waste time closing on *President* he called up all hands to bend on new sails, and splice the rigging to ensure the prize did not escape. He would have sent a boat to secure *President*, but none would float, and at 8.10 he observed *Pomone* and *Tenedos* coming up. Later Decatur would imply – though he scarcely had the gall to claim it openly – that he had defeated *Endymion*. This was simply incredible. Hope was quite certain the American had surrendered.[47] Having adapted his tactics to the situation and defeated *President* he was far too astute to make a mistake on such a cardinal point, and no one ever impugned his integrity.

Never one to miss an opportunity, Decatur kept under way, sliding past the near-stationary *Endymion* at 8.30, and resumed his course of east by north. Hope did not fire; his men were busy aloft and he believed the action was over. However, he had over-estimated his enemy's integrity. Decatur hoped to escape into the night under royal studding sails. Although it was quite dark when *President* started this bid for freedom, the clouds soon cleared and the stars revealed her to the pursuing *Pomone*, which had made up a considerable distance during the action.

Having completed shifting sails, fitting a new main topsail, jib, fore topmast staysail and spanker, *Endymion* trimmed sails and bore up to close on the enemy at 8.52, just after the *Pomone* and *Tenedos* passed. Hope could see *President* heading east, under a press of sail, and at 9.05 observed one of the squadron run up on her larboard beam, and fire into her. *President* then shortened sail, luffed up, and hoisted the light in her rigging higher. Decatur hastily conferred with his two surviving lieutenants, Shubrick and Gallagher, and merchant ship captain Robinson. They concurred that he had no option but surrender, although Robinson was far from happy with the decision.[48] Unaware that the enemy had already surrendered, because *President* was very obviously trying to escape, *Pomone* managed to fire two close-range broadsides into *President*'s larboard bow before Decatur hailed to confirm his situation.[49] The broadsides were ineffective, in part because they were badly aimed, and in part because Decatur had already sent his crew below to attend to their possessions before the British came on board.

Decatur subsequently claimed that *President* had not surrendered to *Endymion*, though this makes it hard to explain his failure to resist *Pomone*. His new opponent was a lightly built 18-pounder frigate, two or three broadsides would have crippled her IF *President* was still in good fighting trim. In truth the American ship was badly damaged. *Endymion*'s steady, accurate fire had smashed the American gun deck and upper deck batteries, killing and wounding officers and men, disabling guns, and damaging masts and spars. With several shot holes between wind and water, and others below the waterline, the hold was filling. *President* was in no state to fight, or to flee. Two days later Decatur acknowledged 'the crippled state of the *President*'s spars' was a factor when he 'deemed it my duty to surrender', hoisting the lantern in his rigging higher to signify the fact. He did not fire even the single shot at *Pomone* that was required for honour's sake.[50]

As *Pomone* came into action *Tenedos* was closing fast, hastily shedding sail to avoid over-running the concluding scene. At 9.45 Hope hailed Hyde Parker to let him know that the enemy had surrendered, but he did not have a boat to take possession. Hyde Parker's men were the first to board *President*. *Endymion* finally caught up with her prize at 12.45 a.m, while *Majestic* arrived at 3.00. Hyde Parker recorded that the captured muster book gave the American ship a crew of 480.[51] Having learnt that he had taken the mighty *President*, Hope ordered the guns secured and beat the retreat.[52] During the day *Endymion* travelled 78 miles on courses steadily shifting from east by north at 1.00 to east-north-east at 5.00, south-east at 6.00, and east at 10.00. The wind varied from north-westerly to north-north-westerly. When the action ended Montauk Point lay north 37 miles, west 95 miles.[53]

The battle had been decided when Decatur changed course and Hope accepted broadside action. While this gave the *President* the opportunity to cripple *Endymion*'s rigging, *Endymion*'s fire left *President* shattered and sinking.

THE *PRESIDENT* TAKEN

After twenty-four hours of action, anxiety and bloodshed, including being knocked to the deck and cut about the head, Decatur must have been exhausted; his men had suffered terribly, his officers falling at a frightening rate. He must have been demoralised by the knowledge that he had been comprehensively out-thought by Hayes, and then out-sailed and out-manoeuvred by Hope. He had no reason to expect the other British ships to be any less dangerous. While Theodore Roosevelt considered Decatur had 'acted rather tamely' in surrendering, Henry Adams suggested: 'anxious to escape rather than to fight, Decatur in consequence failed either to escape or resist with effect'.[54]

By contrast Hope had handled his ship superbly, avoiding the close-quarters broadside action that would have suited the more heavily built *President* for as long as possible. A contemporary British verse celebrating the battle offers the following insight:

'Be Silent, men!' was all his cry. 'Bring all your guns to bear,
And do not fire one shot in vain; both round and grape prepare.'[55]

Once again the battle had been settled by superior gunnery: *Endymion*'s crew fought like professionals, calmly, deliberately, and decisively. They used Broke's system, the state of the *President* after the battle bearing mute witness to their skill. Decatur confessed that *Endymion* fired accurately in the chase; the American casualties indicate she did equally well in the broadside action. Sir Howard Douglas, father of modern naval gunnery, reckoned this was: 'some of the best gun-practice ever effected by British seamen'.[56] Having discussed the action with several of the British officers, William James stated:

Captain Hope, aware of the excellence of the Broke system, had long trained his men to the use of both great guns and small-arms, and many had been the anxious look out on board the *Endymion* for one of the American 44 gun frigates.[57]

Endymion's crew of 346 suffered 11 killed and 14 wounded. Her masts and yards were hit in several places and significant parts of the rigging and sails were cut, but she inflicted far more damage on *President*. On the starboard side *Endymion*'s 24-pounders had smashed through *President*'s hull all along the gun deck and the quarterdeck, causing considerable structural damage, and dismounting or damaging six guns in addition to the heavy human cost. Some shot went straight through the ship.

During the chase and raking action three shot went through the buttock area; one ended up in *President*'s magazine. *President*'s masts were 'crippled'. The damage inflicted by *Endymion*'s guns in the broadside action stood in stark contrast to the 18-pounder shot that simply bounced off the *Constitution* in 1812. Size really did matter: 24-pound shot were far more effective than 18-pounders. Furthermore, they were used with 'destructive precision' which, as the senior officer of the prize reported, left *President* with 'six feet of water in the hold, when taken possession of'.[58] Hayes reported *President* to be in a sinking state, which Hope attributed to 'the steady and well directed fire kept up by His Majesty's ship under my command'.[59] *President* lost 3 lieutenants and 32 seamen and Marines killed, Midshipman Richard Dale died later at Bermuda. Decatur, the master, 2 midshipmen and 66 seamen and marines were wounded, a total of 105 casualties, more than four times the number suffered by *Endymion*.[60] An anonymous British officer reported that after the action Decatur declared to Hope: 'you have out-sailed me, out-manoeuvred me, and fairly beaten me'.[61] John Hayes had equal reasons to be pleased: he had outwitted the best officer in the United States Navy, capturing 'the United States ship *President* – Commodore Decatur, on Sunday night, after an anxious chace of eighteen hours'.[62]

THE PRIZE

The following day Hayes sent the rest of the squadron south towards Bermuda. Hope had his people aloft, replacing the fore topmast and main topgallant yard, knotting and splicing the rigging, assisted by two shipwrights from *Tenedos*. In the afternoon Decatur, his first lieutenant and 213 seamen were moved across to *Endymion* by boat. *Pomone* exchanged 140 Americans for 50 of her own crew; *Tenedos* took 160 and sent her first division across to help man the prize. At the end of the day the easterly wind increased to gale force with occasional rain. The 17th was worse: *Endymion* lost her storm staysails and trysail, began labouring in the heavy seas and 'a great quantity of water was taken in abaft' when the rudder head coat washed away. Hope lightened ship, getting all moveable weight off the upper deck, heaving the quarterdeck and forecastle guns overboard. Soon afterwards the mainmast fell, followed by the mizzen topmast. The foremast and bowsprit did not stand much longer, a legacy of *President*'s fire.

President was also suffering. Shortly before *Endymion* lost her masts *Tenedos* observed the prize flying a distress signal; ten minutes later the fore topmast went over, followed soon after by the main topgallant. As darkness fell *Tenedos* lost sight of the *President* amid the rain showers and gloom of an Atlantic night. Soon after her lower masts were carried away, and, with several imperfectly plugged 24-pounder shot holes between wind and water, she was in danger of foundering, the prize crew being exhausted at the pumps. Only the bowsprit and spritsail kept the ship from lying to in the trough of the ocean. Prize Master William Morgan, first lieutenant of *Endymion*, veered out a sea-anchor made from two hawsers end on from the forward ports, which quickly brought the ship's head to the sea. This manoeuvre enabled the pumps to keep on top of the water in the hold. By the time the sea-anchor gave way, after between eight and ten hours' service, the storm had abated. Jury masts were rigged and the ship limped on to Bermuda.

While *President* and her captors headed south, Hayes worked his way back to New London, arriving on the 22nd.[63] Hotham reported to the Admiralty and Cochrane the following day. His dispatch reached London on 17 February, being read at the Board the following day. Secretary Croker endorsed Hotham's dispatch 'Copy for Gazette' and then:

Own and impress their Lordships' approbation of the judgement with which Sir H Hotham's dispositions were made and of the manner in which Captain Hayes carried them into execution, of the zeal and activity displayed by all the Captains and ships' companies and the gallantry with which Captain Hope brought his ship into action and the distinguished bravery and good conduct maintained by him and all the other officers and ship's company of the *Endymion* and as mark of their approbation they have promoted Lieutenant Morgan to be a Commander and Mr ___ Midshipman to be a Lieutenant and sent Capt. Hope the midshipman's blank commission to fill up for the midshipman. JWC 18.2.1815.[64]

Croker's minutes were invariably works of literary merit and expository power, but good news brought out the best in him.

A few days later Hotham retailed less agreeable news: *Hornet* and *Peacock* had escaped on the 20th 'at which time HM ships stationed off Sandy Hook were unable to keep in with the land. I have no information on which I can rely as to their destination, but always understood they were intended to accompany the *President* and they may possibly proceed to a given rendezvous for meeting her.' To make mattes worse Hotham had no ships he could detach in pursuit, or even to warn other officers.[65]

Unaware of the disaster that had befallen Decatur the sloops pushed on for the South Atlantic. *Hornet* arrived off Tristan da Cunha exactly one month later, where she met and captured HMS *Penguin*, despite Biddle being told that the war was over.[66] *Peacock* went on to capture the East India Company sloop *Nautilus* on 30 June, despite newspapers on board the prize making it clear the war was over. Navy Secretary William Jones finally had his Indiaman, a miserable little sloop that had to be returned, complete with a valuable cargo.

GLORY

President, *Endymion* and *Pomone* reached Bermuda, where the Vice Admiralty Court condemned the American flagship as a lawful prize to the four frigates and *Dispatch*.[67] Bermuda political and commercial leaders hurried to celebrate a striking British triumph, presenting Hope with a public address and a piece of plate, together with an identical silver cup for all future *Endymion*s. When delivered in 1821 the £500 vases featured the bow and stern of the successful ship and the motto 'Old England Forever'.[68] The American crew were treated well, and given their liberty.[69] The heady atmosphere at Bermuda was ruined by the allegation, made by a British officer from the prize crew, that Decatur had concealed sixty-eight armed men in the hold, intending to recover the ship. The allegation appeared in print in the *Bermuda Royal Gazette* of 1 February. Such conduct by an officer who had surrendered would have been utterly dishonourable. It was strenuously denied by the Americans. On Decatur's honour the Governor of the Island compelled the editor, Mr Ward, to retract. Ward obliged, but most unwillingly, repeating the allegation on 16 March. His primary source was Lieutenant George James Perceval of the *Tenedos*, later Captain the Earl of Egmont.[70] Perceval may have misconstrued Decatur's decision to let his men attend to their personal belongings. This was common practice after surrendering. As Perceval had seen the men with his own eyes the editor believed the Governor's demand for a retraction demonstrated undue delicacy.[71] For his pains Ward lost the government printing contract, and received a beating in the street from American midshipman Robert Randolph. Randolph had good reason to be upset: his brother had been captured on board the *Chesapeake*, now he followed suit on the *President*.[72] By this time Decatur was long gone, leaving behind nagging doubts about his honour, his integrity, and his conduct of the battle.

Further disputes arose at Bermuda about the precise course of the action. Decatur had been anxious, for obvious reasons, to claim that he had struck to the entire squadron, that he was outnumbered, and that he had defeated *Endymion*. He stressed that while the British ship bent on new sails and replaced some ropes she did not fire on *President*, despite having a fine view of her stern. In fact Hope understood the lantern hoisted in *President*'s mizzen rigging to be the signal of surrender. Decatur may have been desperate to embellish a defeat, but his officers told a different story. Mr Bowie, the chaplain, swore that the light had been hoisted before *Pomone* arrived. *Pomone*'s officers, considering the light merely a substitute ensign, fired

Victor and vanquished: American naval hero
Commodore Stephen Decatur.

two broadsides. *President* had not replied because, as Decatur
admitted, she had already surrendered. When *Pomone* arrived
he had already sent his men below decks to stow their bags.
Pomone's fire, which Decatur subsequently claimed killed and
wounded many, was, Mr Bowie reported, perfectly harmless.
Only one shot penetrated *President*'s larboard side, the side that
Pomone fired into. All the other hits, on the starboard side, were
from *Endymion*. Another explanation for the sudden surrender
emerged from the testimony of Lieutenant John Gallagher and
Marine Lieutenant Levi Twiggs: in the gloom Decatur mistook
the *Pomone* for the far more potent *Majestic*.[73]

While the precise details of battle, and the integrity of the
officers involved might seem more than a little arcane 200 years
after the event, that would be misleading. Decatur, Hope, Hayes,
Croker and William James knew that this war had been a clash of

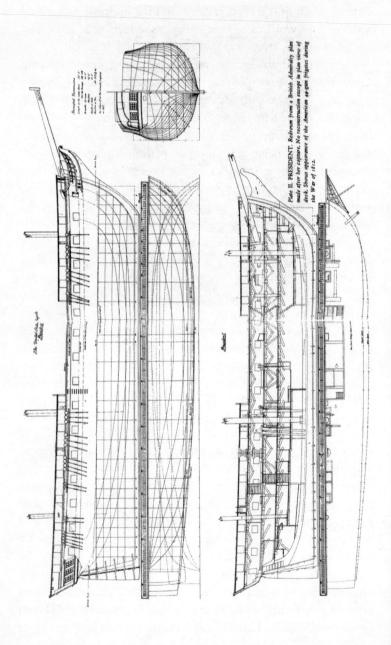

Plate II. PRESIDENT. Redrawn from a British Admiralty plan made after her capture. No reconstruction except in plan view of deck. Shows appearance of the American 44-gun frigate during the War of 1812.

cultures, much of it waged in print, and the impressions created by the printed word would long outlast the facts of the day. The War of 1812 was a very modern war.

Judgements of the action vary. Amid the general rejoicing Henry Hotham provided the most acute analysis of Hope's 'exceedingly gallant and judicious conduct'.[74] In this 'brilliant' action the judgement Hope displayed in holding his position, 'as well as the steady, well directed fire . . . has done him infinite honour'. In sum 'never was an action better sustained; nor more effect produced by any ship's fire. The *President* . . . was in a fair way to be sunk.'[75] Victory was the ideal tonic for Hope, who wrote to his uncle from Bermuda to report the capture of the *President*, observing the severe 'loss and damage she has sustained will shew that we have not been deficient and my brother officers all regret that we had not met single handed. I am confident the result would have been most honourable to *Endymion*.'[76] *Endymion* and *President* were patched up with new masts, but not refitted for service.[77] Then victor and vanquished sailed for Portsmouth, spiritual home of the Royal Navy, in early March.[78]

The British public needed to see the huge 44 for themselves. They arrived at Spithead on the 28th, affording Englishmen 'ocular demonstration of the "equal force" by which their frigates had been captured'.[79] The event was recorded in a lengthy verse by an author with considerable knowledge of the action.[80] One look at the *President* demonstrated that an American 44 was not 'equal force' for a British 18-pounder frigate, despite American claims to the contrary.[81]

Honour restored, fresh laurels gained, the Royal Navy had every reason to be satisfied with the results of its war with America.

CHAPTER 11

Making Peace: War Aims, Strategy and the Balance of Power

The process by which Britain and America made peace was complicated by mutual incomprehension. In 1812 the British government took several months to accept that the Americans would not give way without a serious war. Not only did this policy cripple Warren's attempt to impose an economic blockade, but the timing of every subsequent British policy shift would be driven by the same over-riding imperative – Europe. In 1813 most Cabinet ministers effectively ignored the war, leaving a profoundly unenthusiastic Lord Melville to organise a secondary naval campaign, under the overall direction of Earl Bathurst, another minister with more pressing duties, in his case supporting the war in Spain. Although the *Shannon–Chesapeake* action briefly shifted attention westward, 1813 would be dominated by the crisis and collapse of Napoleon's German empire. Battles at Lützen, Bautzen and Dresden, Austrian accession to the coalition and the titanic battle of Leipzig only emphasised that the American war was a trifling, tedious distraction. The critical turning point for the direction of British strategy was the collapse of Napoleonic Spain. The battle of Vitoria on 21 June 1813 enhanced British diplomatic leverage with other European powers, and ended the need for American grain and flour; soon Wellington's troops would dine in France.

STRATEGY

At any stage before spring 1814 the British government would have settled for the *status quo ante*, terms that would stop America invading Canada, and end their pretension to lecture London on the definition of maritime belligerent rights and the services owed the British Crown by British-born seamen. To secure this end the British adopted a cautious strategy, largely in response to the desperate lack of military resources. Canada would be defended on the frontiers, but the army would fall back to the major fortresses of Quebec and Halifax in the event of defeat, relying on the combination of impregnable fortifications and seaborne supplies to hold these bastions and then recapture lost ground. Governor-General Sir George Prevost proved an adept player of this limited defensive posture, carefully husbanding resources at Quebec to avoid the danger of a sudden reversal of fortune, doling out troops to the porous borders with an economy that suited his Swiss ancestry. The comprehensive failure of every American invasion has obscured the very real danger that the British faced. With the benefit of hindsight some suggest that Prevost might have been more aggressive, but he rightly looked to the other arm of British strategy, the naval offensive, to save Canada. Canada would be defended on the shores of Chesapeake Bay and in the counting houses of American cities.

With this strategy in place the government could ignore the American war because the convoy system reduced commercial risk and loss to manageable levels, while intelligence sharing between Lloyd's and the Admiralty ensured there were no unpleasant surprises. Cockburn's Chesapeake raids began the process of taking the initiative on the littoral, and closing the American cruiser ports. Although they paid the war little attention, ministers were always looking to conclude this annoying sideshow. By late 1813 it was clear that the strategy of isolating and targeting the Southern and Mid-Atlantic states by economic blockade and coastal raids had not broken the Union. In consequence the ministers increased pressure on Washington, translating the vital naval blockade of New England into an economic offensive, and stepping up the scale and tempo of coastal raids. Even so, British options were limited. While Napoleon remained in power few British soldiers could be spared for America. Wellington was always looking for more manpower, while 1813 opened fresh theatres in northern Europe.

As Napoleon retreated westward, the British saw an opportunity to destroy his naval arsenal and fleet at Antwerp. This was the over-riding British strategic interest; in comparison reinforcing Canada or attacking America were insignificant. Antwerp, the *casus belli* in 1793, had become a major French naval base, and the fixed point around which successive Tory ministries of Pitt, Portland, Perceval and now Liverpool developed their war aims. Yet, with the main army in Spain, the Cabinet could only find a paltry 11,000 men for General Lord Lynedoch's force, a stark illustration of the limits of British power. An attack on Antwerp in February, and an assault on the fortress at Bergen op Zoom in March 1814 failed. There were too few men, and they were second-class units.[1] The point is telling. If Britain lacked the military force to secure core war aims in nearby Belgium, there was no prospect whatsoever that men could be found to pursue altogether less important aims in America.

In 1813 British strategists had few options. They had to maintain the naval and economic blockades, to deny the American cruisers and privateers access to the sea, and ruin the American treasury; but limited military manpower meant that anything beyond holding the Canadian frontier, the dominant military effort, and Cockburn's brilliant, extemporised, small-scale high-tempo raiding on the Chesapeake was simply impossible. Too many troops were tied down in West Indies garrisons, ostensibly against the improbable risk of an American attack, but in reality to calm the nerves of politically powerful planters, who feared a slave uprising. A rising tide of insurrection across the Spanish Caribbean and Latin America challenged the security of the British sugar islands, raising questions about the future of British rule that transformed the blundering American filibuster against East Florida into a threatening portent. In the minds of the planters it was not only Canada that was under attack.

The political weight of the West Indies remained strong: the Ministry depended on the planter's votes and their profits, remitted in specie, to retain political power and fund the European war. British strategy would be bound by such calculations until Napoleon had been defeated. Strategy to fight America was bound by chains of sugar and gold to the defence of West Indian commercial and territorial power. West Indies complaints prompted Melville to remove Warren, and replace him with the governor of Guadeloupe. Suppressing the commerce of these ex-French islands to maintain high commodity prices had been critical to retaining the support of British planters. How far the planter interest outweighed other factors in ministerial calculation is hard to ascertain, but the centrality of the sugar economy to British strategy continued a pattern already clear in the War of Independence. The British would not risk the sugar islands for some fleeting advantage on the mainland. In consequence the scale of coastal operations would be severely limited until Europe was at peace.

Over the autumn and winter of 1813 Foreign Secretary Castlereagh spent every waking moment trying to keep the latest European coalition pulling together, using a combination of British economic aid, military hardware and diplomatic pressure. These tools were vital because even Wellington's military successes, crossing the Pyrenees and defeating the French on home soil, paled into insignificance alongside the massive allied armies gathering on the Rhine for the invasion of France. The central European perspectives of Austrian Chancellor Metternich, Tsar Alexander and the Prussians, along with the parochial concerns of Swedish Crown Prince Bernadotte, led them to view Iberia as a sideshow. They saw the American war as a distraction and a weakness they could exploit to limit British influence.

Castlereagh's diplomacy was dominated by Britain's refusal to compromise on the issue of maritime belligerent rights, the core of the American challenge. He recognized that Russia would try to re-open the subject, and not to Britain's advantage, when a post-war Congress assembled to redraw the maps and charters of Europe. Anticipating a future clash, Russia wanted to push the American/French claim that neutral ships made the cargoes neutral – thereby disarming British sea power. This had been the purpose of Rumiantsev's attempt to broker peace in 1813. Castlereagh made the British position very clear, and did not hesitate to issue a scarcely veiled threat: 'Great Britain may be driven out of a Congress but not out of her maritime rights, and if the continental Powers know their own interests they will not hazard this.' At the same time he crushed Napoleon's malicious attempt to divide his enemies with the suggestion that the Americans should be invited to any Congress.[2] In September 1813 Castlereagh restated the British position in a forceful dispatch to the British Ambassador at the Russian court. Maritime rights had never been discussed at any previous congress, and he would not allow them to be raised at the next one. There would be no congress until the subject had been taken off the agenda. He made it equally clear that Britain would not allow the American war to be discussed at a general European settlement.[3] Britain used her power to isolate the wider world from the European settlement. In December 1813 the Cabinet instructed Castlereagh that if the European powers raised the subject he could state that Britain was prepared to make peace with the United States on the principles of the *status quo ante bellum*.[4] These terms had been available to the Americans from the first day of the war – and they were the terms the Americans eventually signed.

To counter-balance the growing power of Russia, Castlereagh carefully built up Austria, making concessions to Vienna on Central European issues beyond the reach of sea power. In essence Chancellor Prince Metternich secured British support for Austrian ambitions in Italy by accepting the British case that the maritime legal code had never been the subject of any European congress, and that Britain had always abided by the law of nations on this subject. It was easy for Metternich, for whom such matters were utterly alien, and effectively irrelevant, to accept the deal. The Anglo-Austrian accord pre-empted French, American, or Russian attempts to alter the rules of war at sea, blocking a diplomatic coalition between the three powers that had challenged British economic war practice over the past fifty years. The following day Castlereagh informed Bathurst, who supervised the Foreign Office while he followed the war across Europe: 'the Allied Sovereigns adhere to the determination which they had previously declared of not permitting that question to be mixed up with any negotiations which may take place'.[5]

Having secured their freedom to deal with the United States and maritime questions without European interference, the British could wait for Madison to recognise the inevitable. American obduracy meant negotiations only began after Napoleon had abdicated. From an American perspective it seemed obvious that once Britain escaped the over-riding demands of the European war a bankrupt, beaten United States could not hope to secure improved terms. It was only common sense to treat, and to reduce domestic expectations of what was possible. Having agreed to talks, the British diplomatic network picked up the American envoys when they arrived at Gothenburg on board the USS *John Adams*. The British Vice Consul forwarded the American mail bag to London, to be opened and deciphered by the Post Office 'Black Chamber'. Reading enemy mail helped ensure diplomatic success.[6]

Although Castlereagh spent much of this period moving round Europe, the Foreign Office kept him up to date with American issues. Face to face discussions in London with Albert Gallatin and James Bayard revealed 'very amicable dispositions', suggesting they hoped to get out of the war 'with a safe conscience, by saying that, the war in Europe having ceased, the causes of their quarrel with us have ceased also'.[7] In effect the Americans conceded Britain's core war aims, maritime belligerent rights and impressment, at the outset. This was logical: having failed to conquer Canada, they had nothing to trade. The only question for the British was how far the blockade and coastal operations could be translated into more positive outcomes. The inner Cabinet showed little interest in anything more, which explains why the Cabinet only sent a small military reinforcement, despite initially planning a far more ambitious programme.

The deciphered American dispatches, and discussions with their envoys, quickly established that American expectations had become more realistic as the European situation turned. When the European war ended the Admiralty pressurised the interim French administration to stop American privateers using their ports.[8] Although American warships were legally entitled to use neutral ports, they could not sell prizes if the host state remained at peace with Britain. Even so, French ports remained a problem for much of 1814 as altogether grander issues preoccupied both Castlereagh and the French government, facilitating a last American naval surge in European waters that summer, distracting British resources from the American coastal zone. The notorious French-owned privateer *Prince de Neufchatel* sold prizes in France months after the downfall of Napoleon, adding insult to injury by doing so more easily than had been possible in the Emperor's day. Melville, rendered cautious by bitter experience, thought new French rules offered only 'a fair prospect' of solving the privateer problem.[9] Foreign Office Under-Secretary Edward Cooke suggested that the restored Bourbon kings of France and Spain might be asked if they were minded to recover Florida and New Orleans, redoubling the pressure on Washington, and ensuring neither power aided the Americans.[10] He had missed the point: Castlereagh had been working hard for months to keep the two conflicts in separate, hermetically sealed boxes. He had no intention of allowing any European power to join this war.

Placing the peace negotiations in Ghent enabled the British to exploit the close proximity to London, and their military occupation of the Austrian Netherlands (modern Belgium). While Austria retained nominal title it had no interest in re-occupying the province, or in maritime rights or America. Castlereagh's close working relationship with Metternich ensured this vital province was now under British control.

By contrast Britain had little ability to influence the negotiations by military force. Three weeks after the end of the European conflict Melville advised Castlereagh that the Admiralty was short of troop ships, Britain's ability to repatriate

French prisoners of war had been compromised by the need to take troops from the Garonne to America, and repatriate the Portuguese army from the south of France to Lisbon.[11] The dull, prosaic troop ship occupied a central place in British strategy: amphibious operations on the American coast would tie down a large fleet of such ships, because the troops had to be based afloat. British troop numbers at Bladensburg and Baltimore were restricted by the logistical demands of a floating army. Armchair generals proposed sending 25,000 troops to conquer Virginia and Maryland, separate them from the United States and emancipate slaves, a strategy to wreck America and ensure peace. The grim realities of shipping and stores left such visionary schemes floating in mid-air.[12] Altogether more intelligent ideas to improve the Canadian–American frontier emerged from discussions between Lord Sidmouth and General Stevenson on 1 March 1814.[13] This prompted the occupation of northern Maine, and influenced the evolution of British war aims.

PEACE TALKS

After Napoleon's abdication, the American war became a source of growing diplomatic embarrassment for the British government. The continued drain of troops and money left Britain looking weak and distracted just as her European partners were about to settle the political future of the continent. Peace would allow the British to focus on the big questions that were to be settled at the Vienna Congress. In his instructions to the British Commissioners – Admiral Lord Gambier, junior minister Henry Goulburn and lawyer Dr John Adams – Castlereagh focused on maritime rights. They should ascertain the American position on impressment and the naturalisation of seamen. He made one point absolute and unequivocal: the right to search neutral merchant ships on the high seas in wartime 'can never be given up'. To give the Americans an easy way out he followed the line discussed with Bayard and Gallatin, that peace in Europe had rendered the subject academic and it should be allowed to drop. By contrast Indian lands, border rectification and the Newfoundland fishery were open for discussion. The British negotiators were to stress that America had started the war, the invasion of Canada being consonant with a 'general system of aggrandisement, in the execution of which they had possessed themselves of Louisiana and a part of the Floridas, in the midst of peace'.[14] Castlereagh refused to discuss blockade, captures made under the Orders in Council and other maritime issues.[15] In this he was entirely successful. The Americans conceded maritime rights and impressment at the outset, even if they had to be reminded of the fact a few months later.[16] The American team would be allowed to draw some small comfort from trifling exchanges over Indian lands and the Canadian frontier.[17] Having set the parameters, Castlereagh left London for the allied headquarters in Europe; day-to-day control of the talks passed to Bathurst, the most hostile Cabinet minister.

Understanding the diplomatic utility of bad news, Bathurst linked reports that Washington had fallen with a hint that, despite their triumph, the British 'wish to terminate the present unfortunate contest on principles honourable to both parties', so far as the terms did not risk the security of His Majesty's dominions.[18] This last point was becoming more important: during his lengthy journey across Europe Castlereagh had studied British economic policy toward America, and 'the growing value of Canada . . . I have acquired by these researches a very increased notion of the value of our North American possession to us as a naval power.'[19] As he worked on the shape of a new Europe, Castlereagh recognised that Canadian timber, forest products and grain would reduce British dependence on European produce, especially from the Russian-dominated Baltic.[20]

By 1 September 1814 the government knew about the financial failure of the American administration. Rather than press their advantage for territorial gain, or humiliating terms, they wanted to restore the European state system, and rebuild Atlantic trade. As Lord Liverpool observed on 11 September, 'I cannot believe that, with the prospect of bankruptcy before them, the American Government would not wish to make peace, if they can make terms which would not give a triumph to their enemies.'[21] The enemies he had in mind were the Federalists. The startling presumption of the American negotiators prompted some ministers to think the whole exercise had been designed to fail, to bolster the war party in Washington. With an eye on opinion in Parliament Liverpool was anxious to ensure the blame for any breakdown fell on the 'impudent' Americans. Anticipating their position would soften as war came home to Washington he was content to wait out the initial posturing.[22] He knew that Britain's room for manoeuvre was limited by the Vienna negotiations, and the widespread feeling among European powers that British interests at the Congress could be ignored because of the American war. Only the occasional victorious sunburst, notably the destruction of Washington, silenced those who wished the Americans well, if only to do the British ill.

The prospect of peace revealed a divergence of opinion in Cabinet. Bathurst, as Colonial Secretary, wanted a buffer state for the Indians. Liverpool, recognising the impossibility of making terms to cover semi-nomadic tribal peoples, preferred a general understanding. In mid-September ministers sensed the circumstances might permit some useful minor border rectifications of a strategic character.[23] In this case Home Secretary Sidmouth's judgement was clear and correct.

We could not sustain the claim to the absolute independence of nations or tribes within the frontier of the United States & never thought we could, but an attempt has been made to consider them as subjects, which is quite novel, & must be resisted at all hazards.[24]

Such opinions reflected the latest intelligence from Paris. Reports of the fall of Washington reached the British Embassy on the last day of September, where Ambassador Wellington was presiding over a soirée. Sidmouth's friend John Beckett stressed there was 'a strong American party in the Town', and hoped the war would end soon:

Rely upon it however that the longer it lasts – the more we shall have reason to lament it, considering the present feelings and dispositions of France. Something formidable may be generated, tho' at present we may have but little to complain of.[25]

Instability in France and uncertainty at Vienna made peace imperative.

In the autumn American operations briefly returned to centre stage. Washington, Baltimore and Plattsburg mattered because Britain needed peace with America to secure the benefits of peace in Europe. The death of Ross and the humiliating fiasco at Plattsburg broke the illusion of triumph, restoring an air of reality to British thinking. Prevost's debacle, abandoning a major offensive without a battle, was hugely embarrassing. His botched combined operation cost the British control of Lake Champlain, either a useful bargaining chip or an additional security for Quebec. Plattsburg wasted all the money and effort put into sending troops across the Atlantic and, far worse, it broke the run of success that was pressurising the Americans into concessions. Victory in Vermont was hardly going to win the war, but it might have been enough to make the Americans concede. Plattsburg cost the British any leverage for border rectification or attempts to create an Indian territory. Strategic choices made in April and May, limiting the military force and retaining Prevost, had produced predictable outcomes. In late October Liverpool accepted the inevitable:

I wish we could get out of this war: but the point upon which I am most anxious is, that we should not get deeper into it, for I fear we shall feel it a most serious embarrassment some months hence; and it is not a contest in which we are likely to obtain any glory or renown at all commensurate to the inconvenience it will occasion.[26]

Sidmouth agreed, lamenting the 'melancholy' affair at Plattsburg.[27] Fortunately the Chancellor of the Exchequer reported a dramatic economic upturn and strong revenue streams, with Europe open for business.[28] Plattsburg encouraged Liverpool to rethink the strategy for securing peace. He moved quickly to limit the damage: the Ghent Commissioners must ensure the Americans understood Britain would rectify any such failure, and prosecute the war with more vigour.

... we can successfully blockade all their ports ... ravage their coasts, ruin their towns, destroy the little commerce which remains to them, and render their agriculture of no profit. They must look, therefore, to the failure of their revenue, to the impoverishment of their country, and probably to a national bankruptcy, from the continuance of the war. Sir A. Cochrane has shown that he will not spare them, and, with the additional military force which will be sent to co-operate with him, the Americans may expect greater disasters than even those which they have already encountered.

Continuing the war would cost Britain about £10 million a year, and require the continuation of the wartime property tax, but, with commerce booming and the economy expanding rapidly as Europe resumed trade, he implied this was not a serious burden.

... there can be no doubt, therefore, that if the Americans are unreasonable in declining the moderate terms of peace which you are authorised to propose, the country at large will feel it necessary to support a war ... the public feeling in this country on the subject of peace with America goes far beyond any proposition which at any period of the negotiation you have been authorised to bring forward.

Nor should America look to Europe for aid. Spain resented the invasion of the Floridas, while Louis XVIII recognised the role the American War of Independence had played in the downfall and death of his brother. British terms were hardly unreasonable, certainly less unreasonable than America would have exacted if 'the circumstances of Europe had enabled her to succeed in the invasion of our North American dominions'.[29]

In truth Liverpool was bluffing; he had many reasons to avoid another year of war. He was not optimistic that the Americans could be brought to see reason, directing the Cabinet to plan on the basis that the war would continue, and especially anxious that Russia and France might exploit the conflict. Nor was he convinced the country would be happy finding another £10,000,000 'for the purpose of securing a better frontier for Canada'.[30] The wartime property tax posed real political problems, and in darker moments he gave voice to concerns that the peace of Europe was not secure. If Europe had been settled he could have faced the American conflict 'with some degree of confidence', but the need to prepare for the new session of Parliament while so much remained uncertain preyed on his mind. The most pressing concern, securing a fresh government loan on suitable terms, would be impossible so long as the American war continued and Europe remained unsettled. Against this backdrop the Cabinet met on 3 November to review the correspondence from Ghent.[31]

Writing from Vienna, Castlereagh tried to bolster the Prime Minister's morale by stressing that while the Ghent process was unfortunate, because it threatened to protract the war, 'it makes little sensation here'.[32] Liverpool's perspective was dominated by the alarming state of France; credible intelligence suggested Bonapartist fanatics planned to assassinate Wellington. To remove the Duke from Paris without exciting suspicion Liverpool considered sending him to Vienna, to provide military advice to Castlereagh, or to command in North America, 'with full powers to make peace or to continue the war, if peace should be found impracticable, with renewed vigour'. While he had little doubt the Duke would prefer the Vienna appointment Liverpool outlined the options to Castlereagh on 4 November.

The Duke of Wellington would restore confidence to the army, place the military operations upon a proper footing, and give us the best chance of peace. I know he is very anxious for the restoration of peace with America, if it can be made on terms at all honourable. It is a material consideration likewise, that if we shall be disposed, for the sake of peace, to give up something of our just pretensions, we can do this more creditably through him than through any other person . . . if we are to have the advantages of his services in America, the sooner it is known and the sooner he can go the better. This appointment will in itself be sufficient to obviate many difficulties and much embarrassment at home.[33]

Although Liverpool hoped for an early settlement, he discussed strategy and policy with Wellington, in case he took the Canadian command in spring. In the interval rumours of his appointment would, Liverpool hoped, have a major influence in Europe and America.[34] While ready to do his duty the Duke was anything but enthusiastic:

... by appointing me to go to America at this moment, you give ground for belief, all over Europe, that your affairs there are in a much worse situation than they really are ... will not my nomination at this moment be triumph to the Americans and their friends here and elsewhere? It will give satisfaction, and that only momentary, in England, and it may have the effect of raising hopes and expectations there which we know cannot be realised. Then I beg to observe that, if once appointed to go to America, your lordship will not find it so easy to take me from that employment for any other on which you might prefer to employ me.[35]

Castlereagh would have agreed wholeheartedly with Wellington's statesmanlike assessment, which had the commendable virtues of being both an accurate assessment of the short-term prospects on the American continent, and a prescient insight into the future. Within months Wellington would be the chief British envoy at Vienna, and then commander-in-chief of an allied army at Waterloo.

CRUSHING THE PRIVATEERS

In attempting to explain the 'victory' of 1812 some American authors have argued that a successful privateering effort influenced British decision-making during the peace process.[36] However, this claim finds no support in the archives. In reality the complex diplomacy under way at Vienna and domestic economic concerns persuaded the British to offer America the *status quo ante*. British insurance rates remained stable, ministers absorbed pressure from commercial interests, and the Cabinet largely ignored privateering. It was not that the problem had gone away; it had never been a significant strategic threat.

In mid-September 1814 Joseph Marryat, Chairman of Lloyd's of London, came to the Admiralty to discuss the problems created by the European peace. Lloyd's opposed licensing ships to sail without convoy. This had led to several losses. He attached a list to illustrate his point that since the end of the European convoy system American privateers had been ranging between the Canaries and the British coast, picking off ships after convoys dispersed. This forced Lloyd's to maintain wartime premiums, putting British ships at a severe disadvantage against neutral competitors. It was, Marryat reminded Lord Melville, the Admiralty's job to deal with this problem.[37] Two months later the political importance of the convoy system became an issue at the state opening of Parliament. On 8 November Melville had to defend himself in the House of Lords against complaints from commercial houses and colonial planters who looked to the Navy for protection, and assumed the Board would shift warships from European waters to defend the Atlantic sea lanes. Melville was blunt: 'It must inevitably be the case when the whole force of an enemy is devoted to privateers, that our entire fleet, wherever stationed, cannot prevent the capture of some of our merchant vessels.' He stressed that some 200 privateers had been taken, along with 900 American merchant ships, while 20,000 American sailors were in detention. As the Americans did not operate a battle fleet there could be no 'splendid victories.' Unwilling to shoulder the blame he pointed out that, of 172 merchant ships missing, 94 were known runners and 38 more had separated from convoys.[38] In reply, opposition leader Lord Grenville could only bluster about the damaging 'impression produced in Europe by this disgrace of the hitherto unconquered Navy of Great Britain'. Such partisan twaddle did him little credit.[39] Seven days later the Admiralty provided the House of Lords with a full report on ships taken and lost. By this calculation the British had taken 1,248 American merchant ships, excluding captures by privateers, or recent success in distant seas. In addition the Navy had taken 34 American warships, and 278 privateers carrying 906 guns, manned by 8,974 men. In total some 20,000 American seamen had been captured. The Royal Navy had lost 16 ships.[40] The United States Navy took only 172 British merchant ships from an American total of 1,613. However 30 per cent of all American prizes were recaptured before they reached port. Even 1,613 ships constituted only 7.5 per cent of the British fleet. By contrast the United States ultimately lost 1,407 merchant ships from a fleet less than half that size. The balance of economic effect very much favoured Britain.[41]

It must be concluded that the kudos accorded privateering reflected post-war American political agendas rather than reality. The Republican Party elevated the privateer to join the militiaman as the bedrock of an economic defence. Confused by the nationalistic fervour that has pervaded the subject, few stop to consider the fundamentally inconclusive nature of commerce-destroying. Post-war the disorderly, unreliable business of privateering became unpopular in some parts of the United States, any strategic benefits outweighed by the concomitant chaos and diversion of seamen. Canadian privateers had also broken the law, and Britain had even less reason to persist with such irregular measures. Later American historians consciously underplayed the darker aspects of privateering to sustain a useful myth.[42] Many relied on the statistics compiled by Hezekiah Niles, unaware that they were created to serve a Republican agenda.

The War of 1812 simply confirmed previous experience: commerce-raiding has never proved decisive – but defence of trade has never been able to eradicate all threats and stop all losses. The safe and timely arrival of most ships has always been the test of successful trade defence, and in 1812–15 this was demonstrated by steady insurance rates. The real danger Britain faced was the loss of a major convoy, or the collapse of the convoy system. However, as Lloyd's and the Admiralty understood only too well, a successful defence was not enough. The enemy could not be allowed to operate with impunity. Therefore it was important to depress the morale of the enemy and keep down the number of predators by capturing cruisers and privateers and imprisoning key personnel. Heavy losses among predators had significant political and economic consequences, dissuading many from taking to the sea, and forcing the American government to adjust their strategy. This is precisely what happened. From the spring of 1813 the Royal Navy steadily gripped and crushed the threat. British success forced the Americans to adjust their strategy. However, commerce-destroying campaigns can never be completely defeated. In both world wars German U-boats carried on to the bitter end, long after they had been rendered irrelevant. It was no different after 1812. Although the war officially ended on Christmas Eve 1814, American privateers were still putting to sea in February 1815, unaware that events in Belgium had ended their careers. This left Lloyd's and the Admiralty dealing with real or rumoured attacks as late as May 1815.

AMERICA CONCEDES

The key to British victory lay not in military might, but in the linked failures of every American offensive and the slow, remorseless pressure of economic blockade. This was a naval victory. After December 1813 American economic warfare, both internal measures to block exports and attacks on British seaborne trade, was simply irrelevant. By contrast the New England blockade beginning in the summer of 1814 immediately pushed up commodity prices by 40 per cent, devastated national revenue, and sent much of the capital into factories or across the border into British government bonds.

In June 1814 Albert Gallatin acknowledged that the best terms available would be the *status quo ante*. The British attacks on Baltimore and New Orleans were quite unnecessary to defeat the United States; the standard British strategy of sea control and economic warfare had been perfectly effective. Gallatin was one of the American diplomats at Ghent who had to balance British entanglement in Europe against their own abject weakness. Furthermore, this was a limited war: Britain had no interest in destroying the United States and compelling it to accept terms after the fashion of Napoleon. While American commerce warfare was still damaging British economic life it was no longer a serious threat, and the balance of economic devastation had long since shifted to favour the British. In addition America was functionally bankrupt, and unable to access European funds: forceful British diplomacy blocked access to Dutch loans.

The capture of Washington was the final straw, leading to a run on the banks that saw large amounts of specie withdrawn and the collapse of the credit system. Attempts to raise money through internal taxes were hampered by Congress, while the obvious solution of an income tax was rejected. On 4 October the United States government was insolvent. On 11 November it defaulted on payments due on the National Debt, and the Louisiana Purchase. At this stage an individual would have had their affairs wound up, their possessions auctioned off, and their family put out on the street. America's credit rating hit an all-time low, the full consequences of which were only avoided by the Treaty of Ghent. The default rose to $2.8 million by the time news of peace reached Washington in February 1815. With a further $15 million of interest payments falling due peace was essential for the United States. It was little wonder that Canada and demands to end impressment and abrogate maritime belligerent rights were sacrificed to secure the *status quo ante*. That this decision was due to the British blockade can be seen in post-war measures to improve inland navigation and develop a fleet capable of breaking a blockade

The detailed history of the Ghent negotiations has been covered at length elsewhere, and the issues that occupied the negotiators were, in truth, trifling. Britain ended an awkward little war without loss, and without even discussing the issues at the heart of the American challenge.[43] When the draft treaty reached London a relieved Liverpool remarked: 'You know how anxious I was that we should get out of this war as soon as we could do so with honour.' By down-playing the prospects of lasting success, aside from punitive amphibious operations, Wellington had collapsed the logic of continuing the war. Canada could not be defended economically because there were 7.5

million Americans and only 300,000 Canadians. Faced with such numbers, changing the frontier would avail little. Liverpool was satisfied because the Americans had abandoned their maritime challenge, and the British public were content: 'As far as I have any means of judging our decision is generally approved.' He remained deeply concerned about the negotiations at Vienna, a consideration 'deserving of some weight in deciding the question of peace with America'. Fortunately the future of the strategically vital Low Countries had been settled by a 'secret article in the Treaty of Paris'.[44] It is indicative of the fundamentally maritime nature of British strategy that Liverpool did not feel it necessary to mention the obvious lesson that Canada would be defended by the Royal Navy, not a rectified frontier, fortresses or an Army.

For the British the War of 1812 had always been a 'tiresome, pointless distraction . . . a nuisance, but not a serious threat'.[45] It was unsurprising that public reaction to the Treaty of Ghent was muted; at least the merchant princes of Liverpool and Bristol were content. With the war at an end the government could focus on Europe and impending domestic battles over taxation and expenditure. The connection between the epic peace process under way at Vienna and the small-scale discussions at Ghent had long been obvious. Castlereagh delightedly observed that news of the treaty altered the Tsar's tone.[46] Sidmouth agreed, expecting it would lead to better news from Vienna.[47] The preliminary treaty was 'a great Relief, tho' not in all respects a subject of exultation. It will however set us on our Legs at Vienna.'[48] Once the treaty had been ratified the British simply forgot the War of 1812 and got back to the business of making money.

Bathurst hurriedly secured the Prince Regent's assent and bundled Anthony Baker, lately secretary at Ghent, off to Washington with the signed draft. Baker's American opposite number, along with the American copy, joined him on board HMS *Favourite*. Only when the American government formally ratified the treaty would the war end. If Washington attempted to alter or qualify anything Baker should publicise the terms, withdraw to Halifax and await further instructions. The British had accepted a compromise peace, but they would not allow the Americans to tweak the lion's tail after the fact.[49] With the treaty safely at sea, Liverpool recalled Castlereagh from Vienna, to meet the mounting domestic political crisis. As the only front-rank government minister in the House of Commons, the chamber that settled budget questions, his presence was essential for the forthcoming session. The country was in the grip of a panic caused by the 'great and unexpected fall in the prices of every description of grain'.[50] News of American ratification reached London in late March, by which time both domestic and international political landscapes had changed beyond recognition.[51]

The Treaty of Ghent upheld British maritime belligerent rights, the fundamental bedrock of British power. While many have seen the British position as overbearing and dictatorial towards neutrals, there was no room for neutrality in a total war; the alternative would have been Napoleonic domination of the continent. By keeping the American war isolated from the European conflict, and accepting the *status quo ante*, British statesmen showed great wisdom, preserving the legal basis of sea power and reducing the risk of future problems. Ghent established a clear distinction between Europe and the outside world, created by the British using their control of oceanic communications and trade. It helped maintain British global power for two generations at very low cost. Above all, British aims at Ghent and Vienna were clear and consistent: the restoration or re-creation of a stable, peaceful world open to trade, one in which the British could prosper while they paid off the mountainous debts incurred waging war with much of the very same world between 1793 and 1815.[52] In the process the British forced the Americans to look at their own internal problems, problems that would keep them divided down to 1865.

On 17 January 1815 the *National Intelligencer*, the quasi-official outlet of the Republican administration, effectively admitted that the declaration of war in 1812 had been foolish, and futile. Three years of war proved that Britain had the cash and credit to wage war with America and France, and defeat both.[53] Such insight would inform the way America dealt with Britain for the next century. British strategic leverage against America was a combination of sea control, economic warfare and small-scale, targeted coastal offensives.[54] The United States had no answer to those threats, beyond an endless chain of massive stone fortresses. As the maritime belligerent rights regime that won the War of 1812 had not been affected by the Treaty of Ghent America remained desperately vulnerable after 1815.

The American challenge failed in the counting house: America lacked the military muscle to win a short war, and once British troops had reinforced Canada the imposition of an effective economic blockade quickly exposed Washington's chronic lack of financial power. America could not pay for a long war, even one conducted on strictly limited terms. The cost of war was a 200 per cent increase in the American national debt, and a decisive shift away from oceanic maritime enterprise.

After the treaty had been ratified, Ghent negotiator John Quincy Adams became American Minister at the Court of St James. He arrived on 25 May, to find everyone in London focused on Napoleon's 'Hundred Days'. On the 29th Adams handed in his credentials to Castlereagh and assured his host that America would honour the treaty, while adopting measures to consolidate peace and harmony. He appealed to British interests by reporting the reciprocal abolition of tonnage duties on goods imported in British vessels, and a Presidential message recommending the exclusion of non-native seamen from the American naval and merchant marines. Evidently the Americans expected the British would renounce impressment. Without a moment's hesitation Castlereagh thanked Adams for the good news, and brushed aside the tired old Jeffersonian promise that America would cripple her own shipping industry to suit Britain: 'no British Government could possibly abandon the right to the allegiance of British subjects'. Adams admitted that as long as the British did not impress American seamen the question would remain moot. Ever the diplomat, Castlereagh even hinted the Admiralty would consider suitable regulations. While none were forthcoming, no one was ever impressed after 1815.[55]

News of peace found the Admiralty desperate to run down the fleet. The draft treaty left England on 27 December; three days later Cochrane was sent new orders detailing the ports at which his ships would be paid off.[56] The sense of relief was palpable. Finally Britain's twenty-two years of war with most of the modern world had come to an end. It was time to pay off ships and men, cut the estimates and resume business as usual. For the British that meant trade with the world, trade networked through strategic bases like Halifax and Bermuda that enabled the Royal Navy to command great swathes of ocean space, to protect British commerce, and crush that of any hostile power.

Elsewhere in Britain peace was greeted with little pleasure, because the treaty did not reflect the reality of British victory. Sir Walter Scott lamented the failure to administer America a stern lesson, but admitted the country was unwilling to wage the war for such a nebulous object. As a world-class creator of fabulous stories he realised the Americans had been given an opportunity to claim victory in print, and convince themselves they might try again.[57] Scott understood the enduring legacy of 1812 would not be territory or rights, but a distinct American culture; he expected American pens would generate the victory that had eluded their swords. This proved to be the case: 1812 was not a second War of Independence in political terms, but it did mark the decisive parting of two cultures. The War of 1812 drove America to acquire a distinctive identity, one that was truly of the New World, privileging its landscape, scale and opportunities over the narrow confines and dusty histories of Europe.

CHAPTER 12

Creating the American War of 1812

Long before the fighting finally stopped Americans began to focus on the way in which history would judge the war. Despite the defeat, it was possible to rewrite the story as a victory, picking up on the ambiguity of the Treaty of Ghent, a *status quo ante* compromise that lacked the absolute clarity that marked the final defeat of Napoleon. By contrast the British were far too busy settling the future of Europe, a problem that was only resolved in late 1815, months after Waterloo. British statesmen had never expressed much interest in the war, and took peace as a good opportunity to ignore it altogether. They had processed the lessons of war and adopted them without any great public fanfare. Very few British accounts of the war appeared in print, and only William James treated the subject in an original manner. This left the Americans free to create an anglophone understanding at variance with reality, largely to serve internal political divisions. This version would occupy a critical role in post-war politics, a contested ground on which Republican partisans erected a substantial victory arch of words and pictures to transform defeat into victory, folly into wisdom. While judgements of the war remain complex they can be summarised by examining the contrasting fates of the *President* and the *Constitution*.

HONOUR AND GLORY: THE BATTLE AFTER THE BATTLE

For all the skill and courage involved, frigate battles rarely exercised a profound influence on international relations. But 1812 was an unusual war. It has often been described as little more than a succession of such Homeric contests, contests in which the new boys challenged the old masters, and whipped them. At the heart of the mythic version lies the USS *Constitution*, the thrice-victorious symbol of American success.

However, there are other ways of reading the naval war. As Henry Adams observed a century ago the War of 1812 was a disaster for the United States:

The worst disaster of the naval war occurred January 15, when the frigate *President* – one of three American forty-fours, under Stephen Decatur, the favourite ocean hero of the American service – suffered defeat and capture within fifty miles of Sandy Hook. No naval battle of the war was more disputed in its merits, although its occurrence in the darkest moments of national depression was almost immediately forgotten in the elation of the peace a few days later.[1]

Perhaps the battle had all been in vain. While the Treaty of Ghent had been signed on Christmas Eve 1814, it took six weeks for the draft to reach the United States for ratification, weeks in which bloody New Orleans was fought, and the *President* taken. Henry Hotham finally received the news on 13 February.[2] The news proved especially timely for some *President* crewmen at Bermuda. Several were recognised as British deserters, but no further action was taken.[3]

With the meaning of the newly concluded war rapidly coalescing, Decatur was well aware that his defeat was open to interpretations that did not add lustre to his reputation. Some argued that he had surrendered to a single, smaller ship, that he had not fought to the finish, and then attempted a dishonourable trick. As Henry Adams observed, 'Decatur was doubtless justified in striking when he did; but his apparent readiness to do so hardly accorded with the popular conception of his character.'[4] In consequence Decatur began to question the merits of his original report. This had been an unusually long, detailed paper, not the brisk seven sentences it once took him to report capturing an enemy frigate.[5] The initial report attributed his defeat to the ship striking on the bar, emphasised the severe losses and damage suffered, and the heroism of the officers and men.[6] He hoped this apparently factual statement would be enough to satisfy his public.

With the ship in British hands any 'damage' suffered on the bar could not be ascertained by American experts. In any case, had it been severe, Decatur had the option at the time of anchoring and waiting for the tide to turn. Furthermore, the fact that his deep-laden ship was able to distance all but one of her pursuers the following day suggests the effect was distinctly limited. Fenimore Cooper was uncertain whether to attribute the *President* being caught to damage received on the bar or 'the manner in which she had been lightened'.[7] Both men missed the obvious explanation. Being caught by HMS *Endymion* at a rate of no more than one knot an hour in light winds proved there was nothing wrong with *President*. *Endymion*, the Royal Navy's crack sailing frigate, excelled in light airs.

A brief account of the action reached new Navy Secretary Benjamin Crowninshield in late January. It was a brief extract from a letter Decatur sent to his wife after the battle, passed on by his friend Oliver Hazard Perry. In it Decatur claimed that he had only surrendered when two British ships were fairly alongside, and the other two close by. This was, of course, complete nonsense, but it satisfied Perry, hero of Lake Erie, who boasted: 'The reputation of the Navy and his own stands yet pre-eminent,'[8] firing the opening salvo in a desperate public relations battle that treated basic facts with complete contempt. The wounded hero arrived at New London on board HMS *Narcissus* on 22 February, conveniently after news of the peace. Decatur feared 'he had lost his lustre with the American public', anxious that his honour may have been tarnished by the Bermudan newspaper account that 'he had surrendered to a single British warship after a less than stout defence'.[9] The adulation of the crowd, a celebratory dinner to mark the peace attended by naval officers from both sides, and a 21-gun salute from Hotham's flagship restored Decatur's spirits.[10] An admiring President would provide him with the perfect stage to re-gild his laurels, and those of his country.

The American government was anxious to restore the reputation of its heroic Navy and its brand leader; they would be the bed rock of post-war diplomacy, the mark of the Republic's standing in the world. The day after Decatur reached New London President Madison sent a message to Congress, calling for war against Algiers. With the Navy on a war footing, and few merchant ships yet at sea it would be timely to settle the Algerian issue. It would also be popular in New England with an election due. The United States had need of Decatur, hero of the last Barbary war, and he had equal need of his country.[11]

Yet so great was Decatur's concern for his reputation that he compiled a second, supplementary report on 6 March. This time he stretched the truth beyond the point of honest mistake, attributing a 'considerable number' of his casualties to *Pomone*'s two broadsides, raising the red herring that fifty of *Saturn*'s crew were on board *Endymion* and laying stress on the fact that he had surrendered to the squadron, as evidenced by his letter of parole. He also took care to blame the mischievous *Bermuda Gazette* for impugning his honour, and his conduct.[12] This was a very different production to the first report, a carefully crafted exculpation based on distinctly dubious 'evidence'. *Pomone*'s wild broadsides caused no casualties – the men were already below deck. The fifty officers and men from *Saturn* were straight replacements for *Endymion* crew killed in the engagement with *Prince de Neufchatel*. As for surrendering to the entire British squadron this may have been true under British prize law, but only *Pomone* was in range when he did so, *Tenedos* was at least 3 miles distant, and *Majestic* much further off. The capture was credited to the squadron because under British prize law every ship in sight when a vessel was captured was entitled to a share in the prize money. By his own admission Decatur had only ever engaged one ship, and surrendered before *Pomone* opened fire. British officers were prepared to be magnanimous; they had the prize they wanted, but Decatur knew that he had not done enough, by his own standards. His public request for a court to investigate was high-risk, but essential if he wanted a command in the Algerian war.[13] In truth Crowninshield was in no mood to quibble. He was happy to call a court, as soon as the *President*'s officers reached America, because the outcome was a foregone conclusion:

... from a conviction of the bravery and skill with which that ship has been defended, and a confidence in the result proving honorable to your high character as an officer, in sustaining a combat so vastly unequal and which terminated in a manner not derogatory to the credit of our Navy, or to the honor of our National Flag.

He closed by wishing Decatur a speedy recovery.[14] On the same day Crowninshield offered him his choice of commands for the war with Algiers, an offer that must have been sanctioned by the President.[15] Significantly Decatur replied by return, and took the first active command:

It would be particularly gratifying to me at this moment to receive an active and conspicuous employment, in Europe it would be seen that my statement had been satisfactory to my Government.

Once the second division of the Mediterranean squadron arrived under Bainbridge, a higher-ranking officer, Decatur would come home.[16] The concern for European opinion is revealing. Well aware that his actions were open to question, Decatur grabbed the first opportunity to resume 'honorable' high-profile public service. Clearly Crowninshield and Madison shared his anxiety: why else would the Secretary of the Navy venture to prejudge the outcome of an investigation required by law. The administration had already appointed Decatur to another command before the court met.

The court of inquiry was a comprehensive whitewash, one that only served to obscure the facts further – adding the *Dispatch* into the mix, and removing *Endymion* from the final scene.[17] Commodore Alexander Murray, Captain Isaac Hull, Captain Samuel Evans and Judge Advocate Cadwallader Colden met on board the USS *Constellation* at New York Navy Yard to consider the case for three short days, beginning on Tuesday 11 April. After reading Decatur's original report into the record they interviewed Decatur, his two surviving lieutenants, four midshipmen, the master, and a sick-berth attendant. To ensure the court received the right message from his juniors Decatur had already offered them appointments on his new ship – he replaced Rodgers in the new *Guerriere*. Furthermore, Decatur was allowed to question his juniors, taking the opportunity to lead them on the key issues. Predictably, the commissioned officers backed their captain, stressing his cool, collected conduct and the inevitability of defeat. This was sensible for young men with careers to make, and the prospect of a Mediterranean cruise. Sailing master James Rodgers proved less willing to follow Decatur's lead, suggesting that the ship might have been better handled. For his pains he found his own honour under attack, forcing him to call a witness in his own defence. Captain Robinson, who had questioned the need to surrender, was not called: he was a volunteer and could be ignored.[18]

The junior officers appear to have overdone their praise, leaving a confused court to produce a perfectly absurd judgment. Murray's report accepted Decatur's exculpatory claims, but then added a new fact, stating that the *President* 'had sustained but little injury', in clear contradiction of Decatur's original submission. Instead, Murray claimed,

they did not give up their ship till she was surrounded and overpowered by a force so superior, that further resistance would have been unjustifiable, and a useless sacrifice of the lives of brave men.[19]

Just in case anyone was minded to question the scale of the whitewash that had been applied, Murray declared that any suggestions Decatur might have done better were 'without foundation, and may be the result of ignorance, or the dictates of a culpable ambition, or of envy'. He went on to impute truly divine qualities to the performance of the ship and her captain. 'In this unequal conflict the enemy gained a ship, but the victory was ours', which beggars belief. Evidently Murray had allowed his brief to exonerate Decatur to run away with him.[20]

Within five months of losing the *President* Decatur had taken the Algerian frigate flagship *Meshuda*, completing a remarkable reversal of fortune. He ended the Barbary War with a display of forceful diplomacy, coercing Tripoli and Tunis into new treaties, before cruising round the Mediterranean to garner fresh plaudits.[21] On his return to America he added the stirring cry 'My Country, right or wrong!' to the national lexicon.[22] The nation needed its heroes, and the elegant, self-assured and well-connected Decatur played the part to perfection.

In complete contrast Charles Stewart brought the successful *Constitution* into New York at a most propitious time. By mid-May the euphoria of peace, combined with the celebration of the last American naval triumph, transformed the three times successful ship into an American totem. The Republican *National Intelligencer* demanded:

Let us keep 'Old Iron Sides' at home. She has, literally become a *Nation*'s ship, and should be preserved. Not as a 'sheer hulk, in ordinary,'[23] (for she is no *ordinary* vessel); but, in honorable pomp as a glorious Monument of her own, and our other naval Victories.[24]

The nation in question was a Republican Party political construct. Just as the Federalist flagship *President* was being measured up for posterity at the Royal Navy's biggest dockyard, Portsmouth in old Hampshire, the Republicans signalled their support for a very specific version of the naval war, one that included the frigate triumphs of 1812, Lake Erie, 'Don't Give up the Ship!', the Pacific cruise of the *Essex*, Lake Champlain, and the last hurrah of 'Old Ironsides', but carefully ignored the loss of the flagship.

Constitution's latest biographer has argued that the American naval victories:

. . . had no direct effect on the course of the war. The losses suffered by the Royal Navy were no more than pinpricks to that great fleet: they neither impaired its battle readiness nor disrupted the blockade of American ports . . . What *Constitution* and her sisters *did* accomplish was to uplift American morale spectacularly . . . The big frigates made Americans proud to be Americans.

Quite why three combat victories over markedly inferior opponents should be such a source of pride is hard to understand. But with the full weight of the party propaganda machine behind the story, *Constitution* was instantly elevated to immortality, while the Federalist *President* was conveniently forgotten. So important was the connection between naval glory and partisan politics that a decade later Commodore Jesse Elliot equipped *Constitution* with a suitably Presidential figurehead of Andrew Jackson.[25] Jackson would use the myth of the United States Navy to browbeat the French into compensating America for commercial losses caused by Napoleon.[26] But by then the force had lost its heroes, and its grip on the national imagination.

THE BITTER LEGACY OF THE USS *CHESAPEAKE*

In 1815 the United States Navy was riding high in public estimation, its achievements boosted to the point of hyperbole by Republican propagandists; it had been far more successful than the Army. Increased budgets, new ships and new missions held out the promise of a bright future. To ensure the money was well spent John Rodgers, Decatur and David Porter were appointed to a three-man Board of Commissioners to administer the Navy. Bringing the leading men of the infant service to the over-heated, hypercritical atmosphere of Washington provided the Navy Secretary with professional advisors, but it also ensured that issues of rank, pride and status would draw the hypersensitive American naval leaders into further disasters. Men more used to the solitary eminence of the quarterdeck found it hard to adjust to collegial working, political intrigue and shore-side temptations. While Rodgers remained a domineering character, the relationship between Decatur and Porter would be complicated: both strove to be the national naval hero, but Decatur always won. Then, in 1818, James Barron returned to Washington, and applied to be restored to the Navy. All three Navy Commissioners had sat on the *Chesapeake* court martial in 1808, and joined almost all serving officers in objecting. Once again Decatur was the most outspoken, something that Barron found curious after the less than glorious surrender of the *President*. After an absurd exchange of stiff unpleasantries Barron issued a formal challenge in early 1820. Rodgers told Decatur to ignore it, but he felt obliged to accept. At first no one would stand as his second, which made it impossible to conduct an 'affair of honour'. Then grim old Bainbridge agreed, although he hated Decatur for stealing his glory on the Algerian coast in 1815. Whatever his motives, William Bainbridge was ill-equipped to reconcile the increasingly threadbare and petty bickering that brought the two men to the field of honour. Barron's second and *agent provocateur*, Captain Jesse Elliot, was a deeply divisive character, best known for failing to support Oliver Hazard Perry at the Battle of Lake Erie. Decatur had supported Perry's damning verdict on Elliot's conduct, and Elliot saw the duel as a chance for revenge.

The seconds arranged for the meeting to be near the humiliating field of Bladensburg, on the usual duelling ground for Washington gentlemen, on the morning of 22 March. They would fire at eight paces, a distance so short that any man with a steady hand was sure to hit his target, even with a smoothbore pistol. Rodgers and Porter knew all about the duel, but did nothing to stop it. They hovered within earshot, but only revealed themselves after the guns had been fired. While the seconds were attending to the details beforehand, one report had Barron declare he hoped they might be better friends in another world, with Decatur graciously replying that he was never Barron's enemy. These remarks were hardly in keeping with Decatur's ferocious rhetoric over the preceding twelve years; the story may be part of a full-scale posthumous whitewash. In this version Bainbridge ignored the remarks, and Elliot hurried the duellists to their positions. Both men aimed at the hip, and both were hit. Barron was knocked to the ground; Decatur's ball had glanced off his femur. Barron's slug also struck the bone, but ricocheted into Decatur's groin, severing the femoral artery. Decatur knew the wound was mortal. As they lay on the damp ground, wracked with pain, the two men were reconciled. For a second time in his sorry career

Jesse Elliot fled in panic, leaving Porter to attend to Barron while Rodgers had Decatur carried in agony from the field of shame.[27] Decatur died that night at his elegant Washington mansion just behind the White House. It might have been unintentional but Decatur, whom many saw as a Presidential contender, had been killed by Andrew Jackson's naval clients.

Newly elected President Jackson restored Barron to the Navy. Although Barron never served at sea, he presided when David Porter was court-martialled for disobedience of orders and conduct unbecoming. Sentenced to a short suspension from duty Porter resigned, ending his career under the American flag. Although a difficult man, ill-suited to peace and political compromise, he deserved better. As Christopher McKee observed Porter was 'both a man of action and intellectual', possessing 'fierce energy and penetrating mind', qualities that first made and then destroyed his career.[28] Decatur's death and Porter's disgrace summed up the post-war decade for the United States Navy, a tragic falling away of wartime glory, mirroring the political misfortunes of the Federalist Party and the ebbing of an oceanic vision of America that linked service and party. Despite the hyperbole, America had not won the war at sea; far from asserting control and upholding American principles, the post-war decade saw the triumph of the Republican continental vision, open plains not open seas.

A CULTURE OF INDEPENDENCE

At the heart of the war lay a profound struggle to define the culture of a new nation, a struggle that divided North from South, and sea from land, one in which the British played a relatively minor role. In 1812 America remained a cultural dependency of Great Britain: art, literature, fashions and manufactures flowed across the Atlantic as if 1782 had not happened. The poverty of American cultural production, widely lamented at home, and not infrequently mocked abroad, constituted a critical challenge to American sovereignty. Americans did not have their own culture; they were still in harness. The search for a culture would take many forms, but war hastened the process, quickening minds and prompting patrons.[29]

America's first millionaire, Salem ship-owner Elias Hasket Derby, made his money privateering during the Revolutionary War, before redeploying ships and capital into the China and India trades. Derby dominated Salem, and Salem dominated Asian commerce. He left a powerful legacy of wealth and interest.[30] By 1800 ninety Salem ship masters had rounded Cape Horn, trading with Canton, Bombay and Batavia. While these voyages constituted only a small fraction of American commercial activity, they were disproportionately profitable at a time when American economic expansion was driven by international trade and shipping.[31] The economic boom led to a marked increase in cultural patronage as the newly wealthy enhanced their lifestyles. Derby commissioned pictures of ships and seamen to decorate his home.[32] The American merchants, ship captains and adventurers who passed through London and Liverpool were part of a general pool of anglophone seafarers and merchants. These men, and their Navy, would fight alongside the British against Republican French privateers in the West Indies between 1798 and 1800, under a Federalist administration, actively supported by merchants and ship-owners. When the French began harassing American shipping in 1797 several ports sponsored the construction of warships to defend their trade. As Navy Secretary Benjamin Stoddert noted in 1798 this included: 'most of the towns distinguished for Federalism, and public spirit'. Elias Derby subscribed $10,000 towards the Salem-built frigate USS *Essex*.[33] It was no coincidence that Federalist President John Adams ordered the *Essex* to escort Salem shipping to Batavia.[34] These warships were 'a compelling cultural expression' of Federalist America. Funded by low-interest loans from the merchants, ship-owners and artisans of seaport towns they epitomised a country where prominent men used private wealth for the common good. The Federalists made little distinction between self-interest and national interest. The leaders of Atlantic America agreed with Alexander Hamilton that a Navy would be both the ideal cultural symbol of the nation, and the guarantee for its commerce. The Navy they created was Federalist, despite a few well-connected, if not always capable, Republican officers.[35] In assuming these were common interests, and that they would remain consistent, both the Federalists and British observers missed a deeper trend in American life.[36]

The War of 1812 had been declared by another larger, more dynamic America, a continentally minded nation of land-hungry expansionists, anxious to push their frontiers westward at the expense of Indians, Spaniards and Britons. These Americans did not share the pan-European cultural notions of the Republican leadership, the international commercial impulse of New England, or a taste for warships. In the South and West a new America of populist democracy, individualism and expansion was taking shape; and it was ready to fight. Victory in war would provide more territory.

AN IDENTITY IN CRISIS

As historians move away from old methodologies that confuse the paper trail of inter-governmental discussion with the deeper motives that underpin the descent to war, 1812 takes on a new role in American history. Clearly expressed contemporary anxieties about the future of the nation, deep-seated fear of enervating sloth, factionalism, avarice and loss of Revolutionary fervour transformed the war from a petty squabble about an ocean of legal niceties into the solution to existential angst. War would solve diseases internal to the American body politic; the unifying patriotism of war would soothe and bind, restoring the virtues of an earlier age, while reconnecting today with yesterday. This line of argument draws great, if unspoken, support from the otherwise singular fact that the main spokesmen for war were entirely unconnected with the supposed 'causes'. Internal concerns propelled the country to war, not Orders in Council or impressment. War Hawks Henry Clay, Felix Grundy and John Calhoun stressed that it would be an opportunity for protectionist economic policies, and a cure for domestic dissent. On 9 May 1812 Jeffersonian journalist Hezekiah Niles, owner-editor of *Niles' Weekly Register*, stressed that the war would give Americans 'a NATIONAL CHARACTER'.[37] Niles's Baltimore paper was the first American weekly to rely entirely on subscriptions for revenue, appearing without adverts. It proved highly successful, largely because the editor's aggressively anti-British views on foreign policy chimed with those of his audience.[38]

For a generation that had grown up in the shadow of the Revolution, war would be a moral tonic, to vindicate the Republican virtues of the Founding Fathers, and 'crusade for Union'. Precisely what kind of republic these men wanted was obvious. In 1799 Albert Gallatin opposed a bill to increase the infant navy, because protecting American overseas commerce was 'a mere matter of calculation . . . a question of profit and loss'. He distinguished 'useful' exports of American produce from 'useless' carrying trades and re-exports. Although the last two made up more than half the national commerce he saw no reason to tax farmers for their protection. For Gallatin, Jefferson and Madison internal trade was the key to America's future, not external commerce. They did not need a navy, only a flotilla of gunboats to collect local revenue. After 1800 manufacturers joined agriculturalists on the list of those approved by the Republicans, but merchants remained outside the pale. Niles stressed that domestic manufacture would end dependence on foreign imports, and reduce international trade. It is no coincidence that modern America is the least globalised trading nation in the G8 group.

In government Gallatin backed investment in roads and canals to distribute domestic goods, seeking advice from ardent Republican steamboat and canal pioneer Robert Fulton. By 1810 domestic manufacturing had reached significant proportions; it was well worth protecting. Industrial protectionism added a significant element to war fever: ubiquitous British manufactured goods undercut domestic production. Catching the steady drift of Baltimore capital from ships to factories, Hezekiah Niles urged an economic model based on domestic manufacturing, arguing that war would end American dependence of foreign production. It was but a short step to post-war protectionism. The growth of domestic production had been a positive, if unintentional, consequence of Jefferson's Embargo. Those with financial interests in the new business model were likely to support war. By 1812 Republican America looked to internal self-sufficiency and continental expansion behind the twin barrier of exclusive tariffs and sea-coast forts; in contrast the British business model relied on an ever expanding network of maritime commerce, sustained by naval dominance. New England, caught between the upper and lower millstones of this ideological contest, would be the main loser. As a result the clash of cultures evident in 1812 had become fundamental by 1815.

MAKING AMERICA REPUBLICAN

For Thomas Jefferson, ideologue of Republican America, the years between 1800 and the Treaty of Ghent were dominated by the need to deal with treasonous Federalists attempting to subvert the Union and ally with Britain. He neither admitted the profoundly divisive effect of his own policies, nor allowed his opponents a scintilla of patriotism. Nor did he reflect on the totalitarian implications of his willingness to wage war on New England once the invasion of Canada had become a fiasco. Crushing New England would enable the Republican administration to purge the nation of wrong thinking and monarchism, using the military methods of the Old World to secure a New World utopia. Although Jefferson's intellectual journey mirrored that of the French republicans in the 1790s, his countrymen were saved from an American 'Committee of Public Safety' by his slightly more pragmatic successor. That said, crushing Massachusetts would remain an ambition for many Southerners, and Jefferson the ideologue of another war. New

England remained the 'enemy' after 1815 because it rejected Jefferson's one-party state.

America's turn to landward expansion was reinforced by the British blockade. Many smaller ports ceased trading abroad, while capitalists switched from shipping to industry. Between 1810 and 1820 American oceanic shipping fell by 40 per cent, while inland shipping rose by 45 per cent, a long-term trend that would only be interrupted by the world wars of the twentieth century. Jefferson's search for internal self-sufficiency collided with a war that emphasised inland, riverine and canalised transport. As Robert Fulton observed, the cost of wartime wagon transport would have paid for a complete internal canal system for the east coast.[39] The post-war canal boom culminated with the high-profile opening of the Erie Canal of 1825; the *leitmotif* of American commercial shipping linked the Atlantic to the Great Lakes. By 1817 coastal, riverine and lake routes were protected markets for American vessels. War and legislation rebuilt America along Republican lines, turning from oceanic commerce to overland expansion. The expansive drive inland dominated the next fifty years of American political life. The British had secured Canada but the Hispanic West and the South-West were wide open. As America changed course it changed culture.

Jefferson's last years would be clouded by the complications of slavery in an expanding Union. Slavery caused Jefferson endless intellectual and practical problems. Much as he disliked slavery, he feared a servile revolt, and the threat posed by black British soldiers and offers of freedom. To square the circle he argued that the South-West had earned the right to extend slavery at New Orleans, while convincing himself that New England abolitionists were to 'blame' for slavery, because they profited indirectly from the proceeds of Southern agriculture.[40] Jefferson's fractured legacy paved the way for new forces to challenge the political leadership of New England and the Middle States.

WESTERNERS AND THE WAR

The War of 1812 was, as J. C. A. Stagg has observed, 'not so much one war as a series of conflicts'.[41] Different sections of the American populace had distinct visions of what a war of 1812 should be about. For the South and West the issues were land, security and an ideology of power based on white, anglophone domination. While the war for Canada and on the Atlantic was primarily against Britain, the real enemies in the South and West were Indians, Spanish colonials and free blacks. The consistent, unifying ideology of American expansionism and the methodology of promoting internal unrest, filibustering and the occasional illegal invasion may have failed in Canada, but it secured major victories here.

For America the cultural legacy of this complex of interlocking wars would be a decisive shift of national identity towards a continental military model, driven by the glorification of a handful of actions, and men. Killing Indians easily outlasted naval glory, because it was more nearly universal. While the North-East made a totem of James Lawrence, the nation elected Andrew Jackson to the highest office.

After 1815 the same land-hungry expansionist political power that helped bring about the conflict hardened into sectionalism, causing a second, far bloodier conflict for the cultural heart of the nation.[42] Unable to control an urgent, dominating Western land hunger, successive administrations were propelled into seizing Indian lands, dispossessing the original inhabitants, and dismantling the last vestiges of Spanish imperium on the continental mainland to satisfy the demands of a politically potent frontier. The War of 1812 boosted the political power of the South and West, laying the foundations for the looming clash of cultures within the United States. Nowhere was this more obvious than in the West, where local political ideas and ambitions took a mighty stride towards the creative and political centre. The elevation of Andrew Jackson and William Henry Harrison – the men who won the war that mattered, the war for land and westward expansion – to cult status and Presidential power transformed the country. The decades after 1815 witnessed the end of austere Republican dreams of small government and agricultural society directed by a civilised, educated elite. Such visions gave way to a tidal wave of levelling democracy, individualism, capitalism and industry.[43] This new America emerged out of the West, a product of inland expansion.

This process began with the Louisiana Purchase, which opened new horizons for American expansion. Roads connecting the Mississippi with the Atlantic were driven through Indian lands, while land-hungry farmers, merchants and speculators increased inter-racial tensions, ultimately sparking the Creek War that co-existed with the Anglo-American conflict.[44] The critical role of naval forces in controlling Southern rivers and harbours, especially the occupation of Mobile in 1813, made the purpose of Jefferson's gunboat navy all too obvious. Only the outbreak of war and the presence of superior British forces stopped the Americans seizing more Spanish territory.[45]

Long before 1812 Western leaders like Harrison had mobilised significant military power to dispossess Indians, by treaty and by force, creating an ill-defined but ever moving 'frontier' that would continue to exert a major pull on American attitudes for much of the century. For Frederick Jackson Turner, historian of the Frontier as a political factor, 1812 would be 'in no inconsiderable degree, the result of aggressive leadership in a group of men from Kentucky and Tennessee', and he picked out leading War Hawk Henry Clay as an exemplary 'Western Man':

The Western man believed in the manifest destiny of his country. On his border, and checking his advance, were the Indians, the Spaniard and the Englishman. He was indignant at Eastern indifference and lack of sympathy with his view of his relations to these peoples; at the short-sightedness of Eastern policy. The closure of the Mississippi by Spain, and the proposal to exchange our claim of freedom of navigation of the river in return for commercial advantages to New England, nearly led to the withdrawal of the West from the Union. It was the Western demands that brought about the purchase of Louisiana, and turned the scale in favour of declaring the War of 1812. Militant qualities were favoured by the annual expansion of the settled area in the face of hostile Indians and the stubborn wilderness.[46]

In the South-West this movement was driven by the economics of plantation slavery, endlessly searching for fresh land to exploit.[47] The introduction of the cotton gin and the explosive growth of American trans-Appalachian trade through New Orleans prompted a drive to secure possession of the coast and ports, while fraudulent and speculative land sales in disputed territory played a critical role in the descent to war.

Driven by Jeffersonian/Republican expansionism, critically linked to the land hunger of key supporters, James Madison followed the futile, internally divisive policy of provoking the only nation on earth that could do America any real harm, over an issue in which right and wrong were far from clear, at a time when the British were engaged a struggle for their very existence. The United States would be lucky to escape the attempt to 'conquer without war' in one piece, yet, by one of history's more ironic twists, the enduring legacy of this brush with disaster would become a ringing endorsement of expansionism and further imperial conquests.

The Anglo-American war gave the Indians their last opportunity to challenge the advance of white settlement and power across the continent. Never again would they have the manpower, or the external support, to do so. Their defeat revealed much about the make-up of the nation that emerged from the shock of war. The onward march of white settlement posed a fundamental threat to native culture, driving hitherto compliant, settled tribes towards Tecumseh's national resistance movement. In reality the Shawnee leader's fiery rhetoric and transcontinental travels did more to rally support for Western leaders, who played on fears Tecumseh could block westward expansion. The results were predictable, but nonetheless tragic. The profound injustice of Jackson's attack on the settled southern tribes, who had secured their rights by treaty only two decades before, was obvious to

Federalist commentators in distant Boston. In the South 1812 would be about the white ownership of land, not a definition of civilisation based on settled agriculture, for the Creeks were already civilised.[48] Pushed into a corner and threatened, Creek society split: some resumed the old hunting way, destroying their fields and livestock before going to war in loose federation with their northern brethren, and the British. This response was not universal; many Indians fought alongside American government forces, against their own people, only to be driven from their lands when the war ended. Andrew Jackson made his intentions clear, justifying the harsh treaties he imposed by observing that the defeated Creeks had 'disappeared from the face of the earth'.[49] It was deeply symbolic that one of Jefferson's derided gunboats ended the last stand of the southern Indians and their runaway slave allies. On 27 July 1816 Gunboat No. 154 fired red-hot shot into a hostile fort, detonating the magazine and killing over 200 people.[50] Nor did western land hunger end with the dispossession of the Creeks. Spanish Florida and the Seminoles would soon follow them into oblivion. No opposition was allowed to stand in the way of the plantation. Jefferson's deluded dream of assimilation had been replaced by Jackson's policy of annihilation, at the behest of land-hungry Southerners. Recognising the political consequences of explosive Southern expansion, parties representing the North and East were 'jealous' of these successes, using their legislative power to block such moves, notably the occupation of East Florida in 1813.

Flushed with confidence after victories at the Thames and Horseshoe Bend, and the fresh lands they had secured, the Westerners had the power to destroy any native societies that stood in their path. The Treaty of Fort Jackson on 9 August 1814 set the pattern. Having annihilated all military opposition, Andrew Jackson stripped the Creek nation of half its land, barred the tribe from intercourse with foreigners, and obliged them to conduct all business with American government agents. Rather than following the policy being set in far-off Washington, Jackson acted as 'the agent of westerners, all of whom wished the treaty to both punish the Indians and reward the white man'.[51] Soon these lands were teeming with settlers; within two decades there was an Indian problem to solve. The victor of Horseshoe Bend became the President, launching an era of expansion which propelled the frontier from Tennessee to the Rio Grande in three decades. The annexation of Texas and the Pacific coast were 'only an aftermath of the same movement of expansion' that began in 1812.[52] Jackson launched the campaign in 1830, driving the Indians across the Mississippi.

Fearing the British would use Indians and blacks to attack Southern property, Jackson had adopted a measure that secured a potent political power base in the West and the South. Many Southerners shared his view that the British were the harbingers of servile revolt. Unifying the ambitions of the many with the political agendas of the elite created Jacksonian America. While land hunger in the South-West was not the sole cause of war in 1812, it provided a powerful impetus and critical votes in the run-up to a conflict that other states profoundly opposed. It was no irony that the policy-makers in Washington lost control of the region to local interests, or that locally raised forces won the decisive battles at Horseshoe Bend and New Orleans. Jackson and his men knew what they were fighting for; they waged war on anyone else with a claim to the region, or opposed their drive for absolute dominion. With the Creeks laid low, the Spanish removed and the British sent packing, the Old South-West ceased to be a frontier, but the frontier kept moving. Western expansion, slavery and ambition set the course for the Civil War that would, once again, reshape American culture.

THE NATURE OF VICTORY

The deeper import of war and peace for America was lost amid the curious euphoria that gripped the nation when it heard, at almost the same time, news of the Treaty of Ghent and Andrew Jackson's victory at New Orleans. This was curious: the war had been strikingly unsuccessful, by any calculation the military effort had been woeful, the navy better, but ultimately futile. Artful propagandists and unthinking patriots were content to see New Orleans as the key to peace because the news reached the East Coast at much the same time as the draft peace treaty, creating a comforting, if entirely erroneous notion that there was a connection between the two events. While the war broke the political power of the Federalists, and the economic primacy of oceanic commerce that had propelled their sectional interest, the Republicans were obliged to adopt key Federalist measures: a bigger state, a national bank, internal taxes, a standing army and an enlarged navy. By a curious coincidence the destruction of Washington, proud symbol of their hopes and dreams, had reconciled the Federalists to the war – creating a consensus around the defence of the nation.

The real American victory of 1812 was against internal opponents, Federalists and Indians alike, building a new identity around the ideal of the self-made man and liberal values. While America's war began with a disaster on land and triumph at sea it ended with victory on land and humiliation at sea. For Americans New Orleans became the defining image; the loss of the *President* was conveniently forgotten, because the sea no longer mattered. But nothing could alter the essential fact that British dominance of the seas remained absolute, utterly unchecked by a few frigate actions, or the treaties signed at Ghent and Vienna. In the rosy afterglow of a lucky escape Henry Clay claimed that the nation had gained honour and standing by waging war. The more hard-headed response took the form of forts, soldiers and warships, while roads and canals reduced American vulnerability to the British blockade. Work began on a canal to link the Delaware River to Chesapeake Bay in 1815. Even Jefferson came to love the American industrialist as a new liberal nation emerged from the war.[53]

The most significant outcome of the War of 1812 was internal, and sectional. Although all Americans saw the Revolution of 1776 as the defining moment in national history they disagreed about the legacy of independence. The partisan ferocity of

Federalist–Republican struggles reflected a deep-seated clash of cultures within America. Men on both sides anticipated that the growing economic, political and cultural divide between North and South would end in divorce.[54] Well aware of the looming sectional crisis the British made it an integral element of their post-war diplomatic and strategic planning. Consequently the most important outcome of the War of 1812 was not 'victory' but the renewal of the Union. War, Albert Gallatin observed:

... renewed and reinstated the national feeling which the Revolution had given and which were daily lessened. The people now have more general objects of attachment with which their pride and political opinions are connected. They are more American; they feel and act more like a nation; and I hope that the permanency of the Union is thereby better secured.[55]

Prominent among those general objects of attachment was the carefully constructed success story of the Navy. Although the United States Navy thus enjoyed a brief period of national esteem, the bubble burst in the late 1820s; the Mexican War, 1846–8 demonstrated a far better way of aggrandising Western land hunger than building ships or blustering about the Canadian frontier. The propaganda triumph of 1812 signally failed to unite: America remained a nation deeply divided along sectional and cultural lines. Those divisions would require a second, far bloodier conflict to resolve them. In 1815 the obvious winners were Southern and Western landowners, many of them slave-owning plantation agriculturalists. Their view of the American future was distinctly different from that of the Atlantic ship-owners and merchants who had borne the brunt of the British blockade on the Atlantic seaboard.

Above all, the war removed the illusory threat of British re-conquest, a useful myth that had obliged North and South to subsume their differences into the national project. When Ralph Waldo Emerson urged his countrymen to generate an American culture, to end the humiliation of cultural dependency on Europeans, his purpose was to bind the sections together. Emerson was equally clear that this meant imposing Northern culture: the South was bereft of culture – it had 'no poets, no libraries, no men of note'. In a narrow, bookish sense Emerson may have been correct, but the South had evolved a potent expansive culture from the experience of 1812. A distinct Southern sectional identity emerged, a thing apart from the Northern states, clearly divided on social, economic, political and international issues. Differing economic interests exacerbated sectional tensions: Southern opposition to protectionist tariffs, designed to promote Northern industry, struck Northerners as unpatriotic.

While the Mexican War provided a temporary boost to patriotism, it also emphasised the deepening divisions within the American identity. A war in the South-West, led by Southerners, was seen by the North as a deliberate extension of slave holding and Southern political power. If Northerners viewed the stability of Southern society with considerable nostalgia they feared the political power of a land-owning class.[56] By 1860 these fears had been translated into political form by a new Northern Republican Party determined to impose a national identity on the South. The North would neither allow the South to leave the Union, nor remain unchanged. To create a political nation one of the 'sectional' identities had to go under.

By a curious logic, one commonly found in deeply divided nations, those seeking to build bridges between North and South frequently blamed the British for slavery. Much of the heated anti-British rhetoric developed by Southerners was a displaced attack on the North, which for patriotic and political reasons they did not want to make directly. Slave owners had been deeply anti-British before 1812, alarmed by the abolition of the slave trade in 1807, and the wider anti-slavery movement. The British decision for complete emancipation in the early 1830s produced a paroxysm of displaced rage. Deeply alarmed Southerners saw the British decision as a deliberate attempt to foster servile revolts; 'thus revenging yourselves on the Americans'.[57] In response the South militarised, using its political power to secure new national forts and warships to defend the peculiar institution. The New England anti-slavery movement might be seen as a belated Federalist revenge for the disasters of 1812.

AMERICAN STRATEGIC CULTURE

Sectional divisions ensured America went to war in 1812 with an utterly incoherent strategy. The administration had failed at all levels to connect aims and means. It had failed to turn political support into taxes, to buy the necessary naval hardware, or mobilise manpower in time to transform it into effective armies. America simply did not have a 'Way of War', a national approach to defence and conflict suitable for a conflict with other developed nations. Any nation professing to act like a great power required professional military forces. Without them America was left to rely on filibuster and bluster. Little wonder Britain and France judged the Republican administrations long on words and sentiments, and strikingly short on the wherewithal to secure their demands. From a European perspective there was something comical about a people who could vote for war, but not the taxes needed to wage it. Confused by such diffuse signals, the British took several months to realise the Americans were serious.

Despite the Churchillian rhetoric of Anglo-Saxon peoples with a common heritage, the reality was, as ever, more complex. Cultural divergence between America and Britain began early, and became substantial long before the Revolution. No sooner had the new nation become independent than its culture was fractured by arguments far more profound than those that had led to the Revolution. If American high arts and polite literature in 1812 were still influenced by British ways, the same could not be said for the American way of war.

In 1812 American strategic culture was dominated by a militia tradition of amateur soldiering, and endemic frontier wars against non-European peoples on open borders. These were wars of savage intensity, directly linked to expansive land hunger, directly benefiting those who fought. Whatever their morality or justice, these were popular democratic wars, propelled by an innate sense of racial superiority.[58] The underlying strategic culture depended on American technological superiority. In such conflicts naval forces provided useful support on rivers and coasts but, in the absence of European opposition, could be extemporised from existing vessels and local personnel.

In 1812 this 'Way of War' resulted in a strategy that relied on largely amateur armies to attack Indians, Spaniards and Canadians, supported by an auxiliary navy at the watery margins, while professional warships and privateers distracted the Royal Navy. In stark contrast to the amateur military tradition the United States Navy was a professional force. In the Revolutionary War the Navy had failed. While American privateers had been successful against British commerce, most regular American warships had been captured and added to the Royal Navy. The new American Navy of the 1790s addressed a very different problem: it was a direct response to piracy and predation against American shipping. The direct link with overseas commerce gave it a strongly partisan character. John Adams's Federalist administration built the cruiser fleet to defend New England oceanic commerce against Barbary corsairs. They gave their new totems suitably important names: the big ships were *President*, *Constitution* and *United States*, names that spoke of American particularism, equipped with majestic figureheads loaded with symbolic meaning.

The Navy fought its first battles in the Caribbean, defending American shipping against French warships and privateers. After 1800 the Republican administrations of Jefferson and Madison used the cruiser fleet, but did not maintain it. They preferred a coastal force of gunboats, to keep America out of the world and the world out of America. Such prosaic craft, and the prosaic mission they entailed, did not sit well with naval professionals, who dreamt of emulating the all-conquering Royal Navy. Jefferson's government replaced the ornate Federalist figureheads with standardised Republican billet heads. These ideologically loaded emblems were in place when *Chesapeake* and *President* were captured. *Essex*'s head was shot away in her final battle.

Rather than expand the regular Navy, and the political power of the Federalists, Jefferson planned to complement his gunboat fleet with a naval militia of privateers. He expected the seafaring community would provide predators, inspired by republican zeal and personal profit. By contrast the regular Navy had no experience of commerce-destroying. Down to 1812 it had been a police force, not a predator. The obvious consequence of this inexperience was the striking failure of the Navy to destroy much British commerce. Most senior officers were obsessed with honour and glory, which they believed should be acquired through single combat with 'equal' opponents. Many cruiser operations would be curtailed by naval battles that, despite the propaganda value of victory, were utterly barren of strategic or economic value. The three frigate victories of 1812 were a classic example: after each battle the victorious frigate went home. The *United States* never got to sea again. Younger, smarter officers realised this was futile: David Porter, William Henry Allen and James Biddle among others switched their focus, with some prompting from Navy Secretary Jones, becoming effective, if short-lived predators.

In 1812 Madison left the largely Federalist Navy to its own devices; Republican ideologues put their faith in privateers, 'the Republic's Private Navy'.[59] It was no accident that the dominant privateer port was fiercely Republican Baltimore, rather than Federalist Boston. The combination of private resources, Republican politics and personal profit solved an otherwise insuperable problem for a state incapable of balancing strategic ambition and national revenue.

The Republican 'Way of War' collapsed at the first test. At Queenston Heights the New York Militia refused to invade Canada; several New England state forces simply refused to mobilise. By 1814 a deeply frustrated Jefferson was left to dream of waging war on Massachusetts, a war Republican America might win. At least America had the beginnings of a professional army by 1814.[60] The privateers proved more effective than the militia because, although few were professional warriors, they were professional seafarers. Yet, after a brief period of windfall profits, the privateers found their ports closely blockaded, and the seas empty of everything but heavily escorted convoys and aggressive British cruisers. When they fled inshore, the British took to their boats and pursued them to the high-water mark, capturing or burning their costly vessels. By 1814 privateers were reduced to bringing in prisoners for head money, and plundering cargo. The British had broken the back of the 'Private Navy', and the state was obliged to buy some of these craft for a new kind of maritime war, true commerce-destroying in which the only object was to deprive the enemy of his ships and cargoes, with no prospect of profiting from their capture.[61] In the summer of 1813 Navy Secretary William Jones ordered his captains to sink or burn, and not to send in prizes.

Despite the harsh lessons of war American statesmen continued to believe in a private navy, basing their strategy for an Anglo-American war on the myth of the privateer for half a century. In 1856 the British exploited this obsession to establish the Declaration of Paris, an international agreement that exchanged acceptance of many long-standing American claims to limit belligerent maritime rights for the complete abolition of privateering. Unwilling to pay for an adequate professional navy, the American administration rejected the declaration. Five years later many of the same men, by now leading the Confederacy, commissioned privateers. Unable to bring in prizes, the private effort failed, obliging the Confederate states to follow William Jones's strategy of commissioning regular warships, the CSS *Florida*, *Alabama* and *Shenandoah*, and repeating the strategy of 1814, the deliberate destruction of enemy shipping, a purely negative form of commerce warfare. In this case the total nature of the conflict lent the policy a coherence that had been hard to find in 1812. In the twentieth century German U-boats and the American submarines that annihilated Japanese merchant shipping followed the same logic.

The most effective critique of pre-war Jeffersonian thinking about strategy was the American 'Way of War' that emerged after 1815. The war created a strong cadre of professional naval and military officers; men like John Rodgers and General Winfield Scott used the war to develop distinct professional 'Ways of War'. The Army emphasised engineering, constructing massive coast defence fortresses; the Navy built up a small battlefleet to challenge the blockade that had throttled the life out of the country in 1814. While the military 'way of war' persisted down to 1861, the naval effort ran out of steam in the 1830s, as political support and funds ebbed away from the ocean towards 'Manifest Destiny' and sectional crisis. Down to 1861 opinion on the Navy was divided: while Northerners wanted a global force to protect and expand their trade, Southerners only began to support the Navy in the 1850s, seeking protection against the British, and a tool to expand slavery into the Caribbean.[62]

Despite the war some elements of Republican ideology persisted. In 1814, when Robert Fulton produced an updated, enlarged version of the Republican gunboat, it was no accident that he named the steam-propelled harbour-defence battery *Demologos*. Thereafter Jefferson's anxiety that oceanic naval power might entangle America in unwelcome external concerns retained political currency long into the twentieth century.

The idea of 1812 as a victorious 'Second War of Independence' won by amateur forces was an illusion created by Republican Party ideologues for partisan purposes. In reality American post-war strategic architecture would be driven by the experience of defeat, and the continuing threat posed by the British. The British had come within an ace of wrecking the United States with a strikingly cheap strategy based on oceanic sea control, a small amphibious army and the menace of servile insurrection. To meet the threat, America needed powerful coastal defences, a militarised population south of the Mason–Dixon Line and enough naval power to divert British effort into the Atlantic sea lanes. While these forces were provided in peace time, an army to invade Canada would, once again, have to be extemporised. The next time America raised such an army it was used to conquer large swathes of Mexican territory; the second such extemporised army defeated the Confederacy. The twentieth century would see more mass armies mobilised as America became a superpower. In the Second World War mass navies and air forces were created as well, and all three services have been maintained at very high levels through long decades of peace. Jefferson's anti-militaristic ideals and amateur 'Way of War' were among the many casualties of the sanguinary little skirmish with the British. In many ways the capture of the Federalist flagship *President*, proud symbol of the hopes and aspirations of the American maritime sector, proved a turning point. It was quickly forgotten because America was abandoning the oceans for the coast and rivers, a process that, with the exception of the two world wars, has continued to this day.[63] The United States was rapidly becoming a continental power; it would need a suitably continental 'Way of War'.

POPULAR CULTURE, IDENTITY AND WAR

The cultural consequences of war would be altogether more telling than the military and strategic. If 1812 resolved little of substance between Britain and the United States, it proved to be a transformational experience for a young nation still searching for an identity. Until then educated Americans took their culture, clothes and habits from England. Native literature and the arts were considered second-rate. Well-intentioned attempts to generate a national literature only demonstrated there were no short cuts to Shakespeare. As the dedicatee of Joel Barlow's ponderous epic *The Columbiad*, Robert Fulton observed that the poem at least proved Americans had mastered the finer points of printing.[64] British reviews, the standard cultural reference across the anglophone Atlantic, were equally unflattering. As Bradford Perkins observed 'because' British critics 'came so close to the truth, they wounded American sensibilities'.[65] The unconscious assumption of British cultural superiority, merited or otherwise, challenged national identity and self-esteem.

Not that British arrogance was solely to blame. The development of a truly American culture had been limited by Republican hostility towards the creative arts, which they associated with monarchs and elites, restricting the ambition of American patrons. Without wealthy patronage there would be little American cultural output, and it was unlikely native talent would flourish. Predictably, Republican taste eschewed allegory, preferring the simple, 'Roman' naturalism of Gilbert Stuart's portrait of George Washington. The great American artist of the era, Benjamin West, founding President of the Royal Society of Arts, moved from explaining why North America was anglophone, with the iconic 'Death of Wolfe', to four versions of the death and transfiguration of Nelson. Pre-war American literature remained equally derivative, preferring Republican concerns for social utility, local issues and land to individual expression. Stories were moral and improving, without much concern for merit, and none whatever for invention. Most were lightly fictionalised versions of recent history. Imported British books were cheaper than native products, while fully three-quarters of American publications were pirated editions. With a copyright system that could not protect native authors, foreigners were fair game for pillaging, either wholesale or by selection. Journals aimed at East Coast elites prided themselves on European merits and rarely lasted long; there was no mass audience for highbrow culture. A native popular culture would emerge during the war, finding new forms to meet a democratic age.[66]

In one area the Americans had already diverged from Britain. American popular culture had a special place for conflict, not the civilised, ennobling war of European nations, but a savage clash of civilisations in the wilderness, a clash that provided a proximate 'other' to solidify identity, and justify further expansion. The right to keep and bear arms, the militia principle and an abhorrence of standing armies melded Roman republican virtue with British constitutional practice in a weird response to

Cromwellian military dictatorship. Nothing summed up these complex emotions better than the affecting economy of Francis Scott Key's hymn to republican virtue and national resolve, which would become the American anthem.[67] After 1783 the history of war occupied a special place in the American imagination; the War for Independence would be retold to generate a sense of identity, of special republican virtue. No one asked awkward questions about the justice of the cause, or expressed doubts about the unfolding divine purpose. Novelists traded heavily on the alleged 'historical' veracity of their material, often interleaving invented characters with the dramatic highlights of the last conflict. Post-war authors Washington Irving and James Fenimore Cooper valued history above fiction throughout their careers. Despite Irving's satirical subversion of the historical genre in his 1809 *History of New-York*, both men would combine the low business of making a living with the higher calling of grand narrative. In America the boundaries of reality were soft and flexible; history had no professionals. The distinction between truth and fiction should not be allowed to spoil a good story. That Irving's subversive account of New York's past is the one that sticks in the memory is more than simple testament to literary merit. It swept away the notion that literature must serve a moral purpose and possess social utility.[68]

And yet the real clash of cultures in 1812 was sectional, not international. The Civil War might have been fifty years into the future but the United States was already a nation divided. Deep-rooted antipathies separated the seafaring, trading, industrial North-East from landed societies in the middle states and the territorially expansionist South and West. These divisions dominated political life, becoming deeply entrenched in 1812. The slave-owning states were petrified of British and Spanish intervention, a nightmarish combination of powerful nations, black soldiers and servile insurrection. The North-East did not share these concerns, nor was it prepared to sacrifice commerce on the altar of 'Free Trade and Sailors' Rights', despite owning and operating most American oceanic shipping. Those who protested most loudly about such abstract notions were the least connected with the ocean, by interest, geography, ambition and culture. Maverick Republican Congressman John Randolph considered America 'a great agricultural nation'; he did not want to be ruled by the commercial interests of seaport towns, or fight Britain over the dubious benefits of the re-export trade.[69]

Not that the process of cultural change was restricted to the Western hemisphere. The Napoleonic wars witnessed a radical transformation in British culture, creating a national consciousness in tune with an existential conflict that pitted continental Europe against insular Britain. Decades of war with Revolutionary and Napoleonic France cut Britain off from the European Grand Tour, polite exchange with foreign gentlemen and the international market in cultural artefacts. War hastened the process of making a shared insular British identity, one that required new cultural icons. In 1798 the figure of Britannia on the reverse of British copper coins had been subtly modified, the old figure bareheaded and holding an olive branch acquired the helmet of Pallas Athene and dropped the foliage to grasp the trident of sea power. When J. M. W. Turner shifted his gaze from the Classical Mediterranean vistas of Claude and Vernet to a sublime native landscape, and re-energised the art of the sea, a medium made luminous by Willem van de Velde a century before, he provided the British with cultural weapons of great power, in forms that could be widely disseminated.[70] The mighty ocean and the genius of Nelson were the ultimate British totems.

Before 1812 much of this new culture had crossed the Atlantic, to a nation starved of heroes and glory. Nowhere was American cultural dependence more obvious than in the case of Lord Nelson. After Trafalgar the dead hero was re-imagined as a classical deity, the war god of a British state waging all-out war with Napoleonic France. His name and deeds became universal possessions. American midshipman Robert F. Stockton's career would be shaped by the Nelson myth.[71] American publishers issued numerous hagiographic eulogies, and they continued appearing throughout the War of 1812. Nelsonic rhetoric had a significant impact on American naval heroics, both Oliver Hazard Perry and Thomas Macdonough employed variants of Nelson's best known motto to encourage their men. There were no suitable American examples; their naval heroes seemed to be tongue-tied in the company of an immortal. James Lawrence was the only American to meet the literary challenge: not only did he die like Nelson, but his line 'Don't Give up the Ship' became a standard. However, it was a later embellishment of less carefully formulated feelings, rather than a composed signal.

IMAGES OF GLORY

If the technique, ambition and intellectual drive of American artists remained tied to the Old World long into the nineteenth century, the evolution of a distinctive American pictorial tradition had been obvious from the early colonial era. American art expressed the expansive dream of a new society. Seemingly endless 'open' land to the south and west created a popular cultural model that challenged the maritime–Atlantic orientation of colonial cities, government and merchant elites. While wealthy merchants commissioned art to represent successful lives, growing families and the ships and ports they used, artists elsewhere tried to record and understand American land, people, animals and plants, seeking scientific rigour in sharp, hard-edged pictures and striking colour. The domestic market could not retain artists of the highest calibre. Both John Singleton Copley and Benjamin West moved to London, using nascent American realism to separate their work from the fading rococo of the English tradition. West's expansive notion of art, and willingness to encourage his fellow-countrymen, effectively created an American fine art tradition. His followers captured the new country, and the new elite.[72] Among them was young miniaturist Robert Fulton, seeking a career in art.

The naval art of the War of 1812 was dominated by aquatints and engravings, a new technology that served popular demand. While individual oil paintings reflected elite tastes, often commissioned to celebrate specific events, the coloured aquatint provided popular representations of the conflict that could be consumed by purchase, or on public display in the windows of print sellers. The aquatint provided a relatively rapid method of transmitting detailed, coloured images to an audience suitably primed by the print media. After two decades of total war, London's dynamic print industry linked successful dealers, skilled engravers and printers with artists and naval officers. The last often provided sketches for chosen artists to develop.[73] Before 1812 the United States had consumed a limited number of British and French prints, alongside the works of a tiny domestic community of marine artists and engravers. In 1812 these men provided pictorial evidence of naval glory, transforming American notions of war and triumph. American naval images of the Quasi-War (1798–1800) had been created by British artist William Birch and American artist-engraver Edward Savage, supported by at least two British prints. Savage's 1799 naval aquatint was the first created in the United States.[74] Interest in an American marine art was sustained by the campaigns against the Barbary powers, which brought American warships into European ports, attracting the attention of French and Italian artists. Some of these artists followed patrons to the United States.

While the War of 1812 would be represented by American, British and French artists, their prints have often been used as innocent productions, devoid of any meaning beyond the literal representation. That not one of the artists involved was present at any of the actions they represent should give pause for reflection. The 'accuracy' of the images varies, reflecting artistic talent and access to reliable sources. The purpose, beyond the obvious profit motive, requires more analysis. American naval glory created a new art market. After capturing the *Guerriere*, Isaac Hull wanted to record his exploits. He consulted portraitist Gilbert Stuart, who recommended local artist Michele Cornè on the strength of a large canvas of a naval battle off Tripoli. Hull commissioned a picture of *Constitution* escaping from Broke's squadron, and four images of the frigate combat, providing details of both actions, and vetting the sketch designs.[75] Elba-born, Cornè arrived in Salem in 1800. His lively, colourful, skilful marine views and battle scenes provided a potent European leaven to a nascent American art. Too skilled to be naïve, and too simple for high art, he found an audience in local sea ports where accuracy mattered more than allegory. Versatile and effective, Cornè produced portraits of ship-owners, sea captains, vessels and families for the homes of newly wealthy New Englanders. His strong, colourful images were ideal for engraving.[76]

The demand for prints during and after the war transformed the American cultural landscape. In 1816 Abel Bowen, one-time dockyard rigger turned woodcut artist, published *The Naval Monument* with twenty-one views of naval battles, engraved and described from Cornè's pictures. Hull's five pictures took a prominent place in the final work, memorialising a major event and the hero of the day. Later Bowen's engravings took on a life of their own, becoming the most familiar images of the naval war, as prints and tableware transfers.[77] Bowen chose his battles carefully: they were either American victories or 'heroic' defeats. Two views, '*Hornet* blockading *Bonne Citoyenne*' and '*Hornet* taking *Peacock*', fed the growing idolisation of James Lawrence, while the 'Capture of the *Essex*' confirmed David Porter's claim of a moral victory

War and the growing economic and political power of the middle class created an art market that privileged native subjects, images and artists. America became the subject of her own art just as the nation took a decisive step away from the sea. A new romantic literature of essays and short stories replaced sermons and tracts; full of expressive, descriptive writing it was an obvious partner for the striking image. American tales needed American pictures. Although connected to the European tradition, the construction of an American marine art was a complex process, reflecting the widespread transmission of great works in engraved form and the achievement of immigrant artists. London-trained Washington Allston developed an American landscape/seascape from European models, notably Joseph Vernet, in which classical allusions featured strongly. A frequent visitor to Europe, Allston spent time in Rome with Washington Irving and English poet-philosopher Samuel Taylor Coleridge; his fascination with Venetian art pioneered an American sublime.[78]

Although imported art and artists brought the traditions of Holland, England, France and Italy to America a truly original American form was emerging. Cornè reached the country as a fully formed artist but Thomas Birch arrived in Philadelphia in 1794 aged fifteen, with his father William, a painter and engraver. Thomas Birch trained on local scenes, many maritime and naval. His models were largely Dutch. He became a professional artist, a member of the Pennsylvania Academy of Fine Arts and the first marine artist to achieve significant public recognition. Birch only slowly relaxed the treatment of detail that could obscure his themes. His War of 1812 canvases dealt with American victories, including several variants of the key oceanic actions produced for sale in Philadelphia. Single-ship action may have been Birch's best form; he addressed the more complex flotilla actions at Lake Erie and Lake Champlain, but only produced a single example of these images. The design and layout of his single-ship actions showed a strong Dutch influence, as did the draughtsmanship and painting. Birch's most important 1812 images were completed within a year of the events they portray, and given the ebbing fortunes of the American Navy most appeared before the war ended. The patriotic, exemplary role of Birch's crisp formally structured work was obvious, helping to explain their success on public exhibition and as mass-consumption prints.[79] He executed more war images into the early 1820s, before turning his focus to the wider national seascape.[80] This sea culture was largely consumed by Northerners. As one might expect in a nation focused on a new western frontier, the post-war market for naval work was limited; while the maritime economy remained dynamic, there were few naval events to commemorate.[81]

The most popular naval subjects were the *Constitution–Guerriere*, and *United States–Macedonian* actions with 31 images each, while the action of Lake Erie dominated the inland naval war.[82] All three actions occurred early in the war, and most images were published before the conflict ended. They represented startling, even shocking events that reversed common expectations.

The aquatints and engravings of Thomas Buttersworth, one of the most important British artists of the naval war, reached the United States in such numbers during and after the conflict that many have assumed he was an American artist. There is no evidence Buttersworth emigrated and, critically, his output focused on British victories, or in the case of *Belvidera* escaping from Rodgers's squadron, fine seamanship.[83] No American artist would have troubled himself to represent the capture of *President*: but Buttersworth produced two fine images for engraving.[84]

French artists produced many of the finest marine images of the war, both oils and engravings, celebrating American naval success. After twenty-two years of defeat and failure the French finally found a way to beat the British, under the Stars and Stripes. They did not bother to picture British victories, a subject with which they were all too familiar.

A LITERATURE OF CONSEQUENCE

If the war created an American art genre it also empowered American literature. As editor of the *Analectic Magazine* between 1812 and 1815 Washington Irving combined well-judged pillaging of British periodicals with original work, notably lives of naval heroes and Francis Scott Key's patriotic anthem. Originally conceived as a vehicle to reprint foreign texts, the *Analectic* was transformed by war. The publisher decided to follow the British *Naval Chronicle*, a record of events at sea, liberally interspersed with the lives of naval heroes. Irving's four naval lives – of James Lawrence, William Burrows (dead hero of the *Enterprise*), Oliver Perry and David Porter – appeared in August, November and December 1813 and September 1814. They achieved a lasting place in naval history, much reprinted and widely, if unwisely, harvested for facts. The essay on Lawrence was re-used six times in as many years; it appeared in John Niles's 1820 life of *Oliver Hazard Perry*, edited to express a more hostile attitude towards the late enemy before a chapter calling for naval increases. Finally the text, with the other naval biographies appeared in Irving's *Spanish Papers*.[85] This extended publication history provided the lives with a wide circulation, exerting unusual influence over subsequent studies of Lawrence, Perry and Porter.[86] The re-use of Irving's work as a historical source exposed a fatal flaw in the making of American culture. Although based on fact and first-hand testimony, the essays were highly romanticised. The Lawrence essay contained serious errors that misled unwary authors for over a century, notably the romantic idea that the *Chesapeake* was an 'unlucky' ship, that the crew was new raised, and created a 'scoundrel Portuguese . . . boatswain's mate'. This 'heroic' treatment elided past the awkward fact that the 'hero' has been trounced in less than fifteen minutes, by a ship of precisely equal force, and significantly smaller crew. Irving's eulogy had Lawrence go into battle under 'disastrous and disheartening circumstances'.[87] Such nonsense made Lawrence look like an imbecile. A month after publication Irving confessed his errors of fact; and apologised for implying Lawrence deserved censure for giving battle to a ship in better order.[88]

Irving's impact on the American 1812 endured. Forty years later Alonzo Chappell's print 'Death of Captain Lawrence: Don't Give up the Ship' appeared.[89] Lawrence's portrait had been engraved for sale in Philadelphia by December 1813, part of a developing print culture of heroic sacrifice. Chappell's picture, like much of his work, had been produced for Jesse Ames Spencer's heavily illustrated *History of the United States* of 1858, where the text described Lawrence's words as 'consecrated in the eyes of his countrymen, and [which] have many a time since been used to animate the spirits of our brave seamen'.[90] Chappell deliberately followed the Nelson tradition, the dying hero posed as Christ's deposition from the cross, a motif that summed up the mood among Lawrence's peers. Washington Irving's hurried biography ensured his fame lived on in popular culture, while the unseemly struggle for control of his mortal remains not only produced three separate burials, but required two tombstones. Fenimore Cooper had also idolised Lawrence, ensuring his name retained its currency into the middle decades of the century. Little wonder the reality of his defeat remains troublesome.

While the flood of self-serving nonsense that followed Lawrence's defeat was brilliantly exposed by William James, it would be revived, for very different purposes, by Theodore Roosevelt and, in part, Alfred Thayer Mahan.[91] By the 1880s a thick veneer of nationalist and racist hyperbole overlay the evidence. Roosevelt blamed the Portuguese bosun's mate for deserting his post, an example followed by the 'mercenary' crew. He did not ask why an American warship needed a 'mercenary' crew, and did not check his facts. The failure of the bugler made no difference; the few Americans left on the upper deck when Broke boarded were overwhelmed by the speed and ferocity of the attack.

Early in the twentieth century Captain Albert Gleaves, USN, loyal advocate of his service and resolute hagiographer, rebutted Washington Irving's more absurd statements, only to generate fresh nonsense. *Chesapeake*, he declared:

. . . was considered the most unlucky ship in the navy, and from the time she was launched until Barron's bullet at Bladensburg, twenty years later, slew the most brilliant sailor officer the navy of the United States has ever produced, she seemed always to exercise a baneful influence upon every one connected with her.

He went on to anthropomorphise an inert thing of wood and iron, claiming that Barron's humiliation 'reflected as much discredit on the ship as it did upon him'.[92] In this he ignored the fact, recorded in his own text, that Lawrence's only objection to the ship was her inferior rate, and his familiarity with the larger *Constitution*. There was no need for luck to explain Broke's victory, nor any dishonour in Lawrence's defeat. Yet even the latest American official publication seems unwilling to concede, arguing that although there is 'merit to the charge that *Chesapeake* was not ready, ultimately *Shannon*'s expertise in broadside gunnery defeated the Americans'.[93] In fact *Chesapeake*'s previous wartime cruises had been moderately successful, and her supposedly 'evil' reputation was entirely posthumous, nothing more than an attempt to preserve the propaganda value of the initial three victories. Such nonsense can be attributed to inexperience and shock. That the United States Navy chose to take its defining motto from a man who had so obviously already lost his ship only adds to the confusion.

Whatever their faults, Irving's essays did not give way to crude nationalism; he stressed that the war was not the occasion to break the relationship between men of commerce and culture. If his heroes were overly romanticised, they were not rabid xenophobes; the enemy was equally brave, and once peace had been restored he expected that good relations, albeit on a more equal basis, would follow. He recorded the fact that Broke had been wounded while saving the lives of American seamen. In such company Lawrence became 'one of those talismanic names which every nation preserves as watchwords for patriotism and valour'. Such names and deeds constituted the naval legacy of war, 'the germ of future navies, future power, and future conquest'. Living heroes proved more difficult, lacking finality and a suitable occasion for hyperbole. Irving's essay on Porter praised his old friend's skill, daring and literary craft, concluding he had 'wreathed fresh honours around the name of the American sailor', in large measure by proving that they could stand and fight amid the slaughter of a battle lost. Once again literary alchemy transformed American defeat into a curious triumph. Once again the facts were less important than the conclusions; even those were suspect, resting as they did on Porter's self-serving account. Irving claimed all three ships had been shot to pieces, and exaggerated British losses. He used heroism to build a national identity free from deference, facing the British as equals.[94]

The *Analectic* failed shortly before the war ended.[95] There was little demand for foreign culture; henceforth American literature would address native subjects. With Porter's *Journal* at the press, Irving agreed to join Stephen Decatur's Mediterranean expedition, only to abandon the idea and head for Britain.[96] In 1817 Decatur tried again, securing Irving a post in the Navy Office with a salary of $2,400. Once again Irving turned down the chance to write naval eulogies; he stayed in Britain to pursue a literary career.[97] In 1819 he created a pioneering fictional treatment of the sea as a sublime romantic spectacle, one that influenced human imagination. His short essay 'The Voyage' inspired a generation of authors down to Herman Melville.[98] While Irving encompassed the process of transforming an oral tradition into mass consumption print media in a single self-referencing career, bringing American letters up to the European standard, meeting an expanding post-war American market for popular culture, he did not create a genuinely American literature. His output remained derivative. He made one last contribution to the history of the war in the 1830s when Astor hired him to write an account of the Astoria affair, and ensured that it blamed William Jones for the costly failure.[99] The way ahead had been charted by *The Port-Folio*, a journal of refined leisure that followed the declaration of war by calling for 'a repository of every thing that may tend to give character to our country, and to cherish in the breasts of our fellow citizens, the holy flame of genuine patriotism'.[100] War opened the floodgates of euphoria; 'the glorious achievements of our navy' had 'kindled a new and holy spirit of nationality, and enabled the humblest citizen among us boldly to say to the world that he too has a country', while 'the remembrance of the old become the cause of future victories'.[101] For the next thirty years America would have a cultural frontier on the ocean, one that waxed and then waned in harmony with the glory days of post-war deep-water commerce, whaling and travel, only to give way to a continental vision in the age of steam and rail. Before 1812 American authors of the sea had been hamstrung by Republican political agendas and a sense of inadequacy in the face of Britannia's awe-inspiring might. Even American naval songs and writings were of British origin, as was the hero of Melville's superb naval narrative *White Jacket*.[102]

Irving gave American literature a strong naval character. The deification of James Lawrence helped create a new national hero and his essays made it difficult for literate Americans to avoid an encounter with the ocean.[103] Irving knew many leading naval officers, and it was no accident that the first to compile a book was one-time room-mate and boon companion David Porter.[104] Porter had returned to New York from the Pacific in July 1814 with a rich fund of exotic tales, and taken a room in Irving's house.[105] With such remarkable material under his own roof it is scarcely surprising Irving published portions of Porter's journal in the *Analectic* a few months later. The book appeared in 1815, though there is no direct evidence of Irving's influence. Having been the subject of an admiring essay by Irving, Porter set the full-length study in an exotic setting as *Journal of a Cruise to the Pacific Ocean by Captain David Porter ... Containing descriptions of the Cape de Verde Islands, Coasts of Brazil, Patagonia, Chile and of the Galapagos Islands*.[106] This energetic, ambitious, and occasionally unreliable account found a ready audience, and remains the outstanding American first-hand naval narrative of the war. It was something rich and strange, mixing art, literature, history and travelogue. Porter described his book as a 'Journal' to create the impression that it was a simple narrative, in the Pacific-voyaging wake of Captain Cook. He used the text to press the case for a new Pacific voyage, to Japan. The idea was excellent, but premature, though the American squadron that finally reached Japan in 1853 could trace its mission all the way back to Porter. Porter's travelogue created an American Pacific, showing American audiences an ocean open for American trade. In his wake sailed Richard Henry Dana and Herman Melville. By way of the whale ship *Essex* narrative, which stressed the connection with Salem, and the Salem-built USS *Essex*, Porter's *Journal* lies at the heart of *Moby Dick*, the ultimate American novel.

Contemporary British reviewers were unimpressed, lambasting Porter's factual inaccuracy and salacious detail. The *Quarterly*

Review, house journal of Lord Liverpool's Tory Ministry, published a scathing 31-page denunciation that compared Porter, unfavourably, to a pirate.[107] While contemporaries attributed the unsigned notice to crotchety anti-American editor William Gifford, the author was Admiralty Second Secretary John Barrow. Something of an expert on travel writing, Barrow had good reason to denigrate the American cruise.[108] Nor, having demolished Porter's character and integrity, was Barrow inclined to believe the central plank of his romantic exoticism, tales of cannibalism on the Marquesas Islands. Cannibalism and lust led William James to dismiss Porter's text as 'filth and falsehood'.[109] In fact Porter's stories were true, providing Pacific literature with its defining metaphors, islands that combined sensual abandon with the cannibal and his feast. Irving, still resident in London, hurried to defend him against the *Quarterly*'s 'spleen and spite'.[110]

Naval service gave one-time Midshipman James Fenimore Cooper an intimate connection with the sea. He had served under James Lawrence and would engage with the naval past across the rest of his career. The social structure of a sailing warship came close to the hierarchical ideal he imposed on the American past, noble leaders, loyal followers, men of character and talent, bound by a common task.[111] Although he resigned from the service in 1811, Midshipman Cooper was swept up in the *President–Little Belt* furore. As Federalists hurried to condemn Rodgers's illegal actions, Republicans like Cooper 'blindly defended' him.[112] A year later, in April 1812, Cooper dined with old naval companions, delighting in their resolve and their confidence. He saw the long shadow of colonial dependence lifting, at least in respect to the arts of war. The heroics of the next twelve months seemed to confirm such hopes, only to highlight the disasters that would follow. Stunned by the dramatic reversal of fortune that saw his friend and hero cut down and the *Chesapeake* lost, Cooper took up *The Port-Folio*'s call for an American literature and identity. Melding maritime nationalism with romanticism, Cooper created a new literary form, setting his heroes in real American landscapes. While he shared Irving's tendency to look backwards to better days, endlessly lamenting the lost virtues of a heroic past of cultured leaders and deferential followers, identifiable figures endlessly re-imagined in an idealised re-working of history as mythic reality, his work met an emerging audience in the decade after the Treaty of Ghent: 'The War of 1812, popularly styled the Second War of American Independence, had quickened national self-awareness.' While Irving moved to Europe, adapting his art to an older tradition, Cooper used the novel 'to demonstrate to American readers that their own country afforded a rich field for the writing of historical fiction'. It was 'patriotic service' to show that 'authentic works of art could grow in indigenous soil'. War obliged artists to address their work to a distinctive national culture. Cooper placed the personal drama of 'Leatherstocking' stories like *The Last of the Mohicans* against familiar historical backgrounds.

Cooper followed the same approach when he wrote naval history, 'serious and respectable' work, emphasising the personal element in historic events.[113] He did not rush into print: if the glory days of his youth, and the heroism of James Lawrence were never far from his thoughts, naval history had to wait for Cooper. Critically he wrote after a political journey that mirrored that of the nation, from Federalist to Republican and by 1825 Jacksonian Democrat. Cooper's may have been a grudging, grumbling progress, but it was inevitable.[114] His naval history began with a masterly essay published in 1821 that focused on 1812. He drew a moral from the American challenge, making British defeats fitting punishment for their condescending treatment of America. He did not mention the loss of the *President*, or the many political meanings that might be drawn from the disaster. While he spoke of the past as history he did so with a strong personal agenda. Rather than trumpet the crudely nationalistic notion that America successfully challenged Britain for the trident of the seas he urged his countrymen to see the Navy as 'our chief defence against wrongs'. Past glories would encourage future achievement, hence the stress laid on Lawrence's famous words, by now understood as 'Don't give up the ship!' At a time when American commercial shipping dominated the Atlantic he had no doubt that the Navy would follow, becoming an integral part of the national identity. Cooper's past was prophecy. America's manifest destiny would be enacted upon the ocean; a suitable space for American enterprise and expansion. America would command the sea because it had demonstrated cultural as well as political independence from Britain.[115]

Cooper's writing played a key role in sustaining cross-party support for the navy 'as the prime instrument of nationalism' for two decades, but by the late 1830s the cultural tide had set against the ocean.[116] It was an older, less confident Cooper who produced the long-matured naval history, just as the glories of 1812 were fading. He attempted to sustain the naval cause, adopting a significantly more balanced historical voice, making judgements on merit, not nationalistic fervour. Although he recognised that frontier concerns had distracted his countrymen from the ocean, he still believed that America's destiny lay in naval greatness.

Cooper's naval history linked hard evidence with his own deeply emotional memories of victory and defeat, retaining the 'eyewitness' quality of his earlier writings to build a moral impression of an age now long forgotten by most Americans. Rather than address William James's precise, number-crunching version of the past Cooper deftly shifted his ground to more general points that served the future of the United States Navy. He rated Decatur's success in bringing home the *Macedonian* above the other frigate victories largely because he had seen the two ships sail through Hell Gate on their triumphant return to New York, and attended the victory banquet on 29 December 1812. The capture of the *Macedonian* acted as psychic compensation for the disaster that befell James Lawrence. The passage of time had not healed the psychological injuries inflicted by Broke's brilliant gunnery: the *Chesapeake* disaster still troubled the old author.[117]

Perhaps the capture of no single ship ever produced so much exultation on the side of the victors, or so much depression on that of the beaten party, as that of the *Chesapeake*. The American nation had fallen into the error of their enemy, and had begun to imagine themselves invincible on the ocean, and this without any better reason than having been successful in a few detached combats, and its mortification was in proportion to the magnitude of its delusion; while England hailed the success of the *Shannon* as a proof that its ancient renown was about to be regained.

Cooper's prose did not disguise the fact that he had shared the 'delusion'; every fresh victory, and the over-wrought celebratory dinners that greeted each new-made hero had reinforced his confidence in his old shipmates and leaders. Having been lionised over his victuals in New York on 4 May 1813 Lawrence's defeat and death less than a month later had coincided only too closely with Cooper's final decision to abandon the sea and take up a new career inland.[118] This was the American journey – and the reality of his cultural career.

Long before his death Cooper must have realised that the ocean frontier had been forgotten, along with the mythology of 1812. His sea fiction would be forgotten, while the frontier tales endured, because continental concerns dominated politics, and the consumption of culture. The Mexican War, primarily an Army campaign, provided fresh glory, the sectional divide a looming, lowering concern. Maritime and naval news was marginalised, and sales of nautical fiction collapsed, leaving Melville's *Moby Dick* hopelessly beached, the author's career effectively over.

Cooper's evocation of landscape and character through dress and appearance linked the instrumental world of fiction with art and, through the new technique of steel engraving, provided items of mass consumption linking text and image. In an age of economic expansion and heightened national consciousness American consumers engaged with high art through the mass-produced engraving, of ships and sea battles, or the strikingly rendered native landscapes of Thomas Cole. Cole illustrated *Last of the Mohicans* in 1827, while his 'American Sublime' quickly became the dominant American artistic genre, linking the words of Irving and Cooper with the expansionist politics of Andrew

Jackson and the notion of an American Empire.[119] The American Sublime directed the gaze of New York and Washington inland and westward, making the frontier into the dominant theme of a new American culture.

EPILOGUE

In 1861 Charles Stewart, the last 1812 frigate captain, retailed a chilling conversation with War Hawk leader John Calhoun in early 1812. He claimed that Calhoun had explained Southern secession in power political terms.

It is through our affiliation with that party in the middle and western states we control our Constitution, the government of the United States. But when we cease thus to control this nation, through a disjoined Democracy, or any material obstacle in that party which shall tend to throw us out of that rule, we shall then resort to a dissolution of the Union.

True or not, Stewart's report of Calhoun's remarks was widely circulated across the North.[120]

A few weeks earlier Stephen Decatur's *United States* had been scuttled at Norfolk Navy Yard. Quickly raised, she served the Confederacy's Navy for a year as a harbour-defence battery. Stewart's *Constitution* served the Union Navy as a training ship, and survives to this day as flagship of the War of 1812 that America won.

CHAPTER 13

The Challenge Answered

While the Republicans were making a totem out of the ever-victorious *Constitution*, the flagship of American victory, that version of events was being neatly subverted across the Atlantic, where her sister ship, the mighty *President*, survived to tell a very different story. At this remove it matters little who 'won' the War of 1812, what matters is that we recognise the fluid, endlessly contested nature of the past. Not the past as fact, but the past as a cultural construction. The War of 1812 as it exists in the modern memory is almost entirely the creation of contemporary and near-contemporary political and personal agendas. Nowhere is this more obvious than in the case of the frigate battles. While the British carefully noted the causes of victory or defeat, and rewarded the successful officers, the American response to defeat, led by the surviving captains and the hagiographers of the third, created a magical reality to obscure unpalatable facts. These versions became enmeshed in the cultural construction of a new national identity; they became foundation myths for an American culture, a new way of being American. Little wonder the language is emotional, rather than rational. That the United States and the United Kingdom hold very different views of 1812 only serves to remind us that history is neither fixed, nor agreed.

The War of 1812 was fought between two literate populations sharing a common language. Partisan accounts of the war were used to sustain Anglo-American hostility long after the causes and aims of the war itself had been forgotten. The American version, the one which concentrated on the three frigate victories and the battle of New Orleans, enabled American politicians to claim that they had 'won' the war. This powerful domestic

449

propaganda was frequently revived for international service. The British response was provided by lawyer turned historian William James, an Admiralty Court officer lately based in Jamaica. When war broke out James and his wife were making their way to a new life at Kingston, Ontario, and had the misfortune to be detained as enemy aliens at Philadelphia. Rendered incandescent by the treatment they received, and incensed by the audacity of the American propaganda that followed their early naval successes, James began to collect the 'facts'. Despite his status he managed to get on board American ships, measure them and interview the crews! In 1816 he rebutted the American version in the booklet, *An Inquiry into the Merits of the Principal Naval Actions between Great Britain and the United States*, pointing out the great disparity in force, of guns and crew, between the British and American ships in the actions of 1812. He followed this with the much enlarged *A Full and Correct Account of the Chief Naval Occurrences of the late war between Great Britain and the United States of America* in 1817. He included much of the argument in his major work, the *Naval History of Great Britain,* and sent the latest edition to Prime Minister George Canning in 1826 specifically to assist him in repelling American bluster based on what he saw as a false version of history. These works remain essential reading, because James discussed the subject with many of the leading officers of the Royal Navy, especially Philip Broke. As he had intended, his stark, precise analysis of guns, tons and manpower confounded all the bluster about 'fair and equal' combat. While generations of American authors have attacked his work, it is important to distinguish between the personal animosities of a man outraged by his treatment, and the dispassionate measure of facts. In his search for the truth James offended more British officers than American, publicly condemning men like George Collier and John Carden for giving the Americans an excuse to boast.

After James, the most ambitious accounts of the war at sea were written by Americans. Theodore Roosevelt sprang to prominence with an attempt to rebut some of James's claims in his *Naval History of the War of 1812* in 1882, while Alfred Thayer Mahan's *The Influence of Sea Power Upon the War of 1812* in 1905 used the reality of American defeat to make the case for an American ocean-going battlefleet. Unsurprisingly, it was the least successful of his major works. Americans didn't want to listen, while the British had lost interest in the war by 1830.

British and American responses to 1812 still reflect the mutual incomprehension evident 200 years ago. While the construction of an American victory was driven by a complex melding of political propaganda, military professionalism, artistic ambition and literary exceptionalism, the British learnt useful lessons about strategy, tactics, discipline and organisation, but they did so in private. Few in twenty-first-century Britain know the war happened; most Britons think the only event of 1812 was Napoleon invading Russia, and by no coincidence at all this was the viewpoint of the men who ran the war. 1812 simply did not resonate in British culture. The British forgot 1812 because they had already created a potent cultural identity fighting Napoleon; with Nelson already enshrined as their war god they had little need of fresh victories and preferred to get back to the business of profitable trade. However, they kept just enough relics to subvert American triumphalism.

Even in 1815 the arrival of the *President* in Portsmouth had been overshadowed by the high drama of Napoleon's Hundred Days. No sooner had Henry Hope delivered the prize than he joined the hastily assembled blockade of the French Atlantic coast, once again under Henry Hotham's command. Shortly after taking the *President*, Hotham's squadron would capture an Emperor – taking custody of Napoleon on board HMS *Bellerophon*.[1] The Hundred Days marked the end of Henry Hope's sea-going career: he paid off his famous ship on 16 August. The empty hulk was laid up in the Hamoaze, in case the country had need of her again.[2] A decade later the Royal Navy rebuilt HMS *Endymion*, a tribute to her fame and her superior sailing qualities: 'the fastest frigate of the late war, which took the *President*', returned to service in 1832, and remained the standard against which the next generation of sailing frigates would be judged.[3] In 1842 she went to war again, this time against China, sailing up the Yangtse River as far as Nanking. Hulked in 1860, the old hero was finally broken up in 1868 – giving her name to fresh *Endymion*s.[4] Hope had been awarded a Naval Gold Medal and gazetted a Companion of the Bath in 1815; he went on to be an ADC to King William IV and then Queen Victoria, dying full of honours and years in 1863.

Having taken one of the American super-frigates the British took care to preserve it, to demonstrate that the defeats of 1812 had been unequal combats. When *President* arrived at Portsmouth John Wilson Croker ordered her lines and dimensions taken off.[5] At the same time the Admiralty renamed the existing HMS *President*, a French prize, freeing up the name for the American *President*, ensuring Hope's victory would never be forgotten. The Admiralty planned to return HMS *President* to service, but she was in poor shape, afflicted by old age and 24-pounder balls, although there was no evidence of any 'damage' from grounding on the bar at Sandy Hook. Yet *President* was far too important a trophy to abandon, so in 1818 Lord Melville ordered the construction of a precise copy, preserving the name and the image.[6]

In stark contrast to the bombast surrounding 'Old Ironsides', the name USS *President* has lain unused since January 1815. Although many Presidents of the United States have had ships named for them, not one ship has been named for the office they hold.[7] The decision not to re-use the name implies there was something dishonourable in her loss, and thus the American flagship, once graced by a figure of the founding father of the country, lives on in another Navy. Taking the *President* mattered because the Americans always had the manpower to invade and conquer Canada. Britain relied on seapower to secure her colonies from American invasion. By reminding Washington who was the master of the oceans the British could exert diplomatic leverage, and strategic deterrence. The reminder necessarily took naval form; and the more potent the image, the more likely it was to be understood. *President* and *Chesapeake*, *Endymion* and *Shannon*, Philip Broke's two sons and other relics of glory would be the key to maintaining the peace between Britain and America. When Anglo-American relations reached a particularly low point in 1833 the First Lord of the Admiralty despatched the new HMS *President*, carrying the flag of Admiral Sir George Cockburn, to the North American Station. It was a clear and simple reminder that the last time America challenged Britain Cockburn had burnt down the White House.[8] In her dotage HMS *President* became the London headquarters of the Royal Naval Reserve, a task she fulfilled until 1903. Thereafter a succession of old vessels bore the prestigious name, until the Reserve headquarters came ashore, to a building close by Tower Bridge that still bears the name. While images of Henry Hope's brilliant action line the corridor of the current HMS *President*, remarkably few officers have ever stopped to look.

By 1812 the British art market, in oils and print, was somewhat satiated by the sheer volume of heroics and glory. Trafalgar, the last great naval battle, was now seven years old, and there were no more Nelsons to laud. An unending diet of success left the national taste somewhat jaded. Even the usually reliable caricature had fallen away: the brilliant career of James Gillray ended in madness in 1811, the year Isaac Cruikshank, his closest rival, died. At first the American declaration of war attracted little attention; popular culture focused on Napoleon heading east, and Wellington's winning ways in Spain. There were new caricaturists, but their images and jokes appeared leaden and dull after the lightning wit of Gillray. His eviscerating insight filled every picture with light and shade, glory and folly, culture and chaos; his successors offered little more than rough images, simple jokes and basic word play. By contrast the new American art of British naval defeat, much of it executed by English emigrants, was taken up with some interest. Then the British developed a variant form, the art of heroic defeat in unequal combat. This version secured the cultural high ground with four aquatints depicting the loss of the *Java* by Nicholas Pocock. Using Lieutenant Buchanan's eyewitness testimony Pocock skilfully subverted American claims that the two ships were equal, making *Java* little more than half the size of her opponent. By the time his engravings were published on 1 January 1814 the fortunes of war had swung decisively in Britain's favour. British naval art returned to more familiar ground with a series of victories, most based on images created by artists working closely with officers who had been present at the action. This anxiety for realism reached a pinnacle in images of the contested single-ship actions of 1812, which remained popular subjects for at least three decades.[9]

Philip Broke's victory led an exhilarated, euphoric nation to demand images and accounts of the battle. Within weeks Broke reported that Captain Edward Brenton of HMS *Spartan* had produced two pictures of the battle: 'they represent one of the happiest moments of my life – as they afford me the privilege of returning with honour to my beloved Loo's arms, conscious of having earned my liberty'.[10] Robert Dodd's print of August 1813 showing the *Shannon* 'hove too, & coolly waiting the close approach of the American', caught the moment when Lawrence took in sail and Broke responded by backing his mainsail and main topsail. A second view represented the moment of boarding. While the prints credited 'information of Captain Falkiner', it may have been based on Brenton's sketches.[11] Another view was dedicated to Admiral the Earl St Vincent, to whom the Navy's discipline was credited. A striking portrait of Broke was commissioned from artist Samuel Lane by the East Suffolk Hospital; it represented the hero, 100-guinea sword in hand, trampling on the Stars and Stripes. Entirely unaffected by his new fame, Broke asked if the pose might not be too ostentatious.[12]

Ultimately the *Shannon–Chesapeake* action generated twenty-five contemporary or near-contemporary images, reflecting both the brilliance of the action, and its fundamental importance in reversing the demoralising trend of American success.[13] In 1830 Broke had the pleasure of sending a set of four new lithographs, engraved from highly detailed drawings by his old lieutenant Richard King and royal Marine Painter John Christian Schetky, to the Duke of Wellington. They have become the standard visual representation of the battle, making Broke's approval highly significant.[14] Prime Minister Wellington was acutely aware of the diplomatic value of the action: 'There is no event of the late war to which I have looked with more interest than that which these prints represent.'[15] The enduring demand for images of Broke's battle demonstrates that, while America slowly dropped the sea, Britain remained a maritime nation and a major consumer of marine art, one where the monarch retained his own Marine Painter. That said, the cultural legacy of 1812 in Britain was limited. While American naval victories tempered an otherwise unbroken run of success, the causes and consequences of the conflict soon faded from the national memory – 1812 was about Napoleon, not Madison. The British memory of 1812 was reduced to a single, exemplary battle, the one in which Philip Broke confounded the American challenge.

The two ships at the heart of that battle had very different fates. *Chesapeake* finally reached Britain in 1814, almost unnoticed amid the euphoria of victory over Napoleon. Unlike *President* she was just another standard 18-pounder frigate, neither large nor fast.[16] By 1820 James Lawrence's ship had been sold for scrap. Her timbers were used to build a watermill at Wickham, not far from Portsmouth. The mill still stands and the stout frames of the old ship are evident from their unusual shapes, shipwrights' marks and the scars of battle.[17] The fiddle head was presented to Broke and owned by the family until recently. In the 1850s a new HMS *Chesapeake* appeared, and she was sent to North America in 1855, commanded by Broke's son George, to remind America who ruled the waves. By contrast the Royal Navy retained *Shannon* as a trophy, a relic of undying glory. In 1833 War of 1812 veteran Admiral Sir John Beresford welcomed Broke's son into the Navy at Sheerness, telling his old friend: 'I show the dear old *Shannon* as a lion here; she is moored near the flagship.'[18] In 1859 the old ship was demolished, her name

The last of the *Shannons*:
Admiral of the Fleet Sir Provo William Wallis.

already re-used on a new ship, ordered at the height of Oregon Crisis in 1844, when Anglo-American relations had taken a down-turn. When the ship was finally broken up her figurehead was presented to Broke's family, and new gates were made for Nacton Hall from her timbers.

After bringing his battered ship home, Broke never went to sea again. The terrible wound to his head and the realisation that he had done his duty allowed him to retire to Suffolk and his beloved Louisa. There was just one, lingering regret, that Commodore Rodgers and his *President* had not come home in

Shannon's wake. However, he took real satisfaction from the fact that the greatest prize had been taken before the war ended, in the approved manner. After the war Broke kept up a lively correspondence with fellow naval reformers, while William James teased out much of what we know about the greatest frigate battle of them all.[19] A bad fall from a horse in 1820 left Broke's left side permanently cold, and he was increasingly confined to the house. His reforms were institutionalised on the gunnery training ship HMS *Excellent* in 1830, teaching gunnery officers and ratings of the Royal Navy to shoot straight and level, hit the target and concentrate fire.

Having answered the American challenge in the most decisive manner, restoring national honour and securing undying personal glory, Broke took up the ancestral duties of a local landowner, living out his days a reluctant national hero. He died on 2 January 1841. His remains lie in the quiet of the family crypt under Nacton church, one of many Brokes to make the last short journey from the old house to a final rest.

The Frigates of 1812

———∞∞∞———

	Shannon	Chesapeake	President	Endymion
Dimensions				
Length lower deck	150 ft 2 in	152 ft 6 in	173 ft 3 in	159 ft 3⅜ in
Length of keel	125 ft 6½ in		145 ft	132 ft 3 in
Extreme beam	39 ft 11⅜ in	40 ft 4 in	44 ft 4 in	42 ft 7 in
Depth in hold	12 ft 11 in	13 ft 9 in	13 ft 11 in	12 ft 4 in
Draft		20 ft	22 ft 6 in	23 ft 6 in
Tonnage	1,065.6 tons	1,244 tons	1,533.5 tons	1,277 tons
Armament (1813 & 1815)				
Main deck	28 x 18-pdr	28 x 18-pdr	30 x 24-pdr	26 x 24-pdr
Upper deck (carronades)	16 x 32-pdr	18 x 32-pdr / 1 x 12-pdr	20 x 42-pdr	20 x 32-pdr
Upper deck (long guns)	3 x 12-pdr / 4 x 9-pdr / 1 x 6-pdr	1 x 18-pdr / 2 x 12-pdr	2 x 24-pdr / 1 x 24-pdr howitzer	1 x 18-pdr
Total	51 guns	50 guns	53 guns	47 guns
Broadside	541 lb	567 lb	816 lb	641 lb

All four ships mounted smaller guns in the fighting tops and on the upper decks.

Crew:	320	387	480	346

See Marquardt, K. H., *The 44 Gun Frigate USS Constitution*, p. 23; Gardiner, *Frigates of the Napoleonic Wars*, pp. 25–6, 43–4; Pullen, H. F., *The Shannon and the Chesapeake*.

Notes

Introduction

1. Adams, H., *History of the United States of America during the Second Administration of James Madison*, Vol. III, p. 63. Adams's thoughtful analysis is far removed from the partisan approach adopted by other nineteenth-century American authors.
2. Martineau, G., *Napoleon Surrenders*, p. 59.
3. Byron, *The Corsair* (1814), Canto 1, stanza 3.

CHAPTER 1: Flashpoints

1. Log book of the *Chesapeake*: 22–23 June 1807: Dudley, W. ed. *The Naval War of 1812: A Documentary History*. Vol. I, pp. 26–8. Tucker, S. C. & Reuter, F. T., *Injured Honor*, provides a full-length treatment.
2. The high self-esteem of the American naval officer corps is evident from the sheer number of surviving portraits of pre-1815 officers who stare serenely sideways and ahead in Christopher McKee's *A Gentlemanly and Honorable Profession: The Creation of the U.S. Naval Officer Corps, 1794–1815*.
3. Long, D. F., *Nothing too Daring: A biography of Commodore David Porter, 1783–1843*, pp. 38–9.
4. Paullin, C. O., *Commodore John Rodgers, 1773–1838*, pp. 174–95. Schroeder, J. H., *Commodore John Rodgers: Paragon of the Early American Navy*, pp. 53–4, 64–7. McKee, pp. 293, 404.
5. Barron to Jones, 22 July 1813: Dudley, W. ed., *The Naval War of 1812: A Documentary History*, Vol. II, pp. 190–1.
6. Presidential Message. 27 Oct. 1807; Dudley I, pp. 32–3.
7. Hill P. P., *Napoleon's Troublesome Americans: Franco-American Relations, 1804–1815*, p. 30.
8. Vice Admiral Sir George Berkeley to Earl Bathurst, 18 July & 17 Aug. 1807: *Report on the Manuscripts of Earl Bathurst*, pp. 63–5.
9. Lewis, E. R., *Seacoast Fortifications of the United States: An Introductory History*, pp. 23–36 & 140.

10. Schroeder, P. W., *The Transformation of European Politics, 1763–1848*, pp. 435–6.

11. Smith E. A., *Lord Grey, 1764–1845*, p. 112.

12. For a classic interpretation by an eminent strategist, see Mahan, A.T., *The Influence of Sea Power upon the French Revolution and Empire 1792–1812*, Vol. II, pp. 271–82.

13. P. W. Schroeder, pp. 307–8.

14. St Vincent to Thomas Grenville (First Lord of the Admiralty), 22 Dec. 1806: H. Craig, ed., 'Letters of Lord St. Vincent', pp. 486–7. Melvin, F. E., *Napoleon's Navigation System*, New York, 1919, pp. 14–15.

15. George Canning to the King, 10 July 1807; King to Canning, 11 July 1807: Aspinall, A., ed., *The Later Correspondence of King George III*, Vol. I, pp. 601–2.

16. Sherwig, J. M., *Guineas and Gunpowder*, p. 189.

17. Nelson to the Admiralty, 1 July 1803: Lambert, A. D., *Nelson: Britannia's God of War*, p. 246.

18. Taylor to Canning, 17 July 1807: Aspinall, p. 602.

19. Napoleon to Admiral Decrès, 4 July 1807: Corbett J. S., 'Napoleon and the British Navy after Trafalgar', p. 246.

20. Mahan, *French Revolution*, II, p. 277.

21. Canning to Gower, 2 Oct. 1807: quoted in P. W. Schroeder, p. 330.

22. Corbett, 'Napoleon and the British Navy after Trafalgar', p. 239.

23. Corbett, 'Napoleon and the British Navy after Trafalgar', quoting G. F. R. Henderson's *Science of War*, London, 1904.

24. Perkins, B., *Prologue to War: England and the United States 1805–1812*, pp. 190–4.

25. Munch-Petersen, T., *Defying Napoleon: How Britain bombarded Copenhagen and seized the Danish Fleet in 1807*. Robson, M., *Britain, Portugal and South America in the Napoleonic Wars: Alliances and Diplomacy in Economic Maritime Conflict*.

26. P. W. Schroeder, p. 436.

27. Perkins, pp. 198–9.

28. North, D. C., *The Economic Growth of the United States 1790–1860*, pp. 17–21.

29. Cannon, J., 'Holroyd, John Baker, first Earl of Sheffield (1741–1821)', http://www.oxforddnb.com/view13608 viewed 09 Mar. 2010. His pamphlet was *Observations on the Commerce of the American States*.

30. North, pp. 22–5, 37.

31. Roland, A., Bolster, W. J. & Keyssar, A., *The Way of the Ship; America's Maritime History Re-envisioned, 1600–2000*, pp. 105–6.

32. North, pp. 30 & 49.

33. Judgment of Judge John Kelsall, New Providence, Bahamas, confirmed by the High Court of Admiralty, 22 June 1805: Dudley I, pp. 16–21.

34. Lord Sheffield, *Strictures on the Necessity of Inviolably Maintaining the Navigation and Colonial System of Great Britain*, London, 1806, excerpted in Dudley I, pp. 21–3.

35. Foreman, S., *Shoes and Ships and Sealing Wax: An Illustrated History of the Board of Trade, 1786–1986*, pp. 1–5.

36. Foreman, pp. 119–20.

37. Onuf, P. S., *Jefferson's Empire: The Language of American Nationhood*, p. 69.

38. Jefferson letter of 13 May 1797, quoted in Onuf, p. 205 n. 64.

39. Jefferson letter of 5 Feb. 1803, quoted in Onuf, pp. 204–5 n. 57.

40. Gallatin to Jefferson, 25 July 1807: Adams, H., ed., *The Writings of Albert Gallatin*, Vol. 1, p. 343.

41. Alexander Cochrane to Thomas Grenville, 20 Apr. 1807: NLS MS 2297, ff. 3–6.

42. P. W. Schroeder, pp. 435–6.

43. For the classical world's hostility to the sea, a theme that was covered by Jefferson's reading: Horden, P. & Purcell, N., *The Corrupting Sea: A Study of Mediterranean History*.

44. Order in Council, 7 Jan. 1807: Dudley I, pp. 24–5.

45. Zimmerman, J. F., *Impressment of American Seamen*, pp. 259–75. McKee, p. 101.

46. Perkins, pp. 94–5.

47. Symonds, C. L., *Navalists and Antinavalists: The Naval Policy Debate in the United States, 1785–1827*, pp. 105–30.

48. For an example of Embargo enforcement orders see Dudley I, pp. 35–6. See also Smith, J. M., *Borderland Smuggling: Patriots, Loyalists, and Illicit Trade in the Northeast, 1783–1820*.

49. Perkins, pp. 165–77.

50. Hill, pp. 37–9, 43, 46.

51. Jefferson letter of 13 Oct. 1785, quoted in Onuf, p. 204 n. 53.

52. The speed with which this ideological aim became an economic fact lies at the heart of Roland, Bolster, & Keyssar's important study.

53. Onuf, pp. 72 & 91.

54. Onuf, pp. 93–5.

55. Onuf, pp. 105 & 110 for 1787 and 1819.

56. North, pp. 52 & 64.

57. Roland et al., pp. 105–6, 110, & 123.

58. Roland et al., p. 122.

59. Onuf, pp. 136–41.

60. Herring, G. C., *From Colony to Superpower: U.S. Foreign Relations since 1776*, pp. 97–101, 107–10.

61. Herring, p. 110.

62. Jefferson Message to Congress, 10 Feb. 1807: Dudley I, pp. 12–15.

63. Smith, G. A., 'For the Purposes of Defense': The Politics of the Jeffersonian Gunboat Program, examines the evolution of Jefferson's thinking on the subject. Tucker, S. C., The Jeffersonian Gunboat Navy, provides a detailed career history of the gunboats, and analyses their wartime role.

64. Perkins, pp. 179–80.

65. Canning to Bathurst, 24 Mar. & 13 Apr. 1809: Bathurst, pp. 86–9.

66. North, pp. 55–7. P. W. Schroeder, pp. 436–7.

67. Dudley I, pp. 37–9; P. W. Schroeder, pp. 438–9.

68. Hill, pp. 89–109.

69. Symonds, p. 141.

70. John Rodgers to Isaac Hull, 19 June 1810: Dudley I, pp. 39–40.

71. J. H. Schroeder, pp. 74–7.

72. Bainbridge to William Jones, 5 Oct. 1812: Dudley I, p. 510. Canney, D. L., Sailing Warships of the United States Navy, pp. 23–41.

73. Sawyer to Bingham, 19 Apr. 1811: ADM 1/501 f105.

74. Sawyer to Admiralty, 29 Feb. 1812, rec'd 6 June 1812; encl Sawyer to John Pasco, HMS Tartarus, 4 July 1811: ADM 1/502, ff. 117–19.

75. Liverpool in House of Lords, 5 Dec. 1811; Liverpool to Sir James Craig, 4 Apr. 1810: Perkins, pp. 5, 13–14.

76. Paullin, pp. 223–30; J. H. Schroeder, pp. 88–90.

77. Bingham to Admiral Sawyer, 21 May 1811: Dudley I, pp. 41–3.

78. Rodgers to Secretary Hamilton, 23 May 1811: Dudley I, pp. 44–9.

79. Hamilton to Rodgers, 28 May 1811: Dudley I, pp. 49–50.

80. British historian William James would have a field day demolishing Rodgers's reputation in the 1820s.

81. McKee, p. 225.

82. Paullin, pp. 239–42; J. H. Schroeder, pp. 88–90.

83. Sawyer to Admiralty, 11 June 1811, rec'd 4 July 1811: ADM 1/501, f. 99, with Secretary's endorsement.

84. Sawyer to Admiralty, 25 June 1811, rec'd 23 July 1811: ADM 1/501, f. 125 et seq.

85. Hill, pp. 124–7.

86. Smith, p. 73.

87. Paullin does not use the prints. J. H. Schroeder does, but warns that they are a 'British view'.

88. Sawyer to Admiralty, 28 June 1811, rec'd 23 July 1811; covering Captain Bradshaw (HMS Eurydice) to Sawyer, 12 June 1811: ADM 1/501, ff. 120–2.

89. Tucker, S., Stephen Decatur: A Life Most Bold and Daring, is the latest biography. See pp. 64–70 for the Tripoli incident.

90. The frigates HMS Spartan and HMS Shannon arrived on 12 and 24 September. Sawyer to Admiralty, 6 Oct. 1811, rec'd 1 Nov. 1811: ADM 1/501, f. 237. Perkins, p. 273.

91. Hill, p. 134.

CHAPTER 2: Going for Broke

1. Brighton, J. G., *Admiral Sir P. B. V. Broke: A Memoir*, and Padfield, P., *Broke and the Shannon*, are the standard biographies.
2. Dickinson, H. W., *Educating the Royal Navy: Eighteenth- and nineteenth-century education for officers*, pp. 40, 43–5.
3. *Shannon* was a standard Leda-class 18-pounder frigate (that is one carrying 18-pounder guns on its main gun deck), built by Josiah Brindley at Frindsbury on the Medway between 1804 and 1806: Gardiner, R., *Frigates of the Napoleonic Wars*, p. 48.
4. Broke to Louisa Broke, 31 Jan. 1811: Padfield, p. 65.
5. Broke to Louisa Broke, 26 Aug. 1811: Padfield, pp. 70–1.
6. Sawyer to Admiralty, 6 Oct. 1811, rec'd 1 Nov.: ADM 1/501, f. 237.
7. Broke to Louisa Broke, 13 Oct. 1811: Padfield, pp. 72–3.
8. Broke to Louisa Broke, 27 Oct. 1811: Padfield, p. 73.
9. Padfield, p. 78 – from Brenton E. P., *The Naval History of Great Britain*, Vol. II, London, 1837, p. 490.
10. Broke to Louisa Broke, 2 Feb. 1812: Padfield, p. 81.
11. Bartlett, C. J., 'Gentlemen versus Democrats: Cultural Prejudice and Military Strategy in the War of 1812', *War in History*, Vol. 1, No. 2, 1994, pp. 140–59.
12. Letters to his wife and mother in early 1812 reveal something of his unease: Padfield, pp. 81–4.
13. Dudley I, pp. 190–1.
14. Perkins, pp. 283–90.
15. Hill, pp. 111–18, 132–4, 138–9, 145–55.
16. Hill, p. 169.
17. P. W. Schroeder, pp. 439–40, & Hill, p. 173 and n. 1, reach broadly similar conclusions.
18. P. W. Schroeder, p. 440.
19. Perkins, pp. 88–94.
20. The half-crown coin was commonly referred to as 'half a dollar' down to British decimalisation in 1967.
21. Dudley I, pp. 68–9.
22. Madison to Congress, 1 June 1812: Dudley I, pp. 73–81, quote p. 80.
23. Cusick, J. G., *The Other War of 1812: The Patriot War and the American Invasion of Spanish East Florida*, pp. 293–301.
24. Stagg, J. C. A., 'James Madison and George Matthews: The East Florida Revolution of 1812 Reconsidered', *Diplomatic History*, Vol. 30, No. 1. 2006, pp. 23–55, esp. pp. 23, 54–5.
25. Hill, pp. 174–6.

26. Woodman, R., *Britannia's Realm: In Support of the State: 1763–1815: A History of the British Merchant Navy Volume Two*, pp. 195–200.

27. Perkins, pp. 324–40, quote p. 359.

28. Perkins, pp. 347, 382–4.

29. Hill, pp. 161–9, 179, 186–7.

30. Perkins, pp. 405–6, 416, 421.

31. Perkins, pp. 361–2.

32. Hamilton to Rodgers and Decatur, 21 May 1812, and Rodgers to Hamilton, 3 June 1812: Dudley I, pp. 117–22.

33. Decatur to Hamilton, 8 June 1812: Dudley I, pp. 122–4.

34. Buel, R., *In Irons: Britain's Naval Supremacy and the American Revolutionary Economy*, pp. 86, 333.

35. Thorne, R. G., ed., *The House of Commons, 1790–1820*, Vol. 1, pp. 325–6, records 110 MPs with West India interests in this period.

36. Arthur, B., *How Britain Won the War of 1812*. Dr Arthur kindly allowed me to read his book in manuscript.

37. Hall, C. D., *British Strategy in the Napoleonic War, 1803–15*, pp. 184–9.

38. Perkins, p. 321.

39. Hall, p. 212. While the Iberian Peninsula contained 60,000 British troops, Canada had 18,000 and the West Indies 20,000. The men in the Canadian provinces were divided between Upper and Lower Canada 12,935, Nova Scotia 4,189, and Newfoundland 708. The West Indies garrison comprised: Jamaica, 3,885, Leeward and Windward Islands 15,248, Bahamas 850, Bermuda 732.

40. Hamilton to Hull, 18 June 1812: Dudley I, pp. 135–6.

41. Rodgers to Hamilton, 19 June 1812: Dudley I, p. 138.

42. Hamilton to Rodgers, 22 June 1812: Dudley I, pp. 148–9.

43. Sawyer to Admiralty, 28 June 1812: rec'd 25 July 1812: ADM 1/502, ff. 294–5.

44. Rodgers to Hamilton, 23 June 1812, and Byron to Admiral Sawyer, 27 June 1812: Dudley I, pp. 154–60.

45. Foster to Sawyer, 22 July 1812, Halifax, ADM 1/502, f. 407.

46. Allen, Consul at Boston, to Sawyer, 18 July 1812: ADM 1/502, f. 443.

47. Foster to Sawyer, 15 June 1812, Washington: ADM 1/502, f. 283.

48. Broke to Sawyer, 16 July 1812, Secret: ADM 1/4538.

49. Dudley I, p. 211 n. 2.

50. Crane to Hamilton, 29 July 1812: Dudley I, pp. 209–10, 235, 524.

51. Admiralty to Sawyer, 13 Oct. 1812: ADM 2/932, pp. 195–6. The British valued *Nautilus* at £3,252.

52. Broke to Admiralty, 30 July 1812, from Lat 40° 44' N Long 62° 41' W, Copy, Secret: ADM 1/4538.

53. McKee, p. 469.

54. Broke to Admiralty, 30 July 1812, from Lat 40° 44' N Long 62° 41' W, Copy, Secret: ADM 1/4538.

55. Broke to Louisa Broke, 21 & 26 July 1812: Padfield, p. 96.
56. Cannell, H., *Lightning Strikes: How ships are Protected from Lightning*, p. 146. Byam (HMS *Thetis*) to Admiralty, 24 Aug. 1812: ADM 1/4538.
57. *Rossie's* Journal: Dudley I, pp. 248–60.
58. Salem merchants to Hamilton, 27 July 1812: Dudley I, pp. 204–5.
59. Dudley I, pp. 225–6. For the Bay of Fundy see: Kert, F., *Trimming Yankee Sails: Pirates and Privateers of New Brunswick*, and Smith. J. M., *Battle for the Bay: The Naval War of 1812*.
60. Sawyer to Admiralty, 17 Sept. 1812: Dudley I, pp. 496–8.
61. Hull to Hamilton, 21 July 1812: Dudley I, pp. 161–5.
62. Hull to Hamilton, 28 July & 2 Aug. 1812: Dudley I, pp. 205–9. Maloney, L. M., *The Captain from Connecticut: The Life and Naval Times of Isaac Hull*, pp. 170–8.
63. Hull to Hamilton, 28 Aug. 1812: Dudley I, pp. 231–3.
64. Maloney, p. 181; McKee, p. 471.
65. Rodgers to Hamilton, 4 Sept. 1812: Dudley I, p. 451. Maloney, pp. 182–91.
66. Gardiner, *Frigates*, p. 42. Hull to Hamilton, 28 Aug. 1812; Dacres to Sawyer, 7 Sept. 1812: Dudley I, pp. 238–45.
67. *Times*, 24 Mar. 1813: Padfield, p. 101.
68. Broke to Dr Hutchinson, 9 Nov. 1812: War of 1812 Collection, Clements Library.
69. Gardiner, *Frigates*, p. 42. Hull to Hamilton, 28 Aug. 1812; Dacres to Sawyer, 7 Sept. 1812: Dudley I pp. 238–45.
70. Admiralty to Sawyer, 6 Oct. 1812 ADM 2/932, p. 192.
71. Sawyer to Admiralty, 17 Sept. 1812: ADM 1/502 f. 530. Rodgers to Hamilton, 1 Sept. 1812: Dudley I, pp. 262–6. Mahan, *Sea Power in its relation to the War of 1812*, Vol. I, pp. 320–7. Paullin, pp. 256–60.
72. Rodgers to Hamilton, 4 Sept. 1812: Dudley I, pp. 450–1.
73. Dudley I, pp. 170–6.
74. Sawyer to Admiralty, 17 Sept. 1812: Dudley I, pp. 496–8.
75. Porter to Hamilton, 2, 8, 15 & 20 Aug. & 3 Sept. 1812: Dudley I, pp. 216–20, 443–7.
76. Dudley I, pp. 490–1. Silverstone, P. H., *The Sailing Navy: 1775–1854*, p. 62.
77. Porter to Hamilton, 5 Sept. 1812: Dudley I, pp. 461–4.
78. Porter to Commodore William Bainbridge, 8 Sept. 1812: Dudley I, pp. 468–9.
79. Sawyer to Admiralty, 17 Sept. 1812: Dudley I, pp. 496–8.

CHAPTER 3: Looking for a Way Out

1. Perkins, pp. 418–19.
2. Keith to Melville, 6 June 1812: Melville Papers, Clements Library.

3. Thorne, Vol. V, pp. 492–3. Warren had been an MP voting with William Pitt, but sat in Parliament in 1807 in the Grenville family interest. In 1812 Lord Grenville led the opposition.

4. Le Fevre, P., 'Sir John Borlase Warren, 1753–1822', in Le Fevre, P. & Harding, R., eds, *British Admirals of the Napoleonic Wars: The Contemporaries of Nelson*, pp. 219–44.

5. Melville to Warren, 30 July 1812: WAR/82, f. 2.

6. Warren to Melville, n.d., draft, & Melville to Warren, 4 Aug. 1812: Warren MS WAR 82, ff. 3–5. Fry, M., *The Dundas Despotism*.

7. Dumouriez, 'Memoir by General Dumouriez upon the American war January 1808': WAR 89.

8. Rose, J. H. & Broadley, A. M., *Dumouriez and the Defence of England Against Napoleon*. Charles Dumouriez (1739–1823).

9. Hurd to Admiralty, 9 Oct. 1812: ADM 1/3558.

10. Admiralty to Warren, 3 Aug. 1812: ADM 2/162, pp. 494–5.

11. Melville to Sir Edward Pellew (Commander-in-Chief Mediterranean), 10 Aug. 1812: Melville at the Clements Library Box August 1812 – February 1813.

12. Morriss, R., *Cockburn and the British Navy in Transition: Admiral Sir George Cockburn, 1772–1853*, see pp. 83–120 for the War of 1812.

13. Admiralty to Warren, 11 & 12 Aug. 1812: ADM 2/162, pp. 519–23. Admiralty to Warren, 10 Oct. 1812: ADM 2/932, pp. 193–4; & ADM 2/163, ff. 123–4.

14. Melville to Pellew, 10 Nov. 1812: Melville at the Clements Library Box August 1812 – February 1813.

15. Admiralty Minute, 15 Dec. 1812: ADM 3/259; Admiralty Special Minute, 10 & 11 Aug. 1812: ADM 3/259.

16. Warren to Admiralty, 7 Aug. 1812, dated London: ADM 1/502, p. 359.

17. Admiralty to Warren, 8, 11 & 22 Aug. 1812: ADM 2/932, pp. 173, 177 & 182.

18. Warren to Admiralty, 5 Oct. 1812: Dudley I, pp. 508–9.

19. Arthur, p. 257 n. 7.

20. Melville to Warren, 21 Oct. 1812: WAR 82, ff. 16–17, explaining Admiralty to Warren, 7 Oct. 1812: ADM 2/163.

21. Warren to Admiralty, 18 Oct. 1812, rec'd 16 Nov.: ADM 1/502, p. 685.

22. Broke to Warren, 31 Oct. 1812: ADM 1/502, f. 717.

23. Broke to Louisa Broke, 26 Nov. 1812: Padfield, p. 114.

24. Warren to Melville, 18 Nov. 1812, encl. Monroe to Warren, 27 Oct. 1812: ADM 1/502, ff. 703–13.

25. Warren to Admiralty, 29 Dec. 1812: Dudley I, p. 650.

26. Admiralty to Warren, 9 Jan. 1813; Dudley II, pp. 14–15.

27. Papers attached to Admiralty to Warren, 9 Jan. 1813: ADM 3/260.

28. Pullen, H. F., *The Shannon and the Chesapeake*, pp. 35–6; ADM 2/1083, pp. 270–3.

29. Hamilton to Rodgers, 9 Sept. 1812: Dudley I, pp. 470–2.

30. Rodgers to Hamilton, 17 Sept. 1812: Dudley I, pp. 494–6.

31. Owsley, F. J., Jr, 'William Jones', in Coeletta, P., ed., *American Secretaries of the Navy*, Vol. I, pp. 100–12.

32. Bainbridge to Jones, 5 Oct. 1812, and Jones to Bainbridge, 11 Oct. 1812: Dudley I, pp. 509–15.

33. Bainbridge to Porter, 13 Oct. 1812: Dudley I, pp. 525–6.

34. Warren to Admiralty, 3 Nov. 1812, rec'd and endorsed 29 Dec. 1812: ADM 1/502, f. 803.

35. Gardiner, *Frigates*, pp. 44–5; Dudley I, pp. 536–41, 580–3.

36. Dudley I, pp. 533–5, 583–4.

37. Commodore Tingey to Hamilton, 7 Nov. 1812: Dudley I, pp. 561–2.

38. Carden, J., ed. Atkinson, C. T., *Memoir of Admiral Carden*, p. 252.

39. Croker to Warren, 30 Dec. 1812, Private: WAR 82, ff. 29–30.

40. Carden to Admiralty, 28 Oct. 1812, & Decatur to Hamilton, 30 Oct. 1812: Dudley I, pp. 548–53. Gardiner, *Frigates*, pp. 46–8.

41. Dudley I, pp. 615–17.

42. Burrows, M., *Memoir of Admiral Sir Henry Ducie Chads*, pp. 11–15.

43. Bainbridge to Hamilton, 29 Dec. 1812, & Chads to Admiralty, 31 Dec. 1812: Dudley I, pp. 639–49; Gardiner, *1812*, pp. 50–3.

44. Warren to Admiralty, 8 Mar. 1813, rec'd 8 July 1813: ADM 1/503, f. 593.

45. Dudley I, pp. 570–7; Symonds, pp. 171–91.

46. Glover, R., *Britain at Bay: Defence against Bonaparte, 1803–1814*, p. 73.

47. Hill, pp. 193–203.

48. *The Times*, 30 Dec. 1812.

49. Warren to Beresford, 10 Oct. 1812: Hulbert Papers HUL/1 NMM.

50. Gwyn, J., *Frigates and Foremasts: The North American Squadron in Nova Scotian Waters, 1745–1815*, pp. 128–52.

51. Warren to Admiralty, 20 Feb. 1813: Bermuda: ADM 1/503, ff. 191–9, & J. M. Smith, *Battle for the Bay*.

52. Warren to Melville, 9 & 18 Nov. 1812: WAR LBK/2.

53. Warren to Melville, 7 Oct. 1812: WAR LBK/2.

54. Bathurst to Admiralty, 21 Nov. 1812: CO43/49, pp. 153–4.

55. Bathurst to Liverpool, 3 Oct. 1812: Add MSS 38250, f. 42.

56. Castlereagh to Admiralty, 12 Aug. 1812: ADM 1/422, p. 169.

57. Dudley I, pp. 566–70.

58. ADM 1/502 1812, p. 389, *re* food and timber for Halifax Navy Yard. Dudley I, pp. 134–5, 202–3, 526–7.

59. See Arthur, pp. 46–63, for discussion of the two economies.

60. Warren to Melville, 30 Dec. 1812: NMM Warren MS LBK/2.

61. Warren to Admiralty, 16 Oct. 1813: ADM 1/504, pp. 417–20, & Dudley II, p. 261.

62. Adams, *Administration of James Madison*, Vol. VII, pp. 262–4.
63. Melville to Warren, 8 Jan. 1813: Admiralty WAR, 82 ff. 39–40.
64. Kert, *Prize and Prejudice: Privateering and Naval Prize in Atlantic Canada in the War of 1812*, pp. 16–203.
65. Burdett, HMS *Maidstone*, to Warren, 17 Nov. 1812: ADM 1/503, f. 87.
66. Warren to Admiralty, 28 Dec. 1812: ADM 1/503, f. 83.
67. Hamilton, C. I., *The Making of the Modern Admiralty: British Naval Policy-Making, 1805–1927*, pp. 92–3.
68. Melville to Pellew, 16 Dec. 1812; Melville Papers Box, August 1812 – February 1813, Clements Library.
69. Draft, Warren to Melville, Bermuda, 19 Feb. 1813, and Melville to Warren, 3 Dec. 1812: Adm. WAR 82, ff. 22–3, 26.
70. Melville to Warren, 3 Dec. 1812: Adm. WAR 82, ff. 18–21.
71. Admiralty to Warren, 30 Dec. 1812: Adm. WAR 82, ff. 29–30.
72. Melville to Warren, 9 Jan. 1813: Adm. WAR 82, ff. 41–4.
73. Glover, pp. 72–3.
74. Admiralty to Warren, 26 Dec. 1812: Dudley 1, pp. 633–4; & ADM 2/1375 (Secret), pp. 337–8.
75. Warren to Admiralty, 29 Dec. 1812: Dudley I, pp. 649–51, & ADM 1/503, pp. 99–102.

CHAPTER 4: Waiting for the *President*

1. 'Representations on Newfoundland 20.3.1813', in Lord Sidmouth's Archive, is an exception: DRO Sidmouth MS OC1.
2. Warren to Admiralty, 21 Feb. 1813: ADM 1/503, f. 209. Beck, J., *The Falmouth Post Office Packet Service 1689–1850*, pp. 169–71. Eighteen packets were taken in this war.
3. Castlereagh speech, 3 Feb. 1813: *Hansard XXIV*, Cols 363–78.
4. Castlereagh, Whitbread, Canning and Alexander Baring, 19 Feb. 1813: *Hansard XXIV*, Cols 593–654.
5. Admiralty to Warren, 10 Feb. 1813: ADM 2/1376, pp. 73–87; Dudley II, p. 19.
6. Admiralty to Warren, 20 Mar. 1813: Dudley II, p. 76.
7. For Bladen Capel (1776–1853), see O'Byrne, *Naval Biographical Dictionary* and *ODNB* entry.
8. Admiralty to Warren, 9 Jan. 1813 & 10 Feb. 1813: ADM 2/1375, pp. 365–73, & 2/1376, pp 73–87: Dudley II, pp. 14–15, 16–19.
9. Melville, Galloway, Bathurst & Liverpool, House of Lords 14 May 1813: *Hansard XXVI*, Cols 173–202.
10. Gardiner, pp. 52–3; Winfield, *British Warships in the Age of Sail*, pp. 122–4, 134.
11. Admiralty to Warren, 26 Dec. 1812: ADM 2/1375, Secret Orders, in Dudley I, pp. 633–4.

12. Warren to Admiralty, 25 Jan. 1813: Dudley II, p. 15–16.

13. Berube, C. & Rodgaard, J., *A Call to the Sea: Captain Charles Stewart of the USS Constitution*, pp. 67–9.

14. Cockburn to Warren, 23 Mar. 1813: Dudley II, p. 326–7.

15. Warren to Admiralty, 20 Feb. 1813, Bermuda: ADM 1/503, ff. 191–9.

16. Warren to Melville, 29 Mar., 19 Apr. 1813: WAR LBK/2, see Ch. 3 above.

17. Warren to Admiralty, 20 Feb. 1813, Bermuda: ADM 1/503, ff. 191–9, *re* Admiralty dispatch of 18 Nov. 1812.

18. James Stirling to Charles Stirling, 15 Nov. 1812, HMS *Brazen*, report on Mississippi and Floridas: copy in WAR 89, ff. 15–21; also cited in Statham-Drew, P., *James Stirling: Admiral and Founding Governor of Western Australia*, pp. 22–4.

19. Warren to Admiralty, no. 78, 21 Feb. 1813, rec'd 20 Mar. 1813: ADM 1/4539 Secret, p. 193.

20. Warren to Admiralty, 8 Mar. 1813, Bermuda, rec'd 8 July 1813: ADM 1/503, f. 593.

21. Warren to Admiralty, 8 Mar. 1813: ADM 1/503, f. 381.

22. North, pp. 57–61.

23. P. W. Schroeder, p. 457.

24. Lieven, D., *Russian Against Napoleon: The True Story of the Campaign of War and Peace*, pp. 69–71, 183. Other Russian leaders shared these sentiments, including Tsar Alexander.

25. Lieven, pp. 285–6.

26. Warren to Melville, 28 Mar. 1813, from Lynnhaven Bay, draft, private: WAR 82, ff. 45–6.

27. Melville to Warren, 4 June 1813, private, Admiralty: WAR 82, ff. 73–6.

28. See WAR 82, ff. 47–55.

29. Melville to Warren, 23 Mar. 1813: WAR 82, pp. 62–3.

30. Melville to Warren, 23 Mar. 1813: WAR LBK/2.

31. Melville to Warren, 26 Mar. 1813, private, Admiralty: WAR 82, ff. 64–5.

32. Warren to Admiralty, 21 Feb. 1813. no. 78, rec'd 20 Mar.: ADM 1/4539 Secret, p. 193.

33. Melville to Warren, 23 Mar. 1813, private, Admiralty: WAR 82, ff. 56–63.

34. Stagg, J. C. A., *Mr Madison's War: Politics, Diplomacy and Warfare in the early American Republic, 1783–1830*, pp. 284–6.

35. McKee, pp. 9–11.

36. Eckert, E. K., *The Navy Department in the War of 1812*, pp. 15–17.

37. Jones to Captain William Bainbridge, 11 Oct. 1812: Eckert, p. 22.

38. Navy Secretary Jones to captains in U.S. Ports, 22 Feb. 1813: Dudley II, pp. 48–9.

39. Eckert, pp. 22–3.

40. Harrington, G. K., 'The American Naval Challenge to the English East

India Company during the War of 1812', in Meister, D. C., Pfeiffer, S. & VanDeMark, B., eds, *New Interpretations in Naval History: The Tenth Naval History Symposium 1991*, pp. 129–52.

41. The key argument of *The Influence of Sea Power upon the War of 1812*.
42. McKee, pp. 299–300, 340.
43. Other comparisons: 198-pound broadside to 297, 38 casualties to 7. Pullen, *Shannon and Chesapeake*, p. 38.
44. Warren, Standing Orders, 6 Mar. 1813: Dudley II, pp. 59–60.
45. For the official letters, see Dudley II, pp. 68–75.
46. Gleaves, A., *James Lawrence, Captain, United States Navy, Commander of the 'Chesapeake'*. The only full length biography. See p. 135.
47. Gleaves, p. 137.
48. Admiralty to Warren, 20 Mar. 1813, & Melville to Warren, 26 Mar. 1813: Dudley II, pp. 75–9.
49. Warren disposition of the Fleet, 28 Mar. 1813: ADM 1/4359, no. 104, & Dudley II, pp. 80–1.
50. See Dudley, pp. 114–21, for the impact of British operations in the Chesapeake and Delaware bays and off New York.
51. Jones to Manuel Eyre (Philadelphia), 12 May 1813: Dudley II, pp. 117–19.
52. Captain Stackpoole to Admiral Cockburn, 8 June 1813: ADM 1/506, pp. 147–50; Dudley II, p. 117.
53. Warren to Captain Stackpoole, 28 June 1813: ADM 1/506, pp. 159–60; Dudley II, p. 121.
54. Warren to Admiralty, 28 May 1813, rec'd 8 July 1813: ADM 1/503, f. 557.
55. Rodgers to Jones, 21 Jan. & 22 Apr. 1813: Dudley II, pp. 5, 104–5.
56. J. H. Schroeder, pp. 120–2.
57. Paullin, pp. 264–5.
58. Capel to Warren, 11 May 1813: Dudley II, pp. 105–6.
59. Petrie, D. A., *The Prize Game: Lawful Looting on the High Seas during the Days of Fighting Sail*, pp. 83–5.
60. Tucker, *Decatur*, pp. 125–7, retails Decatur's version of events, and his claim that Hardy in *Ramillies* was his opponent. Petrie, p. 85, provides a critical corrective.
61. Decatur to Jones, 2, 6 & 18 June 1813; Oliver to Warren, 13 June 1813: Dudley II, pp. 135–9.
62. Tucker, *Decatur*, pp. 128–36.
63. *Constitution* was undergoing a major refit.
64. Canney, pp. 47–8. *Chesapeake*'s designer Josiah Fox disliked Joshua Humphreys's big 44-gun ships.
65. Evans to Decatur, 10 Apr. 1813, & Jones to Evans, 19 Apr. 1813: Dudley II, pp. 98–102. McKee, p. 347.

66. Lawrence to Navy Secretary Jones, 26 Apr. 1813: Gleaves, p. 142.
67. Jones to Evans, 6 May 1813: Pullen, *Shannon and Chesapeake*, pp. 43–4.
68. Pullen, *Shannon and Chesapeake*, pp. 45–6.
69. Lawrence to Jones, 10 May 1813: Gleaves, pp. 147–8.
70. Gleaves, pp. 148 & 169.
71. USS *Chesapeake* log book, 20 May 1813: H.A. 93/877/49, & Pullen, *Shannon and Chesapeake*, pp. 47, 258. The *Chesapeake* log book, a large leather-bound volume, is among Broke's papers. The last ten days cover six pages, including a wealth of detail on the management of the ship, preparations for sea, and for battle. The final, rather poignant entry is dated Monday 31 May 1813, the day before the battle. Such logs were kept on rough paper during the day and written up later. It appears that the rough log of the Chesapeake was destroyed or lost in the confusion that raged on her quarterdeck on 1 June.
72. USS *Chesapeake* log book, 31 May 1813: H.A. 93/877/49. 'Rec'd on board 50 great gun locks. etc.'
73. Lawrence to Jones, 20 May 1813: Gleaves, pp. 167–8.
74. Augustus Ludlow to Commander Charles Ludlow, USN, 28 May 1813: Gleaves, pp. 168–9.
75. Lawrence to Jones, 1 June 1813: Gleaves, pp. 170 & 175.
76. Gleaves, pp. 172–3.
77. McKee, p. 346, citing Gleaves, pp. 172–5.
78. Brighton, *Broke*, p. 41.
79. Broke to Louisa Broke, 20 Mar. 1813, at Halifax: SRO HA 93 9/136.
80. Broke to Louisa Broke, 14 Apr. 1813, at Halifax: SRO HA 93 9/138.
81. Broke to Louisa Broke, 5 May 1813, at Halifax: SRO HA 93 9/139.
82. Broke to Louisa Broke, 9 May 1813, at Halifax: SRO HA 93 9/140.
83. Broke to Capel, 16 May 1813: ADM 1/503, f. 731.
84. Brighton, *Broke*, pp. 42–3.
85. Brighton, *Broke*, p. 51.
86. Broke to Lawrence, June 1813: Dudley II, pp. 128–9.

CHAPTER 5: Many Ways to Die

1. Lawrence to Secretary Jones, 1 June 1813, & Lawrence to Montaudevert, 1 June 1813: Gleaves, p. 175.
2. Commodore Bainbridge sent the original to Secretary Jones on 3 June 1813: Dudley II, pp. 126–9.
3. Brighton, *Admiral of the Fleet Sir Provo W. P. Wallis*, p. 63.
4. George Budd to Secretary Jones, 15 June 1813: Dudley II, pp. 133–4.
5. Brighton, *Wallis*, p. 88.
6. Brighton, *Wallis*, p. 63.
7. Gleaves, pp. 182–4.

8. Brighton, *Wallis*, pp. 64–5.

9. George Budd to Secretary Jones, 15 June 1813: Dudley II, pp. 133–4.

10. Brighton, *Wallis*, pp. 59 & 64.

11. Brighton, *Wallis*, pp. 71–3.

12. Brighton, *Wallis*, p. 83.

13. James (2002), Vol. VI, p. 206. Gleaves, p. 213. Langley. H. D., *A History of Medicine in the Early U.S. Navy*, p. 187.

14. Brighton, *Wallis*, p. 77.

15. Bainbridge to Secretary Jones, 2 June 1813: Gleaves, p. 230, and full text pp. 278–9.

16. Brighton, *Wallis*, p. 96.

17. *Shannon*, killed: George Watt 1st Lt, George Aldham Purser, John Dunn Captain's Clerk; *Able Seamen:* George Gilbert, William Berilles, Neil Gilchrist, Thomas Selby, James Long, John Young, James Wallace, Joseph Brown, William Murphy; *Ordinary Seamen*: Thomas Barr, Michael Murphy, Thomas Molloy, Thomas Jones, Jonathan O'Connelly, Thomas Barry; *Royal Marines*: Corporal Samuel Millyard, Privates James Jaynes, Dominique Sadden, William Young; *Landsmen*: John McLaughlin, Thomas Gorman; *Supernumaries* (Irish emigrants): John Moriarty, William Morrisay. Another four men died of their wounds on board the *Shannon*, and seven at Halifax Hospital.

18. Padfield, p. 185.

19. James (2002). Vol. VI, p. 208. James was told this by the seaman who identified the deserter.

20. George Budd to Secretary Jones, 15 June 1813: Dudley II, pp. 133–4.

21. Gleaves, pp. 296–7.

22. Shea, I. & Watts, H., *Deadman's: Melville Island and its Burial Ground*, pp. 82–9.

23. Broke to Louisa, 19 June 1813: Padfield, p. 192.

24. Capel to Warren, 6 June 1813: ADM 1/503, p. 643.

25. *The Courier*, Friday 9 July 1813, Report of Proceedings in the House of Commons: SRO HA93 6/2/270.

26. Admiralty to Warren, 9 July 1813: ADM2/933, pp. 12–16.

27. Melville to Warren, 23 Mar. 1813, private Admiralty: WAR 82, ff. 56–63.

28. Admiralty General Order to all station commanders, 10 July 1813: ADM 2/1377, p. 154: Dudley II, pp. 183–4.

29. Madison to Navy Secretary Jones, 15 Oct. 1813: Eckert, p. 21.

30. Navy Secretary Jones to Captain John Rodgers, USN: Eckert, p. 21.

31. Melville to Sir Alexander Hope, 14 July 1813, Admiralty: NAS GD364/1/1253, f. 9.

32. Hotham to Broke, 27 June 1813: Padfield, pp. 196–7.

33. Admiralty to Warren, 17 Aug. 1813: ADM2/933, p. 31.

34. Brighton, *Wallis*, p. 89.
35. Dudley II, p. 289, for two of the trials.
36. McKee, p. 399.
37. Padfield, p. 245.
38. James (2002), Vol. VI, p. 206.
39. Gardiner, *Frigates*, p. 129.
40. Brighton, *Wallis*, p. 255.
41. Gardiner, *Frigates*, p. 180. Douglas, Sir H., *Naval Gunnery*, pp. 485, 500–2.
42. James (2002), Vol.VI, p. 209; Padfield, p. 244; Hickey, D. R., *Don't Give up the Ship! Myths of the War of 1812*, pp. 108–13.
43. Brighton, *Wallis*, p. 90.
44. Warren to Admiralty, 22 July 1813: Dudley II, p. 192, and Captain Oliver to Warren, 23 & 30 June 1813: Dudley II, pp. 192–4, & ADM 1/504, pp. 73–7, 271–5.
45. Admiralty to Warren, 1 Oct. 1813: ADM2/933, pp. 42–3.
46. *Chesapeake* muster book: SRO HA93 6/2/259. These records placed more emphasis on physical description and skills than place of birth.
47. SRO HA 93 14/33, *re* Court Martial and Execution, & ADM 1/3459 file on Britons on American ships.
48. Capel to Admiralty, 11 June 1813, 'sent to Secret Dept': ADM 1/503, p. 689 – ADM 1/4539 SECRET, p. 203.
49. Admiralty to Charles Paget, 10 July 1813: ADM 2/1377, pp. 145–8, cited in Dudley II, pp. 164–7.
50. Dudley II, pp. 164–7.
51. Dudley II, pp. 167–78.

CHAPTER 6: Securing the Seas

1. Petrie, pp. 2–9.
2. Garitee, J. R., *The Republic's Private Navy: The American Privateering Business as practised by Baltimore during the War of 1812*, pp. 10–19.
3. Leiner, F. C., *Millions for Defense: Subscription Warships of 1798*, pp. 72–92.
4. Garitee, pp. 20–30.
5. Petrie, p. 9.
6. Garitee, pp. 32–42.
7. Garitee, among the more moderate exponents of this view, provides little evidence.
8. Garitee, pp. 50–4.
9. Garitee, pp. 55–8.
10. The Baltimore Republican paper *Niles' Weekly Register* reprinted these remarks on 3 Apr. 1813: Garitee, p. 46.
11. Garitee, pp. 115–17.

12. Reynolds, J., *Pride of Baltimore II: Renaissance of the Baltimore Clipper*.

13. Chapelle, H. I., *The Baltimore Clipper: Its Origin and Development*, pp. 103 & 86, and Chapelle, H. I., *The History of American Sailing Ships*, especially chapters 3 and 5. Pioneering analyses of sailing-ship design.

14. Garitee, pp. 116–37.

15. Garitee, pp. 145–9.

16. Petrie, pp. 13–30.

17. Garitee, pp. 183–5.

18. Garitee, p. 208.

19. Cochrane to Admiralty, 8 Dec. 1814, no. 166: ADM 1/506 O96, encl. Lloyd to Admiral Brown at Jamaica, 28 Sept. 1814. *General Armstrong: Victory at Fayal*. Horta, Azores, n.d., reprinted from Wilkinson, D., 'Victory at Fayal' *American History Illustrated*, Vol. 13, 1978, pp. 10–19.

20. Chapelle, *American Sailing Ships*, pp. 146–50. Winfield, p. 369, and see pp. 321–3, 367–9 for captured privateers taken into British service.

21. Crowhurst, *The Defence of British Trade*, pp. 75–6. Petrie, Chapters 1 & 3.

22. Harrington, 'American Naval Challenge'.

23. Dudley II, p. 225.

24. Garitee, pp. 193–207, 210–11.

25. Chapelle, *American Sailing Ships*, p. 146.

26. Garitee, pp. 219–31.

27. Crowhurst, pp. 19–22, 29.

28. Parkinson, C. N., *War in the Eastern Seas, 1793–1815*.

29. Admiralty to Warren, Laforey, Stirling, Sawyer and John Lane, Chair of Trade Association, 12 Oct. 1812: ADM2/1107, p. 212.

30. Admiralty to Cochrane, 12 July 1814: ADM 2/933, pp. 172–3. The Board prosecuted the masters of *Orange*, *Boven* and *Jubilee* for sailing without convoy, Cochrane used the information to warn others.

31. Crowhurst, p. 41, cites an excellent example of this practice from 1805.

32. Dudley II, pp. 213–17. Winfield, p. 365.

33. James, *Naval Occurrences*, pp. 127–8.

34. Gardiner, *1812*, pp. 91–3. James, *Naval Occurrences*, has evidence of defects in guns, and poor crew.

35. Crowhurst, pp. 42–80, for convoys.

36. Admiralty Special Minutes, 11 Aug. 1812, to Controller of the Navy, Victualling and Transport Board, & Admiralty to Warren, Laforey and Stirling, 10 Aug. 1812: ADM3/259.

37. Admiralty to Warren, 10 Aug. 1812; ADM 2/1107, p. 82.

38. The Admiralty frequently borrowed the *List*, Lloyd's had to request its return: ADM 1/3393.

39. Crowhurst, pp. 81–95.

40. Lloyd's to Admiralty, 25 May 1812, & 26 May 1812: ADM 1/3393.

41. Lloyd's to Admiralty, 28 May 1812: ADM 1/3393.

42. Lloyd's to Admiralty, 20 July & 3 Aug. 1812: ADM 1/3393.

43. Lloyd's to Admiralty, 2 Mar. 1813: ADM 1/3934.

44. Lloyd's to Admiralty, 25 Aug. 1812: ADM 1/3393.

45. Lloyd's to Admiralty, 14 Jan. & 23 Mar. 1813: ADM 1/3934.

46. Lloyd's to Admiralty, 24 Mar. 1813: ADM 1/3934.

47. Lloyd's to Admiralty, 8 Apr. 1813: ADM 1/3934.

48. *The Naval Chronicle*, Vol. XXXI, p. 165.

49. Lloyd's to Admiralty, 20 Apr. 1813, endorsed for reply 22 Apr. 1813: ADM 1/3934.

50. Lloyd's to Admiralty, 10 Sept. 1812: ADM 1/3393.

51. Lloyd's to Admiralty, 28 Oct. 1812: ADM 1/3393.

52. Lloyd's to Admiralty, 30 Nov. 1812, citing a letter from Nevis of 30 Sept. 1812: ADM 1/3393.

53. Lloyd's to Admiralty, 26 Dec. 1812: ADM 1/3933.

54. Lloyd's to Admiralty, 31 Dec. 1812, enclosing a Barbados letter of 19 Dec. 1812: ADM 1/3393.

55. Sherwig, pp. 233 & 326 for specie shortage.

56. Admiralty to Laforey, 9 Nov. 1812: ADM 2/1107, p. 286.

57. Admiralty to Sir Richard Bickerton, C-in-C Portsmouth, 12 Nov. 1812, & Admiralty to Beeston Long, 18 Nov. 1812: ADM 2/1107, pp. 289 & 307.

58. Admiralty to West India Committee, 27 Nov. 1812: ADM 2/1107, p. 339.

59. Admiralty Minute, 15 Dec. 1812: ADM 3/259.

60. Admiralty to Warren, 2 Dec. 1812, Secret: ADM 2/1107, p. 346, *re* Warren to Admiralty, 19 Oct. 1812.

61. Lloyd's to Admiralty, 8 Feb. 1813: ADM 1/3934.

62. Lloyd's to Admiralty, 9 Feb. 1813 & 1 Mar. 1813: ADM 1/3394.

63. Lloyd's to Admiralty, 22 Mar. 1813: ADM 1/3934.

64. Lloyd's to Admiralty, 27 Mar., 15 & 19 Apr. 1813: ADM 1/3934.

65. Lloyd's to Admiralty, 17 Feb. 1813: ADM 1/3934.

66. Admiralty to Warren, 2 Dec. 1812, Secret: ADM 2/1107, p. 346.

67. *The Times*, 20 Mar. 1813.

68. Warren to Melville, 27 Sept. & 30 Nov. 1813: Warren LBK/2.

69. Admiralty to Warren, 9 Jan. 1813: ADM 3/260.

70. Warren to Admiralty, 20 Feb. 1813, Secret, no. 77: ADM 1/4539, p. 205.

71. Chapelle, *Baltimore Clipper*, p. 100. The destruction of U-boats by Captain 'Johnnie' Walker's Support Group in 1943–4 reflected similar determination.

72. Chapelle, *Baltimore Clipper*, pp. 86–7.
73. Wright, C. & Fayle, E., *A History of Lloyd's*, p. 191.
74. Garitee, pp. 241–4.
75. Mahan, A T., *The Influence of Sea Power upon History, 1660–1783*, pp. 137–8. It should be stressed that Mahan's explicit purpose in writing these lines was to change American naval policy from commerce destroying to sea control.
76. I am indebted to Dr Brian Arthur for rewarding discussion of this subject.

CHAPTER 7: The Price of Folly

1. Corbett, J. S., *Some Principles of Maritime Strategy*, especially p. 14.
2. Melville to Warren, 4 June 1813, private, Admiralty: WAR 82, ff. 73–6.
3. Admiralty to Warren, 13 & 26 May 1813: ADM 2/932, pp. 262 & 265.
4. Kert, *Prize and Prejudice*, p. 4.
5. Kert, *Prize and Prejudice*, p. 6, citing *The Times* of 12 Oct. 1813.
6. Secretary Jones to Allen, 5 June 1813: Dudley II, pp. 140–2.
7. Maples to Thornborough, 14 Aug. 1813: Dudley II, pp. 217–24; Dye, I, *The Fatal Cruise of the* Argus.
8. Petrie, pp. 31–46, esp. pp. 31–9 & fn 29 at p. 174.
9. Tracy, N., *Britannia's Palette: The Arts of Naval Victory*, p. 214. The aquatint appeared in February 1817.
10. J. H. Schroeder, p. 121.
11. Aaron Blewett to Christopher Saverland, Post Office Agent, 23 June 1813: Dudley II, pp. 157–9.
12. Beck, p. 239.
13. Petrie, pp. 24–30, 88–9. Nicoll had also been present three months before when Decatur ran into New London. He decided that all American commodores were either blind or cowards.
14. J. H. Schroeder's account of this cruise at pp. 122–3 identifies *Scourge* as a British schooner!
15. Winfield, pp. 213 & 378.
16. Petrie, p. 16.
17. Captain Charles Napier, who commanded a sister ship, described her as a 'shoe-box'.
18. James, *Naval History* (2002), Vol. VI, pp. 214–15.
19. Rodgers had good intelligence – HMS *Seahorse* was on the American station: Winfield, pp. 144–5.
20. Paullin, p. 270; J. H. Schroeder, p. 123.
21. Hutchison was only promoted commander in 1821: O'Byrne, p. 560.
22. Rodgers to Jones, 27 Sept. 1813, Jones to Rodgers, 4 Oct. 1813: Dudley II, pp. 250–5. & J. H. Schroeder, pp. 123–4.
23. Dudley II, pp. 300–1. Silverstone p. 30.

24. Canney, p. 45. John Smith to Secretary Jones, 14 & 31 Dec. 1813: Dudley II, pp. 300–1.

25. Mahan, *1812*, II, p. 193.

26. Jones to Rodgers, 4 Oct. 1813: Dudley II, pp. 254–5.

27. Warren to Admiralty, 12 Dec. 1813, at Sea, no. 282, rec'd 26 Jan. 1814: ADM 1/506 O17.

28. James, *Naval History*, Vol. VI, p. 282.

29. Warren to Admiralty, 25 Feb. 1814, no. 46, rec'd 25 Mar. 1814, Bermuda: ADM 1/505 O86.

30. James, *Naval History* (2002), Vol. VI, pp. 283–4. Winfield, p. 65. J. H. Schroeder, p. 227 n. 44.

31. *Loire* was an elderly ex-French prize with a standard 18-pounder battery: Winfield, p. 163.

32. Paullin, p. 276.

33. ADM 8/100, in Dudley II, pp. 167–78.

34. Melville to Sir Alexander Hope, 14 July 1813, Admiralty: NAS GD364/1/1253, f. 9; & Pipon to Hope, 6 July 1813: ibid., f. 42.

35. Pipon to Sir Alexander Hope, 10 Sept. 1813: NAS GD364/1/1253, f. 30. Gardiner, *Frigates*, p. 35. James, Vol. VI, pp. 267–8.

36. Admiralty to Warren, 3 June 1813: ADM 2/1377, pp. 65–7, in Dudley II, pp. 139–40.

37. Melville to Warren, 4 June 1813, private, Admiralty: WAR 82, ff. 73–6; see also WAR 82, ff. 66–72.

38. Admiralty to Warren, 28 May 1813: ADM 2/932, pp. 267–8.

39. Warren to Melville, 22 July 1813: WAR LBK/2.

40. Jones to Madison, 7 June 1813: Dudley II, pp. 145–8.

41. Dudley II, pp. 151–5.

42. Jones to Smith, 17 June 1813: Dudley II, pp. 148–51.

43. Cockburn to Warren, 12 July 1813; Dudley II, pp. 184–6.

44. Admiralty to Warren, 9 July 1813: ADM 2/933, pp. 9–10.

45. Warren to Admiralty, 25 Sept. 1813, rec'd 3 Nov.: ADM 1/504, f. 205.

46. Hardy to Warren, 26 June 1813, encl. in Warren to Admiralty, 22 July 1813: ADM 1/504, pp. 49–53; & Warren General Order, 19 July 1813: Dudley II, pp. 162–4.

47. Decatur to Fulton, 5 & 9 Aug. 1813: Dudley II, p. 210–12.

48. Sir Thomas Hardy to Major Benjamin Case, 24 Aug. 1813: Dudley II, pp. 26–7.

49. Madison to Jones, 6 Sept. 1813: Dudley II, pp. 247–8.

50. Admiralty to Warren, 9 Sept. 1813: ADM2/933, p. 34.

51. Warren to Admiralty, 21 Dec. 1813, rec'd 26 Jan. 1814, acknowledging an Admiralty dispatch of 9 Sept. 1813 on torpedoes: ADM 1/506 1814 O8. Warren to Admiralty, 27 Jan. 1814, rec'd 3 Mar., no. 20, Bermuda; & Admiralty dispatches of 16, 10 & 19 Nov. 1814: ADM 1/506 O74. Fulton, R., *Torpedo War and Submarine Explosions*.

52. Admiral Sir Robert Calder to Melville, 11 July 1813, enclosing Taylor to Warden, 25 Dec. 1812: Melville MS at the Perkins Library Box March 1814 – December 1815. Warden had been a Protestant United Irish rebel.

53. Mahan, *1812*, II, pp. 182, 208.

54. Navy Department Circular, 30 July 1813: Dudley II, pp. 204–6.

55. Lewis to Jones, 9 Aug. 1813: Dudley II, pp. 206–7

56. Dudley II, pp. 243–5.

57. Hull to Jones, 24 June 1813: Dudley II, p. 160.

58. Dudley II, pp. 232–42. Smith, *Battle for the Bay*, pp. 75–100.

59. Mahan, *1812*, Vol. I, p. 286, & Vol. II, p. 177.

60. Warren to Admiralty, 4 Sept. 1813, rec'd 10 Nov.: ADM 1/504, p. 167, *re* Admiralty to Warren, 10 July 1813.

61. Warren to Admiralty, 4 Sept. 1813, rec'd 8 Oct. 1813: ADM 1/504, f. 176, encl. Oliver to Warren, 13 June 1813.

62. Warren to Admiralty, 16 Oct. 1813 ADM 1/504, pp. 417–20.

63. Admiralty to Warren, 9 July 1813: ADM 2/933, pp. 6–7

64. Warren to Admiralty, 25 Nov. 1813: ADM 1/504, pp. 525, lists nine tenders: Dudley II, pp. 269–71.

65. Admiralty to Warren, 11 Nov. 1813: ADM 2/933, p. 62.

66. Gutridge, A. C., 'George Redmond Hulbert: A Prize Agent on the North American Station, 1812–1814', *Bermuda Journal of Archaeology and Maritime History*, Vol. 2, 1990, pp. 105–26.

67. Warren to Admiralty, 11 Nov. 1813: ADM 1/504, pp. 699–711, & Dudley II, 277–83.

68. Warren to Admiralty, 13 Nov. 1813: ADM 1/504, pp. 713–15, & Dudley II, p. 284.

69. Warren Declaration of Blockade, 16 Nov. 1813, in Warren to Admiralty, 20 Nov. 1813: ADM 1/504, pp. 551–5, & Dudley II, pp. 262–3.

70. Warren to Liverpool, 16 Nov. 1813: British Library Add. MSS 38, f. 255.

71. Hayes to Warren, encl. in Hayes to Warren, 25 Oct. 1813: ADM 1/504, pp. 733–6, & Dudley II, pp. 273.

72. Bainbridge to Secretary Jones, 31 Dec. 1813: Dudley II, p. 273.

73. Warren to Admiralty, 29 Dec. 1812: ADM 1/503, pp. 99–102.

74. Harland. J., *Seamanship in the Age of Sail*, Conway, London, 1984, pp. 196–8. Hayes club-hauled the 74 HMS *Magnificent* off a lee shore in the Basque Roads in 1812. Gardiner, *Frigates*, pp. 50–3 & 193 fn 28.

75. Admiralty to Warren, 10 Feb. 1813: Dudley II, p. 19.

76. Gardiner, *Frigates*, pp. 48–52.

77. Lecky, H. S., *The King's Ships*, Vol. III, pp. 1–10.

78. Gardiner, *Frigates*, pp. 91–2

79. Gardiner, *Frigates*, p. 145.

80. *American Vessels captured by the British during the Revolution and War of 1812. Nova Scotia Vice Admiralty Court* lists a whaling ship and three privateers.

81. Gardiner, *Frigates*, pp. 52–6.

82. Melville to Warren, 4 June 1813, private, Admiralty: WAR 82, ff. 73-6.

83. Secretary Jones to Master Commandant George Parker, 8 Dec. 1813: Dudley II, pp. 293–6.

84. Secretary Jones to Master Commandant Creighton, 22 Dec. 1813: Dudley II, pp. 296–7.

85. Silverstone, pp. 46–7, 50.

86. Warren to Admiralty, 30 Dec. 1813: ADM 1/505, pp. 87–90, & Dudley II, pp. 307–8.

87. In late 1814 the administration finally created privateer fleets for David Porter and Oliver Hazard Perry, but lacked the credit to buy ships or raise men.

88. Haeger, J. D., *John Jacob Astor: Business and Finance in the Early Republic*, pp.138–50.

89. Garitee, pp. 61–78.

90. Admiralty to Warren, 4 & 15 Nov. 1813: ADM 2/933, pp. 57–9, 65.

91. Admiralty to Warren, 15 Oct. 1813: ADM 2/933, p. 49, approving his decision to reinforce the Lakes, reported in Warren to Admiralty, 21 Aug. 1813: ADM 1/504, f. 189. Warren to Admiralty, 23 Sept. 1813, Halifax, rec'd 3 Nov.: ADM 1/504, f. 210, stripping men from the 74 *Marlborough* then heading home as convoy escort. Pullen, H. F., *March of the Seamen*.

92. For the situation at Charleston, see Dudley II, pp. 242–3.

93. Prevost to Warren, 17 Oct. 1813, in Warren to Admiralty, 18 Nov. 1813, no. 280, rec'd 24 Dec.: ADM 1/504.

94. Warren to Admiralty, 30 Dec. 1813, no. 289, rec'd 26 Jan. 1814, Bermuda: ADM 1/506 O14.

95. Admiralty to Griffith 2 Feb. 1814: ADM2/933, pp. 109–10.

96. Warren to Melville, 9 & 30 Nov. 1813: WAR LBK/2. He raised the same point in the spring. Mahan, *1812*, II, p. 330.

97. Melville to Warren, 24 Nov. 1813: War LBK/2; & Admiralty to Warren, 4 Nov. 1813: ADM 2/1378, pp. 146–51.

98. Warren to Admiralty, 11 Nov. 1813, rec'd 24 Dec.: ADM 1/506 O274.

99. Warren to Admiralty, 16 Aug. 1813: ADM 1/504, f. 187.

100. Warren to Admiralty, 14 Oct. 1813, rec'd 10 Nov.: ADM 1/504, f. 216.

101. Warren to Admiralty, 20 Nov. 1813, Halifax, rec'd 24 Dec.: ADM 1/504, f. 253.

102. Warren to Admiralty, dated Halifax, 16 Oct. 1813, rec'd 10 Nov. 1813 & 20 Nov. 1813: ADM 1/504, f. 223; Dudley II, pp. 261–3.

103. Warren to Admiralty, 11 Nov. 1813, rec'd 24 Dec. 1813: ADM 1/504 O275.

104. Warren to Admiralty, 30 Dec. 1813, Bermuda, no. 292, rec'd 26 Jan. 1814: ADM 1/506 O12.

105. Warren to Admiralty, 30 Dec. 1813, Bermuda, no. 291, rec'd 26 Jan. 1814: ADM 1/506 O11.

106. Stewart to Secretary Jones, 5 & 25 Dec. 1813: Dudley II, pp. 292–3.

107. Whitehill, W. M., ed., *New England Blockaded: The Journal of Henry Edward Napier, Lieutenant in HMS Nymphe*. Salem, Peabody Museum, 1939, p. 23; & Hotham to Cochrane, 14 Nov. 1815: ADM 1/507, p. 440.

108. Warren to Admiralty, 19 Nov. 1813, rec'd 24 Dec., encl. Hayes to Warren, 25 Oct. 1813: ADM 1/504 O282.

109. Griffith to Admiralty, 15 Dec. 1813, no. 18, rec'd 31 Jan. 1814: ADM 1/506 O28.

100. Griffith to Admiralty, 14 Jan. 1814, no. 6, rec'd 8 Feb. 1814: ADM 1/506 O36.

111. Warren to Admiralty, 27 Jan. 1814, no. 21, rec'd 3 Mar., encl. Hayes to Warren, 8 Jan. 1814: ADM 1/506 O62.

112. Warren to Admiralty, 7 Mar. 1814, Bermuda, no. 51, rec'd 15 Apr. 1814: ADM 1/506 O99. James, *Naval History*, Vol. VI, pp. 279–81.

113. Pullen, *March of the Seamen*.

114. Griffith to Admiralty, 19 Jan. 1814, rec'd 9 Feb. 1814: ADM 1/506 O37.

115. Warren to Admiralty, 26 Jan. 1814, no. 18, rec'd 3 Mar. 1814: ADM 1/506 O60.

116. Griffith to Admiralty, 2 Feb. 1814, no. 13, rec'd 25 Feb. 1814: ADM 1/506 O43.

117. Griffith to Admiralty, 28 Feb. & 8 Mar. 1814, Halifax, nos 14 & 15, rec'd 2 Apr. 1814: ADM 1/506 O92–3.

118. Warren to Admiralty, 5 & 10 Jan. 1814, nos 1, 4. & 5, rec'd 3 Mar. 1814: ADM 1/506 O48, 50 & 51.

119. The French frigates were captured in late March: James, *Naval History*, Vol. VI, pp. 261–7. Gardiner, *Frigates*, pp. 30–2.

120. Warren to Admiralty, 27 Jan. 1814, no. 19, rec'd 3 Mar., encl. Nourse to Warren, 24 Jan. 1814: ADM 1/506 O61.

121. Captain's log of HMS *Pique*; Master's log of HMS *Pique*: ADM 53/986.

122. Napier Journal, 10 June 1814: Whitehill, p. 24.

123. James, *Naval History*, Vol. VI, pp. 327–8. Berube and Rodgaard, pp. 73–8, and T. G. Martin, *A Most Fortunate Ship*, p. 186, accept Stewart's version.

124. Tucker, *Decatur*, pp. 130–4.

125. Warren to Admiralty, 2 Feb. 1814, Bermuda, no. 27, rec'd 3 Mar. 1814: ADM 1/506 O64.

126. Admiralty to Warren, 7 Mar. 1814: ADM 2/933, pp. 125–6.

127. Warren to Admiralty, 8 Feb. 1814, Bermuda, no. 34, rec'd 25 Mar. 1814: ADM 1/506 O80.

128. Warren to Admiralty, 18 Feb. 1814, Bermuda, no. 39, rec'd 25 Mar. 1814: ADM 1/506 O81. Warren to Admiralty, 7 Mar. 1814, Bermuda, no. 55, rec'd 15 Apr. 1814: ADM 1/506 O103.

129. Warren to Admiralty, 23 Feb. 1814, Bermuda, no. 40, rec'd 25 Mar. 1814: ADM 1/506 O82.

130. Warren to Admiralty, 7 Mar. 1814, Bermuda, no. 52 rec'd 15 Apr. 1814: ADM 1/506 O100.

131. Warren to Admiralty, 28 Jan. 1814, Bermuda, no. 23 rec'd 25 Mar. 1814: ADM 1/506 O96.

132. WAR 82, ff. 77–94: see f. 82, Melville to Warren, 27 July 1813, for Warren's promotions being disallowed.

133. Rubinstein, H., *Trafalgar Captain: Durham of the Defiance*, p. 237.

134. Melville to Warren, 24 Nov. 1813, Private, Admiralty: WAR 82, f. 96.

135. Warren to Admiralty, 7 Mar. 1814, Bermuda, nos 53–4, rec'd 15 Apr. 1814: ADM 1/506 O101–2.

CHAPTER 8: World-Wide War

1. James Horburgh, Hydrographer to the East India Company, to the Chairs of the East India Company, 11 Nov. 1812: Melville Papers, Clements Library.

2. Coeletta, pp. 101–13.

3. Haeger, pp. 67–8, 89. Table at p. 68 shows the explosion of re-exports, and the collapse of U.S. economic activity under the Embargo.

4. Roland et al, pp. 100–2. Bhagat, G., 'Americans and American Trade in India 1784–1814', *The American Neptune*, Vol. XLVI, No. 1, 1986, pp. 6–15. See p. 17 for George Ropes's 1806 picture of Crowninshield Wharf at Salem, a demonstration of family pride and prosperity at the height of the India trade.

5. Haeger, p. 96.

6. Herring, p. 111.

7. Haeger, pp. 69, 75, 92.

8. Haeger, pp. 99–104.

9. Haeger, p. 107.

10. Haeger, pp. 109–38.

11. Admiralty to Hillyar, 1 Mar. 1813: ADM 3/260.

12. Astor to Jones, 17 June 1813, & Jones to Astor, 22 June 1813: Dudley II, pp. 155–7.

13. Lt William Finch, USN, to Navy Secretary Jones, 13 Feb. 1813: Dudley II, pp. 684–5. For a modern assessment of the voyage, see Brodine, C. E., The Pacific Cruise of the Frigate *Essex*', in Brodine, C. E., Crawford,

M. J. & Hughes C. F., eds, *Against All Odds: U.S. Sailors in the War of 1812*, pp. 1–26.

14. The *Elizabeth* was burned at Rio, being unseaworthy for a passage to the United States. Dudley II, p. 690.

15. Dixon to Admiralty, 5 & 13 Oct. & 10 Nov. 1812: Graham, G. S. & Humphreys, R. A., eds, *The Navy and South America, 1807–1823: Correspondence of the Commanders-in-Chief on the South American Station*, pp. 76–81.

16. Dixon to Admiralty, 10 Mar. 1813: Graham, pp. 85–6.

17. Dixon to Admiralty, 22 Mar. 1813: Graham, p. 86.

18. The instructions arrived on the *Swiftsure* packet at Rio on 30 April.

19. Gardiner, *Frigates*, p. 189. Winfield, pp. 96, 155.

20. Dixon to Admiralty, 30 Apr. 1813 (x2): Graham, pp. 87–8.

21. Heywood to Dixon, 3 Apr. 1813, in Dixon to Admiralty, 11 June 1813, no. 81: Graham, pp. 86–7.

22. Dixon to Admiralty, 30 Apr. & 6 Sept. 1813, Heywood to Dixon, 10 May 1813, rec'd by Dixon 3 June 1813: Graham, pp. 89–91.

23. Intelligence rec'd 3 June 1813, extracts endorsed 'Copy Manley Dixon' from Capt. Heywood of HMS *Nereus*, dated Buenos Ayres, 10 May 1813: Hillyar MSS, NMM AGC/23/7.

24. Extracts of letters sent by Admiral Dixon to Captain Hillyar, addressed to Messrs Brown and Watson of Rio, dated Valparaiso, 8 Apr. 1813, and from a Mr Crompton, dated Lima, 10 Feb. 1813, addressed to Mr Charles Eyes of Buenos Ayres: Hillyar MSS, NMM AGC/23/7.

25. Dixon to Admiralty, 11 June 1813, and Admiralty minute of 6 Aug. 1813: Graham, pp. 92–3.

26. Humphreys, R. A., 'British Merchants and South American Independence', The British Academy Raleigh Lecture 1965, *Proceedings of the British Academy*, Vol. LI, 1965, pp. 151–74 at p. 166.

27. Dixon to Hillyar, secret, 1 & 5 July 1813: Graham, pp. 99–101.

28. Manley Dixon to Hillyar, secret, Rio, 1 July 1813: Hillyar MSS, NMM AGC/23/7, & Dudley II, pp. 713–14.

29. Dixon to Admiralty, 7 Aug. 1813: Graham, p. 105. His son was promoted captain of the flagship.

30. Dixon to Admiralty, 21 June & 12 July 1813: Graham, pp. 93–5, 98–9. See also Tagart, E., *A Memoir of the late Captain Heywood RN*.

31. Bowles to Dixon, 14 Sept. 1813: Graham, pp. 109–10.

32. Winfield, p. 200.

33. Dixon to Admiralty, 1 Dec. 1813, citing Bowles to Dixon, 8 Oct. 1813: Graham, pp. 113–14.

34. Dudley II, p. 711.

35. Commander William Black, HMS *Racoon*, to the Admiralty, 15 Dec. 1813: Dudley II, p. 714. Graham, p. 149.

36. Long, *Porter*, p. 146.

37. Bowles to Dixon, 2 Dec. 1813: Graham, pp. 120–1. Gardiner, *Frigates*, pp. 30–2.

38. Winfield, p. 185. Dixon to Admiralty, 17 Feb. 1814, enclosing Dixon to Pipon, 12 Feb. 1814: Graham, pp. 128–9.

39. Dixon to Admiralty, 16 Apr. 1814: Graham, p. 137.

40. Winfield, p. 200. Bowles to Admiralty, 5 Sept. 1813: Graham, pp. 105–6.

41. Crawford III, pp. 772–80 reproduces the key correspondence. Greg Dening's chapter 'The Face of Battle: Valparaiso 1814', in *Performances*, pp. 79–98, provides a Pacific perspective, but his decision to rename Hillyar as Hillyer prompts some concern.

42. Bowles to Admiralty, 19 Feb. 1814. Bowles's *Aquilon*, a venerable 12-pounder frigate of 1786, was no match for *Essex*, or any other American frigate. Hillyar to Admiralty, 28 Feb. 1814: Graham, pp. 129–33.

43. Porter to Downes, 10 Jan. 1814: Crawford III, p. 711, suggests using the second ship was 'a contingency Porter seems not to have anticipated'.

44. Porter to Navy Secretary Jones, 13 July 1814; Crawford, pp. 715–16. The *ex post facto* nature of the claim raises doubts and the failure of all those on the *Phoebe* to mention the matter suggests that Porter may not have recalled the events precisely.

45. Log book of HMS *Phoebe*, 8 & 9 Feb. 1814: ADM 51/2675, f. 151. Crawford III, p. 712.

46. Dening, p. 87.

47. Hillyar to Admiralty, 28 Feb. 1814: ADM 1/22, f. 214–16. Crawford III, pp. 714–15.

48. Bowles to Dixon, 11 Apr. 1814, in Dixon to Croker, 14 Apr. 1814: Graham, pp. 137–9.

49. Log book of HMS *Phoebe*, 25 Feb. 1814, & British Residents to Hillyar, 25 Feb. 1814: Crawford III, pp. 716–19.

50. Copies of all orders and letters by Captain James Hillyar: MSS NMM AGC/23/7.

51. Farragut, *Reminiscences*: Crawford III, p. 749. Farragut's opinion carries weight: he became the first American admiral – in 1862.

52. Farragut, *Reminiscences*: Crawford III, pp. 749–50.

53. Gardiner, *Frigates*, p. 147, based on contemporary sailing reports. Winfield, p. 189, records that *Essex* became a troopship in 1819, was hulked as a convict ship at Cork in 1823, and sold in 1837.

54. Winfield, p. 166. Dixon to Pipon, 25 Mar. 1814, in Dixon to Admiralty, 30 Mar. 1814, no. 146: Graham, pp. 135–7.

55. Boatswain's report, Crawford III, p. 741.

56. Dening, p. 92.
57. Porter to Navy Secretary Jones, 3 July 1814: Crawford III, pp. 730–9.
58. Hillyar to Admiralty, 30 Mar. 1814 & 26 June 1814, nos 264 & 300: ADM 1/1950. Log book of HMS *Phoebe*, 28 Mar. 1814: ADM 51/2675, ff. 173–4. Log book of the *Essex*, 28 Mar. 1814, as published in the *New York Evening Post*, 8 July 1814: Crawford, pp. 719–30.
59. Carpenter's report & gunner's report: Crawford III, pp. 742–4.
60. Dening, p. 97.
61. Graham, pp. 141–97.
62. Log of *Phoebe*, a small-format volume, probably Hillyar's personal copy, well bound, with coastal views and charts, including Valparaiso, covering the period March 1813 to October 1814: MS87/026 NMM.
63. Dixon to Admiralty, 10 June 1814, encl. Hillyar to Admiralty, 30 Mar. 1814: Graham, pp. 141–2.
64. Dixon to Admiralty, 5 July 1814, encl. Hillyar to Admiralty, 11 May 1814: Graham, pp. 145–6.
65. Dixon to Admiralty, 8 Sept. 1814, encl. Hillyar to Tucker, 14 Apr. 1814: Graham, pp. 147–8.
66. Winfield, p. 166.
67. Dixon to Fyffe, 16 Nov. 1814: Graham, pp. 148–9.
68. Dixon to Admiralty, 24 Dec. 1814, encl. Black to Dixon, 15 Dec. 1813: Graham, pp. 149–50.
69. Admiralty to Dixon, 21 Apr. & 14 July 1813: ADM 2/934, pp. 46 & 52.
70. Admiralty to Dixon, 29 Sept. 1813: ADM 2/934, p. 61.
71. Admiralty to Dixon, 10 Aug. 1813: ADM 2/934, p. 54.
72. Admiralty to Dixon, 11 Oct. 1813: ADM 2/934, p. 63.
73. Admiralty to Dixon, 16 Aug. 1814: ADM 2/934, p. 81.
74. Admiralty to Dixon, 8 Nov. 1814, no. 45: ADM 2/934, p. 84.
75. Admiralty to Dixon, 15 Nov. 1814, no. 46: ADM 2/934, p. 86.
76. Admiralty to Dixon, 12 Dec. 1814: ADM 2/934, p. 91.
77. Long, *Porter*, pp. 160–1. Dening, pp. 88–9.
78. Hillyar to Porter, 4 Apr. 1814: Crawford III, pp. 746–7.
79. Farragut, *Reminiscences*: Crawford III, pp. 757–9.
80. Crawford III, pp. 760–8.
81. Cochrane to Admiralty: ADM 1/507 O281.
82. Porter, D., *Journal of a Cruise etc.* (1815): Crawford III, pp. 708–9.
83. Porter, *Journal* (1822).
84. Long, *Porter*, p. 170.
85. Crawford III, p. 709, admits that the claims were excessive, but accepts the premise that the diversion worked.
86. Dudley II, p. 296.
87. Long, *Porter*, p. 162.

88. Long, *Porter*, p. 159, citing *The Times, Naval Chronicle, The Annual Register* and *Marshall's Naval Biography.*

CHAPTER 9: Burning the White House

1. Arthur, pp. 103–6, 265 n. 60.
2. Cochrane to Admiralty, 17 Jan. 1814: ADM 1/506 O15.
3. Fry, pp. 320–5. Cochrane, A., *The Fighting Cochranes*, pp. 254–63.
4. Lord Melville to Capt. Thomas Cochrane, 30 Sept., 10 Oct. & 12 Oct. 1812: NLS 2264, ff. 233, 237, 240. Chief Baron of Scotland (another Dundas) to Capt. Thomas Cochrane, 14 Oct. 1812: NLS 2264, ff. 244–5.
5. Admiralty Minute, 27 Dec. 1813: ADM 1/504 O287.
6. Admiralty to Cochrane, 20 Jan. 1814: ADM 3/261.
7. Admiralty to Cochrane, 25 Jan. & 22 Feb. 1814: ADM 2/933, pp. 90, 119–20. Cochrane to Admiralty, 29 Jan. 1814, no. 1: ADM 1/506 O24. The Admiralty referred the query to the Board of Trade.
8. Admiralty Minute, 14 Mar. 1814: ADM 3/261. Vale, B., *The Audacious Admiral: The True Life of a Naval Legend*, pp. 73–81, for the Stock Market scandal.
9. Cochrane to Admiralty, 5 Jan. 1814: ADM 1/506 O4.
10. Cochrane to Admiralty, 2 Jan. 1814, Hurd to Admiralty, 7 Jan. 1814, endorsed by Board 12 Jan. 1814: ADM 1/506 O24, f. 153. Day, A., *The Admiralty Hydrographic Service 1795–1919.*
11. Admiralty to Cochrane, 6 Oct. 1814, no. 174: ADM 2/933, p. 236.
12. For example HMS *Epervier.*
13. Codrington to his wife, 10 July 1814: Bourchier, E., ed., *Memoir of the Life of Admiral Sir Edward Codrington*, Vol. I, p. 310.
14. Edward Codrington rated Brown very highly, and lamented his death in September 1814.
15. Rubinstein, *Trafalgar Captain: Durham of the Defiance*, pp. 238–41. The ships were renamed *Iphigénie* and *Gloire*. James, *Naval History*, VI, pp. 259–61.
16. Hotham to Admiralty, 6 Nov. 1813, rec'd 28 Dec., Warren to Admiralty, 8 Nov. 1813, rec'd 24 Dec.: ADM 1/504, f. 263–4.
17. Hotham to Admiralty, 7 Mar. 1814, rec'd 15 Apr., Bermuda: ADM 1/505 O104.
18. Admiralty Minute, 5 May 1814: ADM 3/261.
19. Admiralty to Navy Board, 13 Apr. 1814: ADM 3/261.
20. Admiralty to Cochrane, 30 Apr. & 25 May 1814: ADM 2/933, pp. 146–50; & Admiralty to Cochrane, 16 Aug. 1814: ADM 3/261.
21. Admiralty to Cochrane, 13 Sept. 1814, no. 196, & 25 Oct. 1814, no. 193, *re* his of the 5th, no. 136: ADM 2/933, pp. 214–16 & 256–8.
22. Barrie to his mother, 4 Feb. 1814: Crawford III, p. 17.

23. Cochrane to Cockburn, 9 May 1814: NLS 2333, f. 59.
24. Scott, J., *Recollections of a Naval Life*, pp. 73–348, records the experience of a junior officer serving under Cockburn in 1814. Shomette, D., *Flotilla: The Patuxent Naval Campaign in the War of 1812*.
25. Cochrane to Admiralty, 27 Apr. 1814: ADM 1/505, pp. 273–7.
26. Admiralty to Cochrane, 12 & 22 July 1814: ADM 2/933, pp. 171–2, 182–4.
27. Cockburn to Cochrane, 9 May 1814: NLS 2333, f. 59.
28. Cochrane to Admiralty, 1814: ADM 1/506 p. 42; Cochrane to Melville, 17 July 1814: Crawford III, pp. 132–5.
29. Cochrane to Admiralty, 25 Apr. 1813: ADM 1/505, p. 40.
30. Palmer, M. J., 'The Battle of Lake Champlain', in Brodine, C. E., Crawford, M. J. & Hughes, C. F., eds, *Against All Odds: U.S. Sailors in the War of 1812*, pp. 53–72, is the best modern summary.
31. Renier, G. J., *Great Britain and the Establishment of the Kingdom of the Netherlands, 1813–1815*, a key text that should be read by all students of the War of 1812. Sherwig, J. M., *Guineas and Gunpowder: British Foreign Aid in the Wars with France, 1793–1815*, p. 326.
32. Latimer, J., *1812: War with America*, p. 307. The units were the 1st Battalions of the 4th and 44th Foot, the 85th Light Infantry and 21st Foot. Only the 4th were veterans.
33. Arthur, pp. 181–2.
34. Codrington to his wife, 27 & 31 July 1814: Bourchier, p. 313.
35. Beasley to Monroe, 6 Jan. 1814: Melville Papers Clements Library Box March 1814–December 1815.
36. Napier Journal, 14 May 1814: Whitehill, p. 15.
37. Whitehill, pp. 21–3.
38. Whitehill, p. 35.
39. Whitehill, pp. 3, 27–8 & 67–71.
40. Whitehill, p. 36.
41. Admiralty to Council Office, 31 May 1814: ADM 2/1380, p. 178.
42. Collier to Griffith, 11 July 1814: ADM 1/507, p. 36. *Rattlesnake* 278 tons, 14 guns.
43. Samuel Pym to Cochrane, 15 July 1814: ADM 1/507, p. 40.
44. Campbell, G., *The Road to Canada: The Grand Communications Route from Saint John to Quebec*, has an excellent assessment of the long-term implications of the border and the overland link.
45. Admiralty to Griffith, 16 Aug. 1814, *re* his no. 38 of 19 July with Hardy's report: ADM 2/933, p. 200.
46. Cut down and lengthened from a small frigate in 1812, the *Adams* had taken ten prizes on her only war cruise, beginning in January 1814. Canney, pp. 57–8, Silverstone p. 32.

47. Griffith to Admiralty, 27 Sept. 1814: ADM 1/508, pp. 28–32. Stanley, G. F. G., *The War of 1812: Land Operations*, pp. 357–78, for the land operations.

48. Griffith to Admiralty, 6 Sept. 1814, *Endymion* off Castine: ADM 1/507 O286. Ex-French privateer *Dominica* taken off Charleston on 5 Aug. 1813 by the French-officered and -manned privateer *Decatur*, losing 19 killed and 41 wounded, including her commander. She was retaken by HMS *Majestic* on 22 May 1814.

49. Griffith to Melville, 10 Sept. 1814: ADM 1/507 O287, recommending two officers for promotion. Admiralty to Griffith, 10 Oct. 1814, no. 39: ADM 2/933, pp. 241–3, & Admiralty to Griffith, 31 Oct. 1814, no. 42, *re* report on Machias of 27th ult. approve proceedings of Parker and Pilkington: ADM 2/933, pp. 261–2.

50. Cochrane to Melville, 17 July 1814: NLS 2345, f. 13; & Cochrane to Bathurst, 14 July 1814: Crawford, pp. 131–5.

51. Cochrane to Admiralty, 23 July 1814, no. 70: ADM 1/4360, Secret 1814.

52. Stanley, pp. 331–56; see also Shomette. Marolda, E. J., *The Washington Navy Yard: An Illustrated History*, pp. 8–10, notes that the yard was systematically plundered by locals after the British left!

53. Bartlett, 'Gentlemen versus Democrats'.

54. Bartlett, pp. 144–6.

55. Admiralty to Cochrane, 6 Oct. 1814, no. 173: ADM 2/933, p. 235.

56. Morriss, Chapter 5. Hamilton, pp. 84–115.

57. Codrington to wife, 10 Sept. 1814: Bourchier, p. 319.

58. Cochrane to Admiralty, 23 Sept. 1814, no. 125: ADM 1/507 O318; & Admiralty to Cochrane, 19 Oct. 1814, no. 181: ADM 2/933, pp. 246–8.

59. Arthur, pp. 204–8.

60. Admiralty to Cochrane, 28 Sept. 1814, no. 166: ADM 2/933, pp. 230–3.

61. Codrington to wife, 10 Sept. 1814: Bourchier, p. 319.

62. Cochrane to Melville, 3 Sept. 1814: Crawford, pp. 269–70.

63. Spiers, E. M., *Radical General: Sir George de Lacy Evans, 1787–1870*, pp. 9–10. Codrington to wife, 13 Sept. 1814: Bourchier, p. 320.

64. Cochrane to Admiralty, 17 Sept. 1814: ADM 1/507 O291.

65. Cochrane to Melville, 17 Sept. 1814: NLS 2345, ff. 15–16, & Crawford, p. 289. Bourchier, pp. 312–13.

66. Admiralty to Cochrane, 19 Oct. 1814, no. 180, replying to his no. 116 of 17 Sept. 1814: ADM 2/933, pp. 243–6.

67. Melville to Cochrane, 29 July 1814: Crawford, pp. 329–30 fn 2.

68. Cochrane to Admiralty, 9 Oct. 1814, Halifax, rec'd 1 Nov., no. 141: ADM 1/507 O315.

69. Cochrane to Admiralty, 11 Oct. 1814, rec'd 1 Nov., no. 142: ADM 1/507 O319.

70. Codrington to wife, 4 Oct. 1814, at Halifax: Bourchier, pp. 322–3.

71. Joseph Marryat, Chairman of Lloyd's, to Admiralty, 19 Sept. 1814: ADM 1/3394.

72. Roosevelt, in Clowes, Sir W. L., *The Royal Navy*, Vol. VI, pp. 68–9.

73. Admiralty Minutes, 24 Nov. & 19 Dec. 1814: ADM 3/261, & Griffith to Admiralty, 1 Feb. 1815, no. 5: ADM 1/508 O30. Canney, pp. 87–95. Ordered in January 1813 the American two-deckers were significantly larger and more heavily armed than British 74s, with a broadside one-quarter heavier. However, they were poor fighting ships unable to open their lower deck gun ports in a seaway.

74. Built in 1798 the *Superb* had an unrivalled reputation for speed and seaworthiness. Winfield, p. 66.

75. Hotham to Cochrane, 13 Aug. 1814, *Superb*, off Gardiner's Island: NLS 2327, ff. 60–5.

76. Hotham to Cochrane, 17 Aug. 1814, *Superb*, off New London: NLS 2327, ff. 70–5.

77. Hotham to Cochrane, 19 Aug. 1814, *Superb*, off New London: NLS 2327, ff. 76–9.

78. Hotham to Cochrane, 26 Aug. 1814, *Superb*, off Gardiner's Island: NLS 2327, ff. 82–4.

79. Hotham to Cochrane, 24 Oct. 1814, *Superb*, Halifax: NLS 2327, ff. 89–91.

80. See, for example, three letters from Hotham to Cochrane on 9 Oct. 1814 covering a very long list of ships taken by his squadron, and the capture of the letter of marque brig *Regent* by boats of HMS *Forth*, and of the privateer *Daedalus* (136 tons, two long guns) by HMS *Niemen*, on 18 Sept. 1814: ADM 1/507, pp. 395, 404, 410.

81. Fulton to Decatur, 5 Aug. 1813, & Decatur to Fulton, 9 Aug. 1813: Dudley II, pp. 210–12. Tucker, *Decatur*, p. 130–1.

82. Hotham to Cochrane, 13 Nov. 1814: ADM 1/507, pp. 438–9.

83. Hotham to Cochrane, 13 Aug. 1814, *Superb*, off Gardiner's Island: NLS 2327, ff. 60–5.

84. Hotham to Cochrane, 14 Nov. 1815: ADM 1/507, p. 440.

85. Hotham to Cochrane, 13 Nov. 1814, encl. report by Capt Nash, HMS *Saturn*, 31 Oct.: ADM 1/507, pp. 438–9.

86. Hotham to Admiralty, 19 Nov. 1814, rec'd 11 Dec., encl. Hope to Hotham, 31 Oct. 1814: ADM 1/507 O345. Hotham to Admiralty, 3 Dec. 1814, no. 12, HMS *Superb*, Halifax, rec'd. 14 Jan. 1815: ADM 1/508 O9. Hotham to Cochrane, 30 Nov. 1814, Halifax: NLS 2327, ff. 104–13.

87. Hotham to Admiralty, 23 Dec. 1814, New London, no. 14, rec'd 17 Feb. 1815: ADM 1/508 O23.

88. Tucker, *Decatur*, p. 140. Lieutenant P. Yule to Sir A. Hope, 30 May 1815: NAS GD364/1/1267, f. 4.

89. Hotham to Admiralty, 19 Nov. 1814, rec'd 11 Dec., enclosing Hope to Hotham, 31 Oct. 1814: ADM 1/507 O345.

90. Hotham to Admiralty, 23 Dec. 1814, no. 14, New London, rec'd 17 Feb. 1815: ADM 1/508 O23.

91. Griffith to Admiralty, 2 Nov. 1814, no. 53, rec'd 22 Nov.: ADM 1/507 O322.

92. Griffith to Admiralty, 19 Dec. 1814, no. 68, rec'd 14 Jan. 1815: ADM 1/508 O18.

93. Griffith to Admiralty, 26 Oct. 1814, no. 52, rec'd 22 Nov.: ADM 1/507 O326.

94. Griffith to Admiralty, 13 Nov. 1814, no. 55, rec'd 12 Dec. 1814: ADM 1/507 O330.

95. Collier to John Wilson Croker (private), 29 Dec. 1814, rec'd 24 Jan. 1815: Croker MS at Perkins Library.

96. Hotham to Admiralty, 2 Jan. 1815, no. 2, New London, duplicate, rec'd 17 Feb. 1815: ADM 1/508 O24.

97. Hotham to Cochrane, 2 Jan. 1815, New London: NLS 2327, ff. 114–17.

98. Hotham to Admiralty, 2 Jan. 1815, no. 2, & 6 Jan. 1815, New London, rec'd 17 Feb. 1815: ADM 1/508 O24.

99. Griffith to Admiralty, 10 Jan. 1815, no. 1, rec'd 25 Feb. 1815: ADM 1/508 O27.

100. Griffith to Admiralty, 2 Feb. 1815, no. 7, rec'd 25 Feb. 1815: ADM 1/508 O31.

101. Griffith to Admiralty, 1 Feb. 1815, no. 3, rec'd 25 Feb. 1815: ADM 1/508 O39.

102. Griffith to Admiralty, 24 Feb. 1815, no. 12, rec'd 20 Mar. 1815: ADM 1/508 O82.

103. Griffith to Admiralty, 10 Jan. 1815, no. 2, rec'd 25 Feb. 1815: ADM 1/508 O28.

104. Griffith to Admiralty, 23 Feb. 1815, no. 14, rec'd 20 Mar. 1815: ADM 1/508 O84.

105. Hotham to Admiralty, 14 Feb. 1815, no. 9, rec'd 23 Mar. 1815, enclosing Hotham to Admiral Tyler, 14 Feb. 1815: ADM 1/508 O90, pp. 439–44. Hotham to Cochrane, 21 Feb. 1815, no. 25: ADM 1/508, p. 444.

106. Kastor, P. J., *The Nation's Crucible; The Louisiana Purchase and the Creation of America*, pp. 169–71.

107. Kastor, p. 198.

108. Bunbury to Bathurst, 7 Aug. 1814: War of 1812 Papers, Clements Library. Muir, R., *Britain and the Defeat of Napoleon, 1807–1815*, pp. 107–8.

109. Ross's orders of 6 Sept. 1814 for New Orleans: ADM 1/4360, p. 58; Latimer, pp. 252–3.

110. Cochrane to Prevost, 5 Oct. 1814, Halifax: ADM 1/508. Admiralty to Cochrane, 13 & 28 Sept., 3 Oct. 1814: ADM 2/933, pp. 214–15, 224, 234.

111. Codrington to wife, 4, 20 & 27 Nov. 1814: Bourchier, pp. 324–8.

112. Bathurst to General Lambert, 18 Oct. 1814, Most Secret: ADM 1/4360.

113. Remini, R. V., *The Battle of New Orleans: Andrew Jackson and America's First Military Victory*, p. 69.

114. A point made with great force by Rear Admiral Pultney Malcolm, in charge of the landing and re-embarkation. Malcolm to Clementina Malcolm, 24 Jan. 1815, no. 33: Malcolm MS, Clements Library.

115. Bartlett, p. 158.

116. Kastor, pp. 172–200.

117. Arthur, pp. 119–22, 194.

118. Tucker & Reuter, p. 15.

119. Collier to John Wilson Croker (private), 29 Dec. 1814, rec'd 24 Jan. 1815: Croker MS, Perkins Library.

120. T. G. Martin's account of the cruise, pp. 190–207, is also followed by Berube & Rodgaard.

121. James, *War of 1812* (1817), p. 475.

122. Thomas, H., *The Slave Trade: The History of the Atlantic Slave Trade 1440–1870*, pp. 593–616, 696–7, 715. Marshall, Lt. J., *Royal Naval Biography*, Vol. II, pt. II, p. 536 for Collier.

123. T. G. Martin, pp. 202–5, incorrectly dates Collier's suicide to 1817. Brenton, II, p. 539.

CHAPTER 10: Taking the *President*

1. *Dictionary of American Naval Fighting Ships*, Vol. V, p. 371.

2. Long, D. F., *Sailor-Diplomat: A Biography of Commodore James Biddle, 1783–1848*, p. 48.

3. Tucker, S. C., *Arming the Fleet: U.S. Navy Ordnance in the Muzzle-Loading Era*, p. 183.

4. Tucker, *Decatur*, pp. 128–30.

5. Albion, R. G., with Pope, J. B., *The Rise of New York Port, 1815–1860*, pp. 8–9, 16–27.

6. Secretary of Navy to Decatur, 8 Aug. 1814: *Calendar of the Correspondence of James Madison*, Washington, 1894, p. 428.

7. William Jones to Decatur, 17 Nov. 1814: RG45, CLS (Confidential Letters Sent) 1814.

8. Decatur to Jones, 23 Nov. 1814: RG45 Captains' Letters (CL) 1814, vol. 8, no. 30.

9. Jones to Decatur, 25 Nov. 1814: RG45 CLS.

10. Long, *Biddle*, p. 50.

11. Decatur to Jones, 30 Dec. 1814: RG45 CL 1814, vol. 8, no. 148.

12. Decatur to Jones, 23 Nov. 1814: RG45 CL 1814, vol. 8, no. 30.

13. Dudley, W., *Splintering the Wooden Wall: The British Blockade of the United States, 1812–1815*, p. 127.

14. Admiralty to Admirals, various, 25 Nov. 1814, Secret orders, No. 44: ADM 2/1381.

15. Admiralty to Admirals, various, 26 Nov. 1814, Secret orders, No. 46: ADM 2/1381.

16. Admiralty to Hotham, 19 Dec. 1814, & to Admiral Martin (Plymouth), 19 Dec. 1814: ADM 2/1381 80–4. These urgent orders were sent in a 'fast sailing vessel', directed not to stop on any account, and Hotham was directed to send by return 'the latest intelligence . . . of the enemy's preparations and movements'. However, the timely arrival of orders and intelligence remained prey to wind and weather. The 150-ton Bermudan schooner HMS *Bramble* left Plymouth on the 23rd, endured a tempestuous voyage and ended up stuck on a rock off Bermuda on 2 February. Log book 1814–1815 HMS *Bramble*: ADM 51/2181.

17. Log book HMS *Superb*, December 1814–January 1815: ADM 51/2051.

18. Hotham to Admiralty, 29 Dec. 1814, *Superb* off Newfoundland, rec'd. 2 Feb. 1815, endorsed on decyphered copy 'JWC Feb 1', BEFORE the message was registered as having arrived: ADM 1/508, f. 107. The reply was sent before the letter was registered. Admiralty to Hotham 1 Feb. 1815: ADM 2/1381, p. 165.

19. Hotham to Cochrane, 2 Jan. 1815, off New London: NLS Cochrane MS 2327, f. 114–15.

20. Hotham to Admiralty, 5 Jan. 1815: ADM 1/508, ff. 128–9.

21. Hotham to Admiralty, 16 Jan. 1815, no. 2, rec'd 17 Feb.: ADM 1/508, f. 143, encl. an intelligence report of the 7th.

22. Hotham to Admiralty, 5 Jan. 1815, no. 2, rec'd 17 Feb.: ADM 1/508, ff. 128–9.

23. Hope to Hotham, 11 Oct. 1814, off Nantucket, in Hotham to Cochrane, 15 Nov. 1814, in Cochrane to Admiralty, 16 Nov. 1814, rec'd 14 Dec. 1814: ADM 1/508, no. 10, O344, pp. 263, 422 & 430. The action was on 10 Oct.

24. Henry Hope to Sir Alexander Hope, off New London, 24 Dec. 1814: NAS GD364/1/1267, ff. 21–2.

25. Log book of HMS *Forth*: ADM 51/2397.

26. Gardiner, *Frigates*, pp. 25–6. *Tenedos* was a sister ship of the *Shannon*, built during 1810–12 at Chatham Dockyard. *Pomone* was built as the French *Astrée* at Genoa in 1808 and taken in 1810. These two ships were of almost identical form and size, although the structural plan was distinct.

27. Decatur to Crowninshield, 14 Jan. 1815: RG45 CL 1815, vol. 1, no. 41.

28. Cooper, J. F., *History of the Navy of the United States of America*, p. 430.

29. Hayes to Hotham, 17 Jan. 1815: ADM 1/508, f. 769.
30. Log book HMS *Majestic*, 15 Jan. 1815: ADM 51/2543.
31. Cooper, p. 430.
32. Hayes to Hotham, 17 Jan. 1815: ADM 1/508, f. 769.
33. *Endymion* and *Pomone* logs, & James, pp. 213–14.
34. Tucker, *Arming*, p. 94. James considered these so important that those found on the *President* featured as the frontispiece of his *Naval Occurrences*! Examples are displayed on board the USS *Constitution*.
35. Douglas, p. 480.
36. Douglas, p. 483.
37. Cooper, p. 431.
38. Decatur made his officers swear to this at the court of inquiry. See also 'Autobiography of Commodore Hollins CSA', *Maryland Historical Magazine*, 34, Sept. 1939, pp. 229–30. The charming memories of a first-voyage midshipman, recorded at the end of a long and eventful life are hardly an authority of the first significance.
39. Hollins, p. 230; Cooper, p. 431.
40. *Majestic* log.
41. Tucker, *Decatur*, p. 144.
42. Lieutenant Shubrick, Court of Inquiry Testimony: RG125, vol. 6, no. 202. Harland, pp. 12–13, 33.
43. 'Thessaly', in *The Naval Chronicle*, Vol. 37, London, 1817, p. 194.
44. The decisive moment of the action features in a fine study by Thomas Buttersworth, published as an engraving on 1 June 1815 in London, based on 'particulars and the position of the ships by Lieut [Francis] Ormond, [second] of the *Endymion*'. The picture shows *President*'s spanker in the act of being brailed up, and her lanterns have been put out, which provides a precise time. See Smith, E. N., *American Naval Broadsides*, New York, 1974, p. 191.
45. James, *Occurrences*, p. 385.
46. *Endymion* log.
47. This is quite clear in *Endymion*'s log, and the copy made by the master.
48. The court of inquiry testimony of both lieutenants makes this clear.
49. *Pomone*'s times are roughly two hours ahead of those kept by *Endymion*. I have relied on *Endymion*.
50. Decatur to Crowninshield, 17 Jan. 1815: James, *Naval Occurrences*, pp. 380–1.
51. Captured muster books were used to determine the 'head-money' due to the captors for each enemy combatant taken or slain.
52. There is a copy of Hope's account of the engagement in the master's log book of *Endymion*: ADM 52/3904. In both logs the material has been pasted in as a separate page. ADM 51/2324. Hayes tried to cram the entry into a regular page of *Majestic*'s log; the result is almost illegible.

53. Master's log HMS *Endymion*: ADM 52/3904.

54. Roosevelt, pp. 407–8; Adams, *History*, VII, p. 68.

55. Lecky, p. 9.

56. Douglas, p. 423.

57. James, *Occurrences*, p. 226.

58. Marshall, J., *Naval Biography: Supplementary Volume I*, p. 316.

59. Hope to Hayes, 15 Jan. 1815: James 1817, p. 379.

60. McKee, p. 398.

61. 'Thessaly' letter, dated Plymouth, 15 Jan. 1817: *The Naval Chronicle*, Vol. 37, pp. 193–4.

62. Hayes to Hotham, 17 Jan. 1815: ADM 1/508, f. 769.

63. Log, 22 Jan. 1815, HMS *Superb*: ADM 51/2051.

64. Hotham to Cochrane, 23 Jan. 1815: ADM 1/508, f. 767.

65. Hotham to Cochrane, 12 Feb. 1815, rec'd 20 Mar., no. 17: ADM 1/508, f. 827.

66. Long, *Biddle*, pp. 50–5.

67. Bermuda captures, 26 Dec. 1814–25 May 1815: HCA 49/098.

68. I am indebted to Dr Edward Harris for this information.

69. Decatur to Crowninshield, 20 Feb. 1815 (written on board HMS *Narcissus*): RG45 CL 1815, no. 2, vol. 1, no. 144.

70. O'Byrne, p. 329. James, *Occurrences*, p. 224.

71. James, *Occurrences*, pp. 223–4.

72. Duffy, S. W. H., *Captain Blakeley and the Wasp*, pp. 167, 279–80.

73. James, *Occurrences*, p. 218.

74. Hotham to Cochrane, 14 Jan. 1815, *Superb* before New London: NLS 2327, ff. 121–3.

75. Hotham to Admiral Sir George Hope, 23 Jan. 1815, *Superb* off New London: NAS GD364/1/1267, f. 23. Sir George was Henry's uncle.

76. Henry Hope to Sir Alexander Hope, 2 Feb. 1815: NAS GD364/1/1267, f. 22.

77. Commodore Andrew Evans (at Bermuda) to Admiralty, 19 Feb. & 2 Mar. 1815: ADM 1/1771, ff. 26, 36.

78. Henry Hope to Sir Alexander Hope, 8 Mar. 1815: NAS GD364/1/1267, f. 26.

79. James, *Naval History* (2004), Vol. VI, p. 370.

80. Lecky, Vol. III, pp. 1–10.

81. Cited by Marshall, *Naval Biography* (1827), at p. 317.

CHAPTER 11: Making Peace

1. Renier, pp. 134–6; Hall, pp. 198–203; & Muir, pp. 307–9. The disaster was soon forgotten, and Lynedoch's troops were on the spot to occupy Antwerp when Napoleon abdicated in April.

2. Webster, C. K., *The Foreign Policy of Castlereagh 1812–1815*, p. 147.

3. Webster, *Castlereagh*, pp. 185, 161.
4. Cabinet Memorandum, 26 Dec. 1813, & Memorandum on the Maritime Peace, in Webster, C. K., ed., *British Diplomacy 1813–1815: Select Documents dealing with the Reconstruction of Europe*, pp. 123–6. Webster, *Castlereagh*, dates the latter paper to mid-January 1814, pp. 196–7 & n.
5. Castlereagh to Metternich, 29 Jan. 1814, & Castlereagh to Earl Bathurst, 30 Jan. 1814: Londonderry, Marquess, ed., *Memoirs and Correspondence of Viscount Castlereagh*, Vol. II, pp. 202–3, 214.
6. Newman, Vice Consul at Gothenburg, to Mr Cooke, 15 Apr. 1814: Londonderry, II, p. 464. See also Maffeo, S., *Most Secret and Confidential*.
7. Hamilton to Castlereagh, 18 Apr. 1814, FO: Londonderry, II, pp. 471–2.
8. Hamilton to Castlereagh, 28 Apr. 1814, FO: Londonderry, II, pp. 524–5.
9. Castlereagh to Bathurst, 3 May 1814, Paris, p. 13; Castlereagh to Bathurst, 5 May 1814; Melville to Castlereagh, 9 May 1814, Admiralty: Londonderry, III pp. 4, 13 & 18–19.
10. Cooke to Castlereagh, 29 Apr. 1814, FO: Londonderry, II, pp. 527–8.
11. Melville to Castlereagh, 9 May 1814 Admiralty: Londonderry, III, pp. 18–19.
12. John Harriot (Thames Police) to Sidmouth, 5 May 1814: 152M/C1814/OF 13.
13. General Stevenson to Sidmouth, 16 Feb. 1814: 152M/C1814/OF 11 & note of 1 Mar. 1814.
14. Castlereagh to His Majesty's Commissioners, 28 July 1814: Londonderry, II, pp. 67–72.
15. Castlereagh to Commissioners at Ghent, 14 Aug. 1814, FO: Londonderry, II, pp. 86–91.
16. Earl Bathurst to Commissioners at Ghent, 18 Oct. 1814, FO: Londonderry, II, pp. 168–70.
17. Liverpool to Bathurst, 12 & 14 Sept. 1814: Bathurst, pp. 286–7.
18. Earl Bathurst to Commissioners at Ghent, 27 Sept. 1814, FO: Londonderry, II, pp. 139–40.
19. Castlereagh to Bathurst, 4 Oct. 1814: Bathurst, pp. 295–6.
20. Lambert. A. D., *The Last Sailing Battlefleet: Maintaining Naval Mastery 1815–1850*, pp. 2–16.
21. Liverpool to Bathurst, 11 Sept. 1814: *Wellington Dispatches*, Vol. IX, p. 240.
22. Liverpool to Wellington, 2 Sept. 1814: Yonge, C. D., *Life and Administration of the Second Earl of Liverpool*, II, pp. 24–7.
23. Bathurst to Sidmouth, 15 Sept. 1814, Downing Street: 152M/C1814/OF 15.

24. Sidmouth to Hiley Addington, 7 Oct. 1814: 152M/C1814/OZ 37.
25. Beckett to Sidmouth, 1 & 14 Oct. 1814, Paris: 152M/C/1814/OF 7–8.
26. Liverpool to Sidmouth, late October 1814: Pellew G., *The Life and Correspondence of Viscount Sidmouth*, Vol. III, p. 121.
27. Sidmouth to Charles Bathurst, 18 & 21 Oct. 1814: 152M/C1814/OZ 37.
28. Castlereagh to Nicholas Vansittart, 11 Nov. 1814, Vienna: Londonderry, III, p. 200.
29. Liverpool to Goulburn, 21 Oct. 1814: Yonge, II.
30. Liverpool to Castlereagh, 28 Oct. 1814: Yonge, II, pp. 46–7.
31. Liverpool to Castlereagh, Fife House, 2 Nov. 1814: Yonge, II, pp. 49–51.
32. Castlereagh to Liverpool, Nov. 1814: Yonge, II, pp. 52–3.
33. Liverpool to Castlereagh, 4 Nov. 1814, most secret and confidential, Fife House: Yonge, II, pp. 56–8.
34. Liverpool to Castlereagh, 18 Nov. 1814, most secret and confidential, Fife House: Yonge, II, pp. 62–4.
35. Duke of Wellington to Lord Liverpool, 18 Nov. 1814, Paris: Londonderry, III, pp. 203–4.
36. Garitee, pp. 241–4.
37. Joseph Marryat, Chairman of Lloyd's, to Admiralty, 19 Sept. 1814: ADM 1/39334.
38. Melville speech in House of Lords, 8 Nov. 1814, quoted in Fry, p. 321, from *Hansard XXIX*, Col. 11, & NLS MS 1046, f. 204.
39. Grenville speech in the House of Lords, 8 Nov. 1814: *Hansard XXIX*, Col. 14.
40. List of Ships taken etc., Treasury to Admiralty, 15 Nov. 1814: ADM 1/4297.
41. Arthur, pp. 163–4.
42. Smith. J. M., 'Privateering at the Periphery: Conceptualizing the War of 1812 in the North Atlantic'. I am indebted to Dr Smith for a copy of this paper. See also his book *Borderland Smuggling: Patriots, Loyalists, and Illicit Trade in the Northeast, 1783–1820*, for the wider context of 1812 smuggling and privateering.
43. Perkins, B., *Castlereagh and Adams: England and the United States*, University of California Press, Berkeley, 1964, remains the best account; P. W. Schroeder qualifies the American perspective.
44. Liverpool to Canning, Fife House, 28 Dec. 1814: Yonge, II, pp. 88–90; Renier, pp. 242–9.
45. Muir, p. 240
46. Yonge, II, p. 98 Thompson, N., *Earl Bathurst and the British Empire*, p. 84.
47. Sidmouth to Hiley Addington, 23 Dec. 1814: 152M/C/1814/OZ 37.

48. Sidmouth to Hiley Addington, 27 Dec. 1814, Whitehall: Pellew, III, p. 122; & Sidmouth to Pole Carew, 17 Jan. 1815: 152M/C/1815/OZ.

49. Bathurst to Baker, 31 Dec. 1814: Londonderry, III, pp. 231–2.

50. Liverpool to Castlereagh, 16 Jan. 1815: Londonderry, III, pp. 240–1.

51. Earl Bathurst to Baker, 21 Mar. 1815, FO: Londonderry, III, p. 281.

52. P. W. Schroeder, p. 574.

53. Cited by Arthur at p. 202.

54. Bartlett, p. 159.

55. Willson, B., *America's Ambassadors to England (1785–1928): A Narrative of Anglo-American Diplomatic Relations*, pp. 117–18.

56. Admiralty Minutes, 27 and 30 Dec. 1814, news of peace & details of where ships pay off: ADM 3/261.

57. Bartlett, pp. 158–9.

CHAPTER 12: Creating the American War of 1812

1. Adams, *Madison*, Vol. III, p. 63, a thoughtful analysis, far removed from the partisan approach of other nineteenth-century American authors, who lionise Decatur. Theodore Roosevelt, *The Naval War of 1812*, pp. 401–8, was critical of Decatur, but he was more concerned to score points off William James.

2. Hotham to Admiralty, 13 Feb. 1815, rec'd 20 Mar., no. 8: ADM 1/508, f. 831.

3. James, *Naval Occurrences* (1817), pp. 222–3. James, *Naval History*, Vol. VI, p. 534.

4. Adams, *Madison*, Vol. III, p. 70.

5. In this case an Algerian vessel. Leiner, F. C., *The End of Barbary Terror: America's 1815 War against the Pirates of North Africa*, 2005, p. 101.

6. Decatur to Secretary of the Navy, 18 Jan. 1815: James, *Naval Occurrences* (1817), pp. 379–81.

7. Cooper, pp. 429–32.

8. O. H. Perry to Crowninshield, 28 Jan. 1815: RG45 CL 1815, vol. 1, no. 82.

9. Leiner, *Barbary Terror*, pp. 40–1.

10. Log 22 Feb. 1815, HMS *Superb*: ADM 51/2051.

11. Decatur to Crowninshield, 20 Feb. 1815 (HMS *Narcissus*): RG45 CL 1815, vol. 1, no. 144.

12. Decatur to Crowninshield, 6 Mar. 1815: from NY RG45 CL, microfilm 125, reel 43, no. 16.

13. Decatur to Crowninshield, 6 Mar. 1815: James, *Naval Occurrences*, p. 382.

14. Crowninshield to Decatur, 14 Mar. 1815: RG45; Sec. of Navy letters, microfilm 149; p. 60.

15. Crowninshield to Decatur, 14 Mar. 1815: cited in Leiner, *Barbary*

Terror, p. 56, from the Crowninshield Collection, Peabody Essex Museum.

16. Decatur to Crowninshield, 20 Mar. 1815: cited in Leiner, *Barbary Terror*, p. 56, from the Crowninshield Collection, Peabody Essex Museum.

17. James, *Naval Occurrences*, pp. 213–19.

18. Transcript and Report of the Court of Inquiry: RG125, vol. 6, no. 202.

19. Commodore Murray to Crowninshield, 17 Apr. 1815: James, *Naval Occurrences*, pp. 382–4.

20. Comments by Commodore John Rodgers: Leiner, *Barbary Terror*, p. 59; James, *Naval Occurrences*, p. 383;

21. Leiner, *Barbary Terror*, pp. 87–150.

22. Leiner, *Barbary Terror*, p. 177.

23. A typical use for an old warship, as a harbour auxiliary to lift masts in and out of front-line warships.

24. *National Intelligencer*, 23 May 1815: cited by T. G. Martin, at p. 206.

25. T. G. Martin, pp. 207, 239–47.

26. Gardiner, *1812*, p. 17.

27. Long, *Porter*, pp. 185–8.

28. McKee, p. 202.

29. Perkins, pp. 96–9.

30. Roland et al, pp. 101–2.

31. Leiner, *Millions for Defense*, pp. 161 & 236 n. 5.

32. North, pp. 47–9; & *Michele Felice Cornè* Exhibition Catalogue.

33. Smith, P. C. F., *The Frigate* Essex *Papers: Building the Salem Frigate, 1798–1799*, pp. 32–5.

34. Leiner, *Millions for Defense*, pp. 165–76.

35. Leiner, *Millions for Defense*, pp. 144–6, McKee, pp. 106–7.

36. Leiner, *Millions*, pp. 2–10.

37. Watts, S., *The Republic Reborn: War and the Making of Liberal America, 1790–1820*, p. 216. Brown, R. S., *The Republic in Peril: 1812*.

38. Watts, pp. 246–7, & Garitee, *The Republic's Private Navy*, for Baltimore's politico-economic interests.

39. Mahan, *1812*, II, p. 204.

40. Onuf, pp. 118–31.

41. Stagg, *Mr Madison's War*, p. xii.

42. Clark, T. D. & Guice, J. D. W., *Frontiers in Conflict: The Old Southwest, 1795–1830*, pp. 82, 84.

43. Watts, S., *The Republic Reborn*. Rossignol, J.-M., 'Indians, Settlers and Soldiers: The War of 1812 and Southern Expansionism', in Adams, D. K. & van Minnen, C. A., eds, *Aspects of War in American History*, p. 46.

44. Clark & Guice, pp. 84, 97, 122–3.

45. Clark & Guice, pp. 63–5, 119.
46. Turner, F. J., *The Frontier in American History*, pp. 168, 213.
47. Oakes, J., *The Ruling Race: A History of American Slaveholders*, pp. 76, 87.
48. Martin, J. W., *Sacred Revolt: The Muskogee's Struggle for a New World*, pp. 107–8, 121–6.
49. Rossignol, p. 53.
50. G. A. Smith, p. 125.
51. Clark & Guice, p. 149, citing Remini, R. V., *Andrew Jackson and the Course of American Empire, 1767–1821*, Viking, New York, 1977, p. 227.
52. Turner, p. 168.
53. Watts, pp. 207–9, 229–32, 237–8, 249, 222, 276–84 & 309.
54. Grant, S.-M., *North over South: Northern Nationalism and American Identity in the Antebellum Era*, p. 1.
55. Albert Gallatin to Matthew Lyon, 7 May 1816, quoted in Grant, p. 26.
56. Grant, pp. 46, 69, 1, 27 & 51.
57. Oakes, pp. 137–8.
58. Grenier, J., *The First Way of War: American War Making on the Frontier, 1607–1814*, an important corrective to an old debate.
59. Garitee.
60. Graves, D., *The Battle of Lundy's Lane: On the Niagara in 1814*.
61. See the second USS *Vixen* as an example of a privateer schooner bought into naval service: Silverstone, p. 47.
62. Schroeder, J. H., *Shaping a Maritime Empire: The Commercial and Diplomatic Role of the American Navy, 1829–1861*, Greenwood Press, Westport, Conn., 1985, p. 188.
63. Roland et al.
64. Fulton to Trumbull, 16 Dec. 1806, quoted in Perkins, pp. 97–8.
65. Perkins, p. 99.
66. Bercovitch, S. & Patell, C. R. K., eds, *The Cambridge History of American Literature: Volume 1, 1590–1820*, pp. 541–59.
67. Bercovitch, pp. 372–3.
68. Bercovitch, pp. 664–67, 670.
69. Randolph speeches of 5 & 6 Mar. 1806: Perkins, pp. 111–12.
70. For his engraved views of 'patriotic' locations, see Shanes, E., *Turner's Rivers, Harbour and Coasts*; also Colley, L., *Britons: Forging the Nation, 1707–1837*.
71. Brockmann, R. J., *Commodore Robert Stockton 1795–1866: Protean Man for Protean Nation*, pp. 9–14 & 461–2.
72. Wilmerding, J., *American Art*, Ch. 1–9, esp. pp. 31, 38–50.
73. Smith, E. N., *American Naval Broadsides: A Collection of Early Naval Prints (1745–1815)*; see the foreword by M. V. Brewington, p. xvi.

74. E. N. Smith, p. 51. The pictures were published three months after the action.

75. Maloney, pp. 200–2, 434, 501–2. *Michele Cornè*, pp. 18–20. Cornè lived in Boston between 1807 and 1822.

76. Wilmerding J., *American Marine Painting*, pp. 69–72, see p. 70 for the engraved version of the *Constitution–Guerriere* action. Henceforth Wilmerding 1987.

77. Wilmerding 1987, p. xi.

78. Wilmerding 1987, pp. 64–6, 73. Wilton, A. & Baringer, T., *American Sublime: Landscape Painting in the United States 1820–1880*, pp. 20–1.

79. Wilmerding 1987, pp. 74–7, 81–3, 110–11.

80. Wilmerding 1987, p. 80; see Crawford III frontispiece for Lake Champlain. Lake Erie is on the cover of Dudley II.

81. Foster, K. A., *Thomas Chambers: American Marine and Landscape Painter 1808–1869*, for the career of an English-born immigrant artist producing popular images of sea battles.

82. Brewington, in E. N. Smith, p. xiv.

83. Wilmerding 1987, pp. 86–7. However, the image on p. 86 is clearly mis-captioned. It must be the *Constitution* escaping from Broke's squadron.

84. Wilmerding 1987, p. 88. E. N. Smith, pp. 188–91.

85. Kime, W. R., ed., *Washington Irving: Miscellaneous Writings 1803–1859: Volume I*, pp. 295–309.

86. See the many references to Irving in Gleaves, *James Lawrence*.

87. Kime, pp. 69–70.

88. Kime, pp. xxvii–ix, 73–7, & note from the September issue of the *Analectic* pp. 73–8.

89. E. N. Smith, p. 144. Chappell's print was published by Johnson, Fry of New York: SRO HA 93 13/21.

90. Mitnick, B. J. & Mewschutt, D., *The Portraits and History Paintings of Alonzo Chappell*, pp. 51–2, 58; the quote at p. 51 was taken from Spencer's *History*, Vol. III, p. 196. The picture was bought by President Franklin D. Roosevelt, an enthusiastic War of 1812 collector.

91. Dennis, D. L., 'The Action between the *Shannon* and the *Chesapeake*', *The Mariner's Mirror*, 1959, pp. 36–45 at p. 40; a useful analysis of the historiography.

92. Gleaves, pp. 148 & 150.

93. Dudley II, p. 126.

94. Kime, pp. 132, 94–5.

95. Bercovitch, p. 668.

96. Hellmann, G. S., *Washington Irving*, p. 87. Long, *Porter*, pp. 172–3. Porter sought this command, which may explain how Irving became involved. Decatur recognised the value of embarking a friendly author, seeking to repeat Porter's celebrity.

97. Hellmann, p. 101.
98. Philbrick, T., *James Fenimore Cooper and the Development of American Sea Fiction*, p. 39.
99. Haeger, pp. 210, 263–4.
100. Kime, p. xxix.
101. *The Port Folio* 3rd series 2.115 (1813) cited in Philbrick, pp. 1–2
102. Philbrick, pp. 15, 20–2.
103. For the publication history of the Lawrence biography, see *Washington Irving: A Bibliography*, New York, 1933, pp. 14 & 55.
104. Hellman, p. 82. Long, *Porter*, pp. 35–7, 71–2.
105. Long, *Porter*, p. 171.
106. The second edition *To which is now added an introduction [etc.]* appeared in 1822. See Long, *Porter*, pp. 71–2, & 331–2. Bercovitch et al, p. 763, list it as an 'Important Text on or concerning the New World', the only naval work so noted for this period.
107. *The Quarterly Review*, Vol. XIII, July 1815 (published early December 1815), art 4. Long, *Porter*, pp. 72–3, 331–2.
108. Shine, H. & Shine, H. C., *The Quarterly Review under Gifford: Identification of Contributors*, p. 48.
109. James, *Naval Occurrences* (1817), p. 73.
110. Long, *Porter*, p. 72.
111. Bercovitch, pp. 692–3.
112. Franklin, W., *James Fenimore Cooper: The Early Years*, p. 160, quoting Cooper's *History of the Navy*, Vol II, p. 123.
113. Bercovitch, pp. 676–83, quote at p. 680.
114. Cooper went to Europe in 1826, and only returned to the United States in 1836. In the interval his anxiety to write the *History* was overtaken by pressing financial need. Franklin, pp. 483, 519, 160–1.
115. Franklin, pp. 298–90, 402–3; Philbrick, pp. 45–7, 54, 58.
116. Philbrick, p. 85.
117. Philbrick, pp. 115, 121, 124–7, 134; Franklin, pp. 163–78.
118. Cooper, Vol. 2, pp. 253–4, cited in Franklin, pp. 178–9.
119. Bercovitch, p. 690, and Wilton & Barringer, pp. 14, 20, 23.
120. Berube & Rodgaard, p. 250. As Christopher McKee has noted, Stewart had a long history of inventive recollection, and the quote was pitch-perfect for Northern audiences in 1861:McKee, C., *Edward Preble: A Naval Biography, 1761–1807*, p. 386.

CHAPTER 13: The Challenge Answered

1. Martineau, pp. 102, 140.
2. *Endymion* log: ADM 51/2324.
3. Graham (First Lord of the Admiralty) to Lord Stanley, 18 Sept. 1833: Graham MS 28 Microfilm.

4. Lecky, p. 10. In 1904 Captain Herbert King-Hall asked if the two Bermuda vases could be loaned to his *Endymion* as 'nothing would have a greater effect on the Esprit de Corps of the Ship's company'. ADM 203/9.

5. Sir George Grey (Commander-in-Chief at Plymouth) to Croker, 30 Mar. 1815: Croker MS 1512 Box 1815, Clements Library.

6. Gardiner, *Frigates*, p. 97.

7. The only other USS *President*, a 12-gun sloop operating on Lake Champlain, was taken by the British in 1814 and renamed *Icicle*. *Dictionary of American Naval Fighting Ships*, Vol. V, pp. 371–2.

8. Graham to Cockburn, 24 Jan. 1834: Graham MS 52; Morriss, pp. 210, 222.

9. Tracy, pp. 212–15.

10. Broke to Louisa, 29 July 1813: SRO HA 9 9/150, and Padfield, p. 150.

11. E. N. Smith, pp. 134–7.

12. Tracy, pp. 213–14.

13. SRO HA93 13/ 18–26 contains pictures of the action.

14. Brighton, *Wallis*, p. 179.

15. Wellington to Broke, 17 July 1830: SRO HA 9 9/330.

16. Gardiner, *Frigates*, p. 147.

17. *The Chesapeake Mill* pamphlet.

18. Beresford to Broke, 22 May 1833: Brighton, p. 93.

19. Almost eighty years after the *Shannon*'s great battle Provo Wallis went to his grave an admiral of the fleet and the last of his age. The interment was saluted by a naval firing party from HMS *Excellent* commanded by Captain Percy Scott, who would do for Edwardian naval gunnery what Broke did for that of mad King George. Other mourners included Captain Henry Kane, who took HMS *Calliope* out of Apia harbour in Samoa when the entire American and German squadrons were wrecked in a hurricane, and Geoffrey Phipps Hornby, the greatest of Victoria's admirals. Wallis had been a major contributor to the restoration of Nelson's church at Burnham Thorpe. (Brighton, *Wallis*, p. 295, and information supplied by Mr Michael Tapper, Church Warden.)

Bibliography

ARCHIVE SOURCES

The National Archives of the United Kingdom (TNA)

ADM series Admiralty Correspondence.
  1. In Letters 501, 502
  2. Out Letters,
  3. Minutes
  51. Ship's Log Books
  52. Ship's Masters' Logs
  101. Surgeons' Log Books
  102. Halifax Hospital Log Books.
CO Colonial Office Correspondence
HCA High Court of Admiralty
WO War Office

National Archives of the United States

I am indebted to Dr Michael Crawford for generously providing me with copies of the RG45 papers relating to the capture of the USS *President*. Much of this series will be published in Volume IV of the essential documentary collection *The Naval War of 1812* in 2012.

The British Library

Add MS Additional Manuscripts series
  Liverpool Papers
  Sir James Graham Papers

The National Maritime Museum (UK)

  WAR Warren Papers
  HUL Hulbert Papers
  AGC Hillyar Papers

National Archives of Scotland

  Melville Family Muniments
  Hope Family MS

National Library of Scotland

Alexander Cochrane Correspondence

Devon Record Office

Sidmouth Papers

Hull Record Office

Henry Hotham Papers

Suffolk Record Office

Broke Papers.

William L. Clements Library, Ann Arbor, University of Michigan

War of 1812 Collection
Melville Papers
Croker papers

Perkins Library, Duke University

Croker Papers

OFFICIAL PUBLICATIONS

Hansard British Parliamentary Debates, 1812–1815

Three volumes have so far been published of W. Dudley and M. Crawford (eds), *The Naval War of 1812: A Documentary History* (Naval Historical Center, Washington, 1985, 1992 & 2002). A fourth and final volume is expected in 2012. This excellent collection is the key source for the subject and the quality of the editorial process is immediately evident to anyone who has used the relevant archives. I have cited this source wherever possible, for ease of access for those wishing to follow up references.

BOOKS

Adams, H., ed., *The Writings of Albert Gallatin*, Vol. 1, Lippincott, Philadelphia, 1879

Adams, H., *History of the United States during the Administration of James Madison*, Vol. VII, Scribner's, New York, 1896

Albion, R. G., with Pope, J. B., *The Rise of New York Port: 1815–1860*, New York, 1939

American Vessels captured by the British during the Revolution and War of 1812. Nova Scotia Vice Admiralty Court, Essex Institute, Salem, Massachussets, 1911

Antal, S., *A Wampum Denied: Procter's War of 1812*, Ottawa, 1997

Arthur, B., *How Britain Won the War of 1812: The Royal Navy's Blockades of the United States, 1812–1815*, Boydell & Brewer, Woodbridge, 2011

Aspinall, A., ed., *The Later Correspondence of King George III*, Vol. IV, Cambridge University Press, 1968

Bartlett, C. J., 'Gentlemen versus Democrats: Cultural Prejudice and Military Strategy in the War of 1812', *War in History*, Vol. 1, No. 2, 1994

Bathurst, Earl, Historical Manuscripts Commission, *Manuscripts of Earl Bathurst*, HMSO, London, 1923

Beck, J., *The Falmouth Post Office Packet Service 1689–1850*, South-West Maritime History Society, Exeter, 2009

Bercovitch, S. & Patell, C. R. K., eds, *The Cambridge History of American Literature: Volume 1, 1590–1820*, Cambridge University Press, 1994

Berube, C. & Rodgaard, J., *A Call to the Sea: Captain Charles Stewart of the USS Constitution*, Potomac Books, Washington, 2005

Bhagat, G., 'Americans and American Trade in India 1784–1814', *The American Neptune*, Vol. XLVI, No. 1, 1986, pp. 6–15

Bourchier, E., ed., *Memoir of the Life of Admiral Sir Edward Codrington*, Longmans Green, London, 1873

Brenton, E. P., *The Naval History of Great Britain*, Vol. II, London, 1837

Brighton, J. G., *Admiral Sir P. B. V. Broke: A Memoir*, Hutchinson, London, 1864

——, *Admiral of the Fleet Sir Provo W. P. Wallis*, Hutchinson, London, 1892

Brockmann, R. J., *Commodore Robert Stockton 1795–1866: Protean Man for Protean Nation*, Cambria Press, Amherst, 2009

Brodine, C. E., 'The Pacific Cruise of the Frigate *Essex*', in Brodine, C. E., Crawford, M. J. & Hughes C. F., eds, *Against All Odds: U.S. Sailors in the War of 1812*, US Naval Historical Center, Washington, 2004, at pp. 1–26.

Brown, R., *The Republic in Peril, 1812*, Columbia University Press, New York, 1964

Buel, R., *In Irons: Britain's Naval Supremacy and the American Revolutionary Economy*, Yale University Press, 1998

Burrows, M., *Memoir of Admiral Sir Henry Ducie Chads*, Griffin & Co, Portsmouth, 1869

Campbell, G., *The Road to Canada: The Grand Communications Route from Saint John to Quebec*, New Brunswick Centre for Military History, Fredericton, New Brunswick, 2005

Cannell, H., *Lightning Strikes: How Ships are Protected from Lightning*, Book Guild Publishing, Brighton, 2011

Canney, D. L., *Sailing Warships of the United States Navy*, Chatham, London, 2001

Carden, J., ed. Atkinson, C. T., *Memoir of Admiral Carden*, Oxford University Press, 1912

Chapelle, H. I., *The Baltimore Clipper: Its Origin and Development*, Salem, Mass., 1930

——, *The History of American Sailing Ships*, Bonanza Books, New York, 1935

The Chesapeake Mill pamphlet pub. at the mill in West Wickham, Hampshire, n.d.

Clark, T. D. & Guice, J. D. W., *Frontiers in Conflict: The Old Southwest, 1795–1830*, University of New Mexico Press, 1989

Clowes, Sir W. L., *The Royal Navy*, Vol. VI, Sampson, Low, London, 1901

Cochrane, A., *The Fighting Cochranes*, Quiller Press, London, 1983

Coeletta, P., ed., *American Secretaries of the Navy*, Vol. I, US Naval Institute Press [USNIP], Annapolis, 1980

Colley, L., *Britons: Forging the Nation, 1707–1837*, Yale University Press, 1992

Cooper, J. F., *History of the Navy of the United States of America*, 3rd edn, Philadelphia, 1841

Corbett, J. S., *Some Principles of Maritime Strategy*, Longman, London, 1911

——, 'Napoleon and the British Navy after Trafalgar', Privately printed, London, 1923

Michele Felice Cornè, Exhibition Catalogue, Peabody Museum, Salem, 1972

Craig, H., ed., 'Letters of Lord St. Vincent', in Lloyd, C., ed., *The Naval Miscellany IV*, Navy Records Society, London, 1952

Crowhurst, P., *The Defence of British Trade, 1689–1815*, Dawson, London, 1977

Cusick, J. G., *The Other War of 1812: The Patriot War and the American Invasion of Spanish East Florida*, University of Georgia, 2007

Day, A., *The Admiralty Hydrographic Service 1795–1919*, HMSO, London, 1967

Dening, G., 'The Face of Battle: Valparaiso 1814', in *Performances*, University of Chicago Press, 1996

Dennis, D. L., 'The Action between the *Shannon* and the *Chesapeake*', *The Mariner's Mirror*, 1959

Dickinson, H. W., *Educating the Royal Navy: Eighteenth- and nineteenth-century education for officers*, Routledge, Abingdon, 2007

Dictionary of American Naval Fighting Ships, Vol. V, Washington, 1970

Douglas, Sir H., *Naval Gunnery*, 4th edn, London, 1855

Dudley, W., *Splintering the Wooden Wall: The British Blockade of the United States, 1812–1815*, USNIP, Annapolis, 2003

Dudley, W. & Crawford, M., eds, *The Naval War of 1812: A Documentary History*, Vols I–III, Washington, 1985, 1992 & 2002

Duffy, S. W. H., *Captain Blakeley and the Wasp*, USNIP, Annapolis, 2001

Dye, I, *The Fatal Cruise of the Argus*, USNIP, 1994

Eckert, E. K., *The Navy Department in the War of 1812*, University of Florida Press, 1973

Eshelman, R. E., Sheads, S. S. & Hickey, D. R., *The War of 1812 in the Chesapeake: A Reference to Historic Sites in Maryland, Virginia, and the District of Columbia*, Johns Hopkins University Press, Baltimore, 2010

Everest, A. S., *The War of 1812 in the Champlain Valley*, Syracuse, NY, 1981

Faulkner, H. U., *American Economic History*, New York, 1960

Foreman, S., *Shoes and Ships and Sealing Wax: An Illustrated History of the Board of Trade, 1786–1986*, HMSO, London, 1986

Foster, K. A., *Thomas Chambers: American Marine and Landscape Painter 1808–1869*, Yale University Press, 2009

Franklin, W., *James Fenimore Cooper: The Early Years*, Yale University Press, 2007

Fredericksen, J. C., ed., *Free Trade and Sailors' Rights: A Bibliography of the War of 1812*, Westport, Connecticut, 1985

Fry, M., *The Dundas Despotism*, Edinburgh University Press, 1992

Fulton, R., *Torpedo War and Submarine Explosions*, New York, 1810

Gardiner, R., ed., *The Naval War of 1812*, Conway, London, 1998

——, *Frigates of the Napoleonic Wars*, Chatham, London, 2000

Garitee, J. R., *The Republic's Private Navy: The American Privateering Business as practised by Baltimore during the War of 1812*, Mystic, Connecticut, 1977

Gleaves, A., *James Lawrence, Captain, United States Navy, Commander of the 'Chesapeake'*, Putnam, New York, 1904

Glover, R., *Britain at Bay: Defence against Bonaparte, 1803–1814*, London, 1973

Graham G. S. & Humphreys, R. A., eds, *The Navy and South America, 1807–1823: Correspondence of the Commanders-in-Chief on the South American Station*, Navy Records Society, London, 1962

Grant, S.-M., *North over South: Northern Nationalism and American Identity in the Antebellum Era*, University Press of Kansas, Lawrence, 2000

Graves, D. E., *The Battle of Lundy's Lane: On the Niagara in 1814*, Baltimore, 1983

——, *Red Coats and Grey Jackets: The Battle of Chippawa, 5 July 1814*, Toronto, 1994

Grenier, J., *The First Way of War: American War Making on the Frontier, 1607–1814*, Cambridge University Press, 2005

Gutridge, A. C., 'George Redmond Hulbert: A Prize Agent on the North American Station, 1812–1814', *Bermuda Journal of Archaeology and Maritime History*, Vol. 2, 1990, pp. 105–26

Gwyn, J., *Frigates and Foremasts: The North American Squadron in Nova Scotian Waters, 1745–1815*, University of British Columbia Press, Vancouver, 2003

Haeger, J. D., *John Jacob Astor: Business and Finance in the Early Republic*, Wayne State University, Detroit, 1991

Hall, C. D., *British Strategy in the Napoleonic War, 1803–15*, Manchester University Press, 1992

Hamilton, C. I., *The Making of the Modern Admiralty: British Naval Policy-Making, 1805–1927*, Cambridge University Press, 2011

Harland, J., *Seamanship in the Age of Sail*, Conway, London, 1984

Harrington, G. K., 'The American Naval Challenge to the English East India Company during the War of 1812', in Sweetman, J., ed., *New Interpretations in Naval History: the tenth Naval History Symposium at Annapolis, 1991*, USNIP, Annapolis, 1993

Hellman, G. S., *Washington Irving*, London, 1924, p. 82.

Herring, G. C., *From Colony to Superpower: U.S. Foreign Relations since 1776*, Oxford University Press, New York, 2008

Hickey, D. R., *The War of 1812: A Forgotten Conflict*, Urbana, Illinois, 1989
——, *Don't Give up the Ship! Myths of the War of 1812*, Illinois University Press, 2006

Hill, P. P., *Napoleon's Troublesome Americans: Franco-American Relations, 1804–1815*, Potomac Books, Dulles, Virginia, 2005

Hitsman, J. M., *The Incredible War of 1812*, Toronto, 1965

Horden, P. & Purcell, N., *The Corrupting Sea: A Study of Mediterranean History*, Basil Blackwell, Oxford, 2000

Humphreys, R. A., 'British Merchants and South American Independence', The British Academy Raleigh Lecture 1965, *Proceedings of the British Academy*, Vol. LI, 1965, pp. 151–74

James, W., *An Inquiry into the Merits of the Principal Naval Actions between Great Britain and the United States*, Doull, Halifax, Nova Scotia, 1816
——, *A Full and Correct Account of the Chief Naval Occurrences of the late war between Great Britain and the United States of America*, London, 1817
——, *The Naval History of Great Britain During the French Revolutionary and Napoleonic Wars*, London, 1826. Vols V & VI contain the final, but not the most detailed version of James's account of the Naval War of 1812. They must be read alongside the 1817 text. The 1817 and 1826 texts have been reprinted with new introductions: Conway, London, 2002 and 2004.

Jenkins, B., *Henry Goulburn 1784–1856: A Political Biography*, Quebec, 1996

Kastor, P. J., *The Nation's Crucible; The Louisiana Purchase and the Creation of America*, Yale University Press, New Haven, 2004

Kert, F. M., *Prize and Prejudice: Privateering and Naval Prize in Atlantic Canada in the War of 1812*, International Maritime Economic Association, St John's, Newfoundland, 1997
——, *Trimming Yankee Sails: Pirates and Privateers of New Brunswick*, Fredericton, New Brunswick, 2005

Kime, W. R., ed., *Washington Irving: Miscellaneous Writings 1803–1859: Volume I*, Twayne Publishers, Boston, 1981

Lambert, A. D., *The Last Sailing Battlefleet: Maintaining Naval Mastery 1815–1850*, Conway, London, 1991

——, 'Introduction', in James, W., *The Naval History of Great Britain*, (1828) Conway, London, 2002

——, *Nelson: Britannia's God of War*, Faber, London, 2004

Langley, H. D., *A History of Medicine in the Early U.S. Navy*, Johns Hopkins University Press, Baltimore, 1995

Latimer, J., *1812: War with America*, Harvard University Press, 2007

Lecky, H. S., *The King's Ships*, Vol. III, London, 1910

Le Fevre, P., 'Sir John Borlase Warren 1753–1822', in Le Fevre, P. & Harding, R., eds, *British Admirals of the Napoleonic Wars: The Contemporaries of Nelson*, Chatham, London, 2005

Leiner, F. C., *Millions for Defense: the Subscription Warships of 1798*, USNIP, Annapolis, 2000

——, *The End of Barbary Terror: America's 1815 War against the Pirates of North Africa*, New York, 2005

Lewis, E. R., *Seacoast Fortifications of the United States: An Introductory History*, USNIP, Annapolis, 1993

Lieven, D., *Russian Against Napoleon: The True Story of the Campaign of War and Peace*, Viking, New York, 2010

Londonderry, Marquess, ed., *Memoirs and Correspondence of Viscount Castlereagh*, 12 vols, London, 1848–53

Long, D. F., *Nothing too Daring: A biography of Commodore David Porter, 1783–1843*, USNIP, Annapolis, 1970

——, *Sailor-Diplomat: A Biography of Commodore James Biddle, 1783–1848*, Boston, 1983

McKee, C., *A Gentlemanly and Honourable Profession: The Creation of the U.S. Naval Officer Corps, 1794–1815*, Annapolis, 1991

——, *Edward Preble: A Naval Biography, 1761–1807*, USNIP, 1972

Maclay, E. S., *A History of American Privateers*, New York, 1899

Maffeo, S., *Most Secret and Confidential: Intelligence in the Age of Nelson*, USNIP, 2000

Mahan, A. T., *The Influence of Sea Power upon History, 1660–1783*, Little, Brown, Boston, 1889

——, *The Influence of Sea Power upon the French Revolution and Empire 1792–1812*, 2 vols, Little, Brown, Boston, 1893

——, *Sea Power in its Realation to the War of 1812*, Little, Brown, Boston, 1905

Maloney, L. M., *The Captain from Connecticut: The Life and Naval Times of Isaac Hull*, Northeastern University Press, Boston, 1986

Marolda, E. J., *The Washington Navy Yard: An Illustrated History*, Naval Historical Center, Washington, 1999

Marshall, J., *Royal Naval Biography, or Memoirs of the Services of all the Flag Officers etc.*, 12 vols, London, 1823–35

——, *Naval Biography: Supplementary Volume I*, London, 1827

Martin, J. W., *Sacred Revolt: The Muskogee's Struggle for a New World*, Boston, 1991

Martin, T. G., *A Most Fortunate Ship: A Narrative History of Old Ironsides*, USNIP, Annapolis, 2nd edn, 1996

Martineau, G., *Napoleon Surrenders*, John Murray, London, 1971

Mitnick, B. J. & Mewschutt, D., *The Portraits and History Paintings of Alonzo Chappell*, Brandywine River Museum, Pennsylvania, 1992

Morriss, R., *Cockburn and the British Navy in Transition: Admiral Sir George Cockburn, 1772–1853*, Exeter University Press, 1997

Melvin, F. E., *Napoleon's Navigation System*, New York, 1919

Muir, R., *Britain and the Defeat of Napoleon, 1807–1815*, Yale University Press, 1996

Munch-Petersen, T., *Defying Napoleon: How Britain bombarded Copenhagen and seized the Danish Fleet in 1807*, Sutton Publishing, Stroud, 2007

The Naval Chronicle

North, D. C., *The Economic Growth of the United States 1790–1860*, New York, 1966

Oakes, J., *The Ruling Race: A History of American Slaveholders*, New York, 1982

Onuf, P. S., *Jefferson's Empire: The Language of American Nationhood*, University Press of Virginia, Charlottesville, 2000

Padfield, P., *Broke and the Shannon*, Hodder & Stoughton, London, 1968

Palmer, M. J., 'The Battle of Lake Champlain', in Brodine, C. E., Crawford, M. J. & Hughes C. F., eds, *Against All Odds: U.S. Sailors in the War of 1812*, US Naval Historical Center, Washington, 2004, pp. 53–72

Parkinson, C. N., *War in the Eastern Seas, 1793–1815*, Allen & Unwin, London, 1954

Paullin, C. O., *Commodore John Rodgers, 1773–1838*, Cleveland, 1910

Pellew, G., *The Life and Correspondence of Viscount Sidmouth*, Vol. III, London, 1847

Perkins, B., *Prologue to War: England and the United States 1805–1812*, University of California Press, Berkeley, 1961

Petrie, D. A., *The Prize Game: Lawful Looting on the High Seas during the Days of Fighting Sail*, USNIP, Annapolis, 1999

Philbrick, T., *James Fenimore Cooper and the Development of American Sea Fiction*, Harvard University Press, 1961

Porter, D., *Journal of a Cruise to the Pacific Ocean by Captain David Porter in the United States Frigate Essex, in the years 1812, 1813, and 1814,*

Containing descriptions of the Cape de Verde Islands, Coasts of Brazil, Patagonia, Chile and of the Galapagos Islands, 2 vols, Bradford and Inskip, Philadelphia, 1815

The second edition *To which is now added an introduction, in which the charges contained in the Quarterly Review, of the first edition of this Journal and examined* appeared in 1822 (Wiley and Halstead, New York)

Pullen, H. F., *The Shannon and the Chesapeake*, McCleland & Stewart, Toronto, 1970

——, *March of the Seamen*, Halifax Maritime Museum, 1991

Reilly, R., *The British at the Gates: The New Orleans Campaign in the War of 1812*, New York, 1974

Remini, R. V., *The Battle of New Orleans: Andrew Jackson and America's First Military Victory*, Viking, New York, 1999

Renier, G. J., *Great Britain and the Establishment of the Kingdom of the Netherlands, 1813–1815*, George Allen, London, 1930

Reynolds, J., *Pride of Baltimore II: Renaissance of the Baltimore Clipper*, Baltimore, n.d.

Robson, M., *Britain, Portugal and South America in the Napoleonic Wars: Alliances and Diplomacy in Economic Maritime Conflict*, I. B. Tauris, London, 2011

Roland, A., Bolster, W. J. & Keyssar, A., *The Way of the Ship: America's Maritime History Re-envisioned, 1600–2000*, John Wiley & Sons, Hoboken, NJ, 2008

Roosevelt, T., *Naval History of the War of 1812*, New York, 1882

Rose, J. H. & Broadley, A. M., *Dumouriez and the Defence of England Against Napoleon*, Bodley Head, London, 1909

Rossignol, J.-M., 'Indians, Settlers and Soldiers: The War of 1812 and Southern Expansionism', in Adams, D. K. & van Minnen, C. A., eds, *Aspects of War in American History*, Keele University Press, 1997

Rubinstein, H., *Trafalgar Captain: Durham of the Defiance*, Tempus, Gloucestershire, 2005

Schroeder, J. H., *Commodore John Rodgers: Paragon of the Early American Navy*, USNIP, Annapolis, 2006

Schroeder, P. W., *The Transformation of European Politics, 1763–1848*, Clarendon Press, 1994

Scott, J., *Recollections of a Naval Life*, Richard Bentley, London, 1834

Shanes, E., *Turner's Rivers, Harbour and Coasts*, Chatto & Windus, London, 1981

Shaw, E., *Narrative of his 21 years' service in the American Navy*, Rochester, New York, 3rd edn, 1845

Shea, I. & Watts, H., *Deadman's: Melville Island and its Burial Ground*, Halifax, 2005

Sherwig, J. M., *Guineas and Gunpowder: British Foreign Aid in the Wars with France, 1793–1815*, Harvard University Press, 1969

Shine, H. & Shine, H. C., *The Quarterly Review under Gifford: Identification of Contributors*, University of North Carolina Press, Chapel Hill, 1949

Shomette, D., *Flotilla: The Patuxent Naval Campaign in the War of 1812*, Johns Hopkins University Press, Baltimore, 2009

Shulman, M. R., *Navalism and the Emergence of American Sea Power, 1882–1893*, Annapolis, 1995

Silverstone, P. H., *The Sailing Navy, 1775–1854*, USNIP, Annapolis, 2001

Smith, E. A., *Lord Grey, 1764–1845*, Oxford University Press, 1990

Smith, E. N., *American Naval Broadsides: A Collection of Early Naval Prints (1745–1815)*, Philadelphia Maritime Museum, New York, 1974

Smith, G. A., *'For the Purposes of Defense': The Politics of the Jeffersonian Gunboat Program*, University of Delaware Press, Newark, 1995

Smith, J. M., *'Privateering at the Periphery: Conceptualizing the War of 1812 in the North Atlantic'*, paper presented to the 14th Naval History Symposium at the U.S. Naval Academy, 25 Sept. 1999

——, *Borderland Smuggling: Patriots, Loyalists, and Illicit Trade in the Northeast, 1783–1820*, University of Florida Press, Gainesville, 2006

——, *Battle for the Bay: The Naval War of 1812*, Fredericton, New Brunswick, 2011

Smith, P. C. F., *The Frigate* Essex *Papers: Building the Salem Frigate, 1798–1799*, Peabody Museum, Salem, 1974

Snider, C. H. J., *Under the Red Jack*, Toronto, n.d.

Spiers, E. M., *Radical General: Sir George de Lacy Evans, 1787–1870*, Manchester University Press, 1983

Stagg, J. C. A., *Mr. Madison's War: Politics, Diplomacy and Warfare in the early American Republic 1783–1830*, Princeton University Press, 1985

——, *'James Madison and George Matthews: The East Florida Revolution of 1812 Reconsidered'*, *Diplomatic History*, Vol. 30, No. 1, 2006

Stanley, G. F. G., *The War of 1812: Land Operations*, Ottawa, 1983

Statham-Drew, P., *James Stirling: Admiral and Founding Governor of Western Australia*, University of Western Australia Press, Crowley, 2003

Symonds, C. L., *Navalists and Antinavalists: The Naval Policy of the United States, 1785–1827*, New Jersey, 1980

Tagart, E., *A Memoir of the late Captain Heywood RN*, London, 1822

Thomas, H., *The Slave Trade: The History of the Atlantic Slave Trade, 1440–1870*, London, 1997

Thompson, N., *Earl Bathurst and the British Empire*, Leo Cooper, London, 1999

Thorne, R. G., ed., *The House of Commons, 1790–1820*, Vols. I–V, Houses of Parliament Trust, London, 1986

Tracy, N., *Britannia's Palette: The Arts of Naval Victory*, McGill–Queen's University Press, Montreal & Kingston, 2007

Tucker, S. C., *Arming the Fleet: U.S. Navy Ordnance in the Muzzle-Loading Era*, Annapolis, 1989

——, *The Jeffersonian Gunboat Navy*, University of South Carolina Press, Columbia, 1993

——, *Stephen Decatur: A Life Most Bold and Daring*, Annapolis, 2005

Tucker, S. C. & Reuter, F. T., *Injured Honor: The Chesapeake–Leopard Affair June 22, 1807*, USNIP, Annapolis, 1996

Turner, F. J., *The Frontier in American History*, Holt, New York, 1920

Vale, B., *The Audacious Admiral: The True Life of a Naval Legend*, Conway, London, 2004

Watts, S., *The Republic Reborn: War and the Making of Liberal America*, Baltimore, 1987

Webster, C. K., ed., *British Diplomacy 1813–1815: Select Documents dealing with the Reconstruction of Europe*, Bell & Sons, London, 1921

Webster, C. K., *The Foreign Policy of Castlereagh, 1812–1815*, Bell & Sons, London, 1931

Wellington, Duke of, ed. J. Gurwood, *The Dispatches of Field Marshal The Duke of Wellington During His Various Campaigns in India, Denmark, Portugal, Spain, The Low Countries and France*, Vol. IX, Parker, Furnivall & Parker, London, 1844

Whitehill, W. M., ed., *New England Blockaded: The Journal of Henry Edward Napier, Lieutenant in HMS Nymphe*, Peabody Museum, Salem, 1939

Wilkinson, D., 'Victory at Fayal', *American History Illustrated*, Vol. 13, 1978

Willson, B., *America's Ambassadors to England (1785–1928): A Narrative of Anglo-American Diplomatic Relations*, John Murray, London, 1928

Wilmerding, J., *American Art*, London, 1976

——, *American Marine Painting*, Abrams, New York, 2nd edn, 1987

Wilton, A. & Baringer, T., *American Sublime: Landscape Painting in the United States 1820–1880*, Princeton University Press, London

Winfield, R., *British Warships in the Age of Sail, 1793–1817: Design, Construction, Careers and Fates*, Seaforth Publishing, Barnsley, 2005

Winter, F. H., *The First Golden Age of Rocketry*, Washington, 1990

Woodman, R., *Britannia's Realm: In Support of the State, 1763–1815: A History of the British Merchant Navy Volume Two*, The History Press, Stroud, 2009

Wright, C. & Fayle, E., *A History of Lloyd's*, Macmillan, London, 1928

Yonge, C. D., *Life and Administration of the Second Earl of Liverpool*, Macmillan, London, 1868

Zimmerman, J. F., *Impressment of American Seamen*, Columbia University, New York, 1925

General Index

Page references in *italics* refer to illustrations. Ship actions are listed with the British ship named first.

Index of Ships

Admirals

Britain achieved unparalleled global pre-eminence through one critical advantage – her naval power. While other nations looked to armies for their security, Britain looked to the sea and for more than three hundred years the Royal Navy dominated the ocean. Eminent naval historian Andrew Lambert celebrates the rare talents of the men who shaped the most successful fighting force in world history, from the Armada to the Napoleonic Wars to the Second World War. Through their lives and battles, *Admirals* charts the evolution of naval command across four centuries, while proving that maritime power is a vital and living element of modern Britain.

'An absorbing account of great naval commanders.' *Financial Times*

'Learned, informative, persuasive and sometimes challenging.' *Sunday Telegraph*

'Thoughtful, provocative and based on wide reading and impressive research, this book provides a first-rate assessment of the changing nature of naval command from the Elizabethan era to the end of the Second World War.' *History Today*

ff

Nelson: Britannia's God of War

Nelson explores the professional, personal, intellectual and practical origins of one man's genius, to understand how the greatest warrior that Britain has ever produced transformed the art of conflict, and enabled his country to survive the challenge of total war and international isolation.

'Fascinating . . . Shot through with fresh insights . . . No previous biography has attempted anything so comprehensive.' *Observer*

'A concise, accessible overview of Nelson's career and reputation.' *Spectator*

'Andrew Lambert is the outstanding British naval historian of his generation.' David Cannadine

ff

Franklin: Tragic Hero of Polar Navigation

In 1845 Captain Sir John Franklin led a large, well equipped expedition to complete the conquest of the Canadian Arctic, to find the fabled North West Passage connecting the North Atlantic to the North Pacific. Yet Franklin, his ships and men were fated never to return. The cause of their loss remains a mystery.

Shocked by the disappearance and sickened by reports of cannibalism, the Victorians re-created Franklin as the brave Christian hero who laid down his life, and those of his men. Later generations have been more sceptical about Franklin and his supposed selfless devotion to duty. But does either view really explain why this outstanding scientific navigator found his ships trapped in pack ice seventy miles from magnetic north?

Andrew Lambert re-examines the life and the evidence and discovers a new Franklin: a character far more complex, and more truly heroic, than previous histories have allowed.

'It is an absorbing story and Lambert tells it well . . . the book is intriguing and readable.' *Observer*

'Lambert brilliantly recreates, not just what we know about the events of the expedition, but also how the myth of Franklin as a classic Victorian hero who died for the empire was stage-managed, not least by his widow.' *Sunday Business Post*

ff

Faber and Faber is one of the great independent publishing houses. We were established in 1929 by Geoffrey Faber with T. S. Eliot as one of our first editors. We are proud to publish award-winning fiction and non-fiction, as well as an unrivalled list of poets and playwrights. Among our list of writers we have five Booker Prize winners and twelve Nobel Laureates, and we continue to seek out the most exciting and innovative writers at work today.

Find out more about our authors and books
faber.co.uk

Read our blog for insight and opinion on books and the arts
thethoughtfox.co.uk

Follow news and conversation
twitter.com/faberbooks

Watch readings and interviews
youtube.com/faberandfaber

Connect with other readers
facebook.com/faberandfaber

Explore our archive
flickr.com/faberandfaber